Panorama
of
Psychology

Panorama
of
Psychology

N. H. Pronko
Wichita State University

Brooks/Cole Publishing Company
Belmont, California
A Division of Wadsworth Publishing Company, Inc.

To my sisters
Mary, Anna, Donnie

7 8 9 10   74 73 72

L. C. Cat. Card No.: 69-14579
Printed in the United States of America

Preface

One of the main objectives of this book of readings and essays is to introduce the reader to the broad panorama of contemporary psychology by mapping out significant areas of research, major controversies, and traditional divisions of the field. Another objective is to allow the reader to encounter the challenges, surprises, insights, and ironies that enliven the landscape of psychology.

Can chickens play baseball? Do some songbirds have a Southern accent? Can average people be talked into giving severe electric shocks to helpless victims? Are geniuses born or made? Why do some monkeys wash their yams before eating them? Is a whole brain better than half a brain? What is a memory? Do people learn how to be mental patients? These questions—both the whimsical and the serious ones—are drawn from a few of the collected articles to suggest the wide range of human and animal behavior encompassed by contemporary psychology.

As in most introductions to psychology, this volume is addressed to perennial problems—heredity, development, learning, and so forth—thus suiting it for use as a textbook or set of supplementary readings in a course in introductory psychology. In form and content, however, this book is not at all conventional. In general, books of readings consist of highly technical journal articles, written by professionals for their professional colleagues. Their verbiage is often impenetrable, forbidding, and discouraging to the beginning student. Many of the details so important to the specialized worker are meaningless and boring to the uninitiated. To circumvent these problems, and, simultaneously, to extend the range of coverage, I departed from the common procedure of reproducing only entire articles from technical journals. Instead, wherever feasible, I excerpted, condensed,

and summarized. A few articles that are brief and interestingly written I quoted entirely.* When articles were long, complicated and/or esoteric, I described them, or I rewrote them. In the latter instance, I sent my rewrite to the original author and obtained his approval.

Nor did I limit my selection to technical reports. In delineating fundamental problems, I drew from books as well as journals and from historical and journalistic and even personal documents. Also, I asked fellow psychologists to prepare certain articles specifically for this volume. Furthermore, the articles I selected unabashedly reflect the sometimes intimate relationships between psychology and sociology, biology, zoology, medicine, philosophy, and other disciplines. While most of the articles presented here concern recent theoretical, experimental, and clinical work, some are about older contributions which I feel were simply swamped out and thus neglected in the flood of recent research.

My own frankly admitted preference is for articles discussing raw data that show the variation so characteristic of behavior. However, I did not exclude articles that reflect advances along theoretical or philosophical lines. Although my theoretical preferences undoubtedly show in comments and conclusions and speculations, I have tried to challenge rather than indoctrinate readers, to invite them to develop their own positions and to enter into psychology's lively ongoing debates. It is for this general purpose that I chose to focus attention on areas where problems still abound.

If any guiding principle influenced the

---

*The sources of complete quoted articles and the sources of other extensive quotations are identified in footnotes and are also included in the list of references.

final selection of articles in *Panorama of Psychology,* it was a preference for items reflecting the tremendous potential manifested in the psychological domain. The reader will find illustrations of this sometimes surprising potential in several recent studies—for example, in studies of earliest infancy, in **naturalistic observations** of so-called wild animals, and in reports from the area of **psychotherapy.**[*]

In preparing *Panorama of Psychology,* I also tried to keep in mind such well-founded criticisms of psychological jargon as these pungent observations offered by Robert B. MacLeod in a speech to American Psychological Association members in Los Angeles in 1964 (MacLeod, 1965).[†]

Do you really enjoy reading the psychological periodicals? Can you without blushing assign them to your students? If you can, my point is already made. Sociological jargon may be even worse than ours, and interestingly enough the linguists have recently been achieving a degree of unintelligibility which approaches genius, but among the books the average student is expected to read there are likely to be few that are written with less grace and clarity than are the books on psychology. Read William James again, if only to be reminded that literacy and good psychology are not incompatible [p. 349].

In addition to MacLeod's injunction, these remarks by Peter F. Woodford (1967) offered guidance:

All are agreed that the articles in our journals —even the journal with the highest standards— are, by and large, poorly written. Some of the worst are produced by the kind of author who consciously pretends to a "scientific scholarly"

style. He takes what should be lively, inspiring, and beautiful and, in an attempt to make it seem dignified, chokes it to death with stately abstract nouns. Next, in the name of scientific impartiality, he fits it with a complete set of passive constructions to drain away any remaining life's blood or excitement; then he embalms the remains in molasses of polysyllable, wraps the corpse in an impenetrable veil of vogue words, and buries the stiff old mummy with much pomp and circumstance in the most distinguished journal that will take it. Considered either as a piece of scholarly work or as a vehicle of communication, the product is appalling [p. 743].

I scarcely hoped to achieve a model of stylistic elegance in the present work, nor did I expect to attain the level of excellence and charm found in William James's writings. I did however try to be constantly aware of my purpose, which was to prepare materials designed for reading by non-professionals. Although some jargon and stilted language may have insidiously crept into the following pages, I trust that they are not present in large enough amount to do injury to what should be, at least according to Woodford's standard, "lively, inspiring, and beautiful."

Acknowledgements The writing of a book is a set of interpersonal relations, the most prominent of which, at least, should be noted. First, I am indebted to Bonnie Fitzwater and Charles T. Hendrix of Brooks/Cole Publishing Company for their early espousal and enthusiastic encouragement of the book even when it was in its primitive, amorphous state. And for his perspicuous editing, which transformed the original manuscript into its present improved form, an expression of appreciation is hereby tendered to Robert Mann.

For a reduction of my teaching duties and for their general facilitation of a

---

[*]Terms printed in boldface type are defined in the glossary at the back of this volume.

[†]Each speech, article, or book cited by author and publication date (e.g., "MacLeod, 1965") is fully identified in an alphabetical list at the back of this volume. References follow the style of the *Publication Manual of the American Psychological Association,* 1967 Revision.

research environment at Wichita State University, I am indebted to David Herman, Chairman of the Department of Psychology; Kelley Sowards, Dean of the College of Liberal Arts; and to former President Emory Lindquist. I also want to express appreciation to my colleague Grant Kenyon, with whom I have had a fleeting, though fruitful trade of books, articles, and concepts. I have also enjoyed sharpening my ideas in fierce but friendly debate with another colleague, Robert Borresen. And I thank Robert W. Eichinger of the University of Minnesota, Robert Grissom of San Francisco State College, and Edward L. Walker of the University of Michigan for their most helpful comments on the manuscript.

Thanks are due to Mrs. Steve Hatfield for her conscientious typing of the manuscript and to Marvin Parrish for his faithful and dependable cooperation as an assistant and for his preparation of supplementary materials for this book. I also thank Terry Rae Smith for her speedy and precise work in connection with the index.

Very special thanks are gratefully acknowledged to Mrs. Robert Snyder for her transformation of almost inscrutable scrawls into a meticulously typed manuscript. Beyond that, I am indebted to her for the many painstaking prepublication details that she managed with scrupulous exactitude.

Above all, I must express a sense of deep gratitude to my wife, Geraldine Allbritten Pronko, for her sustained encouragement, moral support, her loyalty, her generous indulgence of what has been labeled a scholarly pursuit and, even more, for her innumerable helps in preparing the manuscript, proofing, indexing, and many other services which summated to a near collaboration.

·N. H. Pronko

Contents

1

Some slants, perspectives, and basic considerations

Some of our most important beliefs about man and his development have changed or are in the process of changing [Hunt, 1964, p. 209].

It seems logical for the first chapter of a book to provide a broad introduction to its subject matter. That is the purpose of the following selections, which discuss science and psychology in broad terms.

The first article makes the basic point that science is a form of concrete human activity and is essentially a way of accurately observing and thinking about various happenings. In order to evoke flexibility in the reader's attitude toward some of the newer concepts presented here, we consider several sources of resistance to their examination. Because everyone is molded by his age, we then consider how limiting are the silent assumptions and intellectual straightjackets of various periods of history. It is easy for us today to think of the earth as a satellite of a relatively small star in the Milky Way galaxy. People have not always found it so.

Not all psychologists are content with the approaches and procedures of the past, for psychology is an active field, one in a state of ferment. For example, the disagreement between the strict **laboratorian** and the **field observer** is reflected in the next two selections, which discuss how psychology should be studied.

Finally, we consider, more specifically, the nature of **scientific method** as applied to our own subject matter and contrast it with nonscientific procedures.

Science is a human enterprise 1

Science is too often treated as a sacred cow, something set apart from the broad spectrum of human activities. We gain a clearer understanding of science when we realize that scientists are not entirely unlike bridge builders, farmers, accountants, or salesmen.

Fundamentally, scientists begin their work by observing gases, liquids, solids, or single organisms or groups of them. Scientists select the particular objects or data that they choose to study and then compare, classify, measure, and think about them. The results are principles, laws, **theories,** and **hypotheses** — "behavioral products" in the same sense as the automobiles or furniture produced by a factory worker, the profits of management, or the compositions of a musician. All are the consequence of people's doing, observing, thinking, and reporting their results to others.

If science can be regarded as one of many kinds of work, we should not be surprised to find that scientists are in many respects similar to other workers. In fact, we should expect them to have ambitions, sensitivities, prejudices, ethics, and morals not unlike those of butchers, bakers, and

candlestick makers. Some welcome progress and change; others are conservative
or even reactionary.

Scientists as objects of psychological study

As living organisms, scientists can be
studied by the biologist in so far as they
manifest the common characteristics of
living things, such as digestion, reproduction, and irritability. However, they are
also appropriate subjects for psychological
investigation while they are observing, classifying, measuring, and speculating about
whatever data they study as scientists.

In the following discussion, we will be
concerned specifically with the way scientists respond to scientific changes in their
own fields. For example, are they open-
minded and tolerant of new discoveries,
procedures, and theories? Opposition to
scientific progress by the church and other
institutions and groups is well known;
astronomy, geology, biology, medicine, and
psychology have all suffered from con-
demnation or suppression. But how have
the sciences fared at the hands of their
own members? This theme is explored in
the following brief discussion of a paper
by Dr. Bernard Barber, who has worked in
the sociology of science. For our purposes,
he is a scientist of scientists.

"Resistance by scientists to scientific discovery"*

The heading above is the title of an
essay by Barber which examines how

---

*Quoted material is from Bernard Barber, "Resist-
ance by Scientists to Scientific Discovery," *Scientific
Manpower Bulletin,* 1960, pp. 36–47.

scientists themselves react to their colleagues' findings and theoretical contributions. While Barber's whole paper is
worthy of careful study, I intend to select
only enough aspects and portions to bear
out the point that science is not a capital *S*
entity, pure and ideal, but as human an
activity as any other. The full realization of
this point should equip us for a more alert
and sophisticated study of **psychology.**

Understandably, Barber (1960, p. 36)
considers it strange that scientists have not
made a systematic analysis of scientists'
own resistance to scientific progress. Of
course, sporadic observations have been
noted here and there. Barber tells how the
famous physicist, Max Planck, suffered at
the hands of his professors when he suggested new ideas on thermodynamics,
ideas that were accepted much later. The
embittering experience caused Planck
(1949) to remark that

a new scientific truth does not triumph by
convincing its opponents and making them see
the light, but rather because its opponents
eventually die and a new generation grows up
that is familiar with it [pp. 33–34].

One of Planck's opponents was the distinguished nineteenth-century physicist
and physiologist, Helmholtz, who had himself met with resistance and expressed his
feelings to Faraday, the British physicist
and chemist, still another victim of the
dogmatists. Helmholtz declared that the
great benefactors of mankind cannot expect
to be properly appreciated in their lifetime.
He also felt that the length of time it takes
for new concepts to be accepted is propor-
tional to their originality (Barber, 1960,
p. 37). Semmelweis, the Viennese physician
who tried to convince his medical colleagues to scrub their hands before
attending women in childbirth, was ridi-
culed, ostracized, and punished cruelly for

his suggestion. Today, of course, his recommendation is standard delivery-room and operating-room procedure. Such clear examples of scientific resistance to change piqued Barber's curiosity. How could it be explained? Barber found part of the answer in the human conditions surrounding the act of discovery; these he divided into cultural and social conditions. Let us examine each briefly.

Cultural sources of resistance

Among the cultural sources of resistance to scientific discovery, Barber (p. 39) includes substantive scientific concepts and theories, methodological conceptions, and religious ideas.

Substantive concepts and theories
Tradition tends to perpetuate the familiar way of thinking about things. Once a theory is established, it is difficult to dislodge. Copernicus, considered the founder of modern astronomy, was savagely attacked by the astronomers of his time, who ignored his discoveries in favor of reality as they knew it. An example closer to our own time concerns Pasteur's discovery of fermentation as a biological process. Pasteur was contemptuously hooted down by scientists who had been taught that fermentation was chemical in nature.

Methodological sources of resistance
Whichever model has become established as a way of studying or interpreting phenomena will tend to be accepted over new ones. Subsequent chapters will demonstrate competing models in psychological inquiry. Now, however, it will suffice to mention a few examples from other disciplines. The discovery of the planet Neptune was rejected by astronomers of the last century. Why? Because the discovery was made on the basis of mathematical calculations, which the astronomers of that period distrusted. (Today, in psychology, mathematical models are quite popular.) Principles of heredity, as worked out by the Austrian monk and botanist, Gregor Mendel, were ignored in 1865 because botanists of that era were antimathematical. When his work was finally rediscovered in 1900, 16 years after his death, botanists had become promathematical and praised his work highly. Other methodological sources of resistance may result from preferences for experimentation over naturalistic observation. The huge successes of the laboratory in physics and chemistry have made it a powerful model for those psychologists who tend to look disparagingly at the **clinician** or the social psychologist, working, as each must, outside the laboratory. Some scientists are antitheoretical, preferring to "do something" in the laboratory. In this connection it is interesting to point out the high status of the theoretical physicist, who may regard the laboratory worker as a mere technician and tester of his theories. Einstein was one of the elite theoreticians.

Religious resistance of scientists
Briefly, "all during the first half of the nineteenth century, resistance to discovery in geology persisted among scientists for religious reasons [p. 43]." The problem was not one of religion versus science but one of religion *in* science. Darwin's work was obviously resisted by organized religion, but several famous *scientists* opposed his theory of evolution on religious rather than on scientific grounds. Barber points out that physics and biology have accommodated themselves to religion fairly success-

fully. But "there is perhaps another story to be told for the resistance from religious ideas among scientists to discoveries in the social and psychological sciences [p. 43]...." To Barber's statement I would add that the conflict in the latter instance is inevitable because human data, in particular, are embedded in a matrix of religious, ethical, moral, political, economic, and philosophical variables.

Social sources of resistance

Resistance due to the relative standing of the discoverer In addition to the commonly shared ideas that discourage innovation, there are sources of resistance that involve the interaction of scientist versus scientist. As in other human enterprises, some scientists belong to the Establishment. Prestige and power operate here as elsewhere. As Barber puts it: "...sometimes, when discoveries are made by those of lower standing in science, they are resisted by those of higher standing partly because of the authority that higher position provides [p. 43]." Barber relates an incident from the life of Thomas H. Huxley, who was once thwarted when he submitted an original and significant paper to a scientific journal. The editor of the journal in question was considered the authority in the field; therefore "the young upstart's" ideas had no chance of publication. Mendel's mistreatment was also partly due to his inferior position in the hierarchy of botanists.

Resistance due to the prevailing pattern of specialization Anyone from another field who attempts to contribute to a specialized field is likely to be treated as an outsider. When Helmholtz announced his theory of the conservation of energy,

it was resisted, partly at least, because, working as he did in physiology and anatomy, he was not considered a bona-fide physicist. The physicists resented the "young medical man [p. 45]." Conversely, medical specialists have a long history of resisting scientific innovations from "the outside." Pasteur's attempt to have his germ theory accepted was violently resisted by medical men of his time (Barber, p. 45).

Scientific organizations may resist innovations in science When someone joins a board of directors of a scientific organization or becomes an associate editor of a scientific journal, he attains a new status. He becomes a member of an "in" group. He may feel subtly pressured to protect established values and views against "outsiders."

Rival "schools" provide opposition to discovery Barber quotes Huxley, who noted only 2 years before his death:

"Authorities," "disciples," and "schools" are the curse of science; and do more to interfere with the work of the scientific spirit than all its enemies [Barber, p. 46].

A contemporary example from the life sciences concerns the crisis precipitated by the quarrel between **molecular** versus **classical biology.** In psychology we shall encounter **"reductionists"** versus **"the hollow-organism" theorists,** clinicians versus behaviorists and Jungians. Sometimes schools tend to guard their reputations and prestige at the expense of their objectivity.

Older scientists generally resist younger scientists As they get older, scientists are more apt to attain positions of higher status, power, and prestige. As a consequence, they may be more liable to become involved in the operation of the other cultural and social sources of resistance that have been suggested.

Summary

The layman is often likely to regard the scientist as an impassioned, objective, open-minded searcher after truth. Barber's analysis, as sketched above, shows the scientist as a human being. Consequently, Barber finds that factors operating within the sciences themselves offer resistance to their growth and development.

Cultural sources of resistance to discovery include certain common ways of thinking. They may involve (1) scientific concepts and theories that enjoy priority because they are already established and will not be supplanted by newer ones; (2) preferred methods, approaches, or **models;** and (3) religious resistance by scientists themselves.

Social sources of resistance may be divided into the following types: (1) the relative social status or standing of the discoverer; (2) the prevailing pattern of specialization (as when the discoverer is considered an outsider); (3) the organization as a reactionary group not readily yielding to novelty and change; (4) rival schools that must guard and perpetuate their positions; and (5) the older scientists versus the younger—who themselves will eventually become older scientists and will form the reactionary element confronting a future generation.

What are the implications of Barber's report? It surely is not meant to inculcate cynicism; rather, it should be the basis for a realistic approach to any and all the sciences that are considered as human enterprises. The achievements of the sciences are beyond dispute. Even psychology, the newcomer, shares in the accumulation of a solid body of knowledge and its applications. It is easy to be satisfied with the accomplishments to date. Indeed, the present book offers a panorama of the studies that psychology has recently made. Nevertheless, we must be alert and aware of possible intellectual pitfalls. We should realize that scientific workers have not always facilitated discovery or helped to continue the progress of their disciplines. It would seem, then, that the student of psychology, perhaps more so than the student of physics, chemistry, or biology, must examine his own behavior for subtle, unwitting obstacles and resistance to discoveries in his psychological venture.

A historical dimension to self-understanding

2

Getting to know oneself may be compared to lifting oneself by the bootstraps. Both operations demand some kind of leverage outside oneself. Understanding oneself only in terms limited to one's own experiences is obviously restricting. (The self-knowledge permitted to the idiot is an exaggerated illustration of the point.) Today even a child has no difficulty conceiving of air as having weight. When the suggestion was first made, however, people thought it absurd and would wave their hands about to prove that air did not, and could not, weigh anything. Other notions evoked a similar reaction. The roundness of the earth is still disputed by certain religious groups, providing us with a pristine specimen of the fossilization of thought.

The following very limited presentation of Erling Skorpen's exciting paper, "The Whole Man,"* stresses the need for getting outside oneself in order to learn about oneself. Skorpen provides a historical dimension to the topic. We might put the question thus: Does every stage of history provide the same opportunity for man's self-knowledge and self-understanding, or do different historical periods furnish different "leverage" and, therefore, different insights into man's potentialities?

A Greek contribution

Among the many contributions that the Greeks made to our civilization, we immediately think of architecture, sculpture, drama, poetry, philosophy, history, government, and a science of sorts. Rarely do we credit the Greeks with shaping our view of man. Yet, according to Skorpen, the Greeks invented the concept of the all-round man, the philosopher-king, "the speaker of words and doer of deeds" as Homer put it. Socrates was a living image of that ideal. In drinking the fatal cup of hemlock, he showed the complete fusion

---

*Quoted material is from Erling Skorpen, "The Whole Man," *Main Currents in Modern Thought,* September-October 1965, **22** (1), 10–16. The discussion here does not do justice to Skorpen's development of an extended and profound thesis, which deserves to be read in its entirety, but the extracted portions serve the present purpose nicely.

and consistency of his logical thinking *and* action. It was that kind of wholeness that Socrates embodied as the Greek ideal, an original conception and "an achievement of the first rank [p. 10]." Another contribution of the Greeks lay in their

perception of the difference between the potentialities for growth contained in man's nature and the rather fixed nature of the material universe men live in. The importance of this innovation is found in the fact that men who lived in mythical times, that is, times prior to philosophical thinking about man and nature, really did not distinguish between themselves and nature; they used the same mythical symbols for both [Skorpen, personal communication, 1968].

Brilliant as they were, the Greeks did not discover the individuality and uniqueness of the person. Although able to see man as distinct from the rest of nature, they did not succeed in freeing themselves from a "we" kind of thinking. Socrates, Plato, and Aristotle were incapable of thinking other than as "we men," "we Greeks," "we whole human beings." The classic Greeks were not able to see themselves as individuals with separate identities. Individuality was as lacking among them as it would be among such colonial organisms as the sponges. If a unit in a sponge settlement could think at all, he could think of himself only as an aspect or phase of the colony that contained him. Separateness is as nonexistent in a sponge colony as it is in a single cell of our skin or bone. So it was in Christendom during the Middle Ages. Men saw themselves only as members of a village, their feudal lord's chattel, a unit of a family, or a race, with emphasis on the group or collectivity without separate identity. They thought of themselves in terms of "we" and not "I" (Skorpen, p. 11).

Individuality discovered
in the Renaissance

Language may furnish a clue to a people's mode of thinking about themselves. At any rate, Skorpen reports that in fourteenth-century Italy men first discovered individuality. They were not afraid to think of themselves as different from their neighbors. For the first time, too, we find such expressions as *uomo singulare* (singular man) and *uomo unico* (unique man) to reflect such thinking. The discovery of the self is further mirrored in such word coinage as self-esteem, self-pity, self-liking, self-love, self-conceit, self-knowledge.

Without the **ego's** recognition of itself as fertile territory for exploration, could it have put sufficient distance between itself and physical nature to supply the objectivity so vital to science? The distinction between the self and the not-self is a crucial refinement of the Greek distinction between man and nature [Skorpen, p. 12].

The Renaissance man

What were the results of the 2000-year-long achievement in man's new insight into his own nature?

Its importance is seen in the fact that, in addition to producing men capable of both intelligent thought and decisive action, this period in Italian history evoked individuals who were gifted and breathtakingly proficient in many fields. With the discovery of the private man in the fourteenth century, "in the following step by step," says Burckhardt, "the number of complete men increased and the ideal of *l'uomo universale* arose." This is the period of such giants as Dante, Alberti, da Vinci, and Michelangelo — men who combined in their persons the talents of poet, philosopher, artisan, artist, scientist, engineer, architect, and even prophet [p. 11].

Such men, inspired by the vision of unlimited human potentiality, labored continuously to become accomplished in the old and new ways of men at their best. We can only pause in admiration before the achievements of such geniuses as Leon Battista Alberti — superb athlete, intellectual, writer, inventor, and artist — who combined all these gifts with a poet's sensitivity so acute that he shed tears of joy at the sight of dignified old men, and was actually healed of his illnesses in the contemplation of nature. Yet his superb attainments are overshadowed, as Burckhardt notes, by the still greater genius of da Vinci, who "was to Alberti as the finisher to the beginner, as the master to the dilettante [pp. 11–12]."

Skorpen (p. 12) notes a fact that is easily overlooked and unappreciated: the Renaissance artist painted and sculpted both Christian and pagan gods and goddesses. This accomplishment resulted from his ability to embrace or assimilate the elements of the Christian religion as well as those of Greek and Roman culture. Skorpen is emphatic:

In considering the great men of the Renaissance, one cannot but be struck by their power of imaginative participation in the materials of their art, which enabled them to see and feel deeply and privately into such elements of Christianity as Christ's passion, the Holy Family, the lives of the saints, and other Biblical figures, as well as the gods, men, and heroic symbols of Greece and Rome [p. 12].

Man's third discovery

The Greeks succeeded in seeing man in clear focus from the rest of nature. Renaissance man discovered his discreteness or uniqueness, but Skorpen considers that modern man has made a further refinement in his distinction of what he calls the inner "I" from the outer "I." In other terminology this might be formulated as the "self-reaction" (Cameron, 1947, p. 97).

According to Skorpen (personal communication, 1968), this third, great discovery of man's reflection upon himself forced him to consider whether his external projects in life were in accord with the needs, aspirations, yearnings of his "inner self." Prior to the third discovery, such questions could never have been formulated.

Has modern man deteriorated?

When this dimension of the Renaissance ideal of the universal man is duly recognized, in the performance of men like Alberti and da Vinci, we may wonder if the human perfection which they instanced does not represent the peak of mankind's development in both theory and practice, such that, apart from improved techniques of scientific discovery and applied technology, little else of importance distinguishes modern man from his Renaissance ancestor. Indeed, we might wonder if modern man hasn't deteriorated in comparison [p. 12].

It is not important for us to determine whether or not humans have regressed since the Renaissance; there are other significant implications of Skorpen's essay. In my view, the following is one. Each person is the child of his age; for this very reason he is handicapped in understanding himself because he is certain to reflect concepts about human nature that he drank in with his mother's milk. Our age looks upon man as being inherently handicapped or advantaged in his development or lack of it. The common conception holds that, prior to birth, a person already possesses or does not possess predisposing factors (**genes**; talents; gifts, as in "the gifted child;" etc.). Surely this concept of what man can make of man has its effect on the rearing and education of our children; just as surely we are unable to recognize it properly and fully, much less evaluate its operation in our lives. Some other age with new conceptions of man's nature will be better able to understand and assess our beliefs, just as we have an advantage over Renaissance man in understanding his view of the universal man. And yet, what if the Renaissance man's conception of man's dormant possibilities is correct?

In one respect the impact is clearly tremendous, since if man's inner self contains infinite resoûrces, the possibility of exhausting them scarcely exists. No man will ever be in a position to complete his life's work if he has construed this work to be the actualization of his potentialities [p. 14].

What a breathtaking view of man's possibilities!

Summary

Our consideration of Skorpen's essay was meant as a kind of Operation Bootstrap. Its aim was to show that a person's understandings of any phenomena are limited by the understandings that he brings to a study of those phenomena. The same applies to an individual's attempts at self-understanding; they can hardly transcend his past experiences in any radical fashion.

Skorpen showed how the Greeks made significant gains when they succeeded in standing aside, so to speak, and examining their own actions and thoughts. The Renaissance man went further in gaining a conception of himself as a discrete and independent individual, free to rise to previously undreamed-of heights. Our age permits the unwitting acquisition of a self-image that views the individual as possessing certain inherent defects or advantages in regard to his development. The crucial point is that the way a person comes to regard himself is very much a function of the particular stage of human history into which the stork drops him. The most exaggerated illustration of the preceding point is to imagine yourself as being born to our caveman ancestors. By contrast, what if you, thoughtful reader, had been born during the Renaissance? And what if you had come to believe, as Leonardo da Vinci and Michelangelo did, that you possessed almost infinite, almost inexhaustible resources for your development? Would you be likely to believe as naturally as you breathe that "No man will ever be in a position to complete his life work if he has construed this work to be the actualization of his potentialities [Skorpen, 1965, p. 14]"?

Sanford: "Will psychologists study human problems?"*   3

As in other scientific disciplines, psychologists show preferences or slants. Some, as we shall see, devote decades to the exclusive study of the lowly flatworm. Others have a predilection for studying ants; still others, human infants. Some pride themselves on being "rat psychologists." Certain psychologists like to work in the laboratory, certain others in the jungles or mountains of Africa. Psychology is, after all, a large field. We offer a particular and definite slant in the following selection.

Psychology is in the doldrums

Psychology is really in the doldrums right now. It is fragmented, overspecialized, method centered, and dull. I can rarely find in the journals anything that I am tempted to read. And when I do read psychological papers, as I must as an editorial consultant, I become very unhappy; I am annoyed by the fact that they all have been forced into the same mold, in the research design and style of reporting, and I am appalled by the degree to which an inflation of jargon and professional baggage has been sub-stituted for psychological insight and sensitivity [Sanford, p. 192].

The preceding quotation from a journal article by Dr. Nevitt Sanford of the Institute for the Study of Human Problems of Stanford University is appropriate here. It follows naturally and logically after our discussion of science as a human enterprise. In fact, it is an example of a methodological factor that, in Sanford's opinion, blocks the progress of psychology as a science. Let us consider his argument at greater length.

Sanford's article began as a letter to the director of the National Institute of Child Health and Human Development. It originated out of a genuine concern for the pattern of research that fund-granting agencies are supporting. His intention was to suggest that the institutes should encourage psychologists to study problems that

*Quoted material is from Nevitt Sanford, "Will Psychologists Study Human Problems?", *American Psychologist*, March 1965, **20** (3), 192–202. Copyright 1965 by the American Psychological Association, and reproduced by permission.

occur outside the laboratory instead of research that derived from psychologists reading about other psychologists' research in the journals. Sanford thinks that fund-granting organizations should foster bolder research designs that confront human problems directly, research that would "examine longer sections of behavior, and larger areas of the person than they usually attend to nowadays [p. 192]...." Instead of being encouraged to devise new methods for solving human problems, psychologists seem to select those problems that can be fitted to existing methods. This is obviously a narrow, limited, and limiting factor in psychology's growth.

Why this state of affairs?

We have produced a whole generation of **research psychologists** who never had occasion to look closely at any one person, let alone themselves, who have never imagined what it might be like to be a subject in one of their experiments, who, indeed, have long since lost sight of the fact that their experimental subjects are, after all, people. (Let us leave the rats out of it for the moment.) They can define **variables,** state hypotheses, design experiments, manipulate data **statistically,** get publishable results—and miss the whole point of the thing. Reading their papers, you get a strange sense of the unreality of it all; the authors' conceptions of variables and processes seem a bit off; and then you realize that the authors have never looked at human experience, they went straight from the textbook or journal to the laboratory, and then into print—and then into the business of getting research grants.

The plain fact is that our young psychological researchers do not know what goes on in human beings, and their work shows it. Not only is it dull, which psychology should never be, but it is often wrong, for that context of processes-in-the-person which they have been trained to ignore is usually doing more to determine what happens in the situation under study than the

variables that have been isolated experimentally [pp. 192–193].

The critique is not of the experimental approach in psychology or of general psychology as a discipline; it is of a state of affairs in which the advocates of a particular kind of psychology — psychology-without-a-person — have been able to gain and maintain power through putting across the idea that they are the representatives in psychology of **true science** [p. 193].

The discipline is still much concerned to establish itself as a science, but the psychologists' naive conception of science has led them to adopt the more superficial characteristics of the physical sciences. This has made it difficult for them to study genuine human problems, for quantification, precision of measurement, elegance of experimental design, and general laws are so much more difficult to achieve once one goes beyond simple part processes [p. 193].

Sanford is quite right. It is easy to design an experiment that will show, for example, the conditioning of an eye blink to a light of a definite measurable intensity. All the other variables can also be controlled and specified in precise terms. Such a laboratory experiment can be neat and exact as well as "scientific," especially if one takes physics as a model of a science. We should rejoice that some psychological data will permit such rigorous manipulation. However, like Sanford, we should recognize that the baby's learning its mother language and the soldier's acquiring a battle **neurosis** also need to be dissected and understood. Psychology has some features in common with the science of astronomy, which cannot take any of its subjects into the laboratory but is limited to observing eclipses and such when *they* choose to happen. Yet, it is not embarrassed, as a science, to do its work exclusively via an observatory. Perhaps Sanford is saying something of the sort in challenging psychologists to attack complex human problems as they occur under natural conditions in the field.

Do isolated processes add up to more complex ones?

To the argument of some that an understanding of simple, part processes "will eventually add up to systematic knowledge that can then be applied to human problems," Sanford makes two points. "One is that the 'adding up' function is rather neglected today, and the other is that many of these findings just do not add up [p. 193]." A **psychosis, anxiety attack,** or a **depression** may have features that do not appear by "adding up" the responses that one gets in a nonsense-syllable learning experiment. An **"inferiority complex"** may be broken down into its component responses, but, as a totality, it has a character of its own that can be related and understood in relation to that individual's **personality** and surrounding conditions.

Truth may be discovered by abstracting parts from the whole and studying them intensively, but the whole truth can never be discovered in this way. It is the whole truth, and particularly the truth about wholes, that is needed for practice. Thus it is that one has to be concerned about a trend in science that seems to put all the accent on the study of abstracted part functions. The main reason for this trend is that it is difficult to study complex processes by existing approved methods. In psychology it seems that theory making itself is often guided by consideration of what can be attacked by such methods rather than by an intellectual involvement with the problems of life. The kind of theory that is needed for the understanding of human problems is different from that which guides most laboratory research or is generated from it [p. 194].

Sanford's holistic approach

It cannot, of course, be claimed that research carried out in accordance with the **holistic orientation** will soon achieve the standards of precision and elegance that are often attained in laboratory experiments involving a few simple variables. Such research can be improved in these respects, but it may never match the best laboratory experiments; it will have to aim at levels of rigor that are appropriate to the task at hand. It cannot be claimed, either, that this kind of research will be other than difficult and expensive. But the criticism of the current strategy of abstracting part functions for experimental study is more serious: It is that because of its very nature it is bound to fall short of the truth. It is not only that it avoids the big problems; it fails to achieve its own chosen goal, which is to establish general laws of behavior. But the main characteristic of such "laws" is their lack of generality. They break down as soon as a new variable is introduced into the picture. And since in real life new variables, or variables not taken into account in the laboratory experiment, are always in the picture, such laws are most limited in their applicability [p. 196].

Summary

Sanford's examination of contemporary psychology impels him to warn psychologists not to let *method* dictate the selection of hypotheses. Such an approach could lead to the investigation of problems that are simple, meaningless, even artificial or unreal. According to Sanford, we should not ignore the rich data that occur all around us, that is, *in nature.* Granted it is not always easy to study them, for one cannot take them into the laboratory. In fact, such data require approaches, modes of attack, and procedures appropriate to their study. Sanford seems to be saying: "Let's not get hung up on only one method, but let us develop whatever methods the various data require, regardless of their difficulty." This point is carried even further in the following selection by Farson.

4

Farson: Behavioral science as a science of man*

Because of our need to compete with the physical sciences, behavioral scientists have skipped over, by and large, the naturalistic stage from which other disciplines developed. We have not been people-watchers as biologists were bird- and bug-watchers. We have moved too quickly into the laboratory and looked only at special populations of people under special circumstances; we have thought we could derive generalizations about human behavior without first gaining the kind of understanding that could come only from years of looking at how normal people behave in normal circumstances, performing normal tasks. Very few of us make any attempt to use our scientific training to investigate what people are really like when they are being themselves. When one examines the literature in the behavioral sciences, one seldom has the feeling, "That's what it's like to be me." The *person* is usually missing and the findings have no reality or meaning for us because we cannot find *ourselves* there [p. 3].

Some psychologists would object strongly to Richard E. Farson's definition of psychology as a Science of Man. But the quotation is included to show the ferment in contemporary psychology. Physicists have not as yet settled among themselves the ultimate number of types of atomic particles. Biologists are presently engaged in a civil war in which "classical" and "molecular" biologists are pitted against each other. Why should psychology be immune to debate and argument? A panoramic view of present-day psychology shows animated intellectual debate. To pretend otherwise would yield a distorted picture. Stated more positively, psychology today accommodates widely discrepant approaches and **theoretical constructs,** as subsequent chapters will demonstrate.

5

Handy: What is scientific method?*

It seems appropriate at this stage to ask how we should go about the business of studying psychology scientifically. Can any general rules be applied?

*Quoted material is from Rollo Handy, *Methodology of the Behavioral Sciences: Problems and Controversies,* 1964. Courtesy of Charles C Thomas, Publisher, Springfield, Illinois.

A book by Rollo Handy, *Methodology of the Behavioral Sciences: Problems and Controversies,* will be highlighted as a way of covering some crucial issues and, simultaneously, of mirroring the pertinent literature in this area. Handy (p. 14) begins with a definition of science that many would find acceptable. The definition covers the following points: (1) the sciences aim at the attainment of *general laws* and (2) prediction and control of the phenomena being studied.

Handy sees problems with the concept of control because high prediction of eclipses, for example, does not necessarily guarantee any degree of control over them. Tornadoes offer another convenient example. However, if "adjustive behavior" is added to "control," then one can run for storm cellars and avoid destruction from the predicted tornado or typhoon by means of behavior appropriate to the situation. In other words, Handy defines control in a less rigid fashion than many scientists. That is why for him:

It seems pointless to ask for some definitely specifiable degree of prediction and control in advance; a contextual approach makes more sense and frees us from unwelcome rigidities [p. 15].

Handy seems to be saying: "Why try to settle such problems from some armchair in advance of inquiry?" Also, to think of the aim of science as the control of nature sounds grandiose and overly optimistic, although Handy has no objection to possible beneficial applications that will permit the modification of nature, including man (p. 16).

As for prediction and achievement of general laws, prediction does not present any special trouble, but, instead of general laws, Handy prefers Dewey's less absolutistic term, "warranted assertion" [Handy, p. 16].

"Warranted assertions" in place of absolute predictions and general laws

"Warranted assertion" has several virtues. It apparently helps to exercise the lingering ghost that science has uncovered (or will uncover) final, fixed, and incorrigible generalizations, or "ideals," or other closures to inquiry. It also helps to concentrate attention on the fact that the assertion in question is warranted by a definite process of inquiry, presumably open to replication and subject to other tests. This also relates to the previous discussion, in which it was maintained that there is both historical and technological relativity as to what is regarded as well-established in a given scientific discipline. Further, one is freed from the only too attractive "problem" of arranging sciences in some type of hierarchy based on the kind of alleged law those sciences have ascertained. A warranted assertion with its ground, justification, or warrant open to inspection and criticism, and with the range of application specified, seems to be the immediate end product of scientific inquiries [pp. 16–17].

For Handy, and for our tentative purpose, we may find it useful to think of scientific inquiry as "the prediction and control (and/or adjustive behavior thereto) of events through the development of publicly verifiable warranted assertions that are subject to continuous criticism [p. 20]." This definition may not be an absolute one in the sense of including everything that was ever done in the name of science, but it will be a convenient one for our purposes.

Webster's New Collegiate Dictionary defines *assertion* as "a positive declaration" and gives as one of the meanings of *warranted* (which, incidentally, has the same derivation as the term, guaranteed) "guaranteed to be as represented." The check on the guarantee is, of course, publicly verifiable, a social check.

The theoretician and the laboratorian

For purposes of contrast, one might be able to find, at one extreme, a laboratorian

—one, who (according to Handy, p. 26) concerns himself with "brute," "rudimentary" *facts*. Some might call him a worshipper of data or, less kindly, one whose chief concern is with "merely descriptive empiricism" (p. 26). Others might think of an extreme laboratorian as one engaged in busy work or functioning as a mere technician. In addition, Handy criticizes the laboratorian for his antitheoretical stand because he is often the victim of some unintentional theoretical position. Handy also raises the point that the mere collection of data does not constitute a science. The interpretation of this data is the essential scientific function. One can't help recalling Poincare's (1946, p. 127) dictum that an accumulation of facts is no more a science than a pile of bricks is a house.

At the other extreme is the **theoretician** who claims that some propositions are not amenable to empirical test or who intuitively elaborates highly formal systems without feeling required to substantiate them. Sometimes complex mathematical schemes that are rigorous, precise, and internally consistent are used, but workers may confuse their mathematical formulae with proof of whatever was assumed in the first place. Handy suggests that "the mere elaboration of complex mathematical structures that do not aid in prediction and (more dangerously) the belief that because internal consistency is achieved, insight into human behavior must follow, are to be deplored [p. 30]."

The role of models

Today there is considerable preoccupation with making models as an aid in developing theories. For instance physics has been cited as an example of a model science

for psychology. The brain as a telephone switchboard and, more recently, as a computer, man as an information-handling system or as a **servomechanism** are some newer models. Several of these models will be discussed in subsequent chapters.

In certain respects, then, models and mathematically formulated theories may share the same defect: much greater ingenuity, work, skill, and effort go into the elaboration of the model than into its alleged use in inquiry [p. 31].

The main point is that models, like airplane models and others, may bring delight and fun to the builder or beholder but permit little in the way of warranted assertion. A crucial commentary about models concerns the analogical reasoning involved. The elementary student in logic recognizes analogy as the lowest form of reasoning consisting of a comparison of two dissimilar things in terms of some superficial factor that they have in common. To say that a living organism is like a drugstore does not greatly advance our understanding of living organisms or of drugstores. Here is the form that Handy's censure of models takes:

Perhaps the major line of criticism encountered in the literature is that an uncritical attitude is often held about the analogies. Far too often, it seems to the critics, the mere discovery of the analogy is taken as having great significance, and unreasonably high hopes are held for what will be found when the analogies are tested [p. 48].

The laboratorian or theoretician—which?

We have examined the rigorous, white-coated, antitheoretical laboratory man who obeys the injunction: "Don't just stand there ("thinking," the cynic might add); do something!" At the other extreme we observed the highly speculative theoretician who freely embellishes analogical patterns or models with little or no warranted assertion. Stated otherwise, there is no way to validate the model-maker's statements because of the gap between behavior and the language couched in terms of the model.

Where does Handy stand in this debate? He favors "a union of theoretical and laboratory work [p. 51]." As for the reader, he must determine his own position. Will he allow himself unbridled speculation, or will he be forever bound to the facts without giving any thought to possible patterns or repeated relationships among them? Or will he look for constructs that are testable in the real world? Will he forge warranted assertions that will be guaranteed by observables, and will his observations through cautious testing yield warranted assertions? As a suggestion, the following diagram represents the intimate and *two-way* connection between the facts or data, on the one hand, and the theoretical constructs on the other.

Theoretical constructs
(i.e., "Warranted assertions")

↑   ↓

Observations of psychological facts or data
(in the laboratory or in nature)

Theoretical constructs are only derived from observations of data, laboratory or extralaboratory. Thus the upward-pointing arrow. If so, then the constructs increase our understanding or explanation of those data; they are referable to them. Thus the downward-pointing arrow. The data, at the same time, support or warrant the assertions or explanatory statements about the data. The aim is to have a close fit between the two levels, observational and theoretical.

Non-science: Ignoring cases that don't fit* 6

When I was a young instructor I awoke in the small hours one morning with a feeling which I had never had before and have never had since: a compelling feeling that something terrible had happened at my parental home. Habitually skeptical about such things, I resolved to record this experience carefully and check it with whatever the reality might prove to be. With that resolution formed but not carried out, I turned over and went to sleep. Upon waking, I was too preoccupied with my teaching to think of the "revealing" experience, and did not think of it again until, within a week, a student asked: "What about those feelings you get that something bad has happened at home, and then you get a message that it has happened?" This reminded me suddenly of my vivid experience and faint resolution, which otherwise I suspect I would have forgotten completely. Thus I was able to cite the experience together with the news, which had come meanwhile, that all was usual at home [p. 910].

Scientific method requires noting negative instances

The charge is often made that people with a strong belief in **mental telepathy,**

---

*Quoted material is from W. S. Taylor, Letter, *Science,* 27 August 1965, **149,** 910. By permission of author and publisher. Copyright 1965 by the American Association for the Advancement of Science.

clairvoyance, and **extrasensory perception** exploit instances that seem to support their belief and ignore cases that do not.

A friend of mine described what, at least superficially, looked like a genuine premonition of her sister's death. She was on a steamship crossing the Atlantic on her way to Sweden to visit a sister whom she hadn't seen for a number of years. One night she awakened suddenly with a strong feeling that her sister was dead. Indeed, when she debarked in Sweden, she learned that her sister had died. She offered the incident in support of her own belief in clairvoyance.

This was her story, but I was not satisfied by it. In a friendly fashion I raised some questions. I asked if her sister had been ill. She replied that her sister had been an invalid for several months. Then I put the crucial question to her: Had she ever had the thought that her sister might die *before* the dreadful anticipation that actually coincided with her sister's death? Being an honest person she admitted that such thoughts had occurred to her on a number of occasions. It was then not hard for her to see that she had unwittingly discounted the negative instances and stressed the single positive instance.

The scientist is required to be scrupulously honest in including all his data. Unlike the layman who unintentionally overlooks facts that do not fit his "theory," the scientist notes negative instances as illustrated in W. S. Taylor's personal experience and the "clairvoyance" incident reported above.

7 Gresham: "Fortune tellers never starve"*

The **pseudosciences** — rod-divining, mental telepathy, clairvoyance, **card reading, precognition, phrenology,** fortune-telling — all have one thing in common, namely, ignorance or neglect of scientific method. All select their data, ignore negative cases, do not rely on a social check or experimental verification, do not develop hypotheses that are subject to test, and do not record their data so as to permit scrutiny by others. Nor can they display any principles or laws. Finally, some practitioners of these pseudosciences are outright charlatans, as the following article will demonstrate.

"Fortune Tellers Never Starve" by William Lindsay Gresham is included here not only for its intrinsic interest but also as an illustration and an expose of one pseudoscience. The article is not a psychological analysis of fortune telling — it is a writer's descriptive account of how fortune tellers and their customers behave individually and in interaction with each other. However, the crude data presented do show how fortune-tellers operate and why their operation works. Two outstanding factors are the practiced skill of the fortune-teller

---

*Quoted material is from William Lindsay Gresham, "Fortune Tellers Never Starve," *Esquire,* November 1949, **32**(5). Reprinted by permission of Brandt and Brandt. Copyright © 1947 by Fawcett Publications, Inc. First published in *Esquire.*

in seizing upon behavioral cues unknowingly furnished by the client (e.g., signs of crying, depression, or the groove left by a wedding ring that was removed prior to the client's entry into the **psychist's** parlor) and the readiness of the victim to believe what he wants to believe. The generality or wide applicability of the fortune-teller's remarks is another common gimmick of the trade. The reader can detect still other procedures of the pseudosciences.

A young woman in a beauty parlor was babbling to a friend. "My dear," she said, "you *must* consult him – I just *know* he can help you. Why, he saved my marriage. You remember when that woman – well, I did just what *he* said, and everything was all right. It's the most wonderful experience. He looks right into your *heart,* and you come away feeling so much better!"

"What's his address?" asked the friend, fishing for a pencil. As she jotted the address down, the beautician, leaning over her shoulder, made a mental note of it; beauticians have their troubles, too.

"If I didn't have him to turn to, I couldn't get along," said the first woman. "He's the most wonderful man!"

Her pastor? Unfortunately, no. Her psychiatrist? She couldn't have spelled the word. No, the lady was talking about her fortune-teller.

No one knows exactly how much money the American public spends yearly on swamis, astrologers, tea-leaf readers, crystal gazers, "character analysts," and "mental-science counselors" – most of them as much fortune-tellers as the old gypsy in her caravan. Fifteen years ago, the "fees" of these people were estimated at $125,000,000, and it may easily have doubled by now.

There was a time when people in trouble automatically turned to the minister. The materialism of our age has cut off this source of aid and comfort from multitudes. There will be a time, no doubt, when the worried automatically turn to a psychiatrist. But that time is not yet. Psychiatry, despite its rapid growth since the war, is still scarce, costly, and a little terrifying to most people. Meanwhile, there is no one to

give comfort and advice to millions of our people except the fortune-teller. For every psychiatrist treating the mind, there are scores of "psychists" reading the mind; for every patient on an analyst's couch, there are a hundred gazing into a swami's crystal ball.

It is usual, but inaccurate, to dismiss the occult worker as a mere swindler, a spiritual confidence man. Some seers, it is true, are out-and-out crooks. But the majority of them depend on "repeat trade," and to bring a customer back again and again you must give him *something* for his money. By trial and error, by shrewd observation of men, many fortune-tellers have worked out long since many of the great truths that official psychology has only just discovered. Before Freud, the soothsayers knew that little boys are often jealous of their fathers; before Adler, they recognized that a brash manner usually conceals a sense of inferiority. As the alchemist preceded the chemist, the herb doctor the druggist, and the midwife the obstetrician, so the average "mind reader" anticipates in technique and knowledge the psychiatrist. He is, in fact, the psychiatrist of the poor; and when he is clever enough he sometimes becomes the psychiatrist of the rich as well.

Bouvier's Law Dictionary defines a fortune-teller as "one who pretends to be able to reveal future events; one who pretends to knowledge of futurity." And this sort of prediction, when done for money, is illegal in many localities. The law, however, leaves room for a multitude of evasions. Even in states where the law cracks down, those throngs who crave "knowledge of the future" find it easy to get.

The most legal method of fortune-telling is also the most efficient. A crystal ball may be seized and produced in court as evidence; the ghost of your grandmother, giving you sage advice in a dark room, may be grasped in the hand revealed as phosphorescent cheesecloth. But the "cold reader" as he is called in the trade, has no gimmicks except his knowledge of men and his colossal nerve. He reads your mind "cold" – when you walk in, he has never seen you before and knows nothing about you. He looks you over, proceeds to pluck out of your mind your past, your troubles, your hopes, and your fears. As long as he remembers to add, "Of course, I do not claim any occult knowledge of the future!" he is usually pretty safe legally.

The cold reader may have started with an M.D. or Ph.D., before he discovered the rich rewards of occultism. I know of a girl trained as a psychiatric social worker now reading palms in a carnival "mitt camp." She is making so much money that she is hardly likely to go back to pounding tenement stairs and bearding drunken husbands in their dens. Her professional knowledge paid very little before she learned to give it an occult disguise.

One "reader" ruefully tells an ironic story on himself. Athirst for more legality, more dignity, he once sought out a struggling young doctor in a small eastern city and made him a proposition. The "mentalist" had many customers, chiefly women in middle life, whose main worry was their health. Could he send them to the doctor — for, of course, a certain percentage of the fee? The young medico thought of his professional ethics; but he also thought of his empty pockets. He accepted and for some time both doctor and reader did well.

But the doctor was still worried about the ethics of fee-splitting. Then he had an inspiration — why split them? He had a legal right to be a psychological counselor himself! Eventually his medical knowledge made him so successful as a reader that the poor fortune-teller, hopelessly outclassed, had to leave town and try his luck elsewhere.

Few secrets are harder to uncover than the "secret knowledge" of the cold reader. Stage magicians, sworn foes of the occult racketeer, speak with contempt of the spirit medium whose tricks they can unmask; but they speak of the cold reader with uneasy wonder. "Just a little applied psychology!" they tell you hastily, and turn the talk to the latest thing in card manipulations. Yet some of them, who began by trying to expose the mind reader, have been fascinated and drawn into his trade. More than one able magician got additional fame by doing mind-reading shows over the radio. A friend of mine, for many years a successful tax consultant, became a mind reader just for the fun of it. He had learned about human nature from the woes of his tax clients.

A successful magician turned mentalist told me, "The first season I went out, working hotels as an entertainer and giving private readings on the side, I took a whole trunkful of gimmicks along. After six weeks I shipped them all back home. I carried on with nothing but the cold reading. I'm telling you, Bill, a lad who can work the cold reading will never starve."

Very little has ever been written about the technique of cold reading. Those who know it have a stake in keeping it unknown by others. But in the catalogue of an occult supply house — dealing in crystals, **ectoplasm,** and brain waves helped out by hidden telephone wires — I found listed a few manuscripts, the "confessions" of old "office mediums" who had, supposedly, "packed the racket in." Half-illiterate, rambling, wretchedly mimeographed, these confessions form the only known textbook of this strange calling. They combine two things: a medium's eye view of human nature and a set of instructions for manipulating it. Using their formulas as a basis, I have been able to read minds for hours on end at charity parties without disappointing a single customer.

Very much compressed, the old manuscripts give the reader's breakdown of human problems somewhat like this:

I. YOUNG GIRL
   A. Wild type
      1. I can't catch, or hold, my man.
      2. My conscience is bothering me.
      3. I'm in trouble.
   B. Home girl
      1. I'm afraid of men.
      2. I'm afraid of life and responsibility.
      3. I'm afraid of Mom.
   C. Career girl (usually jealous of a brother)
      1. Under twenty-five: I'm ambitious. I hate and despise men and marriage!
      2. Over twenty-five: I'm panicky. Maybe no one will marry me!

II. MATURE WOMAN (30–50)
   A. Still wild
      1. Why isn't it as much fun anymore? I'm lonely.
      2. I'm afraid of getting my face scarred, or burning to death in a fire. (This never misses.)

3. I've got to believe in something—the occult, a new religion that doesn't include morals, or you, Mr. Fortune-teller!

B. Wife and Mother
1. Is my husband seeing another woman?
2. When will he make more money?
3. I'm worried about the children...

III. SPINSTER
A. Still presentable
1. When will I meet him?
B. Given up hope
1. My best friend has done me dirt.
2. I'm crushed—a gigolo has got my savings!

IV. YOUNG MAN
A. Wild-oats farmer
1. Is there a system for beating the races?
2. What do you do when you get a girl in trouble?
   a. Is she playing me for a sucker?
B. Good boy
1. Will I be a success?
2. How can I improve my education?
3. Is my girl two-timing me?
   a. She's mixed up with Type A.
4. I'm afraid of Mom!

V. MATURE MAN
A. Wolf, married or single
1. Girl trouble
   a. I can't get her!
   b. I can't get rid of her!
   c. Her male relatives are after me!
   d. Does my wife know?
B. Businessman
1. Where's the money going to come from?
2. Will this deal work out?
3. Did I do right in *that* deal?
4. What does my wife do all day?

VI. ELDERLY PEOPLE
A. Woman
1. Will my daughter get a good husband?
2. Will That Creature be a good wife to my son?
3. Will the children (or grand-children) be all right?
B. Man
1. Will I ever have enough money to retire on?
2. I'm afraid to die.
C. Both
1. Am I going to need an operation?

VII. WISE GUY
A. Toughie
1. Make one false move, fortune-teller, and I bust ya one! (Ease him out quick.)
B. Defensive bravado
1. I'm smarter than most people; I see through you. (Flatter him; he'll end by eating out of your hand.)

This, needless to say, is not all there is to human nature; but it is all most people bring with them to the fortune-teller. The cynicism of this analysis is for many a cold reader's private benefit. What he *tells* the client is full of the milk of human kindness.

The manuscripts follow this up with a set of formula readings designed to cover the basic problems of each type. There is an exploratory opening, followed by a character analysis; then it passes to the main subjects of human interest. Love and money, health and loss, friends and enemies, dangers and dreams. A dash of mystery, a solemn warning, a piece of good advice. Then the close, designed to convince the "mark" of your supernal wisdom and bring him back next week.

Memorizing these formulas may serve an amateur well. I was once asked to help a friend out by reading palms at her party. I memorized a stock spiel for young women and took on about twenty of the girls. They all looked alike to me – so I told them all exactly the same thing. Later I hid in the pantry to overhear them comparing notes in the kitchen, expecting laughter as they saw the joke. They never caught on! Instead, there was a chorus of, "Isn't he wonderful! I just sat there and never opened my mouth, and the things that he told me – my dear, I've never confided them to a soul! The man's psychic!"

In that pantry I learned an important rule of fortune-telling: the human mind is a sieve. It holds what interests it and lets all the rest go. My fortune-teller's rapid twenty-minute spiel gave clients more than they could remember, and they remembered only the "hits."

For those professional readers who are only interested in having the client back, a memorized spiel is only a springboard. He may fall back on it to cover an awkward mistake or to deal with a tough client whose face tells him nothing. Usually, however, he relies on his ability to read faces and to lead the client into unconscious admissions. Both skills take long practice to develop, and a man who has them isn't entirely a fraud – he will know more about you in ten minutes than your husband or wife has been able to figure out in ten years.

Of the skilled cold readers I know, I have found only one who was willing to talk freely – a smooth-tongued old gentleman with a benevolent eye and nerves of cast iron, whom I shall call John Doe, "Doctor of Mental Science."

"Go ahead, son – print anything you like. You'll have a hundred chumps writing in to know where they can get in touch with the wonderful Power. My boy, you can't knock a lop-eared mark!"

This traditional phrase of the con man – it means that a natural-born sucker cannot be undeceived – is no exaggeration. Human gullibility is infinite. There was once in New York City a "materializing medium" who got his hooks into a prosperous investment broker. This hard-headed businessman had a passion for the ballet and had in his youth adored the great Pavlova.

A show girl I know met the medium on the street one afternoon. "I've got a chump upstairs," he told her. "Come on up for laughs."

As the girl tells the story, she and the broker sat side by side on a couch. The medium darkened the room somewhat, but everything remained clearly visible; then he retired into the next room to go into his "trance."

"I *know* Pavlova's going to appear today!" said the mark, trembling with excitement.

Suddenly, his pants rolled up to show his hairy legs, a scarf draped about him, the medium cavorted into the room. He did a pirouette and a few clumsy kicks, then went out.

"Wasn't she wonderful!" breathed the broker. "Pavlova to the life, just as I remember her!"

No, he wasn't nearsighted; but you can't knock a lop-eared mark. Dr. John Doe's clients, whom I watched all one afternoon from behind double doors he left ajar for me, never knew how often they nodded, gasped, or stammered half-finished sentences of information. They left, swearing they'd never opened their mouths.

When I couldn't see how he did his stuff, the Doctor would explain. "Now that little woman with the run-down heels, for instance..."

She crossed the floor toward the Doctor of Mental Science, clutching her pocketbook. On her ring finger there was a telltale mark – she had removed her wedding ring, with a muddled idea of fooling the fortune-teller. By the time she sat down he had her classified.

Wife, probably at least two small children – she had the hunted look. Age, about thirty-five; looks beginning to go; clothes good last year, but this year made over inexpertly (that meant less money this year than last). No servants – the hands gave him that. Conservative, unimaginative, timid – the uninspired get-up and the timorous mouth and eyes gave him that. Strain in the eyes, anxiety and self-pity in the mouth. Probably husband trouble.

"My dear lady," he began, speaking quickly and almost inaudibly. The client, concentrating all her attention to hear him, forgot to be wary. "My dear lady, I am glad you have taken this opportunity to consult me, for I feel I can be of help... you understand, of course, I make no claim to occult powers and do not predict the future in any way..."

That was in case she was a policewoman, though she wasn't the type. Policewomen are easy to spot; they are almost the only women in the world with poker faces.

"Now I see that your *husband* is giving you some anxiety, isn't that so?" Right: the lady's eyes widened, sure sign of a hit. The Doctor fished. "There is another person, a woman..."

Wrong: the eyes narrowed. Try money. Ah, warmer—

"...and this sum of money which must be paid... I see that this is not the main difficulty; there is some anxiety concerning your husband, a lack of will power"—the eyes have widened again—"to stand up for himself to his boss... or is it that he lacks will power in his leisure hours" —aha!—"when his weakness for a few drinks... or gambling... I seem to see cards on a table..."

Whoa! The brows have knitted!

"No, his weakness for these things is not sufficient, as I said, to cause you alarm, but on the other hand there is one temptation which he cannot resist, which takes the money you need, not for yourself—for I can see you are not vain and greedy like so many women"—

Nothing like a little flattery to soften 'em up.

"—but for your young children. And I seem to see crowds, bright colors,... horses, that's it! Madame, your husband is addicted to betting on the races, isn't he?"

The eyes filled with tears. While the lady used her handkerchief, the Doctor continued:

"Now there is no way I could have known this, isn't that right, and you did not speak a word... you see, I just plucked it out of your mind..."

You're in, Doctor, you're in. Treat her kindly now, and she'll tell you her whole life story. When she runs out of breath, you can tell it right back to her, and she'll go away swearing she never opened her mouth.

That is the sort of opening my cold reader friend dreams of, and he gets it more often than a layman would suspect. Most of his clients are women, most of the women have worries, and the more worried a woman is the more she wants a chance to tell somebody about it. Many readings, after the opening has opened up the client, become listenings. At the end my fortune-teller friend comes in with a little common-sense advice, a little sympathy, and a reminder of how great his powers are. The client goes home almost dizzy with relief; next week, when the load is back on her mind, she can always come back to him. The arrangement is ideal for both.

With less-worried clients, a reader may pass from his opening to his character analysis, combining formula material and what he sees in the sucker's face. Of course, what he sees and what he says are two different things!

A spiteful woman has a telltale line at the corner of her mouth. "You have suffered a great deal," says Dr Doe, "from the machinations of malicious and ill-natured people around you. You tend to be too trusting and generous..." That's the way she sees herself.

A bad-tempered man betrays himself in nostrils and lips. "You are naturally passionate and impetuous, easily stirred by unfairness, but the world's lack of understanding has caused you to keep yourself under rigid control..." That's what *he* thinks; his wife thinks otherwise.

The self-righteous of both sexes wear a curious cold smirk. "The baseness of the world was once a great shock to you; you have a fine and sensitive nature; you have had to learn to keep yourself aloof..." The thicker you slice it, the better they like it.

The cold reader, in short, may learn to describe people as they see themselves. He never forgets that every man thinks he's unique, that every woman *knows* she is. The more commonplace the client, the longer it is possible for a fortune-teller to dwell on, "Now I couldn't tell this to every woman, but I can see that you are an unusually sensitive type."

A reader like Dr. Doe does not forget that every wife, sometime or other, muses on the great career she might have had if she hadn't married. If she's intelligent, it was the arts; if she's stupid, it was the screen; and if she's neurotic, it was probably the theatre.

The fortune-teller's most lucrative clients are not necessarily women, however. Financial and political leaders often are the most rewarding. With them, the gambit is money, and there are many prosperous soothsayers peddling market advice in the nation's capital. A story is current about one of them who specialized entirely in financial predictions.

He got his information from one of the hush-hush Washington newsletters, now defunct. He trusted it implicitly; he would read it every week, embroider its bald facts with occult trimmings, add a few scraps picked up here and there, and dish it out to his distinguished clients. They, on their part, trusted *him;* one of them went so far as to take down every word he said in shorthand.

One day the good prophet happened to learn of a financial scandal about to break. No one else knew of it, and he could not resist the temptation to pass it along to his note-taking sucker. When he next picked up his newsletter, there it was, and in his own words!

A little research established the fact that his client with the shorthand was a trusted informant of the newsletter who passed the story on!

"You can't trust anybody nowadays," the fortune-teller complained bitterly. "*Now,* what am I gonna do for my market tips?"

Other significant topics are friends and enemies. To describe a woman's friend, you describe her physical opposite; but for her enemy, you describe the woman herself, and she will identify someone she loathes. Loss is a very important subject, for everyone has lost something — and everyone will react to the word.

Sometimes the reaction is dangerous. Most people, missing a valuable object, think at first that it is mislaid; only later do they suspect theft. Accordingly, when one old-time mind reader who had worked in theatres got the usual "Was my diamond ring lost or stolen?" she answered, "Your first supposition was correct." Her questioner, unfortunately, had begun by suspecting her maid; she walked out of the theatre and had the girl arrested.

The maid was innocent. She was also young, sensitive, and piously brought up; and she felt the disgrace of her arrest so keenly that she hanged herself in her cell. The medium retired from public performances for a few years.

Dr. Doe usually concludes by inviting questions, thus starting the most suspicious sucker talking; and whatever the client says, the reader cuts in with, "Ah, you remember I read that in your mind." His purpose now is to establish something very like what psychoanalysts call a *transference.* The client must be brought to depend on the reader absolutely, to defer all decisions until he can be consulted, to leave all responsibilities in his hands. A qualified psychoanalyst eventually builds up his patient's power of independent action and sets him free; but the technique of Dr. Doe is to try to keep him dependent forever — or until his money gives out.

Thus, it is undeniable that fortune-telling often does serious harm. In addition to those suckers who are simply swindled out of large sums, many others are bled slowly, and the psychological damage may be serious. Dr. Doe frankly admits that, as a cold reader, he encourages his victims, with his talk of occult power, in ignorance and confused thinking and superstition. Thus, even where he does no actual mental harm, the temporary relief he gives may keep a sick mind from treatment until it is too late.

To refute this, it may be pointed out that only an amateur reader will fool around with the psychotic and the seriously neurotic, and even he won't do it after one lesson. An amateur reader, who shall be nameless because she is my wife, learned this at a party. A career woman present was making herself offensive, particularly to a young man too shy to defend himself. With some idea of shutting her up, the amateur suggested a reading, which was eagerly accepted. But the reading never got past one whispered sentence.

Result: pandemonium. Shrieks, hysterics, infinitely embarrassing personal confessions, all accompanied by a desperate clinging to the "inspired psychic." The author of this article looked at his watch, announced that there was just time to make the last train, tucked the frightened cold reader under his arm, and ran. Once safe in Grand Central, he asked, "What on earth did you tell her?"

"Goodness," gasped the "psychic," "all I said was that when she was a baby her mother didn't want her!"

Too true, in this instance, for a neurotic to take without fireworks. No skilled professional would have told the lady that. He wants no hysterics for the clients in the waiting room to hear. When he gets a "disturbed" individual, he dishes out soothing syrup and suggests a visit to the family doctor.

And most people who consult the fortune-teller are, after all, in no great need of psychiatry. They may think they want to know the future. If that is the case, they will often get what they deserve — a lie; there is perhaps no human desire at once so arrogant and so cowardly, so dishonest and so foolish, as the wish to know what's in store — to be God, instead of trusting Him. But most of the reader's clients actually need only a little common-sense advice, a little sympathy, a listening ear, and a few kind words. These such readers as Dr. Doe have in great plenty, and they will go on providing them until properly trained psychological counselors are as common as blackberries.

Until then, the fortune-teller is the only impersonal adviser millions of people have, and though he is far from the best imaginable, he is usually better than nothing. His clients, however muddled in their heads when they leave him, are at least lighter in their hearts and better able to shoulder the burden that waits for them at home.

In his own cynical and mercenary way, even Dr. Doe often helps to make the world a cheerier place; for he has learned too well that "you'll never get rich peddling gloom!"

Chapter summary

We began our introduction to psychology by considering science as a human enterprise subject to the strengths and weaknesses of other human activities. Then, from the widest possible approach and for a possible helpful insight, we examined Skorpen's thesis that the notions prevailing in different historical periods limit man's view of himself. An Operation Bootstrap is required to raise oneself above such cultural impositions for a better view.

Preferences for approaches to psychology manifested themselves in Sanford's and Farson's pleas for a concern with human problems. The topic led naturally to a discussion of scientific method as a way of deriving "warranted assertions" from laboratory or field observations. The resulting "constructs" explained the observations and were, in turn, backed up or validated by them. We concluded with the procedures of the pseudosciences.

The nervous system and psychology

For many centuries the study of psychology has been closely identified with the nervous system, particulary the **brain.** The present chapter constitutes a survey of some recent laboratory, clinical, and theoretical research on the relationship between the functioning of the nervous system and psychological action. Examination of this basic problem which has long troubled psychologists will demand flexibility on the part of the reader. Moreover, while it will not supply final answers, the inquiry will be an interesting intellectual adventure.

We note, in turn, the extreme instability of the nervous system and of the organism as revealed in recent research. Can flatworms cannibalize other flatworms that have learned a maze and profit from that experience without having to undergo learning themselves? Are there pleasure centers in the brain? What happens when large areas of the brain have to be removed surgically? Does the brain "record" memories like a tape recorder? And what are some newer conceptions about the nervous system from contemporary medicine? These are the questions that concern us in the present chapter.

Neurology, unlike the other branches of medicine, has had a unique position. The skin is skin and the heart pumps blood.

But in neurology, and consequently in **psychiatry,** progress was impeded by the notion, metaphysical in the conceptual sense and emotional in its personal connotations, that the organs that are studied in neurology, such as the brain and the nervous-system organs, regulate internally man's organism and externally his relationship with his environment, with God and Nature [Marti-Ibanez, 1960, p. 361].

Experimental observation can determine the function of the skin or heart in the total economy of the organism, but, as Marti-Ibanez (p. 361) points out, "The history of neurology ... has been a gigantic conflict between dogmatic tradition and experimental observation." This is due to the dual function that tradition ascribed to the nervous system alone. Every other organ or organ system has been said to have only a biological function to perform, but the nervous system has been said to carry out its biological work as well as to act as an intelligence bureau that receives messages and sends them much like "a man within the man." Furthermore, for hundreds of years the notion has persisted that in some way the brain is altered when sensing or learning takes place and that the **"brain trace"** causes recall on a later occasion. Much work has been done in an effort to locate the place and nature of the alleged brain traces but without success.

Sperry's brain interference experiments

1

One of the theories explaining the brain integration that is supposed to occur when an organism perceives assumes that an electrical field is at the basis of the integration. R. W. Sperry (1957), among others, put this theory to the test. He first implanted numerous tantalum wires in the visual area of the cat on the assumption that they would effectively short-circuit and so distort the electrical current during perception. The cats wore the metallic inserts for months without any harmful biological consequences, and, what is of far greater interest to us, without disturbing previously acquired, very fine visual discriminations.

In another experiment Sperry (1957) generously filled the visual cortex of his cat subjects with insulating plates of mica with the intention of blocking instead of short-circuiting the supposed electrical brain currents. The results were as negative as the ones in the previous experiment.

Sperry (1957) proceeded more boldly with brain insults carried out by slicing into the visual area of cats "making the cuts as numerous and as close together as possible [p. 5]." Again, his cat subjects performed at almost their presurgical level, making very difficult perceptual discriminations despite their mutilated brains.

The **grey matter** consists of relatively small **neurons** in the top layers of the brain. The largest of the fiber bundles, the **corpus callosum,** connects the two **cerebral hemispheres** (see Figs. 2.1 and 2.2). According to Sperry (1957), it is "somewhat embarrassing to our concepts of brain organization that complete surgical section of this largest fiber tract has consistently failed in human patients to produce any clear-cut functional symptoms [p. 5]." Furthermore, with large areas of destruction of the hemisphere **cortex,** the organism can still retain a previously acquired response or learn

new discriminations "almost as well" as he did with the whole hemisphere (p. 6).

The results of Sperry's experiments are not encouraging. He concludes: "Attempts to localize in the brain the memory traces for particular habits have generally failed. The memory traces, or **engrams,** appear to be extremely elusive and diffuse, and so far have not been specifically localized or demonstrated [p. 6]."

Apparently searching in the brain for spots where perception or learning might be "stored" has been unrewarding. Certain investigators, such as Skinner (1938) and Kantor (1947), support an approach that some have called "the hollow-organism" theory. According to their point of view, it is futile to look anywhere inside the organism for the cause of its learning because nothing can be the cause of itself. They might point out that, in addition to an organism, an outside condition is necessary —that is, a stimulus object, a button to be depressed, a pattern to be discriminated, and so on. Therefore, according to this view, the function of the psychologist is to study how the organism *and* stimulus object come to be related to each other, how they interact or transact. In other words, views that look inside the organism for an explanation are **self-actional** as compared with **interactional** or **transactional** views that look outside and beyond the organism. But with only an indication of alternative points of view, we turn to another aspect of the familiar intraorganismic or self-actional approach to psychological inquiry.

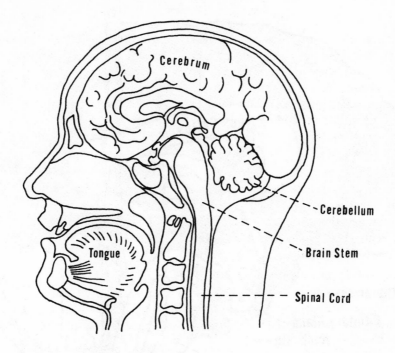

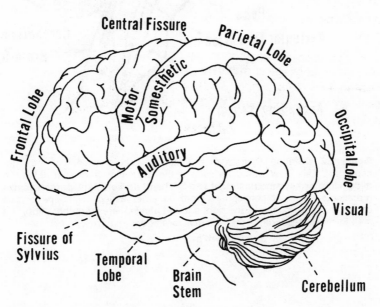

Figure 2.1 Topography of the brain. *Above:* General features, showing relationships between the cerebrum, or brain proper, the cerebellum, brain stem, and spinal cord in relation to the head and spine. *Below:* A "close up" of the cerebrum, showing the location of the motor, somesthetic, auditory, and visual areas in the various lobes of the brain and the two prominent furrows or slits, the Central fissure (also known as the Fissure of Rolando) and the Fissure of Sylvius.

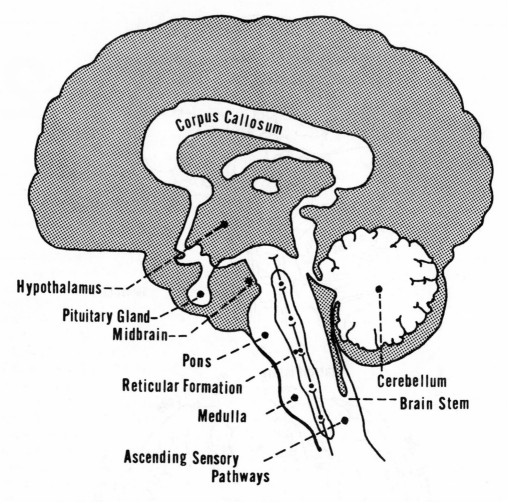

Figure 2.2 Detailed diagram of the mesial (middle) aspect of the right cerebrum. This view would be seen if the organism were split down the middle into two symmetrical right and left hand portions. The portion shown represents the right hemisphere from its inner aspect. Note the corpus callosum, which connects the right and left hemispheres. Another important area in recent research is the reticular formation.

How stable is the organism?

2

So far we have had little success in finding "spots in the brain in which 'psychology' takes place." In Bentley's (1954) terms, the search has been in pursuit of a *"Pseudo-location."* But, dropping that search for the moment, how about the nervous system in general? Does this tissue have properties that would enable it to carry memories, for example, over a long period of time? Can it somehow "register" or "record" impressions and summon them at the appropriate time? This is the question we shall consider now.

One way to study what happens to the components of any tissue in the living organism is to trace the fate of its specific atoms. Suppose you could somehow label or otherwise clearly identify some chemical that plants feed upon. You could then follow that chemical's journey through a cow that fed upon that plant and into the body of an infant who drank that cow's milk or the infant's parents who ate hamburger derived from the same cow.

Recently the creation of radioactive **isotopes** in **cyclotrons** and reactors has made it easy to identify and keep track of batches of atoms of iodine, carbon, sodium, and phosphorus that are otherwise indistinguishable from their nonradioactive twin elements. The radiations that the isotopes emit can be easily discovered by a geiger counter as readily as the fallout from an atomic explosion. Imagine unmasking one-hundred millionth of an ounce of a radioactive element even if it is diluted following

its distribution throughout a cow weighing 1,000 pounds. What a chemical detective a biologist now has for studying what happens to the atoms of an element from one moment to another in an organ or tissue!

Biologists have wasted no time in tracing the destiny of a harmless element injected into a vein or taken by mouth. The track of a **radioisotope** of iodine can be "traced" almost as accurately as the flight of a spaceship in its earthly orbit. Such experiments indicate that sodium can move through the walls of blood vessels at the rate of 50 pounds of salt a day. Within 15 seconds sodium can make a journey from one arm through the heart, lungs, and into the opposite arm. Within another 60 seconds that same element can spread throughout the organism to be excreted from the sweat glands of the opposite arm! Within 75 seconds it has come and gone. Compare this picture with one drawn in our childhood when we heard that "our bodies are completely changed every seven years." Contrast it with the following statement from Aebersold (1954):

Tracer studies show that the atomic turnover in our bodies is quite rapid and quite complete. For example, in a week or two half of the sodium atoms that are now in our bodies will be replaced by other sodium atoms. The case is similar for hydrogen and phosphorus. Even half of the carbon atoms will be replaced in a month or two. And so the story goes for nearly all the elements. Indeed, it has been shown that in a year approximately 98 percent of the atoms in us now will be replaced by other atoms that we take in in our air, food, and drink [p. 232].

Even the teeth are not to be considered permanent. The same holds for the bones and the brain tissue. In fact, the organism should be considered in the same light as the Sorbonne, the U.S. Senate, or the First Infantry. Each may carry the same identity over long periods of time, but its personnel or component parts change constantly. Your local town, city, or university goes by the same name, but change is the only constant feature of each. Consider the university; presidents and boards of trustees come and go, faculty members retire, or die, or resign, and new ones join the staff. As for students, they probably reflect the highest turnover. Surely the name that society bestows on a man over the long span of his life must blind us to the biological and psychological drama that transpires under our very noses. One fact is certain: The biological organism hardly furnishes the permanency and stability required by the conventional brain traces. For, how could "memories" that each of us will recall over as many as 20, 40, 60 or more years reside in such impermanent, perishable matter as the brain?

3 A postscript by a professor of chemistry and molecular biology*

The very nature of matter as we know it today presents a universe in constant motion. The particles which make up my person are never static, whether they be viewed as individual atoms or as an integrated aggregate. The identity which is "me" is only statistically the same as that which existed one moment ago, and the laws of probability infer that it is most unlikely that the precise relationship of atoms which make up my person will ever again be duplicated [Calvin & Calvin, 1967, p. 61].

The preceding is an extract from an address delivered by Professor Melvin Calvin at the Centennial Celebration of Wooster College, Wooster, Ohio, February 18, 1966, in whose preparation Mrs. Calvin collaborated.

Melvin Calvin is director of the Laboratory of Chemical Biodynamics and Professor of Chemistry and Molecular Biology at the University of California, Berkeley. Students and postdoctoral visitors from all over the world come to the interdisciplinary laboratory, which is engaged in solving the most intimate problems of the behavior of a living organism in molecular terms.

Summary

Up to this point in the present chapter, we have considered Sperry's brain interference studies and Aebersold's work at the Atomic Energy Commission's laboratories. Both are unsettling to any theory of brain traces. The first study indicates that learning persists in an organism with a mutilated brain. It also shows that original learning can occur in an organism despite a marked mutilation of its brain. The second study discloses how transitory are the physical elements that constitute the organism. Indeed, the geiger counter has revealed each living thing to be a kind of Grand Central Station, with elements constantly entering and departing. There is nothing static or permanent about living things.

They are dynamic, ever changing systems. So is the brain. As such, it appears to be too unstable to explain the survival of memories over several decades or even over scores of years. The Calvin and Calvin statement underscores the point.

The locus of learning in planaria 4

Most people would boggle at the thought of spending over a decade in research on worms. Not James V. McConnell. While at the University of Texas,* he developed a consuming interest in the lowly flatworm, an organism so low in the evolutionary scale that most people would consider it incapable of any learning whatsoever. The particular worm that McConnell selected for his research was *Dugesia dorotocephala*; it is the highest animal that can regenerate after it is cut into 2, 3, 4, or even 6 pieces. From 10 days to 2 weeks following mutilation, each piece grows into a complete, fully organized animal. The anatomy of planaria and their reproduction by **fission** are shown in Fig. 2.3.

McConnell's early conditioning studies

In his earliest work McConnell (Thompson and McConnell, 1955) kept each worm subject in its own custard-cup living

*McConnell is presently at the University of Michigan.

quarters. When he was ready for experimenting, he transferred the planarian to a maze (see Fig. 2.4) consisting of a plastic trough through which the planarian glided at the rate of a quarter inch per second.

Each conditioning trial lasted 3 seconds. Using two 100-watt light bulbs as the **conditioned stimulus**, McConnell flashed them on for 2 seconds, at which time he administered the subject an electric shock of 32 volts lasting one second. Thus, during the third second both stimuli were operating together. The shock evoked a decided longitudinal contraction of the animal. The light, especially in early training, was neutral. After 150 to 200 pairings of the stimuli, the subjects did not wait for the shock but cringed at the flash of the associated light. They even met McConnell's strict criterion of responding in 23 out of 25 successive trials.

Although there was no longer any doubt about planaria's ability to learn, how about retention? Could the animals retain their lesson? After an interval of about a month, McConnell found that a refresher series of 30 or 40 trials would bring his pupils up again to his former rigid criterion of 23 out

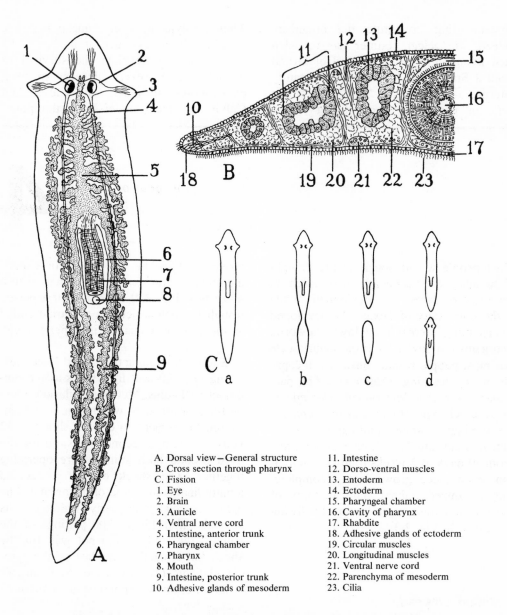

A. Dorsal view—General structure
B. Cross section through pharynx
C. Fission
1. Eye
2. Brain
3. Auricle
4. Ventral nerve cord
5. Intestine, anterior trunk
6. Pharyngeal chamber
7. Pharynx
8. Mouth
9. Intestine, posterior trunk
10. Adhesive glands of mesoderm
11. Intestine
12. Dorso-ventral muscles
13. Entoderm
14. Ectoderm
15. Pharyngeal chamber
16. Cavity of pharynx
17. Rhabdite
18. Adhesive glands of ectoderm
19. Circular muscles
20. Longitudinal muscles
21. Ventral nerve cord
22. Parenchyma of mesoderm
23. Cilia

Figure 2.3 Drawing of a planarian of the species *Dugesia dorotocephala*, used by McConnell, showing (A) general structure, including brain; (B) partial cross section; and (C) reproduction by fission. (Courtesy General Biological Supply House, Inc.; Chicago, Illinois.)

of 25 successive trials. Thus he established the fact that learning in planaria was a relatively stable phenomenon, perhaps more lasting than the hectic and perishable night-before-the-exam cramming of the procrastinating freshman.

Figure 2.4 Pioneer of learning in the planarian, James V. McConnell, observing a subject at the choice point of a T maze. Will the S choose the light or the dark arm of the T maze? The photograph illustrates McConnell's latest research area. (Reproduced by permission of J. V. McConnell.)

McConnell's regeneration studies

The planarian's remarkable power to regenerate suggested an exciting hypothesis to McConnell. Suppose he conditioned planaria and bisected them. In time, as shown in Fig. 2.5, the tail half would grow a new head and the head half, a new tail. How about retention? Would the head end alone, traditionally considered the locus of learning, profit from the experience or would the tail show some retention?

With his hypothesis formulated, McConnell (1959) and his co-workers proceeded as in their earlier experiment, using light as the conditioned stimulus and shock as the unconditioned stimulus. As soon as the animals met the former criterion, the experimenters cut them transversely in half with a sharp razor blade (see Fig. 2.6). This constituted the experimental group.

Controls How much extinction will occur during a 4-weeks' wait for planaria to regenerate and recover completely from possible shock and other effects? Instead of guessing, McConnell conditioned one group of worms to criterion and simply put

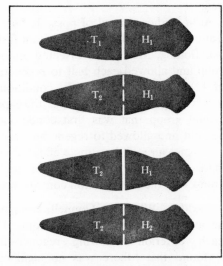

Figure 2.5 McConnell's transection and regeneration experiment. The topmost worm shows transection. The head end was then permitted to grow a new tail (T_2 as illustrated in the worm second from the top). The regenerated animal was again cut in half as represented in the worm third from top. The algebraic creature, T_2 plus H_2 (bottom worm), although not in possession of any of its original organs, seemed to show conditioning. When it was stimulated in the test trough, "it retained a significant amount of the learning acquired by its antecedent, two generations removed." (From *SK&F Psychiatric Reporter,* January-February 1963, p. 4. By permission.)

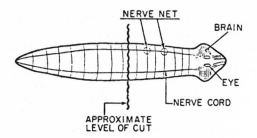

NERVE NET

BRAIN

EYE

NERVE CORD

APPROXIMATE
LEVEL OF CUT

Figure 2.6 The nervous system of the planarian (magnified many times).

them aside *uncut* for the same interval of 4 weeks until he could test for retention by retraining them to criterion the same as the regenerated group. These animals were designated Group TC, the time control group.

As a further control of possible "sensitization" from cutting and a resultant faster conditioning, McConnell bisected another group and allowed each half to regenerate for 4 weeks, at which time he conditioned them. Comparison with Group E, the experimental group that was first conditioned, then cut and allowed to regenerate, would give a measure of the simple effect of cutting as a variable. This group was labeled Group RC, the regeneration control group.

Results When McConnell compared the average number of trials required to reach criterion following regeneration, he found that "there was no significant difference between the head and the tail sections" (p. 3). Comparison of the control group that was cut and allowed to regenerate, then trained to criterion, showed no significant difference in the number of trials required by the head and tail sections either, although both groups required many more trials to reach criterion (a **statistically significant** difference) than the experimental group. Study of the group that was (1) cut, (2) allowed to regenerate, then (3) trained to criterion showed no significant difference

when compared with the experimental group's regenerated head or tail sections.

Perhaps the one most startling result of this study is the fact that the tail sections in the experimental group showed such a great savings of the initial conditioning. The results of Group RC indicate that this phenomenon is not due to any "sensitization" due to cutting and regeneration. Had the tails showed only some slight savings, it might have passed with little notice. That the tails showed at least as much savings as did the heads, and that both heads and tails showed as much retention as did uncut animals, calls for considerable cogitation and perhaps even some reorganization of our thoughts concerning the mechanisms of learning and retention in such organisms as the planarian [McConnell, Jacobson, and Kimble, 1959, p. 3].

Interpretation In considering his extraordinary results, McConnell (1959, p. 4) speculated that while the head end of the planarian is necessary for conditioning to occur at all, it is *not* necessary for its retention. But this finding raises other questions. For example, *how* did the tail sections retain the learned response? If structural changes occurred during conditioning, they must have been diffused throughout the organism. How else could one explain that, even though the tail section had to grow a new head end with its "brain" and eye spots, nevertheless "two of the tail sections in Group E gave this highly complex response in their very first trials! Did the tail sections then regenerate new ganglia with the CR already 'built in' [p. 4]?"

The RNA molecule as a memory repository

In our discussion of heredity in Chapter 4, we will consider the pros and cons of the RNA molecule as the carrier of "the

genetic code." But theorists and investigators have attributed functions other than hereditary to this giant molecule. Reductionistic thinking has also considered that RNA may possibly be responsible for indelibly recording experiences in the brain. The *conceptual* nature of RNA theories of retention is emphasized in the following critical statement by Hilgard. We quote it to contrast (1) the *fact* that organisms learn with (2) *hypotheses* or *constructs* about how they continue to perform whatever they have learned. Traditionally retention of a learned response has been thought of in terms of a "memory trace" in the brain.

Hilgard on the "memory trace" as a hypothetical construct*

Hilgard (1967) commented on the "memory trace" as a **hypothetical construct:**

> The use of the expression *memory trace* . . . requires a word of explanation. The memory trace is purely hypothetical: It is not something known or understood or something we can point to in the brain. It refers to whatever representation persists in our nervous systems of an experience that is subject to recall. We must somehow carry a representation of the experience around with us when we are not recalling it, for someone who has not had the experience cannot recall it as we can. When we say that a memory trace fades or that something else happens to it, all we are really saying is that what emerges when we attempt to recall is something different from the experience that was originally registered.
>
> When the psychologist postulates a hypothetical mechanism to explain his experimental results, he makes what is known as a *hypothetical construct*. This particular hypothetical construct means that the memory trace does

*Quoted material is from Ernest R. Hilgard and Richard C. Atkinson, *Introduction to Psychology* (4th ed.; New York: Harcourt, Brace & World, Inc., 1967), pp. 321–322.

exist and that we may some day discover its nature and perhaps learn thereby the physical processes responsible for remembering and forgetting. Hyden (1959; Hyden and Egyhazi, 1963) has proposed the theory that ribonucleic acid (RNA) might well be the complex molecule that serves as a chemical mediator for memory.

Woodger on the hypothetical construct: an exercise in scientific method

Here we should like to make a deeper and more refined analysis of the use of the hypothetical construct, whether in explaining the facts of heredity or those of learning. For this purpose we lean heavily on Woodger's (1929) perceptive discussion on the hypothetical construct in his own field of biology. Note how he develops his argument in the following summary of his position.

Some biological knowledge is stated in such terms as to be inconceivable in relation to perceptual objects, according to Woodger. The terms are purely conceptual and incapable of representation in imagination. In scientific work it is sometimes necessary to pursue the analysis of a phenomenon to the point where sight and touch give out and access must be had to submicroscopical and imperceptible concepts. Woodger warns that "since such imperceptible entities are invoked to *explain* something which *is* perceived, they cannot be logically prior to the latter [p. 280]." The proposed entities are, and will remain, *hypothetical* and unless they can themselves somehow be demonstrated by further perceptual tests, they "cannot be called scientific [p. 280]." In other words, they continue to enjoy only a tentative and hypothetical status unless and until they can be brought into some kind of relation, however attenuated, to the observed phenomena that set the stage for the observation. Additional dangers exist if we are not constantly aware of the conceptual nature of the entities in question, for we are likely to forget that "we only know such entities 'by description' not 'by acquaintance' [p. 281]." Any statements that we make about the entities in question are based only on our original observations, from which we derived notions about them, rather than on direct observation of the entities themselves. In other words, they are only inferential. "But there is a powerful tendency to forget their conceptual nature and to treat such entities as 'more real' or 'more fundamental' than what is given in perception. This easily leads to all manner of errors [p. 281]." With a last cautionary word about the dangers of reversing the importance and priority of the perceptible over the imperceptible, we once more turn to learning in the lowly flatworm, into which RNA will intrude itself in an obscure, hypothetical role.

McConnell's RNA studies

It is not difficult to see how McConnell's regeneration study of planaria made him try to pinpoint the structural change that permitted the regenerated tail ends to perform the correct response (originally acquired by the head, presumably), sometimes even on the first trial! Recent developments in biochemistry suggested RNA as a memory vehicle and so another hypothesis evolved.

This time McConnell (1962) planned to condition planaria with the same procedure as before, but he would extract RNA from the bodies of conditioned animals and inject the extract directly into the bodies of unconditioned animals. Would there be any beneficial effect of the (presumably) "encoded RNA" on the latter's learning

efficiency? A control group injected with RNA from untrained animals would provide a basis for comparison. He carried out the procedure as planned and found that, apparently, RNA from conditioned planaria injected into naive subjects did facilitate their conditioning as compared with the control group that had been injected with "plain RNA." The results electrified researchers in laboratories in the United States as well as Canada, Austria, Australia, Sweden, and Japan. We shall present a brief survey of some of their findings.

Memory transfer through cannibalism reexamined

Skepticism, dissent, and a double check of one investigator's work by another are as healthy in psychology as in any other discipline. Thus it was not long before Hartry, Keith-Lee, and Morton replicated McConnell's work with finer controls and with contradictory results.

Procedure Essentially Hartry and her co-workers used the same conditioning procedure as McConnell, with light presented as a conditioned stimulus for 2 seconds. The conditioned stimulus overlapped the third second with a one-second shock presented as an unconditioned stimulus:

$$CS \xrightarrow[\qquad US \longrightarrow]{\overset{\text{1sec} \quad\; \text{2sec} \quad\; \text{3sec}}{\longrightarrow}}$$

Their departure from McConnell's experimental method centered in the nature and number of control groups. Altogether they used 12 groups of 12 planaria each, although they did not finish with that number at the end of their study once they, of necessity and by design, introduced cannibalism.

With two worms per group, the entire series took six blocks or replications of 2 days each.*

On the first day of each replication of the experiment, four worms, later to be divided into two groups (Groups C_1 and C_2) were exposed to the light-shock conditioning procedure, and conditioned to criterion. A third group (Group L) was exposed to photic stimuli only, and a fourth group (Group S) to shock only. Each planaria in Groups L and S was matched with a conditioned worm in respect to the number of exposures to stimuli, the intervals between exposures, and the duration and intensity of the stimuli. Thus a planarian in Group L (light only) received the same number, duration, and intensity of exposures to light as a conditioned planarian. Planaria in a fifth group (Group H) received handling only. Whenever it was necessary to handle a worm which was being conditioned (Groups C_1 or C_2) during the procedure (that is, to touch it with a paintbrush or squirt it with an eye-dropper of water to stimulate gliding), the planarian in Group H (handled only) with which it was paired was treated in the same manner. The amount of handling required for any worm varied considerably, as did the intervals at which handling was necessary. On an average, however, handling was required prior to approximately 10 percent of the trials.

At the end of the first day, the conditioned planaria were randomly divided into Groups C_1 and C_2. The planaria in Groups L, H, S, and C_1 were then individually ground up and placed in labeled containers. Four groups of naive planaria which had been deprived of food for 7 days were placed one in each container, and each was allowed to cannibalize the fragmented worm therein. The planaria in the remaining conditioned group (Group C_2) were merely placed, whole and alive, in individual containers so that they could be tested again the following day to determine the number of trials required for a previously conditioned worm to reach criterion. Planaria in two additional groups

were also placed in individual containers at this point. Group F consisted of naive planaria which were each allowed to cannibalize another naive worm, and Group N consisted of naive planaria which remained unfed [pp. 274–275].

Hartry and her co-workers introduced another control at this point. After the subjects were fed, a third investigator 24 hours later transferred every worm of the seven remaining groups and coded them to conceal their identity. The experimenters then went ahead with their conditioning sessions, using the same procedure as before and the same used by McConnell at this point in his work. Independent scoring of the subjects' responses gave an overall percentage of agreement of 96.3 percent.

Results Table 2.1 gives a clear summary of the results obtained under the various experimental conditions although the statistical measures are omitted to save space. The last figures of 157.3, the number of trials on the first day that the original naive, unfed group required to reach the criterion of 23 out of 25 trials, and the mean number of CRs of 7.1 in the first 25 trials, also on the first day, are almost identical with corresponding figures of 153.9 and 7.6 obtained for the control group of naive, unfed worms that were conditioned on the second day (the only difference in treatment). Since the experimenters were working with unidentified subjects (i.e., "blind"), **experimenter bias** was thus eliminated. The fact that both sets of figures are closely similar but radically different from all the other figures lends credence to the general findings.

A point of crucial interest, one comparable to McConnell's findings, concerns the results obtained for the cannibals that ate the preconditioned planaria. These subjects required an average of only 67.5 trials to reach criterion and gave a mean of

*Quoted material is from Arlene L. Hartry, Patricia Keith-Lee, and William D. Morton "Planaria: Memory Transfer Through Cannibalism Reexamined," *Science*, 9 October 1964, **146**(3641), 274–275.

Table 2.1

Results of Hartry, Keith-Lee, and Morton's Experiment

Group number	Experimental condition of subjects	Mean number of conditioning trials to reach criterion of 23 out of 25 CRs on second day*	Mean number of CRs in first 25 trials of second day's retention test
1	Cannibals of planaria exposed to light only	58.0	16.9
2	Cannibals of planaria receiving handling only	60.8	14.7
3	Cannibals of planaria that had been conditioned	67.5	13.9
4	Planaria that had been conditioned only (i.e., not cannibalized)	69.9	12.7
5	Cannibals of planaria exposed to shock only	88.3	11.6
6	Cannibals of naive, unstimulated (i.e., unconditioned) planaria	90.0	10.2
7	Naive, unstimulated, unfed planaria	153.9	7.6
1.2	*Initial* performance of Groups 1 and 2 above on first day (naive and unfed).	157.3	7.1

13.9 CRs out of the first 25 retention trials. This compares favorably with cannibals of naive (unconditioned) planaria with corresponding means of 90.0 and 10.2, respectively. The results seem to support McConnell's conclusion until we compare figures for the cannibals of the planaria that were exposed to comparable amounts of (1) light only and (2) shock only, results even superior to those obtained for the consumers of learned worms. These findings hardly support McConnell's "transfer of memory" concept because retention of conditioning was not involved. Besides, mere feeding alone seems to have a beneficial effect, as indicated by the results of cannibals that consumed naive or "ignorant" worms.

What do the results mean? While Hartry and her associates admit that they have not

*Except for the last figures; these represent the *first day's performance* of Groups 1 and 2, serving as a control for Group 7's conditionability, which was delayed to the second day.

proved that memory transference did not occur, they suggest the more conservative hypothesis that metabolic or nutritional factors somehow sensitized or activated the subjects—no matter what they seemed to do, their subject learned more effectively.

To summarize, the locus of learning in the planarian has not yet been pinpointed, but McConnell's work has certainly stimulated much research and even more controversy. One sometimes thinks that had McConnell's results implicated the planarian brain as the seat of learning, he would have been approved and famous. Instead he outraged the defenders of the brain dogma, who sometimes even question his sincerity. Meanwhile McConnell continues to study worms.

A U.C.L.A. study

Shifting from planaria to rats, Babich, Jacobson, Bubash, and Jacobson (1965) carried out a study that seemed to support McConnell's results. They trained rats in a **Skinner box** to approach a food cup via a click sound produced by the pellet dispenser. No food was given at any other time either in or out of the box. Each rat was given 200 food-reinforced approaches to the click of the food cup for 4 days and 100 more on the fifth day. A control group of rats received the same amount of food as the experimental group but no training.

When the training of the eight experimental rats was completed, they were killed, their brains removed, and RNA extracted from the brain tissue. RNA was also extracted from the brains of the control group. Then 17 new untrained rats were injected, 8 with RNA from trained rats and 9 from RNA from untrained rats. The investigators worked with them "blind,"

not knowing to which group any subject belonged. The procedure involved a total of 25 test trials with click alone (no food) in five sessions spaced out at 4, 6, 8, 22, and 24 hours after injection.

Results The total number of responses per animal (see Table 2.2) shows a preponderant advantage in the case of the experimental rats, who averaged 6.86 responses to the click sound alone without food, compared with a mean response of one for the control group. The differences between the means were statistically significant. The rats injected with RNA extracted from the brains of their click-trained predecessors are distinctly superior to rats injected brain-extracted RNA from untrained rats. Thus McConnell's findings seemed to be confirmed once more. However, the Babich team cautiously suggests that "although it appears most reasonable that the observed effect was produced by RNA, the possibility should not be overlooked that other substances in the extract might have been involved [p. 657]" They also add that *if* there is a coding mechanism, how does "the injected material affect the behavior of the recipient animal [p. 657]"?

Table 2.2
Total Number of Responses to Click Alone (no food) per Animal on the 25 Test Trials

Experimental rats	Control rats
1	0
3	0
7	0
8	1
9	1
10	1
10	2
	3
Mean = 6.86	Mean = 1.00

Another U.C.L.A. study

Encouraged by the results of the above study, Babich, Jacobson, and Bubash (1965) decided to cross species lines. They trained eight male hamsters to approach the food cup when it made the click sound. Eight control hamsters were run simultaneously, but, unlike the experimental group, they received no food at the click sound. After 500 trials, all 16 animals were sacrificed and their brains processed for RNA extraction. The experimenters then selected 16 rats and injected 8 with RNA extracted from the brains of the experimental hamsters and 8 with extract obtained from the control hamsters. The injection was made into the body cavity as in the earlier experiment. Next, they habituated the rats to the Skinner box in four daily 15-minute sessions and ran the test sessions "blind." Results again gave the experimental rats a distinct advantage: a mean of 7.9 responses out of 25 click-presentation trials contrasted with a mean of .6 for the control rats. The difference between the means was once more statistically significant. The results seemed to indicate that learning effects can even cross species lines or at least that the U.C.L.A. rats learned at the expense of U.C.L.A. hamsters' efforts.

Contradictory findings

New theories stimulate new research even though the results do not always provide clear-cut answers to the questions raised. This fact has certainly been true of investigations of a biochemical memory carrier, as these recent studies show.

Walker and Milton's research at the University of Victoria in British Columbia Walker and Milton (1966a) interpreted McConnell's results more parsimoniously in terms of tissue sensitization rather than "memory transfer." In testing the suggested hypothesis, they took ten groups of four planaria each. Five groups constituted the cannibals and five were cannibalized. Four of the cannibalized groups were simply shocked every 30 seconds in blocks of 50 trials per day. They received no conditioning or any other treatment. The total number of shocks varied as follows: Group 50 received 50 shocks; Group 100, 100 shocks; Group 150, 150 shocks; Group 200, 200 shocks. Group 0 was given no shocks. Twenty untreated cannibals were then treated to their shocked colleagues. Results showed an increasing mean number of CRs in 75 trials of the cannibals in increasing proportion to the number of shocks administered to their ingested species members. A CR was defined as

a sharp right or left movement of the cephalic region; or as a longitudinal contraction of the entire body . . . A CR was recorded if either one of these two responses occurred during the 2 seconds of light prior to onset of shock [p. 293].

The 0, 50, 100, 150 and 200 trial-shocked "meals" corresponded to the following mean CRs: 18.00, 18.75, 24.00, 24.50, and 29.50. Walker and Milton suggest that since their subjects were given only shock and not a shock associated to light, McConnell's notion of "memory transfer" could not apply to the "savings" demonstrated by their cannibals. The results did, however, support their sensitization hypothesis, according to which "a tissue change occurs due solely to shock [p. 294]."

Memory transfer as an artifact of the experimental variables This time Walker (1966b) used planaria in 8 groups of six Ss each, 4 groups as cannibals and 4 to be cannibalized. Two groups were matched as closely as possible for the number of trials to reach a criterion of 13 CRs out of 15 consecutive trials. One of the groups, E, was then given 25 extinction trials, followed 24 hours later by an additional 25 extinction trials, after which it was killed and fed to Group EC. The matched control group, X, was killed upon attaining criterion and fed immediately (before **extinction** had a chance to set in) to Group XC. A Group L received exposure to light and Group S to shock. Both were killed and fed to Groups CLC and CSC, respectively. All groups received comparable amounts of exposure to stimuli.

Results The chief data concern the mean number of CRs in blocks of 25 that were made by the cannibal groups over the course of 75 conditioning trials. First, by comparison with the original conditioned Group X (uncannibalized), all the cannibal groups failed to show progressive conditioning effects that Group X Ss showed. But how about cannibals that ate extinguished worms by comparison with cannibals that consumed previously conditioned worms? "The two groups behaved quite similarly with regard to the total number of CRs emitted, but the EC Group (cannibals of extinguished worms) did not show as steep a decline in the number of CRs over blocks of trials [p. 358]." Essentially, however, all the cannibals acted pretty much alike, showing that it made little difference whether they fed on worms full of learning, empty of learning, full of light or full of shock. Again, the facts favor a nonassociative sensitization hypothesis over McConnell's and Babich's memory transfer theory. The early stabilization (or absence of a learning curve) in the alleged conditioning of the cannibals over the 75

trials added additional support to Walker's approach.

Miscellaneous studies

It is obvious that McConnell's original work really stirred things up. In concluding the discussion on the locus of learning in planaria, let us simply note whether findings have been pro or con. Luttges, Johnson, Buck, Holland, and McGaugh (1966) of the University of California at Irvine made an exhaustive study with mice and rats in a variety of learning situations. They report that "findings of 'transfer of learning' via RNA reported by others were not corroborated in our laboratories [p. 837]." Since injection of RNA into the body cavity seemed to show no significant amounts in the brains of donor animals because of a presumed blood-brain barrier, they injected RNA directly into the ventricles of the brain but again no "transfer of learning" effect was noted.

Gross (1965) at Harvard University and Carey at Woods Hole Oceanographic Institute "failed twice to reproduce the results of Babich *et al.*" discussed above.

We have seen that some investigators claimed to have successfully extracted RNA from brains of hamsters and rats while others failed to do so. In an attempt to settle this point, at least, Enesco (1966) relied on radioactive RNA "to determine whether or not exogenous RNA becomes directly incorporated into brain tissue [p. 640]." "The results...show that the radioactive bases of $C_2{}^{14}C_8$-RNA are incorporated into both the DNA and the RNA fractions of liver, kidney, and intestine, but not into muscle or brain [p. 643]."

The final and most eloquent commentary on the role of RNA in memory transfer can be found in the following statement in *Science* (Byrne, 1966): "In 18 experiments no clear evidence of a transfer of any one of these kinds of training from trained donors to recipients was found [p. 658]." The statement is signed by 23 investigators connected with seven institutions from the East and West Coasts of the United States and from McGill University in Canada. Of course, this may not be the last word on the subject.

---

5 *"Pleasure centers" in the brain: James Olds' work with rats*

Although exploration of the brain for possible centers has a long history, our consideration of the topic is restricted to several recent studies. James Olds' (1958) interesting work with rats as subjects will serve as one illustration.

In planning his research Olds was first confronted with the problem of how to get below the brain surface. Even with humans, the cortex has permitted fairly easy access, as the work of Penfield has shown. Work involving the interior of the brain is a different matter. Capitalizing on techniques developed by earlier workers, Olds decided to use a fine needle electrode that could be inserted into the deep portions of the brain and fixed into a permanent position without any harm to the brain or animal itself. Then, whenever he chose, he could use such a rat as subject simply by plugging the electrode into an electrical circuit, which permitted Olds to shock the rat in specific spots within the inner brain. To help him measure the rewarding value of shocking a specific brain spot, Olds adopted the Skinner box, thus arriving at the laboratory setup shown in Fig. 2.7.

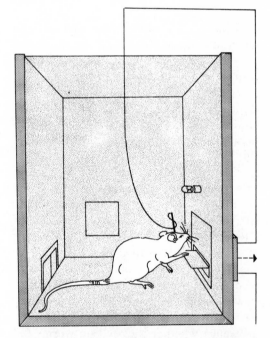

Figure 2.7 Schematic diagram to illustrate self-stimulation in the rat (after Olds). Note the electrode implanted in rat's brain and its connection with one pole of a circuit. When the rat depresses the lever with his foot, he closes the circuit and, thus, administers a shock to his brain at the point of the implanted electrode. Release of the lever opens the circuit and terminates the shock.

Discovery of pleasure centers

Olds was now ready for some unexpected observations. As a base line, he found that the rat would randomly press the bar of the Skinner box about five times an hour without any reward. But when it was given a pellet of food for every bar press, its rate increased to 100 or more times per hour. Different stimuli were found to have different rates.

Early in his work, Olds aimed the electrodes at the rat's **reticular system** in the upper part of the brain stem. However, it was not always possible to hit the target that precisely—a blessing in disguise, for eventually he accidentally hit the **rhinencephalic** nerve instead of the reticular formation. It was this spot that was later confirmed as the pleasure center.

Using a large box with four corners, A, B, C, and D, Olds found that when such a rat was given a mild electric shock after it returned to corner A, it would tend to return to corner A. At the time Olds credited the rat's behavior to curiosity, but he began to think otherwise when he found that he could just as easily shape the rat's behavior into a "fondness" for corner B or C or D by administering a shock when the rat tended to go in a given direction or, for that matter, to any other location in the box.

Further work eventuated in a "do-it-yourself" project for the rat. When the rat happened to press the bar, he thereby administered a shock to himself. After two or three responses of this apparently haphazard sort, the subject soon increased the frequency of bar pressing to one or two per second. The shock was a low-level stimulus lasting half a second. If the rodent continued to hold the pedal longer than half a second, the current went off automatically, requiring release of the pedal and another press in order to obtain another shock. The rat soon learned to shock himself rapidly so that his response rate shot up to an almost incredible 7,000 presses per hour. But when the locus of stimulation was moved forward from the **hypothalamus** and upward toward the cortex, response rates dropped anywhere from 5000 to only 200 per hour. Primary rewarding effects seemed to be "located in a midline system running from the midbrain through the hypothalamus and midline **thalamus** and into the subcortical and cortical groups of the rhinencephalon [1958, p. 324]." According to Olds, the pleasure derived from the rat's self-stimulation of his pleasure center was "in some cases at least twice as strong as a 24-hour hunger drive [p. 319]." When permitted to press the bar for 24 or even 48 hours consecutively, rats kept going to the limit of their physical endurance.

Punishment centers

Electrical stimulation of most parts of the rhinencephalon and many parts of the hypothalamus and related structures (see Fig. 2.2) elicited higher rates of bar pressing. Olds interpreted this as a discharge of the pleasure center which activated the rat's bar-pressing behavior. Further work showed that not all electrode implants produced these results. In fact, some brain areas had the very opposite effects. An attempt at achieving a random sampling of midbrain and forebrain points involved implanting 76 electrodes in a series of rats. Of the total of 76 electrodes, 47 had motivational consequences. Of the 47, 36 yielded approach behavior, 11 produced avoidance behavior. This convinced Olds that "there are anatomically separate mechanisms for reward and punishment in the brain [p. 315]." The latter were located in restricted areas of the midbrain and in certain adjoining parts of the thalamus and hypothalamus. Excellent craftsman that he was, Olds sectioned and stained each brain and verified his findings from a **histological** analysis of the brain specimens. He concluded that the area involved in producing avoidance behavior was much smaller than the area eliciting approach behavior.

An alternative explanation It is questionable if a shock applied to any portion of the brain is dissipated at the point of application and thus confined to a brain center. In fact, it seems reasonable to assume that the shock is transmitted to other portions of the organism that have nervous connection at the point where the electrode is implanted. When the shock comes along, the current travels along the pathway to, let us say, the rat's genitalia, stimulating them to reflex arousal in a manner no different in principle from external stimulation of the same region. The same might be true of tissues and organs involved in thirst and hunger. How about punishment centers? The differential results secured with stimulation of points that did not elicit continuous and rapid bar pressing could be

explained as follows. If electrodes implanted in certain regions are neurologically connected with some peripheral muscle, then the only result of a shock transmitted at the electrode would be a reflex contraction, as in the muscles of the paw, for example. The rat's inevitable response to the muscle spasm induced by the shock is a pain reaction. This simple and alternative theory is proposed cautiously and undogmatically as a suggestion to add interest to our discussion. In fact, the following quotation from Olds could easily be translated into the nonbrain language of the alternative theory proposed here simply by substituting tissue and organ terminology in place of the neurological vocabulary:

Further studies indicate that the electrical brain-shock reward has the effect of a strong primary reward object in several different experimental situations. These studies suggest also that the electric brain shock excites cells which are normally involved in the mediation of the effects of conventional primary reinforcers, such as food and sex objects [Olds, 1958, p. 318].

Perhaps examination of Heath's work on self-stimulation in the following section may throw further light on the question.

6 Heath: "Electrical self-stimulation of the brain in man"*

Olds' brain studies on rodent subjects and Heath's (1963) work with humans are complementary because each was able to get at

*Quoted material is from Robert G. Heath, "Electrical Self-stimulation of the Brain in Man," *The American Journal of Psychiatry,* December 1963, **120** (6), 571–577.

dissimilar aspects of behavior. One distinct advantage that Heath had was a possibility of talking with his subjects and getting their reactions to the total situation.

Subjects Heath's subjects were two male patients, B-7, age 28, and B-10, age 25.

B-7 suffered from (a) severe **narcolepsy,** which precipitated him from alertness to deep sleep within a second and from (b) **cataplexy** or sudden attacks of extreme muscular weakness that left him limp. Because B-7 failed to respond to conventional methods, Heath attempted more radical measures. Profiting from work on intracranial self-stimulation (ICSS) conducted at Tulane on infrahuman animals, Heath adapted the technique similar to that used by Olds and implanted 14 electrodes in predetermined regions of B-7's brain, both in its superficial and deeper portions.

Patient B-10, who carried a diagnostic label of **psychomotor epilepsy** with sporadic brief periods of impulsive behavior, also failed to respond to usual treatments. Like a human pincushion, B-10 walked around with 51 electrode leads implanted into 17 different brain sites, both within the deep layers of the brain and on the cortex. In order to eliminate postoperative shock and other undesirable factors, ICSS was delayed with both patients for an interval of 6 months following lead implantation.

Stimuli Because the two patients presented such different therapeutic problems, they were handled differently. Both, however, carried a specially designed transistorized self-contained unit attached to their belts. Each unit contained three buttons, depression of which delivered a shock via whatever electrodes were connected with the buttons (see Fig. 2.8). Connections could be changed by the experimenter, but control of button pushing and, therefore, of stimulus delivery was in the hands of the patients. A mechanical counter coupled to each button gave a record of the number of presses that the subject delivered to a given brain area. Continuous stimulation was prevented by an internal timer built into the

Figure 2.8 Patient with self-stimulation device capable of stimulating his own brain electrically by means of switch box at waist. (Photo courtesy of Dr. R. G. Heath.)

apparatus; this feature limited stimulus duration (as with Olds' rats) to .5 second for each button press. The three buttons also permitted hooking up various combinations of brain-site stimulation.

In the case of B-7, the three buttons of his unit were attached to electrodes in the **septal** region, **hippocampus,** and **mesencephalic tegmentum.*** He was free to choose whichever button he liked best.

---

*The beginning student of psychology should not be overwhelmed by these terms. It is enough for him to know that they refer to different areas in the deep interior of the brain.

Before he started wearing the stimulator for a 17-week period, a base line was obtained of the amount of time he spent sleeping during an arbitrary 6-hour period each day. This was done to help determine possible improvement in his narcolepsy.

Patient B-10, the psychomotor epileptic, participated in a different experimental design. Since it is incidental to the discussion developed here, I mention it briefly. The main point involved the stimulation of a variety of possible combinations of brain sites, because animal studies indicated that rate of stimulation of a given site was a function of the site that had just been stimulated. However, another part of the study dealt with which brain site was preferred.

Results Patient B-7 pressed almost exclusively the button that delivered a shock at the septum, deep within the brain. Stimulation at another point (the mesencephalic tegmentum) proved aversive. He considered the button for the septal region most rewarding because it overcame his narcolepsy. In fact, his fellow patients soon learned which button roused him, and, when he fell asleep too suddenly to push the button himself, they would push it for him.

Why did he like to push the septal button? Perhaps, in some respects at least, men are like rats. The following quotation from Heath's report tends to relate results of the two studies.

The patient, in explaining why he pressed the septal button with such frequency, stated that the feeling was "good"; it was as if he were building up to a sexual **orgasm.** He reported that he was unable to achieve the orgastic end point, however, explaining that his frequent, sometimes frantic, pushing of the button was an attempt to reach the endpoint. This futile effort was frustrating at times and described by him

on these occasions as a "nervous feeling" [p. 573].

Results with patient B-10, the epileptic, hardly differed from those with B-7, as the following report indicates:

The patient most consistently reported pleasurable feelings with stimulation to two electrodes in the septal region and one in the mesencephalic tegmentum. With the pleasurable response to septal stimuli, he frequently produced associations in the sexual area. Actual content varied considerably, but regardless of his base line emotional state and the subject under discussion in the room, the stimulation was accompanied by the patient's introduction of a sexual subject, usually with a broad grin. When questioned about this, he would say, "I don't know why that came to mind – I just happened to think of it." The "happy feelings" with mesencephalic stimulation were not accompanied by sexual thoughts [p. 574].

Patient B-10 reported several other brain sites as furnishing pleasurable feelings but of lesser degree than his preferred septal point of stimulation.

Another interesting sidelight of Heath's experiment was captured in a 16-mm. sound film involving patient B-10. On one occasion, when the patient was in a violent psychotic state, the stimulus was administered to him without his knowledge. There was an almost instant change from rage and disorganization to a quiet, happy, mildly **euphoric** condition. When questioned, B-10 admitted the beginning of a pleasurable sexual state. According to Heath, similar results have been obtained consistently in a large number of patients (footnote 6, p. 575).

Alternative interpretations As in the Olds study, the question again is: How to interpret the results? Are there "pleasure" and "punishment centers" in the brain? Or do some points of rat or human brains have more intimate and direct connections with rat or human genitalia? Is it really a center that is producing the pleasure or pain, or is the organism responding to an organismic condition at the point terminal to the point of stimulation? Perhaps the question cannot be answered here and now, but perhaps the mere asking is important.

Smith and Burklund: Results of the surgical removal of the left ("dominant") hemisphere*

7

In right-handed and right-eyed people, the left hemisphere is believed to be more important than the right, and thus is referred to as the dominant hemisphere. What would happen if the entire left cerebrum of such a person were to be removed as carefully as possible through surgical procedure? Such an experiment could never be carried out humanely, at least not on a human, but sometimes nature helps out.

E. C., a 47-year-old, right-handed, right-eyed male unintentionally became such a guinea pig. He came to the attention of Doctors Smith and Burklund (1966) with complaints of speechlessness and seizures in the right arm and right face. Five months later a tumor was removed from the sensorimotor area of his left hemisphere. A weakness on his right side pointed to a recurrence of the tumor and so, a year after the first operation, the *entire left hemisphere* was removed in one piece.

The sequelae The immediate results were a paralysis on the right side, loss of sight on the right half of the visual field, and severe loss of speech. His ability to follow simple commands showed that hearing was normal and that there was some comprehension of speech. Later hearing tests showed some bilateral hearing loss above 4000 cycles per second.

Immediately after the operation the patient uttered words and short phrases fairly well, but he took several months to repeat longer sentences on command. "In the fifth postoperative month, E. C. showed sudden recall of whole familiar songs, and he now sings with little hesitation and with few errors in articulation [p. 1280]."

Other responses Learning to print showed some improvement, but writing indicated little subsequent progress. Vocabulary, as tested by the Peabody Picture Vocabulary Test and in conversation as well as in performances demanded on other psychological tests, showed continued improvement. His intelligence test results awarded him a preoperative IQ of 100. Four and five months later and with only half a brain, his IQs were, respectively, 108 and 104. His arithmetic reasoning and ability to multiply, add, and subtract and to count money improved remarkably in the 6-month period following **hemispherectomy.**

Further improvement was noted:

---

*Quoted material is from Aaron Smith and C. W. Burklund, "Dominant Hemispherectomy: Preliminary Report on Neuropsychological Sequelae," *Science,* 9 September, 1966, **153**(3741), 1280–1282.

Marked variability in attention span and in susceptibility to fatigue and distractability, reported following right hemispherectomy in similar cases, was also observed in E. C. shortly after hemispherectomy but gradually decreased. However, "loss of personality values," reported after right hemispherectomy, was not observed. The affective reactions and general behavior that were observed before and after hemispherectomy were appropriate, and they were consistent with the report from the patient's wife that there was no noticeable change in emotional responses or in a basically well-balanced personality.

The patient E. C. can now tell time; he moves about independently in his wheel chair, keeps appointments on other floors in the hospital (requiring use of the automatic elevator) without being reminded, and has been going home for weekend visits since 26 March 1966. **Libidinal** drives were reported normal. Most important, perhaps, he demonstrates a capacity to enjoy and participate in human relationships despite his marked disabilities [p. 1281].

Smith and Burklund (p. 1281) conclude "hemispheric functions would seem to differ quantitatively rather than qualitatively [p. 1281]."

Summary Six months after complete removal of the left half of his brain, a 47-year-old male not only survived but also showed gradual improvement in speech, reading, writing, walking, and IQ with no reported change in emotional response or in "a basically well-balanced personality [p. 1281]." The results point to quantitative rather than qualitative differences in the functions of the right- and left-hemispheres.

Comment Some people would almost anticipate a 50-percent reduction in E. C.'s postoperative IQ following hemispherectomy. They are amazed not only at the lack of radical losses of behavior but also at his gradual improvement. Why? Only because of a culturally built-in set of dogmas about the brain that the facts will not support. Any sound psychological theory must somehow incorporate the data revealed in E. C.'s case as well as those that do show severe behavior disruption.

8

Nielsen and Sedgwick:
Observations on a
brainless monster*

It is a truism that for a child to flourish psychologically it should be as biologically sound as possible. Biological structures are participating factors in psychological events and, as such, condition them. A child born defective "has one or two strikes against it," depending on the abnormality.

*Quoted material is from J. M. Nielsen and R. P. Sedgwick, "Instincts and Emotions in an Anencephalic Monster," *Journal of Nervous and Mental Disease*. November 1949, **110**(5), 387–394.

Sometimes, an infant's embryological development goes amiss to such an extent as to produce a monstrosity (Figure 2.9A, B, C). Nielsen and Sedgwick (1949) report a case that is included here because it shows how an organism maintains its integrity as an organism despite a gross absence of such an important organ as the brain.

The case The infant, a male, was the third of three children; the other two being normal. The most striking feature was the absence of the bony top or vault of the skull, which left its skimpy brain open to view. Inspection showed a **cerebellum** but no **cerebral cortex,** or brain proper. In fact, there was total absence of structures above the midbrain. The brain membranes can be seen (in Fig. 2.9) protuding through the skull at the front in a tumorlike growth **(meningocele).** To the left of it, one can spot an abscess, which was the cause of the infant's death after 85 days of life (including a successful recovery from chicken pox).

Functions observed What can one expect in an infant with such a glaring deformation? After thorough inspection of the visual structures, the examiner concluded that there was no perception of light. However, what is amazing is what happened in other reactive areas, as shown in the following excerpts from the medical report.

Sucking and crying were normal. Loud sounds elicited the **startle reflex,** a fairly organized reaction. The tongue functioned normally, for occasionally the infant was observed licking his lips. He was even observed frequently raising his head off the pillow! He usually kept his arms bent and his legs extended. Painful stimuli applied to hands and legs elicited withdrawal.

Another source of interest to the examiners, shown in the following quotation,

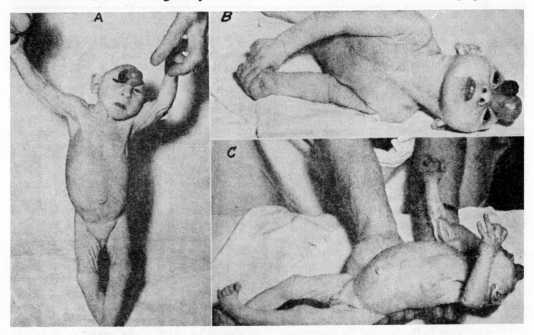

Figure 2.9 (A) With the legs in decerebrate extension the patient hangs from the examiner's little finger by his own strength (grasp reflex). (B) Patient on his left side in repose. Note highlights on tongue as he protruded it to lick his lips. Limbs are not in decerebrate rigidity. (C) Moro "reflex." As the patient is dropped an inch, the arms are thrown up and out. The lower limbs remain in extension. (From J. M. Nielson and R. P. Sedgwick, "Instincts and Emotions in an Anencephalic Monster," *The Journal of Nervous and Mental Disease,* November 1949, **110**(5), 387–394. Reproduced by permission of the authors and publisher.)

was the feelings and emotions exhibited by the infant.

If we handled the patient roughly, he cried weakly but otherwise like any other infant; and when we coddled him he showed contentment and settled down in our arms. When a finger was placed into his mouth, he sucked vigorously. When he was held supine on the extended hands and dropped 2 inches he would throw his arms out in fear then flex them when he again came to rest. He would sleep after feeding and awaken when hungry, expressing his hunger by crying. When the examiner's little fingers were inserted into his grasp, he would hold firmly and hang for at least half a minute (Fig. 2.9A); he was never allowed to fall and hence the total duration of hanging was not determined [p. 394].

Summary and implications We have examined the case of a "brainless" human without a shred of cerebral cortex or related white matter. Despite the gross abnormality, the defective infant showed a number of reflex responses and even more complex and integrated reactions. Such reactions as waking, sleeping, crying, contentment to appropriate stimuli, pain, licking, sucking, and raising the head were observed. The implication of this case seems to be that the organism always presents a united front. Despite the absence of an important organ of integration—namely, the cerebral cortex—the infant acted in ways long thought impossible for a creature without a brain.

9 Thompson, Huff, and Wass: "Migration of bullet in gunshot wound of the brain"*

The patient, a boy 8 years of age, was riding a bicycle, looking back over his shoulder at a companion who, running to catch up with him, tripped and fell, discharging a .22 caliber rifle. The bullet, after traveling a distance of 40 or 50 feet, struck the patient in the right forehead just below the hairline and he tumbled from the bicycle. He was semiconscious when picked up by his mother some 20 or 30 minutes later. About an hour after the accident the patient, stretched out on the back seat of an automobile, was observed by one of the authors. In a state of moderate shock, he was pallid and sweating and the pulse was weak. The patient said he had heard a shot and had fallen from the bicycle.

He was taken to the hospital for treatment, and evidence of shock subsided. Neurological examination was done several hours later and the boy then was conscious and rational. Reflexes were equal and active and the Babinski response was not evoked.

X-ray films of the skull showed the wound of entry in the right **frontal** region and the major portion of the bullet resting in the left **parietal** area, just under the bone. Fragments of the bullet were distributed from the point of entry to the point at which the major portion of the bullet came to rest. Fragments of the bone were present in the right frontal area adjacent to the point of entry.

Antibiotic therapy was administered, and in the ensuing few hours no evidence of progressive neurological involvement developed. Early the following morning, the wound of entry was opened and debrided. Devitalized brain tissue and a few fragments of bone and metal were removed. Then the wound was closed. Antibiotic and **anticonvulsant therapy** was administered and the patient recovered. There was no sign of neurological impairment and the patient was discharged from the hospital.

Anticonvulsant therapy was continued.

*Quoted material is from C. Verner Thompson, Tom Huff, and Warren Wass, "Migration of Bullet in Gunshot Wound of the Brain," *California Medicine,* July 1957, **87**(44), p. 44. Reproduced by permission of the author and publisher.

X-ray films taken at intervals thereafter showed the bullet to be migrating back toward the point of entrance (see Fig. 2.10). Although no attempt was made to keep the patient prone while asleep, he was instructed to lie in the prone position while awake and to jar his head gently against the bedding from time to time. Approximately 5 weeks after the accident, the bullet had returned almost to the point at which it had entered. Thereupon the main portion and a fragment of the bullet and several fragments of bone were removed from a point just inside the skull.

In the next year and a half no evidence of residual injury to the brain developed. No abnormalities were noted upon examination and the parents reported no changes in disposition or in personality. The patient returned to school, where he adjusted to classroom routine and appeared to have no loss of retentiveness.

Approximately 10 years later, the following progress report showed further normal progress. Writes Dr. Thompson:

This young man progressed normally through his school program, and I was recently informed by his father that he was in the process of joining one of the armed forces. The story of this accident, according to him, called for a rather careful evaluation before he could be accepted.

But he made it. A popular notion exists that the brain, as the little black box, is a precious and vulnerable organ. The case discussed above shows the contrary. Even an injury incurred by a bullet migrating through the brain of a boy for 5 weeks produced no apparent psychological defects either soon after or even 10 years later. Apparently, like the heart and other organs, the brain can withstand crises.

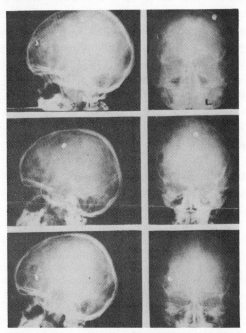

Figure 2.10 *Top row:* X-ray films on day of accident, showing fragments of lead along course of bullet from point of entry in right forehead to point at which major portion came to rest against skull on left side. *Center:* Films taken a week later, after fragments of slug had been removed, showing main body of bullet returned part way along course of penetration. *Lower:* Five weeks after the accident, bullet almost back to point of entry. (From C. Verner Thompson, Tom Huff, and Warren Wass. "Migration of Bullet in Gunshot Wound of the Brain," *California Medicine,* July 1957, **87**(44), 44. Reproduced by permission of author and publisher.)

An excerpt from the report of a stroke victim* **10**

Eric Hodgins has had a distinguished career. As an author he is best known for *Mr. Blandings Builds His Dream House*

*Quoted material is from Eric Hodgins, *Episode: Report on the Accident Inside My Skull* (New York: Atheneum, 1964). By permission of the author.

and *Blandings Way*. He has achieved equal eminence as managing editor, editor-in-chief, and publisher of *Fortune* and as *Time's* general manager. One morning when he was 61 years old and living alone in an apartment in New York, he started preparing his breakfast. While returning the orange juice to the refrigerator, he was bewildered to find that he missed the door by a wide margin. At the same time, he lurched across the kitchen floor, but was able to seize hold of the dishwasher for support.

Nothing more happened until late afternoon of the same day. This time Hodgins was at the phone.

It was then that it happened. To my shock and incredulity, I could not speak. That is, I could utter nothing intelligible. All that would come from my lips was the sound *ab*, which I repeated again and again and again.... Then, as I watched it, the telephone handpiece slid slowly from my grasp, and I in my turn slid slowly from my chair and landed with a softly muffled bump on the floor behind the desk. It all seemed to be happening in slow motion, and in an astronaut's weightless universe. That my universe was not weightless was later attested by a sharply barked shin—the only visible scar on my body as the result of something that had happened, a moment before, inside my skull.... There I was on the floor. I knew instantly what had happened to me: I had "had a stroke" [pp. 7–8].

Hodgins' crushing experience, a cerebrovascular accident, or CVA as it came to be called, left him paralyzed on the left side so that walking and even standing were annihilated. Speech and memory were impaired. Intensive physical and psychological rehabilitation were immediately instituted, but depression and suicidal tendencies delayed rapid recovery, for this was "the deepest hole I ever fell into in my life [p. *vii*]."

"After a CVA you are not the same person as before. The changes may be slight, but they are changes [p. 254]." One of the changes brought an incompetence with buttons and typewriters, but three ballpoint pens later brought Hodgins' unedited version of his report to an end.

...as for CVAs in general a million persons a year have them in the U.S. alone. Of these, 200,000 die, leaving 800,000 alive, with varying degrees of incapacity of course, but think of Reinhold Niebuhr, think of Edward Steichen, think of countless others less renowned who have surmounted what they have had to surmount. From the past, think of Pasteur, think of Handel, think of Walt Whitman. Louis Pasteur was the classic case of cases; his stroke was heavy, yet his very finest work was done after it, and with its burdens [p. 61].

11

The brain as a tape recorder*

As head of Montreal's Neurological Institute, Dr. Wilder Penfield has operated on

*Quoted material is from Wilder Penfield, *The Excitable Cortex in Conscious Man,* 1958. Courtesy of Charles C Thomas, Publisher, Springfield, Illinois.

numerous patients for epilepsy. His usual procedure involves injecting local anesthesia into the scalp before opening the skull (see Fig. 2.11). With the brain exposed and the patient fully conscious, Dr. Penfield explores the surface of the patient's brain, which, contrary to popular opinion, is so insensitive that the patient cannot tell when his brain is touched and when it is not. The surgeon explores the surface of the brain with an electrode that transmits a gentle current to the cortex.

"Interference" and "activation"

In a series of studies Penfield found several interesting results that he could classify either as *"interference"* or as *"activation"* effects. For example, when he applied an electrode to the visual area, the patient reported that he saw "lights, coloured forms or black forms, moving or stationary [p. 11]." The patient also reported simultaneous difficulty in normal seeing of the visual field before him. As Penfield observes (p. 11), the "interference" that he speaks of is considered a local, brain condition at the point of stimulation, while "the activation" applies to the distant portion of the organism that is connected with that **cerebral** part. In the preceding example the patient's "seeing" lights, etc. illustrates "activation," and his inability to see what was actually in his visual field is "interference."

Sensory responses Suppose Penfield were to stimulate the patient in the area of the brain just behind the **Fissure of Rolando.** (See caption for Fig. 2.1). The patient would report a numbness or tingling

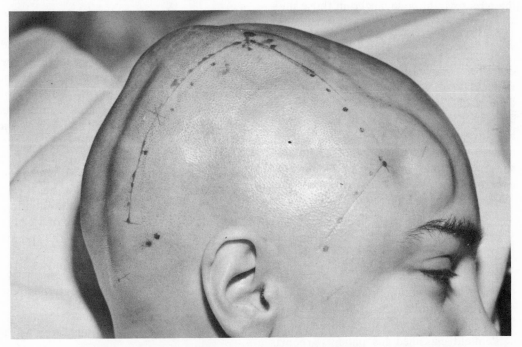

Figure 2.11 The patient M.M. on the operating table. The scalp incision has been outlined after infiltration with nupercaine. (From Wilder Penfield, *The Excitable Cortex in Conscious Man*, 1958. Courtesy of the author and Charles C Thomas, Publisher, Springfield, Illinois.)

on the side opposite to the point of stimulation. It is interesting to note again that the part affected during brain shock was incapacitated as far as use of that body part was involved in some voluntary or required response.

Motor responses   Stimulation of the motor area just in front of the Fissure of Rolando produced movements that occurred despite the patient's attempt to inhibit them. If a portion of the cortex connected with the contralateral hand or a foot were stimulated, that part would move like a reflex. Simultaneous attempts to make voluntary movement of that part would be interfered with if they coincided with application of shock at the brain site concerned. Of course, with stimulation of midline structures such as tongue or jaw, the effect would be localized in those midline parts.

"Psychical responses"   The reactions described above did not at all astonish Penfield and his coworkers. Since the Franco-Prussian War in 1870, when soldiers with open head wounds were available for study, such results have been described. But what came as "a complete surprise [1958, p. 20]" was touching the electrode to the patient's **temporal lobe** (which has connections with the ears) and getting a psychological response instead of the sensory or motor response described above.

Experiential hallucinations and interpretive illusions

Penfield classified his patients' reports into one of two classes: (1) experiential **hallucinations** and (2) interpretive hallucinations.

Case M. M. The patient was a woman of 26 years who was afflicted by recurring cerebral seizures. The first manifestation of each attack was a sudden "feeling—as though I had lived through this all before." At times there was also a feeling of fear. On other occasions she experienced what she also called a flashback...

The initial feeling of familiarity she described as applying to the whole of any experience she might be having at the moment. On the other hand, the flashbacks were experiences from her earlier life. They came suddenly while she retained awareness of her actual surroundings. She gave the following example: Without warning she seemed to be sitting in the railroad station of a small town, which might be Vanceburg, Kentucky, or perhaps Garrison. "It is winter and the wind is blowing outside and I am waiting for a train." This was apparently an experience from her earlier life but it was one she had "forgotten" [pp. 25–26].

The epileptic discharges from the temporal lobe, the site of which was later confirmed by means of diagnostic laboratory procedures, had caused this young woman to duplicate experiences that she had had during her past epileptic seizures. The sense of familiarity illustrated an illusion, the emotion experienced was a feeling of fear, and the reproduction of a previous experience illustrated a hallucination. As a control, sometimes Penfield applied the electrode and sometimes he would not. The subject had nothing to report when the electrode was not applied to her brain although she had no way of differentiating. The following is a sample record of M. M.'s reports from stimulation at the points specified:*

14 (just posterior to 15). This stimulation caused her to say: "The whole operation now seems familiar."

Warning without stimulation. "Nothing."

15   "Just a tiny flash of familiarity and a

---

*Quoted material is from Wilder Penfield, "The Interpretive Cortex," *Science*, 26 June 1959, **129** (3365), 1719–1725.

feeling that I knew everything that was going to happen in the near future." Then she added, "as though I had been through all this before and thought I knew exactly what you were going to do next."

At point 17, an electrode, covered with an insulating coat except at its tip, was inserted to different depths and the current switched on and off at will so as to stimulate in various buried portions of the superior temporal **convolution** and **uncus** (see Fig. 2.12).

17c (1 cm deep) "Oh, I had the same very, very familiar memory, in an office somewhere. I could see the desks. I was there and someone was calling to me, a man leaning on a desk with a pencil in his hand."

Warning without stimulation. "Nothing."

11 (40 minutes after first stimulation of this point). "I had a flash of familiar memory. I do not know what it was."

13 (repeated three times). "Nothing."

11 (after 4 minutes). "Nothing."

Conditions seemed to have changed and stimulation now would summon no experiences [pp. 29–30].

Penfield's theoretical formulation of his observations

From his observations during electrical stimulation of the patient's cortex and the same patient's behavior during an epileptic discharge, Penfield (1958) concludes that "the cortex is rendered more responsive to electrical stimulation by the proximity of a discharging epileptogenic focus for years before the operation. This probably conditions the cortex for readier response here

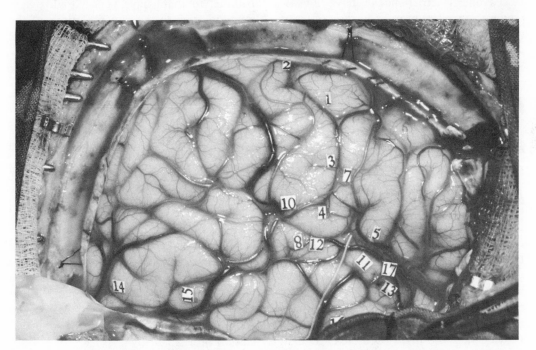

Figure 2.12 Case M.M. Right cerebral cortex exposed; points of stimulations which produced positive responses are marked by numbered tickets dropped on pial surface. (From Wilder Penfield, *The Excitable Cortex in Conscious Man,* 1958. Courtesy of the author and Charles C Thomas, Publisher, Springfield, Illinois.)

[i.e., in the temporal lobe], as it does in the sensory and motor areas [p. 23]." In other words, according to Penfield, the electrode must "trigger" a sorting out of experiences mediated exclusively by the temporal lobe of the brain, never by any other area.

When the neighboring visual sensory area of the cortex is stimulated, any patient may report seeing stars of light or moving colors or black outlines but never "someone coming toward me." Stimulation of the auditory sensory cortex may cause any patient to report that he hears ringing, buzzing, blowing, or thumping sounds, perhaps, but never voices that speak. Stimulation in the areas of sensory cortex can call forth nothing more than the elements of visual or auditory or tactile sensation, never happenings that might have been previously experienced [Penfield, 1959, p. 1723].

"Psychical experiences" have *consistently* occurred only outside the region of the auditory sensory area of the temporal lobe. How are they "stored" and "revived"? Says Penfield (1958): "When we understand the nature of that influence or alteration we will understand the real function of the sensory cortex [p. 13]." We might add that the same holds for the other areas of the cerebral cortex. But where could such a "storage" area be located? Apparently not in the temporal lobe. Why not? Because large areas of destruction here do not interfere with production of "psychical responses." For this reason and still others, Penfield believes that this "storing," "sorting," and "comparing" function is mediated in the midbrain, or centrencephalic area, or in the upper part of the brain stem (1958, p. 38). Recent work has increasingly demoted the "higher centers" so that functions formerly attributed to them have been paradoxically imputed even to the upper portions of the brain stem, a most puzzling development!

12 An alternative interpretation of Penfield's results

Penfield's theory of "the interpretive cortex" is a hypothetical one based on a dualistic view. He frankly admits that neither "the work of Sherrington [Penfield's teacher], Pavlov, or any other scientist has yet proven the complete identity of brain and mind or demonstrated how brain action is converted into thought and thought into brain activity [Penfield, 1958, p. 5]." Proving how the brain "secretes" thought or how thought is "transmuted" into bodily activity remains to be done.

A more economical theory is proposed in competition with Penfield's. This one does not choose to assume that the brain "produces" sensations or thoughts. Instead it assumes that psychological events require a wider field than one confined within the organism, as Penfield's theory demands. Always there are an organism and a stimulus object; for example, in the case of Penfield's (1958) patient M. M., "Vanceburg, Kentucky," "the railroad station of a small town [p. 26]" or a flashback to a scene of "a lumber yard [p. 29]." Why then exclude the factors located outside the organism?

But what role does the brain play in an

alternative theory? A very simple and unglamorous role. Let us return to the situation in which we stimulate various points on the patient's exposed brain. Let us apply a low-intensity shock just behind the Fissure of Rolando and the patient reports tingling and/or numbness in the contralateral hand. What has happened? Is it so preposterous to assume that the current has traveled down the fiber tracts connecting that part of the brain with that hand? Actually, wires between the end points would work as well. Or, is the situation very different from that in which the electrode is applied directly to the hand *externally* rather than via the nerves? I suggest that, as far as the end result is concerned, in both cases the person is interacting with, or responding to, a condition localized in his hand, in other words, a stimulus-response situation. Reflex twitchings as discussed by Penfield above could be handled the same way. Naturally the organism cannot inhibit the contraction of the muscles involved any more than he could if he were unintentionally to grab hold of a "hot wire."

What of the patient who, upon electrical stimulation of his brain's visual area, reports seeing "lights, coloured forms or black forms, moving or stationary" but never actual persons coming toward him? These reports always seem vague and ambiguous. Again I would suggest that if the electrical current involved activates the eyes via the nervous pathways, real sights before the patient must, of necessity, be suppressed and his report takes on the same quality as when the person closes his eyes and presses gently against his eyeballs. Let the reader try this and he will experience "lights, coloured forms or black forms, moving or stationary." Such "**phosphenes**" have been known for centuries but have not been connected with the radical

and rare electrical stimulation of eyes via brain as achieved by Penfield. How else can the organism react when his eyes are stimulated in this (visually) unclear fashion? He does the best he can under the circumstances similar to the way in which he exploits the barren situation under conditions of sensory deprivation.

The same explanation is suggested when electrical stimulation of the auditory cortex "causes the patient to hear buzzing, humming, ringing, or hissing sounds or he may complain only that he is a little deaf [Penfield, 1958, pp. 12–13]." We again seem to have interference as indicated by the subject's complaint of deafness and exploitation of the vague activation of ears. What else can an organism do by means of his ears except hear. "He makes the best of it" and interacts with the condition in terms of past interactions. "Ringing in the ears" is, after all, a common experience, sometimes caused by too much aspirin or other drugs. However, it is questionable that a person without prior experience with actual rings would report "ringing in his ears."

Critique of "psychical responses"

How about "psychical responses"? Penfield (1958) distinguishes clearly between the sensory and motor reports just discussed and the reports that his patients gave of the revival of past experiences. Several comments are necessary. First, it is not clear what role suggestion played, or what controls were made beyond the occasional nonapplication of the electrode followed by a request for the subject's report. We are told that in the latter case the subject reported nothing. Yet in one of the foregoing samples of M. M.'s reports, repeated stimulation with the electrode "would summon no experiences [Penfield, 1958, p. 30]"!

The vagueness of patients' reports also requires comment. How are we to interpret the following statement from the same patient, M. M., upon stimulation of point 17c? "Oh, I had the same very, very familiar memory in an office *somewhere*. I could see the desks. I was there and *someone* was calling to me, *a man* leaning on *a desk* with a pencil in his hand [italics added, p. 30]." Either the "interpretive cortex" is interpreting most inefficiently or the patient is cooperating as best she can to produce what is unwittingly expected of her by the surgeons.

Another criticism is the ready acceptance of the patients' reports as a reliving of his or her past experience. At least, Penfield's report makes no mention of any check on the validity of the patient's recall. Ideally, of course, one should have film and/or tape recordings of at least significant events of the subject's life against which to make comparisons. Some check surely is required.

On one point it is easy to agree with Penfield; that is, when he insists on the differences between his patients' simple sensorimotor reactions, on the one hand, and the complex psychical responses that he elicited by stimulating the superior and lateral surfaces only of the temporal lobe and not the auditory sensory areas that yielded the vague ringings and buzzings. Besides the validity of these reactions as

duplicates of past experiences, let us handle them as responses. A possible clue is furnished in the following comment from Penfield (1958) about psychical responses: "These simple reenactments of experience had auditory and visual elements in them [p. 29]." Could it be that these areas involve more widespread (e.g., *inter*-sensory) portions of the organism? The fact that auditory *and* visual elements are involved would tend to support my hypothesis. The lack of specific interference effects would lend corroborative evidence. The customary vagueness of reports would also fit the argument. Note again M. M.'s comment upon stimulation of her interpretive cortex: "I had a flash of familiar memory. I do not know what it was [Penfield, 1958, p. 30]."

An alternative to the "brain-as-a-tape-recorder" theory suggests that an electrode, whether involving the organism specifically or more generally, furnishes stimulation of one sort or another and not in the insensitive brain (as postulated by traditional brain dogma) but in his sensitive or responsive portions, that is, sense organs or muscles. These activities, acting as substitute stimuli, integrate with other related activities, past or present. The alternative theory does its work by connecting S-R units of the shock situation with other relevant S-R units of the organism. Rather than forcing the brain to carry the entire theoretical burden, it incorporates the stimulus objects involved. Theoretical choices can always be made, for there are no "musts" in scientific explanation.

Some salient comments about the brain by Riese* **13**

One of the most formidable critics of the dualistic notion of the brain's work is Dr. Riese, a neurologist and historian of medicine. The following excerpts and summaries of his work can merely highlight the problems that have puzzled psychologists for hundreds of years.

The flexibility and plasticity of the brain

...contemporary neurosurgeons [have been] performing for therapeutical reasons excisions of entire lobes and even hemispheres in the human subject. The student of cerebral localization remains impressed by the great tolerance of the brain, animal and human, the minimal and often only transient effects resulting at times from maximal destructions and the recovering power of the mammalian brain particularly striking in young individuals [p. 96].

The brain has the same characteristics as any other organ

Can we hope to express what is generally called "higher mentality" in terms of motion and thus relate it to the brain? We have to keep in mind that the brain has no mysterious qualities distinguishing it from other organs and assigning to it an exceptional place relative to other organs. The brain has a definite size, shape, weight, color, consistency, and texture. All those qualities are spatial in character. We cannot expect to detect in the brain other than spatial phenomena [p. 20].

Concerning the argument from structure to function

Though in...[a] most remarkable passage, written about 400 years ago, Vesalius did not refer to Galen, he argued in the same way as Galen, who, 1500 years earlier, was reluctant to derive from the comparative study of mammalian brains any conclusion as to greater or lesser intelligence of animals having more or less complicated brains. Galen taught that it is the quality (of the psychic **pneuma**), rather than the mass and the configuration, that accounts for greater intelligence. In spite of these early warnings, many a nineteenth-century anatomist indulged in painstaking and hopeless efforts to project outstanding abilities on circumscribed areas of the brain surface, if not to explain man's gifts, thoughts, and achievements by over-developed cerebral convolutions. Although nobody would deny to a genius the great importance of his brain, a genius is more than just his brain [p. 82].

The brain has not been the only seat of the soul

The doctrine of the seat of the soul and its numerous variations do not constitute one of the glorious chapters in the history of human search for truth and knowledge. To almost every organ was given the privilege of being the abiding place for the soul and this alone must arouse suspicion against the legitimacy of the doctrine [p. 85].

Is the brain represented in the brain?

In simple terms: if all parts of the body are represented in the brain, where is the area of representation for the brain, which in itself is nothing more than a part of the body? A flat denial of this logical consequence would leave

*Quoted material is from Walther Riese, *A History of Neurology*. (New York: MD Publications, Inc., 1959.) Reproduced by permission of the author and publisher.

to the brain an exceptional if not mysterious power and position among all other organs. In brief, it would pave the way for brain mythology [p. 93].

The frontal lobes as the seat of intelligence

As far as human intelligence or any of its departments are concerned, these are ever-changing functional wholes, whose anatomical counterparts or representations cannot be compressed into small compartments of our brain. Human intelligence not only surpasses the frontal areas, it also includes them as a fraction of human knowledge gained by faithful observation, critical comparison, and intelligible interpretation. After all, we owe it to our intelligence and to our intellectual training that we can study, define, and measure the frontal areas; but these areas do not teach one to be intelligent. Should there be a successful teaching of intelligence, credit should be given to the teachers rather than to the frontal association areas [pp. 112–113].

The argument from a disturbance of function due to injury to its locus in an uninjured brain

Psychic processes as such cannot be localized. Simply to deny the fundamental difference between physiological and psychological, in order to overcome the difficulties experienced at all times by all thinkers dealing with this subject, is but evasion and not solution, since the fact remains that we experience thinking, feeling, emotion as intrinsically psychic and never as physiological states; in other words, we are not conscious of the neuroanatomical and neurophysiological processes underlying psychic states, but of these states themselves. The nature of the hypothetical physiological processes underlying psychic states is unknown.

In so far as an investigator makes positive statements concerning the functions of the frontal lobes on the ground of brain-experimental and brain-pathological experiences, he revives an old error in method, namely, to pass

from disturbed function produced by a local lesion to the seat of the undisturbed function in the same region [pp. 116–117].

What does recovery of function following injury signify?

The phenomenon of recovery itself was no longer compatible with a system operating on a purely mechanical basis. A machine does not repair itself once it has suffered damage and become disordered, but a living individual may regain movement and speech lost after destroying a brain **lesion.** In each of the principles called forth to explain the recovery of lost cerebral functions, the interdependence of the parts is implied as an explanatory principle of greatest power [p. 126].

What does an injured part of the brain teach us about the function of that part when intact?

There has been accumulated from the enormous study of cerebral localization an imposing body of observations allowing the physician to reach a regional diagnosis, that is to localize brain lesions: the refinement of this diagnostic procedure is not equaled by any other organ. The physician may indeed be able to predict with accuracy the local involvement of a few square millimeters of the most intricate cerebral or spinal tissues.

An entirely different problem is raised when we try to localize nervous and mental functions, undisturbed or not. Neither the effect of an artificial stimulation, never occurring under natural conditions and not simulating faithfully the natural function, nor the effects of destruction or removal can teach us the functions of the unstimulated or undestroyed areas. Even the operating of a machine, when deprived of one of its major pieces and still continuing to function, would not teach us the functional significance of the destroyed part in the intact machine; but that is just what the doctrine of cerebral localization was understood to teach [pp. 146-147].

Your brain and our phone system are a lot alike

Figure 2.13 Today, under a prevalent materialistic, mechanistic world view, it seems natural to think of the brain as a mechanism. The analogy of the telephone system depicted in this advertisement furnishes a convenient conceptual model for the brain. This advertisement is an example of the prevalent reinforcement for such analogies present in our culture. Enrollment in an anatomy course is not required to learn to think about the brain in this way. (Reproduced by permission of American Telephone and Telegraph.)

Does recovery of speech following injury argue for a speech center?

It seems that, in a general sense, recovery does not speak in favor of a cerebral localization of functions. If a brain-injured individual recovers movements or speech, one presumes that other areas are "taking over" the functions lost. It is obvious from this assumption that more than one area can perform the same function, whether from the outset or through training. Why not turn to the whole brain as one great single but plastic center, acting always in its entirety, but never in fragments? A given constituent may be the leading one under certain circumstances and constellations difficult to assess in their entirety; the same constituents may be minor under other circumstances, but never the only ones in action. Be this as it may, the assumption of more than just one center implied in substitutional activities is no longer compatible with the basic tenet of cerebral localization, according to which each cerebral area is credited with a function of its own [p. 147].

Not localization of functions but localization of lesions

It seems inescapable to conclude that there is neither localization of functions nor localization of symptoms, which are but disordered functions; the only type of localizations remaining is that of lesions. With this statement, we have reached the maximum of indisputable generalities we may derive from cerebral localization; it is a minimum of novelty and almost a triviality. Instead of speaking of cerebral localization, we should be satisfied with the less prejudiced, less involved, and more cautious concept of vulnerability of a given function or behavior to regional lesions. Thus is saved the regional or local importance of brain lesions, without, however, making the unconfirmed and untenable assumption that nervous and mental functions reside in local areas of the brain [p. 148].

And how about absence of defects following brain injuries?

We let ourselves be unduly impressed by the severe defects that indeed result from brain lesions. We also allow ourselves to underesti-mate, if not to ignore or to leave unanswered, those cases in which serious brain wounds or injuries were not succeeded by corresponding mental disturbances [p. 148].

Summary

Here are the essential points Riese has made about the brain, listed concisely in their proper order:

1. Apparently the brain is not an organ that has a strictly critical construction, as shown by transient or minor results after extensive removal of brain tissue.

2. As an anatomical organ, the brain has features in common with other organs — shape, size, color, etc. — nothing that other organs do not have.

3. The idea that special aptitudes and "talents" are correlated with special brain attributes is no longer common. "A genius is more than just a certain kind of brain."

4. The brain has not always been the seat of the soul or mind. The liver and the kidneys have been so designated, and, for the Greeks, the heart had this special honor, as attested by our linguistic fossil, "learning by heart."

5. If every other organismic part is represented in the brain, where is the brain represented?

6. Should our frontal lobes or our teachers get the credit for our intelligence?

7. Is it proper to argue from (a) a disturbed function due to an injured brain site to (b) the same function undisturbed in the same spot of an uninjured brain?

8. The recovery of speech following brain injury seems to argue for the interdependence rather than the independence of brain parts.

9. We should be most cautious in drawing conclusions about the functions of

the normal brain from brain injuries or from the stimulation of the brain with electrical currents.

10. "You can't eat your cake and have it." If you argue for a speech center and the patient recovers his speech following brain injury, it is not logical to argue that now another center for speech has "taken over."

11. There is not localization of functions in the brain but localization of lesions or injuries.

12. The brain always acts in its entirety, never in fragments.

Some epigrammatic statements by Riese* 14

"The organism cannot be dismembered as long as it has life." *Verbally only,* we can talk *as if* cerebellum, thalamus, heart, or lungs were as detachable as a carburetor, spark plug, or magneto, but in the intact, living organism, they are integral parts of the whole organism.

"Nothing *can't* be the cause of something," quoting Hughlings Jackson. Applicable to a hole in the head as a cause of **aphasia.** How can *absence of flesh* produce speechlessness? Is it rather that an injury has an *interfering* effect on a function?

"No destroyed organ can teach us about the intact organ," quoting the French physiologist, Claude Bernard. An injured brain will teach you about injured brains, but not how that brain functioned when it was whole.

"Speech is not localized anywhere in the brain; it requires the whole brain as its *instrumentality.*" The implication is that the brain is a participating and a necessary or instrumental factor in speaking rather than a cause of speech or a spot that produces speech.

"If cerebral localization of speech were a fact (instead of the hypothesis which it is), how could there ever be recovery of speech?"

*From an address given by Walter Riese before the Sigma Xi Club at Wichita State University, 26 September 1966.

Chapter summary

In considering the relationship of the nervous system to psychology, we first noted the tradition that imputes both a biological and a psychological function to the nervous system. Its described dual duties give it a unique place among all the other systems of the organism.

As a test of the psychoneural doctrine, we examined the brain-insult experiments of Sperry with discouraging results and, as an alternative view, we simply noted the "hollow-organism" theory.

In further pursuit of "brain traces," we considered the instability of the biological makeup of the organism as revealed by radioisotope research.

Regenerating planaria and work in brain centers produced additional problems in attempts to localize learning. It was then logical to inspect the puzzling results of brain injury and of the surgical removal of large amounts of brain tissue.

Finally, we considered some unfamiliar propositions from a medical historian about the nervous system in relation to psychological inquiry. The final outcome? The problem is far from settled.

3

Race and psychology

Our basic question in the following selections centers around the problem of the relationship between race and psychology. The problem is immediately complicated by the failure of anthropologists to agree on a definition of race. Adopting a tentative definition of race as an ethnic group (i.e., one distinguished by common traits of *any* sort), we shall examine such groups as "the black Jews of Harlem" and an "invisible race" in Japan. We shall also discuss the possibility that our ancestors of 100,000 years ago may have had the same psychological potential that we have today, and we shall consider the case of a young American of European ancestry who was a Chinese through and through. How do these topics help us understand the connection between a person's racial membership and all the variety of reactions that he comes to perform? We shall try to find out.

They are "a lazy, apathetic people, eating coarse food and indifferent to the arts and comforts of life." Backward and inferior, they have failed to produce "a good poet, a capable mathematician, or a man of genius in a single art or a single science." These charges sound suspiciously like a racist stereotype of Negro Americans; but actually they were made by influential European writers in the late eighteenth and early nineteenth centuries

against *all* Americans. These assertions were part of a widely accepted theory of "American degeneration," which held that no people could prosper in the severe climate of North America and thus indolence, apathy, ill-health, and stupidity would forever mark Americans.*

The foregoing statement has a modern ring. Yet it is possible that some human group has always thought some other group inferior. Certainly such **sociopathy** is prevalent enough in our own times. Nazi racial dogma is a case in point. Today, the term *racism* is common currency in the American political arena and in our news media. The question of the inherent equality or inferiority of certain races is often raised and is often the subject of heated debate. Thus it seems a legitimate topic for our consideration. Specifically the problem may be stated thus: What is the relationship between race and behavior?

The proper starting point should be an attempt to pin down the term race. Unfortunately, the students of man most closely involved—that is, the **anthropologists**—are themselves in disagreement, as the following excerpts show. Some argue for the concept; others deny the existence of race.

*Quoted material is from *News of Van Nostrand Books,* 17 July 1964.

Coon's defense of race

1

According to Carleton Coon (1965), there has long been, and still is, great confusion about the definition of race. For him, "race is a zoological concept meaning a division of a **species.** A species is a collection of

animals that will breed together when they get a chance and will not breed with other animals—whether they can do so successfully or not—except in desperation or by mistake [p. 5]." Thus all humans are members of one species. On this last point, all investigators agree; beyond this point, there is wide disagreement.

Coon proposes a subclassification of the human species into the Caucasoid, Mongoloid, Australoid, Congoid, and Capoid. The Congoid includes the Negroes and Pygmies of Africa; and the Capoid includes the Bushmen, "and, in a mixed state, the Hottentots, Korana, and Sandawe (of Tanzania). Like the Congoid, the Australoid subspecies is further divided into full-sized Australoids and hereditary dwarfs usually called Negritos [pp. 6–7]." Coon goes on to consider other populations, such as the Maya Indians of Guatemala and some villages in isolated portions of Switzerland, both of which are short statured. However, nutrition and hygienic conditions have practically eliminated the ·condition, and they are not considered "racial dwarfs" (p. 7). Consequently, Coon would raise both the dwarfed Pygmies and the dwarfed Negritos to a subspecies level, which with the other five normal-sized groupings would give us seven races of the human species (p. 7). But because the dwarfed and full-sized Australoids can be combined, as can the dwarfed and full-

sized Congoids, he usually talks about the five races of the human species listed above.

Racial intermediates

Since members of the human species can and do intermarry and breed, this, according to Coon, has led to a complication, particularly between neighboring racial groups. The offspring of such mixed marriages are, of necessity, hard to classify. Where they have appeared with great frequency (as do **mulattoes**), they have given rise to what Coon has labeled, "racially intermediate, or so-called *clinal* populations [p. 7]." The fair skin, blue eyes, and blond hair that appear with greater frequency in northwestern Europe since the retreat of the Ice Age is one such **cline.** Coon suggests that, given adequate time and interbreeding, a "Nordic race" or some other could come into being the same way as the original races did (p. 9). "Thus, if we grant that clinal populations are just as real as populations of nuclear racial regions, we can give everyone a racial name after all [p. 9]."

2 What is a "race"?

When a person sees a Negro and a white man, or a white man and an Indian, standing side-by-side, his eyes seem to "prove" to him that "races" do in fact exist. It is not that simple for the anthropologist, at least not for Ashley Montagu (1963), who makes a painstaking analysis of this concept in his book, *Race, Science and Humanity.*

Montagu's criticism of the "race" concept*

Montagu believes that, as popularly con-

*Quoted material is from Ashley Montagu *Race, Science and Humanity.* (Princeton, New Jersey: D. Van Nostrand Company, Inc., 1963.)

ceived and as defined by some anthropologists,

> The belief in "race" is a widespread contemporary myth in the Western world. It is the modern form of the older belief in witchcraft. I refer here to the popular belief in "race," the belief that "race" is a something about the individual and the group of which he is a member that is characterized by a peculiar and indissoluble union of physical and behavioral traits. These traits are inherited, it is popularly believed, and account for the differences in individual and cultural achievement between the "races." The "races" that have achieved most are obviously biologically "superior," so it is reasoned, to those who have achieved less. There is, therefore, so the argument runs, a natural hierarchy of "races" [pp. *iii-iv*].

Montagu criticizes what he calls the "omelette" conception of "race" as a statistical artifact which has no correspondence to the world of reality (pp. 5–8). The conception is, therefore, artificial and perpetuates error and confusion. Properly used, the term "race" as Montagu sees it applies only to *populations* or *groups of individuals* possessing some common features that distinguish them as a group from other populations. Thus race is a relative and comparative term designating, for example, "white people" versus "black people." There is no harm in referring to them as such as long as one realizes that each group is not homogeneous but is itself variable and overlapping with some members of the contrasting groups. Or, to put it another way, most of the members of each group resemble each other more than they resemble most of the members of the other (comparison) group. The foregoing is a much looser definition of race than the absolutistic notion of the man-in-the-street who sees no difficulty in classifying people because he has no way of knowing when he has misidentified a member of a given "race."

There are no absolutes

If a well-read layman were asked whether James Meredith or Harry S. Murphy was instrumental in the Negro's admission to the University of Mississippi, he would probably recognize and connect the former name with that significant advance in civil rights. But the following quotation from a letter by Fried (1964) to *Science* raises doubts and, at the same time, reinforces the point of the inexactness of "race."

> Harry S. Murphy claims that he, not James Meredith, was the man who broke the color bar at the University of Mississippi. That few people in our society will identify Murphy as a Negro is patent from his acceptance at that institution, but he says he is a Negro and apparently has the genealogical evidence to prove it. "Prove it," that is, by the implicit—and in the legal codes of some states explicit—rule of descent that says that anyone with any Negro ancestor is a Negro. There are good grounds for making the statement that by that standard just about everybody in the United States is a Negro. Marvin Harris (1964) has expressed this very well:
> Genetically speaking, about the only thing any racist can be sure of is that he is a human being. It makes sense to inquire whether a given creature is a man or a chimpanzee, but from the point of view of genetics it is nonsense to ask whether a particular individual is a white *or* a Negro. To be a member of a biological race is to be a member of a population which exhibits a specified frequency of certain kinds of genes. Individuals do not exhibit frequencies of genes; individuals merely have the human complement of genes, a very large but unknown number, most of which are shared in common by all people. When a man says "I am white," all that he can mean scientifically is that he is a member of a population which has been found to have a high frequency of genes for light-skin color, thin lips, heavy body hair, medium stature, etc. Since the population of which he is a member is necessarily a **hybrid** population—actually all human races are hybrid—there is no way to make certain that *he himself* does not owe a

genetic endowment to other populations...The **archaeological** and **paleontological** evidence quite clearly indicates that there has been gene flow between Europe and Africa for almost a million years.... All racial identity, scientifically speaking, is ambiguous. Wherever certainty is expressed on this subject, we can be confident that society has manufactured a social lie in order to help one of its segments take advantage of another [p. 55].

There is only one species of mankind

According to Montagu, although the fact of variability among humans is undisputed, on one point today all anthropologists agree—namely, that "all the varieties of man belong to a single species, *Homo sapiens* [p. 62]." Through migration and isolation over a long period of time, they evolved the attributes (skin color, hair texture, body proportions, etc. that distinguish them today. The following factors (which we need not go into here) are assumed to have played a role in the evolution of such anatomical differences: **natural selection, mutation, isolation, genetic drift,** hybridization, and **sexual** and **social selection.** It is assumed that these factors probably determined the visible variations by which we loosely categorize humans today as "races." But these variations quite obviously do not prevent members of different "races" from interbreeding, which is the criterion of a species. "A species, then, is a group of populations. The group is the species, the populations are the races.... A "race" is one of the group of natural populations comprising the species [p. 15]."

The term race, then, stresses group differences. How about similarities? On this point, according to Montagu (p. 10), research and observation have shown that individuals of *all* the human races carry the same **chromosome** number in their cells, they are all interfertile, and blood from one race can serve as a transfusion for a member of any other race as long as blood types are respected. These features make them all members of the same species.

Ethnic group—not "race"

Having worked hard to refine usage of the term race, Montagu is ready to discard it. *Why?* Because both the concept and the term, originating as they did from common sense and not from scientific inquiry, are "confused and emotionally muddled [p. 64]." As a substitute for race Montagu suggests **"ethnic group"** (p. 64), a more general and noncommittal term. However, this is not a mere changeover from one term to another, for **ethnic group** also calls for a change of viewpoint or conception.

What are the advantages of **ethnic group** over race? Well, for one thing, the latter term points to one of the group of natural populations referred to above but without the absolutistic explanation that goes with the term race. A population can maintain its difference or differences from another population through such isolating mechanisms as geographic or social barriers (p. 67). Montagu's suggestion is appealing because it acknowledges the operation of nonbiological (i.e., historical, social, psychological, or physical) conditions in isolating and thus differentiating a group.

Taking the great white race away from today's racists is like taking candy from a baby. There are sure to be shrieks and howls of outrage. But it will be very hard to take away this piece of candy, because, to drop the metaphor, nothing is harder to expunge than an idea. The white race is not a real, hard fact of nature; it is an idea.

In 1959 a young anthropologist named Philip Newman walked into the very remote village of Miruma in the upper Asaro Valley of New Guinea to make a field study of the Gururumba. It was late that first afternoon when it began to dawn upon his native hosts that he had made no move to leave. Finally, a man of some rank plucked up his courage and said, "How long will you stay, red man?"

Most people are probably amused, but a few will be puzzled and chagrined to know that what passes in our own culture as a member of the great white race is considered red by some New Guineans. But when did anyone ever really see a *white* white man? Most so-called white men are turned by wind, rain, and certain kinds of lotion to various shades of brown, although they would probably prefer to be thought bronze. Even the stay-in who shuns the sun and despises cosmetics would rarely be able to be considered white in terms of the minimal standards set on television by our leading laundry detergents. His color would likely be a shade of the pink that is a basic tint for all Caucasoids. (That, like *"Caucasian,"* is another foolish word in the service of this concept of race. The Caucasus region, as far as we know, played no significant role in human evolution and certainly was not the cradle of any significant human variety.)

No breaks in skin color, only continua

Actually, even the generalization about pink as a basic skin tint has to be explained and

qualified. In some people the tint of the skin is in substantial measure the result of chemical coloring matter in the epidermis; in others there is no such coloring matter, or very little, and tinting then depends on many factors, including the color of the blood in the tiny capillaries of the dermis. Statistically there is a continuous grading of human skin color from light to dark. There are no sharp breaks, no breaks at all. Since nobody is really white and since color is a trait that varies without significant interruption, I think the most sensible statement that can be made on the subject is that there is no white race. To make this just as true and outrageous as I can, let me immediately add that there never *was* a white race.

While at it, I might as well go on to deny the existence of a red race, although noting that if there was such a thing as the white race, it would be at least esthetically more correct to call it the red race. Also, there is not now and never has been either a black race or a yellow race.

To deny that there are differences between individuals and between populations is ridiculous. The New Guineans spotted Dr. Newman as an off-beat intruder as soon as they clapped eyes on him. Of course, they were noticing other things as well, and some of those other things certainly helped to make the distinctions sharper. After all, Newman was relatively clean, he had clothes on, and, furthermore, he didn't carry himself at all like a Gururumba—that is to say like a human being. I was spotted as an alien the first time I showed up in the small city of Ch'uhsien, in Anhwei Province, China, back in 1947. Even after more than a year in that place, there was no question about my standing out as a strange physical type. During the hot summer, peasants who had never seen anything like me before were particularly fascinated by

*Quoted material is from Morton H. Fried, "A Four-Letter Word That Hurts," *Saturday Review,* 2 October 1965, **35**, 21–23. By permission of the author and publisher.

my arms protruding from my short-sleeved shirt, and I almost had to stop patronizing the local bathhouse. I am not a hirsute fellow for some-one of my type, but in Ch'uhsien I looked like a shaggy dog, and farmers deftly plucked my hairs and escaped with souvenirs. Another time, a charming young lady of three scrambled into my lap when I offered to tell her a story; she looked into my eyes just as I began and leaped off with a scream. It was some time before I saw her again, and in the interval I learned that in this area the worst, bloodthirsty, child-eating demons can be identified by their blue eyes.

Individual differences are obvious, even to a child. Unfortunately, race is not to be confused with such differences, though almost everybody sees them and some people act toward others on the basis of them. I say "unfortunately" because the confusion seems so deeply embedded as to make anyone despair of rooting it out.

"Race" is a concept

Most laymen of my acquaintance, whether tolerant or bigoted, are frankly puzzled when they are told that race is an idea. It seems to them that it is something very real that they experience every day; one might as well deny the existence of different makes and models of automobiles. The answer to that analogy is easy: cars don't breed. Apart from what the kids conjure up by raiding automobile graveyards, and putting the parts together to get a monster, there are no real intergrades in machinery of this kind. To get a car you manufacture parts and put them together. To get our kind of biological organism, you start with two fully formed specimens, one of each sex, and if they are attracted to each other, they may replicate. Their replication can never be more than approximate as far as either of them, the par-ents, is concerned, because, as we so well know, each contributes only and exactly one-half of the genetic material to the offspring. We also know that some of the genetic material each transmits may not be apparent in his or her own makeup, so that it is fully possible for a child to be completely legitimate without resembling either side of the family, although

he may remind a very old aunt of her grand-father.

The phenomenon of genetic inheritance is completely neutral with regard to race and racial formation. Given a high degree of isola-tion, different populations might develop to the point of being clearly distinguishable while they remained capable of producing fertile hybrids. There would, however, be few if any hybrids because of geographical isolation, and the result would be a neat and consistent system.

Much too neat and consistent for man. Never in the history of this globe has there been any species with so little **sitzfleisch.** Even during the middle of the **Pleistocene,** way down in the Lower **Paleolithic,** 300,000 or more years ago, our ancestors were continent-hoppers. That is the only reasonable interpretation of the fact that very similar remains of the middle Pleisto-cene fossil **Homo erectus** are found in Africa, Europe, and Asia. Since that time movement has accelerated, and now there is no major region of this planet without its human popula-tion, even if it is a small, artificially maintained, nonreproductive population of scientists in Antarctica.

Mobility and variability

The mobility so characteristic of our **genus,** Homo, has unavoidable implications, for where man moves, man mates, (Antarctica, devoid of indigenous population, is perhaps the only exception.) This is not a recent phenomenon, but has been going on for one or two million years, or longer than the period since man became recognizable. We know of this mobility not only from evidence of the spread of our genus and species throughout the world but also because the fossils of man collected from one locality and representing a single relatively synchronic population sometimes show extra-ordinary variation among themselves. Some years ago a population was found in Tabun Cave, near Mt. Carmel, in Israel. The physical anthropologists Ashley Montagu and C. Loring Brace describe it as "showing every possible combination of the features of **Neanderthal** with those of modern man." At Chouk'outien, a limestone quarry not too far from Peking, in a cave that was naturally open toward the close of the Pleistocene geological period, about 20,000 years ago, there lived a population of diverse physical types. While some physical anthropologists minimize them, those who have actually pored over the remains describe differences as great as those separating modern Chinese from Eskimos on one hand and Melanesians on the other. All of this, of course, without any direct evidence of the skin color of the fossils concerned. We never have found fossilized human skin and therefore can speak of the skin colors of our ancestors of tens of thousands of years ago only through extrapolation, by assuming continuity, and by assuming the applicability of such zoological rules as **Gloger's,** which was developed to explain the distribution of differently pigmented birds and mammals.

The evidence that our Pleistocene ancestors got around goes beyond their own physical remains and includes exotic shells, stones, and other materials in strange places which these objects could have reached only by being passed from hand to hand or being carried great distances. If our ancestors moved about that much, they also spread their genes, to put it euphemistically. Incidentally, they could have accomplished this spreading of genes whether they reacted to alien populations peacefully or hostilely; wars, including those in our own time, have always been a major means of speeding up hybridization.

Even phrasing the matter this way, and allowing for a goodly amount of gene flow between existing racial populations, through hundreds of thousands of years of evolution, the resulting image of race is incredibly wrong, a fantasy with hardly any connection to reality. What is wrong is our way of creating and relying upon **archetypes.** Just as we persist in thinking that there is a typical American town (rarely our own), a typical American middle-class housewife (never our wife), a typical American male ("not me!"), so we think of races in terms of typical, archetypical, individuals who probably do not exist. When it is pointed out that there are hundreds of thousands or millions of living people who fall between the classified races, the frequently heard rejoinder is that this is so now, but it is a sign of our decadent times. Those fond of arguing this way usually go on to assert

that it was not so in the past, that the races were formerly discrete.

In a startlingly large number of views, including those shared by informed and tolerant people, there was a time when there was a pure white race, a pure black race, etc., etc., depending upon how many races they recognize. There is not a shred of scientifically respectable evidence to support such a view. Whatever evidence we have contradicts it. In addition to the evidence of Chouk'outien and Tabun mentioned above, there are many other fossils whose morphological characteristics, primitivity to one side, are not in keeping with those of the present inhabitants of the same region.

Dangers of stereotyping

Part of the explanation of the layman's belief in pure ancestral races is to be found in the intellectually lazy trait of **stereotyping,** which is applied not only to man's ancestry but to landscape and climate through time as well. Few parts of the world today look quite the way they did 15,000 years ago, much less 150,000 years ago. Yet I have found it a commonplace among students that they visualize the world of ages ago as it appears today. The Sahara is always a great desert, the Rockies a great mountain chain, and England separated from France by the Channel. Sometimes I ask a class, after we have talked about the famous Java fossil *Pithecanthropus erectus,* how the devil do they suppose he ever got there, Java being an island? Usually the students are dumbfounded by the question, until they are relieved to discover that Java wasn't always cut off from the Asian mainland. Given their initial attitudes and lack of information, it is not surprising that so many people imagine a beautiful Nordic **Cro-Magnon,** archetypical White, ranging a great Wagnerian forest looking for bestial Neanderthalers to exterminate.

Has the "cave man" vanished?

Once again, there is no evidence whatsoever to support the lurid nightmare of **genocide** that early *Homo sapiens* is supposed to have wreaked upon the bumbling and grotesque Neanderthals. None either for William Golding's literary view of the extirpation of primitive innocence and goodness. The interpretation that in my view does least damage to the evidence is that which recognizes the differences between contemporary forms of so-called Neanderthals and other fossil *Homo sapiens* of 25,000 to 100,000 years ago to have been very little more or no greater than those between two variant populations of our own century. Furthermore, the same evidence indicates that the Neanderthals did not vanish suddenly but probably were slowly submerged in the populations that surrounded them, so that their genetic materials form part of our own inheritance today.

Then, it may be asked, where did the story come from that tells of the struggle of these populations and the extinction of one? It is a relatively fresh tale, actually invented in the nineteenth century, for before that time there was no suspicion of such creatures as Neanderthals. The nineteenth century, however, discovered the fossils of what has been called "Darwin's first witness." After some debate, the fossil remains were accepted as some primitive precursor of man and then chopped off the family tree. The model for this imaginary genealogical pruning was easily come by in a century that had witnessed the hunting and killing of native populations like game beasts, as in Tasmania, in the Malay peninsula, and elsewhere. Such episodes and continuation of slavery and the slave trade made genocide as real a phenomenon as the demand for laissez-faire and the Acts of Combination. It was precisely in this crucible that modern racism was born and to which most of our twentieth-century mythology about race can be traced.

In the vocabulary of the layman the word "race" is a nonsense term, one without a fixed, reliable meaning, and, as Alice pointed out to Humpty Dumpty, the use of words with idiosyncratic meanings is not conducive to communication. Yet I am sure that many who read these words will think that it is the writer who is twisting meaning and destroying a useful, common-sense concept. Far from it. One of the most respected and highly regarded volumes to have yet been published in the field of **physical anthropology** is *Human Biology,* by four British scientists, Harrison, Weiner, Tanner, and Barnicot (Oxford University Press, 1964). These distinguished authors jointly eschewed the word "race" on the ground that it was poorly defined even in **zoology**, i.e., when applied to animals other than man, and because of its history of misunderstanding, confusion, and worse, when applied to humans.

The non-existence of human races

Similar views have been held for some time and are familiar in the professional literature. Ashley Montagu, for example, has been in the vanguard of the movement to drop the concept of human race on scientific grounds for twenty-five years. His most recent work on the subject is a collation of critical essays from many specialists, *The Concept of Race* (Free Press, 1964). Frank B. Livingstone, a physical anthropologist at the University of Michigan, has spoken out "On the Nonexistence of Human Races" (*Current Anthropology,* 3:3, 1962). In the subsequent debate, opinions divided rather along generational lines. The older scientists preferred to cling to the concept of race while freely complaining about its short-comings. The younger scientists showed impatience with the concept and wished to drop it and get on with important work that the concept obstructed.

Criticism of the concept of race

Quite specifically, there are many things wrong with the concept of race. As generally employed, it is sometimes based on biological characteristics but sometimes on cultural features, and when it is based on biological traits the traits in question usually have the most obscure genetic backgrounds. The use of cultural criteria is best exemplified in such untenable racial constructs as the "Anglo-Saxon race," or the "German race," or the "Jewish race." Under no scientifically uttered definition known to me can these aggregates be called races. The first is a linguistic designation pertaining to the Germanic dialects or languages spoken by the people who about 1500 years ago invaded the British Isles from what is now Schleswig-Holstein and the adjacent portion of Denmark. The invaders were in no significant way physically distinct from their neighbors, who spoke other languages, and in any case they mated and blended with the indigenous population they encountered. Even their language was substantially altered by diffusion so that today a reference to English as an Anglo-Saxon language is quaint and less than correct. As for the hyperbolic extension of the designation to some of the people who live in England and the United States, it is meaningless in racial terms—just as meaningless as extending the term to cover a nation of heterogeneous origin and flexible boundaries, such as Germany or France or Italy or any other country. As for the moribund concept of a "Jewish race," this is simply funny, considering the extraordinary diversity of the physical types that have embraced this religion, and the large number that have relinquished it and entered other faiths.

The use of cultural criteria to identify individuals with racial categories does not stop with nationality, language, or religion. Such traits as posture, facial expression, musical tastes, and even modes of dress have been used to sort people into spurious racial groups. But even when biological criteria have been used, they have rarely been employed in a scientifically defensible way. One of the first questions to arise, for example, is what kind of criteria shall be used to sort people into racial categories. Following immediately upon this is another query: how many criteria should be used? With regard to the first, science is still in conflict. The new physical anthropologists whose overriding concern is to unravel the many remaining mysteries in human evolution and to understand the role that heredity will play in continuing and future evolution are impatient with any but strictly genetic characters, preferably those that can be linked to relatively few gene loci. They prefer the rapidly mounting blood factors, not only the ABO, Rh, MNS, and other well-known series, but such things as Duffy, Henshaw, Hunter, Kell, and Kidd (limited distribution blood groups named for the first person found to have carried them). Such work has one consistent by-product: the resultant classifications tend to cross-cut and obliterate conventional racial lines so that such constructs as the white race disappear as useful taxonomic units.

Some scientists argue that a classification based on only one criterion is not a very useful instrument. On the other hand, the more criteria that are added, the more abstract the racial construct becomes as fewer individuals can be discovered with all the necessary characteristics and more individuals are found to be in between. The end result is that the typical person is completely atypical; if race makes sense, so does this.

Race as a statistical abstraction

That racial classification is really nonsense can be demonstrated with ease merely by comparing some of the most usual conceptions of white and Negro. What degree of black African ancestry establishes a person as a Negro? Is 51 percent, or 50.1 percent, or some other slight statistical preponderance necessary? The question is ridiculous; we have no means of discriminating quantities of inherited materials in percentage terms. In that case, can we turn to ancestry and legislate that anyone with a Negro parent is a Negro? Simple, but totally ineffective and inapplicable: how was the racial identity of each parent established? It is precisely at this point that anthropologists raise the question of assigning specific individuals to racial categories. At best, a racial category is a statistical abstraction based upon certain frequencies of genetic characters observed in small samples of much larger populations. A frequency of genetic characters is something that can be displayed by a population, but it cannot be displayed by an individual, any more than one voter can represent the proportion of votes cast by his party.

The fallacy of racial classification

The great fallacy of racial classification is revealed by reflecting on popular applications in real situations. Some of our outstanding

"Negro" citizens have almost no phenotypic resemblance to the stereotyped "Negro." It requires their acts of self-identification to place them. Simultaneously, tens of thousands of persons of slightly darker skin color, broader nasal wings, more everted lips, less straight hair, etc., are considered as "white" without question, in the South as well as the North, and in all socioeconomic strata. Conversely, some of our best-known and noisiest Southern politicians undoubtedly have some "Negro" genes in their makeup.

Why is it so hard to give up this miserable little four-letter word that of all four-letter words has done the most damage? This is a good question for a scientific linguist or semanticist. After all, the word refers to nothing more than a transitory statistical abstraction. But the question can also be put to an anthropoligist. His answer might be, and mine is, that the word "race" expresses a certain kind of unresolved social conflict that thrives on divisions and invidious distinctions. It can thrive in the total absence of genetic differences in a single homogeneous population of common ancestry. That is the case, for example, with the relations between the Japanese and that portion of themselves they know as the Eta [Cf. below].

In a truly great society it may be that the kinds of fear and rivalry that generate racism will be overcome. This can be done without the kind of millenarian reform that would be necessary to banish all conflict, for only certain kinds of hostilities generate racism, although any kind can be channeled into an already raging racial bigotry. Great areas of the earth's surface have been totally devoid of racism for long periods of time and such a situation may return again, although under altered circumstances. If and when it does, the word "race" may drop from our vocabulary and scholars will desperately scrutinize our remains and the remains of our civilization, trying to discover what we were so disturbed about.

4

DeVos and Wagatsuma: Japan's Invisible Race

It is a truism that human populations differ in skin color, hair texture, size, and other less noticeable anatomical characteristics. What is the relationship between these attributes and human temperament, skills, and other behavioral potentials?

If we could manipulate humans as we do rats, we could design an experiment to help answer the question. In our experiment, we would want to control *every condition but one* and simply observe the effect of varying that single factor.

We might care to select skin color as the one variable. For example, let two groups of people, one with black skin and the other nonblack, each be equally segregated, equally deprived of educational opportunities, equally hated and mistreated. Other things being equal, the outcome, if different, could be attributed to the skin-color variable. If there were no differences in outcome, we would be justified in concluding that the skin-color variable made no difference.

The thought of designing such a monstrous experiment is revolting. Yet sometimes "nature's experiments" furnish valuable knowledge about humans even though they are not as carefully controlled

*Quoted material is from George DeVos and Hiroshi Wagatsuma, *Japan's Invisible Race*. (Berkeley: University of California Press, 1966.)

as laboratory experiments. The following report of an ingenious study is only remotely analogous to the experiment proposed, but it is the best we have and it does shed light on the relationship between race and psychological inquiry.

The fact of white prejudice against the Negro in the United States is an explosive issue today. Its counterpart in Japan concerns a group of two to three million real or imaginary descendants of an untouchable pariah caste known as the Burakumin. In a book that provides the substance of the present article, DeVos and Wagatsuma tell how "radical" prejudice has forced the Burakumin into ghettos of inde-

scribable poverty, wretchedness, and suffering in such representative cities as Osaka, Kobe, Kyoto, and Nara, although they have banded together in rural areas as well.

Officially the Burakumin were emancipated in 1871, at which time they were free to discard the special prescribed garb they had been forced to wear and the occupations that had identified them for over a thousand years. Yet, despite recent radical economic and social changes that have placed Japan among the top four or five countries of the world, the condition of the Burakumin remains unchanged and they suffer the same indignity and lack of opportunity as the Negro in America or the 50

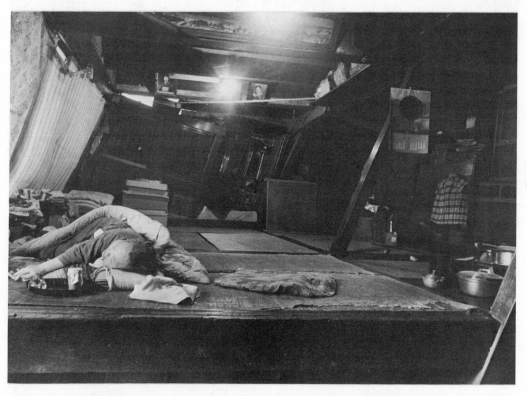

Figure 3.1 Death comes for an old Buraku woman. Note house which is about to collapse also. The broken and twisted furniture won't function. (Photo courtesy of Mr. K. Fukumoto, Kobe News, Japan.)

Figure 3.2 A Burakumin wedding. Even though inbreeding is considered undesirable, Burakumin must intermarry. Even marriage between partners of two different Burakumin settlements is frowned upon. (Photo courtesy of Mr. K. Fukumoto, Kobe News, Japan.)

million untouchables in India. Japanese see no inconsistency in their repugnance at any familiarity or contact with a Buraku.

Life in the outcaste ghetto

Marriage The tight, geographical confinement of the Burakumin would obviously limit mate selection. Consequently, intermarriage occurs on a much more "local" basis than in nonoutcaste communities. However, in more recent years inbreeding is very gradually breaking down. For example, according to DeVos and Wagatsuma, although less than 10 percent of Buraku men over 50 years of age married outside their caste, 38 percent of men under 30 have done so. Similarly, of Buraku women over age 30, less than 5 percent married men from the majority population as compared with 30 percent of women under 30 (p. 119).

Occupation Historically the outcaste group has been connected with the building and guarding of tombs, undertaking, butchering, tanning, leather-working, including shoe- and sandal-making, working in armor, fur, bowstrings, basket making and tea-whisk manufacture. How one's occupation can readily identify one's social position is illustrated effectively in the case of one such outcaste who preferred to live in his ghetto. When asked "If you were to live elsewhere, can you think of any sort of undesirable conditions you might face?" His reply: "Because I am a shoemaker, everyone would know of my Buraku origin [p. 167]."

Food In a Buddhist setting, meat eating is unthinkable, but the consumption of the internal organs of cows and horses is even more abhorrent. By this conspicuous practice, many Burakumin have succeeded in segregating themselves further from the majority population.

Dress The Burakumin tend to dress carelessly within the ghetto, but in the

Figure 3.3 A Burakumin toilet. Because of bad sewage, the filth overflows. Since housing is so concentrated, sewage disposal is a serious problem— where will you dig? (Photo courtesy of Mr. K. Fukumoto, Kobe News, Japan.)

larger community they impose greater formality. Weather permitting, children under six are allowed to run around completely naked.

Speech Vocabulary, such as special or secret words, ruder speech, and identifying accent also tend to set off a person reared in a Buraku ghetto from the majority as well as from the other lower (i.e., non-Buraku) segments of the Japanese population. The Cockney of London offers a parallel example.

Identifying the Burakumin

The people whom Buraku outcastes choose for their mates, their occupations, their food, dress, and speech are all very conspicuous and *visible* "things." And yet DeVos and Wagatsuma refer to the Burakumin as "the *invisible* race." How so? The whole point, one of utmost significance in considering the relationship of biological factors and psychological events, is this. "It is not widely known that Japan has discriminated in the past and continues to discriminate against a pariah caste that is completely indistinguishable *in any physical sense* from the population as a whole, whose segregation nevertheless has long been justified *in racial terms* [italics added, p. *xx*]." For a special emphasis of this point, the following statement regarding Japan's pariahs is quoted from Wagatsuma (1967):

Not racially different in any way from the majority Japanese, they can be identified with certainty only by the registry of place of birth and residence. Nevertheless, many Japanese believe that they are in some way or other visibly identifiable [p. 118].

Most Negroes in America manifest a skin color that permits instant recognition and a resultant expression of any existing prejudice toward them. The black skin triggers the prejudiced response. However, undress a representative outcaste and a representative upperclass citizen of Japan and they are indistinguishable from each other. Ask about the locality where they were born, listen to them talk, eat, note their dress, and once more you can segregate them. "The concept of caste remains a social force because it exists in the emotional structure of individual Japanese [p. *xxi*]." The point of our discussion is that prejudice can always find food to feed upon. If no distinctive **anthropomorphic** feature exists between human groups, one can *create* some cultural feature that will serve the same purpose as kinky hair and pigmented skin. A yellow star of David worn on the sleeve will serve equally well. If you herd people into strictly bounded areas, restrict their manner of earning a living or their opportunities for education, if you contrive appropriate historical, economic, and religious factors, and spell out their diet and dress and whom they can marry, you will find that skin color is not indispensable. Skin color is only more obvious.

DeVos and Wagatsuma seem to agree with this thinking:

Outcaste status and attitudes about untouchability developed within medieval Japanese culture because of a complex set of economic, social, political, and ideological conditions. And once established, outcaste status has had great staying power. The formal rational explanations and protests on the parts of members of the majority society, or by the outcastes themselves, have had little effect on hastening change in outcaste history [p. 13].

Does "passing" occur among Burakumin?

The answer to the above question, as applied to the Negro in North America, is clear cut. Because the vast majority of Negroes cannot erase their distinguishing skin color, they cannot merge into the white population. In Japan, however, since "No scientific fact substantiates the myth that there are hereditary biological factors that separate ordinary Japanese from the former pariahs [p. *xxi*]," the transition seems easier. Not having a different skin color or other distinguishing anatomical characteristic, the Buraku should be able to blend into the majority population; this is physi-

cally possible to them on a much wider scale than for the colorful Negro.

DeVos and Wagatsuma tell us the secrets of "passing." In order to escape completely from the stigma of his past, a Burakumin must make a complete geographical and occupational break with his ghetto and "forge for himself an entirely new identity and in some cases fabricate a past so that he will not be disadvantaged by his lack of ancestry [p. 241]." However, such a step would require extreme challenge and motivation that would be blocked by difficult procedures, steps, risk of discovery, and lack of money, opportunity for employment, and so on.

Buraku individuals who marry across

Figure 3.4 A winding, narrow alley in a Burakumin settlement. Rain is a calamity if your occupation is road building. (Photo courtesy of Mr. K. Fukumoto, Kobe News, Japan.)

the caste barrier may establish successful and lasting happy marriages *unless* and *until* they are identified by a person out of their past. The result often spells rupture, anguish, guilt, and a break-up or suicide. The consequences of discovery may match the tragedy of *Madame Butterfly*. The following poignant story from DeVos and Wagatsuma makes the point emphatically:

A Buraku woman, named Niwa Mariko, sent her letter to the journal *Buraku,* describing her painful experience.

"I was born in a Buraku, as a youngest daughter. Although my family was relatively well off in the Buraku, I had to work hard as soon as I finished junior high school. I found a job...in Kyoto, where I met my future husband. We fell in love with each other, and after talking it over with my brothers and sisters, I married him...A few years after our marriage, my husband was promoted to a position of supervisor in his factory. I was happy.

"Last year, I went to the factory to see my husband, and there I happened to meet a former acquaintance who knew I was a Buraku girl. She showed in an exaggerated manner her surprise at the fact that my husband was a factory supervisor. I felt disgusted at the expression on her face, but I did not realize fully that the woman thought it was simply too much for a Buraku girl like me to be married to a factory supervisor. About ten days later, my husband came home sullen and morose.... From that night on my husband became a changed person.... He said, finally, that I was from a Buraku, and that it was all wrong. It may sound too naive, but until that time I had not fully realized what it meant to be a Burakumin to those who are not. I had never been told very clearly that I was a Buraku woman, and was therefore the subject of discrimination. I later discovered that my old acquaintance had told everyone at the factory that I was from a Buraku. My husband finally forced me to leave his house. By that time, my previous intense love toward him changed into hatred.

"I received a letter from my husband's brother telling me to sign a divorce paper so that my husband could marry someone else. I wrote back a letter that I would not consent to the divorce unless I was fully persuaded it was best for me. I went to my husband's house anyway to pick up my belongings.... There I found my bedding thrown into the garden like some objects of filth. While married, I had made for us bedding of the finest quality, but only the poorest set was given back to me. We also found two suitcases in the garden, which had been filled with the things I had used before my marriage. I could not meet with my husband; he was out. I had been thrown out of the house, like filth. I trembled with anger and returned to my sister's home, angry, sad, and exhausted.

"My husband and his brother still insisted that I sign the divorce document. I hated them, and had no intention of remaining his wife. And yet, I did not like to consent to a divorce, because the stated reasons for divorce...were all untrue. I did not believe that my husband had had any feelings of discontent before his discovery of my identity.

"I had an opportunity to meet the man who was secretary of the Kaiho Domei. He told me that discrimination against Burakumin would never end unless Burakumin themselves fought back. He said I should overcome my own depression and fight for all the Burakumin, who were sufferers from discrimination. Also, one of my sisters, married to a non-Buraku man, wanted to keep our background hidden from her husband. If I stood up to fight, my sister's marriage would probably be threatened. I talked with the secretary of the Domei several times, and being ashamed of my indecisive attitude, I still cannot make up my mind. I know that eventually I will have to get over this conflict in myself and stand up and fight [pp. 255–256]."

Some final comments on Japan's "invisible race"

First, it is interesting to note the origin of the DeVos and Wagatsuma study. They were impressed by the high delinquency rate among Negro youth in the U.S. Would they find an analogous relationship in Japan between, on the one hand, the status of a minority group segregated by caste barriers and barred from easy assimilation into its modern industrial society and delinquency on the other hand? Evidence from their inquiry showed a positive relationship between boys' residence in a Buraku ghetto and joblessness, school absenteeism, dropout, low IQ, and a rate of delinquency which was three times that of non-Buraku boys (pp. 258–272). A direct parallel existed in these respects between Buraku youth in Japan, on the one hand, and American-Negro and American-Mexican youth on the other.

Within the context of our discussion, the crucial question is: What is the psychological significance of the black skin of the American Negro? Apparently the kinds of sociopathologies and **psychopathologies** connected with crime and other forms of deviance do not demand skin color or any other discriminable anatomical factor; in the two groups compared, the latter is present in the United States but absent in Japan. Is it not a mere coincidence that skin color is a badge of the Negro's caste status and that the Burakumin simply wear nonanatomical but equally visible badges? The common factors related to social deviance in both groups appear to be registry of birth in a certain locality, their residence in common ghettos, lack of social, educational, and occupational opportunity, discrimination and other barriers to their involvement in the full life of the community.

The fundamental question that the reader must answer for himself is this: How does "race" enter into our understanding of a person's psychological nature? What does the individual's skin color, hair texture, limb-to-body-height ratio or any other hereditary, anatomical characteristic have to do with his or her attainment of excellence as a Metropolitan Opera star, an atomic scientist, a chemist, violinist, conductor, composer, military strategist, or poet? Today the evidence for high attainment is occurring on a global basis, irrespective of continent, nationality, religion, or "race."

Brotz: The Black Jews of Harlem **5**

In *The Black Jews of Harlem,* Howard Brotz discusses a group of people who constitute an ethnic group, to use Ashley Montagu's term. Despite their black skin color, they dissociate themselves from Negroes, upon whom they look with scorn and derision. In addition to adopting the Star of David as a symbol, they speak Hebrew and teach their children to do so. Their manners and customs are as orthodox and their diet as kosher as that of the most orthodox Jew (Brotz, 1964, p. 22). Here, as with the Buraku population of Japan (DeVos and Wagatsuma, 1966), we can make interesting comparisons and contrasts. As an ethnic group the black Jews can, anatomically, be matched with other Harlem populations. They cannot be matched culturally because they themselves choose to identify with certain white citizens of New York who call themselves "Jews."

An attempt to understand the religious and dietary customs and manners of the black Jews of Harlem requires a different dimension from the one that makes understandable the similarity of their skin color with the skin color of their Negro neighbors. The former dimension demands space-time boundaries that span historical time, contacts with other ethnic groups, assimilation of certain customs and manners, a given individual's residence in assimilated groups, and similar acculturation. Ethnicity via skin-color resemblance calls for a genetic (i.e., biological) space-time dimension known more simply as heredity. Ethnicity via religious and dietary ways of behaving demands a time dimension that begins with the individual's birth. It should be emphasized that anatomical factors do not have priority. Certain customs like scarring the skin, molding the head, enlarging ear lobes, and creating saucer lips practiced by various African tribes are not the result of genetic (i.e., biological) conditions but of practices

adopted by a given human population. Montagu (1963) seems to be in agreement with this position when he argues that the phrase "ethnic group"

avoids the reductionist or "nothing but" fallacy, that is, the notion that men are nothing but the resultant of their biological heredity, that they are what they are because of their genes. The phrase "ethnic group" is calculated to provide the necessary corrective to this erroneous viewpoint by eliminating the question-begging emphases of the biologistic bias on purely physical factors and differences and demanding that the question of definition be left open until the necessary scientific research and answers are available. The emphasis is shifted to the fact that man is a uniquely cultural creature as well as a physical organism, and that under the influence of human culture the plasticity of man, both mentally and physically, is greatly increased—indeed, to such an extent as to lead anthropologists to the creation of races upon the basis of physical traits which were subsequently discovered to be due to cultural factors, as, for example, the head forms of the so-called **Armenoid** and **Dinaric "races"** [p. 67].

6 A final point about race

Is it possible that all members of the human species, regardless of "race" or ethnic group, are equipotential at birth? Is any group of humans "endowed" at birth, thus giving it a head start over any other? Again Ashley Montagu's (1955) clear answer supports the belief in a genetic unity of mankind:

From the point of view of the capacity for social development, every individual possesses all the necessary potentialities, and this is true for human beings in every ethnic group and has certainly been true of our species for many hundreds of thousands of years. In their capacity for social development within the range

of the normal, all men fall within the range of equality at birth [p. 86].

There is no good evidence that any human group differs from any other in the nature of its gene potentials for mental or social development. Hence, until evidence to the contrary is forthcoming, we may rule out any effect of a genetic factor in differentially determining any of the cultures in the great range of human society known to us [p. 87].

These are strong words, encompassing. as they do, not only contemporary human populations but also those spanning millenia. Such a view would be denied by most people, who find it hard to believe that

Aristotle or Confucius (if brought to life today) could learn to drive a Jaguar, to enjoy contemporary music, philosophy, or painting, or become an atomic physicist. Implicit in popular thinking is an inadvertent imposition of an evolution of mankind from a former, inherently more stupid state to the present "advanced" one. In addition, one notion that colors such thinking is the belief that present-day human groups were arrested at different stages of evolutionary development. On this point Jean Rostand (1959), France's distinguished biologist and pioneer researcher on artificially induced **parthenogenesis** (virgin birth) and induced mutation, adds his voice. Stressing first "the fundamental stability of our species," a point too often underrated, he goes on to say:

Contrary to popular belief, man has long since ceased to evolve. Present-day man, the human being of the twentieth century, the human being that we are, does not differ essentially from the human being who lived in the caves of the Quaternary Age some 100,000 years ago, whose bony traces and rudimentary tools have been exhumed by the paleontologists. The whole of that part of man's history which has gone by since those faraway ages has not, or has scarcely, altered the **morphological** and **physiological** outfit of our species. The enormous difference which nonetheless exists between the ancient flint-chipper and his modern heir is entirely the work of civilization — that is, of the culture gradually accumulated and transmitted by social tradition. Already at the origin of the species man was equal to what he was destined to become. He carried within him, potentially, all the things that were destined gradually to expand and fructify in industry, in technical skill, in science, in art, in philosophy, and in religion. So much so that if, by some miracle, it were possible to fetch a newborn child of that past age into our time and to bring him up and educate him as one of ours, he would become a man exactly like us: a man whom nothing, either in his appearance or in his conduct or in his private thoughts, would single out as a stranger among us, as a ghost from the past;

a man who would meet with no particular difficulty in initiating himself into the complexities and refinements of our customs; a man who, finding himself on the same footing with the most advanced manifestations of thought or of aesthetics, would be able to argue about existentialism, or explain the paintings of Picasso, as well as anybody else [pp. 75–76].

It would be a gross misrepresentation to give the impression that all students of man agree with Montagu and Rostand. As in all fields of learning, differing points of view exist. One reason lies in the different assumptions that each investigator starts with. Their examination of the facts convinces Montagu and Rostand that all the varieties of present-day mankind derived from a common stock. Both think that all people belong to the same species and have the same remote ancestry. One member of the opposition, Carleton Coon (1962, 1965), thinks otherwise. He postulates that about a half-million years ago

man was a single species, *Homo erectus,* already divided into five geographic races or subspecies. *Homo erectus* then evolved into *Homo sapiens,* not once but five times, as each species, living in its own territory, passed a critical threshold from a more brutal to a more sapient state [1962, p. 656].

Space limitations prevent further comments on Coon's alternative view, but extensive arguments against Coon's position are available in Montagu's (1964, pp. 83–91) *Man's Most Dangerous Myth: The Fallacy of Race.* Certainly a critical analysis of the discrepant views of man's origin and evolution are required in an attempt to answer the question whether all human groups have the same or different potentialities for psychological development. The following case provides an opportunity to test several of the points raised in this section on the relationship between a person's "racial" or ethnic membership and his psychological status.

7 A test case

Clyde Kluckhohn (1960) describes a young white American who through fortuitous circumstances had been culturalized in a radically different manner from that of most American children. Consequently, he was a stranger in his own land. Kluckhohn's statement follows:

> Some years ago I met in New York City a young man who did not speak a word of English and was obviously bewildered by American ways. By "blood" he was as American as you or I, for his parents had gone from Indiana to China as missionaries. Orphaned in infancy, he was reared by a Chinese family in a remote village. All who met him found him more Chinese than American. The facts of his blue eyes and light hair were less impressive than a Chinese style of gait, Chinese arm and hand movements, Chinese facial expression, and Chinese modes of thought. The biological heritage was American, but the cultural training had been Chinese. He returned to China [pp. 21–22].

What did "race" have to do with making the young Caucasian American psychologically, at least, a "Chinese"? Conversely, what does Chinese morphology and skin color have to do with making a native-born citizen of that country a Chinese in his diet, dress, religious and political beliefs, customs, manners, and so on?

Chapter summary

For a potentially helpful insight into the relationship between psychology and race, we first unsuccessfully attempted a definition of the term race. We found anthropologists disagreeing on the proper use of the term. Adopting as a substitute Montagu's looser conception of "ethnic group," we noted that human groups can be isolated *even anatomically* by stretching of lips or tattooing of skin, clearly a social rather than hereditary set of conditions. In fact, we later noted the contradictory situation of a self-segregated group of black-skinned individuals, identified by others as American Negroes, refusing to be so identified. The black Jews of Harlem have resigned from the Negro "race" and declared themselves Jews.

We also inspected "Japan's invisible race," a minority group anatomically indistinguishable and segregated as pariahs by means of certain behaviors, index behaviors that allowed them only minimal psychological development because of restrictions imposed upon them. A parallel was drawn to the easily-visible American Negro minority and equally disastrous psychological consequences deriving from prejudice based on that visibility. We then considered the exciting hypothesis that, not only contemporaneously but also possibly even for the past 100,000 years, all members of the human species have had the same psychological potentiality at birth. However, we also noted the dissident voices opposing this view. Finally, we presented a test case with which to judge the points raised in this chapter. Our final assessment, however, is that "race," however defined, furnishes no clue to the richness and diversity of behavior that we find among various scattered groups of the single human species. It is suggested that not any specific group has any peculiar psychological advantage or handicap resident in its biological constitution.

4

Heredity and psychology

"Heredity" is a simple and convenient answer to many puzzling questions about people's behavior. And yet what is heredity and how heavily can we lean on this idea to explain behavior? These are questions we shall consider as we look at the relationship between heredity and psychology.

Semantically considered, the term "heredity" is a muddled one. Elsewhere I have shown that this term did not originate from scientific inquiry but has been in recorded use for at least 400 years. In fact, it was uncritically borrowed from uncritical common sense, which considered the following as heritable: right of succession (to the crown or to a title), sin, sickness (the gout, the stone, and until comparatively recent times, even tuberculosis and syphilis), and "a fixed hereditary hate between the crowns of Macedon and Thrace [Pronko, 1957, p. 46]." Obviously the word has had a rich and varied, thus unclear, usage.

Because of the widespread belief that (to some degree or other) at least certain behaviors have a hereditary basis, we now examine the broad question of the relationship between heredity and psychology. We start by raising doubt about the existence of a clear causal relationship between biological inheritance and behavior. A highlight of the chapter is an older but still fresh and, in my opinion, a classic statement on biological heredity. For how can we settle the problem of heredity and psychology if we don't have a clear notion of how heredity works in biology? Then, we consider a critical analysis of the doctrine of psychoheredity, which is an attempt to impose biological theory upon psychological facts. Finally, we examine some common myths concerning the inheritance of psychopathology and other deviances, like laziness, licentiousness, and feeble-mindedness.

Critique of the heredity doctrine 1

The notion that people inherit disposition, temperament, ability, or even lack of it, dies hard. Let a man excel in some area, and, if his father also excelled in the same way, the son is "a chip off the old block." Successive generations of craftsmen, musicians, or artists are easily fitted into a hereditary theory, according to which part of the explanation for a given individual's outstanding performance is attributed to the germ plasm contributed by a parent similarly distinguished.

Implicit in this layman's theory is the belief that the excellence acquired by the parent during his lifetime (for example, excellence in pianistic performance) has somehow become indelibly impressed upon his germ plasm; at conception the distinguishing characteristic of the parent is somehow transmitted to the child. However, the theory of the inheritance of acquired characters was long ago demolished. The persistence of this ready-made explanation of the man-in-the-street is another evidence of "cultural lag"—the uneven flow of various parts of our cultural stream.

At this point, the reader may feel impelled to ask: "But how about the Bachs? Didn't musical ability 'run' in their family?" Terry's (1929) study of 14 generations of the Bach family covers a span from 1561 to 1929 and includes 229 persons! The answer is clear. The alleged inheritance of musical talent shows a remarkable pattern. The number of professional musicians in each of the 14 generations follows: 0, 1, 3, 3, 10, 18, 23, 6, 0, 0, 0, 0, 0, 0. Starting from zero in the first generation, excellence gathers momentum, rising to a crescendo of 23 individuals in the eighth generation, diminishing to six in the ninth, and disappearing in each of the succeeding six generations. It is pertinent to ask what strange principles govern the erratic distribution of musical talent displayed in the Bach family.

And where did these so-called inherited capacities originate? Did Adam and Eve contain within their germ plasm all of the capacities for artistic, musical, and mathematical activities invented or discovered in subsequent ages? Or, assuming an evolutionary theory, were all the capacities there from the start, or were they introduced into the germ plasm at different times? When? From where? How? Do we all carry genes for as-yet-unheard-of and unknown capacities?

We finally come to the most fundamental problem, one involving analogical reasoning that attempts to see likenesses in two unlike things—namely, psychological activities and anatomical structures. As Montagu suggests:*

---

*Quoted material is from Ashley Montagu, *Biosocial Nature of Man* (New York: Grove Press, 1956).

The fallacy is to assume that because the biological heredity of man is transmitted by mechanisms similar to those operative in other animals and in plants, the same mechanisms are responsible for fundamental human behavior. What is true in the purely biological context becomes a dangerous fallacy when it is applied to human material [pp. 42–43].

Montagu sees man as being "free of all those predeterminants which condition so much of the behavior of nonhuman organisms [p. 42]."

Nonreflex automatic behavioral responses, except for crying under conditions of distress, the response to the sudden withdrawal of support, and the response to a sudden loud noise, are acquired by learning in man, and not inherited by genotype. The evidence indicates quite clearly that everything human beings do *as human beings* they have had to learn from other human beings.

Man is not born with a built-in system of responses to the environment, as are most other creatures. On the other hand, man is born with a built-in system of plastic potentialities which under environmental stimulation are capable of being caused to respond in a large variety of different ways [p. 42].

Biological heredity

The term biological heredity is obviously redundant. If the reader were to enroll in a course in heredity or genetics, he would find it listed in biology, where it properly belongs. Genetics is the branch of biology that studies the similarities and differences of successive generations of organisms. In attempting to find the possible relationship between heredity and psychology, it seems appropriate to turn to the biological specialist who studies genetics. In doing so, we

FIRST GENERATION

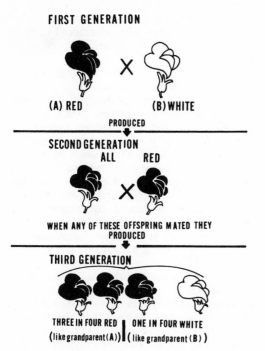

(A) RED   (B) WHITE

PRODUCED

SECOND GENERATION
ALL   RED

WHEN ANY OF THESE OFFSPRING MATED THEY
PRODUCED

THIRD GENERATION

THREE IN FOUR RED | ONE IN FOUR WHITE
(like grandparent (A)) | (like grandparent (B))

Figure 4.1 How biological principles of heredity operate. In the first generation, red snapdragons (A) were crossed with white snapdragons (B). The offspring were all red (A). But when any of these red offspring were cross-bred, their offspring, the third generation, showed a ratio of three red snapdragons (A) to one white one (B). These results are said to follow Mendelian principles, which are interpreted in terms of dominant and recessive "genes."

enlist the aid of one who might be termed the father of American genetics. The date of his paper would cause a young reader to classify the document as ancient history. Yet I believe it has a modern ring because Jennings (1924) saw things clearly and sharply, although occasionally with slips. The following extensive quotation is meant to provide a base of operations by delimiting the operation of heredity in determining the organism's anatomical structures.

Jennings: "Heredity
and environment"*

2

What happens in any object—a piece of steel, a piece of ice, a machine, an organism—depends, on the one hand, upon the material of which it is composed; on the other hand, upon the conditions in which it is found. Under the same conditions, objects of different material behave diversely; under diverse conditions, objects of the same material behave diversely. Anything whatever that happens in any object has to be accounted for by taking into consideration both these things. Neither the material constitution alone, nor the conditions alone, will account for any event whatever; it is always the combination that has to be considered.

Organisms are like other objects in this respect; what they do or become depends both

on what they are made of, and on the conditions surrounding them. The dependence on what they are originally made of we call heredity. But no single thing that the organism does depends alone on heredity or alone on environment; always both have to be taken into account.

What an organism is first composed of comes directly from its parents; this is the reason why dependence on that composition has been called heredity. But this habit of speech has led to conceiving heredity as something in itself, an

*Quoted material is from H. S. Jennings, "Heredity and Environment," *The Scientific Monthly,* September 1924. By permission of the publisher.

entity, a "force," something that itself does things—an error that has induced clouds of misconception. Possibly we should be better off with no such concept as heredity: then analysis would be correctly directed toward understanding, in organisms as in other things, in what ways there is dependence on the stuff they are made of: in what ways on the conditions in which that stuff is found.

As to the dependence on the stuff that they are made of, research has shown that the substances passed from parent to offspring, giving rise to the phenomena of inheritance, are a great number of discrete packets of diverse chemicals, imbedded in a less diversified mass of material. The masses formed by the grouping of these packets are visible under the microscope as the chromosomes. The number of different kinds of packets that go into the beginning of any individual is very great, running into the hundreds of thousands. They are not massed in a haphazard way, but are arranged in a definite manner; so that the young organism is like a well-organized chemical laboratory with many reagents so arranged in containers as to react with each other in an orderly way, producing a definite and harmonious result.

Development we know consists in this orderly interaction of these substances—with each other, with the rest of the cell body, or cytoplasm; and with the oxygen, food, and other chemicals brought into the cell from outside; all under the influence of the physical agents of the environment. The final result—what the individual becomes—is dependent upon all these things; a change in any of them may change the result [pp. 225–226]....

The only way to grasp the laws of inheritance is to arrange a set of objects in the way the genes are arranged and to put them through the simple movements followed by the genes; attempts to understand them in any other way are futile. The laws of inheritance are not immediate consequences of some fundamental physiological principle, but of the arrangement of the packets of chemicals and their method of distribution. Where the arrangement is different, there are other laws. For many kinds of reproduction, on this account, nothing resembling Mendelian inheritance occurs. But as the rules work out in most cases of biparental inheritance, every germ cell gets a different combination of these packets of chemicals from that obtained by any other, so that in consequence every individual starts out as a differ-

ent combination of chemicals from every other; this makes prediction of results more hazardous in this field than is sometimes represented [p. 227]....

These facts—the relation of single packets to particular later characteristics—gave rise to a general doctrine, a philosophy, of heredity and development—a doctrine which has had and still has a very great influence on general views of life. It is to this doctrine that the prevailing ideas as to the relation of heredity and environment, as to the relative powerlessness of environment, are due. But it has turned out to be a completely mistaken one. This fact has not come to general consciousness: the doctrine continues to be a source of mystification and error. Its complete disappearance would mean a very great advance in the understanding of life.

From the fact that the "unit characters" changed when a single gene changed, it was concluded that in some ill-defined way, each characteristic was "represented" or in some way condensed and contained, in one particular gene. There was one gene for eye color, another for stature, another for feeble-mindedness, another for normal-mindedness, and so on. Every individual therefore came into the world with his characters fixed and determined. His whole outfit of characteristics was provided for him at the start; what he should be was preordained; predestination, in the present world, was an actual fact. Environment might prevent or permit the hereditary characters to develop; it could do nothing more. Heredity was everything, environment almost nothing. This doctrine of the all-might of inheritance is still proclaimed by the popularizers of biological science.

But this theory of representative particles is gone, clean gone. Advance in the knowledge of genetics has demonstrated its falsity. Its prevalence was an illustration of the adage that a little knowledge is a dangerous thing. The doctrine is dead—though as yet, like the decapitated turtle, it is not sensible of it. It is not true that particular characteristics are in any sense represented or condensed or contained in particular unit genes. Neither eye color nor tallness nor feeble-mindedness, nor any other characteristic, is a unit character in any such sense. There is indeed no such thing as a "unit character," and it would be a step in advance if that expression should disappear.

What recent investigation has shown is this:

the chemicals that were in the original packages derived from the parents — the genes — interact, in complex ways, for long periods; and every later characteristic is a long-deferred and indirect product of this interaction. Into the production of any characteristic has gone the activity of hundreds of the genes, if not of all of them; and many intermediate products occur before the final one is reached. In the fruit fly at least 50 genes are known to work together to produce so simple a feature as the red color of the eye; hundreds are required to produce normal straight wing, and so of all other characteristics. And each of the cooperating packets is necessary; if any one of the fifty is altered, the red color of the eye is not produced [pp. 228–229]....

Heredity is not the simple, hard-and-fast thing that old-fashioned Mendelism represented it. Further, more attentive observation has revealed that any single one of the genes affects, not one characteristic only, but many, probably the entire body. The idea of representative hereditary units, each standing for a single later characteristic, is exploded: it should be cleared completely out of the mind.

The genes then are simply chemicals that enter into a great number of complex reactions, the final upshot of which is to produce the completed body. The characters of the adult are no more present in the germ cells than is an automobile in the metallic ores out of which it is ultimately manufactured. To get the complete, normally acting organism, the proper materials are essential; but equally essential is it that they should interact properly with each other and with other things. *And the way they interact and what they produce depends on the conditions* [p. 230]....

In producing these structures, the genes interact, not only with each other, with the cytoplasm, with the oxygen from the surrounding medium, and with the food substances in the cytoplasm: but also, what is most striking and important, with products from the chemical processes in neighboring cells. Necessarily, then, this complicated interaction depends upon many conditions, a dependence that becomes manifest as methods of experimentation become precise. The process of development shows itself not to be stereotyped, as at first appears to be the case; it varies with changes in conditions. What any given cell shall produce, what any part of the body shall become, what the body as a whole shall become — depends not alone on

what it contains — its "heredity" but also on its relation to many other conditions; on its environment.

This is well shown in the development of our close relatives, the amphibia. The frog or salamander begins as a single cell, which divides into two. Usually one of these two produces the right half of the body, the other the left half. But this depends on the relation of the two cells to one another; separate them, and each produces an entire animal instead of half a one. Somewhat later in development the young salamander has become a sphere of many small cells, differing in different regions. Under usual conditions it is possible to predict what later structure each cell, each region of the sphere, will produce. The cells that will produce brain, eye, ear, spinal cord, skin, can be pointed out. The predicted process occurs with such regularity as to appear stereotyped.

But study shows that this is because the effective environment is usually the same for any given cell. What any cell shall become depends in fact on the conditions surrounding it: on its relation to the other cells. Development, it turns out, is a continual process of adjustment to environment. The recent brilliant work of Spemann shows that at a certain point in the developing mass of small cells (just in front of the blastopore) there begins a differentiating influence, whose further nature we do not know. This creeps from cell to cell, forwards and sideways, determining the type of chemical processes that shall occur in each cell, in such a way as to fit and conform the structures produced by that cell to those produced by the cell differentiated just before it. In this way the whole mass of cells diversifies into the pattern of the later structures. Here the cells differentiate into spinal cord, next into medulla, next into midbrain, here at the side into eye, here into ear; still farther on into skin. But if before this has happened the disk of cells is cut off and turned sideways, or completely around, the differentiating and adjusting influence creeps through it from the same point as before, but now in a different or reversed direction, so far as the cells are concerned. The cells that were to have formed skin produce spinal cord; those that would have produced eyes may form midbrain, or skin or ear, depending on just how they are placed with reference to the spreading differentiating influence; and so of the others. Or, transplant a small piece of prospective skin to the center of the eye-producing region; it now transforms into eye instead of into skin; transplant a prospective ear to another region, and it becomes skin or spinal cord, as its place in the pattern requires. It is proved that any particular cell may become part of any one of these structures, depending on its relation to the other cells, its relation to the "pattern." There comes a time, after the wave of differentiation has gone over them, when they can no longer be altered; their fate has been accomplished. But until then development is adjustment to the conditions. What part of the body a cell shall produce is not determined alone by its genes, by what it contains, but equally by the conditions surrounding it.

In later stages we know something of the nature of the cell products which help determine what other parts of the body shall become. There are a vast number of such intermediate products, necessarily produced before the adult structures can be made; some of them are the internal secretions, hormones, or endocrine products which are now the reigning sensation in biology. Their production, their distribution, their action, and the consequent method of development of the organism are subject in high degree to change by the surrounding conditions.

Not only what the cell within the body shall become, but what the organism as a whole shall become, is determined not alone by the hereditary materials it contains but also by the conditions under which those materials operate. Under diverse conditions the same set of genes will produce very diverse results. It is not true that what an organism shall become is determined, foreordained, when he gets his supply of chemicals or genes in the germ cells, as the popular writers on eugenics would have us believe. The same set of genes may produce many different results, depending on the conditions under which it operates. True it is that there are limits to this; that from one set of genes under a given environment may come a result that no environment can produce from another set. But this is a matter of limitation, not of fixed and final determination; it leaves open many alternative paths. Every individual has many sets of "innate" or "hereditary" characters; the conditions under which he develops determine which set he shall bring forth. So in man, the characteristics of an educated, cultured person are as much his inherited characteristics as are any that he has.

These sweeping statements are substantiated by precisely known facts in many organisms. In that animal whose heredity is better known than is that of any other organism, the fruit fly, individuals occur with hereditary abnormalities. The abdomen is irregular, deformed; the joints between the segments are imperfect. This is sharply inherited as a sex-linked character, so that it is known to be due to a peculiarity of one of the genes in the x-chromosome. If the father has this abnormality, all his daughters inherit it, but none of his sons do so. The daughters hand it on to half their sons and half their daughters, and so on.

But the fruit flies in the laboratory usually live in moist air; this inheritance appears under those conditions. If they are hatched and live under dry conditions, the abnormality doesn't appear — even in those daughters which indubitably inherit it. Clearly, it is not necessary to have a characteristic merely because one inherits it. Or more properly, characteristics are not inherited at all; what one inherits is certain material that under certain conditions will produce a particular characteristic; if those conditions are not supplied, some other characteristic is produced [pp. 231–233]. . . .

Many years ago there was discovered in Mexico a salamander that lives throughout its life in water; has a heavy, broad body, a tail flattened for swimming and external gills. In this condition it becomes mature, lays its eggs in the water; produces young that inherit its characteristics and finally dies. This continues for generation after generation. A number of these axolotls were kept for years in the zoological garden at Paris; they showed the inherited characteristics above set forth. Breeding experiments on these animals would show these characteristics to be inherited in the usual Mendelian manner.

But after years in which these were the only inherited characteristics that they were known to possess, certain different environmental conditions were brought into action, and thereupon, to the astonishment of the observers, the axolotls developed a new set of inherited characteristics, a new and diverse personality. The external gills disappeared, the body became smaller, slender, and of a very different shape, the animals came out on the land and remained there, breathing air. They now became mature in this amblystoma condition, laid eggs, and produced offspring—which again, under these conditions, developed into land animals of the same sort; and this, too, may continue for generation after generation. The inherited characteristics are now these land characters; these are, in detail, inherited in the typical Mendelian manner.

Here we have two extremely different sets of inherited characters; which one shall appear is determined by the environment under which the organism develops. Both sets are hereditary characters; both sets are environmental characters. Any character requires for its production both an adequate stock of hereditary chemicals and an environment adequate for its production through proper interaction of these chemicals with each other and with other things [p. 234]. . . .

Every creature has many inheritances; which one shall be realized depending on the conditions under which it develops; but man is the creature that has the greatest number of possible heritages. Or, more accurately, men and other organisms do not inherit their characteristics at all. What their parents leave them are certain packets of chemicals which under one set of conditions produce one set of characters, under other conditions produce other sets. In man, the number of diverse sets that may thus be produced is very great; although it is of course not unlimited. But what the limitations are cannot be stated from general biological principles or from what we know of any other organisms; they can be discovered only by concrete studies of man himself [p. 236].

Analysis of the doctrine of "psychoheredity"   3

The basic error involved in imposing heredity on psychological data has been referred to above. Granted that yellow or wrinkled peas beget, respectively, yellow (and not green ones) and wrinkled (not smooth) progeny or other lawful proportions when they are crossbred. Granted that Negro parents do not produce white offspring and white-skinned parents do not beget black children. Yet what has this to do with psychology, which deals not with the shapes, sizes, and colors of organisms but with their tastings, hearings, strivings, dreams, despairs, loves, hates, fears, agonies, guilts, discoveries, and creative acts? Montagu (see above) has already warned us of the fallacy of analogizing from principles that have valid application in the understanding of anatomical features of plants and animals to complex psychological activities of humans. Let us con-

sider certain other related points in an expanded analysis of heredity in psychological investigation.

1. *Imposition of theory derived from one kind of data upon totally different data* Suppose an investigator became an expert in his study of mechanical things. Suppose that he finally decided to delve into the nature of living things. Suppose further that even prior to any observation or experimentation, he should list the theories and laws that he had derived from his previous study of levers, fulcrums, engines, and other mechanical devices? Would it be proper for him to impose such explanations onto the irritability, reproduction, metabolism, and other manifestations of *living* things? We see the scientific inappropriateness of indiscriminantly applying theories derived from the study of one

kind of phenomenon to a very different kind of phenomenon. This same kind of transposition is evident in the ages-old reasoning by analogy from the inheritance of physical characteristics to the inheritance of neurotic or psychotic behavior, or the inheritance of talent or genius. A mother and daughter acting in a paranoid or anxious manner or two generations of Bachs performing musically or composing music is, according to this overly simple view, just like a man and his son having black skin. Is it necessary to point out that "acting a certain way" is thus *reduced to* the status of a biological quality like skin color?

2. *The layman's unfounded belief in the inheritance of superior organs* "But can't one person start with sharper ears, or eyes, or a faster reaction time than another?" students commonly ask. The student fails to recognize that he has only stated a hypothesis that requires testing and substantiation or rejection. He believes that it is so. On this point, we offer an alternative to the hereditary theory in the following quotation from Norman Cameron.*

Not so long ago the belief was almost universal that sensitivities were usually a matter of delicate sense-organs and nerves. Thus, composers and performers of music were supposed to keep their hair long to protect their hypersensitive ears. The clear superiority in visual perception that an experienced sailor shows at sea was likewise held to mean superior optic sensitivity, and few doubted that slender, hypersensitive fingers were basic equipment for skillful surgery.

Today even children know that Beethoven was deaf during most of his career, and no serious music-lover would be disturbed if news leaked out that Shostakovitch would soon be as bald as Sibelius. Under the uniform condi-

tions of an eye clinic or a psychological laboratory, any number of landlubbers can be found who test higher in visual acuity than the average seaman, even though they are unquestionably inferior to him in detecting a landfall or ships on the horizon. As for surgery, some of the world's most proficient and eminent operators have short stubby fingers and yet, though wearing rubber gloves, they can still feel things that the most slender-fingered layman could not detect with his bare hands.

No one, of course, questions the basic fact that skilled, experienced persons actually do perceive things clearly, within the range of their professional work, which remain imperceptible to others. But if their sense-organs are not necessarily hyperacute, and if in some cases of unusual excellence the sense-organs involved are actually inferior, to what are we going to ascribe their selective sensitivity? The answer seems to be that a person, whose receptors give no evidence of being in any way unusual, can still be rendered highly sensitive by his own reactions, by the organized special attitudes and responses he acquires. He is, in other words, not receptor-sensitive but *reaction-sensitive*. In behavioral terms, the acquisition of special reactions, in relation to certain situations, gives the excitants of those reactions prepotence when such situations arise. The special organized attitudes and responses, in short, leave an individual selectively sensitized to whatever stimulation habitually arouses them.

We may now define *reaction-sensitivity* as *a selective readiness-to-react to certain components of a stimulating situation and not to others, which is the result of one's having acquired a system of related attitudes and responses* [pp. 65–66].

Cameron, then, suggests that the reason why one person perceives pitch more precisely than another is not due to sharper sense organs but to sharper *reactions* that he has built up during his lifetime.

3. *Organ functions versus psychological responses* A comparison stemming from the directly preceding point involves organ functions and the psychological reactions of an organism. In the turtle, a heart can be removed and still go on beating rhyth-

*Quoted material is from Norman Cameron, *The Psychology of Behavior Disorders* (Boston: Houghton Mifflin, 1947).

mically in its lonely existence. Here is clearly an instance of *organ functioning.* Not so when one places a violin in the hands and under the chin of a naive person. Hands, arms, and chin do not automatically elicit ecstatic sounds from the instrument. A long series of organism-stimulus-object interactions are required for such an eventuality. Another dimension is involved following the individual's birth and his confrontation with a violin. Events involving the two are essential in describing the career of a violin virtuoso. Granted that hands, arms, and a chin are essential; nevertheless, they are not *causal,* only *instrumental.* Without them, obviously, a concert career is doomed, but their presence does not guarantee success. They appear to be a necessary condition, but without a violin a concert career is also doomed.

Man cannot, by means of his own organic equipment alone, hope to fly as expertly as the hawk or sea gull. Is it not correct, then, to say that man's heredity has "predestined" him to an earthbound condition? Heredity has prevented him from learning to fly. But, on the other hand, is it proper to say that heredity "predestines" that man should walk at all— simply because heredity has endowed him with two legs? If a child should "up-and-walk" the way he "up-and-sneezes" when his nose is tickled with a feather, then we could call both acts organ functioning. But a child must first kick, crawl, stand, etc., before walking *finally* evolves. Then, too, children isolated for long periods or autistic children who have inherited two good legs are not assured upright walking. Some never walk. In short, psychological acts should not be equated with organ functioning whether or not the latter are conceived to be allotted among humans on a superior or inferior basis.

4. *Genetics as a comparative newcomer to the sciences* Leucippus said: "Where ignorance exists, there theories abound." When nothing was known about gout, tuberculosis, or syphilis, we blamed heredity. The Juke myth in the next section is a case in point. But lack of scientific evidence has had little effect in inhibiting the construction of pedigree charts of short-sightedness, right-handedness, or epilepsy in successive generations of hypothetical families. Certainly the layman's belief in the power of heredity will flourish for decades to come, despite absence of scientific proof or disproof.

Summary

This section constituted a critical analysis of the biological concept of heredity applied to psychological inquiry. Taking up the layman's notion of talent allegedly "running in families," the following points were made: Turning to the proper discipline for a clear definition of the term heredity, we gave extensive consideration to the classic statement by Jennings, who sees the packet of chemicals contributed by each parent and that packet's *interaction* with surrounding conditions as explaining the completed organism. Jennings rejected a *predestined* set of unit traits residing in unit genes. The packets obviously set limits but so do surrounding conditions. We considered criticism of "psychoheredity" on the grounds that a theory derived from a study of one kind of data (biological) was superimposed upon a totally different kind (psychological). Next, we attempted to explain the traditional, hypothetical "inheritance" of "sensitive organs" in terms of Cameron's "reaction sensitivity." We then considered the notion that, in psychology, organs are *instrumental* rather than *causal* and not comparable with mere organ functioning as in biology. Finally, attention was called to the fact that genetics is a new and young science, only recently applied to the relatively long-lived and slow-breeding human species.

---

4 Adams: The Juke myth*

No other family in American annals is so well and unfavorably known as the Jukes. The name is a synonym for depravity. What the Rothschilds embody in finance, the Jukes represent in misdemeanor. If there were an International Hall of Ill Fame, they would get top billing.

And they never existed otherwhere than in the brain of an amateur criminologist. Richard L. Dugdale did not precisely invent them; rather he compiled them from an assortment of human derelicts whom he collected after a method peculiarly his own, for the purpose of bolstering his theory of criminal heredity. He passed on his findings to posterity in his *magnum opus,* "The Jukes: A Study in Crime, Pauperism, Disease, and Insanity."

This classic has permeated the sociology of nations. Geneticists like Giddings, East, and Walter have swallowed it whole. The New York State Prison Association sponsored it. Putnam's brought out three large editions, which were accepted as sociological gospel. Dugdale became the recognized authority on crime. His qualifications as an expert are peculiar. When the Dugdale family came to this country from England in 1851, Richard was ten years old. It was intended that he should go to college. After three years of schooling in New York something went awry in his education. He left school and became assistant to a sculptor. In the evenings he attended classes at Cooper Union, where he won something of a reputation as a debater on social topics.

His career, if such it were, was interrupted by the departure of the family to try farming in the Middle West. The venture was unsuccessful. The Dugdales returned to New York and Richard turned his hand to manufacturing. He was then twenty-three. The business failed. Richard had a nervous breakdown and withdrew from active endeavor. "For four years I could neither earn nor learn," he records. Such was his technical equipment as a sociologist.

The Jukes came into his life quite by chance. He happened to be in a Kingston, N.Y., police court in 1873, where a youth was on trial for receiving stolen goods. Five relatives were present as witnesses. They came of a breed, to quote the incipient investigator, "so despised that their family name had to come to be used generically as a term of reproach." They were alleged to live like haggards of the rock, in the caves of a nearby lake region. "Crime-cradles," our author calls the locality. He was a neat hand at a phrase.

He invented the name Juke for the clan.

The fact that the Juke at the bar of justice was acquitted in no wise discouraged young Dugdale. He made inquiries about the others present. An uncle of the accused is set down as a burglar. No proof is adduced. Two male cousins had been charged with pushing a boy over a cliff, one of whom was convicted. The remaining witnesses, two girls, he lists as harlots. By the Dugdale method, "under the heading of harlots are included all women who have made lapses, however seldom." This is fairly indicative of his standards of investigation and attribution.

With this auspicious start, he canvassed the neighborhood for further specimens.

"With comparatively little inquiry," he writes, "it was found that out of twenty-nine male adults, the immediate blood relations of

---

*Quoted material is from Samuel Hopkins Adams, "The Juke Myth." First published in *Saturday Review.* Copyright 1955 by *Saturday Review, Inc.* Reprinted by permission of Brandt and Brandt.

the six, seventeen were criminals and fifteen others convicted of some degree of offense."

Impressed by this suggestive ratio—as who would not be by thirty-two out of a possible twenty-nine?—Dugdale went sleuthing back through the generations until he came upon an old Dutch reprobate who kept a turnpike hostelry in Orange County about the middle of the eighteenth century. Old Max appears to have been a sporting character. Several illegitimate children were imputed to him. He enjoyed a local reputation for drinking, gaming, and wenching, divertissements fairly general in those lusty pioneer days. He became Exhibit A in the Dugdale rogues' gallery, though nothing criminal appears in his record.

Max had two legitimate sons who married into a family of six sisters. With the discovery of the sisterhood, Dugdale really hits his stride. The family line of the six is obscure; it "has not been absolutely ascertained," he admits. "One, if not all, of them were illegitimate," he surmises, on what grounds he does not explain. Delia is recorded as a "harlot before marriage," and Belle as a "harlot after marriage," Clara, he notes (presumptively with reluctance), was "reputed chaste." She did, however, marry a man who shot a neighbor. Effie's reputation was unknown to author Dugdale, which was certainly a break for Effie.

Another sister *circa* 1760 is Dugdale's prize specimen. "Margaret, Mother of Criminals," he calls her, although her name was Ada. Apt alliteration's artful aid again! To her goes the credit for "the distinctly criminal line of the family." But, what family? For all that he reveals, Margaret-Ada, of unascertained parentage, may have been a Van Rensselaer, a Livingston, a Saltonstall, a Biddle, or the granddaughter of the original Joe Doakes. To be sure, he later characterizes the whole lot as "belonging to the Juke blood." Pure assumption. As their derivation was unknown and they were suspectedly illegitimate anyway, how could Dugdale or anybody else know anything of their ancestry?

As a "Mother of Criminals" Margaret (or Ada) hardly lives up to her name. Her daughter is designated as a harlot, but, by way of palliation perhaps, our author adds, "not industrious." One son was a laborer, "somewhat industrious." The other, a farmer, is stigmatized as having been "indolent" and "licentious in

youth." The same might be said of some eminent non-Jukes, including Robert Burns and the Apostle Paul.

Margaret-Ada was married to one of old Max's sons. She had a son of her own, whom Dugdale holds to be co-responsible for the evil Juke inheritance. But this son was a Juke only in name. He was illegitimate. Dugdale says so.

Thus, the notorious criminal-Juke strain derives on one side from a progenitor who was not criminal (Old Max) and on the other from a line which was not Juke except by Dugdale fiat. (Margaret-Ada through her illegitimate son.)

It sufficed Dugdale. He had his theory; now he set out after supporting facts. He made a year's tour of prisons, almshouses, and asylums, collecting Jukes. The result he published in 1875. It is still regarded by those who have not read it, and even by some who have, as an authoritative document. It established the Jukes as the type-family of degeneration.

Dugdale invented a terminology to go with his Jukes. His thesis is based, so he states, upon "Positive Statistics and Conjectural Statistics... Conjectural Statistics consists in Political Arithmetic and the Theory of Probabilities." This recondite process "reduces the method of study to one of historico-biographical synthesis united to statistical analysis," which sounds as if it might have come out of Lewis Carroll.

Applying this yardstick, Dugdale lists 709 alleged Jukes, of whom 507 were social detrimentals. Such conventional crimes as murder, arson, rape, and robbery, quite lacking in proof for the most part, are cited. But there were not enough of them to support satisfactorily the Dugdale political arithmetic and theory of probabilities. So he fattens up the record with entries like the following:

Reputed sheep-stealer, but never caught.
Thief, but never caught.
Petty thief, though never convicted.
Guilty of murder, but escapes punishment.
Unpunished and cautious thief.
Bastardy prosecution.
Supposed to have attempted rape.
Cruelty to animals.
Habitual criminal.
Impossible to get any reliable information, but it is evident that at nineteen he was a leader in crime.

And such scattered attributions as "pauper," "harlot," "brothel keeper," "vagrant," "lazy," "intemperate," "drunkard," "immoral," "lecherous," etc., etc., etc. There was also a "contriver of crime," and a hardened character who, in addition to frequenting a saloon, was accused of breaking a deaf man's ear-trumpet. Like the Juke who started it all, he was acquitted. It did not matter to our investigator; the non-breaker of the ear-trumpet comes down the ages, embalmed in criminal history.

All this might seem rather attenuated evidence on which to indict an entire family. It sufficed Dugdale. He followed the long and proliferating branches of the clan through the generations and worked out a diagram as framework for the composite portrait. This he calls "Leading Facts."

Consanguinity

		F		
C	Prostitution	O	Illegitimacy	P
		R		A
R		N		U
		I		P
I	Exhaustion	C	Intemperance	E
		A		R
M		T		I
		I		S
E	Disease	O	Extinction	M
		N		

Not Consanguineous

In other words, *fornication* (the italics are his), either consanguineous or not, is the backbone of their habits, flanked on the one side by *pauperism,* on the other by *crime.* The secondary features are *prostitution,* with its complement of *bastardy,* and its resultant of miseducated childhood; *exhaustion,* with its complement, *intemperance,* and its resultant, unbalanced minds; and *disease,* with its complement, *extinction.*

Dugdale's investigations into hygiene and morality are on a par with his criminological efforts. Insanity, epilepsy, deformity, impotency, and tuberculosis appear to have been as typical Juke phenomena as thievery, bastardy, and general lawlessness. Some of the evidence cited is calculated to astonish students of heredity. For example, it is recorded that the original Max went blind and transmitted the affliction to his posterity. As he lost his sight late in life, after his children were born, it is difficult to see how he can be held responsible for their blindness unless he poked them in the eyes with a burnt stick.

Our author's figures on tuberculosis are confident, but where he found them is left a mystery. Nobody bothered to keep statistics in those days. Still more difficult would it have been to gather reliable data on venereal disease. Yet our conjectural statistician specifies, in one branch of the Jukes, forty harlots who contaminated 440 men, presumably eleven per harlot. In another genealogical line he states that 23½ percent of the females were immoral. That ½ percent is fairly awe-inspiring.

Not until long after the author's death did anyone rise to challenge his thesis. The late Thomas Mott Osborne, of prison-reform fame and at one time president of that same prison association which certified the Dugdale revelations, studied the Juke records with growing skepticism. Himself a practised investigator, he raised questions about the Dugdale methods which that author might have found awkward to answer.

Whence, Mr. Osborne wished to know, did Dugdale derive those cocksure figures on disease, insanity, and death? Vital statistics at the time of his inquiry were practically nonexistent. How did he acquire his data on criminality when court records for the period were notoriously unreliable, if, indeed, they were available at all? What genealogical method did he use in tracing back the Juke line through the mazes of its prevalent bastardy, for a century and a quarter? Legitimate family lines, Mr. Osborne pointed out, were difficult enough to trace; illegitimate were flatly impossible, beyond a generation or two. Further, the objector indicated, a specially trained sociological investigator would have required at least years to do the work which Dugdale completed in one.

Analyzing the indicated method of investigation, Mr. Osborne suggested that Dugdale based it on a formula of retroactive hypothesis as follows:

That every criminal was a putative Juke. That every Juke was a presumptive criminal.

By the system which Dugdale employed in tracing down his Jukes, Mr. Osborne concluded, it would be possible to asperse the morality, sanity, and legitimacy of any family in America. As for the Jukes, they were "pure folklore."

Another dissident raised objections in *The Clinical Review* for April, 1902. Was it credible, Edmund Andrews asked, that Old Max possessed "such a miraculous energy of vicious propagation that, by his sole vital force, he begat and transmitted the degeneracy of all the Jukes for five generations?" Each descendant in the fifth generation, the critic pointed out, had fifteen other progenitors. Why assign his or her lawless, shiftless, or bawdy habits to Max any more than to any other of the uncharted Jukes

or Jakes or Jeeks or Jenkins? A sturdy breeder like Max might well be the ancestor of a couple of thousand great-great-grandchildren, 1,500 of whom, for all that Dugdale knew to the contrary, might have been missionaries.

"It is sheer nonsense," Mr. Andrews contends, "to suppose that he (a fifth-generation Juke degenerate) got them all (his vicious proclivities) from that one lazy, but jovial old Rip Van Winkle, the original Juke."

These were but voices crying in a wilderness. To scotch a good, sturdy historical fake, once it has got its growth, is impossible. Nine-tenths of America devoutly believes that Robert Fulton invented the steamboat and that Abner Doubleday was the founder of baseball. So the Jukes will doubtless continue to furnish texts to trusting sociologists, and no great harm done.

But they are in the wrong category. The proper place of a Juke is not in criminology. It is in mythology.

Jastrow: The inheritance of psychopathologies* 5

As etiology of the mental diseases, heredity has been given the first place, not only by a few thoughtful observers in the Greek period and the Middle Ages, but especially since the biological conceptions achieved their great publicity and importance. Starting with the observation which is forced upon any man of experience that mental disease "runs in families," there was developed a school of thought which gave to heredity transmission the first place in the causation of the psychoses and which merely changed its form in the twentieth century by taking on a Mendelian coloring....

In studying the inheritance of epilepsy he [Charles B. Davenport] makes up a list of characters all of which are given equal hereditary weight in reaching the conclusion that the patient's condition rests on a hereditary basis. These characters are all vague, may arise from a number of causes; furthermore, their hereditary weight is the point to be proven. Yet with

an appalling sangfroid their hereditary potency is assumed. The list starts with A (which equals alcoholism), proceeds with apoplexy, blind, Bright's disease, criminalistic, cancerous, deaf, etc., and goes blithely enough through the alphabet to V or vagrant. The final criticism of such a list as that which Davenport here uses is this: By extending the list of conditions that may be declared hereditary, one finally extinguishes all differences, comes down to the fact that man is mortal, has sickness and weakness, and is sinful, A linking-up thus can be made of the vicissitudes and misfortunes of life and the psychiatric diseases.

---

*Quoted material is from Joseph Jastrow, *The Story of Human Error* (New York: Appleton-Century, 1936). By permission of Appleton-Century, affiliate of Meredith Press. Copyright 1936 D. Appleton-Century Co., Inc.

This kind of work, which assumes that a sausage-mill will take care of meat, paving-stones, old clothes, and soap and turn out good sausages, is the absolutely untenable basis of the work done not only by Davenport, but by those who have portrayed with gusto and alarm the royal families of the feeble-minded, the Nams, Kallikaks, the hill-folk, Zero tribe, etc.

The errors in this whole theory, which dates back to a period of medical knowledge before there was any definite understanding of medical knowledge, before there was any definite understanding of brain physiology, spinal-fluid chemistry, reflex pathways, serology endocrinology, X-ray study, may be thus enumerated:

First, the fallacy of the positive instance dominates. If, for example, it turns out that the non-insane have more cases of apoplexy in their ancestry and collaterals than do the insane, as is the case, then apoplexy in an ancestor is merely coincidence and not related to insanity. If it is assumed that alcoholism in an ancestor or relative is a hereditary psychopathic character, how is the fact explained that the children of the alcoholic Scotch are no worse so far as feeble-mindedness, etc., is concerned than the children of the non-alcoholic Scotch, as shown by the study of Elderton and Pearson? Headache, fainting spells, epilepsy – all these are terms of varied clinical meaning and etiologic value; they are not specific and may relate to such diverse matters as brain tumor, fractured skull, bad teeth, sinusitis, heart disease, indigestion, nervous instability, and malingering. At least 90 per cent of the work done on the heredity of mental diseases has been wasted, and a large part of it is merely a bolstering of preconceived theory by specious figures.

Second – and this error is as bad on the other end of the situation as the weighting of the psychopathic ancestors and relatives – any approach to the problems of psychiatry that makes a unity or even a unit of "insanity" or feeblemindedness or crime is based on a fallacy of the overgeneralization type – so common when little is known about a subject. The "all cats look gray in the dark" axiom aptly fits the case. Insanity is a legal term and merely means that the person labeled as insane needs incarceration or must have his affairs managed by others. Mental disease has quite a different connotation, though a false unity is implicit in the word mental. What links together, for example, the case of general paresis, due to syphilis, with the alcoholic hallucinosis; or either or both with the case of dementia praecox, which rests very likely on some hereditary disorder; or all of these with senile dementia, which comes to everyone who lives long enough to have his brain disordered before his body dies? Similar with feeblemindedness – this is merely the name of a symptom, just as cough is. No more than the cough of pneumonia, tuberculosis, aneuryism of the aorta, nasal spur, hay-fever, hysteria, and embarrassment links these diseases and conditions together does "feeblemindedness" link together cretinism, mongolism, microcephaly, brain injury, and the perhaps hereditary group of the feeble-minded.

Where little is known in medicine, heredity is invoked as a cause, just as in tuberculosis the early clinicians called it a family or hereditary disease on the same basis that we now speak of the familial psychoses, namely, that brothers and sisters, ancestors and descendants, had tuberculosis. Then came Koch and the discovery of the tubercle bacillus, which knocked out heredity and placed the blame on an environmental organism. The ground then shifted to predisposition – that is, patients acquired tuberculosis because they were predisposed to get it. While it cannot be denied that there may exist a predisposition and that some persons resist forces to which others easily succumb, there is a good bit of *petitio principii* in the general use of the word. A skull can be fractured by a falling brick only if it is thin enough – that is, predisposed to be broken; otherwise it would crack the brick, in which case the predisposition would be with the brick. Predisposition, constitution, these are logically necessary inferences; but they are not facts, nor until the whole world of variables is taken into account can they be shown even mathematically to exist.

The whole subject of the heredity of mental disease needs a fresh start. The nineteenth-century work can be discarded almost completely, and most of the twentieth-century researches make a jump from genetics, which is limited in its application and deals with simple characters of simple creatures, to the mentality of man, which, whatever weight we may give to heredity, is certainly in a part a product of social and cultural forces. There is some hereditary background for a few of the mental diseases, apparently for manic-depressive psychosis, perhaps for dementia praecox, and for many of the cases of feeble-mindedness. To infer that these are Mendelian characters is to proceed without the slightest possibility of proof—certainly at the present time [430–435].

A contrary view
on inheritance
of psychopathologies

6

Jastrow's paper above is hardly current and not well known. However, a book of the same vintage with wide appeal even today is Kallmann's *The Genetics of Schizophrenia* (1938). In it Kallmann studied the ancestry and descendants of 1087 schizophrenics, the total population of a Berlin Hospital admitted between the years 1893 and 1902. After reviewing the case histories of 15,000 patients in the hospital's archives, Kallmann made his own diagnosis of schizophrenia. The fact that his diagnosis differed from that in the hospital records did not seem to bother him.

Having secured his base, Kallmann began calculating the expectancy of developing schizophrenia in the case of the patients' children, their siblings, and their parents. The figures obtained were then compared with the figure for the general population. The figure of .85 percent shows that slightly less than one out of 100 people in the general population develops schizophrenia. How does this compare with Kallmann's expectancy figure for relatives of his schizophrenic population? He states a figure of 10 percent occurrence of schizophrenia in the immediate ancestry of his subjects. But he reports "a predisposition to schizophrenia...of at least one third of the parents, uncles, and aunts [p. 42]."

For various subgroups of schizophrenia among the children of his schizophrenic subjects, Kallmann reports figures of between 10 and 20 percent (p. 107). But when he included "schizoidia or eccentric borderline cases [p. 104]," he reports total expectancy figures of from 30 to 35 percent!

Criticism of Kallmann's work

Kallmann's work is used to support a hereditary basis for schizophrenia. For example, it is defended in a recent, prestigious book on behavior genetics that is discussed in the next section. Still, according to some students of the field, Kallmann's methods are considered very loose. Pastore (1949) has written an objective and systematic criticism of Kallmann's near-classic work. Here are a few objections raised against his procedure.

1. Kallmann took it upon himself to make the diagnoses. He should have had other experts make independent judgments (p. 288).

2. Kallmann himself pointed out that his data were "limited to case histories that were made decades ago and described according to obsolete medical methods and psychiatric conceptions [Kallmann, p. 22]."

3. In diagnosing the relatives of the patients, hospital criteria were absent. "Consequently, many individuals must have been diagnosed on the basis of 'anecdotal' materials. This would be especially true for the parents and grandparents of the probands — individuals who probably matured in the first half of the nineteenth century and late eighteenth century. Establishing a particular type of diagnosis for these individuals, almost a century later, seems to be quite risky [Pastore, p. 289]."

4. One category that Kallmann used, the spouses of his cases, was labeled "schizophrenic or suspicious of schizophrenia" (p. 289). Is any comment necessary?

5. Another questionable category listed 16 "doubtful schizophrenic cases" with 92 classified as "definite schizophrenic cases [p. 290]." Should not the 16 have been followed up to determine that they *did* become schizophrenic?

Pastore continues with a thorough but devastating dissection of Kallmann's work. However, the book continues to buttress the argument of the pro-hereditarian.

7 A preview of things to come

The preceding articles regarding heredity have been largely orientational or theoretical. Specificities have been omitted. Recent work has gone into details that are beyond our present level. The following statement from the preface of a pioneering textbook in *Behavior Genetics* by Fuller and Thompson (1960) warns that "this book is written for a readership of advanced undergraduates and graduate students in biology and psychology" (p. v). The treatise is too complex and abstract to discuss here but is mentioned briefly as an indication of the direction that developments are taking in the area.

The student should not, however, expect to read all about the inheritance of human behavior in *Behavior Genetics*. As a matter of fact, Fuller and Thompson are somewhat embarrassed about the dearth of human materials in their book because of the "difficulty ... in selecting suitable materials for citation, especially when these fell short of exacting scientific standards [p. vi]." They had considered omitting human studies entirely, "but did not do so because of the primary interest of many readers in human problems [p. vi]."

An excursion into the biology of inheritance would lead us still deeper into a biochemical jungle and would simultaneously plunge us into the civil war being waged among biologists over DNA. The more courageous reader may wish to sample the intellectual fare in such works as Barry Commoner's (1964) timely paper on the "Roles of deoxyribonucleic acid in inheritance."

A more moderate stand on the heredity-environment question has been spelled out by Anastasi (1958), who correctly points out that "the heredity-environment problem is still very much alive [p. 206]." It can be ignored but it is not necessarily a dead issue.

Chapter summary

We examined the relationship between heredity and psychology and found a lack of data to substantiate the common belief that characteristics like musical ability are inherited. Some other fallacies implicit in the popular conception of heredity were indicated. Essentially, the errors involve (1) a misapplication of theory derived from biological data to psychological materials, (2) the belief that superior performance is *caused by* constitutionally superior organs, and (3) an approach that equates complex pianistic performance, for example, with mere finger-, hand-, and arm-functioning.

As a reference point, we used a clear statement on biological heredity by Jen-nings, the father of American genetics. With this basis of operation, we were able to detect the error in scientific procedure of applying biological heredity to psychological subject matter.

"The Jukes and the Kallikaks" are often quoted in support of the inheritance of psychological traits. Consequently, we showed the mythical basis of such reports and concluded with a critical examination of the notion that psychopathology is inherited.

Unable to provide final answers, we closed our discussion with the suggestion that the heredity-environment issue is still a live one.

5

Instincts (?), tropisms, and imprinting

Between the living and the nonliving lie the viruses. They puzzle the biologist because, as a transitional form, they have some characteristics of each. A similar problem arises in connection with an absolute distinction between plants and animals. If you offer the criterion that animals locomote and that plants produce food by photosynthesis, where will you place *Euglena,* which does both? Nature prefers continua or gradients that show gradual changes between various distinctive levels rather than jumps or discontinuities.

This and subsequent chapters are meant to reflect such a natural continuum – one ranging through unlearned and learned acts. We start by considering simple, repetitive but unlearned acts and then move on to more complex acts that appear under conditions of learning and imprinting.

Kellogg's classic
view of instinct*

1

I believe that the following selection deserves to be regarded as a classic. In it Vernon L. Kellogg describes the nest-building of the female Ammophila wasp in clear, unforgettable style. On first impression, the wasp's behavior seems to show uncanny foresight.

Along the western shores of the long southern arm of San Francisco Bay there stretch broad salt marshes, through which tide-channels run, but which embrace considerable areas that lie above all but the very high spring tides, and which are mostly covered by a dense growth of a low-fleshy-leaved plant called samphire or pickle-weed (*Salicornia*). Here and there, however, in these areas there are small, entirely bare, level sandy places which shine white and sparkling in the sun because of a thin incrustation of salt over them.

Each September these bare places are taken possession of by many female wasps of a species of Ammophila, which is a long, slender-bodied "solitary" or "digger" wasp, that is somewhat gregarious in habit, but is not at all a "social" wasp like the hornets and yellow-jackets, the *Vespas*, more familiar to us. Now, watching closely any one of these female Ammophilas flitting about these bare places, one can see the following performance take place.

First, the Ammophila, after various flights – flights of survey, we may call them – over the salt-encrusted ground, will settle down somewhere on it, and, with her sharp jaws, cut out a small circular bit of the salty soil crust, which she gets out unbroken, and drags off a few inches to one side. Then she digs out, by means of her jaws, bit by bit, a little vertical well about three inches deep and slightly less in diameter than the circular bit of salt crust. Each pellet of soil dug out is carried away by the wasp, flying a foot or two from the mouth of the hole in any direction, and dropped. She does not plan to

*Quoted material is from Vernon L. Kellogg, *Mind and Heredity* (Princeton: Princeton University Press, 1923). By permission of the publisher.

have any tell-tale pile of soil near the mouth of that precious hole in the ground. In emerging from the hole she always backs upward out of it, and while digging she keeps up a low humming sound. We might imagine this to be the joyous song of the homemaking mother — but as we are scientific observers we had better restrain, if not our imagination, at least our unverifiable interpretation of things. Let us be properly matter of fact.

After the hole is about three inches deep our energetic Ammophila, climbing out with the last pellet and flinging it to one side, seeks for and finds the little circular bit of salt encrustation which was so carefully removed and put to one side at the beginning of this hole-making performance. This she now drags to the hole and with it carefully covers the hole's mouth. Then she flies away over the surrounding pickleweed and disappears in it.

We must wait a few minutes now, sometimes only a few, sometimes as many as fifteen or twenty. If we like, we can look around us in the little bare space and we shall see other Ammophilas digging holes, going in head first and backing out, flipping pellets of soil away, humming their nest-building songs and altogether doing just what our first Ammophila did and in just the same way. But now, silence and immovability! For the first Ammophila is back, flying low and heavily with what seems to be a looper or inch-worm (larva of a Geometrid moth) about an inch and a quarter long, held in her jaws. She comes directly to the covered hole — how does she tell where it is, with its salt-crust cover making it look like all the rest of the ground? — puts the limp inchworm down by it, carefully removes the salt-crust cover, and then drags the inchworm down into the hole, going in head first and then coming up and out backwards. Then she re-covers the hole with the salt-crust lid, and flies away again. After a while, she is back with another limp inchworm which she puts into the hole, going through just the same performance as she did the first time. And so on until she has put in five inchworms. If we watch other Ammophila mothers, we shall see that they vary a little in number of inchworms put into their holes. The number runs from five to eight, or, rarely, ten, but is usually five or six.

Now, what next? After taking the fifth inchworm down into the hole, Ammophila does not come out as soon as she has after putting each of the others down. After several minutes, however, she does come out, but instead of flying away she now begins to fill the hole with pellets of soil which she scrapes up here and there with her sharp strong jaws. Some of the pellets are the ones she scattered a foot or two away while she was digging the hole. If they are close by, she scrapes them in with her forefeet. If farther away, she brings them in her jaws. She works rapidly, running and jumping about, making little buzzing leaps and flights, until she has quite filled the hole.

Then she does a clever thing. With her forefeet she paws and rakes the surface of the filled hole until it is quite smooth, and then with jaws and horny head she presses and tamps down the bits of soil on top until they are a little below the surface of the salt crust around the hole. Finally, she gets again the circular salt-crust lid and neatly puts it into the depression on top of the filled-in hole so that it fits perfectly with the hard continuous salt crust around the hole's edge! Without saying anything about intention on the part of Ammophila, it is certain that by this performance she has almost perfectly concealed the whereabouts of the hole. In fact, if we take our eyes off it, we shall have difficulty in finding it again: and yet *we* know, to start with, just where it is. How about the various predaceous birds or insects who would like to find it with its store of luscious inchworms?

And now Ammophila is finished with this hole, at least. But we are not. Let us dig it up and have a look at those apparently dead inchworms, and also see if we can find out what kept Ammophila so long in the hole after taking down the fifth worm. So we dig up and examine the five inchworms. Sticking to the body of the last one put in there is a little, shining white, seed-like thing. It is an egg which Ammophila has laid and glued on to the worm's body. And the worms themselves instead of being dead are alive but paralyzed. If we prick any one of them near head or tail, it will wriggle just a little. If we prick one in the middle of the body it does not wriggle. Ammophila has stung each inchworm in one or more of the middle tiny ganglia or body-brains which are ranged segmentally along the under side of the body; a very exact and useful surgical operation. For the worms, which are, of course, to serve as food for the Ammophila grub that will hatch from the single egg, if dead would soon decay and be useless to the grub, and if not paralyzed would promptly dig their way up and out of the hole before the egg even hatched. So down in the darkness of the filled-in hole there will soon begin the tragic eating alive of the worms by the Ammophila grub which soon hatches from the egg and which will find in the inchworms enough food to last it until time to pupate, when it takes no more food. Then, later, it will issue as a full-fledged new Ammophila, to dig its way out and find another and mate, and, if a female, go through this same performance next September. And it will do all this without ever being taught by its mother or any other Ammophila. In fact, it will never see its mother or father, nor will they ever see it [pp. 1–6]. . . .

Is Ammophila's action as clever as it appears?

. . . although Ammophila's egg-laying and food-providing performance is very elaborate and seems very clever, it is about the only elaborate performance she does in her whole life. Most of the rest of Ammophila's activity in life is to avoid as well as she can by good flying, and a use of her sting, the various predaceous birds, lizards, toads, or large insects that would like to catch and eat her, and to hunt about for some food for herself, which isn't difficult, as she, and all other wasps, are almost omnivorous; practically anything in the way of animal food as well as various kinds of vegetable food will do. In the second place, we can find by a little experimenting that even in the accomplishment of her elaborate and wonder-compelling egg-laying and food-providing performance there is a quickly-reached limit to her cleverness.

Suppose we interrupt Ammophila in her clever performance and give her a few difficulties, to overcome [pp. 8–9]. . . .

Interrupt her chain of activities in the nest-making and provisioning performance and she is lost. If, for example, we quietly remove one of the inchworms, after she has brought it and laid it on the ground near the nest, and place it a few inches farther away while she is engaged in getting the salt-crust cover off of the hole, what happens? When she turns about to seize the worm to drag it down into the hole and does not find it just where she placed it, she is non-

plussed. She moves about distractedly. She doesn't search. She simply flutters about, perhaps happening by chance on the worm; perhaps not. She doesn't seem to use her powers of sight and smell, which she has certainly used in finding the same inchworm in the pickleweed, to find the nearby worm now on the ground in plain sight or smell of her. So if she doesn't happen to find it promptly by chance she simply gives up further work on this burrow. If she goes on with her nest-making at all, she starts a new hole. In other words, she starts the chain of performance all over again from the beginning. Fabre found in the case of another kind of solitary wasp which stores its burrow with individuals of a certain kind of wingless ground cricket, that if he merely turned around one of these crickets brought by the wasp to the side of the hole, and which she deposited with the long hind legs nearest the hole so that she always seized the cricket by these legs preparatory to dragging it down, that the wasp failed to put the cricket in the hole although the antennae projecting from the head, which was now nearest the hole, were about as good handles to seize it by as the legs.

We get an enlightening idea from this. This wonderful and apparently most sensible and even reasoned performance of burrow-building and provisioning is obviously a series of separate but connected successive performances, each single act being the necessary stimulus for the next in the chain, the whole chain being started by the stimulus of egg-production in the body and all of it possible to the Ammophila by inherited endowment without any learning. And it is as possible to any one female Ammophila as to another. There seems to be no, or at best but little, possibility of variation in the performance [pp. 9–11].

In the first part of his description of the Ammophila's action, Kellogg presents the digger wasp as a foresightful, conscientious mother. In the next section he exposes her "stupidity" and reflexlike action. According to Kellogg, the wasp's activity is similar to the egglaying of the silkworm moth. If you were to capture this creature soon after its mating and cut off only the posterior part concerned, you could elicit egg-laying action by rubbing the ventral portion of the remnant!

The performance of egg laying will be carried on just as it would be by an unmutilated female. In other words, the interesting and useful egg-laying behavior of the adult female moth—which is practically all of its behavior in its whole adult life—is, the mechanists would say, simply an inevitable physical or mechanical reaction by a small mass of living substance to a group of physico-chemical stimuli [p. 21].

The same holds true for the mating activity of the male moth. A pair of scent glands in the posterior end of the female evokes a mating response from the male. But suppose you were to cut out the exciting scent glands and place a normal male

...equidistant between the female moth and the removed glands, or even much nearer the female than the glands...the male will inevitably move toward the glands and reaching them remain there and go through the motions of an attempt at mating. It doesn't distinguish the difference between the cut-out glands and the female moth, and it thus doesn't mate at all. The male silkworm moth is, say the mechanists, positively chemo-tropic: its movements are simply a positive and inevitable physical reaction to a chemical stimulus. That accounts for practically all of the behavior of a male silkworm moth through all of its adult life [p. 20].

Kellogg seems to have felt a need to classify the reactions of the Ammophila's nest making, the silkworm moth's egg laying, and her mate's sexual activity as reflexes rather than as complex psychological acts so commonly performed by the human. "Tropism" is the term applied to such reflexive activities.

Tropisms

Plants and animals display positive or negative tropisms to light, to gravity, to chemicals, and so forth, from birth onward, without any sign of learning. An indoor plant growing toward a window shows a positive phototropism; and a beetle on its back, struggling to right itself, shows a positive geotropism; a male silkworm moth pursuing the odor of a female's scent glands shows a positive chemotropism. For Kellogg these tropisms are "all inevitable physical reactions to physical or chemical stimuli, all mechanistic behavior [p. 23]." A more up-to-date statement would be that, apparently as the result of a certain evolutionary development, living organisms are structurally organized to react in highly specific ways to certain kinds of physical or chemical conditions. These *unlearned* acts are impressive, but what a far cry from composing a symphony or designing a dress or a bridge. Interrupt Ammophila's "chain reaction" and she must start from scratch or give up the entire enterprise.

In the next selection we take a closer look at pheromones—chemical excitants—which, without prior learning, elicit highly specific (e.g., mating) reactions from members of the species concerned.

2 Pheromones

On a certain day ant A (in Fig. 5.1), a foraging ant, set out from home to discharge her social duties. Fortunately, she found a rich source of food for the colony,

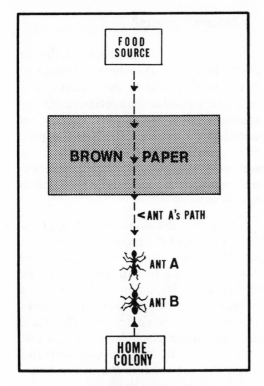

SCENE NO. 1

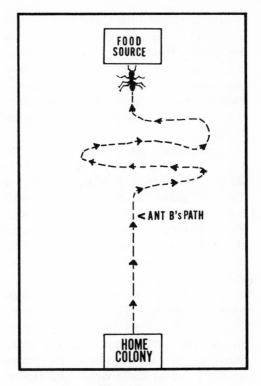

SCENE NO.2

Figure 5.1 "Chemical communication." Ant B's attempt to follow in Ant A's footsteps was frustrated by the Experimenter's removal of a piece of paper on which the trail was laid. But random movements brought the story to a happy conclusion.

loaded up, and began her return trip home. As she approached the colony's residence, she met ant B. Instantly ant B showed a radical change in her action. She set out energetically in the direction from which A had just come. Straight as an arrow, she marched over the ground as if walking in A's footsteps, until she reached a certain point. Suddenly her path ceased to be a straight line and she began wandering to and fro. Eventually, though, B's march resumed its earlier straightforward direction, and, like ant A, her foraging ended with a rich find. As the figure reveals, the secret behind B's interrupted course lies in the absence of a piece of brown

paper. After ant A had passed over it on her return trip home, we removed the paper. Obviously ant B had difficulty in staying on course *only* over the territory that the brown paper had previously covered. It is apparent that ant A must have laid down the trail that ant B retraced just by "following her nose." Where the trail was missing, B's movements were random and ineffectual.*

The incident illustrates what has come to be known by the formidable term, *phero-*

---

*A recent study by B. P. Moore (1966, p. 746) has confirmed the trailing by parent termites of artificial trails made from extracts of trail-laying glands or even of whole insects.

mone. Of recent origin, the term derives from the Greek, *pherein* (to carry) and *horman* (to stimulate or excite). It designates substances secreted by organisms that have an effect on other organisms. Pheromones are essentially built-in, reflex-like reactions to simple physicochemical stimuli.

In discussing the silkworm moth, we noted the mating response of the male to the fragment of the female moth possessing the scent glands. Jacobson (1965) reports that the female scent may attract a male from a distance as great as 3 miles (p. 8)! He also confirms the male's attempt to make genital connection with the severed abdomens of female clothes moths (p. 22). Bees, cockroaches, beetles, the cotton bollworm, and the Hessian fly are among the numerous insects used in the study of pheromones. The control or even destruction of whole classes of undesirable animal species (such as cockroaches and clothes moths) depend on the momentous consequences of sex-attractant pheromones (Jacobson, 1965, Chapter 12). Soon, no doubt, the stimuli for many pheromones will be chemically identified and even synthesized (Jacobson, 1965, and Silverstein et al., 1967).

What are instincts?

According to a dictionary definition (1939), the term *instinct* means "a tendency to actions that lead to the attainment of some goal natural to the species.... As distinguished from habit, *instinct* is not dependent on the individual's past experience... As distinguished from a reflex, it is more complex, more adaptable, and less stereotyped, and may involve a conscious impulse to activity."

The above definition, which approximates the popular conception of *instinct,* certainly points away from tropisms and pheromones and toward complex innate psychological adaptations. That instincts are independent of past experience implies that the organism comes into the world with ready-made psychological equipment. Is this so? In an effort to deal with this basic issue, we shall, in the next articles, ask such questions as these:

Do lemmings have a "suicidal instinct" as folklore would have it? Do swallows return to Capistrano with deadly regularity? Are certain animals "man-eating beasts" by instinct?

---

3 Krebs: The so-called "suicidal instinct" of the lemmings

According to folklore, the lemming—a small furry rodent species native to the Arctic region—periodically manifests a strange and fatal "instinct." When a population explosion expands its numbers beyond the food supply available to maintain the species, lemmings are said to start moving in "mass migrations" across vast stretches of land. Like an army on the march, they move straight across the landscape, swimming across rivers or lakes that lie in their path. When they reach the sea, according to the traditional story, their "suicidal instinct" compels them to jump in and start swimming. Inevitably fatigue overcomes them, and they drown by the millions. All ends well, however, because the population density has been restored once more to match the available food supply until the situation is again unbalanced at some later time.

What are the facts?

The lemming story is an apt illustration of myths handed down from generation to generation and accepted as factual by otherwise enlightened people. While no facts exist to support the legend, neither were there any to contradict it. Recently, however, Dr. Charles Krebs of the Department of Zoology of Indiana University studied the story of the sporadic "death march" of lemmings.

For four long years, Krebs (1964) stationed himself on the west side of the Hudson Bay near the Arctic Circle. Here, in an area of three square miles, he conducted a fine-tooth comb study of population changes in lemmings. He live-trapped and snap-trapped brown and varying lemmings. (The latter are white in winter and grey in summer.) Among other techniques, he performed 4000 autopsies on captured animals. He discovered that their gestation period was about three weeks, that the litter size varied between three and nine pups, and that the young matured in three to four weeks. Apparently, biological conditions yielded a rapid succession of generations as well as rapid increases (or decreases) in the population. Krebs stayed long enough to observe a complete cycle of population change. It started with an increase from very low numbers in the first summer to a tremendous population growth over the first winter of the study. There was very little further increase in the next peak summer, but a great decline set in over the following winter, and this decline continued through the third summer. The final winter of the study again showed little change in numbers. Then an increase in population size began once more in the fourth and last summer of his study. Thus, whatever criticisms might be made of Krebs' study, one cannot say that he failed to observe a cycle over time that included extreme variations in the population density of lemmings. For, during the first winter of his study, crude estimates of the increase were of the order of 25- to 50-fold expansion in brown lemmings and 5- to 10-fold in the varying type. During the second winter, a severe decrease in population density occurred, estimated at 90 to 95 percent in the brown species and 70 to 80 percent in the other. These are radical variations! Certainly he had witnessed firsthand an extraordinary swelling and a shrinking of the population.

Krebs observed that a lengthened summer breeding season and winter breeding were both correlated with the population increase and that a shortened summer breeding season and absence of winter breeding were correlated with the population shrinkage. He found a similar relationship in fall and winter weather conditions and population changes. Slightly higher adult mortality rate and extremely high juvenile mortality also occurred in the period of population decline. However, Krebs ruled out both food supply and predatory animals, such as the weasel, as factors in the population changes.

There is no question that lemmings do move individually on sea ice, lakes, and the land during the spring melt-off in peak years and that they may move quite long distances on ice.

There is no question that one may see ten or fifteen lemmings at a time on the bare patches of ground during the melt-off and that sled dogs may gorge themselves on lemmings while travelling across country. But these are not solid masses of lemmings marching in a particular direction. I have been told by people at Baker Lake that during the 1960 spring there were "millions" of lemmings marching across the tundra toward Hudson Bay and that there were "thousands" of lemmings all over the lake ice, when, in fact, fewer than 50 lemmings were actually seen by the persons involved. The Eskimos of the Barren Grounds have no legends of mass lemming migrations, and it is difficult to believe that they would overlook such an event if it ever occurred. I therefore do not believe that mass migrations of lemmings occur in North America [pp. 55–56].

Krebs (pp. 56–57) quotes Scandinavian writers who strengthen his own observations. The striking facts in the various studies reveal the lemming as almost an antisocial creature rather than the fantastically gregarious one created by folklore. When observed in local movements, they are seen "always singly or some few near together, never in close formation [translated from Collett; Krebs, p. 56]."

In Spring, the lemmings ran singly on the ice, never forming groups, and only in a few cases were more than three animals seen simultaneously [translated from Nasimovich; Krebs, p. 56].

It is indeed surprising to find that there is no objective evidence for mass migrations of the Norwegian lemming. Until evidence to the contrary becomes available, it seems best to regard mass lemming migrations as a fiction and to confine our attention to the individual movements found sometimes at peak densities [Krebs, p. 57].

A popular movie, widely accepted as a nature documentary, depicted a suicidal mass migration of lemmings. When Dr. Krebs was queried about this photographic evidence, which seemed to contradict his findings and other scientific findings, he replied that as far as he had been able to gather, the lemming scenes had been staged with several hundred lemmings purchased from Eskimos. According to Krebs, "I have not yet seen an authentic picture of lemmings taken in the wild which showed more than two individuals [personal communication, 1968]."

Moral: A good story may be as widely believed as a true story.

4 Mayhew: The swallows of Capistrano

There is an old California legend about the swallows of Capistrano: On every March 19th, St. Joseph's Day, the swallows arrive at the mission of San Juan Capistrano from their winter quarters in South America. The annual event has occurred ever since 1776, when Father Junipero Serra established a mission there. The mysterious phenomenon began when townspeople destroyed the swallows' nests and a kindly priest at the mission opened the doors to the mission and invited the swallows in.

An investigation spanning 8 years, 71 bird colonies, 15 counties in California, and one in Nevada could hardly be considered a trivial venture. The total number of cliff swallows in the study, including those banded or recaptured in the same or subsequent breeding seasons, came to 27,112! Most of the work was done in the Sacramento Valley area by Dr. Wilbur W. Mayhew (1958) of the Division of Life Sciences of the University of California at Riverside.

Of greatest relevance to us is the date of arrival of the cliff swallows. Without going into the tempting descriptive features of their migration, we reproduce a "schedule" of arrivals at various localities in California (see Fig. 5.2).

The most striking feature of the schedule of arrivals, is the *absence* of *simultaneous*

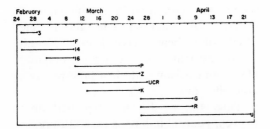

Figure 5.2 Extreme dates for first arrival of Cliff Swallows at some representative colonies. Legend: 3 = 5 mi. E Folsom, Sacramento County; F = 7 mi. S Sacramento, Sacramento County; 14 = 4.5 mi. SE Florin, Sacramento County; 16 = 1 mi. N Elk Grove, Sacramento County; P = 4 mi. W Davis, Yolo County; Z = 2 mi. NE Davis, Yolo County; UCR = University of California campus, Riverside, Riverside County; K = 7 mi. W Davis, Yolo County; G = 6 mi. NW Davis, Yolo County; R = 5 mi. NW Davis, Yolo County; J = 7 mi. W Davis, Yolo County. (From Mayhew, Wilbur W. "The Biology of the Cliff Swallow in California," *The Condor*, 1958, **60**(1), 7–37. Reproduced by permission of author and publisher.)

arrival of swallows at *any* of the eleven places represented there. The duration of arrival periods varies from as few as 4 days to as long as approximately one month. The results hardly match the precise arrival dates claimed for the swallows of Capistrano. But how about them? According to Mayhew (personal communication), "these birds are no more precise in their time of arrival at Capistrano than at any other site I have studied. There seems to be considerable variation as to the time the great bulk of the birds return." Furthermore, the swallows of Capistrano are even "abandoning the mission as a nesting site. The last time I visited the mission (1965), there were only about half a dozen active nests there [Mayhew, personal communication, 1967]. It would seem that all disciplines must do battle on two fronts. They must guard against (1) unwarranted theory and (2) false data. We have found the latter applicable in both the lemming story and the story of the swallows of Capistrano. Both cases involve *alleged* facts or data rather than genuine ones. Lemmings do not commit suicide via mass migrations and the swallows of San Juan Capistrano not only do not arrive on precisely the same date each year, but they have even "defected" from the mission to another nesting site. It seems that the criterion of *warranted assertion* needs to be applied to the raw data of psychology as well as its theories.

Caras: The alleged ferocity of animals

5

"The first point is that there is no such thing as a *dangerous animal*, only animals *potentially dangerous* [Caras, 1964, p. *xviii*]."

The quotation at left comes from a book entitled *Dangerous to Man: Wild Animals: A Definitive Study of Their*

Reputed Dangers to Man. In it, Roger A. Caras surveys the whole animal kingdom, smashing 2000 years of fiction, legend, and rumor about the ferocity of wild animals. We learn, for example, that although the great cats (lions, tigers, leopards) can run as fast as 40 miles per hour, thus easily overtaking man, few become maneaters (p. 3). Tigers find "man's proximity quite threatening and do not generally linger long in any place near men [p. 8]." Lions "never molest men unless suddenly startled, bullied, wounded, or driven to regular man killing by disease, excessive hunger ...etc. [p. 15]." "An ingredient of the 'wolf as dangerous to man' problem is man's own need to fictionalize the subject" (p. 35). Regarding the killer whale, we are informed (p. 67) that this is indeed a large and formidable creature, one that can "snap a seal or a porpoise in half with a single bite [p. 67]," but "why, in thousands of years, has there not been one single authenticated attack by an animal whose appearance in the vicinity of small craft could be reported daily from some place on the oceans of this planet? [p. 68]." Caras thinks that the story of the killer whale's ferocious nature stems entirely from its huge size and its large, conical, dangerous-looking teeth.

Although the black widow spider is acknowledged to be venomous, it is not a deliberate foe of man. In fact, it "is shy and retiring like most spiders and will seldom seek issue. If trapped in your shoe, it will, of course, attempt to defend itself [pp. 290–291]." But, surely, the hairy tarantula is an exception. No; we discover that "the tarantulas are calm, docile, very mildly venomous animals of no appreciable menace to man [p. 293]." So the story continues. The grizzly bear is "peaceful and goodnatured, whose temper is defensive, not aggressive [p. 42]." An interesting quotation from the famous hunter, Theo-

dore Roosevelt, asserts on this point: "No grizzly will assail a man now unprovoked...though if he is wounded or thinks himself cornered he will attack his foes with a headlong fury that renders him one of the most dangerous of wild beasts [Caras, p. 42]." Yet, what about newspaper stories on the seemingly unprovoked attacks by grizzlies? One possible hypothesis concerns the habitat of such animals, who do not live under natural conditions, conditions where they would normally fend for themselves. They receive handouts from tourists in our national parks. Failure to receive expected food from a human could provoke an attack by a hungry, irritated bear. Such bears have been "contaminated" by man and live a most unnatural life in comparison with their brethren living in a wild state.

Thus the myths are exploded about wolves, peaceable hippos (p. 102), ponderous rhinoceros, which like most wild, hoofed animals are "shy" (p. 97). As for boa constrictors, who are said to break every bone in a person's body and crush the life out of him, "they do *not* crush the life out of their prey [p. 134]." Indeed, there is not one authenticated case of a human being killed in the coils of a giant snake (p. 134). Man has certainly been attacked by members of numerous species, but only when the animal concerned is defending his territory, protecting his young, is startled, feels overwhelmed, trapped, or otherwise threatened. Exceptions are the occasional wild animal who has developed a genuine taste for human flesh or the rare, solitary, "rogue" animal (Caras, pp. 76 and 230), which, though little understood, seems to be pathological, killing wantonly. In general, the infrahuman animals prudently avoid encounter with man whenever possible.

Every year in the United States there

are approximately 10,000 murders, which means that every year in this country about 10,000 humans kill about 10,000 humans! No wild animal could touch this record. Nor are man's motives unpremeditated (by the very definition of the term) panic reactions to surprise, threat, or defense as are the simpler, subhuman ones. With malice aforethought and for lust, greed, or hatred, man compounds the motive to kill, making murder, like war, a peculiarly human institution. If someone were to compile statistics for murder on a worldwide basis and compare, or rather contrast, them with the number of humans killed by all the rest of the animal kingdom combined, we would have an impressive study.

Summary We examined the facts about the alleged ferocity of wild animals, as presented by Caras, and found them largely fictitious. When infrahuman animals are in the vicinity of man, they avoid him by retreating. When surprised, threatened, or attacked, they become defensive and aggressive and attack the human. We also found that man is a potentially dangerous animal to himself — more dangerous, it would seem, than all the wild animals put together.

Adamson: The two faces of Elsa, a lioness*

6

No consideration of the temperament of animals is complete without a brief account of Elsa, a lioness with a split personality. The story, a true one, comes out of Africa and has been reported by Joy Adamson, Elsa's nurse, "mother," and "friend." The story of Elsa begins in Mrs. Adamson's (1960) fascinating book, *Born Free,* which was also made into a popular movie.†

One day Joy's husband, George Adam-son, a game warden in Kenya, had to shoot a mother lioness who attacked George and his companion in defense of her babies. The mother's death placed the responsibility for the three orphaned cubs on George, who took them home. Mrs. Adamson took over their feeding and finally had three flourishing, bouncy cubs. Realizing that they could not keep three energetic baby lions forever, they gradually adapted two of them for travel and eventually sent them to a zoo in Holland. Elsa was the one selected to stay with the Adamsons.

Separation from the cubs resulted in a greater attachment toward Elsa's two remaining friends. She followed them everywhere, even sleeping in their bed,

†In the film, Elsa's role was played by still another tame lioness. A total of 18 lions was used. Africa, U.S.A. — a 260-acre California ranch — trains animals for parts in television and movie productions. On the training methods that he uses, Ivan Tors, Africa, U.S.A.'s director, is quoted as follows (*Life,* September 29, 1967): "Animals we raise from babies are easiest to train. Others are tamed with sponge-tipped petting sticks gradually reduced in length until the trainer can stroke the animal with his bare hand. With animals you cannot love without touching. Animals going on to big-time acting get extra training in an obstacle course where they get used to the confusion of movie sets [p. 42]."

*Quoted material is from Joy Adamson, *Born Free* (New York: Bartholomew House, Inc., 1960). By permission of the author.

often wakening them by licking their faces with her rough tongue. She went on safari with them, riding on top of the cabin of their truck. The Adamsons developed an intimate, affectionate relationship with Elsa, much as they might with an only child. At first Elsa greeted her surrogate parents with an enthusiasm that landed them on their backs into the sand, water, or mud. To inhibit her overpowering demonstrations of affection, they taught her, with the judicious use of a small stick, to obey the command "No."

How spoiled by civilization Elsa became is indicated by an incident that took place when the family went camping at an altitude where the nights were cold. Mrs. Adamson kept Elsa in her tent, made her a nest of lichens, and covered her with her warmest blanket; then she spent most of the night replacing the covers that kept falling off Elsa causing her to shiver (see Fig. 5.3). Elsa responded by licking her benefactress' arm. In explanation of the lioness' gentle nature, Joy Adamson writes:

Her good-natured temperament was certainly due in part to her character, but part, too, may have come from the fact that neither force nor frustration was ever used to adapt her to our way of life. For we tried by kindness alone to help her to overcome the differences that lie between our two worlds [p. 108].

As she grew in size, strength, and experience, Elsa also broadened her

Figure 5.3 Highly-civilized Elsa. Shown as a member of the family who must be tucked in to bed with a blanket to keep her warm. (Photo courtesy of Mrs. Joy Adamson.)

experience by pushing out on her own. She stayed away from home more often and for increasingly longer times. At the time, she was 27 months old, fully mature, and ready for mating. The Adamsons knew that a decision would soon have to be made about Elsa's future, particularly since they would shortly be going on leave. Elsa complicated matters by not allowing anyone else to look after her. They felt, at times, like prisoners. They considered sending Elsa to a zoo also, but her love of nature and of her freedom ended that plan. They decided, instead, to return her to nature. Consequently, they spent their leave "uncivilizing" Elsa.

With great ingenuity the Adamsons proceeded to transform their humanized lioness into a wild one with all the skills necessary to maintain her in that condition. On one occasion, instead of feeding her cut-up meat, they gave her a whole animal, a young buck. She promptly opened the animal and ate her fill. The next step was to teach her to kill for herself. Driving to a remote area, they would leave her for days at a time, hoping that hunger would force her to find and kill her own meat. However, on their return she was always waiting, hungry and affectionate. Finally, they moved to another location, where Mr. Adamson could teach the lioness to hunt and to experience the feel of pulling down the kill, a procedure her lion mother would have taught her had she raised her.

At last, Mr. Adamson and Elsa cooperatively killed a waterbuck. George Adamson shot it, but, before it fell, Elsa lunged at its throat and suffocated it. This was her first attack on an animal of her own weight. Matters proceeded quickly after that.

Thus, Elsa evolved into an expert huntress. However, she did not lose her gentleness. The following scene occurred immediately after Elsa had killed a 1200-pound buffalo in a hard and bloody battle.

When I joined her a few moments later she licked my arm, embraced me with her paw, and hugged me to her wet body. We relaxed after the morning's excitement. I felt very touched by her gentleness and the care with which she treated my skin and avoided scratching me with claws that only a few minutes ago had been so deadly to the thick skin of a powerful buffalo [pp. 194–195].

After more than 3 years of living with humans, Elsa was free. She disappeared for longer and longer intervals, obviously accepted by some lion pride as one of their own. The Adamsons arranged reunions every few weeks, however, and, after firing a gun as a signal, would see Elsa come bounding joyfully out of the bush, sometimes 15 hours later.

In a follow-up story, entitled *Living Free,* Joy Adamson (1961) describes what happened next. The mating with a wild lion resulted in three cubs, which, in good time, Elsa introduced to the Adamsons. Photographs (Figs. 5.4 and 5.5) show how the two-generation family got along. In time the cubs learned to obey the word "No" even without reinforcement with a stick (p. 122). The trust that Elsa still had in her foster parents was shown by her entrusting the cubs with Joy Adamson while she went to the river to drink.

Mrs. Adamson tells how, on one occasion, Elsa came into camp accompanied by her babies. "... she walked up slowly, nubbed herself gently against me, rolled in the sand, licked my face, and finally hugged me. I was much moved by her obvious wish to show her cubs that we were friends [p. 38]." And later, "We all sat together on the grass, Elsa leaning against me while she suckled her family [p. 39]." During all this time, she expected handouts of meat exactly as in her past life.

Figure 5.4 Elsa and cubs with "foster mother-grandmother," Joy Adamson. The cubs learned to respond to vocal and gestural "No." (Photo courtesy of Mrs. Joy Adamson.)

Figure 5.5 A peaceful "family" scene. Two-generation lion-family at ease with Joy. (Photo courtesy of Mrs. Joy Adamson.)

On one visit Joy Adamson found a large thorn embedded deeply in Elsa's tail. "It must have been very painful, and when I tried to pull it out she became irritable [all 300 pounds of her]. Luckily, I did eventually manage to extract it; then she licked the wound and afterward my hand, by way of thanking me [p. 62]." In one instance, "persecuted by tsetse flies," writes Mrs. Adamson, Elsa "flung herself in front of me, asking me to dispose of these pests [p. 53]."

In an introduction to Joy Adamson's *Living Free,* the English biologist, Sir

Julian Huxley, describes how impressed he was with the sight of Elsa bounding into camp with her cubs, how she "sprang toward Joy Adamson as toward an intimate friend, putting her great paws on Joy's shoulders and almost knocking her over with the vigor of her greeting [p. *xxi*]."

One must agree with Sir Julian's comment that the story of Elsa surely "demonstrates the wealth of potentialities in higher mammals, waiting to be drawn out and elicited into actuality [p. *xxii*]." However, her split personality should not be overlooked either. What was remarkable was not that gentle Elsa became a ferocious, deadly beast. The psychologically significant point is that she had two distinct personality organizations appropriate to two distinctly different situations. She continued to be loyal, warm, affectionate, trusting of the Adamsons, and dependent on them for food and for their civilizational accoutrements. She also learned to stalk and to kill her own prey when George and

Joy were gone. Elsa's scars testified to the battles she must have fought with other lionesses. Furthermore, she mated with a wild lion, had three wild-born cubs, and continued to live with her mate in between visits to her foster parents. There was no question of Elsa's being tame *or* wild; it is a fact that she was both tame *and* wild.

Summary We examined the case of Elsa, a female lion cub, raised as a child might be in a family of two human adults with much patience and affection and without corporal punishment and frustration. The result was a warm, intimate, dependent relationship. After 3 years of such civilized life, the foster parents decided to return Elsa to the wild. They taught her to stalk prey, to kill, to mate, and to live with other wild lions. The latter development did not suppress or otherwise interfere with the earlier. In fact, Elsa is offered as a case of split personality, of a coordinate tame *and* wild organization of personality responses.

Recent work of the young ethologists **7**

The twentieth century has seen a prodigious number of field studies of the reactions of infrahuman animals. These investigations have been conducted where the action is. In the nineteenth century, by contrast, students of animal behavior contented themselves with trading wild, unsupported anecdotes of animal cunning, revenge, etc., or with reports on caged animals in zoos or at home. By analogy, how much would a Martian learn about human society from a

human imprisoned in a cage on Mars?

The comparative ethologists have gone into the field and observed animals living under natural conditions. The freedom and greater range of stimulation of their home milieu provide opportunity for a much richer development of behavior than that permitted by the prisonlike, unnatural zoo cage of the infrahuman (as well as the human) inmate. Studies of animals in their own milieu also show them in a much better light. The following sections are representative of studies that challenge not only the "instinct" doctrine but also much current "knowledge" about the infrahuman animals. In place of the theory that allowed "the lower species" a ready-made ferociousness and rigid, innate modes of action, modern studies demand a theory that acknowledges shyness, gentleness, wide flexibility, spontaneity, and abundant potentialities for learning, problem solving, and "memory" in man's evolutionary kinfolk. Although the gap between the human and the infrahuman still exists, that gap narrows. Today what is "human" and what is "animal" require redefinition.

Schaller's work on the gorilla*

The Year of the Gorilla by George B. Schaller is a remarkable book about the world's largest primates, the mountain gorillas of Africa.

Dr. George Schaller, a young American zoologist, went to the high rain forests of East Central Africa to observe gorillas in their natural habitat. Here, alone and unarmed, he literally lived among the free-roaming gorilla tribes for weeks at a stretch.

Day after day, he observed gorillas at close hand; he saw them feeding, playing, sleeping, mating, and caring for their young. He describes their ways of expressing anger, curiosity, fear, and affection—and their reactions to him. He came to know them as individuals and was permitted to approach them closely and even to bed down in their sleeping area at night [Schaller, 1965, frontispiece].

Before leaving for Africa with Dr. John T. Emlen of the University of Wisconsin's Zoology Department, Schaller (1964, p. 10)

---

*Quoted material is from George B. Schaller, *The Year of the Gorilla* (New York: Ballantine Books, 1965); and George B. Schaller, *The Mountain Gorilla* (Chicago: University of Chicago Press, 1963).

read hundreds of popular books, newspaper stories, as well as textbooks and scientific articles, but, as he soon discovered, most of what he read proved sensational, exaggerated, or false.

The exploratory study

Even his very first encounter (p. 44) with a group of contented, feeding gorillas was an anticlimax to the bloodcurdling accounts he had read of gorillas instantly capturing humans and strangling or crushing them. When the two researchers were within 30 feet of the gorillas, the latter peered cautiously at them. Then, as Emlen raised his hand, "the animals screamed and walked away [p. 44]." No murderous attack, no fury, no snarling rage of the sort displayed by King Kong, the movie monster, or by Gargantua, the ferocious gorilla exhibited in a circus sideshow for many years.

The two researchers followed the group and caught up with them again, observing this time from a distance of 200 feet. A 400-pound adult male gorilla watched the two humans intently with suspicion and then roared (p. 44). The gorilla next rose to his feet, beat a rapid tattoo on his bare chest, and sat down. Threat and bluff appear to be common techniques of control among the infrahuman animals. Gradually the gorilla group became more accepting of the two pale hairless creatures and although they still watched them, says Schaller, "I was amazed at their lack of excitement [p. 45]."

Once more the gorilla band was frightened and fled, and once more Emlen and Schaller followed, finding them 2 hours later. Sight of the humans generated some excitement, but soon the gorillas settled down and paid little attention to them. The center of interest this time was a female

Figure 5.6 Specimens of *Gorilla gorilla,* whom Schaller (1963) describes as being of "an outwardly placid nature which is not easily aroused to excitement," with facial and body expressions which are, "even in disturbing situations,...ones of repose." They "have a markedly shut-in or introverted personality" and are "stoic or aloof" (pp. 80–81). Chest beating, at least in response to man, serves "intimidating functions" (p. 234) or, in every-day terms, bluff. (Photo courtesy of George B. Schaller.)

gently holding an infant to her breast. Then the two men observed the mother, the infant in her arms, leaning against a male who "leaned over and with one hand fondled the infant [p. 46]."

For 6 months the researchers followed groups of gorillas in their exploratory or general survey. Up and down the mountains of the eastern Congo, Ruanda-Urundi, and western Uganda, they trudged after their elusive scientific quarry and became convinced that a more intensive study of gorillas at close range by Schaller (and his wife) would be profitable. The two stayed on for an additional year of work, which yielded, besides *The Year of the Gorilla,** a more technical monograph entitled *The Mountain Gorilla* (Schaller, 1963). The former included many of the Schallers' personal experiences, feelings,

*Hereafter *The Year of the Gorilla* will be abbreviated as YOG and *The Mountain Gorilla* as MG.

and reactions to their experiences. The latter is a fascinating compendium of factual observations on the mountain gorilla.

The gorilla's behavioral repertoire

The gorillas' behavioral repertoire as it is reported in the monograph includes their fairly continuous, but leisurely and ungreedy, eating; their building of tree nests for siestas and night nests for extended nighttime sleeps, and their fouling of the nest. However, this barely begins the catalogue of their behavior. We learn that, despite extensive use of hands in foraging, they rarely manipulate objects or transport them, perhaps because of the very fact of the abundance of food in easy reach. In contrast to chimpanzees, Schaller saw "no tool-using in gorillas [MG, p. 200]."

Sneezing and coughing, and particularly yawning, closely resembled their human counterparts. Self-grooming was observed, as was grooming of the young by adults, but grooming between adults was infrequent (MG, p. 245). Gorillas do scratch often and pick their nose and teeth (MG, p. 208). Schaller describes their facial expressions and vocalizations. We learn that

Males roar and the other members of the group scream when angry. I have heard males roar only in response to the presence of man, and when swooped at by ravens. Females often scream when quarreling with each other [MG, p. 218].

Chest beating, which is an element of a complex display including hooting, rising, running, throwing, leg kicking, slapping, and tearing and which occurs in moments of great tension and excitement, has its human counterpart.

Man behaves remarkably like a chimpanzee or a gorilla in conflicting situations. Sporting events are ideal locations for watching the behavior of man when he is generally excited and emotionally off guard. A spectator at a sporting event perceives actions which excite him. Yet he cannot participate in them directly, nor does he want to cease observing them. The tension thus produced finds release in chanting, clapping of hands, stamping of feet, jumping up and down, and the throwing of objects. This behavior is sometimes guided into a pattern by the efforts of cheerleaders who, by repeating similar sounds over and over again, channel the displays into a violent but synchronized climax. The intermittent nature of such behavior, the transfer of excitement from one individual to the next, and other similarities with the displays of gorillas are readily apparent [MG, p. 235].

Social behavior of the gorilla

Leadership exists as it does among most higher animals and determines and regulates much of the group's activity. So do dominance-submission relationships. And though copulation may be termed "brutish" or "animal-like," it is surprising how infrequently Schaller observed mating behavior among gorillas. "In 466 hours of observation I witnessed only two copulations and one invitation to copulate [MG, p. 275]." And again:

Since most females are either pregnant or lactating, the silver-backed male or males in the group may on occasion spend as much as a year without sexual intercourse, for they seem to make no overtures to the females unless these indicate their receptivity [YOG, p. 137]...

Sex is of little importance here. Gorillas always give me the impression that they stay together because they like and know one another [YOG, p. 137].

Schaller's data, plus supporting evidence from Kinsey (1948, 1953), tend to identify a stress of sexual activity as more of a human than a gorilla characteristic.

*The alleged fierceness
of the gorilla*

Schaller (MG) remarks that when he surprised a lone male at 60 feet, "he [the gorilla, not the man] emitted a sharp grunt and a scream as he fled [p. 315]." He tends to agree with other reputable authors that a gorilla will not attack a man unless attacked and "will not attack a man who stands his ground and faces the advancing animal [p. 308]." If a man flees, however, the gorilla pursues and bites like a dog. Again, we read that "gorillas are basically not aggressive and that they tend to retreat if given the chance" (p. 308). Particularly to single observers (but even to two), gorillas "usually become used to the presence of a single observer sitting quietly and in full view near them day after day [p. 311]."

The following brief quotations from *The Year Of The Gorilla* complete our study of the mountain gorilla. Perhaps they may help to correct the twisted reputation that this gentle, "introvertish," primate relative of man has carried ever since his discovery in 1902 (MG, p. 15).

In all the months I spent with the gorillas without a gun, none attacked me [YOG, p. 128].

And, finally,

The gorilla is by nature reserved and shy, and, whenever it can possibly do so, it avoids contact with its human neighbors [YOG, p. 114].

Summary The primary function of Schaller's work is to set the record straight. One finds no elaborate theory here, only much needed crude data about the quiet, dignified, well-behaved gorilla, instead of distorted myths. In general, after a year and a half's observation, Schaller found the mountain gorilla afraid of man but willing to tolerate him at a safe distance. If threatened, he roars, gestures, and bluffs in similar ways. Sexually, gorillas are restrained, compared to humans, and seem to band together because of other social ties. A quiet monotony pervades the life of the huge but shy and gentle gorilla.

---

*Goodall's life among the
chimpanzees** **8**

Until recently, despite their ready availability, chimpanzees have not been studied at first hand and in their natural habitat. Not until June 1960 did a young British ethologist, Jane Goodall,† begin a pioneer study of chimpanzee behavior.

---

†In 1964, Jane Goodall became Baroness Jane van Lawick-Goodall by marrying Baron Hugo van Lawick, her photographer-collaborator.

Near the heart of Africa, on the shore of Lake Tanganyika in Tanganyika (now Tanzania) lies the Gombe Stream Chimpanzee Reserve. Accompanied by her mother, Jane Goodall set up a base camp near the lakeshore, aided at first only by an

---

*Quoted material is from Jane Goodall, "Chimpanzees of the Gombe Stream Reserve," in Irven DeVore (Ed.), *Primate Behavior* (New York: Holt, Rinehart and Winston, 1965).

African cook and his wife. After several years, however, she expanded her organization and, today, in addition to her husband, who is an expert photographer, she has two European helpers and a staff of six Africans. Here, since 1960, in a study area of 15 square miles, via still and moving-picture photography, plus other aids, she and her staff have observed and recorded the life activities of the eastern or long-haired chimpanzee, *Pan satyrus schweinfurthi.* Steep-sided valleys and ravines and open spaces in the otherwise wooded area provided Jane with opportunities for observing her infrahuman subjects. This report limits itself to the more complex forms of behavior that she has reported.

Getting close to the chimps

Her (Goodall, 1965a) earliest attempts to get close enough to the chimps to make observations were fruitless and frustrating. At the mere sight of the strange, hairless primate, the chimpanzees scattered. Despite days of 12-hour stints, there were few notes to record at first. Nevertheless, Jane persisted, for she realized that she must accustom the chimps to her presence if she ever hoped to make closeup observations.

Habituation was a long, drawn-out process. At first, when the chimpanzees detected her even from 500 yards away (Goodall, 1965a, p. 428), they scattered; but within 8 months the distance narrowed to 50 feet under certain conditions. After 10 months most individuals would tolerate her at 100 feet, but Jane made real progress after 14 months, when the chimps would carry on their everyday activities of eating, sleeping, and mating with Jane only 30 or 50 feet away. Finally, three mature males

became so tame that they accepted food from the hand of their first human friend.

Observations

As Goodall followed the chimps about on their travels, she learned that they were nomadic in the sense that they slept in a different place each night. Their daily travels in search of food necessitated moving about in shifts of about 3 hours' duration before they settled down to another feeding and a siesta. She also discovered that their diet was largely vegetarian and included 73 varieties of fruits, leaves or leaf buds, blossoms, seeds, stems, and 2 different kinds of bark (1965a, p. 440). Eating occupied about 6 or 7 hours a day. Insects offered an occasional change from a vegetarian menu, as did meat of the red Colobus monkey and of the bushpig; but meat eating occurred only nine times in 2 years and thus must be considered rare.

Mothers and their infants form the only enduring relationships among the chimps. No stable families are formed. Even groups are not permanent; rather, they have a loose membership and on occasions two groups may coalesce and split again after a day or two. Introvertish isolates (hermits?) have been observed. Toleration for each other's actions are the rule. Chimps appear to be gentle, peaceful animals, entirely lacking in violence. In one observation during the mating season, Goodall (1965a, p. 455) noted their patience and lack of aggression when seven males took their turn in copulating with one female. Tolerance toward infants is common on the part of the mature as well as the adolescent individual. Children engage in gentle wrestling, patting, tugs of war, and tickling. They also engage in thumb sucking.

Figure 5.7 One of the many touching mother-infant relationships, play, is shown here. Mothers play with their babies, as their human counterparts do, by swinging them, tickling or engaging in gentle "rough house" with them. (© National Geographic Society, Courtesy National Geographic Magazine.)

According to Goodall, "Instances of attack were seldom observed [p. 466]." In 2 years she saw only one fight: "Huxley" hit "William" on the shoulder for taking a bite out of the former's meat. However, she never saw any visible signs of injury, even in these rare instances. Hostility seemed to be easily resolved or ventilated.

The sociability of chimps

In a later account Goodall (1965b) stresses the more intimate aspects of (by this time) her friendly subjects. In fact, some of them fully trusted and accepted her as one of them, proving that even wild chimpanzees can be tamed. She came to know some 50 chimps (1967, p. 21) and named many. With certain ones, she attained a mutual grooming status. Personality differences and individuality, even in appearance, were the prevailing pattern. Soon the chimps walked into camp, helped themselves to bananas, or ran off playfully with towels and blankets. The regular customers would bring new ones into camp and the "Banana Club" flourished.

Mutual grooming

One of the activities that may occupy as much as 2 hours of the chimp's day is mutual grooming (see Fig. 5.8). One ape minutely examines small patches of the other's skin, looking through the hair for flakes of dried skin or grass seeds. The grooming posture is quite likely to elicit a grooming response in another ape. If ignored, a chimp "may reach out and poke the other [1965a, p. 470]." Mutuality is the keynote, for if X enjoys being groomed too long, Y gets fed up, stops, puts his hand on X's shoulder and points to an area on himself where *he* wants to be groomed. Mutual grooming, with its prolonged close contact, is one of the most important social activities, one which Goodall considers a prototype of altruism in the human. Grooming also protects the individuals involved against ectoparasites and dirt and helps in the shedding of hair.

Greetings

Friendly greetings are the rule. Like their human cousins, chimpanzees "pat

Figure 5.8 "You scratch my back and I'll scratch yours." Three pairs of chimps (and an odd solitary) shown in *mutual grooming,* in a session which may last as long as two hours. (© National Geographic Society, Courtesy National Geographic Magazine.)

each other on the back, embrace, kiss, and even, quite commonly, hold hands" (1965b, p. 825). After long separations, greetings can be as enthusiastic as in the case of two Latins embracing. One day Goodall was fortunate in viewing a domestic scene. After a day's separation from his mother Flo, a juvenile by the name of Figan "approached Flo in his typical cocky fashion and brushed her face with his lips. How similar to the peck on the cheek that is all a human mother can expect from a growing son!" (1965b, p. 825) Later the Goodalls witnessed David and Goliath in a dramatic, mutual embrace. Standing face to face, they flung their arms around one another, vocalizing with apparent pleasure and agitation (p. 825). Another social gesture, the laying on of hands, is extended as a

comfort to a member of the group who is jumpy or nervous (1965a, p. 472). A gentle touch on the arm or shoulder has a quieting effect. Appeasement, ingratiation, and submission, as well as dominance, can be communicated via gestures. In addition, responses can be conveyed vocally; however, space limitations prevent our treating that subject here.

So how about instincts?

The lemming story showed that the mysterious and elaborate instincts propounded by folklore do not rest on facts. Indeed, they can flourish despite facts to the contrary. Studies of California swallows show that not only are the birds not prompt in arriving at Capistrano but that they have virtually stopped arriving at all. As for the instinctive ferocity of grizzlies, killer whales, and other man-eaters, their danger to man except under very special conditions seems largely fictitious. The story of Elsa, the lioness, demonstrated that a lion cub could be shaped into a gentle, tame creature. Then, when circumstances required it, her human foster parents deliberately taught Elsa reactions that ordinarily characterize "wild" lions. The training provided her simultaneously with a

"civilized" and a "wild" personality organization. Next, we considered the work of ethologists like Schaller and Goodall on gorillas and chimpanzees, respectively. Instead of the expected fierceness and hostility toward humans, we found only shyness and early avoidance of humans and, later, with Jane Goodall's chimpanzees, even mutual grooming and comfort between human and beast. May the reader draw his own implications about instincts from these studies.

Goodall: Fishing for termites* 9

One of the classic distinctions between man and the other species concerns the making and use of tools. This characteristic was once said to be totally absent in all the rest of the animal kingdom. Only man was believed capable of fashioning and using tools. However, recent studies show that tools are used by such widely varied species as chimpanzees, vultures, mongooses, and finches.

Since we have just been discussing Jane Goodall's work, let us continue with a presentation of her findings in this area.

Termites abound in the Gombe Stream Reservation. Both baboons and chimps consider them a delicacy. However, the baboons must wait until the termites attain their winged form and fly out to start other colonies. Under the circumstances, it is a short season and a "catch-as-catch-can" business. Not for the chimps, however, who have often been observed working at termite nests and successfully extracting their catch from it.

Goodall (1964, pp. 1264–65) describes the procedure. The cue that initiates the chain reaction is a visible sign, a freshly sealed-up spot on the surface of the termite hill that indicates termites immediately under the surface awaiting favorable conditions for flight (Goodall, 1965a, p. 442). Goodall has often seen individual chimps examining termite nests for the recently sealed openings (see Fig. 5.9). Sometimes, equipped with a tool, they look, give up, throw the tool aside, and hunt for a better termite nest. If they see the telltale sign (Goodall, 1965a, p. 442), they pick the seal with index finger or thumb and carefully insert a short stick, vine, or twig with the leaves stripped off into the nest. They leave the stick in the nest for awhile, then withdraw it slowly. Clinging to it are some termites, which the chimp picks off with

---

*Quoted material is from Jane Goodall, "Tool-using and Aimed Throwing in a Community of Free-living Chimpanzees," *Nature,* 28 March 1964, **201**(4926), 1264–1266.

Figure 5.9 Chimpanzees of Tanzania's Gombe Stream Reserve "fishing" for termites at a termite mound. As observed by Jane Van Lawick-Goodall, they strip off the leaves from a stem, bite a piece from one end, make a small opening in the termite nest and carefully insert the stem into the nest. After a while, they just as carefully withdraw the stem and eat the ants clinging to it. (© National Geographic Society, Courtesy National Geographic Magazine.)

his lips. Since its hands are clumsier than man's, the ape is sometimes forced to support the end of its tool on the wrist of the other arm (see Fig. 5.10). If the tool gets bent, it is turned around or another one is procured.

Planning seems to enter the picture, too. In many instances Goodall saw chimpanzees pick up a grass stalk and proceed to a termite hill that was out of sight and about 100 feet distant. "One male carried a grass stalk (in his mouth) for half a mile, while he examined, one after the other, six termite hills, none of which was ready for working [Goodall, 1965a, p. 443]." Does this mean that the chimp can "think ahead"?

Other uses of sticks Goodall (1964) saw sticks used to catch an ant mass from a species of ants that builds underground nests. The sticks were inserted and adhering ants transported to the mouth via the stick, which was now used as a spoon. Furthermore, once the apes were tame enough to enter her camp openly, she found three adolescents independently using sticks to open boxes containing bananas (1964, p. 1264).

A sponge for drinking water

On a number of occasions Goodall saw chimps drinking water from a natural water bowl in a tree. She also reports another investigator (1964, p. 1265) who saw a chimpanzee dip its hands into such a water bowl and lick the water from its fingers. To provide easier observation of the phenomenon, she hollowed out a bowl in one of the trees in the area and watched five individuals drink from it on 26 different occasions, but they used a "sponge" for sopping up the water (p. 1265).

What the chimps did was to strip (by hand or mouth) from one to eight leaves from a convenient twig. They put them into their mouth briefly, crumpling them. Then

Figure 5.10 Chimp enjoying appetizing snack of termites on a stick, the "fruit" of his patient labor of fishing for them. Monkeys and baboons must wait until termites leave the nest on their migrations, but the chimps enjoy the benefits of a more effective tool-using tradition. (© National Geographic Society, Courtesy National Geographic Magazine.)

they dipped the leaf mass into the water bowl and drank the water retained in it. Goodall next carried out the following procedure:

A simple experiment showed that this drinking tool was more efficient than the licking of water from the fingers. I chewed three leaves and then dipped them 10 times into a glass of water, sucking out the liquid after each dip. I then repeated the test with only the fingers of one hand dipped into the glass. The result showed that 7 to 8 times as much water was removed by the first method [Goodall, 1964, p. 1265].

Using leaves for wiping the body

The following quotation illustrates both the neatness of apes and the use of a natural object (leaves in this case) for personal purposes.

Leaves were also used for wiping the body. Once a female stripped a handful of leaves to wipe mud from her foot. An adolescent picked leaves to wipe off drops of urine which had splashed on to him from a juvenile sitting above. Another juvenile, after carrying sticky bananas, pulled leaves towards him, rubbed his chest with them, then broke off a leaf spray and rubbed again. After handling bananas which had been smeared with honey in a feeding experiment, two individuals used leaves to wipe themselves: an infant pulled leaves toward her and rubbed her sticky lips with them, and an adolescent stripped off a handful of leaves with which to rub her other hand [Goodall, 1964, p. 1265].

Aimed throwing

Bombs, bullets, and bricks—all are projectiles aggressive humans direct at one another. Did Goodall's chimpanzees ever react to situations in this "human" way? Yes. Aimed throwing of handy objects occurred—but it was infrequent. Goodall noted some instances of aimed aggressive throwing directed against humans and baboons, but she feels that her scanty data do not permit drawing any definite conclusions about the ape's use of objects as tools of destruction. What observations she has made suggest that this capacity is not as highly developed as the other tool-using behaviors. She did note that sticks, stones, and handfuls of vegetation were frequently thrown *at random* in a social context of frustration or excitement.

Is the chimpanzee's tool-using learned or instinctive?

Goodall (1964, p. 1266) believes that there is some evidence on the answer to the above question. It comes from her observations of tool use by infants. For example, she never saw infants termite fishing before 18 to 22 months of age, and at this stage, their attempts were "clumsy and inadequate [p. 1266]." Proficiency was not attained before 3 years of age. Secondly, Goodall observed many instances of infants watching closely when adults engaged in termite extraction with twigs. In fact, her 1967 publication has captured one of the teacher-apprentice learning opportunities in an interesting photograph on p. 49. And she often saw infants pick up discarded "tools" and attempt to use them. Here is Jane Goodall's answer to the question whether such tool-using as she observed is instinctive or learned.

It therefore seems probable that the use of sticks, stems, and leaves for the specific purposes described here represents a series of primitive cultural traditions passed on from one generation to the next in the Gombe Stream area. [Goodall, 1964, p. 1266].

10 Goodall and van Lawick: Use of tools by the Egyptian vulture*

Goodall and van Lawick have inquired into the use of tools by species other than chimps. While in Tanzania they witnessed the Egyptian vultures' use of stones to break open ostrich eggs. It is true that, altogether, they saw only five vultures, one pair in Serengoti National Park and three other birds near the Olduvai Gorge about 60 miles away. However, they observed a similar pattern in all five subjects, so their report is included here as an exploratory study. With a burning desire to get at the ostrich egg contents, the vultures used the following procedure.

Each individual picked up a stone in its bill [obviously one whose thickness would accommodate the bird's bill], raised its head high with bill pointing upward [almost skyward], and then projected the stone in the direction of the egg with a forceful movement of head and neck until the shell of the egg was broken; the bird used one stone or several in succession [p. 1468].

The very first time that the young couple

*Quoted material is from Jane van Lawick-Goodall and Hugo van Lawick, "Use of tools by the Egyptian vulture, *Neophron percnopterus*," *Nature*, 24 December 1966, **212**, 1468–1469.

observed an "egg-scrambling," they noted that other vultures—of a species different from the egg-breaking Neophron percnopterus—had gathered around an abandoned ostrich nest and had repeatedly (and unsuccessfully) tried to break the eggs open by pecking at them. The second incident occurred when the observers positioned two eggs, one at a time, near their three other subjects in the Olduvai Gorge.

Two of the four eggs were opened after four and six direct hits respectively; each of these eggs was broken by a single vulture in just under 2 minutes. The other two eggs were broken after eleven and twelve hits respectively; one by a single vulture (which twice moved away from the egg before finally opening

it) in approximately 8 minutes; and the other by two birds, each throwing stones at the same time in 5 minutes. These two birds aimed wildly, often pausing to threaten each other, and many hits only just touched the egg. During the process of breaking all four eggs the vultures threw stones approximately twice as often as they hit the eggs [p. 1468].

At Seronera, the stones that the vultures used weighed a little more than 4 and 6 ounces, respectively. The eight stones used at the second site (Olduvai) to crack the first egg ranged in weight between a little more than 2 ounces and a bit over 5 ounces. The stone that broke the second egg weighed a little more than 10 ounces.

Eisner and Davis:
"Mongoose throwing and
smashing millipedes"*

11

Millipedes of the order Glomerida (also called Oniscomorpha) have the peculiar habit— shared with certain armadillos, pangolins, and some of the familiar isopod Crustacea known as "pillbugs" or "sowbugs"—of coiling into a tight sphere when disturbed (Lawrence, 1953). The behavior is usually assumed to be defensive, but this had never been tested with millipedes. We recently obtained from South Africa mature specimens of two large glomerids of the genus *Sphaerotherium,* and offered these to several caged predators. In most cases the millipedes proved invulnerable, as expected. Nevertheless, they did fall prey to one particular enemy, which was singularly adapted to cope with them.

Both species have an unusually hard skeletal shell. The slightest provocation, even a mere tapping of the cage, causes them to coil. Coiling, plus the possession of armor, are the only noticeable means of protection. *Sphaerotherium* lacks the defensive glands found in some other glomerids (Meinwald, Meinwald, & Eisner,

1966) and in most millipedes of other orders (Eisner & Meinwald, 1966).

When a *Sphaerotherium* was offered to ants (*Pogonomyrmex badius*), they swarmed over the coiled millipede and attempted to bite and sting it, but without success. With the millipede's legs and antennae inaccessibly tucked away, the ants could not secure the necessary hold with their mandibles. A blue jay (*Cyanocitta cristata*) and a grasshopper mouse (*onychomys torridus*) were equally unsuccessful.

The blue jay pecked repeatedly at the millipede, but its bill merely glanced off the hard shell of the prey, flipping it aside. The mouse, a voracious insectivore capable of subduing cockroaches of nearly its own size, seized the millipede in its front paws and attempted to bite

---

*Quoted material is from Thomas Eisner and Joseph A. Davis, "Mongoose Throwing and Smashing Millipedes," *Science,* 3 February 1967, **155**(3762), 577–579. Reproduced by permission of author and publisher.

it, but had difficulty clamping its jaws on the smooth-shelled sphere; the prey was eventually abandoned, uninjured.

Figure 5.11 Three consecutive stages in the hurling and smashing of a "pillbug" by the banded mongoose of Africa. The millipede is part of its diet. (Drawing by Mrs. Margaret Menadue. From T. Eisner and J. A. Davis, "Mongoose Throwing and Smashing Millipedes," *Science,* February 1967. Copyright 1967 by the American Association for the Advancement of Science.)

The unexpected occurred in tests with a banded mongoose (*Mungos mungo*). The predator responded instantly to the glomerid, sniffing it, and rolling it about with the paws. It seized it in the jaws, biting upon it with its sharp teeth, but the millipede was neither pierced nor crushed. Suddenly the millipede was dropped from the jaws and grasped in the front paws. The mongoose backed against a rocky ledge in the cage, assumed a partially erect stance, and — with a motion so quick as to be barely perceptible — hurled the millipede backward between its legs, smashing it against the rocks (Fig. 5.11). Fatally injured, with its shell broken and its body torn apart, the millipede was promptly eaten.

All told, nine *Sphaerotherium* were offered to the mongoose, on two separate occasions, almost a year apart. The results were virtually identical in every instance. The mongoose was inconsistent in its choice of target surface, but it invariably selected an appropriately hard background and oriented itself properly toward it just before the throw. Sometimes the millipede was not smashed until the second or third attempt.

The banded mongoose lives throughout most of Central and South Africa, and its range overlaps that of *Sphaerotherium* and other glomerids (Lawrence, 1953; Ellerman, Morrison-Scott, & Hayman, 1953). It has a diversified diet and is known to feed on insects, larvae, molluscs, young birds, small rodents, berries, and seeds (Roberts, 1954). Millipedes may also be taken, and it seems likely that glomerids are thrown and smashed in nature as they are in the cage. Mongooses also eat eggs, and captive specimens have been known to break these by hurling them (Kinloch, 1965). We found that snails, including such hard-shelled forms as *Neritina reclivata,* and even hazelnuts, are successfully dealt with in the same way. The behavior may occur whenever preliminary pawing and mouthing of a hard "attractive" object fail to yield the edible contents.

Millikan and Bowman: "Observations of Galapagos tool-using finches in captivity"*

12

Is it possible that our definitions limit what we see or do not see? The present survey has already shown that tool-using is not restricted to humans or even to apes. Birds also indulge in it. Perhaps ingenuity is an ubiquitous property of life, and we are only beginning to observe things that have always been there to see.

So far we have considered numerous field studies, but Millikan and Bowman (1967) did an imaginative study on tool-using finches under laboratory conditions. They captured six *Cactospiza pallida* on Indefatigable Island in the Galapagos and kept them for a year in a large communal cage with such facilities as crevices and twigs. Then they began an analysis of the bird's responses and of the controlling stimuli.

The earliest phase of the finch's response involved searching by cocking† its head, the better to see into nooks and cracks. It even managed to perch sideways and to hang upside down to peer into every possible part of its surrounds.

Shaping or selecting a tool The finches were never seen to pick up a twig from the ground, apparently preferring to investigate only high perches, even if they

had to fashion a tool. They broke a twig off a branch and sometimes snapped it in two, selecting the shorter and more manageable part. Millikan and Bowman (p. 25) provided miscellaneous objects for their captured birds, including weird configurations of toothpicks glued together, cactus spines, metal rods, wooden dowels and applicators, flexible wires, green pine needles, coping saw blade, hairlike fibers, and a 20-cm "stick" of spaghetti (uncooked, of course). One finch attempted to probe with the last item. Another used a wooden dowel 8mm in diameter, and still another resorted to a strong, round applicator 3mm in diameter.

Using a tool Whenever food was visible but unattainable by means of the beak, the bird would resort to use of a tool. But, quite often, a finch was seen to pick up a twig in the absence of food. Occasionally it even carried a tool, perhaps by a circuitous route, to a crack 5 or 6 feet from the point where it picked it up. In one experiment, finches carried tools through a complex maze made up of three overlapping partitions and finally placed them beside some cracks at the end of the maze. They were also seen to use tools in crevices not previously explored with the beak, as if searching or exploring, rather than probing, for food with their tools.

---

†According to Millikan and Bowman (p. 25), the popular notion that birds, such as the Robin, cock their heads to *listen* for worms has been disproved. Their finches were able to locate even dead worms, which could hardly have been making any detectable sounds.

---

*Quoted material is from George C. Millikan and Robert I. Bowman, "Observations on Galapagos Tool-Using Finches in Captivity," *The Living Bird*, 1967, **6**, 23-41.

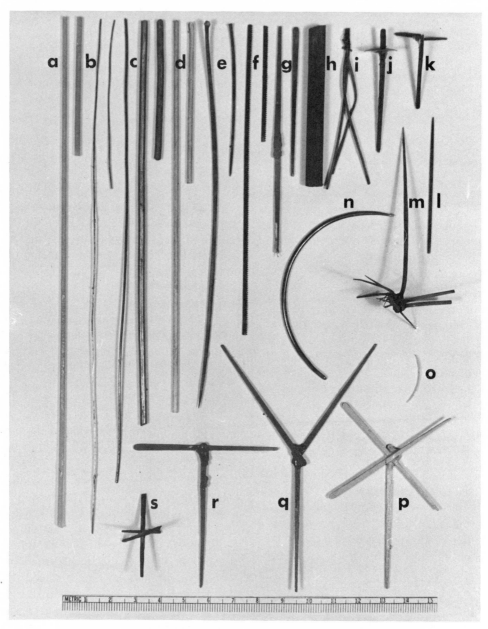

Figure 5.12 "Tools" made available to *Cactospiza pallida*, the Woodpecker Finch, in experiments described in the text: (a) spaghetti; (b) flexible wires; (c) metal rods; (d) wooden applicator sticks; (e) cactus spines; (f) coping saw blades; (g) toothpicks; (h) wooden dowel; (i) pine needle fascicle; (j) toothpick with circular metal shield near one end; (k) 3 toothpick pieces glued together at right angles to each other; (l) metal needle; (m) cactus spine cluster; (n) upholstery needle; (o) wood shaving; (p, q, r, and s) configurations made of toothpicks glued together. Scale shown at bottom, 153 mm. (Photo courtesy of Robert Bowman.)

Figure 5.13 *Cactospiza pallida* manipulating a fascicle of pine needles. *Above:* Warding off another finch approaching the food table. *Below:* Attempting to insert ends of needles in a baited slot. (Photo courtesy of Robert Bowman.)

The efficiency of the finches   In studying Millikan and Bowman's photographs and reading their description of the finches' use of tools, one cannot help being impressed with their skill and efficiency. The finches made precise adjustments, depending on the tool they were working with at the moment:

With a very short tool the bird bent forward so that its beak was almost on a level with its

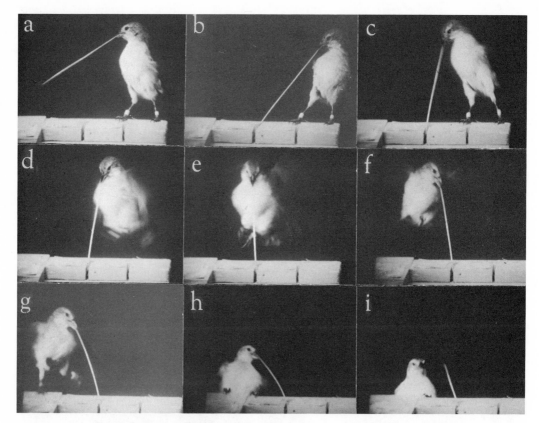

Figure 5.14 *Cactospiza pallida* using a tool in flight. Holding a six-inch cactus spine lengthwise in its bill (a), the finch leans backward with legs fully distended and head forming an acute angle with the neck (b); as the distal end of the cactus spine engages the crevice (c), the bird rocks forward and stretches its legs and neck to the utmost. Unable to insert the spine to the bottom of the crevice, the bird takes flight (d) in a semicircular path, pivoting on the tool (e, f), which has now penetrated the depths of the slot. As the bird prepares to land on the opposite side of the food table (g), the spine, now bending under the weight of the bird, is still firmly grasped with the bill. Finally missing a foothold on the food table (h), the bird relinquishes its hold on the tool, which falls from the crevice (i). (Enlarged from frames of 16 mm motion-picture film. Photo courtesy of Robert Bowman.)

feet; with a long tool the bird stood very high and stretched its neck to the utmost. Test birds usually held their tools at one end so that they projected straight in front of the beak. However, they sometimes effectively shortened both long, rigid tools, such as cactus spines and applicator sticks, and flexible tools, such as pine needles and brass wire, by holding them near the middles, which, in the case of flexible objects, gave the tool more rigidity. On one occasion a bird attempted to probe with a 15-cm cactus spine held by one end. Unable to insert the free end of the spine into the crack, even with legs and neck fully extended, and failing to change its hold on the spine to nearer the middle, the bird made a short, semicircular flight and, while on the wing, successfully used the tool to dislodge the mealworm from the crevice [p. 29].

Figure 5.15 *Cactospiza pallida* using a six-inch cactus spine as a tool for probing at prey far out (*above*) and close in (*below*). Note how the tool is aligned with the "tomial axis of the bill" which intersects the eye posteriorly (Photo courtesy of Robert Bowman.)

Our birds performed a variety of motions with the tools. Mealworms in cracks were levered sideways or pulled toward the body; mealworms in transparent tubes were poked through to the far end. At least once a mealworm was slowly levered up the inclined surface of a slippery plastic container in an extraordinary display of motor coordination. One of the most remarkable, and least frequent, behaviors was the use of a tool as a weapon. In one instance, a bird with a probe in its mouth moved toward another bird and drove it from the feeding tray. In another instance, when an unarmed bird, engrossed in foraging at a baited crevice, was suddenly confronted by a weapon-wielding bird, the unarmed bird was more aggressive and forced the armed bird to retreat.

The holes in which our finches probed varied in size. The birds inserted toothpicks into round holes, almost large enough to accommodate their heads, and into cracks barely wide enough for a toothpick. They also inserted twigs into small holes (2mm in diameter by 10mm deep) and into the mouths of medium-sized test tubes [pp. 29 & 31].

A slow learner   One bird was not seen to probe with a twig, *not even once* during a whole year's intensive study. When Millikan and Bowman inquired further, they discovered that he was the single subject who, upon capture at a young age, had been raised isolated from the other finches. Later association with tool-using companions had no apparent effect on his ability to probe for food. The writers consider the possibility of a "sensitive" period (p. 31), as we will observe in discussing imprinting. However they cannot conclude that contact with other tool users is necessary because "this bird may have suffered another deficiency of experience or inheritance which impaired its performance [p. 31]."

I would go beyond Millikan and Bowman and suggest the hypothesis that tool-using may well be a tradition handed down

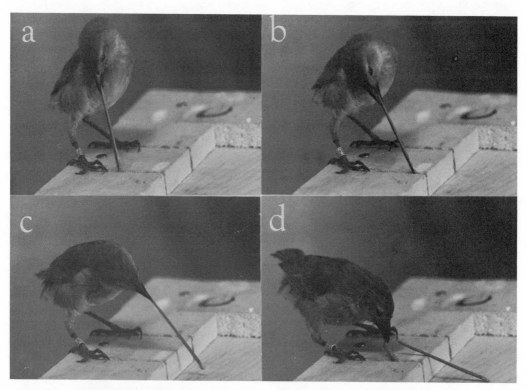

Figure 5.16 *Cactospiza pallida* using a toothpick tool to dislodge a meal-worm from a slot. Note that the finch moves the tool in the direction of the open end of the slot. (Photo courtesy of Robert Bowman.)

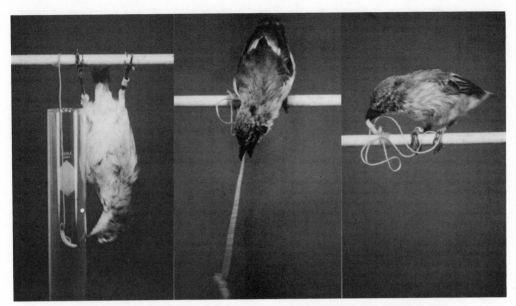

Figure 5.17 *Cactospiza pallida* reacting to a mealworm suspended on the end of a string. *Left:* The finch hangs upside down from its perch, its legs fully distended, and pecks at a mealworm enclosed in a glass tube. *Center:* Holding several loops under its toes, the bird prepares to take a new bite on the hanging string. *Right:* The bird has just succeeded in reaching the mealworm by pulling up the last portion of the eight-inch-long string. (Photo courtesy of Robert Bowman.)

from generation to generation. A crucial experiment is not hard to design. Why not interrupt the contact of baby finches with tool-using finches by hand feeding one generation and see if they use tools? Such a study needs to be done.

String pulling   Since the finches were found to be expert probers, how would they do in manipulating strings with a mealworm attached to the other end? One end of the string was attached to the perch upon which the bird sat. The mealworm on the far (i.e., lower) end of the string was out of reach of the bird's bill. Sometimes, to prevent the bird from flying down and picking the worm off "on the wing," they shielded the worm by means of a glass tube.

For comparative purposes, they used other bird species, such as the titmouse and the shrike. Despite the finches' expert-

ness with twigs and sticks as probes, they were not superior to other bird subjects. Without using its feet, a hand-reared shrike expertly pulled on the base of the string by using the hooked end of its upper bill as a kind of pulley. Other birds used coordinated movements of bill and feet in their string pulling, holding the pulled-up portion under a foot, at the same time pulling up another portion of string. The job was done in installments.

Summary

Man is no longer regarded as the exclusive tool user. The few studies we have reviewed force him to share the distinction with chimpanzees, vultures, mongooses, and finches. Jane Goodall, for example, found chimpanzees using leaves

Figure 5.18 Reactions of a hand-reared Plain Titmouse to a mealworm suspended on the end of a string. *Left:* The titmouse hangs upside down from its perch, legs fully distended, attempting to reach a larva with its bill. *Center:* The titmouse holds under both feet a short loop of string that it pulled up to the perch with its bill. *Right:* Occasionally, the titmouse attempted to seize the worm directly with its bill while in flight. (Photo courtesy of Robert Bowman.)

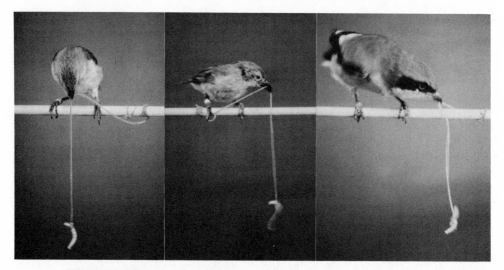

Figure 5.19 String pulling by two species of Galapagos finches and a Loggerhead Shrike. Wild-caught individuals of *Camarhynchus psittacula (left)* and *Cactospiza pallida (center)* show a basically similar neuromuscular coordination of bill and feet in string-pulling behavior. Without using its feet, a hand-reared shrike *(right)* obtained the suspended larva by pulling on the base of the string, causing the pendant portion to slip under the hooked end of the upper bill. (Photo courtesy of Robert Bowman.)

Figure 5.20 The Plain Titmouse *(above)* of western United States and *Camarhynchus parvulus (below)* of the Galapagos Islands are ecological and behavioral equivalents. Here both species are shown after sidling along the perch. The mealworm, obtained by string-pulling, is held with one foot during feeding. (Photo courtesy of Robert Bowman.)

to wipe themselves and as a sponge, using sticks to fish for termites, and using stones and other natural objects for throwing. The most significant observation is that chimpanzee tool-using is a part of their primitive culture transmitted from generation to generation.

We also noted the use of stones by the Egyptian vulture, whose head movement in throwing is similar to the motion of the human. The mongoose proved itself a formidable enemy of the millipede. Other predators were stopped by the millipede's impenetrable armored coil. The mongoose, by hurling millipedes, snails, and hazelnuts against rocks, succeeds in breaking them and making them available as food. Only

further work can show how complex such problem-solving is and how such behavior originates.

For retrieving worms and grubs from highly inaccessible crevasses, the efficiency of the species of finch studied by Millikan and Bowman seems unmatched. Roundabout detours with tool-in-mouth for a distance of 5 or 6 feet testify to the goal-orientation involved. Use of a stick for effective leverage and another instance of flying while trying to extricate a mealworm indicate the complexity involved. Also significant is the observation that one finch reared in isolation for 3 months never learned to use sticks as tools. Is this another indication of cultural transmission?

13

Chemosensory perception in the migration of fish

Down through the centuries, the migrations of fish have aroused man's interest and curiosity about their precise but obscure movements. Only recently, with the development of suitable techniques, has research revealed some of the factors concerned. The fundamental problem has involved man's attempt (as a land air-breathing animal) to follow the movements of an organism adapted to living in water. The laboratory approach and its modification for field studies have been a tremendous help toward a partial solution of the puzzle.

At the University of Michigan, Bardach and his associates (1967a, 1967b) have been successful in pinpointing fishes' chemical sensitivity as the basic reaction involved in migration. They actually photographed the tracks of fish in such reactions by using fluorescent tags and ultraviolet light. They attached a small oval piece of plastic to the center of a fish's head. Since the plastic had been sprayed with fluorescent paint, it reflected the ultraviolet light so that the fish could be photographed from above the shallow laboratory tank in which it was studied. The reflection from the disk yielded a photographic trace of its path, as shown in Fig. 5.21.

Fundamentally, the Michigan group has been interested in chemosensory perception of the bullhead, a fish commonly found in streams and lakes near Ann Arbor. They trapped bullheads, blinded them by simply putting a drop of phemerol in each eye, thus eliminating vision, and started to test their taste sensitivity. They found bullheads fantastically sensitive to minute

amounts of attractants. Anatomical studies showed that the bullhead is endowed with taste buds by the thousands, located in the mouth and all over its body but concentrated heavily in the barbels or whiskers (see Fig. 5.22).

Figure 5.21 Orientation by taste in fish. Bullhead bearing a fluorescent tag approaching the release point of dilute liver extract mixed with fluorescein. (Time exposure, with final flash by P. Davis. Photo courtesy of John E. Bardach.)

To observe the sense of taste alone, without the complications of smell, the Michigan investigators severed the fish's olfactory nerve or cauterized the nostrils. Most bullheads still continued to follow a

straight path in still water and a figure-S, figure-8 course in flowing water to the source of the attractant. Even more interesting to the student of psychology, Bardach and associates applied their method to the social behavior of the bullhead, which Thomas J. Way has described:

Bullheads create hierarchies and territories and have various social disputes, and they can distinguish strangers from members of their own communities. Moreover, they live in dark waters and are usually active only at night. The sense of smell, so strangely uninvolved in the finding of food, may play an important part in their social behavior; one goal of current behavioral work is to test this hypothesis. So little is known of how fish that live in dark waters or the depths communicate, select their mates, and care for their young that the results of these studies may well have far-reaching implications, extending to the commercial fishing industry [Way, 1967, p. 4].

---

*Hasler: The migration of salmon**

14

The Chinook salmon of the Pacific Northwest presents a baffling life cycle. It breeds in the small headwaters of a large river like the Columbia or Yukon. Its birthplace also becomes its home for a year or two. After a certain stage of maturity, it migrates downstream to the Pacific Ocean. Once in the ocean, it may roam as far as 2500 miles and take from 1 to 7 years for its oceanic trips. Eventually it returns to the river, fighting its way back upstream against heavy odds. After swimming as far as 2500 miles upriver against water, falls, and formidable man-made dams, it seeks out

the rivulet of its birth and breeds. Thus it starts and finishes its life in the same stream. How, over such large distances and after so much time, can it so unerringly find its way home? That is the question we shall examine here.

In a stimulating book, *Underwater Guideposts: Homing of Salmon,* Arthur D. Hasler reports his investigations of the

---

*Quoted material if from Arthur D. Hasler, *Underwater Guideposts: Homing of Salmon* (Madison, Wisconsin: The University of Wisconsin Press, 1966). Reprinted with permission of the copyright owners, the Regents of the University of Wisconsin.

final and most dramatic phase of the salmon's total migratory journey, its "stream homing [p. 13]." Older theories held that temperature and CO_2 content of the stream were the pertinent variables, but, as Hasler points out, as inconstant as these factors are, how could they identify the salmon's home stream?

Hasler's odor hypothesis

The preceding discussion of the bullhead's keen chemoreception paves the way for Hasler's odor hypothesis. From previous work of his own and of others, Hasler was inclined to think that the salmon identified the stream of its birth by its characteristic odor.

The odor may be organic in origin, possibly derived from the unique plant community of the stream's drainage basis and the flora within that stream. In short, the fish smells its way home from the coastline of the sea, tracking a familiar scent like a fox hound [p. 16].

Since there is variation in the flora and fauna and in the geological strata that constitute different portions of mountain streams, that variation could very well provide the basis for the specificity of conditions that the odor hypothesis required. Besides, Hasler (p. 16) had already convinced himself of the keen sensitivity that fish displayed in detecting industrial pollutants and other odorous substances dissolved in the water.

Laboratory tests

Hasler first built special aquariums in his laboratory; then he obtained two varieties of water, one from Otter Creek, which runs mostly over quartzite rock, and another from Honey Creek, whose bed is 95 percent sandstone. One water sample was admitted into one end of the tank, the other at the opposite end. Fish (blunt-nose minnows) from two aquariums were rewarded with food when they entered the Otter Creek end zone and punished when they swam toward the Honey Creek end zone. Fish from two other aquariums were given inverse training. To avoid a position habit, Hasler randomized the end from which the stimuli were presented as well as each day's first order of presentation of the two stimuli.

After a month's training, the minnows clearly discriminated between the two samples from the different streams. However, training continued for two more months in order to achieve the maximum level of discrimination as manifested by a plateau in the learning curve. Another answer that Hasler sought concerned seasonal factors on streams. In other words, would the trained minnows distinguish between the samples from Otter Creek and Honey Creek regardless of season? The fish responded in accordance with their training, no matter what season the samples were collected, showing that streams maintain their distinctive identity throughout the year.

Was the learned discrimination a function of odor? To check this hypothesis, Hasler (p. 26) anesthetized the trained minnows and destroyed their olfactory capsules by cauterizing them. The results? Their performance matched their purely random pretest scores. More significant still, they were hopeless in achieving any degree of retraining, again pointing to odor as the principal factor involved in the original learning.

How about retention of learning? To answer this question (p. 27), Hasler stopped all further daily training and presented the two stream samples weekly without reward or punishment. After 6 weeks' testing, the discriminatory responses were extinguished. Hasler criticizes his own procedure, realizing that he was actually "detraining [p. 27]" his subjects for 6 weeks. The age of the minnows was another significant factor. "Because the average life span of blunt-nose minnows is only 2 years, these fish were approaching senescence when their training was begun [p. 27]." By contrast, baby salmon get their contact with the odor of either Otter Creek or Honey Creek (or other) from birth or earlier. In a biochemical sense their natal stream even becomes an integral part of them. How could one start any earlier than that? And Hasler realizes full well the importance of early conditioning (pp. 27–29).

Confirmation of the minnow studies
Although Hasler proved that minnows could learn to make the smell discriminations demanded by his odor hypothesis, the experiment did not necessarily prove that salmon were capable of making comparable perceptions. Consequently, he carried out similar experiments with very young salmon. The young salmon did not survive the kind of study that would yield statistical analysis, but they did respond in accordance with their training. "... the character of their reactions in tests after brief conditioning seemed to verify that salmon do have the ability to detect different waters and to discriminate between them [p. 34]."

Field tests of the odor hypothesis

Hasler's laboratory studies of minnows and salmon established that fish can react selectively to a specific stream odor through conditioning. However, this did not prove that salmon, under natural conditions, located their home stream in the same manner. Therefore Hasler shifted to naturalistic observation, plus experimentation, in the streams where the salmon lived.

A little thought will show how important it is for the homing salmon, returning upstream, to make the correct choice at each point where a tributary joins the main stream. A wrong choice means backtracking, an occurrence that has been noted. Obviously certain sensory systems must be crucial in facilitating the correct choice. Because odor proved an important factor in the laboratory experiments, it was used again.

Experimental methods Hasler (p. 38) selected a point of confluence of two streams in Washington state, the Issaquah Creek and the East Fork of the Issaquah, for his experimental site. He constructed fish traps, one about a mile above the junction and the other about one and a half miles upstream from the same point but on the smaller tributary. Now he could catch the mature coho (silver) salmon that had presumably returned to their native streams.

After the salmon were captured, they were tagged according to a code system that indicated whether they belonged to the experimental or the control group and where they had been caught.

The experimental subjects were first anesthetized, then cotton plugs were inserted into the olfactory pit, thus eliminating smell as a cue. As a special precaution, Hasler surgically severed the olfactory nerve just behind the olfactory pit in some subjects. The control animals consisted of unmutilated, tagged salmon. Both groups were released three-fourths of a mile below the junction of the two streams. Their recapture was eagerly anticipated at the two traps where they had originally been captured, for it would show if they were able to retrace the earlier route from the junction point.

Results   Analysis of the data showed that *all* the control (unmutilated) subjects originally taken from Issaquah were captured in the Issaquah traps on their second attempt! Of the recaptured East Fork controls, 71 percent returned to it on their second attempt! Of the experimental (smell-deprived) salmon originally captured on the Issaquah and then recaptured, 23 percent took the wrong East Fork turn on their second attempt. Of the experimental subjects originally captured at the East Fork trap and later recaptured, only 16 percent made the correct turn at the East Fork junction (p. 41).

The data indicate that the normal fish were readily able to repeat their original choice at the stream juncture, thus furnishing additional support for the home stream theory. Those with olfactory occlusion, however, were unable to select accurately. Interference with olfaction seriously disrupted their orientation and reduced their ability to retrace their original route; this is interpreted to mean that salmon with plugged noses were unable to differentiate between the two streams and consequently distributed themselves in what may be considered a random fashion if one makes allowance for easier entry into the larger stream. These experimental findings are consistent with the results which would be expected if the fish were relying on their sense of smell to differentiate and select between streams [pp. 41–43].

Hasler's studies on salmon migration did not end here. He followed the above work with inferences from studies by others and from his own laboratory, all of which, according to him, "have continued to verify the odor hypothesis [p. 44]." In addition, he became interested in the salmon's oceanic movements and found some support for a sun-compass orientation, both by ingenious field work and by laboratory investigations. His delightful book can be enjoyed by layman or scientist.

Summary

We started with Bardach's laboratory work on the chemosensory perception of bullheads, which provided an easy shift to Hasler's odor hypothesis of the upstream migration of salmon. We then considered his laboratory check of said hypothesis with blunt-nose minnows and young salmon. A combination of experimental and naturalistic methods further confirmed his theory. A final point will permit a natural transition to the following topic, namely, imprinting.

Hasler (pp. 46–47) reports studies in which salmon eggs were removed from their ancestral stream and placed in a different stream. A few years later, when the salmon returned to spawn, they passed up the ancestral stream in favor of the adopted stream where they had hatched and developed. Other extensive studies show similar results. Hasler's conclusions: "that the odor characteristics of the stream are learned through an imprinting process — that is, a learning of environmental factors — rather than through any hereditary mechanism [p. 46]." The story that salmon migrated because of an ancestral memory is only a myth. These studies reveal how knowledge based on scientific investigation discloses the specific factors involved even in such complex reactions as migration. Hoary folklore about mysterious migration instincts can flourish only in the absence of scientifically derived facts such as those uncovered by Bardach and Hasler. No doubt future research will further clarify the salmon migrations.

As an application and a test of Hasler's theory of salmon migration, it should be pointed out that "coho salmon have been planted in a number of streams of the Great Lakes in the past 3 years and turn out to be a highly successful conservation project. This is a massive application of knowledge acquired in migration studies" (personal communication).

Imprinting **15**

The phenomena of imprinting have been observed for about a hundred years, but the field has been systematically studied and understood only within recent years. In his historical introduction to the field of imprinting, Sluckin (1965) reports observations by a zealous student, Spalding (1873). Spalding made many observations on newly hatched chicks. By keeping his subjects hooded and in a state of blindness for a period of up to 3 days, he could condition them to follow, say, his hand as persistently as other chicks pursued their hen mothers.

Spalding made another trial-and-error observation. He discovered that when he removed the hood from his chick subjects after 4 days, they dashed away from him in great terror. Thus Spalding had stumbled onto what later came to be known as the *critical period* for imprinting. Certainly it is significant that a chick will follow a certain object if imprinted within its first 3 days and that it will avoid the same object if imprinted after that period. Could the critical period explain what happens when the so-called wild animals become man-shy? Is this the explanation of Elsa's behavior? She was imprinted early on George and Joy Adamson and thus approached them. Generally lion cubs are not confronted by humans within the first 3 days; they avoid humans when they do meet them later. Sluckin (1965) says something similar in the following statement:

> The view that timidity gradually develops in the very young animal, and that it eventually overcomes or inhibits the tendency to approach and follow moving objects, might be substantially true [p. 3].

The implication of such findings seems to be that imprinting can achieve either approach or avoidance to the same stimulus object, depending on the *timing* of its initial appearance.

Lorenz's pioneering work
in imprinting* **16**

One of the acknowledged leaders among contemporary ethologists is Konrad Lorenz, who feels strongly that animals should be

*Quoted material is from Konrad Z. Lorenz, *King Solomon's Ring* (New York: Thomas Y. Crowell Company, 1952). Reprinted by permission of the author and publisher.

studied in their wild state whenever possible. His home in lower Austria was a naturalist's paradise where ducks, geese, jackdaws, and other animals lived in their natural habitat and at the same time enjoyed the run of his house. In the following section "the father of imprinting" describes an early attempt to imprint mallard ducks on himself as an appropriate "mother."

In the study of the behaviour of the higher animals, very funny situations are apt to arise, but it is inevitably the observer, and not the animal, that plays the comical part. The comparative ethologist's method in dealing with the most intelligent birds and mammals often necessitates a complete neglect of the dignity usually to be expected in a scientist. Indeed, the uninitiated, watching the student of behaviour in operation, often cannot be blamed for thinking that there is madness in his method. It is only my reputation for harmlessness, shared with the other village idiot, which has saved me from the mental home. But in defence of the villagers of Altenberg I must recount a few little stories.

I was experimenting at one time with young mallards to find out why artificially incubated and freshly hatched ducklings of this species, in contrast to similarly treated greylag goslings, are unapproachable and shy. Greylag goslings unquestioningly accept the first living being whom they meet as their mother, and run confidently after him. Mallards, on the contrary, always refused to do this. If I took from the incubator freshly hatched mallards, they invariably ran away from me and pressed themselves in the nearest dark corner. Why? I remembered that I had once let a muscovy duck hatch a clutch of mallard eggs and that the tiny mallards had also failed to accept this foster-mother. As soon as they were dry, they had simply run away from her and I had trouble enough to catch these crying, erring children. On the other hand, I once let a fat white farmyard duck hatch out mallards and the little wild things ran just as happily after her as if she had been their real mother. The secret must have lain in her call note, for, in external appearance, the domestic duck was quite as different from a mallard as was the muscovy; but what she had in common with the mallard (which, of course, is the wild progenitor of our farmyard duck) were her vocal

expressions. Though, in the process of domestication, the duck has altered considerably in colour pattern and body form, its voice has remained practically the same. The inference was clear: I must quack like a mother mallard in order to make the little ducks run after me. No sooner said than done. When, one Whit-Saturday, a brood of pure-bred young mallards was due to hatch, I put the eggs in the incubator, took the babies, as soon as they were dry, under my personal care, and quacked for them the mother's call-note in my best Mallardese. For hours on end I kept it up, for half the day. The quacking was successful. The little ducks lifted their gaze confidently towards me, obviously had no fear of me this time, and as, still quacking, I drew slowly away from them, they also set themselves obediently in motion and scuttled after me in a tightly huddled group, just as ducklings follow their mother. My theory was indisputably proved. The freshly hatched ducklings have an inborn reaction to the call-note, but not to the optical picture of the mother. Anything that emits the right quack note will be considered as mother, whether it is a fat white Pekin duck or a still fatter man. However, the substituted object must not exceed a certain height. At the beginning of these experiments, I had sat myself down in the grass amongst the ducklings and, in order to make them follow me, had dragged myself, sitting, away from them. As soon, however, as I stood up and tried, in a standing posture, to lead them on, they gave up, peered searchingly on all sides, but not upwards towards me, and it was not long before they began that penetrating piping of abandoned ducklings that we are accustomed simply to call "crying." They were unable to adapt themselves to the fact that their foster-mother had become so tall. So I was forced to move along, squatting low, if I wished them to follow me. This was not very comfortable; still less comfortable was the fact that the mallard mother quacks unintermittently. If I ceased for even the space of half a minute from my melodious "Quahg, gegegegeg, Quahg, gegegegeg," the necks of the ducklings became longer and longer, corresponding exactly to "long faces" in human children—and did I then not immediately recommence quacking, the shrill weeping began anew. As soon as I was silent, they seemed to think that I had died, or perhaps that I loved them no more: cause enough for crying! The ducklings, in contrast to the greylag goslings, were most demanding and tiring charges, for, imagine a two-hour walk with such children, all the time squatting low and quacking without interruption! In the interests of science I submitted myself literally for hours on end to this ordeal. So it came about, on a certain Whit-Sunday, that, in company with my ducklings, I was wandering about, squatting and quacking, in a May-green meadow at the upper part of our garden. I was congratulating myself on the obedience and exactitude with which my ducklings came waddling after me, when I suddenly looked up and saw the garden fence framed by a row of dead-white faces: a group of tourists was standing at the fence and staring horrified in my direction. Forgivable! For all they could see was a big man with a beard dragging himself, crouching, round the meadow in figures of eight, glancing constantly over his shoulder and quacking—but the ducklings, the all-revealing and all-explaining ducklings were hidden in the tall spring grass from the view of the astonished crowd [pp. 40–43].

Lorenz's experience as a surrogate (or substitute) mother to the mallard ducklings is an appropriate introduction to the topic of imprinting. It illustrates the strong bond that is formed between a newborn organism and the conditioning stimulus object which henceforth will serve as its parent companion.

It is well known that lambs follow those who bring them up on the bottle. It is said that even after such animals have been weaned and have joined the flock, they approach the keeper and stay near him whenever given a chance. In cases of this kind, "cupboard love" could be the main factor in the animals' attachment to people; but imprinting may not be altogether discounted. Grabowski described a case of the close devotion of a lamb to its human keeper. Scott reported that a lamb raised by himself

and his wife on the bottle for the first few days of its life became very attached to people. Hediger quoted earlier reports of two young moufflons which followed the girl that looked after them. He also quoted cases of buffalo calves which, when separated from their mothers, followed the huntsmen's horses. A new-born zebra foal was said to have attached itself once to a moving car, running behind it and refusing to be chased away. There have also been reports of following responses in young red deer. More recently, Altmann described a "heeling" tendency, imprinting-like in character, in young moose calves. There are, too, reports by Hess and by Shipley of imprinting in the domestic guinea pig [Sluckin, pp. 13–14].

The early view of imprinting

Often, in scientific work, the earliest formulation of a given phenomenon forces it into a rigid framework that proves quite resistant to subsequent modification. In my opinion a self-actional view determined the interpretation that early workers such as Thorpe (1963) gave to the data of imprinting. Thorpe emphatically speaks of "an innate releasive mechanism, which is the inborn counterpart of the releaser..." (p. 130). Consequently, he sees imprinting as restricted to a certain very brief period in the organism's life, and as being, in its early stages, a recognition of kind or as a general attachment to the animal's species rather than to individuals (p. 128). Also, once imprinting is established, he sees it as being extremely fixed and "Perhaps totally irreversible [p. 129]."

Laboratory studies of
imprinting

17

The original formulation of imprinting generated great interest in the topic and

produced a veritable avalanche of laboratory work in which both zoologists and psychologists have participated. As a result, a vast literature has accumulated in the last ten years. In the book mentioned earlier, Sluckin (1965) provides a keen and critical evaluation in a comprehensive coverage of the work. His work will be referred to at appropriate points in the following discussion.

First, we examine an experiment designed to test the conception previously mentioned, which asserted that imprinting is the process by which the newborn learns its species. According to this view, *species* recognition was said to be necessary precursor of *individual* recognition. Yet Gray and Howard (1957) believed that earlier work supported their hunch that the infant animal's first attachment was to the individual (i.e., imprinting) stimulus object with a subsequent possible generalization to that *class* of stimulus objects. Evidence from studies by Ramsay and Hess (1954) and by Hess (1957) with ducklings had demonstrated a discrimination between male and female facsimiles of ducks after imprinting was established to the male model of the pair. Similar work with chicks also fitted the Ramsay and Hess findings. Apparently earlier workers who had formulated *the-species-first, then-the-individual* characterization of imprinting had based their conception on the apparent failure of imprinted birds to discriminate one human from another.

Imprinting chicks to individual humans

Gray and Howard (1957) obtained chicks from the hatchery 24 hours following incubation and kept them in their "essentially lightless and cramped shipping carton until 31 hours after removal from the incubator [p. 301]." Gray and Howard served as makeshift mothers, each imprinting six chicks.

Procedure The experimental procedure involved releasing a chick from its box and evoking a following response in a separate room. Five minutes was the maximum time required for imprinting a following response; the rest of the time was spent in conducting the chick about the room. A second imprinting session was conducted 6 hours later; each chick participated in a 10-minute session and all followed immediately. Uniform treatment was accorded all subjects, who were kept visually and tactually isolated from each other.

Results Results on the crucial tests carried out 24 hours after the first imprinting session proved that Howard was a more acceptable mother image than Gray. All of the chicks imprinted to Howard correctly identified their mother. Four of the 6 imprinted to Gray chose him correctly, but 2 chose a wrong person. In other words, 10 out of 12 subjects made a correct choice while only 2 failed the test.

All tests required that no imprinting sound be used, only vision was involved. Gray and Howard conclude as follows: Our data invalidate any assumption that birds imprinted to a human do not know that human from another. Since imprinted chicks are able to recognize their human parent-surrogate, one must conclude that previous theorizing about imprinting has been shown to be unwarranted by simple tests [p. 303].

Why had Lorenz failed? After reading Howard and Gray's study, I went back to Lorenz's (1952) humorous incident of imprinting the mallard ducks. The kind of procedure he used in that instance may well explain his failure to achieve imprinting to individual humans with his mallard ducklings. Apparently he failed to imprint them even to himself when he presented himself under two vastly different conditions of sitting on the ground and standing.

Lorenz-standing and *Lorenz-sitting-on-ground* certainly must have presented such different aspects of Lorenz to the ducks as to constitute two different stimulus objects to them. A solid object when he sat on the ground, presenting trousers and a shirt, suddenly vanished and gave way to two "columns" that one could see through. After all, ducklings are not geared to "rubber-neck" at "skyscrapers." When Lorenz arose and assumed a standing position, the imprinting stimulus object may well have been out of range. (Apparently Gray and Howard had more uniform and, therefore, more successful imprinting to individual humans.) They do state that they wore similar clothes on both conditioning days (p. 302).

Experimental tests of a "social-releaser mechanism" in birds

An early study by Tinbergen (1948) seemed to show that several species of birds manifested an innate reaction. The subjects were confronted with an ambiguous silhouette figure that resembled a predatory bird when moved in one direction but not when moved in the other direction. Even birds raised in isolation gave an avoidance reaction when the figure was moved so that it resembled a predator. Movement in the opposite direction did not bother the birds. The results agreed with Tinbergen's theory of species-evolved innate releasing mechanisms which simply fire off when triggered by certain adequate stimuli in the animal's surroundings. In a sense, according to Tinbergen's theory, the organism comes into the world "pre-adapted" to flee (without learning) from his natural enemies but not from harmless animals.

McNiven (1960) decided to reproduce the conditions of Tinbergen's study to see if he got the same results. The project was all the more significant because Tinbergen's findings were being quoted in the literature. As a test stimulus, McNiven used an ambiguous design that resembled a hawk when moved to the left and a goose when moved to the right. The first was meant to mimic the hereditary enemy; the second, a barnyard friend. Would chickens, ducks, and pheasants crouch or run from the first and ignore the second? That was the question. McNiven also introduced two different types of movement of the stimulus object, a sailing movement and a swooping one. As subjects, McNiven used domesticated chickens, undomesticated mallard ducks, and undomesticated pheasants. The test area was a wire enclosure 10 feet in diameter. At a height of 15 feet, a wire allowed affixing Masonite silhouettes, one unpainted and the other painted black. The former had a wing span of 28 inches with a 14-inch body, and the latter a 20-inch wing spread and a 10-inch body. With the short neck leading, the figures resembled hawks. Pulled in the opposite direction, they resembled geese.

After a 10-minute orientation in the relatively shadow-free room, a silhouette was sailed over the birds in one direction, then the other. Each group experienced six trials of figure presentation in each direction, with order of presentation rotated. The same procedure was involved for the swooping condition. Swooping trials followed sailing trials except for one group of chickens which received *only* swooping trials and another group which received *no* swooping trials. Swoops were simulated with the aid of a 12-foot wire to which the silhouettes were attached. Responses of the subjects were tallied under (1) escape response, (2) crouching response, and (3) no response categories.

Results With the short neck leading, the proportion of escape and crouching responses combined was 32.50. With the long neck leading, the figure is 32.26! When tested statistically, the figures indicated "no differences in the number of escape responses elicited by the silhouette when pulled in the short-necked direction and when pulled in the long-necked direction" (p. 263). This finding held true for all the experimental groups, showing no differential response to the hawk versus goose stimuli. The sailing versus swooping results yielded figures of 5.29 and 59.29 escape and crouching movements, respectively (p. 263), thus indicating that the type of movement was a significant variable in the experiment. In other words, "goose" or "hawk" sailing above normally created no particular problem. However, either stimulus involved in a sudden downward plunge caused crouching reactions on the part of the subjects. On the main question concerning the innate fear of predator in birds, McNiven* concludes:

Tinbergen's results concerning a hypothetical 'social-releaser mechanism' were not supported in this study [p. 263]...
"How could these results differ so markedly from those obtained by Tinbergen?" Perhaps

---

*Quoted material is from Malcolm A. McNiven, "Social-releaser Mechanisms in Birds—A Controlled Replication of Tinbergen's Study," *The Psychological Record*, October 1960, **10**(4), 259–265.

the answer lies in the different approaches to studying a problem demonstrated by American comparative psychologists and their European counterparts. Tinbergen's statement of the results merely indicated that young gallinaceous birds, ducks, and geese reacted in a frightened manner to the silhouette when moved in the "hawk" direction, but showed no escape responses when the silhouette was moved in the "goose" direction. No data were reported and no description of the details of the procedure was reported. A request to Tinbergen for specific information about the experimental procedure was not answered. The answer to the question of why the results differ may lie in the details of procedure, in the details of the subjects' environment prior to the trials, or in many other aspects of the study. But, unless these are reported by the experimenter, we will never know. Writers in America have given wide circulation to the studies of the Lorenz-Tinbergen school without demanding corroborative evidence of the adequacy of the experimental work. Several individuals have worked closely with members of the Lorenz-Tinbergen school and have reported on their work. One such report by Lehrman (1953) criticized Lorenz's theory of instinct for the following reasons:

1. It is rigidly canalized by the merging of widely different kinds of organization under inappropriate and gratuitous categories.

2. It involves preconceived and rigid ideas of innateness and the nature of maturation.

3. It habitually depends on the transference of concepts from one level to another, solely on the basis of analogical reasoning.

4. It is limited by preconceptions of isomorphic resemblances between neutral and behavioral phenomena.

5. It depends on finalistic, preformationist conceptions of the development of behavior itself.

6. As indicated by its applications to human psychology and sociology, it leads to, or depends on (or both), a rigid, preformationist, categorical conception of development and organization. [p. 264].

The indifference of chickens, ducks, and pheasants to a hawk silhouette is one thing. Yet when one notes the intense fear response of an adult quail to a hawk, the mere thought of imprinting a baby quail to its mortal enemy sounds preposterous. This is exactly what Kenneth B. Melvin, F. Thomas Cloar, and Lucinda S. Massingill (1967) attempted to do, despite the fact that Tinbergen's "social-releaser mechanism" attested to its futility.

Procedure   The procedure varied somewhat so that the end result was a series of five subexperiments. The variations are not crucial to the main hypothesis and are omitted here out of space considerations. Essentially what the Melvin experiments did was to train an adult female sparrow hawk to ride on a perch suspended over a circular runway 8 inches wide and 4 feet in diameter with walls 5 inches high. The hawk's perch was an arm radiated from the center of the apparatus and set to move at a rate of a half foot per second. Although the species of hawk used in the experiment preys on mice and insects, it is also reputed to eat young quail. An event during the experiment tended to corroborate the last report.

Imprinting involved placing the subject in the apparatus behind the moving, live hawk for 20 minutes. A similar session occurred 6 to 8 hours later. Approximately 20 hours later the subjects were given a 20-minute testing session. The criterion of imprinting required following within one foot of the hawk for 70 percent of the first

8 minutes, a seemingly stringent criterion.

Results   Seven birds satisfied the criterion for imprinting. Three other subjects showed a moderate amount of imprinting but not to criterion level. However, the imprinted birds acted like baby chicks who are out of sight of the mother hen. They gave "distress" calls when the hawk was out of sight, ran to it as soon as it appeared, positioned themselves under the hawk's tail and pecked at it! In a test run on the second day, nonimprinted birds ran in the opposite direction at sight of the hawk. In another test on Day 3 three imprinted birds, placed equidistant between the live hawk and a model of a female, showed unanimous preference for the hawk by approaching it! In general, then (with wide individual differences), the bobwhite quail can be imprinted to a bird that normally would be its predator and from which it would normally flee. In support of the concept of the critical period, however, three subjects on whom imprinting was attempted at 30 hours after hatching "showed strong escape behavior and were given only one session [p. 236]."

An untoward event   Ordinarily, shortly before each imprinting session, Melvin and his fellow experimenters fed the hawk some beef. They did this as a precaution against the hawk's feasting on the quail subjects. On one occasion they forgot to feed the hawk, which took advantage of the first opportunity to remedy the error. After following the hawk in the runway for 5 minutes, the quail subject ran just ahead of the hawk and stopped. The "imprinting object" then seized the bird by its neck feathers. Instant intervention by the experimenter caused a disturbance that sent the quail in an accidental spill to the floor. Soothed during a 2-minute rest interval, the quail was replaced in the runway, whereupon it "resumed following and showed very strong imprinting during sessions 2 and 3 [p. 237]."

The "paradoxical punishment [p. 237]" observed here and in other experiments is considered a distinguishing feature of imprinting in contrast to associative learning. Melvin and his collaborators, however, offer a reasonable explanation for the *apparent* paradox. If punishment (the quail's fall to the floor) increases fear, why should not nearness to the imprinting object or the goal box reduce that fear, thus reinforcing the response of following the hawk? In short, the quail acted consistently by running toward its "beloved" hawk "mama."

Summary Using a circular runway, an attempt was made to imprint 18 bobwhite quail chicks, 8 to 20 hours after hatching, to an adult female sparrow hawk, the quail's natural predator. Seven subjects were strongly imprinted, and three moderately so. Three subjects on whom imprinting was attempted 30 hours after hatching showed only strong escape behavior. Tinbergen's results were not replicated and his notion of a "social-releaser mechanism" not supported.

19 Scott's lamb and critical periods in imprinting*

A number of years ago I was given a female lamb taken from its mother at birth. My wife and I raised it on the bottle for the first 10 days of life and then placed it out in the pasture with a small flock of domestic sheep. As might have been expected from folklore, the lamb became attached to people and followed the persons who fed it. More surprisingly, the lamb remained independent of the rest of the flock when we restored it to the pasture. Three years later it was still following an independent grazing pattern. In addition, when it was mated and had lambs of its own it became a very indifferent mother, allowing its offspring to nurse but showing no concern when the lamb moved away with the other members of the flock [p. 949].

John Paul Scott was impressed by the permanent behavior modification in the lamb as the result of a very brief experience. The event centered Scott's attention on the critical period in the organism's development. Arguing from embryonic development, Scott (p. 957) points out how fluid an embryo's development is up to a certain point. For example, a cell that normally gives rise to an eye can be transplanted to a belly region and become part and parcel of the belly, but when a certain critical point in development is reached, the same transplantation will not conform to the new region. As Scott puts it: "organization inhibits reorganization [p. 957]." In Scott's opinion, the same principle holds for behavioral development.

Scott feels strongly about the importance of the critical period and sees it largely as a matter of maturation. Others,

*Quoted material is from John Paul Scott, "Critical Periods in Behavioral Development," *Science,* 30 November 1962, **138**(3544), 949–958.

like Schneirla and Rosenblatt (1963), see the matter in a more developmental light. Sluckin (1965) cites evidence indicating an *optimal* period for learning rather than a *critical* one (p. 71). Sluckin would generalize the notion of a most favorable period for learning to human situations such as learning to speak, read, or walk. While he regards the concept of critical periods less absolutistically than others do, nevertheless, he does see it as being more applicable to imprinting than elsewhere. The difference between animal and human optimal periods for imprinting may be due to the relatively simple psychological setting of the newborn animal. Relevant variables are more numerous and therefore less prominent, in the more complex human situation. Even here, however, one cannot help speculating that what happens *behaviorally* conditions what happens *behaviorally* later. The research that Sluckin (1965) noted indicates that normally reared chicks raised in a group will follow a moving object only up to the third day of life, not after that. Yet chicks raised in visual isolation from each other, or from any other visual object, will still approach and follow moving objects after the third day. Why the difference? Because, being unimprinted, they follow any moving object indiscriminately. On the other hand, normally (i.e., group) reared chicks become imprinted upon each other, stick to their own, and hence become indifferent to any new figures (pp. 78-79). Again and again, it seems that the earliest formulations of imprinting may have forced investigators to see the facts in accordance with those formulations. As a result, they overlooked other happenings occurring right in front of them, or, to be more charitable, let us say that the question of the critical period has not yet been answered finally.

Moltz and Rosenblum on the "irreversibility" of imprinting

20

A distinguishing feature of imprinting, in comparison with associative learning, is the irreversibility of the former. Howard Moltz and Leonard Rosenblum (1958) had noted that evidence from earlier investigators showed that the "following response" of coots and moor hens was *not* irreversible, but they wanted experimental evidence. What would happen to the strength of a following response with experimental conditions held constant from trial to trial?

Procedure Peking ducks, individually housed, saw no moving object prior to their exposure to the moving test object. An alley, 10 feet long and 2 feet wide, constituted the apparatus, which also had a leather belt suspended above the floor and passed around two pulleys 9 feet apart. The test object, a green box 9 inches long, 4 inches wide, and 4 inches deep, was suspended from the belt. A motor drove the pulleys and could be set to move the imprinting green box at a constant rate of .4 foot per second. The arrangement permitted the duckling to follow in pursuit of the imprinting object up and down the alley. With head covered, the duckling was transferred from the cage to the apparatus and presented visually to the green box set in motion after an interval of 30 seconds. A single test trial consisted of a 10-minute run. Only one test trial was given each day for 15 days. Neither food nor water was made available to the subjects in the apparatus. Exploratory study showed that, in addition to following the green box while it was moving, the ducklings also walked beside it or, as all ducklings have done down through the ages, they frequently ran ahead and waited for "mama" to catch up.

Results Because Moltz and Rosenblum's purpose was to study the picture of imprinting over a period of time, they naturally needed solidly established imprinting as a base. Had they worked with varying degrees of imprinting as a starter, this would have obscured and confused the results. Consequently, they rejected as a subject any bird that did not follow the imprinting object at least 60 seconds on the second trial and 500 seconds on the third trial. Of the 20 birds run, 13 met the criterion.

What about irreversibility? The experimenters obtained a following score in terms of seconds for each subject. They computed a median following, or moving, score for each bird. Their results showed a fairly strong following between trials 2 and 8, but quite a sharp drop in the number of seconds that subjects followed the green box during Trials 9 through 15 (see Fig. 5.23).

The results in the early part of the experiment show following near maximum strength, but certainly no continuous plateau is apparent throughout the 15 trials. Figure 5.23 shows a decreasing trend as early as the sixth trial, after which there is a progressive decrease in strength of imprint-

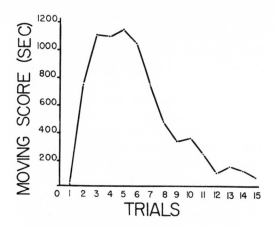

Figure 5.23 Reversibility of imprinting. Median moving-scores as a function of trials. Scores are in terms of seconds, 1200 seconds being the maximum possible because that was the total time that the green box moved. The trials are one per day for 15 days. While each animal showed following of near maximal strength in Trials 2 through 8, continued exposure to the imprinting object showed progressive and rapid extinction of the following response during Trials 9 through 15. Conclusion: Imprinting is as reversible as other kinds of learning. (From Howard Moltz and Leonard A. Rosenblum, "Imprinting and Associative Learning: The Stability of the Following Response in Peking Ducks," *The Journal of Comparative and Physiological Psychology*, October 1958, **51**(5), 580–583. Figure reproduced by permission of author and publisher.)

ing. According to Moltz and Rosenblum, "every bird included in the study exhibited this decrease" (p. 581).

By the fifteenth trial, nine subjects either failed to follow their "mama" or gave less than 200 seconds of following out of the total of 1200 seconds that the imprinting object moved. One subject, which showed a moving score of 1182 seconds in Trial 5, deteriorated to a mere 28 seconds in Trial 15.

It is obvious that, at least with respect to the Peking duck, the present study offers no evidence in support of Lorenz' contention that following is irreversible. Indeed, when neither primary nor secondary reward is associated with the object followed, and when experimental conditions tend to remain constant from trial to trial, imprinting appears to be a very unstable phenomenon [Moltz and Rosenblum, 1958, p. 582].

Our discussion of imprinting began with Lorenz's mallard ducklings and with Scott's lamb; in both cases, ducklings and lamb scorned members of their own species. We then noted an early view of imprinting, which explains the phenomenon as an innate self-releasive mechanism. This self-acting mechanism is characterized by a critical period and irreversibility. It also is thought, according to this early view, to serve as a means of facilitating *species* attachment first, then *individual* attachment. We next examined laboratory studies that showed imprinting to *individuals* first rather than species, a test of the theory of the "social-releaser mechanism." We found the theory contradicted by McNiven's study and that of Melvin and his colleagues, who imprinted a following response of bob-

white quail to its presumably innate enemy.

We then considered the critical period, both as a maturational and as a behavioral condition limiting further behavior development. We also discussed Moltz and Rosenblum's study, which showed a fairly rapid extinction of imprinting, thus disproving its irreversibility.

Finally, the small sample of recent research on imprinting seems to justify Klopfer's (1967) comment on a series of studies showing a relationship between imprinting and the kind of stimulus used.* "Our present results suggest imprinting is far more complex a process than suggested by the *tabula rasa* model [p. 1396]." And the reader should bear in mind this statement from Sluckin's critical review of the field. "There is little that can be said by way of defining imprinting that cannot be challenged or queried [Sluckin, 1965, p. 15]."

---

*If imprinting is only learning, then why shouldn't different kinds of stimuli produce different results? After all, why should we expect different stimuli to have equivalent functions or values?

Chapter summary

A basic concern of the present chapter has been: Is there such a thing as unacquired behavior? Starting with the wasp and moth, we observed reactions that were definitely unlearned. Yet we saw nothing of the properties of the psychological in them. Instead we perceived undeviating, rigid, routine, mechanical-like actions — tropisms. They remind us of reflexes except that large portions of the organism are involved. We found pheromones to be unlearned, primitive responses to physicochemical stimuli.

Pursuing the problem of instincts further, we found that many alleged instincts rest on the basis of folklore of fiction. On the other hand, turning to the studies of the young ethologists, we found evidence of complex activities in chimps, gorillas, and finches. We also saw evidence of learning and even of a primitive culture in these species.

Selections on the migration of fish illustrated that homing or migration occurs on a basis of a sensitive reaction to significant chemical substances, plus imprinting factors. Finally, Sluckin's analysis of imprinting suggests that it is itself a form of learning. In his 1937 pronouncements, Lorenz saw none of the features of learning in imprinting. More recently he expressed the idea that "imprinting tapers off into learning" and that "imprinting is definitely a type of conditioning [Sluckin, 1965, pp. 8–9]."

All the evidence considered in the present chapter strongly implies that, when there are unacquired reactions, they are not psychological; that when there are definite psychological reactions, they are acquired.

There are a number of ways to enlarge on the difference between the two. One way is to characterize the nonpsychological as simpler and the psychological as more complex. All we are saying is that physiologically, because the organism is constructed a certain way, certain stimuli can have one, and only one, outcome. For example, what else can the pupil in the human eye do except contract when light stimulates it? By contrast, the human vocal apparatus may be used in speaking any one or more of the hundreds of languages spoken on our planet, or none of them, depending on a person's history following birth.

Another way to differentiate between the psychological and the nonpsychological is to point out that nonpsychological actions do not require a temporal dimension to develop following the organism's birth. A child who addresses his father may learn over a period of time to call him "daddy," "baba," or "vater," depending on the country in which that child lives following its birth.

The temporal characteristic leads us naturally to the next distinguishing property of the psychological, that is, its specificity. A knee jerk or sneeze is universal among humans (even among some nonhumans), but not language, religion, diet, or manner of dress. The latter partake of the same specificity as the infant's name for its father; the former are built-in or "ready-made" reactions that are evoked by a number of a general class of stimuli. A reflex sneeze response can be elicited by sunlight, pepper, a feather, or a pollen grain. But only one specific person can call forth the response "papa," "Mr. President," or "Mayor X."

Still another difference between the two classes of phenomena can be summed up with the term *evolution*. Psychological actions evolve during the lifetime of the organism. He must learn to speak, to dance, to skate, to fiddle, to paint. He does not have to learn to burp, to vomit, to urinate (reflexly), or to produce a knee jerk.

Further differentiation between the psychological and the physiological is possible. Among others, Kantor (1933) and Mahan (1968) offer additional properties beyond those considered above.

6

6

Beginnings, origins, nascencies, and sequences

The preceding chapter discussed the origin and evolution of psychological action outside a biological matrix. It attempted to show that if organisms performed actions that were unlearned, such actions were rigid and mechanical chain reactions to physicochemical stimuli. On the other hand, where we did observe the more complex, psychological, responses, we also witnessed a set of circumstances labeled imprinting, conditioning, or learning. The present chapter explores the role of learning in the earliest stages of the newborn's life.

We shall first go behind the scenes, so to speak, and examine the very beginnings of life, for it appears that some behaviors *seem* to spring forth at birth, without prior learning. Is this a fact, or could such reactions have an unseen but definite developmental sequence in utero? The studies on human and duck embryos included here will shed some light on that question.

Secondly, it has long been thought that the newborn infant is too young to learn.

Is this a fact, or should such notions be discarded? A sampling from a mass of studies shows the tremendous complexity of behavior development even in the earliest days and hours.

The new approach involves a shift from the earlier, obsolescent view of developmental stages or norms. Even smiling and crying, once considered almost "instinctive," will be seen to have a complicated history. So with attention, head turning, sucking, smelling, crying, and vocalization as the earliest fundaments of speech.

Finally, massive enrichment studies versus deprivation studies will show the possibilities for tremendous behavior development or its near absence in the case of autistic and feral children. As a preview, the reader should be aware of the readiness and speed with which young life begins its psychological career. If given a chance, the infant seems to be an eager learner from the very start.

Gesell:
The Embryology
of Behavior*

1

He who sees things from their beginnings will have the most advantageous view of them." So said Aristotle, who wrote the first great compendium of embryology, and who looked upon living nature with a breadth of vision far in advance of his time [Gesell, 1945, p. 1].

*Quoted material is from Arnold Gesell, *The Embryology of Behavior* (New York: Harper & Row, 1945). While I accept Gesell's findings, I reject the materialistic, theoretical orientation in which his data are embedded.

The Embryology of Behavior, a classic contribution replete with many patient observations and astute inferences about behavior origins and early behavior development, was written by a child specialist at Yale University, Dr. Arnold Gesell. The phrase, *the embryology of behavior,* is a metaphor, because *embryology* refers to the formation and development of the biological organism. Still, the title is used with full awareness of its correct meaning. It is applied to the origin and change in behavior development by analogy with the origin and change in organic forms. Another reason for relating behavior with embryology is that behavior is never seen apart from living organisms. Furthermore, a still better reason lies in the fact that origins of behavior *may* be closely connected with the origins of the organism. Where you see one, you may see the other. Certainly studying behavior at a later stage may cause us to overlook its earlier phases and origin and to interpret it as if it appeared full-blown. Finally, we have the word of Gesell (1945) that we "now have sufficient data to trace in outline the remarkable organization of behavior which occurs prior to birth" (p. *viii*). The following brief and kaleidoscopic account of Gesell's findings is merely offered as a lure to a lengthier and more thoughtful examination of his work.

The search for beginnings

Gesell had earlier studied children from 4 months to 6 years of age. He even drew up tables of norms for behaviors that were typical at different stages of maturity (p. 4), but he never seemed to get to the origins of behaviors. Then he decided to go farther back toward the point of conception. His studies convinced him that "an extraordinary amount of behavior organization takes place in the ten lunar months which precede birth" (p. 9).

How did Gesell get his data? By studying prematurely born infants. Some had been surgically removed and thus could be observed only for a brief period. However, most of his observations were made on premature infants who did live, and these ranged in age from 28 to 40 weeks from conception. Both spontaneous and responsive activities were recorded by means of cinematographic and stop-action photography. The data, arranged into normative inventories, brought the developmental picture up to normal birth (fetal age, 40 weeks).

The overall impression of Gesell's elaborate study concerns the *continuity* of development. Everything proceeds by gradual degrees; there are no jumps from embryo to fetus to infant and child. Only "beginnings, origins, nascencies, and sequences" (p. *viii*) are emphasized against the background of continuous progression. Note the embryonic drama revealed in the following series of scenes.

Movement before nerve connections

The common conception of the nerve connection as an *indispensable* agent of response is not supported in our first view of the embryo as provided by Gesell.

The major components of both trunk and limb musculature are in evidence in the anatomy of the embryo at the close of the second lunar month. During this period, the embryo floats in a fluid sphere contained by the amniotic membrane. Presumably it floats quiescently and passively. Muscles, however, are peculiarly sensitive to environing influences. They tend to twitch at an early stage of their embryonic development when the ions in the surrounding medium are unbalanced. They may contract feebly and intermittently, without the stimulus of nervous impulses. In the heart, as we shall see, this contraction becomes a peristaltic sweep and settles into a rhythmic beat before nerve connections are established. Smooth muscles of intestine, stomach, and blood vessels are capable of similar myogenic activity [p. 30].

*Experience with gravity
prior to birth*

It is easy to think that humans must begin their encounter with gravity *after* they are born; this is certainly the time when the largest and most sudden displacements, such as falling and being dropped, can and do occur. However, to consider the matter seriously, one must realize that the fetus must bend over every time the mother bends over, the fetus must also turn to the right every time his mother turns to the right, lies in a different direction from the immediately preceding position when she turns on her back, and so on. Here is how Gesell describes this area of experience.

Equilibrium...is not a general ability which is mastered once and for all. It always functions in relation to the motor system which is operative at the time. In the postnatal period, specific equilibrium patterns must be acquired for the maintenance of head station, sitting posture, standing, and walking. The human infant does not balance himself independently on his two feet until he is about 56 weeks of age. The equilibrium of the embryo has a different economy, but in part it depends upon the same mechanisms which will be used by the infant in the assumption of the upright posture. Man begins his lifelong contest with gravity even before he is born. All told, it takes about a hundred weeks before he stands and walks erect. Most of the basic organization of this distinctively human posture is laid down during the fetal period [p. 32].

The above incident once more emphasizes the continuity in the elaboration of the organisms patterns of action.

*A "snapshot of the
fetus at 12 to 16 weeks"*

Twelve lunar months hence, at the postfetal age of 20 weeks, he will rotate his head repeatedly and avidly, through an arc of 180 degrees. This pattern comes to a peak of intensity at that age. But it is anticipated and to a modest degree actually fabricated in the fourth fetal month.

This month is in many respects the most remarkable in the embryology of behavior because the fetus exhibits (even though he does not yet command) an extremely varied repertoire of elementary movement patterns. Almost his entire skin is sensitive to stimulation. Crude generalized responses give way to specific reactions. Arms and legs show more motility at every joint and make excursions into new sectors of space. Within the confines of the amniotic sac, these movements are probably mild, and vary from episodic twitches to variably prolonged tonic contractions which wax and then wane into nothingness. Their vigor and incidence must also vary with constitutional and with passing biochemical conditions. As in all growth patterning, the primary impulses come from within.

The daily course of these natural activities is not conspicuously ordered by rhythms of work and rest. It must depend rather on the meandering distribution of the metabolic foci of growth. Accordingly, now the head and mouth, now the feet, now the hands, emerge into action, somewhat as ripples rise here and there upon a placid surface. Reactions seemingly detached are nevertheless patterned and all have their morphogenetic determination in a unitary growth plan. So this fetus in the course of a day or a fortnight (between 14 and 16 weeks) would display a changing succession of patterns with successive intervals of quiescence.

He moves his upper lip. When a little more mature, he moves his lower lip. Later he moves both lips in unison. Still later he opens and closes his mouth [see Fig. 6.1]. He swallows with closed mouth, but at times he also swallows amniotic fluid. His tongue moves, or he moves his tongue. (We have no semantics to take care of this distinction.) He may also rotate his head in association with the "oral reflex," for complex patterns of feeding behavior are in the making. Peristaltic waves sweep over his lengthening digestive tube [pp. 68–69].

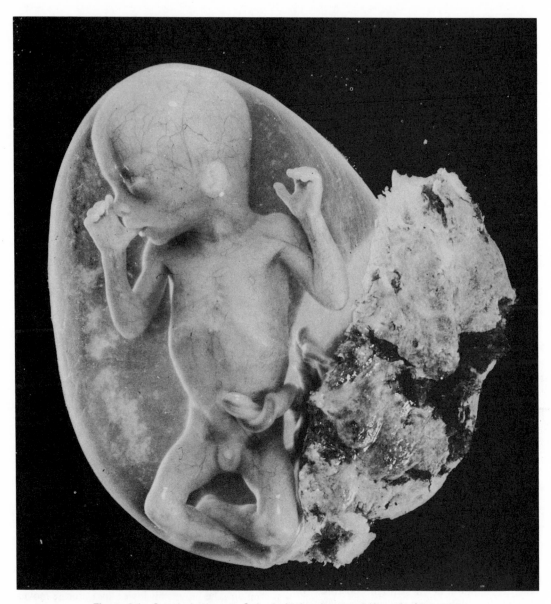

Figure 6.1 Caught in the act. Only six inches long and 18 weeks from conception, this infant is already started on a precocious career of sucking his thumb. We once thought that thumb-sucking was a built-in response ready to function at birth. However, recent work shows the gradual evolution of this response and others out of earlier and simpler acts during the child's nine-months' residence in his mother's uterus. (Photo © Lennart Nilsson; courtesy *Life* magazine.)

Another "snapshot" of the fetus at 28 to 32 weeks

The eyeballs move conjointly both laterally and vertically. But positive visual responses are scanty or quite absent. The fetal-infant will, however, make mild avoidance responses to a bright light, blinking, frowning, and flinching slightly. Even this response, however, soon peters out and diminishes to a tired blink, or the eyes simply remain closed.

The reaction to sound, when a small hand bell is tinkled near the ear, is similar. There may be a slight frown, a "squinch" with a blink, followed by a short wave of activity which soon subsides. On repeated stimulation, the fetal-infant rapidly becomes impervious to sound. Inaction again supervenes. It is as though the action system were a toy with a weak spring which readily runs down. A mild jolt of the table on which the fetal-infant lies may also produce a small wave of activity which presently sinks into a drowsy quiescence [p. 112]. . . .

All things considered, the most important developmental advance achieved by the mid-stage fetal-infant is his capacity for brief periods of wakeful alertness. They are the growing germs which will elaborate into the complex cycle of diurnal wakefulness and sleep. The early-stage fetal infant gives virtually no sign of this cycle because neither sleep nor alertness is discernible in his state of amorphous dormancy.

Out of this amorphous anlage, true wakefulness first begins to differentiate during the mid-stage of fetal-infancy. Again and again during the day (and night) he pricks the surface of mere being with movements of true wakefulness. The frank, though as yet only occasional, open-eyedness, the hunger cry even though feeble, the stirrings of discomfort are so many glimmers of wakefulness. Sleep, however, remains indecisive; he is, on the whole, an indisputably drowsy individual.

His present behavior equipment represents an intermediate stage of maturity. He is no longer profoundly apathetic and flaccid. Nor is he yet a lusty, active, competent neonate [pp. 121–122].

Summary

The preceding sketchy account of human embryological development lacks the richness found in Gesell's book, but it is meant to convey, at least, the unbroken continuity in the melding and elaboration of organismic functioning that provides the building blocks for the infant's continued extrauterine development. Gone is the notion of the *tabula rasa*. Psychological development starts with the organism's rich stock of materials waiting to be related to numerous stimulus objects in the newborn infant's surroundings.

Gottlieb and Zing-Yang Kuo: A window in a duck egg*

2

Ordinarily the development of a duck embryo into a newly hatched duckling goes on unseen by human or any other eyes. Gilbert Gottlieb and Zing-Yang Kuo, however, were determined to view the opaque, internal proceedings in the egg.

They ingeniously shifted the air space in the egg from the blunt end to the middle of

---

*Quoted material is from Gilbert Gottlieb and Zing-Yang Kuo, "Development of Behavior in the Duck Embryo," *Journal of Comparative and Physiological Psychology*, 1965, **59**(2), 183–188.

the egg, cut off the shell over the latter, and thus obtained an inside view of developments. In order to observe the embryos beyond 12 days of development, they cut the shell off over the blunt end and applied warm, liquified Vaseline to the opaque membrane underneath, making it transparent. Altogether, Gottlieb and Zing-Yang used 250 Pekin duck eggs.

Behavioral development

The researchers were looking for more detailed aspects of embryonic development than we require, so only certain of their results will be given here.

Passive head movements With its head bent toward the region of the heart, rhythmic cardiac movements induced "passive vibration or nodding of the head and stimulation of the region of the presumptive bill" (p. 185). These movements were observed between the third and fifth day. After this time, the duck embryo's head became larger and the heart took a more internal position, which eliminated passive head nodding by Day 9.

Active head movement Three varieties of head movements were observed: lifting, bending, and turning. The lifting movement was observed before head turning. Interestingly, head bending toward the heart region preceded head lifting, but as the head became larger and heavier and the neck longer and thinner, head lifting gave way to head turning. The experimenters observed that the direction in which the head was turned was a function of local conditions. When the duck embryo lay with its left side to the yolk sac, the head turned more frequently to the right. When the condition was reversed, so was the direction of head turning, thus showing that the embryo's movements are a function of stim-

ulus conditions impinging upon the organism.

Oral movements Opening and closing of the bill showed relationships similar to those of the other bodily parts. After the ninth day, when its wings or legs touched or scratched its bill, the head was turned away in response to the self-stimulation.

Movements of the forelimbs Action involving forelimbs or wings appeared on the sixth day even before the limb buds developed digits. By the tenth day, the forelimbs had the appearance of wings, and flapping movements of a definite sort first appeared on this day.

Movements of the hindlimbs or legs Development of leg movements was similar to that for the wings. On Day 10, paddling movements appeared. Stretching of the toes and alternate movements of the feet also occurred.

Combination movements The above analysis of movements involving various bodily parts suggests that the duck embryo acted in a disjointed fashion with each part moving on its own. Such was not the case, for we are assured that throughout the incubation period (p. 187) the independent movement of a single bodily part was rare. Combinations of movements involving two or more parts were the rule rather than the exception.

Responsiveness to external stimulation

The above description of the behavior of the duck embryo suggests that the animal is responsive to external stimulation. For example, even in the earliest stages, the bird's head was seen to lift and turn away from the heart. After the heart retreated into the thorax and the embryo lay with its left side in contact with the yolk sac, the embryo's head turned more frequently away from the yolk sac than towards it. As early as Day 10 of incubation, whenever the bill or the chin was touched by the tip of the wing or scratched by the toes, the head turned away from the source of stimulation. When the touch was relatively light, one found a clapping movement of the bill instead of the head turning away. In all such cases there was no obvious indication of a refractory period, possibly because stimulation was not persistent but intermittent.

However, in the case of ocular responses to light and some other responses to persistent auditory, vibratory, or tactile stimulation, there was a noticeable refractory period (the actual length of which has not been quantitatively determined).

This study has revealed five facts, which, owing to their theoretical significance, are recapitulated here.

1. In the duck embryo, as in the chick embryo, each organ begins to function when it is in only the most rudimentary form. (Whether the physiology of the nervous system develops in the same manner requires investigation.)

2. During the embryonic period, the shape and relative size of the bodily structures are important determinants of the action patterns observed at any given stage.

3. The action patterns of the embryo are also influenced by extra-embryonic factors, such as amnion contractions and movements of the yolk sac.

4. In the duck embryo, as in the chick embryo, every organ or part of the body has been involved in a certain amount and certain kinds of activity before incubation is half-completed.

5. The embryo is constantly subject to stimulation throughout the course of prenatal development, whether through its own activities or otherwise. Nodding of the head from the beating of the heart, head-turning from tactile stimulation imparted by the limbs, swinging of the body in relation to amnion contractions, and aural stimulation from its own vocalizations are a few diverse examples of this point.

The above facts would seem to support the view that the ontogeny of behavior is gradual and continuous and that sequences of action occurring *in embryo* are significant precursors to the "preadapted" quality of action patterns in postnatal life. However, these conclusions

cannot be accepted without experimental (as contrasted with descriptive) support. In seeming to favor the probabilistic* rather than the predetermined epigenetic view of behavioral development, we are not asserting that standing, walking, pecking, flying, and swimming are learned or acquired in the egg. Rather, we consider the traditional conception of innateness as far as the study of the ontogeny of action patterns is concerned. In any stage of development there is no "innate" action pattern without historical antecedents, nor is there any "acquired" pattern that is free from elements which have not been active in the history of the developing organism. At best the innate-acquired dichotomy is an oversimplification of behavioral development and at worst a barrier to experimental analysis.

We would like to stress, with Holt (1931), Lehrman (1953), and Schneirla (1956), the concept of *self-stimulation* as a factor which may contribute to (facilitate) the establishment of action (motor) patterns and, possibly, certain perceptual preferences. It is not anticipated, however, that the effects of self-stimulation must mimic those of learning or conditioning (Holt, 1931). Musculoskeletal as well as kinesthetic and proprioceptive self-stimulation may be essential to the normal development of action patterns and "sequential ordering" of the embryo's behavior may be due to the developmental dynamics of the growing embryo *and* the changing mechanics of the amnion-yolk sac—embryo relationship.

Though there is a great deal of evidence for the general proposition that stimulation is a requirement for growth and function in behavioral development (Riesen, 1961), there is as yet no evidence to show that conventional learning theory is relevant to the prenatal development of behavior or to the relationship between prenatal and postnatal behavior. (Lehrman, 1962, has raised essentially the same point in relation to certain phases of postnatal development.) Furthermore, certain other conclusions may unintentionally impede both the analysis of

---

*"*Probabilistic epigenesis* stresses the importance of (1) stimulational factors in actualizing the various potentials of embryo, which occurs (2) gradually and continuously throughout development. *Predetermined epigenesis* stresses (1) invariant schedule of neuro-muscular growth and differentiation in determining behavior, with emphasis on (2) abrupt transitions or changes in behavior throughout development [original footnote]."

prenatal behavior and the progress of developmental theory: "What is happening inside the egg when we detect movements of the embryo is, mainly if not entirely, a process of maturation of the innate behaviour patterns" (Thorpe, 1956, p. 311).

Though we make no pretense concerning the completeness of our "theoretical" formulation, we do believe that emphasis on self-stimulative processes partially rectifies two important deficiencies of developmental theory. First, *self*-stimulation calls attention to the observable and testable aspects of the *organism's* contribution to its own development and, second, "stimulation" avoids the empiricistic bias of the global term "experience" [pp. 187–188].

Summary

Gottlieb and Zing-Yang's study of the development of the duck embryo supports Gesell's findings on the evolution of the human fetus. Again, there appears to be an unbroken sequence of movements and their elaboration and differentiation, but also integration, into more complex organismic action. The phase of functioning achieved at birth prepares the way for an adequate postnatal functioning and continued growth. The new notion that the researchers contribute is the interactional view of self-stimulation, which agrees with the probabilistic conception of behavioral epigenesis, a more dynamic view than the passive and self-actional view of maturation as completely determining behavior. Whenever behavioral development is studied, it is necessary to try to synthesize the stimulative and maturational contributions in order to achieve a more adequate picture of the developmental process.

3 Grier, Counter, and Shearer: "Prenatal auditory imprinting in chickens"*

The present study follows naturally the work of Gesell and of Gottlieb and Kuo. It is a further illustration of the continuity of development, particularly of the transition from mere physiological action to genuine psychological responses. The article stresses the point that nothing springs forth *de novo* and that whatever occurs *now* has had a past.

*Quoted material is from J. Brown Grier, S. Allen Counter, and William M. Shearer, "Prenatal Auditory Imprinting in Chickens," *Science* 31 March 1967, **155**(3770), 1692–1693. Copyright 1967 by the American Association for the Advancement of Science.

As long as one ignores Aristotle's stricture to look for the origins of things, one can convince himself that a chick "instinctively" follows its clucking mother-hen upon hatching. However, if one reads the report of J. Brown Grier, S. Allen Counter, and William M. Shearer, one is forced to question such traditional ideas.

Grier, Counter, and Shearer's study

Is it possible that prenatal auditory learning (imprinting) might play a role in the chick's "immediate postnatal recognition [p. 1692]" of its mother's cluckings? In other words, is the chick, upon hatching, merely continuing to respond to the sounds that its mother uttered as she hovered over the eggs in her nest? Does the chick emerge ready to react to the same sound that it learned while still in the egg? Perhaps following is a unit of action easily grafted on to the prenatally acquired auditory response that is ready-to-go upon hatching.

Procedure In order to determine the earliest point in its embryological development that the chick shows auditory sensitivity, the experimenters tested the incubated eggs, one each day, from Day 4 to Day 18. Subjecting the series to bursts of a 1000-hz (cycle) tone, they discovered a consistent movement response to the auditory test stimulus after Day 12.

Now they were ready for the experiment proper. They incubated two groups of White Rock chicken eggs. Next they subjected an experimental group of 15 chicks prenatally to a patterned sound and raised a control group of 12 subjects in a quiet, sound-attenuated room. Within 6 hours of hatching, the experimenters tested *every* chick for recognition and response to two stimuli: (1) the tone that had been presented prenatally only to the experimental group and (2) a novel test sound. The experimental sound was a series of one-second beeps of a 200-hz tone separated by one second of quiet. The novel stimulus had the same pattern but at 2000-hz. The experimental group heard the former sound pattern continuously between Day 12 and Day 18.

Testing All testing was carried out on a circular table with concentric lines painted on it to facilitate measuring the

chick's movement to the auditory stimulus. The latter proceeded from either of two loudspeakers placed opposite each other on the periphery of the table.

Shortly after it hatched, each chick was placed in the center of the test board, and either the experimental or novel sound was turned on for 45 seconds. Only one speaker was active at a time. At the end of 45 seconds the distance the chick had moved toward the speaker was measured, the chick was returned to center, and the other tone was given. The order of presentation of the two sounds and the order of use of the two speakers were counterbalanced. The sound was approximately 65 db at the center of the table [p. 1692].

Results The results are stated in terms of the average distance that both groups of subjects moved toward a stationary sound source. Taking the control group first, these chicks, hatched in a quiet incubator, traveled an average distance of 13.72 cm when the 200-hz pattern was used and 13.46 cm toward the 2000-hz sound. Thus the control group subjects do not react differentially to two sounds quite different in frequency. How about the experimental group? The 2000-hz tone elicited an average of 11.84 cm distance traveled to it, but the 200-hz prenatally administered pattern gave an average of 25.22 cm. The difference that the experimental group traveled in response to the two tones is highly significant statistically, with a P value greater than .01.

A second experiment

In a second experiment chicks in the experimental group were tested for following behavior. At the end of the discrimination test each chick was returned to the center of the table and a child's pull-toy model chicken was moved in front of it by hand from one edge of the table to the other at a rate of about 1.2 meters per minute. Every chick was tested under each of three conditions: two passes with the model quiet, two passes with a small speaker on its back emitting the novel sound, and two passes emitting the experimental sound. The order of presentation of the conditions was counter-balanced from chick to chick. When the model reached the edge of the table, the trial was terminated. The chick was considered to be following as long as it was within 10 cm of the model. The average amount of time that the chick spent following the model out of a maximum of about 30 seconds was: no sound, 5.35 seconds; novel sound, 10.07 seconds; and experimental sound, 15.21 seconds. An analysis of variance of these scores showed a significant difference ($F = 10.15$, 2–26 *df*, $P < .005$). The 5 percent least-significant difference between the means is 4.71, indicating that each of the three conditions differs significantly from the others.

Newly hatched chicks seem to find any sound attractive, but a sound heard during the prenatal period proved more attractive than a novel one in two tests. In the second test the imprinted chicks even occasionally tried to jump on the toy model to get to the speaker. The results of these tests do not seem attributable to a natural preference for lower-frequency stimulation, since chicks in the control group found both the 200-hz and 2000-hz patterns equally attractive. Thus, young chicks are able to respond differentially to a sound heard prenatally. One possible explanation of the results of the following test could be that the sound merely called attention to the model, so that the following was primarily a response to a visual form. But since the model was passed directly in front of the chick several times, it is unlikely that the chick could not see it. These studies indicate that the auditory system functions considerably prior to hatching, and perhaps more important, that auditory events during the prenatal period can influence immediate postnatal preferences and behavior. To the extent that the term "imprinting" implies the ability to use this earlier exposure to stimuli

as a basis for later behavior, such as recognition, attraction, or following, we believe that the experiment demonstrated prenatal auditory imprinting [pp. 1692–1693].

Summary

Acting on the hypothesis that the chick's following response is, in part, a function of prenatal auditory imprinting, Grier, Counter, and Shearer set up an experiment to test it. They hatched a control batch of chicken eggs under quiet conditions in a soundproofed incubator. They also hatched an experimental batch of chicken eggs under continuous presentation of a 200-hz sound from Day 12 to Day 18 of incubation. Tests with the experimental sound and a novel sound showed no difference in travel distance for the control group. However, the experimental group showed twice as much travel distance to the experimental sound as to the novel sound. The results support the notion that the following response is, in part, learned as a *prenatally acquired* recognition which needs only to be grafted on to the part of the response that involves a movement toward the source of the discriminated sound.

He who does not "see things from their beginnings" can easily convince himself that behavior arises "from scratch," whereas even the beginnings of certain things themselves have their own origins in certain prior stages. A child may suck its thumb at, or shortly after, birth, but we know now that the response had an opportunity to develop while the infant was in utero.

Lipsitt: The post-
"developmental age" era*

4

As a student of the development of the embryo, Gesell has deservedly earned the status of a pioneer for his keen observations, but his work in devising tables of developmental norms (Gesell & Ilg, 1949) for children of different ages is another matter. In the latter work, he was not interested in discovering the underlying processes involved but only in establishing their actuarial or statistical derivatives. In other words, he sought an answer to the question: At what age does the "average child" crawl, stand, walk, etc.? What do developmental tables do except reflect the existing state of affairs? They tell *what is,* not how it got that way or how it could be.

Lipsitt's views

Lewis P. Lipsitt has questioned why it is that everyone celebrates the significance of early childhood and yet "systematic empirical study of the child in his crucial first year has been an on-again, off-again affair [p. 45]." He sees two major historical factors as having discouraged studies of the very young child: (1) a traditional over-concern with the biological basis of child development and (2) a rather "pervasive pessimism with respect to the *potentialities* of infants [p. 45]." It seems to me his statement provides an incisive commentary on how theory guides action, and as a preview of things to come, how it blinds us to facts right in front of us and determines not only whether we do experiments but also what *kind* we do.

The maturational bias

In expounding further, Lipsitt (p. 45) points out how the child developmentalists and professional educators of 30 or 40 years ago believed that "the young organism harbors the maturational or genetic determinants which will dictate the appearance of certain behaviors at certain stages of development and that experiential circumstances have only minimal influences [p. 46]." With such a view, one simply waited.

The concept of "reading readiness" was one such state believed to be essentially determined by time, as if after the mere passage of so much time, the child was ready to learn to read. Undoubtedly many of our educational practices still encourage the notion of time-bound stages, after the analogy of the child's physical development. In fact, the norms established for various behaviors lead to usage of a *developmental age* analogous to *mental age.*

Effects of the maturational bias

The close tieup of child development with "structural or morphological biology" had two effects on the study of children's development in the period from 1920 to 1950. (1) The field was slow in moving toward the adoption of experimental manip-

*Quoted material is from Lewis P. Lipsitt, "Learning Processes of Human Newborns," *Merrill-Palmer Quarterly of Behavior and Development,* 1966, **12** (1), 45–71.

ulative techniques despite the use of these methods in other areas of psychology. (2) Its maturational slant "inhibited the extensive study of environmental or experiential factors as they affect behavior, most specifically, learned changes in behavior. An ancillary effect of this maturational bias was the premature acceptance, or at least overvaluation, of certain data and propositions concerning the limitations of the human organism [p. 47]...." In general, with a few exceptions and until very recently, it was believed that the young infant could not learn.

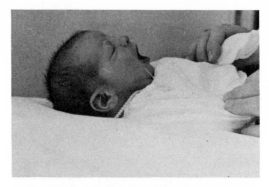

Figure 6.2 The Babkin reflex. The response is elicited by pressing on the palms of the hands and consists of turning the head to midline and opening the mouth widely as in a yawn. The response has been conditioned at Brown University. (Photo courtesy of Lewis Lipsitt.)

Lipsitt's stand

I have...a certain zeal about the feasibility of an experimental psychology of infancy which takes into consideration but is not obsessed by the age determination of child behavior. In my own laboratories we have done some research which is of a rather strictly developmental nature. For instance, one study (Lipsitt and Levy, 1959) showed that infants become increasingly sensitive to tactual stimulation within the 4-day lying-in period, and that female newborns are somewhat more sensitive to such stimulation than are males. Another such study [Lipsitt, Engen, and Kaye, 1963] showed that the neonate's sensitivity to olfactory stimulation improves sharply within the first four days of life, and that odor reception and discrimination are present even in the first day of life. [See Fig. 6.2 and 6.3].

But it is not so much about these developmental-assessment studies that I wish to speak; rather, I want to concentrate on our studies of behavioral *processes* in newborns; studies of behavioral change in the earliest days of life as a function of how we stimulate the babies. These studies are in the tradition of Marquis (1931), Wenger (1936), Wickens and Wickens (1940), and Kantrow (1937), a tradition which is too often ignored (Kessen, 1963) when the psychological competency of the very young child is at issue. I think that it will become apparent that I have confidence that the human newborn is a learning organism [p. 47].

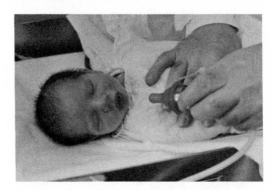

Figure 6.3 Automatic sucking apparatus. Note the continuation of strong sucking movements after nipple is removed from the mouth. Age of infant 3 days. (Photo courtesy of Lewis Lipsitt.)

Lipsitt's program and laboratory

At Brown University Lipsitt has set up an elaborate newborn laboratory to study various aspects of child behavior within the first few days of life. The laboratory, which is supported by the National Institute of Neurological Diseases and Blindness, is equipped with stabilimeter cribs to record movement or startle, a six-channel polygraph, an audio-oscillator for producing tones via a speaker, a physiological stimulator and interval timer for precise timing of stimuli. Sucking behavior can be recorded by means of a polygraph and breathing by means of a pneumograph. Everything is automatically recorded. The most admirable aspect, however, is the positive attitude and determined attack on fundamental problems concerning the neonate. Lipsitt's purpose is

to explore the full behavioral repertoire of the very young child, to try to discover new features of infant behavior if there are any to be documented, and to always keep in mind the possibility of developing some measures of individual differences in infant behavior which might be useful either in the detection of present aberrations or in predicting later behavioral or neurological deficits [p. 48].

Some findings at Brown University

The newborn's response to olfactory stimulation With continuous measurement of body movement and breathing, the Brown University experimenters presented olfactory stimuli such as asafoetida on a cotton swab and a dry (nonodorous) cotton swab as a control. They discovered that repeated stimulation with, let us say, asafoetida, caused a gradual decrement in the infant's response to the constant stimulus. They used this very habituation as a technique for testing recovery of the infant's olfactory response, for, after such habituation, they would introduce a novel stimulus. Now, if the baby showed recovery of response, it was indicating that it was discriminating between the asafoetida and the novel stimulus (p. 53). Further experimentation with families of odorous substances convinced Lipsitt that "the human neonate is indeed a remarkably

competent behaver," for his infants discriminated components of odorants from the compounds of which they are members. Moreover, concerning the infant's discriminative abilities, the infants lined the odors up in terms of similarity just as adult observers do (p. 55–56). How did they know? By the strength of response as measured on the polygraph records (see Figs. 6.4 and 6.5).

Conditioned sucking in the newborn
To determine whether classical conditioning could occur in the first days of human life, Lipsitt and Kaye (1964) tried the sucking response. They used a tone as a conditioning stimulus (CS) and insertion of a nipple in the baby's mouth as an unconditioned stimulus (US). If more sucking occurred after the paired presentation of CS and US, then conditioning would be demonstrated. A control group received the same amount of intraoral stimulation and tonal stimulus but unpaired.

Procedure involved an initial presentation of five basal trials of tone or CS alone. Then the experimenters administered 25 training trials, followed by between 10 and 30 extinction trials. The differences in the results of the experimental and control groups (which had received unpaired presentations of the same stimuli) showed that infants in the third or fourth day of life do learn.

Another study of sucking by Lipsitt, Kaye, and Bosack (1965) corroborates the above study. Instead of a nipple, they used a tube which was known from a previous study to be inferior in eliciting the sucking response. Briefly, they used a dextrose-and-water solution to reinforce sucking in a group of 20 infants between 2 and 4 days of age. A control group received the same amount of stimulation but it was unpaired. Results showed a reliable difference in

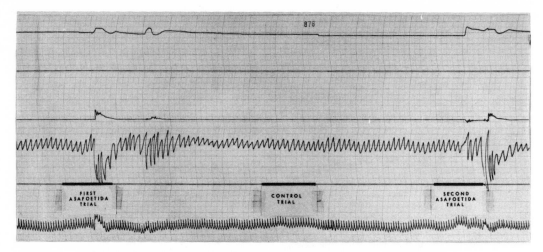

Figure 6.4 A sample polygraph obtained from a newborn's response to asafoetida stimulation. Note absence of response in control trial. (Photo courtesy of Lewis Lipsitt.)

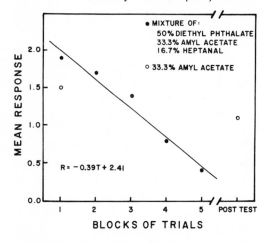

Figure 6.5 A newborn's habituation curve. Evidence of recovery is shown in the post-test responding to a component of the previous habituation mixture. (Courtesy of Lewis Lipsitt.)

conditioning, although the differences in reconditioning fell short of significance. The experimenters concluded that infants 2 to 4-days old could learn to suck more on an inferior tube following a conditioning procedure.

Conditioned head turning in infants
(See Fig. 6.6.) Siqueland (1964) studied three groups of ten 4-month-old human infants. One group of ten subjects, reinforced according to a randomized schedule, served as a control. The control group received milk reinforcements without reference to any pattern of head turning and showed no changes in behavior. The two remaining experimental groups were reinforced with milk as a reinforcing stimulus, one group for turning their heads to the right and the other for turning their heads to the left.

At the start of the experiment, there was no significant difference in head turning between the control and two experimental groups. The selective conditioning separated the two conditioned groups from the control group even though the latter had been given the same number of presentations of milk stimuli. The conclusion was that the head turning response of 4-month-old infants can be conditioned selectively using a standard nursing bottle as a reinforcing agent.

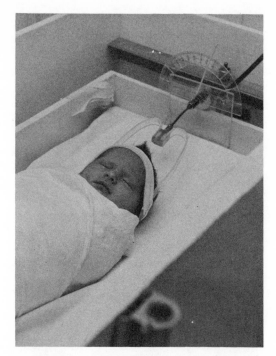

Figure 6.6 Conditioned head-turning apparatus. A newborn with head attachment that permits measurement of extent of head turning in conditioning experiments. (Photo courtesy of Lewis Lipsitt.)

Conditioned head turning in the newborn This time Siqueland and Lipsitt (1966) used touch as "an already *partially* effective unconditioned stimulus" and also younger subjects ranging in age (over the three experiments) from 24 hours to 116 hours! In Experiment I, they gave each of their 36 neonates 30 conditioning trials and from 12 to 30 extinction trials. Conditioning involved presentation of a buzzer for 5 seconds, during the last three seconds of which the experimenter administered three light strokes of the finger near the baby's mouth. The response to be conditioned was a turn of the head to the side of the touch stimulus. Reinforcement consisted of a 2-second presentation of a 5 percent dextrose

solution upon the infant's prescribed head turn. The control group got the same number of dextrose reinforcements but always 8 to 10 seconds after tactile stimulation.

The results, as indicated in Fig. 6.7 show a clear separation of experimental versus control groups. The latter show a relatively stable base rate of response as compared with a shift of the experimental group from a base of a 30 percent probability of response to one of 83 percent and after only 30 conditioning trials presented in a single brief session! The two groups are also widely separated at the end of the extinction series.

In Experiment 2, Siqueland and Lipsitt (pp. 363–367) used the same setup and procedure as before with the following modifications. They gave the tactile stimu-

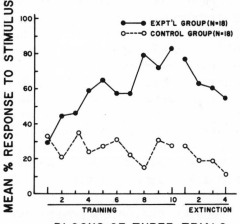

BLOCKS OF THREE TRIALS

Figure 6.7 Changes in head-turning for experimental and control groups represented as mean percent responding to tone-touch stimulations. The experimental group received reinforcement consequent upon response to the training stimuli, while the control group received the same stimulation and reinforcement non-contingently. (From Einar R. Siqueland and Lewis P. Lipsitt, "Conditioned Head-Turning in Human Newborns." *Journal of Experimental Child Psychology*, 1966, **3**, 356-376.)

lus on opposite cheeks on alternate trials. Furthermore, right-cheek stimulation was preceded by a buzzer and left-cheek stimulation by a tone (counterbalanced for the entire series of subjects), so that right- and left-sided cheek stimulation was consistently paired with a distinctive auditory stimulus. The response (ipsilateral head turning) required left rotation to left-sided stimulation and right turn to right-sided stimulation. As before, dextrose solution was the reinforcement. Experimental subjects received reinforcement for ipsilateral response to one of the two stimuli, but not to the other. Control subjects got the same number of reinforcements, but 8 to 10 seconds after tactile stimulation rather than contingent upon head turning.

Briefly, results again clearly separated experimental and control subjects after only 48 training trials, and extinction effects were demonstrated over 36 extinction trials. The *reinforced* ipsilateral response showed learning by increased frequency of occurrence, while the nonreinforced ipsilateral response showed habituation. Extinction results also distinguished the two groups. Side of stimulation was, of course, counterbalanced and the initial base line trials showed that the two groups were comparable at the beginning of the experiment.

In Experiment 3, the two auditory stimuli — buzzer and tone — served as positive and negative cues for reinforcement, each in association with right-cheek stimulation. For half the subjects, tone was the positive stimulus; consequently, turning right to right-sided stimulation while the tone sounded was reinforced. However, if the subject turned right to right-sided stimulation while the buzzer sounded, he was not given reinforcement. The remaining half of the subjects got the buzzer as positive stimulus and the tone as negative.

Results were consistent with those of previous experiments. These babies, all under 4 days of age, showed an increase in probability of response over the training trials to the positive stimulus and a negligible change to the negative stimulus. But, more interesting was the shift that was observed with reversal of the positive and negative stimuli. During a reversal phase of the experiment, the previously positive stimulus was now made negative, and the previously negative was made positive. The infants' performance shifted so that by the end of reversal training they were responding more to the now-positive than the now-negative stimulus. Thus discriminative ipsilateral turning was brought under stimulus control in the first phase of the experiment. The extent of the control was further demonstrated through production of reversal behavior requiring extinction of a previously learned response. Therefore, even within the first four days of life, babies not only learn but they show that they *can* change course, as shown in their shift of discriminatory responses following reversal of cue-reinforced contingencies.

Conditioning of vocalization,
smiling, and crying in the
infant 5

Vocalization*

A now classic study of vocalization brought under control in 3-month-old infants via operant conditioning was conducted by Rheingold, Gewirtz, and Ross (1959). Apparently they were stimulated by the observation that, by three months of age, the infant often gives a definite response to the action or appearance of adults. The response may be a smile, a vocalization, or other action.

The subjects The subjects were 21 infants institutionalized almost from birth at Saint Ann's Infant Asylum in Washington, D.C. Their median age was 3 months; all were healthy and responsive.

The method The procedure involved three sessions of two days each. The first two days provided the base line; conditioning was carried out on the following two days, and extinction on the last two experimental days.

Base line

In experimental Days 1 and 2 (first and second base line days) *E* leaned over the crib with her face about 15 inches above *S*'s and looked at him with an expressionless face, while *O* tallied vocalizations, out

---

*Quoted material is from Harriet L. Rheingold, Jacob L. Gewirtz, and Helen W. Ross, "Social Conditioning of Vocalizations in the Infant," *Journal of Comparative and Physiological Psychology*, February 1959, 52(1), 68–73.

of *S*'s sight. *E* moved her head as necessary to remain in *S*'s line of vision, a condition which obtained throughout the experiments.

Conditioning

During experimental Days 3 and 4 (first and second conditioning days), *E* again leaned over the crib with an expressionless face except that when *S* vocalized, *E* made an immediate response and then resumed the expressionless face until the next vocalization. The response, or *reinforcing stimulus*, consisted of three acts executed by *E* simultaneously, quickly, and smoothly. They were a broad smile, three "tsk" sounds, and a light touch applied to the infant's abdomen with thumb and fingers of the hand opposed. No more than a second of time was required to administer the reinforcer.

At the beginning of the conditioning periods, each vocalization was reinforced. Sometimes, as the rate of vocalizing increased, only every second, and later, every third, vocalization was reinforced. In Experiment I, 72% of the reinforcers occurred after *each* vocalization; in Experiment II, 94%. Less frequent reinforcing seemed to depress the rate, at least initially, and, because of the rather severe time restrictions, was abandoned altogether by the end of the study.

Extinction

Experimental Days 5 and 6 (first and second extinction days) were the same as Days 1 and 2; *E* leaned over the crib with an expressionless face and made no response to *S*'s vocalizations [p. 68].

The vocal response All clean-cut voiced sounds were counted as vocalizations by two observers, whose counts showed a median percentage agreement of 96. The unit used for statistical analysis was the number of vocalizations produced by the subject in a 3-minute period. Every-day nine 3-minute sessions were held.

Results The results are most clearly shown in Fig. 6.8. First, the remarkable similarity in the two curves from two different experiments conducted by different experimenters with different subjects proves, by statistical analysis, lack of significant differences. Apparently the response that the experimenters were dealing with was a relatively stable characteristic of 3-month-old infants.

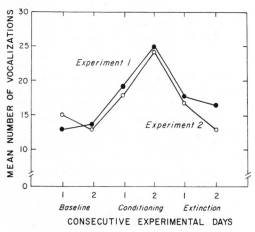

Figure 6.8 Mean number of vocalizations on consecutive experimental days. (From Harriet L. Rheingold, Jacob L. Gerwirtz, and Helen W. Ross, "Social Conditioning of Vocalizations in the Infant," *The Journal of Comparative and Physiological Psychology,* February 1959, **52**(1), 68–73.)

Under base line conditions, the subjects gave about 13 or 14 vocalizations per 3-minute period. Social reinforcement for Day 1 raised the frequency to 18 vocalizations, or an increase of 39 percent. Day 2's conditioning raised the rate to 25, an additional increase of 34 percent. Altogether, conditioning in only two sessions of 27

minutes each yielded an increase of 86 percent. The end of the first day's extinction series lowered the rate to 17 vocalizations and the second day's extinction to 15, so that the experiment ended about where it began.

Conclusion The 3-month-old infant's vocalization can be brought under control in a social situation by means of operant conditioning. The authors point out (p. 72) that, by extension to life situations, the results suggest that mothers can increase or decrease their babies vocalizations, their going to others or turning away from them, their showing interest in strangers or fearing them, and so on.

Social and nonsocial conditioning of infant vocalizations

The foregoing account of Rheingold, Gewirtz, and Ross' (1959) experiment on the social conditioning of vocalization in the infant seemed to point conclusively to the fact of increase in vocal behavior as the result of the infant's contact with people at the moment that it vocalized. Yet how can one be sure that the mere presence of the experimenters did not serve as a social "releaser" (whatever that is)? In fact, the Rheingold team of workers offer that theory as an alternate explanation and suggest that "the decisive answer to the question must await an experiment in which the reinforcing stimulus is administered with equal frequency, but never directly after the infant vocalizes [p. 71]."

Paul Weisberg (1963) decided to find a definitive answer to the above question. Fortunately he was able to conduct the study at Saint Ann's Infant Asylum, the identical one where Rheingold and her associates had worked.

Subjects and procedures Thirty-three 3-month-old healthy infants served as subjects. A base line of vocalization was established for each infant, after which it was randomly assigned to one of six groups.

1. *No experimenter present.* The experimenter was hidden behind a partition 5 feet to the left of the subject but could see the latter via a transparent part of the partition.

2. *Experimenter present* but maintained a "blank expression" and made no movement whatsoever.

3. *Noncontingent social stimulation.* Under this condition, the experimenter, on a prearranged schedule, provided the subjects with essentially the same type of social stimulation as Rheingold and her colleagues did but without reference to the infant's vocalizations, that is, randomly.

4. *Noncontingent nonsocial stimulation.* A door chime sounded on the same schedule as in condition 3, that is, randomly.

5. *Contingent social stimulation.* This time social stimulation (touch, smile, and talk) was given only when the infant vocalized. When it did not vocalize, the experimenter returned to his "blank expression" state.

6. *Contingent nonsocial stimulation.* Every time the infant vocalized, the chime was sounded.

Results Days 1 and 2 were control days for mean vocalization prior to instituting the various controls. Lack of any significant group differences showed absence of any bias in the original group's selection. All subjects in Group 5 showed considerable gains in their rate of vocalization and substantiated the findings of the Rheingold study, indicating that social stimulation provided on the occasion of

the infant's vocalizing acted to reinforce that response. The results also indicated that an unresponding adult in the environment did not reliably increase rate of responding.

Conditions other than social reinforcement (e.g., presenting the reinforcing stimulus noncontingent upon vocalizing and giving an auditory stimulus in the presence of an unresponding adult both independently of and contingent upon vocalizing) did not seem to control infant vocal behavior [Weisberg, 1963, p. 388].

Conditioning of the smiling response in the infant

Yvonne Brackbill (1958) conducted an experiment on smiling parallel with that of Rheingold and her associates. She used eight normal infants ranging in age from 3½ and to 4½ months.

Brackbill (p. 117) ran her subjects in two or three sessions a day for from 8 to 16 days per subject, depending on how long they stayed awake. After securing a base level of smiling in her infant subjects, she carried out the conditioning sessions under conditions similar to those of the Rheingold vocalization study. During these sessions she stood motionless and expressionless 15 inches above the subject. As soon as *S* smiled, *E* smiled in return, began to speak softly, and picked it up. After holding, jostling, patting, and talking to *S* for 30 seconds, *E* put it back in its crib. Brackbill put one group of four subjects on a schedule of regular reinforcement and the other group of four on intermittent reinforcement. The extinction interval was conducted in the same manner as the base line period.

Results Since the two groups did not differ in a statistically significant way in either mean operant response rate or in total number of responses, scores were combined. The resultant cumulative curve shows a steep rate of acquisition for the infants subjected to conditioning. By contrast, a "cumulative" curve plotted for a control subject, who was run, but *without reinforcement,* for 19 conditioning periods or three times longer than the experimental subjects, showed no acquisition. So, apparently, the social factor or mere presence of the experimenter was not the crucial factor. Reinforcement must have come from the experimenter's action at the time of the subject's smiling. Incidental to our main point are the results of the extinction series, which showed a much greater resistance to extinction by the intermittently reinforced group than by the regularly reinforced group.

Summary The smiling response of eight normal infants between 3½ to 4½ months old was brought under control. A base line of operant smiling was obtained in eight 5-minute sessions when the experimenter stood motionless and expressionless about 15 inches above the subject. In the conditioning period, when S smiled, E began to speak softly to it, picked it up, jostled, patted, and talked to it for 30 seconds before replacing it in the crib. A nonreinforced control subject showed that the social factor of the experimenter's mere presence was not instrumental in conditioning. Conditioning with intermittent reinforcement was more resistant to extinction than with regular reinforcement. Conclusion: Infants 3½-months old "can be taught" to increase the frequency of their smiling.

Babies are taught to cry: A hypothesis

As long ago as 1954, Dr. Saul Rosenzweig of the Community Child Guidance Clinic at Washington University suggested the hypothesis that "babies cry largely because they are taught to do so" (1954, p. 81). According to him, at first the response occurs to pain or distress but generalizes to other conditions when parents ignore other unconditioned responses. For example, if hungry, the baby may put out his tongue or lick his lips; if cold, he may tremble or squirm; if wet, he may sneeze. Although Rosenzweig used a Pavlovian framework at the time, we can say, in terms of reinforcement theory, that if the parents attend to his lip licking, squirming, etc., they are increasing the frequence of *these* responses *rather than* the response of crying.

The following quotation from Rosenzweig makes clear

the possibility that crying is a form of communication used by the infant on a general basis — rather than specifically in situations of distress — only if no alternative has been learned. One may restate the hypothesis thus: Crying as a generalized form of expression or communication is learned. There are actually other modes of unconditioned response by which the baby attempts to make his wants known, and the sensitive and alert adult can learn this language. In the event of successful learning on the part of the parent, the infant does *not* learn to cry as a generalized language. Instead, there is established between the parent and the baby a warm and sympathetic relationship that plays an important part in the entire development of the child [1954, p. 84].

The changing pattern of crying in the infant*

Ordinarily one gives little thought to the infant's crying and even less to its analysis. However, Karelitz, Karelitz, and Rosenfeld recorded and analyzed 1300 record-

---

*Quoted material is from Samuel Karelitz, Ruth F. Karelitz, and Laura S. Rosenfeld, "Infants' Vocalizations and Their Significance," *Mental Retardation,* 1965, 439–446.

ings of normal and brain-damaged infants through their first two years. Along with tape recordings, they also made clinical and psychiatric evaluations. The following quotation from their notes illustrates the normal longitudinal development of the crying of one infant over a 2-year period.

Two days The first recording... was made at the age of 2 days, shortly before feeding. The crying response came immediately after flicking the sole of the infant's foot with a finger. The duration of each burst of crying lasts as long as the infant's exhalation, and is followed by a sharp intake of breath. The rhythm is rapid but regular, and the intensity great for the size of the child. The cry diminishes in frequency and intensity until it stops. This is repeated with each painful stimulus.

Four days The cry at 4 days is similar to but perhaps a little stronger than that at 2 days.

One month At one month the cry is still rapid and rhythmic, and coughlike sounds introduce the actual crying.

Two months The cry at 2 months is still rhythmic, but this rhythm pattern is somewhat slowed by the lengthening of the inhalation and the cry.

Three months Inflectional variations and a plaintive quality are evident at 3 months.

Six months The repetitive rhythmic pattern, which is evident in the younger infant's cry, is no longer characteristic of the cry at 6 months. There are pauses, rising and falling inflections, and a mouthing of the cry sounds.

Nine months At 9 months the cry is inflected and plaintive with greater variations in pitch, and the distinct syllable *ah-ha* occurs throughout.

Twelve months At 12 months the qualities of the 9-month cry are still present but are somewhat intensified.

Eighteen months Recognizable words are now interspersed throughout the crying at 18 months.

Two years At 2 years the child communicates with words as well as with the cry [p. 441].

Later effects of social reinforcement on operant crying*

Changes in crying are not limited to developmental changes in the pattern of the crying response. Obviously they can also occur in terms of the relationships built up to their correlated stimulus objects or to the dissolution (i.e., extinction) of such relationships. It is such relationships that Hart, Allen, Buell, Harris, and Wolf discovered and manipulated under real-life conditions in the schoolroom.

The Hart team (as it will be termed hereafter) points out how readily most teachers and parents can identify the two classes of crying, respondent crying and operant crying (p. 145). The first occurs to sudden, unexpected and/or painful stimuli, such as a hard fall, a blow from another child, or being caught or squeezed in some apparatus. By contrast, operant crying occurs in situations that yield attention, comfort, affection, or some other personal gain to the crier. Eye contact may initiate crying or increase its volume. We should also note that what starts out as respondent crying may change and become operant crying.

With the above as an introduction, we return to the Hart team's report of a series of observations on the vicissitudes of crying in only one of two cases that they observed.

Procedure With the aid of a pocket counter, a teacher recorded each instant of operant crying. First, the observer obtained a base line record of operant crying over a period of 10 days at the end of the first month of school. Here is the subject.

---

*Quoted material is from Betty M. Hart, Eileen K. Allen, Joan S. Buell, Florence R. Harris, and Montrose M. Wolf, "Effects of Social Reinforcement on Operant Crying," *Experimental Child Psychology,* July 1964, **1**(2), 145–153.

...Bill was 4 years and 1 month old when he entered school (the Laboratory Preschool at the University of Washington). He was a tall, healthy, handsome child with well-developed verbal, social, and motor skills. Outdoors he ran, climbed, and rode a tricycle with energy and agility; indoors, he made use of all the available materials, though he appeared to prefer construction materials such as blocks, or imaginative play in the housekeeping corner, to activities such as painting or working with clay. His verbalizations to both teachers and children were characterized by persuasive and accurate use of vocabulary, and frequently demonstrated unusually sophisticated conceptualizations. He and many of the other children who entered nursery school at the same time had been together in a group situation the previous year and were thus fairly well acquainted. His former teachers had described Bill as a child eagerly sought by other children as a playmate. His capability and desirability as a playmate were immediately evident at the beginning of the second year. He moved almost directly into play with two other boys, and with his many good ideas structured one play situation after another with them, situations which often lasted an entire morning. Bill was frequently observed arbitrating differences of opinion between his playmates, insisting on his own way of doing things, or defending his own rights and ideas; nearly always, he did so verbally rather than physically.

In the first few days of school, teachers noted that in spite of Bill's sophisticated techniques for dealing with children, he cried more often during the morning than any other child in school. If he stubbed his toe while running or bumped his elbow on a piece of furniture, he cried until a teacher went to him. If he fell down, or if he was frustrated or threatened with any kind of physical attack by another child, he screamed and cried; all play, his and his companions', stopped until Bill had had several minutes of comfort from a teacher. In view of his advanced verbal and social skills, teachers questioned whether his crying was due to actual injury or maintained by adult attention [pp. 146–147].

Results   The base line for Bill showed that, at the beginning of the study, he was crying five to ten times every morning at school. An extinction period followed, during which his teachers completely ignored Bill's crying, reinforcing it in no way whatsoever. However, they were to assure themselves with a surreptitious glance that he was out of harm. If the subject behaved in any way deemed superior to crying, the teacher was instructed to give him much attention and approval. The procedure resulted in a striking decrease of operant crying, within five days of introduction of extinction, to between zero to two episodes per day.

Recondition   If crying is truly extinguished, then it should be possible to reinstate it through use of the opposite condition of reinforcement. By reinforcing successive approximations to crying, for only 4 days, they seized upon such reactions as sulking and whimpering and succeeded in reestablishing the full-blown crying response at the former or base line rate.

Reextinction   The experimenters again introduced the extinction procedures that had practically eliminated crying in the first such period above. Four days later "the behavior was practically eliminated [p. 149]."

Substitute responses   As the second extinction progressed, the teachers were instructed to shape other desirable social responses in situations that had previously evoked crying. Such expletives as "Stop that," "That hurts," or "Ouch," in frustrating or painful situations were reinforced with favorable attention. No harmful side effects of extinction were noted. However, favorable results like more cooperative, constructive absorbed play with an apparent oblivion for adults in the environs and a greater acceptance by peers were observed.

Conclusions Operant crying can be brought under control as evidenced in two alternating reinforcement-extinctions series on a 4-year-old child in a schoolroom situation. The studies indicate that "fre-quent crying may be largely a function of adult attention [p. 145]," a confirmation of Rosenzweig's hypothesis of ten years earlier.

Additional studies of early childhood **6**

The experimental work of Lipsitt and his colleagues reviewed above hovered around the psychological zero point, that is, the point at which behavior begins to emerge, e.g., smiling, vocalizing, crying, etc. The studies briefly described here go beyond earliest infancy into later infancy and early childhood. They are not offered as a comprehensive review, but rather as a sampling intended to show the renewed interest in the area of infant development. They illustrate the point made by Michael Lewis (1966) in the following statement at a conference on research and teaching of infant development.

The fact that we are at a meeting on research in infant behavior, the fifth such meeting in an equal number of years, that journal articles on infancy are increasing yearly, and that formal committees are being organized to discuss the problems in infant research speaks for the growing interest in infant behavior [p. 1].

Attention

Because attention is the initial phase of every response, we begin with it. The most appropriate starting point is a paper by Peter Wolff (1965), who reported the devel-opment of the infant's capacity for attention during the first month of life. In fact, his interests were even more fundamental, for Wolff was intent on distinguishing the "background" state from which attention arises. His emphasis (p. 815) was on the internal factors (such as fatigue, organic need, and arousal) which determine that attention occurs at all rather than on the child's response itself during the time he is alert. The general background of arousal states that supported or facilitated atten-tion — the background out of which attention arose or from which it was differentiated — is what concerned Wolff.

Wolff's paper reports his findings from observations of ten infants during the first month of life. Within a psychoanalytic framework, Wolff points out that (1) the infant's total period of alertness within a day is extremely limited (p. 824), (2) attention is present at birth (p. 824), (3) it becomes progressively independent of hunger and other "disruptive visceral stimulations [p. 825]," (4) it becomes a "wakefulness of choice" rather than "of necessity [p. 826]," (5) it occurs in the face of other motor activity, and (6) arousal of interest can delay sleep and prolong attention.

Individual differences in attention

How are we to understand the variation in attention among babies even within the first year of life? Obviously, what happens to them psychologically will, in part, determine that variation. Is that all? Lewis, Bartels, Campbell, and Goldberg (1966) sought an answer in the infant's physical condition. Specifically, they looked for relationships between variation in attention among infants and their biological status at birth. As a measure, they relied on the widely used Apgar score, which evaluates heart rate, respiratory effort, muscle tone, reflex irritability, and color as judged 60 seconds after delivery.

Subjects consisted of 20 girls and 21 boys selected from the population of a longitudinal project on attention on the basis of availability of their Apgar scores. The conclusion was that, within the first year at least, efficiency of attention is partly a function of the birth condition as measured by the Apgar birth score.

Distribution of attention

Kagan and Lewis (1965) were curious about the stability and distribution of attention as between auditory and visual stimuli. They felt that such information would throw light on the infant's learning in the opening months of life. As subjects, Kagan and Lewis used 32 infants (16 boys and 16 girls) and observed them at 6 and at 13 months of age.

In a most general way, their results showed that the bases for differential attention were not the same at 6 months as compared with 13 months. At 6 months photographs of human faces were preferred over symbolic representations of a person,

but at 13 months schematic faces won the infant's attention over the realistic forms. However, at both ages, human faces were more effective in holding the infant's attention than geometric designs. Sex differences favored girls, who showed more mature attentional habits as indicated by "sustained attention and a preference for deviation from the familiar [p. 126]."

As for stability, this aspect of attention showed no stability between 6 and 13 months of age as far as visual stimuli were concerned, but Kagan and Lewis attribute this finding to a lack of interesting stimuli. The auditory mode did show some stabilization for the same period, especially for the girls. As for locomotor activity, there was no relationship between this variable "at one year and attention at six months for boys, whereas, for girls there was a negative relationship between these variables" (p. 123). The authors think that if further work supports this finding, it may indicate that "individual differences in complex attentional phenomena in a school age child are influenced, in part, by constitutional variables or very early experiences that influence degree of spontaneous motor activity [p. 126]."

Other studies continue to a consideration of attention as it functions developmentally. Lewis, Campbell, Bartels, and Fadel (1965) investigated the infant's changing responses to facial stimuli during the first year of life. An anatomical study of attention in 24-week-old infants was carried out by Lewis, Kagan, Campbell, and Kalafat (1966a and 1966b). They found that the longest and the first fixations were better indexes of discrimination than was total fixation. In the second study they discovered that the cardiac response was a correlate of attention in infants, showing a deceleration with increased attention.

Plasticity of sensorimotor development in the human infant

As an extension of the basic study by Wolff reported above, Wolff and Burton L. White (1965) investigated attention as revealed by visual pursuit (i.e., a coordinated head-eye rotation) in 48 healthy 3- to 4-day-olds. The following is Wolff and White's own account of their study.

Infants were tested for visual pursuit of a moving target under the following conditions: (1) alert and inactive; (2) waking and active; (3) vigorous pacifier sucking; (4) satiated pacifier sucking.

We found that (1) pacifier sucking generally inhibits head rotation and thereby reduces the range of over-all pursuit movements; (2) infants pursue by conjugate eye movements more persistently when alert and inactive than while waking and active; this effect is not found when coordinated head and eye rotations are compared; (3) infants pursue with their eyes as well as or better while sucking on a pacifier than during alert inactivity, and consistently better than during waking activity; (4) after sucking the pacifier for at least 3 minutes, infants pursue a moving object with their eyes more consistently than right after they begin to suck [p. 483].

White and Held's study of visual attention*

By means of weekly observation periods that allotted each subject 3 hours, White and Richard Held (1966) attempted to discover the sheer amount of visual exploration shown by 63 infants born and reared in an institution. All were judged physically normal.

---

*Quoted material is from Burton L. White and Richard Held, "Plasticity of Sensorimotor Development in the Human Infant," in Judy F. Rosenblith and Wesley Allinsmith (Eds.), *The Causes of Behavior: Readings in Child Development and Educational Psychology* (Boston: Allyn and Bacon, Inc., 1966).

Figure 6.9 shows the extent of visual attention from birth through 4 months of age. The difference between White and Held's study and that of the constructors of tables of norms of a past era is that the former related what the child did at certain stages to changes in stimulus variables.

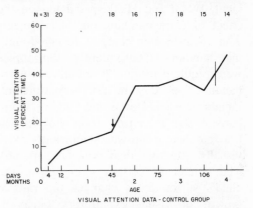

Figure 6.9 Note: The arrow at 45 days indicates the median age at which sustained hand regard appeared. The vertical bar at about 110 days indicates relocation to large open-sided cribs. (From Burton L. White and Richard Held, "Plasticity of Sensori-Motor Development in the Human Infant," in Judy F. Rosenblith and Wesley Allinsmith (Eds.), *The Causes of Behavior: Readings in Child Development and Educational Psychology*, 2nd ed. Boston: Allyn and Bacon, Inc., 1966. Reproduced by permission of author and publisher.)

For example, the sharp increase in slope at about 2 months (*c.* 50 days) of age occurs at about the same time as the onset of sustained hand regard (visual regard of the hands). [See arrow in Fig. 6.9.] For the next 6 weeks or so, the child spends much of his waking time observing his fist and finger movements. The next major change in the visible environment occurred for these infants between 3½ and 4 months (*c.* 105 to 120 days; see vertical line in Fig. 6.9). They were transferred to large open-sided cribs. The combination of greater trunk mobility, enabling them to turn from side to side, and the unlined crib sides provided a new and considerably more variegated visible environment. At about this time, the slope of the curve again shows a sharp increase [p. 63].

White and Held also made observations on visual accommodation, but these are omitted in favor of a brief mention of their findings on visually directed reaching. Having noted the stimulating effect of postnatal handling of laboratory animals (dogs, mice, and kittens) on their subsequent development, White and Held speculated on the effect of extra handling on their subjects who, as institution charges, received minimal handling. Consequently, the nurses were required to give 20 minutes of extra handling per day to ten (experimental) infants between Day 6 and Day 36. Comparison with a control group showed that the "handled group was significantly more visually attentive than controls" (p. 66). Thus changing certain variables in the child's surroundings changes the rate of growth of visual exploratory behavior.

Massive enrichment study

Encouraged by the change in rearing conditions mentioned above, White and Held decided to introduce greatly enriched environmental conditions for their institutionalized subjects (see Figs. 6.10 and 6.11). Accordingly, between Day 6 and Day 36, they provided the infants with 20 minutes of extra handling again. Starting on Day 37 and continuing through Day 121, they placed the infants in a prone posture for 15 minutes following the 6 A.M., 10 A.M., and 2 P.M. feedings, thus forcing them into *self-induced* movements. Opaque crib liners were replaced with transparent plexiglass, allowing visual inspection of ward activities. Above the crib the experimenters placed a special structure, a stabile, with highly contrasting colors and a variety of forms against a dull white background. These infants were at first slowed somewhat with respect to the development of visual attentiveness, onset of sustained

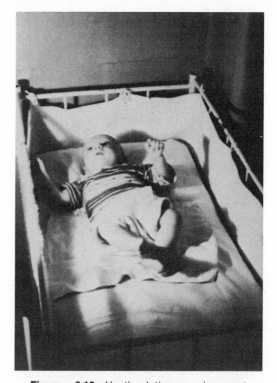

Figure 6.10 Unstimulating environment comparable to an institutional situation. Note bleak walls and shielded crib. (From Burton L. White and Richard Held, "Plasticity of Sensori-Motor Development in the Human Infant," in Judy F. Rosenblith and Wesley Allinsmith (Eds.), *The Causes of Behavior: Readings in Child Development and Educational Psychology,* 2nd ed. Boston: Allyn and Bacon, Inc., 1966. Reproduced by permission of author and publisher.)

hand regard, and related behaviors. Starting at 2½ months, however, they accelerated rapidly and exhibited precocious visually directed reaching as well as unusually high visual attentiveness.

Modified enrichment study

A new group of infants was reared under somewhat different conditions in an attempt to produce more consistently positive results. The experimental conditions were

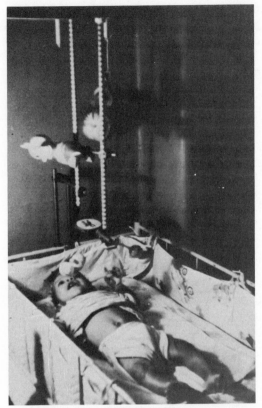

Figure 6.11 Infant in an environment showing "massive enrichment." (From Burton L. White and Richard Held "Plasticity of Sensori-Motor Development in the Human Infant." In Judy F. Rosenblith and Wesley Allinsmith (Eds.), *The Causes of Behavior: Readings in Child Development and Educational Psychology,* 2nd ed. Boston: Allyn and Bacon, Inc., 1966. Reproduced by permission of author and publisher.)

similar to the massive enrichment study except that from Day 37 to Day 69, instead of the stabile overhead, etc., the only enrichment consisted of two pacifiers mounted one on either side of the crib. They were designed so as to be easily viewed and struck by the infant, with due regard for his accommodative limitations and his postural habits. These infants were consistently more precocious than all previous subjects in the behaviors studied.

The significance of the age range from 1½ to 5 months of age

The first major conclusion derivable from our research is that the age range from 1½ to 5 months (*c.* Days 45 to 150) is a time of enormous importance for early perceptual-motor development. According to our findings and those of others, human infants reared under natural conditions show a dramatic surge in both visual activity and development at the middle of the second month of life (*c.* 45 days). During the next 3½ months the following events occur: (1) the development of flexible accommodative function culminating in virtually adultlike performance at 3½ months (*c.* 105 days), (2) discovery of the hands and gradual development of manual control by the visual system culminating in true visually directed reaching, (3) the initiation and complete development of the blink response to an approaching visible target, (4) the initiation and complete development of visual convergence, and (5) the onset of social smiling.

Plasticity in human visual-motor development

The studies reported above demonstrate that aspects of early visual-motor development are remarkably plastic. As yet we know neither the limits of this plasticity nor the range of visual-motor functions that fall within this classification. At the very least, the onset of hand regard and visually directed reaching and the growth of visual attentiveness are significantly affected by environmental modification. Infants of both Group B and C developed top level reaching in approximately 60% of the time required by the control group, a result very much in line with the theory that self-initiated movement with its visual consequences is crucial for visual-motor development. Whether or not visual accommodation, convergence, pursuit, and blinking to an approaching target share this plasticity remains to be seen. Assessment of the extent to which various types of mobility and specific environmental factors contribute to these and other perceptual-motor developments is the goal of our continuing research [pp. 70–71].

Visual scanning of triangles
by the human newborn

Much of the contemporary research on infant behavior deserves credit not only for its goals and results but also for the ingenious devices designed to accomplish experimental purposes.

At Yale University, Salapatek and Kessen (1966) were interested in pursuing the problem of why, even during the first few days of life, human infants prefer certain visual patterns over certain others. The question was even more intriguing in the light of discrepant results reported by different investigators.

Subjects The Yale experimenters randomly selected as subjects 20 awake, alert, newborn infants under 8 days of age. The experimental group consisted of 5 males and 5 females ranging in age from 23 to 177 hours with a mean age of 68.1 hours. The control group included 6 males and 4 females with an age range of from 23 to 137 hours and a mean of 77.6 hours.

Procedure and apparatus Each subject participated in a 20-minute session before its regular feeding at 9:30 A.M. or 5:30 P.M. in a quiet room moderately lit. The experimenters then showed the experimental subjects a solid black equilateral triangle 8 inches on a side and centered on a circular white background. The triangle stimulus, painted on wire window screen, appeared to be solid from the baby's side, a distance of 9 inches from the screen. However, sufficient light passed through the screen to permit photographic recording of the eyes by a camera positioned behind the screen and directly over the baby's eyes (see Fig. 6.12). The control group of ten subjects underwent the same conditions as the experimental group except

that they looked at a homogeneous circular black field. Other technical variations are omitted in the present brief report.

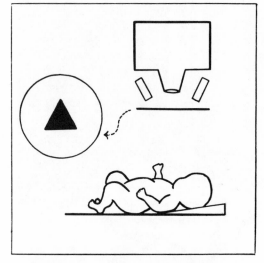

Figure 6.12 Schematic representation of the apparatus used in determining ocular orientation. (From Philip Salapatek and William Kessen, "Visual Scanning of Triangles by the Human Newborn," *Journal of Experimental Child Psychology*, May 1966, **3**(2), 155–167. Reproduced by permission of author and publisher.)

Results The corneal reflections photographed by means of infrared photography showed differential results for the two groups of subjects. The orientation of the eyes for the control subjects shown a homogeneous black field were widely distributed through the visual field. Not so with the ten subjects in the experimental group who saw a black equilateral triangle on a white field. "Relatively few orientations were directed toward the center of the triangle. It seems clear, from a comparison of figures, that the ocular orientation of the human newborn is to some degree controlled by visual form [p. 164]." They did not look at the figure as a whole.

Summary Photographic recording of eye movements in ten experimental and ten control subjects showed differential results in ocular orientation of the former to a black triangle and of the latter to a homogeneous circular black field. The control group showed a wide distribution of ocular orientation throughout the field, whereas the experimental group did not orient toward the center of the triangle or toward other portions of the visual field but tended to orient toward the vertices of the triangle.

Results are related to three possible theoretical interpretations. A fourth simple explanation is possible in terms of the stimulus objects. What reason is there for believing that all stimulus objects should be equivalent? Why should a circular field be expected to play a psychological role identical with that of a triangle? In other words, differential aspects of different stimulus objects are correlated with different reactions of responding organisms. These are lawful and adequate relationships and fit an interactional or transactional view. A self-actional interpretation looks inside the organism for hypothetical explanatory mechanisms. There are always choices.

Watson:
"Situational learning in the second month of life"*

An examination of the literature has revealed no existing studies involving the experimental longitudinal approach required to test the question of transfer or generalization of response-reward learning in early infancy. In the absence of such studies, a set of observations will be presented here which I made on one subject during the infant's third month of life. These data should be allotted little supportive value, for they were collected in a fairly uncontrolled setting by an observer potentially subject to paternal bias. Yet, since the preceding theoretical paradigm was largely stimulated by these data, they are at least worth reporting for illustrative purposes.

While preparing to carry out a laboratory experiment focusing on the operant conditioning of eye movement in 3-month-old infants, I was in the fortunate position of having a young infant at home. The temptation to do some pilot work was strong yet prohibited by incomplete construction of apparatus. Finally, a game-like analogue to the prospective experiment was hit upon just after my son turned 2 months of age. The observations reported below were then begun.

A fixation contingency game

The "game" was as follows: The arms of the observer (O) were extended toward the subject (S) so that O's closed fists were about a foot apart and about 2 feet from S's eyes. S was seated in a commercial, hammocklike bouncing chair. Depending on O's choice of contingency, one of his hands would open and close (this involving about one second) upon being visually fixated by S. The other fist would not respond to fixation. The reoccurrence of the visual stimulus of hand-opening was contingent on S's looking away then looking back at the designated fist.†

Observation No. 1—0;2(2): The observer had no success in obtaining fixation on his fists due to S's strong interest in O's face. After covering his face with a cloth, O obtained some fixation on his fists, but the frequency of fixation was only slightly greater to the responsive fist and so O's sense of having observed learning was very weak.

0;2(3): The observer's sense of observing

*Quoted material is from John S. Watson, "The Development and Generalization of 'Contingency Awareness' in Early Infancy: Some Hypotheses," *Merrill-Palmer Quarterly of Behavior and Development,* 1966, **12**(2), 123–135. Reproduced by permission of author and publisher.

†This paper follows the fairly standard system of age designation wherein "0;2(2)" refers to zero years, 2 months, and 2 days; "0;2(3)" refers to zero years, 2 months, and 3 days, etc.

learning in this session was notably stronger than at the end of the preceding session, though still uncertain. The amount of directed fixation on *O*'s fists was noticeably increased, and the relative frequency of fixation on the responsive fist was greater than in the first session.

0;2(4): The observer's judgment of learning was again increased in the feeling of certainty. Two things seemed to be occurring. The frequency of fixation on the responsive fist appeared to increase relative to fixation on the nonresponsive fist, and the time *S* spent fixating the responsive fist after it had responded seemed to diminish across trials.

0;2(5): This session provided *O* with a very strong sense of having observed learning. After establishing what appeared to be an acquired preferential frequency for *O*'s responsive right fist, the contingency was changed to the left fist. After a brief period of "confused" fixations, *S* established a fairly clear preferential distribution of fixations to the left fist [pp. 128–129]....

The behavior and its consequence in the next observation are a natural contingency. The sequence of responses required to turn from prone to supine position is not uncomplicated, but it is related to the nature of physical reality such that it results in certain stimulus events without intervening adult cooperation.

Observation No. 3—0;2(12): The subject was observed successfully turning from his stomach to his back on the first occurrence of this act. He was immediately returned to his original prone position. He reestablished a near-successful position and after a bit of a struggle finally rocked past the fulcrum of balance with a swinging movement of his leg. He was again returned to prone position. His speed of turning was faster than previously. Again he was returned to prone position and this time his turning was essentially instantaneous. Again he was replaced and again he turned immediately.

While the sequence of increasing articulation of behavior in Observation No. 3 surely would have done no more than exhilarate *O*'s paternal pride under other circumstances, in the setting of the present case *O* could not help considering an hypothesis of transfer. If the previous learning games had increased the temporal limits of *S*'s contingency awareness, this could have contributed to the rapid mastery of turning following its initial occurrence.

Observation No. 4—0;2(17): Following the seemingly complete mastery of a few fixation learning games, *S* was provided a structured but yet natural contingency situation. A cradle gym was hung in front of *S* while he was seated in the bouncing chair. The gym was at a distance which would allow *S*'s occasional extended arm movements to contact the gym. Within 20 minutes it appeared that *S* had clearly established a stable response to striking the gym as its movement ceased. *S*'s eyes were fixed on one of the shiny supporting springs of the gym.

Observation No. 5—0;2(24): During the preceding 6 days, fixation games were played and two new variations were introduced. One variant provided a vocal "beep" from *O* when the designated fist was fixated by *S*. The other variation provided tactile stimulation to *S*'s legs for correct fist fixation. Learning seemed to be clearly apparent under both of these new modalities of reward.

On this occasion *S* was seated in his bouncing chair near the table where *O* and Mrs. *O* were finishing dinner. Suddenly *O* noted that *S* was making gross contortive archings of his body (similar to a wrestler's "bridging" exercise) which when relaxed caused the bouncing chair to react with extensive bouncing. While *O* worried about the neurological implications of these periodic contortions, Mrs. *O* proposed that the bouncing effects of this behavior might be rewarding the response. It was true that *S* had previously "enjoyed" being bounced, but he had never systematically bounced himself. *O* then proposed that if Mrs. *O*'s hypothesis was correct, *S* should eventually refine his behavior if the notion of least effort had any merit.

0;2(26): At this time *S* was systematically bouncing his chair by use of rhythmic arm and leg movements.

0;2(27): Now *S* was bouncing the chair consistently with use of rhythmic leg movement alone [pp. 130–131].

What dramatic and effective learning and at such a tender age!

Implications of experiments on learning in the neonate

The traditional notion among laymen, even among psychologists, has been that newborns are too young to learn. In the work just cited, John S. Watson notes the discrepancy between the findings of such laboratory work as reviewed earlier with those of Piaget who "has discovered no evidence of this kind of behavioral modification prior to about three months of age for infants in their natural setting [p. 126]."

Watson's reply is that in the natural environment during the first 3 months of life, the infant possesses few, if any, responses that "elicit rewarding stimulation directly from the physical environment and at the same time possess recovery speeds sufficient for the infant's level of contingency awareness [p. 127]," the kind that Watson provided for his filial subject in the records of his observations above.

As a result of the successful learning of neonates, Watson believes that it is a safe assumption that "the human organism is structurally ready to process contingency information from the very beginning of his interaction with the external world [p. 133]." But what if his surroundings are devoid of reinforcement opportunities? What could be "the long-term consequences of this initial period of 'natural deprivation' [p. 133]."

The final answer can come only if controlled experiments could be made with human infants under natural conditions and under conditions of enriched stimulation during the early months of infancy. In the absence of such findings, Watson speculates about the outcome of such an experiment. "For instance, this comparison might indicate the presently 'natural' course of human development, involving this natural deprivation period, produces a permanent loss in intellective potential [p. 133]." What if future research were to substantiate Watson's bold speculations? Would humanity suffer untold guilt for having so long suppressed human self-actualization and for having actively (even though unwittingly) discouraged the full attainment of human potentiality?

Stimulation versus deprivation 7

We have considered the ready conditionability of attention, head turning, smiling, crying, and vocalization in infants from the earliest hours, days, and months. The research reviewed demonstrates how quickly and easily each newborn child meshes with the persons, things, and conditions in its surroundings. We should have been impressed with how early the infant can be launched on its psychological career, compounding reaction upon reaction. In contrast to the richness, complexity, and earliness with which behavior can develop cumulatively, we next examine its failure to develop properly if at all. We shall examine various areas for interfering or preventive conditions. Because developmental conditions furnish the earliest possible factors, we return to the womb.

Emotional factors in prenatal environment

Folklore and superstition have long held that the condition of the pregnant mother may affect the child she is carrying. Only recently, however, has this belief in "material impressions" been subjected to scientific inquiry. Antonio Ferreira (1965) has written a paper whose purpose is "to review the evidence for a prenatal environment, and document the importance of emotional factors upon the mother-fetus continuum, from conception to delivery, particularly insofar as they may become etiologic to abnormal patterns of behavior [p. 108].

Emotional factors (according to Ferreira) may have an interfering effect on the process of pregnancy itself or on its product, the fetus, but obviously "any interference with the process is an interference with its product" (p. 109), so Ferreira does not separate the two.

Briefly, some of the interfering variables include: emotional factors in conception as manifested in infertility or pseudopregnancy; interruption of pregnancy through stillbirth, miscarriage or abortion (p. 109); prematurity, which in 50 percent of cases shows no discernible physical cause; complications of pregnancy, such as prolonged pregnancy and labor; mother's smoking; her use of drugs; her undergoing severe emotional stress; her acceptance or rejection of her pregnancy, etc. (pp. 110–113).

The supporting evidence that Ferreira gleaned from the literature is available in his extended report. Many of the studies that he cites are substantial contributions to the body of psychological research on infancy. In essence, they illustrate the factors that operate in a negative way to hinder behavior development.

Incubator isolation

A theoretical paper that leads more in the direction of our present goal has been contributed by Barbara Rothschild (1967). Her concern starts with the report of an apparent "higher incidence of emotional disturbance among individuals born prematurely as compared with full-term babies" (p. 287). Why should this be so? No one previously had considered the possibility of incubator isolation as a factor; Rothschild did.

Summarizing Mary Shirley's early study (1933) of those born prematurely, Rothschild lists the following six factors to which Shirley attributed the premature infant's emotional disturbance:

unfavorable prenatal environment, traumatic birth, overprotection and then overstimulation by the mother, the lag in motor development as compared with sensory development, and the deprivation of any opportunity for breast feeding. Nowhere does she discuss the possibility of the early weeks of isolation for the prematurely born child in an incubator being a contributing factor to the later high incidence of emotional disturbance. Is it not possible that the lack of early visual cues, which are not provided by incubator living and which the full-term child usually receives almost from birth, might contribute to the subsequently slow motor development in the "preemie" and thereby to his low frustration tolerance, his unusually high dependence on others, and his low degree of perseverence [p. 290]?

Surveying the recent literature on sensory and emotional deprivation among infants of the lower animal species, Rothschild notes how consistently the data from primates, dogs, and birds show that a lack of visual stimulation early in life seems to hamper subsequent behavior so that adequate response is not developed even when stimulation does become available on a later occasion.

Bettelheim: Feral children and autistic children* 8

At a laboratory school of the University of Chicago—namely, the Sonia Shankman Orthogenic School—exciting observations have been reported (Bettelheim, 1950, 1955) and treatment methods have been developed in connection with severely disturbed children. Some of the 34 children, ranging in age from 6 to 14, have been as wild as the wildest feral children (see e.g., Singh and Zingg, 1940) in spite of having no contact with any animal but the human and of being reared by none but human beings.

Having observed much savage behavior among the children of his school, Bruno Bettelheim (1959) was fascinated by the wolf children of India as reported by Singh and Zingg (1940). A Christian missionary, the Reverend Singh, described the discovery of two girls, Amala and Kamala, in a jungle ant mound huddled with two wolf cubs after he had flushed three grown wolves out of the hollow. Briefly, the two girls walked on all fours; ate and drank by lowering their mouths to the plate like a dog; refused to wear clothing and were insensitive to heat and cold; were shy, frightened, and aloof; avoided all contact with human beings; prowled at night; and howled like wolves.

Comparison of the two groups

The following quotation from Bettel-

heim's (1959) account of his autistic charges is eloquent testimony to the similarity of their behavior with that of the wolf children.

Many times when we have described the behavior of some of our extremely autistic children—how they urinated and defecated without so much as knowing it as they walked or ran about; how they could not bear clothes but would run about naked; how they did not talk but could only scream and howl; how they ate only raw food; how they would bite us so often and so severely as to require frequent medical treatments—even persons quite familiar with disturbed children would react with polite or not so polite disbelief. But later, when they met these children, their doubts changed to complete belief, so that they would have been willing to believe almost anything told them about the children or their pasts [p. 456].

Let us meet some of the autistic children in the generalized descriptions that follow. Some of them "kept their wild looks for months [p. 457]." The tidy hair of one autistic girl could, like Kamala's, be transformed, within hours, into a " 'hideous ball of matted hair,' glued into a mass by saliva, remnants of food, dirt, and what-not. One of our autistic girls kept her face well hidden for months behind a curtain of hair [p. 457]." Anna continually applied saliva

---

*Quoted material is from N. H. Pronko *Textbook of Abnormal Psychology* (Baltimore: The Williams & Wilkins Company, 1963). Reproduced by permission of the publisher.

to every part of her body and bit and chewed her toes like an animal. Anna also inflicted bites on an attendant who, in one year, required medical attention a dozen times. Some children would prowl around at night, remaining quiescent in the daytime. Raw food, especially raw vegetables such as onions, held a peculiar fascination for some and they would go to any lengths to procure them. Others would lick salt from their hands by the hour. Still others would build a cave or den in some dark closet and hole themselves up in it; here they would also carry their food and eat it, shoving it into their mouths without utensils. Upon seeing a dog, one girl got very excited, jumped down on all fours, cried or howled like an animal, and made biting gestures like a dog. Had Bettelheim (p. 458) believed in this girl's feral origin, he could have convinced himself that the girl recalled her former feral companions upon seeing a dog and that she had reverted to her former existence. But this was impossible because this child's complete life history was well known to him.

It is obvious that the wolf children and the Chicago autistic children show a remarkable resemblance. This striking similarity convinced Bettelheim (p. 456) of the authenticity of Singh's description of Amala's and Kamala's behavior, but he believes that Singh only imagined their feral origin because he saw no other way to explain their wild behavior. Therefore the story of their origin is false, the record of their action accurate and well substantiated by Bettelheim's own observations. As an alternative to Singh's fantastic account of Amala's and Kamala's origin, Bettelheim (p. 457) suggests that the children were emotionally and physically abandoned because they were autistic children who soon came to someone's attention.

Summary

Study of the so-called feral children, and comparison of them with known and well-observed wild autistic children, suggests strongly that their behavior is due in large part, if not entirely, to extreme emotional isolation combined with experiences which they interpreted as threatening them with utter destruction. It seems to be the result, as was assumed, of animals'—particularly, wolves'—humanity. To put it differently, feral children seem to be produced not when wolves behave like mothers but when mothers behave like nonhumans. The conclusion tentatively forced on us is that, while there are no feral children, there are some very rare examples of feral mothers, of human beings who become feral to one of their children [p. 467].

Chapter summary

A significant highlight of the present chapter lies in the behind-the-scenes view afforded by Gesell's work. Important for us is the full realization of the close interrelationship between biological development and activity. Behavior emerges gradually out of biological reactivity until it has its own developmental sequence. Gottlieb and Zing-Yang's as well as Grier, Counter, and Shearer's work on the imprinting of the duck embryo is a confirmation of the conception that everything that happens, psychologically as well as organically, has a natural history. Perhaps still more important is their demonstration that, if an organism manifests behavior at birth, such behavior had a prebirth developmental history. It does not appear full-blown without a prior development.

Next, we examined the present-day intensive examination of the field of infant learning, which departs from studies made during the "Developmental Age" era—studies that stressed norms. Current research opens up exciting vistas of the tremendous potentialities in early learning in the infant. Formerly we said that the earliest years are the most important. We should change that to "The earliest days and even hours are the most important." Finally, we considered the devastating effects on early development of such factors as unsatisfactory prenatal environment, incubator isolation, and sensory and emotional deprivation. Our outstanding exhibits were the wolf children of India and the autistic children studied by Bettelheim. Each showed a near or complete irreversibility of their behavior deficiency. Do these studies show that humans have "a critical period for imprinting"? Does the development of human behavior have an optimum sequence and timing?

... if the behavioral sciences have discovered anything that approaches, in significance for human welfare, the antibiotics and the contraceptive pills of biochemical science and the atomic energy of the physical sciences, it may well be this new evidence of great plasticity in infantile and early child development [Hunt, 1967, p. 11].

7

The reactional biography, or psychological history

The technological advances of physics and chemistry constitute a brilliant success story among the sciences. The technological applications of psychology have just begun. Why the lag? Is it because psychology is a relatively new science, or is the lag at least partly a result of outmoded theories? It seems to me that recent but delayed successes in psychological applications are the result of a breaking away from traditional theory. The concepts already discussed, both in biology and in psychology, are limited in their applicability. A self-actional view of the limitations of various racial groups is one example. Within any given race, the notion is prevalent that some fundamental inherent property of the individual circumscribes his development. If a person achieves excellence in some field, retrospective explanation is that he possessed the capacity at the start. If he does not excel, his lack of development is explained by a relative lack of that inherent potential. Such a view implies extremely limited possibilities for the modification of behavior through experience. In general, human potential is so incompletely realized that one is tempted to speculate whether any anatomical or social limitations are absolute or even highly significant.

Current research points to the extreme significance of this psychological history in determining the individual's behavioral potential. Nevertheless, only one approach makes any real effort to fit early psychological experiences into a general theoretical framework—the **interbehavioral theory** of Kantor, which is examined below with special attention to his concept of the **reactional biography.**

A final point. Existing theories in psychology deal in terms of body and **mind** or body minus mind. The first are mentalistic or **dualistic,** the latter **reductionistic.** All are limited and limiting. Kantor's interbehavioral approach takes a much broader view of psychological events. In the hope that it may provide a more fruitful method of analysis and of application, we now examine Kantor's general "**field**" theory and his concept of the reactional biography or psychological history. The basic question is: Do Kantor's theoretical tools provide insights about a proper understanding of human and animal behavior?

The interbehavioral approach

1

After the decline of Watsonian (Watson, 1930) behaviorism in the 1930's, a new system appeared, one that has often been improperly identified with behaviorism. Perhaps its name, **interbehaviorism,** was partly to blame. However, its approach was radically different. Instead of reducing psychological happenings to hypothetical muscular, neural, and glandular processes, it took a completely different approach. From the interbehaviorist point of view, psychological occurrences are *events* in which both organism *and* stimulus objects mutually and reciprocally participate.

According to this view, the organism assuredly plays a role in a given psychological event, but so does the **stimulus object,** for without it the event would not occur. The proponent of this modern interbehavioral approach was J. R. Kantor (1926).

A distinctive feature of Kantor's approach lies in the equal emphasis it gives the organism and the stimulus object—the two main factors, or variables, in the psychological event. Unless one allows the stimulus object a role in psychological events, one must not go outside of the organism to explain the events. For this reason, traditional theories have explained behavior in terms of hypothetical internal superstructures such as the brain and the mind, plus elaborations of the latter like the **id, ego,** and **superego,** or the **conscious, preconscious,** and **unconscious.** When theoreticians had tucked the whole psychological drama within the skin of the organism, they were forced to invent "actors" on that internal stage, "men" within the man—all hypothetical entities presumed to be carrying out certain jobs.

Kantor sees the organism as an entity, not as a bifurcated creature consisting of a body *and* a mind. What others see as happening inside the person (i.e., within his mind), Kantor sees as involving both the person and the stimulus object. Kantor's system belongs with the interactional or transactional views rather than with the self-actional view of conventional "body-mind" theories. If we must use the term "mind" to apply to Kantor's system, then instead of locating mind *within* the organism, we would put it outside the organism, and, more specifically, in the relationship *between* the organism and the stimulus object. Yet why should we redefine old terms? Why not use new terms for new approaches?

The nature of the reactional biography

According to Kantor, whatever activities the organism performs at birth, such as reflex sneezing, regurgitating, and knee jerking, are "built into" the organism, so to speak, and are viewed as "structure-function" interactions. A sensitive tissue, triggered by an adequate physical or chemical agent, goes into operation. The event is a biological reflex in a class with **tropisms** or **taxes.** All are distinguished from psychological events through an absence of a psychological *history.* (No child needs to learn how to sneeze, defecate, or urinate.) As long as the organism develops normal structures during its uterine existence, those structures will function appropriately upon first contact with the adequate **stimulus.** However, a different dimension is required if the child is to utter "Daddy," "Mama," "Bonjour," or "Guten abend." A series of contacts between infant and certain stimulus objects is necessary. No infant ever says "Daddy" at the first visual or other contact with its father. The class of reactions to which "Daddy" belongs requires an explanation in terms of a reactional biography, or psychological history. One of Kantor's chief (but unrecognized) contributions has been his insistence on distinguishing between biological and psychological events as described above. Figure 7.1 (Kantor, 1933, p. 48) attempts to show the relationship between the biological evolution of organisms and their psychological evolution.

The complexity of reactional biography

"The complete behavioral experience of the individual is called his reactional biogra-

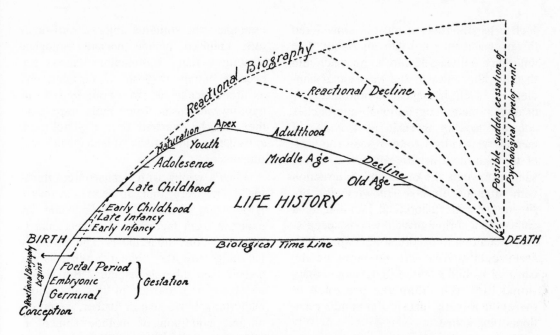

Figure 7.1 Diagram suggesting development of reactional biography in relation to biological life history. Note especially the following points. The biological life history has an earlier start than the reactional biography. Soon after birth, the two correspond closely, because certain behavior development must wait for growth. However, later phases of reactional biography can show continued expansion even after biological decline or even old age. (From J. R. Kantor, *A Survey of the Science of Psychology*. Bloomington, Indiana: The Principia Press, 1933, p. 48. Reproduced by permission of author and publisher.)

phy [Kantor, 1933, p. 44]." Even a cursory statement impresses one with the immensity of the reactional biography. A complete listing of behavioral experience would note each instance that one scratched his ear, saw a sparrow flit across the yard, heard the doorbell, sat down in a chair, and so on. The sheer number of reactions inventoried would constitute an astronomical aggregate, but fortunately, for most practical purposes, every reaction need not be included. After all, neither **astronomers** nor **entomologists** have been able to count every star or species of bug. The former have established a recognized science with-

out defining the boundaries of the cosmos, and entomologists have yet to catalogue and name all of the existing species of insects. As for psychopathology, it is surprising how much insight a therapist can gain from a sporadic but connected series of relevant behaviors that constitute delinquency or crime, neurosis or psychosis.

The role of biological factors

Biological factors influencing behavior cannot be ignored. Injury, disease, hunger, drugs, or other biochemical conditions, such as **hypothyroidism,** must be considered (if and when they are demonstrable). The difference between Kantor's approach and that of others lies in the *theoretical* handling of such biological conditions. For example, many conventional approaches consider lack of **thyroxin** as a *cause* of mental retardation. Kantor sees the lack of thyroxin as a negative factor, one that simply prevents the organism's interaction with stimulus objects. His view is consistent with his theoretical handling of a child with a normal **thyroid** who is successfully acquiring a reactional biography. The absence of thyroid can no more be the cause of a child's failure to develop a reactional biography than the presence of thyroid can be the cause of a child's reactional biography.

To state the argument another way, lack of a thyroid *precludes a child from being the kind of a biological organism* that can come into contact with stimulus objects and acquire reactions toward them. In the case of the hypothyroid child, absence of a thyroid deprives the child of a status that would permit stimulus objects to "get through" to it. As a result, psychological development is at a stand-still. The hypothyroid child's biological development would continue, but not its psychological history, unless and until we inject thyroid extract into it. Now we see the baby start to learn, and he continues to do so as long as we continue the injections. If we were to withhold them, the child would become a vegetable once more. This example shows the biological conditions to be participating factors, or necessary conditions, and not *causal* ones. In addition to the thyroid gland's proper functioning or the injection of that gland's secretion, another set of variables is

essential — the stimulus objects. **Autistic** or **attic children** having **normal** biological structures (e.g., Bettelheim's cases) can become "lumps of flesh" as certainly and as dramatically as the brain-injured or hypothyroid cases. Even more important, they can be recalled to a psychological existence without being injected with any substance.

What's wrong with "cause-effect thinking"? The worst thing to be said against it is that it oversimplifies. Consider an example from medicine. A young man in India develops tuberculosis. The lesions in his lungs are the "effect." What is the cause? The tubercle bacillus? But almost everyone is a carrier of this ubiquitous bacterium. If we search further, we note a chronic condition of malnourishment in our young Indian! Is this, then, the cause? Or is the cause to be found in his Hindu repugnance at eating available beef that might have kept him well nourished? Or could primitive, inefficient, and unproductive farming methods be the cause? Or the government's indifference? Or are they all "causes"? If so, then the term *cause* loses its potency as a label for a single determinant of tuberculosis. The tubercle bacillus now becomes only one antecedent (but essential) factor, which takes its place alongside several other factors in the constellation. But all the factors or variables play a part in the event referred to as "a young Indian has tuberculosis."

Among others, Skinner (1953) has raised objections to "cause" and "effect" as conceptual tools. He indicates that the terms are no longer widely used in science because "they mean more than scientists want to say [p. 23]." But popular thinking still adheres to the "cause-effect" paradigm. As Skinner shows, astrology looks to the position of stars for causes of people's behavior. Physiognomy considers the shape of the head, color of hair, and the features of the face as causes, and temperament and character as effects. If fat men are jolly, can one be sure that fat men are jolly because they are fat? Or are they fat because they are jolly? Or are they fat as a result of other variables?

Skinner points out that "heredity" as the layman uses the term has often been used as a purely fictional explanation or cause of behavior (p. 26). Skinner has much more to say in a critical analysis of internal causes of behavior such as "exhausted nerves," "id, ego, and super-ego," and "intelligence." The earnest reader will be repaid by an examination of Skinner's essay.

In place of "cause," Skinner prefers "a change in an independent variable" and for "effect" he would substitute "a change in a dependent variable." In his scientific procedure, Skinner looks for "functional relationships" among the different variables. The following quotation from his work shows Skinner's general approach to the study of behavior, an approach which has a close kinship with that of Kantor.

The practice of looking inside the organism for an explanation of behavior has tended to obscure the variables which are immediately available for a scientific analysis. These variables lie outside the organism, in its immediate environment and in its environmental history. They have a physical status to which the usual techniques of science are adapted, and they make it possible to explain behavior as the other subjects are explained in science. These independent variables are of many sorts and their relations to behavior are often subtle and complex, but we cannot hope to give an adequate account of behavior without analyzing them [Skinner, 1953, p. 31].

Summary

Our examination of the rapidity of learning in early infancy led us naturally to an examination of a modern framework for psychology, namely Kantor's interbehavioral approach. We discussed Kantor's concept of the reactional biography, a concept quite compatible with contemporary psychology's approach. The distinctive feature of his theory is an emphasis on the relationship between the organism and the stimulus object. In this respect he differs from others who rely upon real or hypothetical happenings inside the organism. However, Kantor does not ignore biological factors; he considers them as participating or necessary conditions but not causal ones. Kantor contends that the essential feature of an organism's life history is the evolution of psychological interactions and the interconnectedness of those interactions. "Cause-effect thinking" has no place in his system.

The following selections are intended to illustrate various phases of the reactional biography hypothesis. Several examples of psychological history will stress the pervasiveness and persistence of certain conditions that maintain the organism's status or level of functioning over a long period of time. Other examples focus on the importance of the early years, months, and days that give the organism a slant or direction in its psychological development. The following article by Dorothy Lee, for example, shows the influence of the home in shaping the attitudes of schoolchildren toward education and scholarship. Despite poverty, wretchedness, brutal teachers, and similar factors that, at first glance, seem to contradict every principle of modern learning theory, children have learned to value education deeply.

2

Lee: "Developing the drive to learn and the questioning mind"*

As an anthropologist, I am concerned with the **cultural** factors that may inhibit or encourage the development of the potential to learn. Such factors reach the individual through the society of which he is a member, through the family and community, on the one hand, and, on the other, directly through the school.

Cultural factors are built into the experience presented to the growing child; and their strength lies in this. For instance, if a school does not value effort particularly, a low demand for effort is built into the curriculum itself. Even if it does value effort, it may find itself in conflict with a community which does not. The child will read the advertisement of an electrical vibrator, for instance, which urges its readers to "exercise without effort." All around him, he will see technology used to spare people from putting forth effort—from bending, walking, lifting; from exerting their minds to calculate; and from exertion in general.

I have chosen this instance advisedly because for me *develop* and *development* are active words, active concepts. To develop, I have to do something about it. I have to engage myself in the experience, exercising my capacities and exercising them with effort. So I have posed to myself the question: What are the factors that motivate the individual to develop his capacity to learn?

This question has apparently concerned the Western world from ancient times. Plutarch suggested that the growing boy be "led" and "urged" to excellence through admonition and reasoning, praise and blame, but "not, in heaven's name, blows and torments." St.

Augustine described an education that was enforced by punishment. And reflecting on how he hated Greek, which he had learned through being "urged vehemently with cruel threats and punishments," and on how he loved the study of Latin, which he learned "without pressure of punishment...for my heart urged me to give birth to its conceptions," he concluded that "a free curiosity has more force in our learning these things than a frightful enforcement."

Saint Augustine's description of his own education, however, raises a question which will concern me in this paper. He says that learning to read and write was a "burden and penalty"; that "one and one, two; two and two, four" was "a hateful sing-song"; that he was beaten because he played ball instead of studying. Yet he did learn the hated Greek; he did learn reading and writing and arithmetic; and if he hated them, he overcame his hatred. There is no doubt that he went on studying eagerly, going on his own initiative much farther than he was required or expected to. All this "frightful enforcement" did not interfere with the development of his capacity to learn. If it did not motivate him, neither did it stop him. It did not make him hate all learning, all intellectual development, perhaps because in itself it did not have the power to stop growth or because there was a powerful motivation which nothing could stop.

Motivation as culturally derived—and all important

It is with such a powerful motivation that I concern myself here—with the cultural factors, and particularly the factor of values, that incite the individual to develop his potential to the utmost. I have purposely chosen to speak of a society where the motivation is strong, spurring the individual to put forth all he has. Such a motivation sweeps away all that might have

*Quoted material is from Dorothy Lee, *Freeing Capacity to Learn* (Washington, D.C.: Association for Supervision and Curriculum Development, 1960), pp. 10–21. Reprinted with permission of the Association for Supervision and Curriculum Development and Dorothy Lee. Copyright © 1960 by the Association for Supervision and Curriculum Development.

been interferences under different circumstances....

In my study, I have found children consistently learning to read before, according to our notions, they can be biologically ready; and to show the ability to concentrate before they can possibly have a long enough **attention span.** I have found originality valued and exercised where learning was acquired by imitation and repetition with hard discipline and a multitude of regulations....

To show how cultural factors support the development of capacity, as expressed in the community as well as through the curriculum and the methods of teaching, I shall write of... a highly literate society, the Jewish *shtetl* of Eastern Europe — the tight Jewish communities found in small towns or villages until World War II....

*Everything wrong in these
schools — according to us*

In the culture of the Eastern European Jews, the strong value supporting the pursuit of learning was absolutely necessary if there was to be education at all because, according to our theories, everything was wrong with the educational system. The children went to school long before their eyes could focus properly on the tiny marks on the page; they were offered an uninteresting curriculum, in a strange language; the teaching was pedagogically unsound, the teachers with no compassion or understanding; the days were too long, the schoolrooms unpleasant.

Only boys were sent to school; and they were practically torn from their mothers' arms at infancy. It was not unusual to start school at three, and usually boys started before five. The **kheder** to which the little boy went is described as "crowded, noisy, and unventilated," small and ill-lit — a room with a long table flanked by hard, backless benches on which the little boys sat for ten hours a day, five and a half days a week.

The first books for the little student were prayer-books, in ordinary print, without pictures to attract the child's attention. Through these, he had to learn the letters and then the words of an unknown tongue — Hebrew — and later to memorize each word, through endless mechani-

cal repetition. Only later was he given the meaning, which he also had to memorize; and eventually he learned to understand the meaning of a sentence. But at this time, no attempt was made to help the boy to understand the meaning of the whole.

In a few months, as soon as he had mastered the mechanics of reading, he was graduated to the **Pentateuch.** This was full of interesting stories but not for the little four-year-old. He had to learn to master the ritualistic detail of the Leviticus.

There were few diversions in the ten-hour school day. In the afternoon, the teacher went to the synagogue for about an hour, and the children were free to play, perhaps even outside in the school yard. Sometimes the children went home after nine hours and came back for a two-hour session at night. And there was a break for lunch, when the poorer children ate their piece of bread dry while the others might buy syrup to dip their bread in or hot soup from a peddler.

There were no educational games to help the child learn and "relieve the tedium." The children did not even have pencil and paper to play with. Writing was not a part of the curriculum, playing was not considered necessary, and, in addition, many of the children could not afford to buy paper and pencils. Besides, it would be a distraction; and the child had to learn to pay unwavering attention. If his attention wandered, if he was not ready to pronounce the word at which the teacher's stick pointed, he was usually severely punished.

To this school the children often went barefoot, out of poverty. They had to take their own candles to school for the hours of dark and a lantern to light their way back through the unlighted streets. And there were not always enough books to be shared among the children, though none of the reports I know mentions the extremity that was found among the Jews of Yemen, many of whose children, when they arrived in Palestine, could read upside down only, having learned to read while sitting across the table from the teacher who held the sole book in the kheder.

Perhaps all this would not have mattered if the teacher had been filled with enthusiasm for learning, with the love of teaching, with tenderness and empathy for the little boys who were struggling through this difficult curriculum. But in most cases, the teachers in these schools are described as ignorant, miserable, unjust, cruel to the children. Sholem Aleichem reports that whippings were so usual in his school that there was no feeling of shame attached to them; the resulting sores were painful, but the boys said, "They'll heal before we are married." The teacher is generally described as having taken up teaching through default, "fallen into his profession because he failed elsewhere."

Yet lifelong learners were so educated

Yet, out of this miserable schoolroom came people whose one desire was to be a scholar for life; who, when the path of secular studies was open to them, became great philosophers or teachers or men of letters or scientists. Not only in adulthood but even in childhood, we find this burning, self-directed application to study. A Lithuanian Jew tells how, at the age of nine, he left home and moved in with a teacher because the only time this man could give him instruction in the **Talmud** was at 5:00 A.M. After two years, he and a friend decided that they could get better instruction in another town, and they went there, without even consulting their parents. A gunny-sack filled with straw and laid on a bench in the synagogue made an adequate bed; and meals were probably provided by the different households in the Jewish community, which usually undertook to feed the students who came from elsewhere. These were small boys of eleven, acting on their own initiative.

Morris Cohen, who is remembered by many as a brilliant professor of philosophy in New York, also speaks of such initiative in pursuit of learning at an early age. His education had been Talmudic; so when, at eleven, he found someone who had a manuscript on arithmetic, he copied this by hand for his own use. At this time, too, he discovered books on history and the history of civilization which could be had for rent; and, on his own initiative, he started a small business that netted enough money to pay the rent on such secular books. These are only a few of the many reported instances I have found showing the readiness for total involvement, total effort, in developing the potential to learn.

Learning deeply valued by culture

How did this love of learning, this personal search for knowledge, survive the miserable schoolroom? "Were you very miserable?" I asked a student of mine, a Bessarabian Jew who had gone to school at the age of three under conditions that I found appalling. "Miserable?" he answered. "I was learning the language of the ritual. I was learning to say the chants like my father and my older brother. I was proud." And this statement, with variations, is repeated in many of the reports.

Much of the father's time was spent at home over his sacred books. Even if he did not devote all his time to study, he studied in the morning before he went to work or in the evening. Or at least he would devote the Sabbath to study. Perhaps the only time that the father paid attention to his little boy was over this subject of studying. As he read the sacred books, he would often take the baby boy on his lap, swaying with him as he chanted, and pointing out reverently the black marks on the pages. When the boy learned to read and understand Hebrew, he was initiated into this, his father's world; it was actually his initiation into male adulthood. At the end of a year or so of schooling, when he passed, amidst great celebration, the examination showing that he had mastered the mechanics of reading, he received recognition from his father; and all the community accorded him the first marks of the kind of respect accorded to adult men.

So to the little boy learning to read Hebrew meant identifying himself with his father and the valued male role; it meant the awakening of respect from others and a recognition of his status as a male. As he grew older, he found out that the value of learning went beyond that. To study meant to obey the command of God; only through studying the Scripture could one be a good Jew.

From early babyhood the child was exposed to the value of learning. The mother, lulling her baby, sang of her hopes of scholarship for the boy and of a scholarly bridegroom for the girl. A baby's hairline was sometimes shaved back to give him the appearance of intellectuality. When a four- or five-year-old was ready to take his first examination to prove his ability to read, the occasion was of tremendous importance for family, relatives, friends. And afterwards, when he was introduced to the study of the commentary of Rashi, his father, as well as visiting scholars, would engage the little boy seriously in learned argument. Later, a bearded man might bring a difficult Talmudic question to a boy of thirteen. Thus, on the one hand, learning was presented as of infinite value; and, on the other, it earned, not condescending praise, but true respect and a welcoming acceptance into the fellowship of men.

The value of education was manifested in another way. All boys, except perhaps orphans with no relatives, went to school, though education was neither compulsory nor free; the schoolteacher had to be paid a fee for each child. And this tuition fee was the most important item in the budget. Food costs would be cut, jewelry pawned to raise the fee. Morris Cohen speaks of how his mother, who at the time was supporting a number of children with her peddling, could yet manage to raise enough to engage a teacher to teach him to write, since writing was not a part of the school curriculum for which she was already paying a fee. At this time, young Morris was going to school barefoot and was practicing writing on sand with his finger or a stick because there was no money for writing materials. The people of his village "wore rags on their feet and ate white bread only on the Sabbath, but no child went without schooling."

A learned man was a valued man, the pride of the community; he had authority and status. He was a *sheyne* Jew, a "beautiful" Jew, and able to sit closest to the east wall of the synagogue, the place of highest honor. There were in the community the few manual workers who, as unfortunate orphans, had had no one to pay their school fees and were doomed to a low status. But many of the manual workers did have some basic learning so that they could at least spend the Sabbath in the synagogue pursuing their studies. There were those who spent much of their time in business, who were well-to-do. They considered it a privilege to endow a daughter with a large dowry so they could acquire a learned son-in-law; they considered it a privilege to support him in his further studies or to give money to a **yeshiva,** a school of higher learning. There were the women, whose highest

function was to enable men to continue their scholarship; many wives earned the livelihood for the family while their husbands devoted themselves to their studies. And there were the people of small means, who, if they lived in a town which had a school of Talmudic studies, invited the students to as many meals a week as they could afford...

Kind of learning also significant

In itself, though, this value is not enough to account for the *kind* of scholarship we find among the Jews, for the inquiring spirit, the incisive, challenging mind that enabled a man to pursue his Talmudic studies throughout his life, attacking the book with fresh vigor and inquiry every time he started a new reading of it, making an original interpretation which he was able to defend against all opposition. What accounts for this, I believe, is the emphasis on individual difference, on unique personal quality, which was expressed in the kind of education a boy had after he left the primary school I have previously described, an education supported and echoed in the home and the attitudes of the community.

In the earliest school, for the first few months, the child had merely been mastering the mechanics of reading through repetition and memorization, without understanding. At the next stage, he learned to translate. Now, as he read the Pentateuch, he was also given a commentary to read and study so that he could become acquainted with the search for hidden meanings and the value of individual interpretation. From now on, and particularly when he was graduated to the study of the Talmud, the entire emphasis was placed on the searching for one's self, on the exercise of individual imagination, on the making of an original synthesis, on the raising of questions which were peculiarly one's own; and, above all, on never accepting a statement without a search for its assumptions and implications—not even the statement of a rabbi or of the *Torah.*

Even in the earliest school, individuality had been given some recognition; each child read aloud at his own rhythm, pitching his chant at his own individual level. But it was in the Talmudic studies that his autonomy of opinion was given full scope. The students were encouraged to compare different interpretations, analyze all possible facets of each, weigh opposing opinions, and finally to come through with a unique solution. To do this the student must be involved at his fullest, drawing on memory and imagination, on logic and wit, attacking every statement the teacher makes, arguing with subtlety and incisiveness. An eyewitness describes students pressing against the teacher's platform, shouting contradictions, challenging every sentence. "This mental activity combines the pleasures and satisfactions of high scholarship and of high spirit," writes Zborowski, who grew up in a **shtetl**. The teacher himself enjoyed and encouraged these vociferous attacks....

Summary and conclusion

I have given here a biased view of learning in [another culture]. First, as I said earlier, I deliberately selected the...Eastern European Jews for presentation because they exhibit so strongly values making for the development of this capacity to learn. I do not present them as a random sample; these values are not present in all societies.

Second, I have not spoken of the boys and men who could not involve themselves in the highly demanding process of learning; if they have written their autobiographies, these were not available to me. I have not mentioned the wives, who, while taking on the responsibility of maintaining the household, upbraided their husbands for laziness and impracticality.

Third, I have not raised the question as to the mental health of adults who were introduced to such severe discipline at what we would consider infancy.

Fourth, I have not dealt with the question which you all have a right to raise: What does the teacher do when the cultural values do not offer incentive or support for the high development of the potential to learn?

I have had to limit myself. Therefore I have concentrated on bringing out the following major points: *first,* that the values in these societies were so influential because they were consistently expressed and because they permeated all life; and, *second,* that in their strength they overcame possible drawbacks in the educational system. It follows that the interference with development of inherent potential comes, not through the presence of obstacles but rather through the absence or weakness of such values or through inconsistency among the various aspects of the culture.

3

Sherman: Freed from Watts*

I

The year 1965 marked a change in many people's lives. For some, it was a year of tragedy; for others, it was just a passage of time. But for the people of Watts, it was the year that was. The year that had to be and finally came. It was the year that all patience wore thin, and Watts burned to the ground.

For many people, it marked the beginning of

---

*Quoted material is from Jimmie Sherman, "From the Ashes: A Personal Reaction to the Revolt of Watts," *The Antioch Review,* Fall 1967, **27**(2), 285–293. Reprinted by permission of author and publisher. Copyright 1967.

a new day—a new era. An era that was such a long time coming, and a long time cried for. An era in which Watts would start to progress along with other communities in this fast-moving society. Prior to August of that year, Watts, like other ghettos in this land, stood motionless in a world that sped by too fast and too unconcerned to even take notice. While rockets were being launched for Mars and the moon, and the Vietnam situation was taking a new shift, and the budgets were reaching new heights by the day, we of the ghettos went hungry and were dying in filth and poverty.

Crime was as common as unemployment, and need was always present. Young men stole and sold dope, and young ladies went into shoplifting and prostitution, in order to survive. Teen-agers hung around on street corners in packs, smoking weed, drinking wine, and fighting, because there was nothing to do and no place to do it in. And the schools? Schools were just institutions that even the teachers cared little about.

When our cries for better schools, better housing, fair employment, a hospital, and better police community relations were ignored, our many frustrations mounted. Then, after a period of years (each year worse than the last) we exploded. It was like a keg of dynamite that only took one match—one incident—to set it off, and any one thing or anybody could have lit the fuse.

When it happened, tempers burst and buildings went up in flames. Cars were smashed and turned over in the street. People crusaded through the night, burning, looting, throwing rocks, bricks, and Molotov cocktails, and screaming, "Burn, baby, burn!" Sirens cried out everywhere, speeding from one uprising to another, fire to fire, and casualty to casualty. And for four straight days the city was in a state of shock and confusion.

II

The facts were there
The dreams were gone
The deadly viper listened on.

I never thought that I would become a writer. I never really believed that I would ever be anything. I only knew that I wanted to be something.

As a child I used to dream of being a great man when I got big. I wanted to be a general, a lawyer, a man who flew those big shiny planes. I wanted to be lots of things—not just one. I even wanted to be President. But sadly enough, dreams withered with time, and age brought me closer to reality—a reality I wanted no part of. I began to notice many things around me—things I did not like, but could do nothing about. I noticed my mother going out to the white folks' houses, scrubbing their floors and serving their food everyday. I realized that my father, the man I idolized and imitated, had been cleaning sewers all of his life and getting nowhere. I even heard a white man call him "boy" a couple of times. That really made me mad. It made him

mad, too. But what could he do but take it? I noticed the old shacky house we lived in—the cold splintered floors, the torn curtains, the broken chairs we sat in, the pie pans and jelly jars we ate and drank from. I noticed the roaches crawling on the walls, across the floors, and breeding all over the house, and the junk and the trash that piled up and scattered in the yard. And for the first time, I realized that I was in poverty.

Then I discovered that we weren't the only family in that bag. My friends were in bad shape, too. Their parents were also servants, and they were living on beans and grits and hand-me-downs, just as we were. And I discovered that being black had something to do with it.

I became angry—very angry. I started to rebel. I rebelled against everybody—parents, teachers, anybody—I didn't care. School no longer meant anything to me, and home was just another place to get away from. I started smoking cigarettes—both kinds, tobacco and marijuana. I drank wine, picked fights, and learned to gamble. I did everything that I possibly could to say, "I don't care."

People tried to talk to me but I didn't want to listen, because they were talking that same ole stuff about going to school and being somebody some day. To me, that was just a bunch of bull, and they couldn't tell me nothin'.

The only person who could talk and make me listen was my grandmother, an old lady who needed an ear to fill. We used to talk all the time, for hours, sometimes a whole day. She used to tell me of the old days and of how things were then. She told me of old superstitions that she and people of her day believed, and stories of strange things that happened to her and those she knew. It was just like being there, and she had my undivided attention. After the story or lecture she would conclude with a wise saying. She would say something like: "So that jus' goes t' show yuh, boy—never whip a dawg an' pet a cat," or, "A man ain't free when somethin's ailin' 'em." Finally she would ask, "What's ailin' you today?" And I would tell her. She always had a remedy or a ready-made solution, and her advice was nearly always good.

Immediately after turning seventeen I took her advice and joined the service. I had to get away for a while, because even I knew that I had to change. I spent three years in the army—

three years of changing, and three years of learning that a black soldier had it rough and that discrimination was in there, too.

When my three years were finally over, I was honorably discharged and ready to take another stab at civilian life. I had decided while I was in that when I got out I would get two jobs, make a lot of money, and go into business for myself. But I was soon disillusioned. I looked all over town for work. I searched the want ads through and through. I phoned places, wrote places, and went for scores of interviews, but no one was hiring. Those who were, weren't hiring Negroes. And those who were hiring Negroes wanted experience. No one wanted a man who had no skills.

III

"You's a good boy, Sammy Lee,"
Missa Charley said.
Den 'e rubbed and patted me
Ri' chea on dah head.
I grinned an' showed em all my teeth
An' said, "Y' thank yuh boss."
I kept my feelins down beneath
Dis happy shinin' gloss.

I nevah lakt dat good boy stuff
'Cause I knows what 'e means.
Long as I can mop an' buff
An 'cept a plate of beans,
Long as I say, "Yassm boss,"
An' make lak um in joy,
Wit' dis happy shinin' gloss
Den um a good boy!

Finally I found a job at a downtown clothing factory. I worked as a shipping clerk, making minimum wages. I worked there for two weeks and found that I couldn't save any money, so I quit and found another low-paying job, then another. Within the span of one year (from February 1964 to February 1965) I went from shipping clerk to stock clerk to used car salesman to janitor to unloading potato trucks. Then I weakened and went to the unemployment lines. I had completely given up.

I abandoned all plans for going into business. I started drinking wine and smoking pot again, and hanging around the pool hall all day with other guys who had also given up. I found myself bumming pennies, nickles, and dimes from people passing on the street, not for wine or dope, but for a candy bar or something sweet to spoil my appetite. I felt pretty low. I felt like a dog who had no bone, or a boy who had never graduated to manhood. I felt sorry for myself— very sorry and very ashamed and unnecessary. I felt mistreated, because this country owed me something—the white man owed me equality and should give me a taste of the good life too. And I was stupid enough to sit and wait for it.

I grew weak and weary waiting, and all ambition died with patience. I was destined to live and die as my fathers did before me, in ignorance, filth, and poverty—a "good boy."

IV

I'm here!
At last, I'm here.
Despite the pain, despite the fear,
I'm here!
Here to meet another soul and chat
    a while,
At last, I frown, I cry, I smile,
I'm here!
I'm glad, I'm here, despite the bitter
    pain and fear.
The pain feels good—Good I'm here!
Thanks to life and hail to birth,
I cheer!
At last, a life—mother earth,
I'm here!

Then came salvation! It came with the flames of the Watts revolt and changed my life completely.

The revolt had such an impact and so much meaning that it made me start thinking again. I mean seriously thinking. I spent nearly a week after the revolt in my room, thinking and feeling every drop of anger that had built up within me over the years. Each thought made me angry, each thought brought resentment. I was angry about many things. I couldn't understand why I was hungry and couldn't get a decent job, or why I had been ashamed of myself for all these years and ashamed of being black. And the main thing I resented and the least I understood was the fact that I was still a slave in the twentieth century.

On my last day in that room I said to myself: My forefathers slaved in the masters' fields. Many black men have fought hard and died in this country's wars to preserve its freedom. Black men have sweated endless hours in the laboratories inventing the "American brand." We have added a new beat to this nation's culture. Our literary contributions have been tremendous, ranging from novels to poetry to the blues. And for this and much more, all we've received in return was the "blues."

After those thoughts, I felt the deepest desire to protest. I felt the need to sing the blues and the compulsion to just say, "God damn that wicked man whose foot's on my neck!"

I wanted to scream it out and let the whole world hear—especially that Southern bigot and that Western politician and the Northern liberal who boasts about the leftovers he gave the maid —I wanted to tell them all that,

This is the home of my fathers.
They helped win this land.
They've conquered the fields of your fathers
With a strong, black helping hand.
In chains, they've suffered sharp pains
    of a whip
And strenuous work of a slave.
In protest I've cried,
You're hurting my pride
When they've earned and you claim
    you gave.

This is the home of my fathers.
In all of your wars they have died;
In every battle they've risked their lives,
And for what?—Freedom being denied!
They've toiled and strained with muscle
    and heart,
Their bodies all covered with sweat,
And with sad weary eyes
They protested the lies
That stated, "We give what you get."
I am the son of my fathers.
I deserve what they never got.
That's a chance to excel
In the things I do well

Without being hanged or shot.
This is the home of my fathers,
Soon it will be of my sons
I hope by that time
They'll be able to climb
'Cause oppression may lead them to guns!

Instead, I wrote it. I wrote it not only for myself, but for my people as a contribution to the cause. It was the first time I had ever thought of it like that—as a contribution—and it was the beginning of a new outlook. I didn't care about the pains, the fear, the ups and downs in life anymore. I had a job to do and I was ready to accept all of the pains that went with it. I was ready to make a new start.

I wrote more, much more—poems, songs— you name it, I wrote it. My work began to pile up. Soon I had stacks of it, enough pieces to present to anyone, and I was ready to, as my good friend and colleague, William Marshall, might say, "Straighten up the backbone—stick out the jaw bone—throw away the wishbone— and step on it!" I gathered up everything that I had written and hurried down to the State Employment Office, hoping that they could help me find a job as a writer. I showed them my work and they seemed to like it but they couldn't help me. They referred me to the Urban League. I went to the Urban League and they sent me to the NAACP. The NAACP referred me to the *Sentinel* newspaper. So I tried the *Sentinel.* Though they weren't hiring, my trip was not in vain, for they encouraged me to keep trying the different newspapers, even the smaller ones, and to accept anything to start with, even if it was sweeping the floors. They assured me that I was heading in the right direction, and I left happy and full of confidence.

I was in luck. I landed a job selling advertise- ments for the *Star Review,* a Watts weekly newspaper. The editor was a very understanding person who liked to see young people trying. He knew that I wanted to write and that I had never written a newspaper article before, but he gave me a chance to prove myself. He sent me out on a story, a big story. I was to report on the First Annual Community Beautiful Parade in Watts. I was very excited, and so thankful for the opportunity that I wrote much better than he and I had anticipated. A week later, I was promoted to Business Manager. And two weeks after that, I was appointed Co-

Chairman of the Citizens for Good Government Committee. Things were happening fast and I was beginning to get deeply involved in community affairs.

The following month I, along with Mr. George Crawford of Crawford's Men's Store, and a few other merchants up and down 103rd Street, and with the help of Westminster Neighborhood Association, got together and reorganized the Watts Business and Professional Association, and they elected me secretary. Shortly after my twenty-second birthday, I resigned from both the newspaper and the Business Association (in good standing, of course) to have more time to help form the Watts Happening Coffee House. I felt that I would be able to help a few guys like myself, who needed some form of direction. So I pitched in and became the Publicity Director of the Board. While serving on the Board, I met Budd Schulberg, who was down in the area trying to help young writers like me get a start. He told me of the classes he was teaching, and he said that he would be glad to have me as a member. So I joined. It was an honor to be able to learn from such a great and genuine person as Budd Schulberg. I attended every class.

Then, two months later, there came a tragedy in the family. My grandmother passed on. At her funeral, I learned a fact she had never told me. I learned that in her younger days, while teaching at a little country school in Texas, she wrote a play. I also learned that it was stolen because it had not been protected by copyright. Upon hearing this, I grew angry again, and through my anger I was inspired to write a play—my first play. I wrote it in verse and folk dialect, in memory of her, and filled it with slavery, oppression, protest, and revolt. I built it around two poems: "The Home of My Fathers," which I already quoted, and "Negro History," which goes like this:

A ship
A chain
A distant land
A whip
A pain
A white man's hand
A sack
A field

Of cotton balls
The only things
Grandpa recalls.

I called the play "A Ballad from Watts." I took it to Budd Schulberg, and he liked it. He advised me to find a group and have it performed. That was a good idea; I had never thought of it. So I did as Budd said and took it around town to different theatre groups; but everyone was busy doing other plays. It would have been at least two months before any of them could get around to mine, and I couldn't wait. So with the encouragement of Budd Schulberg and William Marshall, I formed my own theatre group—The Theatre of Watts—and produced and directed the play myself.

The following month we performed at the Watts Summer Festival and were successful.

From then on there was no stopping us. We went from UCLA to the Elks Hall, and each time we performed we picked up new members. We grew from a nucleus of sixteen to an organization of forty, and we're still growing. Our main goal is to make Watts the Broadway of the world. And we will do it.

So, if one should ever ask me what I believed in, I would have to say, "I believe in progress through unity, self-help, and determination—this I believe." And it is for this I am fighting. If I were asked the same question before the revolt, I would have answered, "Burn, baby, burn!"

Well, the burning is over, thank God. People are beginning to progress, and there is a lot being done now, though still very much more to be desired.

I don't regret what happened in August—not in the least. My only regret is that it was necessary. I'm letting the oppressor regret the rest. I benefited from it, it opened my eyes, and for once I realize that "I'm here."

The dead has finally awakened;
A soul has found its way
And I'm a writer now!
Born through flames of August chaos
Into an era of self-help and progress...
From the ashes, I came,
And with me, many others....

From an embittered, frustrated drifter, Jimmy Sherman was transformed into a writer and poet, not by changing his heredity, skin color, or other anatomical factors but through changes in his reactional biography.

An audacious thought
from a biologist*

4

In an article entitled "Where Is Biology Taking Us?" Robert Morison (1967) makes some points that concern the concept of the reactional biography, particularly the earliest or basic phase of it.

He argues that as institutionalized education gains in effectiveness and respect, "the prestige and influence of the family will continue to decline [p. 430]." Of paramount concern to us is the fact that the family, which served in the past to transmit "conventional wisdom in a relatively static society, is relatively poor at assimilating and transmitting new knowledge essential to survival in a rapidly moving world" (p. 430).

To illustrate, take the situation in the modern farm home.

The young boy or girl on the farm no longer looks to mother to learn about the setting of hens or to father to learn how to plow, fertilize, and harvest; instead he joins a 4-H club to learn about inbred and hybrid strains, **antibiotics,** hormones, and **artificial insemination** [p. 430].

...a type of assault on the integrity and authority of the family is almost certain to grow out of our increasing knowledge of the biology and psychology of infancy and early childhood. Although relatively little is known in this area with any real certainty, all the evidence we have points to the importance for future development of influences brought to bear during the first 5 or 6 years of life. These are the years which the child ordinarily spends in the bosom of his family, and evidence is accumulat-ing that it is this fact that is primarily responsible for the relative fixity of the socioeconomic class structure of a country like the United States.

Just as a wider appreciation of the science of genetics has made a pleasant 18th-century fantasy of the stirring phrase "all men are created equal," growing knowledge of the plasticity of the human **nervous system,** of critical periods in development, and of the phenomena of imprinting and releasing as well as of conditioning and **stimulus-response learning** has made it quite clear that it is idle to talk of a society of equal opportunity as long as that society abandons its newcomers solely to their families for their most impressionable years. The institution of such programs as **Head Start** testifies to the growing awareness that society must in effect invade the sanctity, or at least usurp some prerogatives, of the home if it is to assure equal opportunity for all. As society itself becomes more complex and demands an even higher standard of emotional and intellectual competence from all its members, it seems increasingly unlikely that at any level it can rely exclusively on the haphazard educational procedures provided by home environments during the most impressionable first 6 years of life.

I am not advocating that the family be abolished. I am merely pointing out that some of its functions have already been taken over by other social agencies and that more are likely to follow.

We have already accepted, with only a minimum of protest, the principle that children who

---

*Quoted material is from Robert S. Morison, "Where Is Biology Taking Us?", *Science,* 27 January 1967, **155**(3761), 429–433. Reprinted by permission of the author and publisher. Copyright 1967 by the American Association for the Advancement of Science.

don't get enough food at home should be properly fed at school (though it must be admitted that this social advance was facilitated by the fact that many normally Republican states were at the time producing excessive amounts of grain and dairy products). There is still some difficulty in providing sex education in school for the children of parents too dogmatic or too squeamish to provide it at home, but the opposition is crumbling. Somewhat curiously, the major public opposition to invasion of the home by the State seems to center at present on the right of the parents to decide whether or not their children shall have dental caries....

As evidence accumulates that infants who have mobiles floating over their cribs develop hand-eye coordination faster, and that those who have books at home learn to read earlier, than those who don't have these amenities, it seems inevitable that society will provide aids to development, just as it now provides vaccination and school lunches.

Certain other functions of the family—notably the maintenance of a reasonably stable emotional atmosphere, with some more or less regularly available mother figure for the child to cling to in time of stress—are likely to be most effectively and economically provided, for some time to come, by the family as we have traditionally known it. Presumably, some inventiveness will be needed to preserve and, if possible, enhance these roles while allowing for the inevitable decline of familial function in other areas.

Although I believe it to be a matter of great importance that those functions which the family can perform better than any other social mechanism be defined and strengthened, it is not my purpose to propose how this may be done. What is equally important is for society in general to recognize what is happening and to become more conscious of the need to develop

a new mechanism for supplying the individual rewards and satisfactions, and for strengthening the ties between human beings, which used to be provided almost wholly through family life [p. 432].

In an article entitled "Early Learning In the Home" Benjamin Bloom (1965) corroborates and extends Morison's remarks. He makes the following salient points.

1. The most significant human characteristics appear in the first five years of life, in the bosom of the family. That's why the family is so important.

2. The schools must build on a foundation, built by the home. The child is not a *tabula rasa* when he comes to school. In fact, much of the variation observed in the first grade is a reflection of variation in the children's homes.

3. Human development is sequential. What can happen at a given point in the child's development depends on what happened earlier.

4. Early learning is related to later academic achievement. The "dropout" actually begins his career in the home rather than in the school.

The psychological implications of Bloom's analysis point to the basic personality and character that advantaged homes build early in their children and to the fact that such conditions are missing in the homes of disadvantaged children. The latter are, consequently, psychologically "predestined" for academic failure.

---

5 Are geniuses born or made?

Perhaps the most commonly held theory of **genius** is that it is a self-actional occur-

rence. The notion is that somehow genius occurs because of some inherent quality that may or may not be aided by environment. Consequently, genius becomes obscure and puzzling, even, perhaps, a freak of nature. One cannot help remembering the Greek notion of the inspired poet as being seized by a "divine frenzy." All through history people have resisted a naturalistic explanation of genius; hence, the genius has been placed beyond the jurisdiction of the psychologist.

The following remarks on the subject of human potentiality are taken from an address that I gave on the occasion of the Twelfth Annual Honors Convocation at Wichita State University, 11 May 1966. They were made to an essentially lay public and are therefore not as technical as a strict psychological analysis requires. The material is included, however, in the hope that it throws a different light on the traditionally obscure subject of genius.

Early manifestation of genius

Research on the early careers of people of great ability shows, as a rule, that their excellence was observable even in childhood. It has been demonstrated over and over that youngsters who show early promise tend to perform better in later life than youngsters who do not show early promise. In their 30-year follow-up study of so-called gifted children, Terman and Oden found that children with an IQ of 135 or higher who had been accelerated 1, 2, or even 3 years were more successful in later life than equally bright children who were held in lock step. However, there is no implication here of pushing children, which is always and inevitably a disastrous program.

The notion that the work of the genius just pours out

Here we meet another piece of folklore: a work of art simply pours out of the genius in one steady gush. What are the facts? Exhibit A is that giant of composers, Beethoven, whose sketchbooks and notebooks have been studied by Leonard Bernstein. We quote a few excerpts from his analysis. According to Bernstein, Beethoven went through

...a gigantic struggle to achieve the rightness as we know his Fifth Symphony today....We know from his notebooks that he wrote down fourteen versions of the melody that opens the second movement of this symphony. Fourteen versions over a period of eight years... Beethoven struggled with all his force. The man rejected, rewrote, scratched out, tore up, and sometimes altered a passage as many as twenty times. Look at those agonized changes, those feverish scrawls. Beethoven's manuscript looks like a bloody record of a tremendous inner battle. And yet before he began to write this wild-looking score, Beethoven had for three years been filling notebooks with sketches.

Bernstein summarizes: "Imagine a whole lifetime of this struggle, movement after movement, symphony after symphony, sonata after quartet after concerto. Always probing and rejecting in his dedication to perfection." In my opinion, here is the psychology of genius laid bare before us.

The case of G. B. Shaw

Beethoven is not an isolated case, for wherever one finds excellence, one also finds heroic effort, dedication, struggle, perseverance, endurance, and striving for perfection. George Bernard Shaw quit the dry goods business, left Ireland and nearly starved for 5 years in London while serving an apprenticeship as a writer. He produced five novels in those years, five books that were not published until 40 years later and that were far more important biographically than as literature. Yet that early work—at the constant rate of 500 words each and every day of those 5 years—underlay Shaw's career as a great playwright.

The genius of Newton

Geneticists have found nothing in the ancestry of Isaac Newton to explain his productive genius. His father was a ne'er-do-well and his mother, whom he adored, was undistinguished from her village farm neighbors. In his old age, when praised for his contributions, Newton remarked: "I had no special sagacity, only the power of patient thought." He made his discoveries, he said, "by always thinking unto them. I keep the subject constantly before me and wait until the first dawnings open little by little into the full light."

Report from the geniuses themselves

What do other geniuses have to say? Do they throw any light on the supernatural versus natural theory of genius? Commenting on his own accomplishments, Thomas Edison said: "Genius is 1 percent inspiration and 99 percent perspiration." When praised for his contributions to physics, Einstein pooh-poohed his own efforts in his laconic statement: "I have stood on the shoulders of giants."

Bach was asked about his organ playing and replied: "You have only to hit the right notes at the right time, and the instrument plays itself." Many a music critic has looked at Bach's productions with amazement, and spoken of them as something superhuman. To which Bach answered, "I had to be diligent. Anyone who works as

hard will get as far." He set the highest values on industry and held himself up as an example in this respect.

Rachmaninoff tells how from the age of 12 he went to study and live in the home of a stern piano teacher, Sverev, who worked 12 hours a day and expected his pupils to do the same. The boys were rarely allowed to go home for a visit, even during holidays.

Debussy led the existence of a **recluse** and rarely showed himself. He devoted himself entirely to his work, yearning for a perfection that was never satisfied.

Haydn, whose family tree showed not a single musician or intellectual for three generations back on both sides, had words of praise for his first teacher, Franck: "I shall be grateful to that man as long as I live for keeping me so hard at work."

In his brief lifetime Mozart made days do the work of years: "You know that I am swallowed up in music," he wrote his father. "I am busy with it all day long—speculating, studying, considering." He died at 35 in Vienna, leaving an incredible testament of 600 works. Music is his monument.

Hard work and concentration are the outstanding characteristics every time.

Buffon, the great naturalist, considered that genius was nothing else than a greater aptitude for patience than that possessed by other men, which is rather like Carlyle's well-known dictum that "genius is first of all a transcendent capacity of taking trouble." And another writer, Brewster Ghiselin, referring to "the self-surrender so familiar to creative minds," says: "The concentration of such a state may be so extreme that the worker may seem to himself or to others to be in a trance [Jones, 1957, p. 39]."

All those writers who have commented on their craft agree that a work of art is work. According to Paul Engle, "Pilots on the river at Rouen would see the light in Flaubert's study very late at night as he utterly shut himself away from the world to worry two pages of prose a week into the ruthlessly purified and perfected shape he demanded. At times, 15 to 20 pages would be reduced to four. Thus, when Flaubert said that he spent a week over two pages, he meant over the two finally perfected pages out of many more. Why this enormous care?

Returning to our own time and place, we find Truman Capote devoting the equivalent of one-fourteenth of a normal life span to one book. For five years he lived and breathed *In Cold Blood*. Day in and day out, month after month, year after year, he worked at his craft. Why shouldn't the book be outstanding and a best seller after such a heavy investment of self?

In an article, "How to Tell Your Friends from Geniuses," Ernest Jones, the famous English disciple of Freud, begins by asking if there really is such a thing as genius. Does a genius possess some attribute that differs essentially from those attributes that are present in all human beings? He answers decidedly in the negative and holds the view that the manifold differences between the genius and the rest of mankind are quantitative rather than qualitative. On occasion, this quantitative difference may be so striking as to give the impression of something qualitative and absolute. Jones' view coincides with my own, which sees the genius' act as earthly rather than supernatural and as a reactional superiority rather than an inherent superiority. Of course, it is comforting to any member of an elite group, whether artistic, musical, or mathematical, to consider himself one of the annointed few. Some accomplished people resent having their excellent work placed on a continuum even if it is toward the reactional superiority end of the spectrum. Several famous "hams" and "prima donnas" come to mind as members of this self-proclaimed unearthly elite.

The work of Suzuki

A hundred years ago in Japan a violin was neither seen nor heard. In fact, it was unknown, along with Western music in general. The Japanese, their ears tuned to their "weird Oriental strains," were considered incapable of mastering Occidental music. Recently 6000 children ranging in age from 3 to 15 gave a violin concert in a stadium in Tokyo. They played Vivaldi, Bach, and Mozart. Today throughout Japan there are 16,000 young violinists who have been taught by a genius teacher, Suzuki, or by one of his disciples. Suzuki has the bold idea that he can take any child from any continent, or any skin color, or any ancestry and teach him to play the violin well. There is one and only one condition: that the pupil can speak his own native language. Some of us were privileged to hear ten of Suzuki's students in this very auditorium [at Wichita State University], children 5 years of age who had already devoted half their lives to playing the violin. Professors from the Juilliard School of Music, from the Eastman School of Music, and from our own School of Music, were unbelieving at what the Talent Education Institute of Japan accomplished effortlessly, naturally, and without pushing. Some teachers shook their heads and asked each other, "What have we done wrong?" I would like to suggest that we have espoused a false theory of the nature of genius or excellence.

Consequences of bad theory

This false theory has caused us two kinds of mischief, which I have time only to mention, not to develop. First, as a teacher, what can you do if you believe that some students "have it" and some don't?

Figure 7.2 Children taught to play the violin by Suzuki's methods. (United Press International Photo)

Not much. As a result, effective pedagogy goes by the board. Secondly, suppose that as a pupil you believe that you are endowed with talent or are not. One can only speculate at the tragedies that result from false expectations of students who ask "Why should I crack a book? I'm naturally smart." Or, on the other hand, "Why try? I just don't have it." What a far cry from Alfred Adler's declaration, "Every person (i.e., biologically normal person) is equal to his life task."

Significance of Sputnik

Now for an example from another area. For a good many years many Americans thought of the Soviet citizen as a dull peasant, fit only to till the soil, certainly incapable of mastering science and tech-

nology. Sputnik should have exploded once and for all the notion of the natural inferiority of certain groups. The view I am presenting implies that there is no such thing as a stupid country.

We should not be surprised at the idea of a South American or African Sputnik. I predict that such things will come inevitably, and that out of "darkest" Africa, for example, will emerge great engineers, atomic physicists, composers, writers, and statesmen if it is true, as I am arguing, that regardless of so-called racial or national origin, all humans are **equipotential.** In my view, the United Nations as a **microcosm** offers some support to my statement and gives an indication of the shape of things to come.

I would also dare to predict that some day such terms as the "gifted child," the "inherently stupid child," the "naturally bright child," the "talented child" will be linguistic fossils. It will (and must be) admitted that not all children have the same psychological status at any point in their development. Some are ahead, some are behind. It is this advanced or retarded status of each child that determines what can be accomplished at any given stage rather than some inherent potency or lack thereof.

In conclusion, I am proposing that the excellence that is shown among those students whom we are honoring here today was achieved and was not the result of something thrust upon them. This does not make their attainment any less admirable or remarkable. In fact, I like to think that many have something in common with Michelangelo, who experienced both the agony and the ecstacy of genius but who, at the same time, could say as I hope they can say, "If people knew how hard I have had to work to gain my mastery, it wouldn't seem wonderful at all."

Martin: An experiment with the "talking typewriter"* 6

Preview

Twenty kindergarten children, five years old, were taught to read on Edison Responsive Environment machines over a period of five months. The level of reading proficiency for the group as a whole was near second grade at the close of the experiment in June 1964. The average time of exposure to the automated self-instruction was less than thirty hours—ranging from twenty-two to thirty-six hours per child. One of the peculiar virtues of the E.R.E. machine is its capacity to provide tutorial attention and response to every action of a child: Instrumentation such as the E.R.E. can help significantly to solve many of the problems in the public schools today.

Background and setting

In the summer of 1963 the Thomas A. Edison Laboratory and their associates, the Responsive Environments Corporation, invited the Freeport Public Schools to conduct an experiment to determine the validity of their E.R.E. Instrument as a teacher of reading to kindergarten and **mentally retarded** children.

After discussions with the Commissioner of Education for the State of New York, Dr. James

E. Allen, Jr., and members of the State Department of Education, it was decided to proceed on a local basis with some State research funds being made available if needed. The Freeport Board of Education supported the entire project without stint and with unanimous agreement.

Freeport, Long Island, is a suburban village of 40,000 population some 35 miles from New York City. The public schools have a population of 7,000 with approximately 4,000 in five elementary schools. In July 1963, the Board of Education directed that a sixth elementary school, over 90% Negro, be closed, and the children be distributed to the other schools in the district. The Atkinson School where this experiment was conducted, one of the five remaining schools with a population of over 600 children, thus became approximately 20% Negro. This school contained the only classes in the Freeport Schools for mentally retarded children of elementary school age. Thus, the Atkinson School made available a comprehensive sample of a general public school population.

---

*Quoted material is from John Henry Martin, *Freeport Public Schools Experiment on Early Reading using the Edison Responsive Environment Instrument* (New York: Responsive Environments Corporation). Reproduced by permission of the author.

Its four kindergarten classes divided into two morning and two afternoon groups contained 115 children. The one primary class for mentally retarded consisted of 14 children.

The experiment

A statement of the problem was: "Could a technological device teach five-year-olds to read?" Simple analysis of the problem revealed several subsidiary questions. Over what intelligence range would the instrument have any consequences? Would Negro children from a recently closed segregated school respond? Would mentally retarded children learn to read from an instrument?

Twenty-two children were selected, eleven for each of the two available machines. A matching control group was simultaneously identified. These groups were matched over a range of criteria covering age, sex, race, intelligence, left- and right-handedness, hearing, vision, language maturity, and socio-economic status as measured by parental job classification. Binet intelligence tests were made of every individual in the experimental and control groups by qualified psychologists. All pretesting was completed in November 1963. By June 15, 1964 two subjects were lost to the experiment by moving from the district.

The classroom environment

Two years ago, the kindergarten teachers were invited by the supervisors of reading to use reading materials within the regular program of their classrooms. It was generally agreed that too doctrinaire an adherence to child development views in the past had isolated some able kindergarten children from learning to read. In the kindergartens of the Atkinson School were two mature and superior teachers, each with more than ten years of teaching experience, with advanced degrees in elementary school education and reading. Both classrooms were richly equipped and were well supplied with materials of instruction.

The control group

Under these circumstances, the general assumptions underlying a **control group** could not obtain. It became apparent that our control

children would not be in a standard kindergarten where formal or informal reading instruction would not take place. Nor would it be possible to isolate our **experimental group** from some exposure to classroom instruction. It was possible to anticipate that a reverse **Hawthorne effect** could develop. At the Hamden Hall Country Day School, Hamden, Conn., where O. K. Moore conducted the first research into the applied theory which led to the development of the **Edison instrument,** one or more members of the teaching staff were reported to have revealed competitive antagonism to the withdrawal of their children to receive half-hour reading instruction in Professor Moore's research program. Similarly, in the year and one-half before the automated Edison instrument had appeared, Moore-trained reading teachers from the Freeport staff had observed the same reaction when they taught children to read from regular kindergarten and first-grade rooms using a modified electric typewriter in a tutoring situation identical to the Moore pattern. Under these circumstances it was reasonable to expect that the arrival of technological instruments of a complexity never before seen in a common school would generate competitive anxieties in teachers possessing a high degree of professional competence and pride. We were not to be disappointed.

Faced with these situations we could not offer the control subjects a **"placebo"** of nothing while we administered a new E.R.E. — medication to the experimental group. Rather, we were confronted with the difficult situation where we could be reasonably certain in advance that our control children would receive the best primary reading program that stimulated teachers could devise while maintaining the best aspects of a good child-centered kindergarten. Nor would the research picture remain clear of the effects upon the experimental group of their being withdrawn from their kindergartens daily for one-half hour or more (approximately one-quarter of their day), to return to some incidental exposure to the reading instruction being given tutorially and in small groups to the other children in the class. We recognized that until pre-school children from essentially impoverished environments without tutorially minded parents are used as experimental subjects, we shall not be able to completely eliminate certain factors which influence results.

But given these circumstances, which in one form or another affect all studies conducted within social institutions, our results would have to be examined against a restatement of the purpose of the experiment. "Could the E.R.E. instrument teach children to read better than a matched control group who would be taught to read under the best of conditions through the use of regular reading materials and procedures?" In effect, it was possible to anticipate that the normal Hawthorne effect which stimulates the participants in an experimental situation to higher energy output (because of the sense of being part of something special) would in this situation more likely accrue to the control children and their teachers to a degree seldom found or accounted for. On the contrary the sense of being "special" would occur to our experimental group as well. Albeit, that they would be the ones who would leave their classes to go to a distant room voluntarily to enter an isolation booth to play and work with a "talking typewriter."

The nature of the E.R.E.

The Edison Responsive Environment Instrument, E.R.E., is a computerized typewriter that reproduces several of the sensory responses of a human being. That is, it talks, it listens, it accepts, it responds, it presents pictorial or graphic material, it comments or explains, it presents information, and it responds to being touched. It can be orchestrated to do each of these things in a straight-line sequence or in planned parallels of these different sensory behaviors.

For the purpose of this experiment, very limited exploitation was made of the instrument's capacities. We frankly have only now, after five months' work, gained some insights into "feeding" the mouth of this benign and neutral machine. Programming, as the term is currently used, is largely a linear concept of the presentation of printed material in planned sequences with or without pictorial material, with or without audio, and with or without branching materials based upon a limited anticipation of the learner's responses. The E.R.E. differs from this concept of programming analogously to the difference between an old-time player-piano and a symphonic orchestra which has been computerized. The first is a mechanical device which can be activated by punched rolls of paper. The second will make different instrumental sounds to produce a symphonic effect as simply or complexly as the score which can be

written to activate it. In other words, the E.R.E. is not fixed to any sequence of behavior or responses. The key to a fuller utilization of its many capacities will come from seeing it as *Multi-Sensory Methodology open to simple and varyingly complex behaviors as well as responses from the learner who uses and controls it.*

E.R.E. — a working description*

A few examples to illustrate the Multi-Sensory Methodology capabilities of E.R.E. are:

In its simplest operation, the depressing of any key by the pupil will result in the immediate pronunciation of the particular key-symbol and also in the instantaneous typing of that symbol on the typewriter paper in extra large type-style.

Not only must the keyboard be "jam-proof" but, most important, once a key has been depressed, no other key of the total keyboard can be depressed until the audio-pronunciation is completed. Otherwise, this would lead to "wild-typing" and jibberish audio-pronunciation.

Even in this simple form of operation, a number of variations were proven to be essential; of particular importance is the ability to pre-record the keyboard in "several languages" even for the teaching of reading and writing of the "natural language." In order to teach sound analysis of the spoken word resulting in written (typewritten) symbols, one should be able to record the alphabet-keys in their phonetic equivalents as well as their letter names. For example, "t" (tee) or "t." A third variation may consist in the combining of phonetic equivalents and letter names, such as "tee-t." One must be able to switch from one language to the other effortlessly, dependent upon the student's own requirements.

It is further necessary to be able to delay the audio response to give an advanced student an opportunity to "beat the teacher" with the pupil's own pronunciation of the key-symbol.

In an advanced stage of teaching, E.R.E. adds to these functions the visual exhibition and accompanying audio explanations of single letters, words, sentences, and stories. The

---

*"This section appropriately was prepared by Richard Kobler, the technical creator of the Edison Responsive Environment Instrument."

Figure 7.3 Little girl sits at an E.R.E. There is a transparent shield behind the keyboard. Through the shield, the learner sees printing on a paper roll and a picture projected on a screen. (Photo courtesy of Responsive Environments Corporation of New York.)

Pointing Mechanism must be such as to gradually expand the visual focus of the pupil: thus, single letters can be exposed and pointed to, either in complete isolation or gradually coupled with other letters to form words; later on, a whole printed line is exposed, and lastly, several lines may be exposed.

Probably one of the most important features of the E.R.E. System is the fact that any symbol pointed to by E.R.E. is also "encoded" in its keyboard. This means that this particular key is the *only one* which can be operated by the pupil and which will type its symbol on the typing paper, while all other keys are inoperative (blocked).

Because incorrect responses cannot be completed on the "blocked" keyboard, this approach has aptly been called the "trial and success" method.

A typical operation would be for E.R.E. to point out a particular letter, to pronounce this letter to the pupil, and to free the one single,

particular key corresponding to this symbol for manual operation by the pupil. The moment the pupil depresses this key, the pointer will move to the next symbol, pronounce it, and free the corresponding key on the keyboard. Here, again, it must be possible for the E.R.E. to pronounce symbols in the before-mentioned two or three modalities (letter names and phonames) dependent upon the program.

Suppose that E.R.E. is pointing to a letter, has pronounced it, and has freed the corresponding key for operation by the pupil. If at this moment, the child's mind "wandered away," a *stalemate* between child and instrument would develop which would call for the intervention of a human teacher and probably end in the termination of the pupil's session with E.R.E.

E.R.E. avoids such a stalemate by audibly repeating the pronunciation of the last letter every few seconds until the pupil operates the corresponding key.

As the pupil proceeds from letters to words, an *additional* audio system takes over, which, although it can be programmed to take effect at *any* time or special point of the program, is frequently activated when the "space-bar" is depressed by the pupil. Since the depression of the "space-bar" indicates the end of a word, E.R.E. will at that point pronounce and spell the word just typed. Similar rules hold true of the audio-recapitulation of a total sentence after "period" and even of total paragraphs or stories.

Usually after the pupil has become familiar with a number of words, the audio pronunciation of *individual letters is cut out* because pupils want to proceed at a faster pace and start to resent audio repetitions of things they know in whole word form.

At this point we shall give another example of the *purposeful withdrawal* of a sense-modality (the withdrawal of a "letter audio" was one example). This time we shall *cut out the visual exhibition* of words or sentences and E.R.E. must be able to *ask the pupil* to type certain words or letters based only upon the pupil's audio-reception. This, of course, is "writing" and furnishes proof of the pupil's absorption of material. The only "help" given is that the keys are sequentially encoded.

Finally, in order to give precisely controlled "**gestalt**-illustrations" of orthographically presented materials, pictures can be shown to the pupil in close relation to the rest of the program. This is accomplished through an automated rear-projection-instrument built into E.R.E.

As powerful as these multi-sensory, synchronized activities of E.R.E. may be, they frequently are insufficient, if it were not for the ability of E.R.E. *to record the pupil's voice and to automatically play it back to him* in such a manner as to compare his own talk with the *models prerecorded in the E.R.E. System.* All these functions have to be totally synchronized with all other visual and audible as well as tactile stimuli. Having built a word from its visual, tactile, and audible components, having summarized it phonetically, having spoken it and compared it with the pronunciation of the E.R.E., a perceptual ring has been closed which not only results in the learning of the *reading* skill of the natural language, but also in the *writing* skill, based upon the *phonic analysis* of the pupil's own speech and therefore results in a *re-learning of the spoken natural* language on a higher plane.

All of these functions must be easily programmed by electronically and mechanically unskilled personnel. The mere typed copy of the text of a card by an attendant and the operation of a few auxiliary keys will automatically program E.R.E., using a simple card containing not only the visual information but the total encoded program as well as all audio explanations. Each single card may contain as many as 120 words accompanied by 20 minutes of audio explanations.

Testing schedule

Because the delivery of the two machines was originally scheduled for December 1963, pre-test data on the children was undertaken in November 1963. At that time the experimental group was fixed in size at twenty-two, the estimated capacity of the two machines in the typically short kindergarten school day. Among the tests used to establish the equivalency of the control group were the **Binet I.Q.**, and two reading tests, the **Lee-Clark** and the **Wide Range Achievement Tests.** The IQ distribution of both the experimental and the control groups ranged from the 140's to the 50's. The original groups were arranged in matched pairs in five categories of intelligence from Superior (120–140), Bright (112–118), Average (90–107), Dull (80's), to Retarded (50's to 70). The forty children who remained in June 1964, divided into twenty Experimental and twenty Control, were distributed in threes, fours, and fives in each of the above five intelligence categories.

The scores achieved on reading tests in November 1963 were used to refine the matching of the pairs and the total group, and to provide the bases for comparative measures.

Final testing was done during the weeks of June 8th and 15th, 1964. At that time, the **Gates reading test** was administered to both groups.

The administrative program

The twenty-two children in the experimental group, eighteen from four different kindergartens, and four children from a special primary class for mentally retarded children, came voluntarily for thirty-minute sessions, the maximum time permitted to work with the two E.R.E. instruments. After the first introductory week, the children left their rooms and found their way to the second-floor classroom into which had been built two demountable, sound- and air-conditioned, plywood booths approximately eight feet in cube that housed the E.R.E.'s and provided isolation from distraction and adult intrusion. The booths were monitored through one-way vision glass and intercom phones by trained teachers or clerks.

Training of the adults consisted primarily in teaching them how to establish a non-directive relationship with the children. Children could signal a desire to leave the booths or ask a question by raising a hand. Prompt response was expected and given provided it was non-instructional. Special note should be made of the successful effort to produce a calm and tranquil atmosphere in the experimental center. Mrs. Dorothy Johnson, Director of Primary Reading in the Freeport Public Schools, as well as Associate Director of the E.R.E. Project, not only did this, but in her manner and person contributed beyond measure to every aspect of the program. No one ever spoke in loud tones. Hurry was forbidden. A generally pleasant hush was maintained in order to keep the children in a neutral atmosphere. We wanted neither tensioned-fright nor over-stimulated excitement. The staff achieved this goal despite the almost continuous flow of visitors.

Results

Without going into technical details, the average of the scores of the experimental group exceeded 90 percent of the scores achieved by the control group!

Observations

1. The E.R.E. instrument has scarcely been exploited as a Multi-Sensory Methodology of teaching.

2. The material prepared during this project for the instrument represents less than twenty hours of instruction time. There is subjective evidence to indicate that only a fraction of these cards carried the major burden of the learning consequences.

3. Additional research is needed to explore the coordinations of the various sensory modalities of the instrument.

4. Exclusive E.R.E. instruction of the very young should produce results superior to those presented here.

5. The predictions that children over four would do poorly with the instrument were not substantiated by our findings.

6. The one case of the 18-year-old Negro boy with a "sight reading vocabulary of less than thirty words," three months ago, who now reads as the unique contribution of the E.R.E., is not generalizable. But the temptation and need to test this field are as immense as the problem.

7. Certain techniques are of importance and were too little used in this project. Desk top slates for tactile confirmation of letter and word learning are of presumptive value. Books distributed to the participants early after their exposure to the instrument should add to the consequences if the one-week experience at the end of this project is an indicator.

8. There is strong subjective feeling that the E.R.E. may make its greatest contribution as a rapid, three to five months "gestalt-producer" for early reading. Our associate director, chief psychologist, and the other research personnel associated with the project, all suggest that long drawn-out reading programs may be overlooking the phenomenon that learning to read well is the consequence of *early success* followed by much reading.

Conclusions

1. The E.R.E. instrument taught within five months (actual time at instrument ranged from 22 hours to 36 hours) twenty kindergarten and mentally retarded young children to read significantly better than twenty children carefully matched by a series of criteria who were taught by enriched traditional reading methods.

2. The children with less intelligence scored as significantly superior as did the brighter children.

3. Negro children in the group were indistinguishable by their scores from the remainder of the group.

4. Sex differences were not apparent in the scores.

5. The mean difference for the experimental group in reading score at the end of the five month period was 1.7 months over the control group.

6. There is evidence to indicate that the difference between the experimental group and the control group would have increased had the experiment continued.

The world of Nigel Hunt* 7

Imagine the anguish of parents who discover that their newborn child is a Mongoloid. The usual reaction is to consign the infant to an institution. As for the infant, his development is aborted, for how could much growth be expected even in a normal child in the light of results obtained from institutionalized children reared in physical and psychological sterility?

When Mr. and Mrs. Douglas Hunt heard the ominous diagnosis of **Mongolism** attached to their newly arrived son, they experienced the grief and tragedy of other parents of deformed children. However, their reaction differed from that of most other parents. About 2 weeks after Nigel's birth, the prediction was made that

...no matter how much love and care we gave Nigel, he would be an idiot and that nothing we could do would alter the fact.
If we had accepted this, it would have become true [Hunt, 1967, p. 22].

Another **self-fulfilling prophecy** would have come to pass. The child would have been institutionalized and destined to attain a state of profound retardation after a number of years' residence with other retarded children and adults. The Hunts, particularly Mrs. Hunt, refused to accept the dire prediction. Instead she treated her deformed baby as if it were normal.

Mongoloids can learn to read

With infinite patience, as a game, Grace Hunt spelled out words phonetically for her baby as soon as he could talk. In fact, we are told that "no child in his primary school could read better" (p. 23)! Grace's devotion to her son was rewarded, for in time he became the first Mongoloid to write a book, *The World of Nigel Hunt,* the very book that forms the basis of my report.

Two points are important here: (1) the Hunts, like most parents, exaggerate their child's performance. (2) Perhaps he is not a "genuine" Mongoloid.

Both points are covered in a foreword to the Hunt book written by the distinguished English neurologist and student of mental retardation, Dr. L. S. Penrose. Penrose refers to Nigel's "autobiographical essay, written spontaneously [p. 9]." He speaks of "Nigel's astonishing knowledge of words," of his "acute powers of observation," and his extremely good memory of separate events (p. 10). On the debit side, Penrose reports Nigel's limitation to concrete thinking, being unable to make any generalization. To offset that deficiency, he tells about Nigel's "vivid powers of description [p. 12]" and

often an unexpected phrase which shows a charming blend of childishness and sophistication.... Punctuation and spelling are surprisingly good throughout the typescript, and very few corrections were necessary [p. 12].

Penrose addresses himself to the doubting Thomases who question if Nigel really

---

*Quoted material is from Nigel Hunt, *The World of Nigel Hunt* (New York: Garrett Publications, 1967).

Figure 7.4 Nigel Hunt with his father Douglas Hunt. (Picture courtesy of Thames Television's *This Week* programme.)

wrote the manuscript himself. On this point, he adds, "Anyone who had met him, however, would find any such doubts quickly dispelled [p. 12]." When one learns that Penrose knew the boy since he was 3 years old, that he considers him "remarkably well adjusted" (p. 12), and that he believes that "his mental development has been phenomenal" (p. 12), we can accept the characterizations in the context of Penrose's scientific training and work. The second point referred to above on the genuineness of Nigel's diagnosis as a Mongol is covered in Penrose's disclosure of an "extra chromosome" in the boy's cellular structure (p. 13), notwithstanding which, he predicts that young Nigel "will go on learning ... and will no doubt proceed to further triumphs [pp. 12–13]."

"No Mongol has ever written a book before"

The above heading is a quotation (p. 15) from the father's (Douglas Hunt's) preface to the book written by his 17-year-old son. The following excerpt is a further elaboration:

All but the most enlightened of the medical profession would hoot with laughter at the very idea that a Mongoloid could write much more than his name, even after years of training. They will say that this book is just a stunt.

It is not.

This book was actually written by Nigel Hunt, who, as he says in the first chapter, taught himself to type. I showed him how to use the shift key for capital letters, and that is all. He still makes mistakes, but the photostat of a page of his typescript—his own unaided and spontaneous effort — will show you that he does not make a great many [p. 16].

Additional interesting details about Nigel's reactional biography are provided in the passages quoted from the father's contribution.

Like any normal child, he is very fond of doing what Daddy does. I spend a good deal of time at the typewriter, and one day I let Nigel have a go at it. I showed him how to press down the key which gives capital letters; that is literally all. The rest he learned by himself and he can now type as fast as I can, though, like myself, he uses only two or three fingers of each hand.

The time came when Daddy was constantly finding his typewriter monopolized, so Nigel had to have his own. He has written this book with it [p. 28].

For 2 years, to our subsequent deep regret, we allowed him to go to a special school for educationally subnormal children. Here he associated with children considerably more

Figure 7.5 Nigel Hunt, playing a recorder. (Picture courtesy of Thames Television's *This Week* programme.)

retarded than he and was constantly told, "No, you can't do that, Nigel; that's too difficult for you."

This, of course, is the worst possible attitude to take to any handicapped person, and when we saw that our efforts were being undermined we took him away and were fortunate enough to be able to place him in a private school where he received strict and loving discipline and excellent teaching. If he did not do his work, he was kept in until he did. It never took him long then [p. 29].

In many ways we have faced far fewer problems than do most parents of modern teen-agers. In many ways he is far more capable of looking after himself. And he has started his first book at the age of 17.

We can take him anywhere, and he makes friends wherever he goes. As you will read in his book, he has been abroad with us and he is quite capable of going into any foreign shop alone and coming out not only with what he wants, but often with a little extra gift as well [p. 31].

This, above all, is the message we, his parents, would like to give to our readers. MONGOLOIDS CAN LEARN AND GO ON LEARNING IF THEY ARE GIVEN THE ENCOURAGEMENT [pp. 32–33].

Here is an excerpt from Nigel's autobiography:

On my mother's birthday in August we went to Salzburg to celebrate with a drink somewhere. After that we went to have a look round the shops to get some souvenirs and a picture postcard for ourself to imagine you are in Austria. Then we went to St. Peter's Square [*Cellar*] for a drink where my Dad went to christen it; he always says he must and then to have a snack at the restaurant. There we had a real meal, Salzburger Knockel, which was very good with roast.

After a while we went to visit Mozart's birthplace, which is quite quaint with a crested shield over the door where he was born. He wrote his music there. Then to Salzburg Castle, which was over the river. It is right over the bridge on the left. We started in when I bought a picture of it, or rather my father did; the castle was very beautiful with a portrait of Mozart. [Nigel is here thinking of the Mirabellen Garten.] After that we were exhausted, so we had a bit of a rest. Herbert took us to Salzburg. Then it was time to leave Salzburg. We had a long ride ahead of us. We went past Innsbruck and through Wilten back to our hotel [pp. 78–79].

A final word from Nigel's father:

May I conclude by telling you one more true story to illustrate the fallibility of the experts and to encourage you if you have a child like Nigel.

Before Nigel was 5, I was summoned to the senior officer concerned with mental affairs (in a certain county). My wife and Nigel and I went to see this "expert," who was to help decide our child's fate.

The first thing the good lady said to us—in Nigel's hearing, of course—was, "Oh, yes, a little Mongoloid. Quite ineducable. Do you want him put away?"

Had we been more easily impressed by "experts," we might have said "Yes" [Douglas Hunt, pp. 125–126].

8 A psychological lesson about sex from hermaphroditism

A boy's a boy and a girl's a girl. The matter seems simple enough and yet contemporary research shows that one's psychological sex role is not absolutely determined by one's anatomical sex. In fact, a boy is not always a boy and a girl is not always a girl. Work at Johns Hopkins University reveals that girls can become boys and vice versa.

As long as a phenomenon—such as the acquisition of a sex role—continues according to expectations, we may overlook the essential factors in its development. Let it misfire and it may reveal much that we have taken for granted or oversimplified in our prior understanding and interpretation of the given phenomenon. The newer insights concerning sex identity come from studies of **hermaphrodites.**

Obviously our discussion up to this point is confused and confusing, for example, when we talk about "boys *becoming* girls." We need more precise terms if we are to make any progress in our analysis. An adequate technical vocabulary has been provided by Money (1955a, 1955b, 1956, 1960, 1961) and his associates at Johns Hopkins University in their research over the past several decades.

A technical vocabulary

Money (1955a) has surveyed the literature of hermaphrodites in an examination of over 300 cases in the English literature ranging from 1895 to 1951 (p. 286). In addition, together with his associates (Money, Hampson, and Hampson, 1956), he has directly studied 94 cases of *hermaphroditism,* which brings us to the first term requiring definition. A thorough treatment of the topic would lead us too far into anatomy. Therefore only the highlights will be sketched in the following brief discussion.

True hermaphroditism

A true hermaphrodite is defined as a person with both ovarian and testicular tissue present. The two tissues may be combined as in an ovotestis or as a separate **ovary** and a separate **testis** or in two ovo-testes, although the production of both egg and sperm cells is not required by the definition. Since only an operative procedure would provide the necessary knowledge, it is not surprising that "no more than 60 cases have been reported in the European and American literature of the last century" (Money, Hampson and Hampson, 1965a, p. 287).

Other classes

Female pseudohermaphrodites may appear as females with almost normal female sex structures but with hairiness and other signs of precocious masculinity. The disorder may be controlled or corrected with **cortisone therapy** (p. 286). *Female pseudohermaphrodites with phallus, normal ovaries, and normal Mullerian structures* provide further ambiguities to an easy two-category classification of organisms on an anatomical basis. Apparently, since this type of sexual development only begins to encroach upon male sexuality in a superficial way, the organism concerned is considered essentially female, hence the prefix *pseudo*. Similar deficiencies, accents, or exaggerations in the male yield several categories of *male pseudohermaphrodites*.

Chromosomal pattern and hermaphroditism

Another anatomical criterion that has recently been discovered to help distinguish males from females is the chromosomal pattern as revealed under the microscope via a skin **biopsy**. The components of the person's cellular structure may help to categorize him into the male-female categories.

Hormonal sex

As Money, Hampson, and Hampson (1955b) point out, the mere presence of ovaries or testes in an individual does not guarantee maleness or femaleness in appearance "for ovaries do not always make **estrogens,** nor testicles **androgens** [p. 304]." Sexual structures may be upset as by hyperfunctioning of the **adrenal glands,** which may masculinize a woman, or by an overabundant secretion of estrogens by the testes of a male, which would have a feminizing influence on his otherwise masculine body. Thus contradictions between the sexual organs and their glandular output add additional complications to any easy sexual cataloguing of people. Money, Hampson, and Hampson (1955b) found 27 cases among their patients who were embarrassed and worried by a contradiction between the sex with which they had been identified and the sex that began to manifest itself during **puberty** (p. 305). Twenty-three of the patients were treated successfully with **glandular therapy** or **plastic surgery.** However, four cases in the series who had been reared as girls became ambivalent sexually. One, on his own initiative, decided to live as a man from the age of 16 on. The other three, although continuing to live as women, showed some degree of bisexual inclination. Concerning the relationship between the secretion of the sex glands and anatomical maleness or femaleness, Money, Hampson, and Hampson (1955b) conclude:

Like **gonadal** sex, hormonal sex per se proved a most unreliable prognosticator of a person's gender role and orientation as a man or woman, boy or girl [p. 305].

Internal accessory organs

What is the relationship between the female's **uterus,** so closely allied with

menstruation and femaleness on the one hand, and the **prostate gland** in the male with its secretion of **seminal fluid** and maleness on the other? How determinative are these seemingly sexually distinctive internal organs in making a male a man and a female a woman? Money, Hampson, and Hampson (1955b) reach the following conclusion on this point:

So far as the evidence goes, there is no reason to suspect a correlation between internal accessory organs and maleness or femaleness of gender role [p. 306].

A complicating factor in this area should be indicated. As Money et al. point out, in hermaphroditism, unless there is medical intervention, rarely does the uterus or the prostate reach full functional maturity. However, in their series of cases, three patients with fully functional uteri "had been reared as boys and had a thoroughly masculine gender and outlook [p. 306]."

Gonadal sex

Mere mention of gonadal structure should be adequate because we already covered this point in our definition of hermaphroditism. We noted then that a true hermaphrodite, by definition, has both male and female sex glands although not necessarily producing both ova and sperm. It should be no surprise, then, that "gonadal structure per se proved a most unreliable prognosticator of a person's gender role and orientation as man or woman, boy or girl. By contrast, assigned sex and rearing proved a most reliable one" (p. 304).

External genital appearance

The most basic of all criteria are, of course, the external sex organs. From time immemorial the medical attendant or midwife has proclaimed to expectant fathers, "It's a boy!" (or "girl," as the case might be) on the basis of a quick and superficial inspection. Pink or blue blankets and similar distinctions by parents, relatives, and others follow. Thus, the child becomes a boy and a man or a girl and a woman. Surely the correlation here, at least, is safe and certain. Not according to Money, Hampson, and Hampson (1955b), for 23 out of 76 of their hermaphroditic patients for two-thirds of their life lived a sexual role the *opposite* of that indicated by their external genital organs. The patients did not get surgical correction of the deformity during infancy but learned to live with the sex organs of the opposite sex. Whatever sex they had been labeled with and reared as, they followed despite the evidence of their own senses. This was true in all but one case.

Money et al. (1955) are careful to explain that their hermaphroditic patients with contradictory sex organs were certainly not perfectly adjusted. On the contrary they did suffer anxiety and distress. Difficulties were most grievous in the case of patients whose external sexual structures blatantly contradicted the sex role that had been assigned to them and in which they grew up. When plastic surgery made anatomical correction more in accord with assigned sex and sex role, patients benefited from the procedure. Even here, however, not every patient saw surgery as a panacea. One patient reared as a girl for 16 years spontaneously changed his birth certificate and started to live as a man. Instead of seeking surgical procedures that would aid his belated change of sex role, he retained his feminized sexual structures while playing a male role.

To summarize, we have reviewed the relationship between five organismic conditions and the pattern of behavior that society identifies as that of a man or a woman. We considered, in turn, chromosomal sex, hormonal sex, internal accessory organs, gonadal sex, and external genital structures. The results are disappointing in terms of any expectations of a correlation between anatomical or physiological factors and masculine or feminine ways of acting.

Other factors in hermaphroditism

Had Money, Hampson, and Hampson stopped with their investigation of biological conditions, their study would have produced only absurdities. Fortunately, they considered two other nonanatomical factors: (1) assigned sex and sex of rearing and (2) gender role and orientation as male or female, established while growing up (1955b, p. 302).

The first term, *assigned sex and sex of rearing,* is simple enough, referring to the classification as male or female that a child is given at birth. Under "normal" conditions *assigned sex* and *sex of rearing* are identical, for a boy is reared as a boy and a girl is reared as a girl. Not always, though, because sometimes a mother, for example, *recognizes* the fact that her newborn infant is a boy; still she rears him the way other mothers rear their girl babies. The case would illustrate an *incompatibility* between assigned sex and sex or rearing.

For a definition of *gender role and orientation* I quote directly from Money, Hampson, and Hampson (1955b).

By the term gender role we mean all those things that a person says or does to disclose himself or herself as having the status of boy or man, girl or woman, respectively. It includes but is not restricted to sexuality in the sense of **eroticism.** Gender role is appraised in relation to the following: general mannerisms, deportment and demeanor; play preferences and recreational interests; spontaneous topics of talk in unprompted conversation and casual comment;

content of dreams, daydreams, and **fantasies;** replies to oblique inquiries and **projective tests;** evidence of erotic practices and, finally, the person's own replies to direct inquiry [p. 302].

The above definition is psychologically satisfactory because it deals in specific reactions that society considers either masculine or feminine categories.

Now, if we ask about the relationship that Money, Hampson, and Hampson (1955b) discovered between sex rearing (i.e., whether a child was reared as a boy or girl) and his gender role (i.e., whether he acted and identified himself as a boy or girl or man or woman), we find that

In only 4 cases among 76 was any inconsistency between rearing and gender role observed, despite the many inconsistencies between these two and the other five (i.e., anatomically based) variables of sex [p. 308]!

Summary

Starting with hermaphroditism, we noted the possibility of a single organism's playing a dual role anatomically or physiologically. We then sought possible correlations between (1) an individual's assigned sex assignment and sex rearing and (2) his gender role and orientation *and* biological factors. We found no reliability in any of the following indices: chromosomal pattern, hormonal sex, internal accessory organs, gonadal sex, and external sex organs. The significant factors discovered in research of hermaphroditic (as well as "normal") children showed a reliable relationship between a person's behavior as a man or woman and his identification as one or the other *and* the sex assigned to him at birth and continued by him as a role afterward. In fact, sex assignment and rearing contradicted the anatomical facts. In reality, both psychologically and anatomically speaking, a boy can be a girl and a girl a boy, once again demonstrating the extent of human potential.

9

*Seitz: "Basic reactions in rats"**

From naturalistic observations we are quite certain that a traumatic event occurring early in the life of an organism can have lasting effects. It would be preferable if we could experimentally, under controlled conditions, demonstrate such effects, but obviously such experiments with humans as subjects are impossible. However, we can do such work with infrahuman animals, which is exactly what Philip F. D. Seitz did with the Wistar strain of albino rats as subjects. His review of the literature in the following quotations from his report (Seitz, 1954, p. 916) serves as background and introduction to his own study.

Review of the literature

Hunt (1941) studied the effects of feeding frustration during infancy upon adult "hoarding" in the rat. He found that rats which had been exposed to feeding frustration early in their lives (after weaning) "hoarded" significantly more food pellets than their controls in adulthood. He also demonstrated that the earlier the feeding frustration, the greater its effect upon adult "hoarding."

Alexander Wolf (1943) investigated the effects of interference with vision and hearing during infancy in the rat. He found that animals exposed to interference with vision and hearing during infancy exhibited significantly poorer performance than their controls on learning tests involving visual and auditory cues in adulthood.

*Quoted material is from Philip F. D. Seitz, "The Effects of Infantile Experiences upon Adult Behavior in Animal Subjects: I. Effects of Litter Size during Infancy upon Adult Behavior in the Rat," *American Journal of Psychiatry*, 1954, **110**, 916–927. Copyright 1954, the American Psychiatric Association.

Bernstein (1952) reported an experiment with rats in which he found that amount of handling (following weaning) was correlated with adult behavior in a learning situation.

Levy (1934) reported an experiment on the sucking reflex and social behavior of dogs. This investigation was not concerned directly with the problem of infantile experiences in relation to adult behavior but with more immediate effect of infantile experience.

Levy (1939) also reported investigations of pecking behavior in chickens. Chicks raised on wire beginning at 10 days of age were unable to peck the ground in satisfaction of pecking needs. These animals subsequently developed the habit of feather-pecking, which did not occur in animals raised on the ground.

Zing-Yang Kuo (1930) demonstrated experimentally that rat-killing behavior in the cat is influenced by early-life experiences of seeing the mother kill rats.

Bayroff (1936) studied the effect of early isolation of white rats upon their later reactions to other white rats. He concluded that the experiment did not offer definite evidence on this problem.

Biel (1939) found that rats subjected to severe inanition [food and water deprivation] during infancy exhibited normal maze-learning ability in adulthood.

Pattie (1936) investigated the gregarious behavior of normal chicks and chicks hatched in isolation. Whether the two groups differed in terms of gregariousness is not clear from his data.

Patrick and Laughlin (1934) found that wall-seeking behavior in adulthood is influenced by the size of the enclosure in which infant rats are raised.

Kahn (1949) reported an experiment on the effects of severe defeat at various age levels upon adult aggressive behavior in mice. He found that severe defeat early in life resulted in less aggressive adult behavior. As was the case in Hunt's experiment, he found that the earlier the experience of severe defeat, the greater its effect upon adult behavior.

Scott (1945) separated infant lambs from their mothers at birth and raised them in a human environment for the first 10 days of life. He found that such lambs showed a permanent change in their behavior toward other sheep.

Hall and Whiteman (1951) investigated the effects of intense auditory stimulation during infancy upon adult emotional stability in the mouse. They found that the infantile experience of intense auditory stimulation resulted in adult emotional instability.

Scott, Fredericson, and Fuller (1951) reported experiments demonstrating some effects of infantile experiences upon adult behavior in dogs.

Fredericson (1951) found that mice exposed to competition for food shortly after weaning exhibited competitive behavior for food, even though not hungry, in adulthood [pp. 916–917].

Hypothesis

Seitz (1954) had an interesting hypothesis to check. He wanted to know if reactions established in the infancy of a rat would have a lasting effect on the adult. He decided to test his hypothesis by controlling litter size, thereby inducing variation in maternal care and nurture during the suckling period of the rats' earliest days.

Procedure

A female rat has 12 nipples although several are usually not functional. Thus a mother rat with 12 babies would obviously have both her hands and her nipples full. Only the most aggressive members of the litter would succeed in the competition for the mother's nurture and other maternal care. So Seitz divided 120 newborn rats into litters of 12 and litters of 6. Seitz randomly selected 10 rat mothers who were

assigned foster litters of 6 and 5 rat mothers who were given foster litters of 12. When the rat subjects reached adult status at 3 weeks of age, Seitz carried out tests to determine whether behaviors induced by the variable of litter size had any lasting effect. The tests were made periodically between 1 month and 2 years: The life span of the rat strain used is about 2 years; hence it is obvious that Seitz pursued his testing program into the advanced old age of his rats.

Results

The results were as follows:

1. *Body weight* Seitz weighed the animals periodically to see if litter size in infancy was correlated with body weight in adulthood. He found that although the subjects of the two groups did not differ significantly at the start of the experiment, at 3 weeks when they weaned spontaneously, rats raised in small litters weighed significantly more than pups raised in large litters. This was true for males as well as females. However, at 3 months, Seitz found a sex difference between males and females of the small-litter group. The trend for small-litter males to weigh more than large-litter males "continued far into the adulthood of these animals [p. 919]." After about 1 year of age, small-litter males weighed about 13 percent more than their large-litter counterparts and appeared flabby and obese.

2. *Food and water consumption* The only significant difference was in food consumption by females. Small-litter females ate significantly more than those from large litters. This was at age 1 month. This finding supported the hypothesis that small-litter animals tend to eat more as adults than animals from large litters.

3. *Hoarding* At 2 months and again at 9 months, Seitz conducted tests of hoarding. Every morning for 10 days he filled the food hopper with pellets. Twenty-four hours later he counted the number of pellets that the rat subjects had removed from the hopper and hoarded somewhere about the cage. Results showed that "both male and female animals from large litters 'hoarded' significantly more pellets than the rats reared in small litters [p. 920]."

The difference between the two experimental groups was so striking and consistent that statistical analysis was not really necessary. The large-litter animals had usually emptied their food hoppers after each 24-hour period, whereas the animals from small litters had hauled only a few pellets each day. This striking difference occurred in both sexes, and was strongly evident far into the adulthood of the animals.

These findings indicate that although the large-litter animals eat less and weigh less than rats from smaller litters, they "hoard" more [p. 920].

4. *Food-getting behavior when hungry* What differences, if any, would there be when, after a 23-hour fast, rats from the two groups were tested in a single-unit **T maze?** Each animal was tested separately to determine how long it took to reach food that was always placed at the end of the left arm of the T. Seitz also counted the number of wrong turns made in getting to the food. Results showed that both male and female small-litter subjects took less time to reach the food than the large-litter subjects. However, no differences occurred between the two groups in the number of errors made in reaching food.

5. *Food consumption after fasting* In addition, Seitz measured the amount of food that his rodent subjects ate after 23 hours of fasting. Both male and female subjects from small litters ate more food

in the test-feeding periods than subjects from large litters.

These findings coincide with the results of previous tests in which the small-litter animals exhibited heavier body weight, greater food consumption when food was available continuously, and greater speed in reaching food when hungry [p. 921].

6. *Reaction to a novel situation* Could differences in the infantile experience of rats appear in adulthood as differences in anxiety and in exploration of new situations? When the rats were 7 months old, Seitz put rats singly into an **open field test** and again compared the two groups. He observed the distance that each rat traveled in the circular area 9 feet in diameter; he also counted the number of fecal **boluses** dropped by the subjects after 2 minutes' exposure in the open field. The former measure is considered an index of exploratory behavior and the latter a measure of degree of tension or anxiety. Results showed that both male and female subjects from the small-litter group defecated significantly less than animals from large-litter groups. They also traveled significantly greater distances in the open field than the large-litter animals. We might say that the small-litter rats seemed "better adjusted."

7. *Competition for food between pairs of animals living together* Suppose one were to test pairs of animals from the two groups in competition for food after 23 hours of fasting. This is exactly what Seitz did when his subjects attained 15 months of age. He paired animals from the small and the large groups against each other, male against male and female against female. He allowed them to compete for food for one hour following 23 hours of food deprivation. Seitz noted which animal reached the food first, the number of times that each animal pushed its competitor, and the

amount of time each managed to eat. Seitz also noted and recorded "rooting" behavior, an act in which a rat noses under an animal and flips it over his back, thus pushing him away from the food. Seitz found that "rooting seemed to be used almost exclusively by the rats reared in large litters" [p. 922]. Male animals raised in large litters reached the food first and held on to it for a significantly longer time than the small-litter rats, showing that the former tend to be more successful competitors for food than rats raised in small litters.

8. *Qualitative observations*   When handled, small-litter rats were "more docile, quiet, and passive when picked up" (p. 923) than their large-litter counterparts. Squealing and struggling characterized the large-litter subjects. Viciousness and biting were also more frequently noted in the latter, as were "startle" and "alert" when the cage door was open.

A further control experiment

The present experiment demonstrated that litter size during infancy affected adult behavior in the rat. The question then arose whether a similar experience in adulthood would influence subsequent behavior. To answer this question, the following additional control experiment was done.

A group of 84 adult albino rats were selected randomly from an **isogenic** colony raised in our laboratory. The animals were 9 months old and had never been used in any experiments. They were separated according to sex and then placed in groups of 6 and 12. Among the females, there were two groups of 12 and four groups of 6. Fewer males were available, and we had only two groups of 12 and two groups of 6. These groups were put in living cages, where they stayed for 3 weeks. Since all cages were the same size, the groups of 12 were more crowded than those of 6. Only one food hopper

and drinking tube were placed in each cage. The purpose of this arrangement was to duplicate for adult rats an experience similar to the litter-size variable in infancy. After these adult rats had lived in groups of 6 and 12 for 3 weeks, they were placed in individual cages. Tests were begun immediately to determine whether the experience of living in large or small groups influenced their subsequent behavior.

First test

The "pellet hauling" (hoarding) test was carried out twice following the 3-week period of living in groups: (1) immediately, and (2) 2 months afterward. The reason for choosing this test was that it gave the largest differences between groups in the main experiment. Immediately following the experience of living in large (as opposed to small) groups during adulthood, a significant difference was found in pellet hauling by males. The males from small groups "hoarded" significantly more pellets than males from large groups. This trend is the opposite of that observed in the main experiment.

Two months following the experience of living in large as opposed to small groups during adulthood, no significant difference in pellet hauling was found. We conclude from these findings that, in the rat, the experience of living in groups of 6 and 12 during adulthood does not have comparable effects upon subsequent behavior as the experience of being reared during infancy in litters of 6 and 12. This suggests that the infancy period is characterized by greater susceptibility of the organism to long-term effects of experiences.

Second test

The other test used at this time was the "open field" test. The two groups did not differ significantly. Since tests that discriminated the large- and small-litter animals in the main experiment did not reveal significant differences in this control experiment, we generalize tentatively that infantile experiences appear to have greater effects upon subsequent behavior than do similar experiences [p. 924].

The variable of litter size during infancy was found to be correlated in adulthood with several behavioral traits having to do with body weight, eating, food-getting, "hoarding" of food, reaction to fasting, and competition for food. Animals raised in small litters tended to eat more, weigh more, and go after food more quickly when hungry than rats from large litters. On the other hand, the large-litter animals "hoarded" more and were more successful in competition for food.

How can these correlations be explained? The results appear to suggest that the greater the amount of maternal care and nurture during infancy, the more "eating-oriented" the organism is in adulthood. Within the framework of psychoanalytic theory, Fenichel (1945) proposed five kinds of experiences which favor the development of **"fixations"**; the first is: "...excessive satisfactions at a given level ...." The relatively little competition for suckling and maternal care among the small-litter animals may possibly have induced "excessive satisfaction" from eating and consequent "fixation" upon this kind of behavior. Some justification for considering eating behavior to be "excessive" in these animals is seen in the fact that they tended to become overweight in adulthood. Why this phenomenon was confined to male animals cannot be explained at this time but must await further investigation.

The tendency for rats from large litters to "hoard" more and to be more successful in competition may have resulted from the fact that these animals were exposed to considerably more competition for food early in their lives, and from this experience developed greater skill and practice in competing. Why the infantile experience of feeding frustration and competition should result in a greater tendency to "hoard" food is more difficult to explain. Fenichel (1945) listed as a second cause of "fixation": "...excessive **frustrations** at a given level." If the "hoarding" behavior is explained on the basis of "fixation" resulting from infantile feeding frustration, the question arises why the animals "hoarded" food instead of eating it. The hypothesis is suggested that specific behavioral consequences of "fixation" depend in part upon the type of infantile experience giving rise to the "fixation." Behavior resulting from fixation due to overgratification may tend to differ from that resulting from fixation based upon frustration. Applying this theory to the results of the present investigation, the following formulas would result:

Overgratification of suckling in infancy → Fixation of behavior on **eating** → Subsequent tendency to **overeat.**

Frustration of suckling in infancy → Fixation of behavior on **storing-up** food → Subsequent tendency to **"hoard"** food [p. 925].

Summary

To test the hypothesis that differences in infantile experience will have an effect into the adult stage of the rat, Seitz divided 120 newborn rats into litters of 6 and 12 each, thus introducing greater frustration and competition in the early experience of large-litter subjects. When the rats reached adulthood, comparative tests that yielded the following results were made:

1. Although small-litter male animals at the start of the experiment did not differ significantly in weight from the large-litter subjects, at 3 months they began to weigh more — a difference that continued well into adulthood.

2. Small-litter females ate significantly more than large-litter subjects.

3. Hoarding occurred significantly more among both male and female animals from large litters.

4. Following a 23-hour fast, small-litter subjects took less time to reach a food-box goal and ate more than their large-litter counterparts.

5. However, in competition for food, males from large litters were, in adulthood, more successful in reaching the food first and maintaining hold of it for a significantly longer time than the rats reared in small litters.

6. Also, in adulthood, large-litter rats were more vicious, struggled, bit, and fought more when handled than small-

litter rats. The former also distinguished themselves in adulthood by showing greater "startle" to new stimuli than the small-litter subjects.

7. A control experiment with adult rats living together in groups of 6 and 12 "did not result in sustained behavioral differences between the two groups [p. 927]."

Conclusions

The results of this investigation support the hypothesis that experiences during the infancy of a mammal can influence the subsequent behavior of the organism throughout its life. The following additional hypotheses were proposed to explain the results of the present experiment:

1. The infant **mammal** is more susceptible to long-range effects of experiences than the adult animal.

2. There is a litter size above which additional offspring negatively **reinforce** maternal behavior in the mother.

3. The three variables of litter size, maternal behavior, and behavior of the offspring are related and influence each other as chains of interacting events....

4. Although both overgratifying and overly frustrating infantile experiences may result in behavior "fixations," the types of "fixated" behavior resulting from such infantile experiences tend to be specific and different [p. 927].

*Kaufman and Rosenblum: "Depression in infant monkeys separated from their mothers"**

10

In children severe and serious effects are known to follow separation from mother for more than a brief period. Higher organisms, who are not precocial, require parental care to develop normally. The relationship between infant and mother is thus crucial and the consequences of its disruption are momentous.

In our study of infant pigtail monkeys *(Macaca nemestraina)* we found two striking effects of a one-month separation: (1) three of four infants developed a severe depression and (2) in all four there was a marked and long-lasting intensification of the mother-infant relationship after the mother and infant were reunited.

The subjects were four infant monkeys, 4.8 to 6.1 months of age at separation, who were born in the laboratory and raised from birth by their feral mothers in a group which also included their sire and an infantless adult female. The group, which had been together for over 2 years at the start of the study, was housed in a pen 2.4 m wide, 4 m deep, and 2.1 m high. Observations, made through **one-way vision windows,** began 1 to 2 months before separation and continued for 3 months after reunion. They were spread over 3 to 5 days per week, for a total of about 2 hours per week for each dyad pair in the month before and after separation, and for each infant alone during separation. Observation time was reduced by half in the second and third months after reunion. With a keyboard-clock counter device the observer recorded the total duration and frequency of a wide variety of behaviors by the mother and the infant; they included, for the infant, both filial and nonfilial behaviors and, for the mother, both maternal and nonmaternal behaviors.

The physical separation of mother and infant was done outside the pen with a minimum of handling and trauma. The mother was placed

*Quoted material is from I. Charles Kaufman and Leonard A. Rosenblum, "Depression in Infant Monkeys Separated from their Mothers," *Science,* 24 February 1967, **155**(3765), 1030–1031. Copyright 1967 by the American Association for the Advancement of Science. Reproduced by permission of the authors and publisher. Various useful references and notes have been omitted (see original article).

Fig. 7.6 Depression in an infant monkey. A motherless pigtail infant monkey following separation from its mother. After about one day's agitation, the response changes to the posture shown. Play ceases, as does movement, and response to social invitation occurs rarely. The depression gradually lifts after 5 or 6 days in a social environment. (From I. Charles Kaufman and Leonard A. Rosenblum, "Depression in Infant Monkeys Separated from their Mothers," *Science,* 24 February 1967, **155**(3765), 1030–1031. Copyright 1967 by the American Association for the Advancement of Science. Reproduced by permission of the authors and publisher.)

in a separate location, and the infant was returned to the group. After 4 weeks the mother was returned to the group. There was a 3-week overlap in the separations of the first two infants, and again in the separations of the second two, approximately 10 weeks later.

The reaction during separation, in three infants, fell into three phases: agitation, depression, and recovery. The fourth infant showed only the first and third phases. During the first phase, pacing, searching head movements, frequent trips to the door and windows, sporadic and short-lived bursts of erratic play, and brief movements toward other members of the group seemed constant. Cooing, the rather plaintive distress call of the young macaque, was frequent. There was an increased amount of self-directed behavior, such as sucking of digits, and mouthing and handling of other parts of the body, including the genitals. This reaction persisted throughout the first day, during which time the infant did not sleep.

After 24 to 36 hours the pattern in three infants changed strikingly. Each infant sat hunched over, almost rolled into a ball, with his head often down between his legs. Movement was rare except when the infant was actively displaced. The movement that did occur appeared to be in slow motion, except at feeding time or in response to aggression. The infant rarely responded to social invitation or made a social gesture, and play behavior virtually ceased. The infant appeared disinterested in and disengaged from the environment. Occasionally he would look up and coo.

After persisting unchanged for 5 or 6 days, the depression gradually began to lift. The recovery started with a resumption of a more upright posture and a resurgence of interest in the inanimate environment. Slow tentative exploration appeared with increasing frequency. Gradually the motherless infant also began to interact with his social environment, primarily with his peers, and then he began to play once

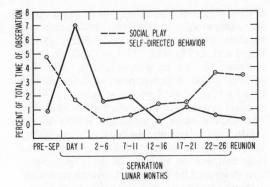

Figure 7.7 Mean duration of self-directed behaviors and of social play for all four infants during the month before separation, successive periods of the month of separation, and the month after reunion. (From I. Charles Kaufman and Leonard A. Rosenblum, "Depression in Infant Monkeys Separated from their Mothers," *Science,* 24 February 1967, **155**(3765), 1030–1031. Copyright 1967 by the American Association for the Advancement of Science. Reproduced by permission of the authors and publisher.)

again. The depression continued, but in an abated form. Periods of depression alternated with periods of inanimate-object exploration and play. Movement increased in amount and tempo. Toward the end of the month the infant appeared alert and active a great deal of the time; yet he still did not behave like a typical infant of that age.

The fourth infant, the offspring of the dominant female, did not show the phase of depression. During the agitation phase, unlike the other infants, she spent a great deal of her time with the adult females in the group. As she recovered, she became actively involved in exercise play and in exploration of the inanimate environment, followed later in the month by social play. However, the nondepressed infant showed many of the same behavioral changes as the other infants.

During the separation month, all four showed a significant increase in self-directed behavior ($P < .05$) and exploration of inanimate objects ($P < .01$) and a significant decrease in play ($P < .01$), both social and nonsocial. The early reaction to separation included a drastic fall in social play and a great rise in self-directed

behavior, whereas recovery was accompanied by a gradual rise in social play and normal levels of self-directed behavior.

When the mother was reintroduced to the group, another dramatic change occurred. There was a tremendous reassertion of the **dyadic relationship** with marked increases in various measures of closeness in all four pairs. Clinging by the infant [Fig. 7.8], protective enclosure by the mother, and nipple contact all rose significantly ($P < .01$) in the month after the reunion as compared to the frequency of these actions in the month before separation. Even in the third month after the reunion this trend was evident. This significant rise in measures of dyadic closeness is particularly striking in view of the

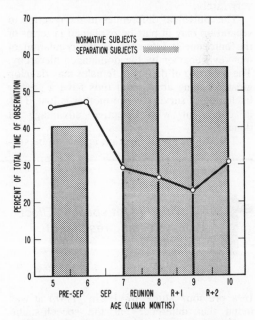

Figure 7.8 Results of separation in pigtail infant. Average duration of ventral-ventral (or vis-a-vis) contact between 9 normative, or control, mother-infant pairs indicated by the line of points and the same measure for 4 mother-infant pairs that were separated during the same period (indicated by the columns). (From I. Charles Kaufman and Leonard A. Rosenblum, "Depression in Infant Monkeys Separated from their Mothers," *Science,* 24 February 1967, **155** (3765), 1030–1031. Copyright 1967 by the American Association for the Advancement of Science. Reproduced by permission of the authors and publisher.)

fact that ordinarily, for the age periods involved, these particular behaviors fall considerably.

The increased closeness was manifest in other ways as well. A measure of mother-infant physical separation that we have found valuable in our normative studies concerns departures (usually by the infant) to another level of the pen. The frequency of such departures during the month after the reunion fell to 20 per cent of the departures in the month before the separation. Furthermore, the mean duration of these departures fell from 60.5 seconds to 34.4 seconds. Finally, maternal behavior, which normally discourages dyadic cohesiveness at this age, such as punitive deterrence and nipple withdrawal, appeared very rarely.

The individual differences in the reaction to separation may in part be explained in terms of the ontogenetic influence of the regulation of monkey behavior by the dominance hierarchy. The offspring of dominant females may develop greater coping ability and thus have a greater likelihood of survival if the mother is lost. This is consistent with selective advantage of dominance.

The stages of the reaction appear to be suc-

cessive efforts at adaptation. The first two stages are comparable to the two basic response systems proposed by Engel (1962a, 1962b; Engel and Reichsman, 1956) as available to the organism for dealing with mounting stress. The agitated phase, which appears to coincide with Engel's "flight-fight" response pattern, is likely to effect reunion with mother, if she is available. The second stage is strikingly similar to the syndrome of **"anaclitic depression,"** reported by Spitz (1946), in human infants separated from their mothers, an example of the response pattern described by Engel as "conservation-with-drawal, [which] involves inactivity... and **withdrawal** from the environment," and which appears to conserve energy and avoid injury. The striking similarity between the early stages of the reaction to separation of pigtail infants and children suggests that the mediating central nervous response systems may be common to both species. The third stage, recovery in the continued absence of the mother, which was not reported in the human infants, may in the monkey infant be attributed to his greater loco-motor ability, which enables him to reengage the environment actively on his own.

---

11 Irwin: "Infant speech: Effect of systematic reading of stories"*

In a previous study by Irwin (1948) it was found that differences in the speech-sound status of two groups of infants exist when they are categorized according to the occupational level of their fathers. The fathers of one group of babies were in business and the professions, the fathers of the other group were skilled, semi-skilled, or unskilled workers. The influence of occupational level was found to be negligible during the first year and a half, but during the period from about 18 months to 30 months the

speech sound superiority of the former group of infants over the latter was statistically significant.

The present study was designed to test the hypothesis that in the homes of working families systematic reading of stories to infants during the year-and-a-half period between the ages of 13 and 30 months will increase the amount of their phonetic production.

Subjects

Two groups of infants were selected from families whose fathers were engaged in occupations which fall into the following categories: day laborer, truck driver, fireman, policeman,

*Quoted material is from Orvis C. Irwin, "Infant Speech. Effect of Systematic Reading of Stories," *Journal of Speech and Hearing Research,* June 1960, 3(2), 187–190. Reprinted by permission of the author.

mechanic, delivery man, electrician, printer, ambulance driver, nurseryman, tavern keeper, carpenter, barber, tentmaker, and butcher. The experimental group included 24 infants, the control group 10. All of the children were considered physically normal; all were from Iowa City homes which, with only a few exceptions, were **monolingual.**

Method

Mothers of the 24 infants in the experimental group were instructed to spend 15 or 20 minutes each day reading stories to their children from illustrated children's story books, pointing out the pictures, talking about them, making up original, simple tales about them, and, in general,

furnishing materials supplemental to the text so that the speech sound environment impinging upon the children would be enriched. In order to insure that the regimen was carried out by the parents, frequent consultations were held with them. Two or three books were brought into each of the homes during each two-month period beginning when the child was 13 months of age and continuing until he was 30 months old.

Books were not furnished to the parents of the 10 children in the control group and no reading regimen was prescribed for the group. This, of course, does not mean that the control group children did not receive the customary stimulation characteristic of these homes.

The children of both groups were regularly

Table 7.1

Comparison of mean phoneme frequency scores of two groups of infants at 2-month intervals during study of effect of systematic reading of stories on their speech sound production. The experimental group (E) of 24 children was under a regimen of enriched reading; the control group (C) of 10 children was not.

Age Level (months)	Group	Mean	SD	Difference	t*	Significance Level
13–14	E	78.7	–	−2.5	–	–
	C	81.2				
15–16	E	84.5	–	−1.7	–	–
	C	86.2				
17–18	E	90.9	12.1	6.2	2.21	.02
	C	84.7	11.3			
19–20	E	93.9	12.9	9.7	3.62	.01
	C	84.2	11.2			
21–22	E	107.8	29.2	12.0	1.77	.10
	C	95.8	18.4			
23–24	E	117.2	29.3	16.4	2.13	.05
	C	100.8	15.4			
25–26	E	131.1	32.0	25.4	2.73	.01
	C	105.7	21.1			
27–28	E	144.3	40.9	36.7	4.03	.005
	C	107.6	11.6			
29–30	E	152.5	30.1	31.1	4.26	.005
	C	121.4	12.5			

*One-tailed test. Beginning with the 21- to 22-month level, a modified t test that allows for unequal variances was used.

paid an afternoon visit during each two-month period, and their spontaneous speech was recorded by paper and pencil in the international phonetic alphabet rather than by a tape recorder. As a rule, one parent was present. No effort was made to stimulate the child's vocalization. It has been demonstrated by Irwin (1947) and Irwin and Chen (1946) that infants' articulation may be measured in terms of phoneme type or frequency. A phoneme type is one of the individual sounds listed in the international phonetic alphabet. **Phoneme frequency** is defined as the total number of times a particular type occurs in a given speech sample. An infant who vocalizes a single phoneme would receive a type count of one and a frequency count equal to the number of productions of that type. The present report is concerned with the amount of vocalization as measured by the total phoneme frequency of all types. It has been found in Irwin (1945) that a satisfactory unit for observing phoneme frequency is one breath. The reliability of the observer who recorded the sounds live by paper and pencil in the international phonetic alphabet has been demonstrated and reported elsewhere, Irwin (1957) and Irwin (1948). The vocalizations of sounds on 30 breaths constituted the sample taken at each visit. The phoneme frequency score for each child at each age was his total score at that age.

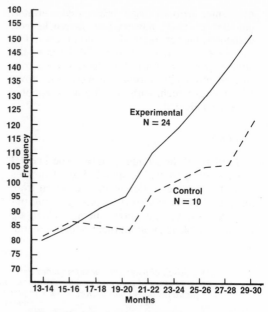

Figure 7.9 Graphic presentation of mean phoneme frequency scores of two groups of young children. Children in experimental group were under a regimen of enriched reading. Children in control group were not. (From Orvis C. Irwin, "Infant Speech: Effect of Systematic Reading of Stories," *Journal of Speech and Hearing Research,* June 1960, **3**(2), 187–190. Reproduced by permission of the author.)

Results

Data were grouped into two-month age levels for analysis. Mean phoneme frequency scores (Table 7.1 and Fig. 7.9) show that from the thirteenth until about the seventeenth month there is little difference between the experimental and control groups. Soon after the seventeenth month the curves for the two groups separate, and thereafter the means of the experimental group consistently exceed those of the control group until the age of two and a half years, the age at which the experiment was terminated.

Table 7.1 gives the phoneme frequency scores for the two groups and the significance of the differences between them. Except for the first two age levels, all differences are in favor of the experimental group. (The differences at the first two age levels were not tested.) A one-tailed **t test** was applied. It will be noted that,

for the experimental group, not only the means but also the variances increase with increase in age, whereas the variances for the control group remain about the same. The effect is to render the variances for the two groups unequal beginning with and after the 21- to 22-month level. For evaluation of differences beginning with the 21- to 22-month level it was thus necessary to use a modified *t* test, Cochran (1950), which can be applied regardless of the sizes of the variances. All differences are significant at or beyond the 5 percent level except that of the 21- to 22-month age. The differences between the experimental and control groups increase markedly after this period.

The results of this study suggest that systematically increasing the speech sound stimulation of infants under two and a half years of age in homes of lower occupational status by reading and by telling stories about pictures will lead to an increase in the phonetic production of these infants over what might be expected without reading enrichment.

Summary

This study was designed to test the effect which systematic reading of stories would have on phonetic production of very young children. Subjects were 34 children: the experiment began in their thirteenth month and ended in their thirtieth month. During this period, books were furnished weekly and a regimen of reading was prescribed for the children in the experimental group ($N = 24$), but not for the children in the control group ($N = 10$). Spontaneous vocalization of each of the 34 children was recorded by paper and pencil in the international phonetic alphabet in home visits during each two-month period throughout the experiment.

Little difference was found between the groups in the **mean** scores for phoneme frequency until about the seventeenth month; from then on the difference increased consistently with the experimental group having higher scores than the control group.

Chapter summary

Chapter 7 has criticized conventional, pessimistic, limited, and limiting views of psychological potential. An interbehavioral approach stressing the role of reactional biography was examined. The hypothesis was suggested that the life history of the organism furnished the crucial factors in explaining achievement. This concept is in contrast to traditional theories, which stress presumed innate or self-actional factors. The variety of selections in the rest of the chapter were offered as a test of the reactional biography conception.

In these selections we learned that (1) ghetto children in wretched, unlit schools, but from homes where learning is appreciated, do become scholars. (2) A young drifter can become a poet and playwright in spite of the squalor and degradation of Watts. (3) The school "dropout" may well begin his career in his earliest years *in the home*. (4) Geniuses sweat and toil for their achievements; things don't come easy for them. (5) After relatively brief exposure to talking typewriters, even 5-year-olds, even those from the lower IQ levels and from the ghetto, can learn to read. (6) "Pre-destined" by diagnosis to perpetual, hopeless idiocy, a Mongoloid has written his autobiography. (7) The human psychological sex role can circumvent the anatomical reality, for boys can "be" girls and vice versa. (8) By manipulating the early life history of rats, one can make them into "hoarders of food" or compulsive consumers. (9) Through separation of monkey infant and mother, severe pathology can be induced. (10) Extra stimulation of children of working class families does increase their phonetic production.

Jewish ghettos produced scholars, a Negro dropout from Watts can become a poet, a Mongoloid can write his autobiography—these facts speak eloquently for the reactional biography hypothesis stated at the beginning of this chapter. It would seem that our conventional concepts of biological and social limits on the psychological potential require radical revision. A suitable theoretical framework must be adopted; one that will place all relevant factors in their proper place in relation to the individual's life history.

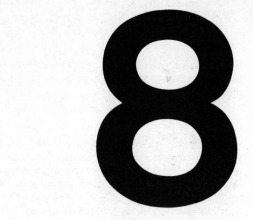

Conformity, or shared responses

It is common knowledge that no animal lives, from birth on, in solitary fashion as if in a vacuum. Characteristically, animals live in groups. In fact, the widespread grouping of animals in flocks, herds, schools, packs, droves, or colonies so impressed psychologists of a bygone era that it produced the familiar concept of a gregarious instinct. Since we prefer interactional explanations to self-actional ones, let us state the issue as follows. What happens to an organism born into a community of other organisms having certain existing modes of action? This is the question that concerns us in the present chapter.

We begin with an attempt to define the shared, or, as it is sometimes called, the social psychological **response.** Next, we observe the patterns of culture in various human groups and their effect on the behavior of the individual born into the group. For example, posture appears to be rooted in **anatomy,** and yet a closer look will show that it too, is shaped by the particular group's ways. Other patterns are examined, such as how culture determines whether one eats or starves in India, as illustrated by the article on the "sacred" cow.

The impact of culture in determining human behavior is beyond doubt. However, what about the lower animals? Do monkeys and chimps have a culture? Does it condition the individual's action? As for birds, do their songs show any social psychological pattern? Do birds demonstrate any individualistic or **idiosyncratic** pattern? These and similar questions are discussed in the following selections.

Bucklew: "The social psychological response"*

1

Conceptions of social psychology

Current writers on **social psychology** regard it as the study of the individual living in groups or as the influence of groups on the development of the individual. Sometimes social behavior is considered as responses made to other *people* or in a social setting. Although these conceptions satisfy the ordinary use of the word "social," they fail to isolate a distinctive subject matter for the science of social psychology. Consequently, the data usually included in the subject seem heterogeneous and badly organized. Basic to this confusion is the lingering idea, itself a reflection of popular thought, that psychology can divide behavior into hereditary and environmental categories. Thus social psychology, as the study of the latter, has increasingly come to include a vast collection of data garnered from several fields of psychology, such as **developmental** and **abnormal psychology,** and from neighboring sciences, such as sociology, anthropology, and **ethnology.**

Two criteria for the social response

It is axiomatic in science that orders of data must be distinguished as well as related. For the distinction of social psychology from its neighbors, we thus require the isolation of some type of behavior which can be studied and related to other things. As psychologists we

---

*Quoted material is from John Bucklew, Jr., "The Social Psychological Response." Reprinted with slight revision from N. H. Pronko and J. W. Bowles, Jr. (Eds.), *Empirical Foundations of Psychology,* (New York: Rinehart, 1951), pp. 120–122.

should keep our attention centered upon specific behavior of organisms, and as *social* psychologists we should note how such behavior is related to those aspects of living which we call "social." If we consider psychology as an objective study of certain events occurring in nature, there exist two criteria by means of which we can isolate a subject matter for social psychology. On the side of the organism, we note whether or not the response function being performed is essentially the same as we can see other people making—in other words, whether the behavior being observed is shared by sets of people. For example, if we watch men removing their hats upon entering an elevator we may be sure we are observing conventional, or social psychological, behavior. Sets of people can be observed performing such actions, but not everyone performs them.

The second of our criteria is obtained by shifting our attention to the action of the stimulus instead of the action of the responding organism. Here we note whether or not the stimulus functions in the same way for groups of people. If so, we have isolated the counterpart of the conventional response—the conventional **stimulus function.** A mouse running through the living room will stimulate strong feelings of aversion, disgust, and fear among the seated company because mice have been endowed with that stimulus function in our society. A dog in the living room will not elicit comparable reactions. People have learned to accept one as a pet but not the other; thus the two animals represent different types of institutional stimuli.

The difference between the two criteria stated above is one of emphasis only. In one case, we single out the action of the organism; in the other, the action of the stimulus. It depends upon the one in which we are most interested at the moment—the psychological institutions which exist at any given time or the groups of people who share certain conventional actions. Stimuli and responses, of course, are integral parts of unitary events and are separated from one another only for the sake of convenience.

Nonsocial or idiosyncratic behavior

It is not possible to classify the entire behavior of the individual as social psychologi-

cal in origin. Individuals may evolve personal ways of responding to things which they do not necessarily share with someone else. The behavior has not been taken over from others and, therefore, is not social psychological. Individualistic contributions of painters, writers, and others illustrate such distinctive ways of responding. Beethoven's *Fifth Symphony* is a unique affair. In contrast to conventional or shared reactions, let us agree to call the uniquely individual reactions *idiosyncratic*.

An illustration of the social psychological response

The following social psychological test may serve to clarify the distinctions outlined above and at the same time will illustrate some of the outstanding characteristics of social psychological behavior. Other characteristics will be illustrated in the selections which follow. It is only because the reader possesses conventional ways of responding to various stimuli that he is able to complete any of the phrases or sentences listed below.

A social psychological test*

See if you can complete the following phrases or sentences:

1. Haste makes _____.
2. Neither rhyme nor _____.
3. You have hit the _____ on the _____.
4. I escaped by the _____ of my teeth.
5. Into each life some _____ _____.
6. Revenge is _____.
7. The flower of our young _____.
8. Fools rush in where angels _____ _____.
9. When a rich man becomes poor, he becomes a _____.
10. No one teaches a cat how _____ _____.

The first eight of the above phrases are products of Western European culture, and it is by virtue of membership in this cultural tradi-

---

*The answers can be found on page 251.

tion that one is able to complete them. The last two come, respectively, from China and Africa, and it will be only very rarely that anyone living in this country can complete them. The phrases are mostly artificial metaphors, but to the person knowing them they possess a "natural," familiar sound. Some of them are quite old, and others are comparatively recent in origin, although the individual usually cannot tell either where or when they originated, or at what time in his life he came into possession of them.

All this is generally true of social psychological behavior. It seems natural, almost inevitable, and its origin or distribution over the world is unknown to the individual performing it unless he is educated in such matters. Insight into the conventional nature of his behavior is achieved only when the individual becomes aware of other possible ways of behaving which various groups display. For this reason, the study of social psychology is closely related to, although distinct from, **cultural anthropology,** a science which has undertaken the study of *groups* as such living throughout the world [pp. 120–122].

The following selections will serve to illustrate still other characteristics of conventional behavior.

Cultural ways in different parts of the world

2

It has been said that if fish were scientists, the last of all their discoveries would be water. Since the social scientist is first a product of his own culture, and only much later a social scientist, detecting the operations of his cultural milieu is as difficult as discovery of water by the fish. But we must try.

The force of culture in determining human behavior has been glimpsed in the following quotation from Ruth Benedict's *Patterns of Culture* (1934).

The life history of the individual is first and foremost an accommodation to the patterns and standards traditionally handed down in his community. From the moment of his birth the customs into which he is born shape his experience and behaviour. By the time he can talk, he is the little creature of his culture, and by the time he is grown and able to take part in its activities, its habits are his habits, its beliefs his beliefs, its impossibilities his impossibilities. Every child that is born into his group will share them with him [p. 2]....

Commerce

Whatever the hour of the day, the American is accustomed to jump into his car, drive to the nearest shopping center, and get whatever he needs to carry on his domestic functions—that is, if the American is in the United States. However, if he is residing in one of the countries around the Mediterranean, a similar intention meets with frustration unless and until he learns to conform to the ways common in that part of the world. In the Mediterranean region and the Tropics generally, the midday rest or siesta precludes practically all business transactions. In Spain, Italy, Israel, or Egypt an American soon learns to follow tradition and rests or reads between 1 P.M. and 4 P.M., for during those hours stores pull down their metal shutters and shopkeepers lock up and go home. Streets are deserted; everyone is having his leisurely midday meal and siesta. After 4 P.M. the business world comes to life once more. Even the banks reopen from 4 to 6 or 7 P.M.

Hello and goodbye

A man from another planet might understandably be confused if he watched people departing on passenger liners in different parts of the world. Departure customs in New York differ markedly from customs in the Mediterranean countries, for example. People taking leave of one another in the United States execute the gesture that says goodbye with the palm of the hand open toward the other person, making up-and-down or side-to-side movements of the hand with the wrist acting as a hinge.

The Turk, Italian, or Greek, by contrast, finds it just as natural or normal to wave goodbye in the opposite direction from that of the American. The palm of the hand is open toward the person who is waving goodbye and the predominant direction of the hand is toward the person executing the movement.

Generally handshaking is much more prevalent in Europe than in the United States. Friends who see each other every day shake hands when they first say "hello." European women, too, offer their hand naturally to either sex. In America, however, handshaking seems to be disappearing. It takes a considerable absence among friends to evoke a handshaking response. Moreover, the American woman seldom initiates this gesture.

Observe friends at a railroad station in Japan parting from one another and all one sees is an endless repetition of bows and smiles, no handshakes, no touching—another example of how inevitably culture shapes behavior.

Eating

Most Americans have three meals a day. Many Europeans prefer four, even if one is called "tea." Certainly the Britisher would feel cheated if he missed his tea and biscuits, a repast that permits him to postpone the evening meal to a later hour. Dinner time itself shows tremendous variation. For example, an American, accustomed to eating his evening meal as early as 5:30 or 6:00, may wait impatiently for the dining room of his hotel in Spain to *open* at 9 P.M. Should he wish to mingle with and observe the Spaniards while they are dining, he must wait still another hour or two at least. The ultimate in varied meal times is illustrated by the Indians of Bolivia, who simply have no set times. Eating, as well as sleeping, shows no regularity; each depends on the individual's specific needs. As a rule, division of meals into breakfast, lunch, and dinner is nonexistent.

Food

As for food, there is an immense diversity even within our own culture. Fried foods, cokes, and candy are staples for some people. At the other end of the spectrum, some Americans have eclectic and cosmopolitan tastes.

Can you imagine a housewife shopping for snakes to serve as the main course for her family? You could if you lived in Singapore, for the snake is a common item of diet there. In Korea peasant women like eels, which they catch in the streams. As soon as they have caught one, they pop it into their mouths and behead it with one swift bite. Japanese commonly eat flaked fish raw; many consider it a gastronomic sin to cook it, and thus to spoil the flavor. Frenchmen, among others, consider snails a delicacy, and in Marseilles a tiny sardinelike fish is "French-fried" whole, in the state in which it is caught (i.e., without being "cleaned") and eaten without the slightest qualm.

A Turk went to England and was shocked when he saw the English ordering such items as kippered herring, sausages, and baked beans for breakfast. His usual breakfast was bread, cheese, and tea. And, like everyone else, he found the coffee undrinkable and sadly missed the tiny but potent cup of Turkish coffee he enjoyed six to ten times a day at home.

An incredulous Frenchman once asked an American if it was true that in America people drank coffee (not wine) with their meals. For him coffee was a demitasse to be sipped after dinner. As for the preparation of coffee itself, the process varies from country to country and many think that another's product is unfit to drink. Often people believe that their own diet, dress, customs, and ways of doing things are superior to those of others. Thus an American, whose first choice is probably steak, is surprised to find on his initial trip to Europe that most Europeans prefer other meats — veal, lamb, and so on.

Clothes

Generally, for most Americans as well as Europeans, the skirt is strongly linked with the female sex and pants with the male sex. Although jeans and slacks are fairly common feminine attire and even pantsuits are frequently worn by women, there is virtually no masculine equivalent to the skirt. Even the Scotsman's kilt is denied identification as a skirt. The mere thought

of a man's wearing a skirt is repugnant to our custom and to our legal system; yet a woman's wearing trousers as part of a uniform may not only be approved but also required in certain government positions.

What is the correlation between sex and the skirt in the rest of the world? As with other human activities, customs vary widely. For example, in modern Japan, there are still Japanese who cling to the old order, men as well as women who wear the

Figure 8.1 The arbitrariness of custom pertaining to dress is illustrated in this photo. If you had told a visitor from another planet that, at least in Western culture, women wore skirts and men, trousers, how would you go about explaining the apparent contradiction shown here? (Photo courtesy of British Travel Association.)

traditional kimono. In China, on the other hand, available information shows that both men and women commonly wear a pajamalike costume. In Cairo, a traveler might see his dining room waiter wearing the *galabiya,* which is essentially a night shirt and therefore closer to a skirt than to a pair of pants. The robe of the Mandarin of ancient China and the robe of the priest in various religions are additional examples of a lack of correlation between the skirt and sex.

3 Henderson: Male sopranos

People have a ready way of categorizing the human voice into such discrete categories as child and adult, high and low, male and female. The distinctions seem valid, even biologically given. Yet if we consider what man has done with his voice in different periods of history, our belief in the absoluteness of the above categories is shaken. The following brief account is based on Henderson's *Early History of Singing* (1921), particularly his chapter on "Male Soprani and Other Virtuosi."

In the early seventeenth century, male sopranos frequently rose to great heights. In fact, one of them, Loretto Vittori, became so famous and so venerated that a statue was erected to honor him. Both male and female virtuoso singers were held in such esteem that they were accorded a social status worthy of nobles (p. 134), but it is the male soprano who interests us here.

Nothing in the history of this period and the Handelian era so astonishes us as the glory of the male soprano. It seems inconceivable that Caffarelli, Carestini, Farinelli, Senesino, Guadagni (the original Gluck *Orfeo*), and other immortal names were the appellations of men who sang with boys' voices and even sometimes wore petticoats and assumed women's parts. Yet such was the fact and these artificial and unreal singers were the idols of the public [p. 135].

The earlier falsettists

The earlier history of the male soprano **(evirato)** has its origin in the falsettists who were used to give greater range to polyphonic church music, thus closing the door to the female voice. This was in the fifteenth century. The Spanish developed the falsetto to such a clever degree that it attracted attention in Rome, where it was adopted for use in the Sistine Chapel. Gradually the male soprano began to supplant the falsettist, and by the seventeenth century he had won a position of honor.

The male soprano in opera

In time opera provided an opportunity for the male soprano to show his wide-ranging capabilities. Assignments of roles were capricious, with no concern for sex appropriateness or dramatic fitness.

Composers, inspired by the brilliant execution of florid music by the evirati, composed for them and thus further fanned their popularity. Some of these sopranos enjoyed careers as distinguished as the finest contemporary artists, and their audiences were moved to shouting, screaming, and even fainting. Police lines were sometimes broken, as when the populace "broke into the Palace of the Jesuits at one of his (Vittori's) appearances and literally chased out nobles and Cardinals [p. 141]." Another famous evirato, Padre Girolamo Rossini, was the first male soprano to be appointed to the Papal Choir (p. 140).

In summing up the virtuosity of the male sopranos of the seventeenth century, as reported by musicians and writers of every variety, Henderson writes, "These male sopranos and contraltos all sang with exquisite technical finish, with thoroughly equalized scales, with suavity and elegance [p. 143]."

The opera of the seventeenth century was written especially to permit singers to display their skill in embellishing and ornamenting the music written for them. Technical competence was expected and admired. "Touching expression" and "pathos" but not "tumultuous passion" (p. 171) were all that was called for and appreciated. It was the entrance of the latter and closer adherence to truth and reality, especially as regards character portrayal, that eventually established the custom "of giving the role of the hero to a tenor, that of the heroine to a soprano, while the darker voices of the contralto and the baritone were habitually employed to either the sentiments of the unfortunate or wicked personages in the story [p. 178]."

Today's countertenor

Fashions change in all things. The male soprano went out of existence about 130 years ago, but recently he has been rediscovered — in what amounts to the rediscovery of a lost art. The stimulus has been furnished by a revival of interest in baroque music. Sir Henry Purcell, a countertenor, composed numerous hymns, madrigals, cantatas, operas, and carols especially for the high male voice. At 31, Alfred Deller, started a renaissance that carried him to the heights of success, a success he has enjoyed for the past quarter of a century. The new movement has produced half a dozen other countertenors, including an American, Russell Oberlin.

Neither Russell Oberlin nor Alfred Deller considers his voice to be "artificial or unreal."*

Thus we have another example of a recurrent theme manifested in contemporary psychology, namely, the rich potential of human behavior. And again we see how behavior can transcend conventional limits — including those based on anatomical sex and other biological categories.

---

*The difficulty of identifying the sex of a singer by his or her voice alone can be demonstrated by presenting portions of the following three albums and asking the hearer to identify the voice as male or female: Vanguard, Everyman Classics, Stereolab SRV-141 SD (*Album of Beloved Songs: The Deller Consort and Alfred Deller*); Decca Stereo, DL 710032 (*A Russell Oberlin Recital*); and Capitol T299 (*Yma Sumac: Legend of the Sun Virgin*).

Answers to social psychological test on page 246

1. Haste makes waste (English proverb).
2. Neither rhyme nor reason (Shakespeare, *As You Like It*).
3. You have hit the nail on the head (Rabelais, 1495–1553).
4. I escaped by the skin of my teeth (the Bible).
5. Into each life some rain must fall (Longfellow, 1807–1882).
6. Revenge is sweet (Byron, 1788–1824).
7. The flower of our young manhood (Sophocles, 496–406 B.C.).
8. Fools rush in where angels fear to tread (Pope, 1688–1744).
9. When a rich man becomes poor, he becomes a teacher (Chinese proverb).
10. No one teaches a cat how to steal (proverb of the Ashanti tribe).

252 / Conformity, or shared responses

4

Levy:
Culturally imposed "clubfoot"

A glance at fashions and customs shows that man has often tampered with his "natural condition." Examples are numerous: the tranquilizing opium pipe of the Orient and the modern sleeping pill; high-heeled shoes, worn by Louis XIV as well as by some modern housewives; pierced ears and tattooed skin. The list seems endless.

It would make an interesting document to chronicle how man has attempted to change his biological shape by stretching, twisting, shrinking, coloring, or amputating. Yes, deliberate crippling, too, for this is what Chinese foot-binding achieved. We shall briefly examine this custom, which persisted in China for a thousand years. As our source, we use Howard Levy's work, *Chinese Footbinding: The History of an Erotic Custom* (1966).

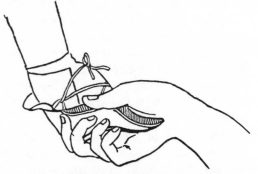

Figure 8.3 Footbinding and sexuality. "Grasping the golden lotus" took on a highly erotic coloring. (Reprinted from Howard S. Levy, *Chinese Footbinding: The History of a Curious Erotic Custom,* p. 150, with the permission of Walton H. Rawls, publisher.)

Even before the days of Confucius small feet were admired because they resulted in small, dainty, graceful steps in walking. Large feet were considered low class and vulgar. The palace dancers probably originated foot binding in the tenth century (p. 30), which suggests that originally squeezing the foot was not severe enough to interfere with dance movements. Later the custom spread and changed in meaning, and compression was increased to the point of crippling. As a result, the upper-class woman's chastity was safeguarded by making it virtually impossible for her to move outside her home. In other words, it was a restraining device. Another factor entered into the persistence of this custom for an entire millenium, that is, its sexual appeal to the Chinese male.

What tortures a young girl of 7 would undergo in order, as her mother would assure her, to be attractive and thus win a fine husband! Her toes were bent toward

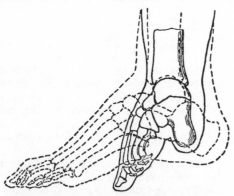

Figure 8.2 An example of institutionalized clubfootedness. The results of Chinese footbinding are vividly shown in the comparison of a non-bound foot with an overlay of one deformed by the custom. (Reprinted from Howard S. Levy, *Chinese Footbinding: The History of a Curious Erotic Custom,* p. 217, with the permission of Walton H. Rawls, publisher.)

the sole and bandaged tightly, forcing the toes backward so that her foot would not grow to be more than 3 or 4 inches long. Pus, inflammation, and bleeding occurred. The unbearable pain made walking impossible. "The pain continued for about a year and then diminished until at the end of 2 years the feet were practically dead and painless [p. 26]."

But what delight the tiny foot brought to the Chinese male! The mere thought of seeing his beloved's foot sent him into ecstacy. If he were permitted a touch, it meant that the woman was his or sometimes it meant the equivalent of a "shot-gun marriage." The rituals and procedures connected with the bathing and binding of the woman's feet in the strictest privacy of her boudoir, and the **fetishistic** reaction of the male to her feet, are another interesting but incidental story. Our main purpose here is to emphasize how clubfeet were institutionalized in a human society and perpetuated for a thousand years.

One way to have a clubfoot is to experience the unfortunate accident of a failure in embryological development. Another way is to have it thrust upon you following birth. For a thousand years the Chinese culture created clubfootedness on a wholesale scale by binding little girls' feet. Whether the process is an accident of birth or an enforced custom, walking is painful or impossible. Since foot-binding was abolished in China only in 1928 (p. 205), there may still be middle-aged women who show the residuals of culturally created clubfootedness.

Bucklew: Features of conventional behavior* 5

We are now in a position to summarize some of the prominent features of conventional behavior. These are not all the possible features that could be named, nor does every specific example display all the characteristics enumerated. But all conventional behavior will exhibit some of them.

1. The responses are distributive. They can be found in definite geographical regions. Even in so restricted a region as that represented by a small town, not all of the conventional behavior will be shared by all. Instead, there are innumerable groupings and cleavages.

2. The responses are diffusive. They may spread from one individual to another and from one region to another. The custom of coffee drinking is an example.

3. The responses are historical in origin. They arise at some definite time and place and often seem to be perpetuated by mere chance.

4. The responses are often correlated with one another. Head scratchers were an adjunct to huge headdresses in France, and to the menstruation rituals in Indian tribes. This is one characteristic which makes conventional behavior seem so important and indispensable to the person performing it. He cannot conceive of one action being changed without changing many others, too. Whether the whole conglomerate is essential to his life usually falls beyond the scope of his understanding.

5. The responses are powerful. They tend to remain as permanent features of the individual's equipment and to resist change or modification. Consequently, changes, when they do

*Quoted material is from John Bucklew, Jr., "Conceptions of Social Psychology," in N. H. Pronko and J. W. Bowles, Jr., *Empirical Foundations of Psychology* (New York: Rinehart, 1951).

come about, are usually accomplished in a protracted series of small steps. Resistance gives way to partial tolerance, and finally to acceptance.

6. The responses are nonrational. The person possessing them has not "thought them out" or compared them to any objective standards.

Social psychological behavior is an important item in the study of human behavior. This type of behavior can be encountered in any of the general categories of psychology, such as perceiving, feeling, reasoning, recalling, and so forth. Social psychology really cuts across the other branches of psychological science, and a proper orientation in it is essential to an adequate study of almost all other topics [pp. 126–127].

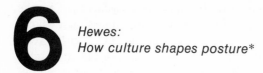

6 Hewes: How culture shapes posture*

An American crossing a street automatically looks to the left before stepping off the curb, and, again, before reaching the middle of the street, he looks to the right. The whole series of reactions occur in a mechanical fashion, certainly without forethought.

Let such an American go to Scotland, where the flow of traffic is reversed, and the anatomy of the reflexlike looking-while-crossing-the-street is laid bare. He becomes aware of what he took for granted for so many years, particularly if he barely escapes with his life from too close an encounter with a tram or automobile. Such near-fatal encounters happened to me on several occasions in Glasgow and impressed me with the lesson that my own automatic habitual acts could be worse than useless in another culture.

Our automatic behaviors—simple acts like crossing the street—are set by the culture in which we grow up and are appropriate to that culture. The same applies to gestures and postures, as the following excerpt from Hewes' article, "World Distribution of Certain Postural Habits," will show.

*Quoted material is from Gordon W. Hewes, "World Distribution of Certain Postural Habits." *American Anthropologist*, April 1955, **57**(2), 231–244.

Human postural habits have anatomical and physiological limitations, but there are a great many choices, the determinants for which appear to be mostly cultural. The number of significantly different body attitudes capable of being maintained steadily is probably on the order of one thousand. Certain postures may occur in all cultures without exception, and may form a part of our basic hominid heritage. The upright stance with arms at the sides, or with hands clasped in the midline over the lower abdomen, certainly belongs in this category. A fourth of mankind habitually squats in a fashion very similar to the squatting position of the chimpanzee, and the rest of us might squat this way, too, if we were not trained to use other postures beyond infancy. **Anthropoid** postures may shed some light on the problem of which human ones are most likely to be "natural" or precultural, although ape limb proportions would deter us from relying too heavily on such evidence.

Of factors which affect postures, aside from the biological substrata, we might start with sex-differentiating conditions, such as pregnancy and lactation, which possibly render certain sitting positions more frequent among adult females, and nutritional conditions (not wholly independent of culture), which may determine the amount of fat accumulated in posturally strategic parts of the body. Fear of genital exposure, whatever its etiology, seems to play an important role in postural customs (or at least in their rationale) in many cultures. Clothing and footgear, such as heavy boots and tight-fitting skirts, doubtless exert their effects on ways of sitting. Artificial supports—whether logs, rocks, stools, pillows, backrests, benches, or chairs—are highly significant, with complex histories and manifold cultural interconnections. There is also a relation of types of house construction to posture.

The influence of techniques and activities like textile weaving, fire making, wood carving, food grinding, playing of musical instruments, canoe paddling, or the use of gaming devices, all requiring the maintenance of particular bodily attitudes, cannot be denied. Nearly every new tool or machine must be adjusted to some body posture or sequence of postures. The push button represents the ultimate attenuation of environmental control through postural adjustments; vocal cord vibration to actuate servomechanisms, though still neuromuscular, cannot be described as postural.

Terrain and vegetation may influence out-of-door sitting or standing habits. In some regions the existence of high grass may force herdsmen to watch their flocks from a standing position, whereas in a short-grass or tundra region, herders may watch the stock while squatting or sitting down. In our own culture, moist, snowy, or muddy ground clearly inhibits sitting down, whereas a reasonably dry lawn may invite us to do so (Mauss, 1935, pp. 280, 286).

Habitual excretory or burial postures may become tabooed in other situations. It is altogether possible that the rarity of the deep squat in our culture is due to this kind of repression.

Finally, several writers suggest that infant-carrying customs may affect the postural maturational sequence, and the ease or difficulty with which children or adults can assume certain postures. If tight swaddling or cradling can influence later postural habits to anything like the degree that some authorities have claimed is the case with personality, the effects on sitting and standing behaviors should be indeed remarkable [Hewes, 1966, pp. 231–232].

"The human body or a reasonable facsimile thereof may be regarded as a mechanical system of movable parts with finite possibilities of angular displacement [Hewes, 1966, p. 108]." There are fourteen or more independently movable segments (p. 107) but, as Hewes pointed out above, culture has an invisible hand in fixing their combinations into patterns of movements.

Hewes' collection and classification of postures

Finding little data on posture in the literature, Hewes (1955) decided on a pioneering effort in this direction. He amassed a tremendous number of photographs from 480 different cultures or subcultures (p. 234) and classified them in much the same way as a botanist would a collection of plants or an entomologist an assemblage of insects. From a study of the postures in photographs, Hewes drew sketches of them and recorded information on the ethnic group of the person represented. From these data, he plotted the geographic distribution of postures on 13 world maps, two of which are reproduced in his (1955, p. 239) report. The postural typology is represented in part in Fig. 8.4. Let us consider it briefly.

Nilotic one-legged resting stance (Fig. 8.4: 23–25.5) This storklike manner of resting on one leg occurs in regions like the Sudan and is especially used by herders in regions where the grass is tall. It is not limited to such areas, however, for we learn (p. 237) that the men of the Walpi pueblo in Oregon assume this posture as a resting position while hoeing. Geographically, it occurs in scattered regions of the earth.

Chair-sitting postures (Fig. 8.4: 30–38) There are 11 common ways of sitting on chairs, 6 of which are sketched in Fig. 8.4. However, sitting on chairs is not universal but shows a scattered distribution over the world. It came late into Chinese culture and never quite displaced the custom of sitting on the floor, still common in Japan and Korea (p. 238).

Deep squatting postures (Fig. 8.4: 54, 58, 114) Squatting with the soles of the feet flat and the buttocks either actually resting on the ground or floor, or only an inch or two above it, has a very wide distribution except for European and Europe-derived cultures. Absence of

Figure 8.4 A sample of the world's postures. Some of the approximately 1000 different bodily postures into which culture molds the human form. The data are based on examination of photographs in ethnographic literature covering 480 different cultures or subcultures. (Reproduced by permission of the American Anthropological Association from Gordon W. Hewes, "World Distribution of Certain Postural Habits," *American Anthropologist*, April 1955, **57**(2), 231–244.)

reports of the deep squat from northern Asia probably can be attributed to the general weakness of my data on that area. The only European examples I found were ancient—on a Greek metal vessel and on a La Tene Iron Age vessel based on the same motif. Significantly, the squatting figure represented a daimonic individual playing a Pan's pipe, which suggests that the original Greek artist regarded the posture as uncouth or primitive. In the culture of the contemporary United States, the deep squatting posture is reliably reported to occur among males in the backward mountain communities of the southern Appalachians and the Ozarks.

In the world at large, women seldom use the deep squat, at least in public or in situations likely to be photographed. The role of taboos against female genital exposure in determination of acceptable or nonacceptable feminine postures is presumably important, but the evidence is slight. The deep squatting posture is, of course, a near-universal defecation position outside of a few Occidental cultures, and is often used when urinating, sometimes by one, sometimes by both sexes.

A posture resembling the squat, but in which the legs are only partly flexed (Fig. 8.4: 53,59, 59.6), has nearly worldwide distribution, again chiefly among males. It is frequently assumed by males (and by trousered females) in our own culture when the customary chairs or benches are unavailable [Hewes, 1955, p. 238].

Sitting with legs stretched out (Fig. 8.4: 70–72) A typically feminine posture, particularly among Melanesian women who may be resting in this position while their husbands may be sitting in a deep squat or with their legs partly flexed as in the sketch numbered 59.

Cross-legged or "tailor-fashion" (Fig. 8.4: 80–89.5) "Tailor-fashion" or "Turk fashion," with eight or nine different versions, has wide although not universal distribution. It occurs with highest frequency in India and Southeast Asia and rarely in Western culture.

The religious diffusion of some of the cross-legged postures from India with Hinduism and Buddhism seems to be unquestionable; thus in Japan one finds the *hanka-fuza* (Fig. 8.4: 83) and *kekka-fuza* (Fig. 8.4: 84) practically restricted to the Zen Buddhists. It is therefore of considerable interest to find the *hanka-fuza* position as a well-established Samoan custom—apparently uniquely in Polynesia. Sitting cross-legged so that the sole of one foot lies on the opposite thigh occurs in Samoa, Japan, Bali, Cambodia, Thailand, and in India—where it is one of the Yoga *asanas*.... Such postures seem to be quite unknown in western Eurasia, Africa, and the Americas [p. 240].

Kneeling on knees and feet or knees and heels (Fig. 8.4: 102–104.5) Sitting with the feet under the buttocks in a "deep kneel" can be commonly seen in any Moslem mosque. In Japan it is also the formal sitting posture for both sexes. I once

saw an elderly woman on a train in Japan eat her breakfast and go to sleep in a posture of "deep kneel." Three hours later she awakened and extricated herself from the position with the greatest of ease and without any creaking of joints.

The remaining postures sketched in Fig. 8.4 further illustrate how culture sculpts the jointed human into a variety of configurations. They seem as proper, right, and natural as breathing. It is not difficult to agree with Hewes' conclusion concerning the world distribution of postural habits.

In spite of the tentative nature of my information, I think there is good reason to believe that many postures are not only culturally determined, but will exhibit the kinds of geographic distributions we have come to expect for other features of cultural behavior [p. 241].

Summary

We started with a simple response—crossing the street—to show how culture interpenetrates every phase of behavior. We broadened our survey to include the variety of a thousand or so postures that man is capable of assuming. We noted a few and observed that the way a person sits, stands, rests, or lies is fashioned by the culture in which he lives from birth on. We also noted that particular configurations were diffused in the same way other cultural items were distributed. The Hewes study is of psychological importance in its implications for the **setting factors** that operate in a given individual's acquisition of behavior.

7 *The sacred cow of India*

Famine is no stranger to India. It is a recurrent theme throughout her history. Adequate crops are rare because of an exploding population, capricious rains, lack of irrigation, and dependence on primitive farming methods. It is difficult for an American or European to reconcile the widespread malnutrition and starvation he sees with the common scene of cows ambling freely about even in the most congested sections of the chief cities of India (see Fig. 8.5). Cows are everywhere, blocking traffic, dropping excrement, scrounging competitively with humans for scraps of garbage.

If a cow were to appear in the center of a busy city on any other continent, it would surely be removed. In India, however, the cow is considered sacred by the Hindu religion, which is the most prevalent in the land. The devout Hindu regards the cow as an object of veneration, with a special status far beyond the demands of the Hindu religious principle of *Ahimsa*, which unifies all living things. He accepts the cow's gift of life-sustaining milk and cheese and he depends on it for a beast of burden. However, he would never slaughter it or eat its flesh; this would not only be abhorrent but even sacrilegious. Accord-

Figure 8.5 Typical street scene in India's capital of New Delhi. Free-roaming cattle tie up traffic, but no one gets emotional about the common condition depicted here. (National Observer photograph by John F. Bridge.)

ing to Williamson and Payne (1959): "The ...Hindu would rather starve to death than eat his cow [p. 137]." As a result of his rearing, the whole cluster of attitudes, practices, and feelings connected with the Hindu's "Holy Cow complex" appears natural, normal, and proper to him.* For precisely the same reason—the way he was reared—the typical American finds the Hindu's attitude unbelievable. He considers the Hindu's reactions bizarre, irrational, ludicrous.

An American visiting India, may ask about the cow population and be told that there are anywhere from 85 to 250 million (Griffiths, 1967, p. 483) cows in India. At this point his capitalist mentality, stimulated by the underlying and correlative profit-making motive, will cause him to see, not cows but so many billions of hamburgers ambling about India in search of potential (and famished) Hindu customers. When he returns to reality, how can his own rearing permit him to see the situation other than as senseless and cruel? The sight of starving humans, including children, existing side by side with cows is a difficult one to accept.

Superficially at least, the Hindu's response to cows appears to Western eyes to be an inflexible, irrational, traditional institutionalization of a state of perpetual hunger or starvation in the presence of food!

Prior to the middle of the nineteenth century, the tomato was widely regarded as a curiosity and not as an *edible* object. Many people rejected it as food, not because of scientific tests, but merely

Figure 8.6 Malnutrition twists the limbs and dulls the skin of young famine victims of Bihar. (Photo by Alexander Low; reproduced by permission of *The Daily Telegraph* of London, England.)

---

*Miss Vijayalakshmi Shastri, a Hindu who read this article, asked a difficult question about George Washington's troops. While on a tour of Valley Forge, she was told that they starved during the severe winter of 1777-78. She wants to know: "Why didn't they eat their horses? That would have nourished them as it does people in various countries today." What would you say?

because they were *told* that it was poisonous. Of course, its social psychological status has been reversed since then; we now know it to be "an excellent source of vitamins A and C." The tomato's earlier status with humans offers a less dramatic example of unreasonable social behavior in contrast to the Hindu veneration of cows, with its apparently far more drastic results.

So far the consequences of India's institutionalization of the cow as a sacrosanct object seem to be entirely negative. For the benefit of the student of social behavior, we consider next an alternative interpretation, mindful of Whitehead's injunction: "Seek simplicity and distrust

Figure 8.7 The successful are untouched by famine. Scene from Benares showing a well-to-do business man. (Photo by Alexander Low; reproduced by permission of *The Daily Telegraph* of London, England.)

it [Woodger, 1929, p. 18]." One of the most fundamental of scientific rules, the principle of *parsimony,* recommends choosing the simpler of two competing interpretations for a given observation. It is possible that our attempt to follow the principle of parsimony may have led us astray in properly interpreting one of India's perennial problems.

Marvin Harris (1966) offers an alternative interpretation of India's sacred cattle. He starts with the premise that the theolog-

ical, irrational, exotic, and noneconomic aspects of Hindu behavior toward cattle have been "greatly overemphasized at the expense of rational, economic, and mundane interpretations [p. 51]." Instead, he suggests seeking the explanations in what may have evolved as "adaptive processes of the **ecological** system of which they are a part, rather than in the influence of Hindu **theology** [p. 51]." Furthermore, he considers that the interrelated customs, taboos, and rituals may serve some "positive functions"; that is, they may have some beneficial consequences. His main arguments, presented as briefly as possible, follow:

Milk production While milk production is a minor aspect of the Indian cow's economic contribution to the economic system, nevertheless almost 50 percent of the country's dairy products comes from cow's milk (p. 53). This bovine contribution should not be overlooked.

Cows as tractors When one considers that 80 percent of human caloric intake comes from grain crops and that the cow serves in the capacity of a tractor, here is another "positive function" served by the sacred cow. In fact, instead of the alleged excess of cows, we learn of the scarcity of draft animals, which even borrowing and lending cannot solve because of the short period for plowing in relation to the critical rains (p. 53). The cow is important in contributing the bullock as a tractor substitute.

Dung The chief source of domestic cooking fuel comes from cow dung. The BTU equivalent of dung consumed for the baking or boiling of grain crops is the equivalent of "35,000,000 tons of coal or 68,000,000 tons of wood"! Should one rashly suggest replacing plow animals with tractors, where will oil for the tractors come from, much less oil for cooking fuel? As long as cows are available, the Indians need only wait and gather their fuel on top of the ground. In addition to its usefulness as fuel, 340,000,000 tons of dung enters the ecological energy system as manure (p. 54), giving the cow an important place in India's economy as a cheap source of precious fertilizer.

Beef and hides India's population includes 55 million non-Hindus (Untouchables and outsiders) and several million Moslems and Christians, many of whom will eat beef if they get a chance. The chance does come because 25 million cattle die naturally or otherwise. "Indeed, could it be that without the Orthodox Hindu beef-eating taboo, many marginal and depressed castes would be deprived of an occasional, but nutritionally critical, source of animal protein [p. 54]?" In addition, the slaughter taboo does not interfere with "India's huge leather industry — the world's largest . . . [p. 54]."

Harris' analysis includes other important points, but the foregoing are sufficient to show that the cow in India is a multipurpose animal. It provides proteins in the form of dairy products to the higher classes and carrion beef to the lowest classes, constituting an efficient and comprehensive distribution system that provides benefits to a great number of people. Furthermore, we should mention in addition to the use of bullocks for plowing, dung for cooking fuel and fertilizer, and hides as raw material for the leather industry, that cows scrounge for their food in the fodder and other agricultural by-products of no use to man. Thus, instead of competing with man, the cow maintains a **symbiotic** or mutually advantageous relationship with man.

The crucial point here concerns the complexity of social forms of behavior, particularly their origin and manner of functioning, and the extreme caution required in understanding and interpreting them.

In China mothers once bound their daughters' feet because tiny (deformed) feet in young women had a high social premium placed on them. Such feet were erotically pleasing and a distinct advantage in the girl's competition for a husband. It is logical to place a starving Hindu's repugnance to the sight and smell of roast beef under the same category of the shared response. An individual born into either group behaves unquestionably like the other members of his group, and his behavior (to him, at least) seems natural. Consider the common stimulus value that various groups attach to the following stimulus objects: a crucifix, a Star of David, a national flag, the latest dance, the newest hairstyle, a Pope, a President of the United States, a *Playboy* bunny.

Itani:
Culture among monkeys* **8**

A vacation in Europe with its many small countries vividly illustrates the abrupt changes in patterns of language, dress,

Quoted material is from Junichiro Itani, "The Society of Japanese Monkeys," *Japan Quarterly,* 1961, **8(4).

manners, diet, religion, and political and economic conditions in different human groups.

In Chapter 5 we discussed the work of the young ethologists in regard to "instincts." Even in that discussion it was impossible to ignore the force of tradition in the use of tools, diet, etc., in different animals. Here we look for responses among Japanese monkeys that are distinctive enough to set groups apart on a psychological rather than anatomical basis. We might anticipate dietary preferences, vocal utterances, gestures, or rituals. The criterion that must be met in our examination is that a particular behavior be widespread in a given group, X, and that it distinguish Group X from Group Y. A comparable case would be stopping at the Italian Customs and being confronted with a language, dress, and so on differing from what one had just left behind in Yugoslavia. We start by inspecting Japanese monkeys via the research of Junichiro Itani of the Japan Monkey Center of Kyoto University.

Dr. Itani tells a discouraging story of the early days (in Japan in 1950) of the Primates Research Group, which was created to study monkeys native to Japan. For 2 years Itani and his co-workers ranged over pathless mountains with little success, for the monkeys scattered at the first sight of their human investigators. Then Itani and his group decided to set out sweet potatoes and barley (the technical term is **provisioning**), which provided the breakthrough. The monkeys' greed for food eventually overrode their fear and suspicion of humans. Moreover, because they experienced no harm at the hands of humans, the monkeys soon ignored them. In time the free lunch counters were reduced to one. Now, instead of running through dense forests to get a passing glimpse of a monkey, the Primates Research Group could look continuously, with unobstructed view, at a whole family, group, or population. We continue with Itani's report on several aspects of their social behavior.

Paternal care

An example of a troop activity to be seen in the Takasaki-yama troop is "paternal care."

The society of Japanese monkeys has mothers but no fathers. During the breeding season, which lasts for 3 or 4 months in the winter, pairs of monkeys, one male and one female, are to be seen at many points in the troop. However, these relationships, known as "consort relationships," last for about a week at the most, and when they break up both the male and the female seek new partners. Since this kind of relationship between the sexes is only known during the breeding season, the babies that are born have no recognized father. Despite this, the adult males show a type of behavior exactly identical with that of the mother to her own child, and it is this that is known as "paternal care."

This behavior is observable only during the delivery season from May into August, and it is only the elite of the troop's males, from the leader class and subleader class, who look after the young monkeys instead of their mothers. The infants who are thus looked after are all either 1 or 2 years of age: Up to 1 year the males and females are lumped together, but on reaching the age of 2 the males gradually go out from the center to the periphery, which means that females are more numerous than males among infants of 2 [years] receiving protection. It is the infants of 1 year, however, who are the chief objects of such care, most of them children whose mothers cannot look after them because they are bearing or rearing their next offspring.

Paternal care is characteristic only of the troops at Takasaki-yama and at Takahaski in Okayama Prefecture. This way of behaving, then, sets these two groups apart from the other monkey populations of Japan.

Dietary preferences

Paternal care is not the only difference of custom existing between troop and troop. Our studies of the kind of food eaten by different troops have revealed all kinds of variations. The monkeys of Takasaki-yama are very fond of the fruit of the *muku (Aphananthe aspera)* tree; the hard stone inside they either throw away or swallow whole to be excreted later. The monkeys on Arashiyama, however, break the stone with their teeth and eat the albuminous matter inside. The monkeys at Mino'o dig up the roots of the yam to eat, and also eat snails. The monkeys at Taishaku-kyo eat the bark of pine trees. Monkeys on Mount Ryozen in the Suzuka range are known to catch and eat the flesh of hares while the snow is on the ground in the winter. Some of the monkeys in troops living on the coasts of Wakasa and two or three other places eat shellfish. These are all habits which cannot ordinarily be observed in other troops.

Thus one troop will eat things which other troops will not. This means that Japanese monkeys do not simply eat anything that seems likely as food but that the troop has its own fixed ideas of what is edible and what [is] inedible. Obviously these ideas are handed down within the troop. Such behavior and customs are referred to as **"protoculture."** Other characteristics besides food habits that are looked on as cultural phenomena include sexual behavior and social organization.

Finger bowls and sweet potatoes

At some time in the past someone originated the custom of a finger bowl after dinner, a practical custom for people who eat with their fingers. The tradition survived among the upper classes, and people continue the ritual of dipping their fingers into the bowls even when their hands are perfectly clean. This is the proper point at

Figure 8.8 Japanese monkey running to the shore to wash its sweet potatoes. Note how fully occupied arms exact bipedal locomotion. Other monkeys shown in repast presumably after washing their sweet potatoes. (Photo by Mr. Sugio Hayama, Laboratory of Physical Anthropology, Kyoto University, Kyoto, Japan.)

which to introduce the story of how the custom of washing sweet potatoes was started and perpetuated in the Ko-shima troop of Japanese monkeys.

In 1953 a young female in the Ko-shima troop began to wash in the sea the potatoes that we set out on the beach. Little by little the habit spread to other monkeys in the troop, until today a full two-thirds of all the individuals in the group invariably wash their potatoes before eating them, and the practice is more or less completely established as an element in the troop's cultural life. The washing of the sweet potatoes spread gradually, to the first young female's playmates, to her brothers and sisters, then to their particularly intimate associates.

The origin and spread
of caramel eating

We once experimented to see how the habit of eating caramels — an entirely unfamiliar food — would spread among the Takasaki-yama troop. The trial, conducted over a period of more than one year with one hundred individuals whom we recognized by sight, produced the following conclusions: Infants under 3 were extremely positive in their attitude toward new things and were quick to start eating the caramels. The acquisition rate dropped considerably with age, however, and elderly individuals proved most conservative of all. As in the case of washing the sweet potatoes, the habit spread from the individual to those particularly close to him. The acquisition rate of female monkeys with infants thus was quicker than that of adult males, while that of leaders and subleaders who practiced paternal care was quicker than that of the peripheral males who did not. The channels for the spread of new cultural elements which were thus revealed were probably also followed in the first place by the old-established elements, being transmitted from senior to junior members of the troop.

However, this spreading and handing down of customs is a completely one-sided form of communication. The individual learns by observing another individual, with whom it has an extremely close relationship, performing some unfamiliar action. The latter never tells him "This tastes good," or "You should try this," or "The sand comes off if you wash it."

The incest taboo

We intend to pursue our studies of the Japanese monkey still further yet. We are hoping, for example, that provisionization will yield many further harvests. This is obviously a heresy viewed in the light of natural history's traditional prohibition against disturbing the objects of study in any way. How otherwise, though, could we have peered into the innermost workings of their society? With a number of troops, we have worked out blood relationships between the members, and are carrying out research on this basis. Using such methods of study, we have so far observed no instances of sexual relationships between mother and son; discoveries such as this are undoubtedly of the greatest importance in considering the evolution of our own human society.

Summary

Studies of Japanese monkeys show that various isolated groups are distinguished from other isolated groups through shared behavior. One group practices what we might call baby sitting, but a closely adjacent group does not. Dietary preferences characterize different groups as they do various national or religious human groups. Whether monkey or human, the organism born into a given group comes to behave like other members of that group. It would be interesting to study what would happen among their monkey friends, relatives, and neighbors if a few monkey leaders could be persuaded to use finger bowls — were they made accessible. We can only speculate, but we need not speculate about the presence and transmission of shared reactions. They are quite real.

Students frequently ask: If man and the apes are so closely related biologically, why has man alone developed culture? Why haven't the apes also shown some degree of cultural evolution? Difficult as these questions are to answer, Dr. Adriaan Kortlandt of the University of Amsterdam has a hypothesis to offer after long years of study of chimpanzees.

In its simplest terms, Kortlandt's (1967) "dehumanization hypothesis" states that around the pre-Glacial and Glacial periods, the ancestors of today's African apes lived chiefly in semiopen woodlands and savannas that favored primitive humanlike forms of behavior, such as walking on two feet, social cooperation, a semicarnivorous diet, and the use of crude weapons against natural enemies. According to a second assumption of Kortlandt's hypothesis, when manlike creatures appeared on the scene with spears that could kill at a distance, the apes were forced to withdraw and to live in the more protective woods. Here they largely lost the semihuman characteristics that they had gained in the grassland regions.

In order to test his hypothesis, Kortlandt and some associates traveled throughout Africa to find forested and savanna regions in order to compare the behavior of the apes in both. His team found an ideal spot to test his hypothesis in Guinea. They discovered an area with many open plains where chimpanzees in large numbers had dared to emerge from the small forests along streams to repopulate the savannas once more. Why? Because the natives were

Muslims, whose religion prohibited them from eating chimpanzees.

Realizing their opportunity for experimentation, Kortlandt's team designed a stuffed leopard (the chimp's natural enemy) whose mechanism had a device that moved the head and tail in imitation of a live animal. Camera crew and observers hid in the bush and waited until the chimps came into view; then they animated the mechanical leopard. Their records and motion pictures revealed the following.

The savanna-dwelling chimpanzees versus the forest dwellers

In a single trial the wild chimps of the savanna attacked the leopard

many times by means of heavy sticks up to 2.10 meters [about 7 feet] which attained hitting speeds up to 90 kmh [approximately 50 to 60 miles per hour], and by prods, blows, and kicks with the hands and feet. Eventually the remnants of the leopard were dragged away into the bush. On the other hand, in none of the nine trials conducted with forest-dwelling chimpanzees was the beast of prey ever hit by a potential weapon, and only once it received a prod with a bare fist.

When Kortlandt and his team compared the motor pattern of attack shown by the savanna chimps with similar fighting techniques shown by humans using clubs, they found a remarkable resemblance. Not so with different subspecies of forest dwellers both in Guinea and in the Congo. Only aborted remnant responses occurred; the latter were simply ineffective in handling clubs as weapons of attack. On two occasions a forest-dwelling ape tore off a large tree branch, stripped it of leaves, and casually dropped it just in front of the leopard.

Another difference between the two groups of chimpanzees showed a more cooperative group attack by the savanna subjects than by the forest dwellers. Also, in support of Kortlandt's hypothesis, the former "behaved much more **bipedally**" than the latter.

The Kortlandt group interprets the results as indicating that the savanna chimps show "a form of true armed fighting with real weapons, intended and effective enough to disable their predators, whereas in forest-dwelling chimpanzees, it is essentially a form of mobbing with intimidation tools intended to harass the enemy out of the area."

In one of the forest experiments a team member, Jo van Orshoven, began to charge at the leopard in the chimp way, emitting chimp calls. The apes came nearer, very soon "some sort of vocal communication could be established," and after half an hour the apes lost their shyness of man.

Conclusions

From this and other evidence, Kortlandt and van Zon conclude that "a forest habitat 'dehumanizes,' and that a savanna habitat 'humanizes' chimpanzee behavior." In addition to the study reported above, Kortlandt uses evidence from observations made on zoo animals and from field studies. In another paper (1967), he refers to Jane Goodall's observations of the occasional killing and meat eating by her chimpanzee subjects in a savanna in Tanzania as confirming his hypothesis. The implication seems to be that, although vegetarians because of their present habitat, the chimpan-

zees have an evolutionary hangover derived from their savanna ancestors that drives them, as it were, to kill and eat meat if necessary.

An alternative interpretation

Although I do not intend to pursue the matter to its end, I suggest a simpler interpretation than Kortlandt's evolutionary hypothesis. Surely it will be readily granted that behavior is not independent of the organism's surroundings. Environmental surroundings facilitate or deny opportunities for individual and/or group behavior development. If man becomes a threat to savanna-dwelling chimps, they retreat into a forest where they learn to survive by simply reaching for shoots, fruit, and leaves of plants found there. However, if they no longer fear man because man's religion forbids him to harm or kill apes, then the apes in question will venture forth into the new (i.e., savanna) environment. A cultural transmission of fearlessness is made possible. The open spaces, lack of abundant vegetation, and presence of a different animal life thus provide opportunities for developing new tastes, skills in provisioning of food, bipedal walking, defense, and attack. Even the banding together is more natural in the open grasslands than in the easily obscuring, dense forests. The chimp's development of behaviors in the savanna and their cultural transmission are no more than an accident of the conditions provided by the savannas. The "humanization" that Kortlandt sees may be simply a coincidence of similar patterns of behavior between the human and ape species. For example, absence of thick forests also means absence of swinging from tree to tree and, therefore, a greater resemblance between the chimp and the nonswinging human. Successive generations of chimps and humans acquire whatever behavior patterns are available. The alternative suggested here would seem to be more parsimonious than Kortlandt's hypothesis.

One final point concerns the question raised at the beginning of this article—namely, why haven't the apes developed a culture? Part of the answer would appear to lie in the condition which Jane Goodall (1967) pointed out in her observations of chimpanzees, that is, their nomadic life. A constant change of population from day to day is hardly conducive to the initiation, stabilization, and accumulation of ways of behaving. Instead, their highly transient state would facilitate a simple society geared closely to nourishment, rest, reproduction, and security from the common enemy.

Summary

This section considered the question of why apes have not acquired a culture.

In an attempt to find an answer, we discussed Kortlandt's "dehumanization hypothesis" as applied to the African chimpanzee. According to it, when the savanna-dwelling apes were threatened by man, they retreated to the forests and lost their ability to band together for the purpose of killing their predators or other animals for food. They also lost other human characteristics. Recently, with man no longer a threat, at least in Muslim Guinea, the chimps have emerged and become "humanized" again. A simpler, alternative suggestion is proposed: the ape's failure to build a complex culture is explained partly by the transient unit groups and their respective behaviors and partly by the condition of easy subsistence and absence of language. The fact that a protoculture among apes exists and is passed on to successive generations is beyond doubt.

Marler and Tamura: Culturally transmitted patterns of vocal behavior in sparrows

10

One song sparrow sounds like any other song sparrow or so it seems. Yet modern research shows the error in lumping seemingly similar things together too readily. Patient analysis shows that it is possible to note differences that did not seem to be there prior to analysis. As the following discussion will show, different populations of song sparrows show distinctive variation in their song. In fact, we are going to compare the similarities of song in a given population with that of another population but of the same species. The data derive from some striking field and laboratory studies by Peter Marler and Miwako Tamura (1962, 1964), which show that

sparrows have "dialects" in their song just as humans have in their speech. A Bostonian, a Texan, and a Kansan show easily identifiable speech habits—so do sparrows. Furthermore, both kinds of "dialects" seem to be transmitted from one generation to the next.

Song "dialects" in three populations of sparrows

Marler and Tamura (1962) were attracted to the study of the white-crowned sparrow (*Zonotrichia leucophrys*) because for a long time investigators had noted and commented upon its variation of "dialect" in different geographical regions. They selected the three following study areas in California: (1) Sunset Beach State Park (about 100 miles south of Berkeley), (2) the central part of the city of Berkeley and (3) an area 2 miles northeast of the center of Berkeley. They recorded bird songs on a tape recorder, played the recordings on a Sonagraph, and made measurements on the resulting **sonagrams.** (A later but similar study is depicted in Figure 8.9.)

The Sunset Beach population

Sonagrams from birds recorded at Sunset Beach and reproduced in Marler and Tamura's (1962) study "reveal a relatively homogeneous sample [p. 371]." The songs of their 18 subjects as represented physically in the sonagrams show a remarkable similarity.

It would be interesting to know how stable the Sunset Beach "dialect" is. The idea occurred to Marler and Tamura and so they returned to the same area one year later. They found a striking correspondence with very little statistical variation from the figures of the previous year for song duration, number of notes and syllables, and maximum and minimum frequencies. Their "conclusion is that the song characteristics are stable within this population over a period of 2 years [p. 373]." The sonagrams of the birds of the repeat study (p. 372) are indistinguishable from those of the earlier one. Apparently young birds adopt the prevailing patterns of the population in which they live.

The Berkeley population

In an overall way, the species resemblances between the Berkeley and Sunset Beach populations were apparent, but even qualitative inspection of the sonagrams showed that "there are striking differences between the two populations in the structure of the syllables which make up the trill [p. 373]." Marler and Tamura conclude that while in some respects the two populations have certain common features in their respective songs, "nevertheless those differences which exist are unambiguous and consistent, so that the home locality of a single bird chosen at random could be accurately assigned on the basis of its song pattern [p. 373]." Only 2 miles apart and already distinguishing dialectal differences appear! The finding is reminiscent of what one hears in going from Brooklyn to Manhattan or from Piccadilly to the Cockney district of London. Note the radical nationalistic differences to be observed in passing through the small countries of Eastern and Northern Europe.

The Inspiration Point population

Similar findings obtained for the third population, (1) a homogeneous sample, (2) similar in most respects with the other two. However, in their possession of more syllables and phrases per song than the Sunset Beach population, they show a closer resemblance to their Berkeley neighbors. And why not? In going from Elizabeth to Plainfield in New Jersey, one should not expect to hear radical language differences in the human populations involved. Neither should we expect large dialectal differences between the Sunset Beach and Berkeley sparrow populations, for they are only 2 miles apart. Yet dialectal differences between the adjacent populations are apparent in their respective sona-

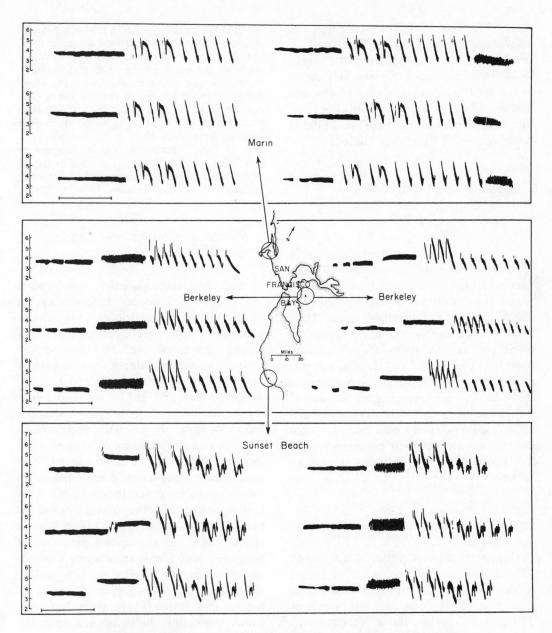

Figure 8.9 "Dialectal" map of California White-Crowned Sparrow's song. Three populations, two of them only several miles apart and one about 100 miles distant (Sunset Beach) are represented by distinct "dialects" in the sonagrams reproduced above. Even nearby populations showed distinguishing features in their song and stability over the two-year interval during which they were studied. (From Peter Marler and Miwako Tamura "Culturally Transmitted Patterns of Vocal Behavior in Sparrows," *Science,* 11 December 1964, **146**(3650), 1483–1486. Copyright 1964 by the American Association for the Advancement of Science.)

grams (Fig. 4, p. 374). The similarities and differences in the songs of three populations of white-crowned sparrows from three localities in the San Francisco Bay Area, as reported in a later study by Marler and Tamura (1964), are apparent in Fig. 8.9. The results represented there are a kind of corroboration of the earlier findings.

Effects of rearing experiences of fledglings captured from different populations

If one were to capture young male sparrows from populations with different "dialects" and raise them together, what would the results be? This is a question that Marler and Tamura (1964) asked. They found it to be a relative one. It depends on when you capture them. If you capture them between 30 and 100 days of age and raise them in pairs, their songs manifest the "dialect" of their parents. However, if they are taken at 3 to 14 days of age and all are raised together under one roof, then they do not sing as their parents sang. In fact, "some birds from different areas have strikingly similar patterns [p. 1483]."

Effect of differential training

One group of birds, captured at between 30 and 100 days of age, were subjected to different auditory training, which was started at 100 days of age with some, at 200 days with others, and at 300 days with still others. Only training begun at 100 days of age had any effect on the adult song. Apparently the earlier the training, the better the results. The following quotation would tend to support this proposition.

Two males were placed in individual isolation at 5 and 10 days of age, respectively, and were exposed alternately to the songs of a normal white-crowned sparrow and a bird of a different species. One male was exposed at 6 to 28 days, the other at 35 to 56 days. Both developed fair copies of the training song which was the home dialect for one and alien dialect for the other. Although the rendering of the training song is not perfect, it establishes that the dialect patterns of the male song develop through learning from older birds in the first month or two of life. Experiments are in progress to determine whether longer training periods are necessary for perfect copying of the training pattern [Marler and Tamura, 1964, p. 1484.].

Individual differences among sparrows

With their **anthropocentric bias,** humans are prone to consider individuality an exclusively human attribute. Yet several years ago Marler (1960) proved that songs among sparrows can be idiosyncratic enough to plainly identify an individual bird (p. 354). He made a dissection of the songs of some 70 individuals and found that "no two of them were identical [pp. 354–359]." Is this not comparable to the idiosyncratic signature of humans, even though all write in the same language? In fact, some of the more contrasting songs "were so different that it was at first difficult to believe that they came from members of the same species [p. 359]." Even in species that are considered monotonous songsters, individuals show some variability from time to time. However, just as we accept the variation in the pitch of human speech that distinguishes Britishers from Americans, birds appear to make population identifications despite variations among individuals of particular groups.

One would think that individual variation would obliterate the species character of the sparrow's song. However, the fact that Marler and his co-workers could usually recognize the species of the most varied singers suggests that the birds themselves are at least as discriminating (p. 361). In fact, each bird's departure from the species' patterns is more like a variation on a theme. It might be compared with a human individual's signature or calling card. His song pattern serves as his calling card when he utters it and as a call for him when uttered by someone else, especially if that someone is out of sight. Such sparrow communications depend on a phenomenon called antiphonal singing.

Thorpe and North: Antiphonal singing in birds* 11

The term *antiphonal singing* refers to a type of church music in which the priest and choir (or congregation) respond alternately and serially to each other's chant. However, the term is also used to refer to a type of singing evolved by birds in intimate relation with each other as, for example, bird mates. Thorpe and North (1965), among others, have discovered antiphonal singing in birds, both in the field and in the laboratory.

It is common for humans to admire the split-second timing demanded by Beethoven's Ninth or Choral Symphony. The choir, singer, and instrumentalist must each fit his brief contribution in the instant required or the whole pattern is ruined. Still, it is hard to believe that birds could achieve equal complexity and critical timing in the duets and trios that contemporary research shows them capable of performing. For several years Thorpe and North (1965) and others have studied antiphonal singing in a number of species. They have discovered that the female can respond to the male within 150 milliseconds (about 1/7) of a second.

Duets and trios among the boubou shrike

For some years Thorpe and North (1965) have been studying the tropical boubou shrike *(Laniarius aethiopicus)*, both in the field in Kenya and Uganda and in the laboratory at Cambridge University. Their results show that the male and the female each have an extensive tonal repertoire with which, in time, they evolve a series of duet patterns. If one bird is out of sight, they can nevertheless recognize each other if the second bird chimes in appropriately at the exact instant demanded by the duet pattern.

Some essential steps

While solitary practice is involved during the bird's maturational period, "the duet is worked out during a long practice period (probably of many months) between two birds in their territory [pp. 220–221]." The timing, phrasing, and pitch of the duet can be performed with precision after such extensive rehearsal. Several other interesting findings are as follows: (1) Either sex can start the pattern and the other complete it. (2) If the partner is absent, the single bird can do the duet alone, carrying out the other's role flawlessly. (3) Should the partner return, they can carry on *dupli-*

---

*Quoted material is from W. H. Thorpe and Myles E. W. North, "Vocal Imitation in the Tropical Boubou Shrike Laniarius Aethiopicus Major as a Means of Establishing and Maintaining Social Bonds," *Ibis*, 1966, **108**, 432–435.

cating the duet "in perfect time [p. 221]" or, which is more common, singing antiphonally again. Apparently during the learning sessions each bird learns the role of its partner and the relation of both roles to the pattern of the whole. Thorpe and North (1965) have analyzed the songs of their subjects by means of sound **spectrographs,** but with the boubou shrike the tones have been found pure enough to be recordable in musical notation. The complexity and precision of timing demanded can be seen in Fig. 8.10

Variability in patterns

So far Thorpe and North (1965) have recorded 135 different patterns of duet for the *major* race of the boubou shrike (p. 222). They speculate whether certain races show more flexibility and variability in their tonal repertoires or whether the finding is related to the fact that "this is the race which it has so far been possible to examine most intensely [p. 222]." Another variation that has been noted involves a third party, or a trio. A third bird has been observed to make his contribution with the same precision and timing as the other two. Although the meaning of the trio is not clear, the essential function of antiphonal singing seems to be a cohesive one, one that permits the establishment and perpetuation of the pair bond. The fact that either bird of a given pair can sing his role *or both* serves as a compelling signal to summon the missing partner. When one thinks about it, the specificity involved is no different from that implicated in the family dog or cat "answering to his name." The difference is that we are accustomed to think this way about cats and dogs but not about birds.

Figure 8.10 Seventeen different chaffinch duet patterns. *L. aethiopicus,* Reed Inlet, Lake Nakuru, Kenya, 5 September 1963. The separate figures (a) to (q) show the seventeen different duet patterns produced by a single pair of *L. ae. major* during the course of a single day. The last four patterns were transcribed in notation (see Myles North, 1950). All the rest were recorded directly on tape. All were presumed to be duets, but the distribution of the parts between "x" and "y" is only inserted where the evidence is clear. The expression "chatter scold" denotes a characteristic harsh pulsed sound of wide frequency distribution. The term "snarl" is expressive of a common note, not markedly pulsed, but with the energy, though widely spread, showing a peak at the frequency indicated by the wavy line. (From W. H. Thorpe, and Myles E. W. North, "Origin and Significance of the Power of Vocal Imitation: With Special Reference to the Antiphonal Singing of Birds," *Nature,* 16 October 1965, **208**(5007), 219–222. Photo courtesy of Dr. W. H. Thorpe.)

An observation of the evolution of antiphonal singing in the laboratory

In the summer of 1965 one of us (W. H. T.) had, in one of the tropical aviaries, two hand-reared boubou shrikes. The first bird ringed "W" (for "white") had been hand-reared by Mrs. Avril Royston in the spring of 1964 at Sotik in Kenya and sent to us on 15 July 1964. During the following 12 months it had not developed its vocalizations very notably, although the two single notes that it was in the habit of producing were fully mature in tonal quality. On 10 December 1964 another bird (ringed "M" for "mauve," a female) also reared in the same way and the same place, was received from Kenya. This bird, being somewhat delicate, was kept for the greater part of the time in a separate cage indoors in the laboratory at room temperature. During this period its voice developed somewhat and it was in the habit of producing, in addition to its single notes, a series of four notes, still rather juvenile and of quavering pitch. On 8 July 1965 this bird was transferred to the **aviary** in which W was established, and in the course of the subsequent month, W and M together had developed a simple antiphonal song—beginning with one or two single notes from W followed immediately by the juvenile four-note performance of M. During this period these birds were constantly recorded and W was never heard to give anything but its normal one or two notes. On 10 August 1965 M died suddenly from an obscure infection. Immediately W started to behave in a very agitated manner, searching continually around the aviary as if looking for its lost companion, all the while uttering the full duet pattern; namely, its own introductory note followed by four—or more often five—quavering juvenile notes characteristic of its former companion. The bird continued to behave in this remarkable way for some days, but the frequency of production of the combined duet pattern gradually declined and it was not heard much after 20 August. On 24 August it was given another shrike as a companion, but since then little in the way of song has developed, for the period of declining day length of the English autumn, even though supplemented by artificial light, does not appear to be favourable for the vocalizations of these tropical birds in their aviaries.

We submit, then, that this result constitutes an unexpectedly dramatic confirmation of the view that one of the major functions of the imitative ability of birds is to establish and strengthen the social bonding [pp. 434–435].

The talking birds

Imitation or at least the acquisition of the prevailing pattern in a given population has been demonstrated in both the field and laboratory studies of bird songs considered up to this point. What of the "true" talking birds, such as the parrots and mynah birds? The flexibility that they show is impressive. No matter where they are shipped, they manage to learn to speak phrases in the language of the host country and with an "accent" indistinguishable from that of the native of that country.

Thorpe and North (1965) note how the parrot and the mynah "can imitate not only human speech to astounding perfection but also a seemingly endless variety of other noises [p. 219]." Horns, bells, squeaking doors, musical tones, sneezes, clicks, and whistles have been reproduced with dazzling virtuosity over a range far surpassing any human accomplishment. However, as Thorpe and North point out, this extreme imitative ability looks much like a "preadaptive" evolutionary mechanism but one "which conditions of life in the wild never require of it...since it appears not to be used at all except under conditions of domestication" (p. 219). While the phenomenon is not yet clearly understood, it does seem to fit into the general pattern of antiphonal singing as we have discussed it. It seems to be most highly developed in the Tropics and gives extra scope to the specificity demanded under the conditions of dense growth of the jungle for "social recognition and cohesion [p. 219]."

Summary

Contemporary research shows an interesting feature of bird song; namely, that it differs from population to population to such a degree that a given bird's song pattern will identify the specific group with which he was reared. "Dialects" of a species' song are as characteristic as they are for the speech of humans reared in different human populations. Training experiments and consideration of the "true" talking birds, such as the parrot and the mynah, illustrate the flexibility and the wide range of *potentiality* in this as in many other areas of psychological research.

Within a given population of sparrows, instead of a monotonous sameness in the song, research shows the same law of individual differences that applies to human personality. The specificity is especially marked in the intimate development of antiphonal singing among bird pairs, which serves the function of social recognition and cohesion as shown by laboratory as well as field observations. So with birds, at least with respect to their singing, we find the presence of shared reactions and idiosyncratic responses.

Chapter summary

The present chapter considered the psychological effect of group living on the behavior of the individual, human or animal. Focusing on the behaviors that individuals had in common, we found them to be distributed to specific groups. Foot-binding here, institutionalized starvation there, and dress, posture, and gesture everywhere. Turning our attention to apes, we found the same process of introduction, diffusion, and transmission of cultural traits as we did among humans. Even the lowly song sparrows show dialectal differences that characterize human language groups. Not only that, but individualistic or idiosyncratic responses are prevalent also. What a wealth of knowledge recent research has uncovered! The outmoded instinct doctrine with its self-actional, internal "springs-to-action" approach had the same opportunity for interpretation or theory construction of an alternative sort except for a view that made it blind to the very same facts. New theories provide new perspectives.

9

9

Personality

The selections in the present chapter fall naturally into three main areas: defining **personality,** applying learning principles to personality development, and measuring and evaluating personality. We shall also consider a discussion of drug addiction and personality.

First we turn to the central problem of definition. In daily gossip, as well as in more objective discussion of people, the layman is constantly involved in evaluating and understanding the personality of friends, relatives, colleagues, and so on. The term personality baffles many people. It is often a vague and mystical business. Sometimes it is thought of as a general but elusive quality, such as charm or magnetism, or as something that is not an individual's thoughts, actions, or feelings but that somehow affects his thoughts, actions, or feelings. Obviously such a concept does little to help in understanding personality. As an alternative, we shall consider a formulation by Mahan (1968), a formulation based on the objective approach of J. R. Kantor discussed earlier. We shall then note the fluidity and complexity of personality in a brief excerpt by the great American psychologist, William James.

The second group of articles in this chapter deal with learning principles as applied to normal and abnormal personality development. The first of these articles shows how behavior in normal children can be shaped through imitation. The topic is relevant to the prevalent habit of American children—watching television. With preschoolers reportedly putting in 56 hours a week in front of the TV screen, there has been some justifiable concern about the effect of the content of television programs on children's personality. A second article describes operant conditioning principles applied in the treatment of seriously disturbed children. The procedures used are as striking as the results. The third article focuses on factors that reinforce chronic psychopathology and offers a guideline on how to make mental patients perpetual patients.

How to measure and evaluate personality constitutes the third area of our concern. Opinions vary. "Doctors disagree" on the best way to assess individual differences. However, the problems involved are presented in a nontechnical fashion by a prominent **psychometrician.**

There are many hearsay reports about the personality effects of **LSD,** pot, and other drugs. Because of contemporary interest in the problem of drug addiction, a survey article of the topic is included at the end of the chapter.

Mahan: Personality from the standpoint of scientific psychology*

1

What...is personality from the standpoint of scientific psychology? The answer is that we cannot consider personality to be anything other than the individual's system of inter-

*Quoted material is from Harry C. Mahan, *The Interactional Psychology of J. R. Kantor: An Introduction* (San Marcos, California: Project Socrates Press, 1968). By permission of the author.

actions with particular stimulating objects, persons, situations, and events. This set of interactions we may refer to as the repertoire of behavior equipment of the individual. What we are referring to here are the actual response patterns which the individual shows when he is in contact with particular items in his surroundings. For example, each person has his own repertoire of knowledge and skill reactions, which are presumably at his command when he cares to use them.

It is variations in behavior equipment which result in the principle of individual differences in psychology, and the first characteristic of personality is that every person is unique. Such differences apply to virtually every trait of personality, and when the many traits of an individual are brought together in his makeup, the differences from person to person are very great indeed. Such differences prevail with respect to every kind of knowledge, to skills, to talents, to attitudes, and to all of the other traits which make the person what he is. It is a question of whether individuals possess, in their storehouse of behavior equipment, the appropriate reaction systems for responding to the demands of potential stimulating situations. The essential fact here is that all of the knowledge, skills, capacities, and abilities that we have constitute specific forms of reaction systems to particular stimuli. These reaction systems are integrated into even broader patterns of activity, which, together with their coordinated stimulating situations, constitute the adaptive interactions of the individual. Personality, then, from the psychological standpoint, may be summed up as being the totality of a particular individual's reaction systems; in short, everything that the person does or can do. No phase of the individual's behavioral equipment can be omitted; his entire repertoire must be included. This brings us to a second characteristic of personality, which is that the personality is integrated into a single unitary entity.

As the psychological personality consists of the behavior equipment of the individual, it follows that the status of any particular person at a given time must result from the development and organization of his reaction systems. This development we will call his interactional biography, or the behavior history of the individual. From earliest infancy, the individual must begin to acquire specific types of reaction systems, resulting in adaptational contacts with the great complexity of objects, persons, situations, and events with which he is surrounded. It is exceedingly important to observe that every phase of distinctly human behavior equipment must be acquired during the behavior lifetime of the person.

A third characteristic of personality is, therefore, that the personality is continuous throughout the individual's behavior history. Whatever we are at any given moment is determined by what has gone before, and the old saying that the boy is father to the man contains considerable truth. Influences which were present at a very early age are still being felt at a much later period of life, even though thousands of behavioral events may have transpired in the meantime.

A fourth characteristic of personality refers to a point already made. It is that the personality is consistent over a period of time to enough of an extent to permit predictions to be made with respect to an individual's behavior. Granted that such predictions may be far from perfect, they are at least significantly superior to those based on **chance** alone. Not only is some consistency shown from one time to another, but consistency is thought to be present to at least a limited extent from one behavior pattern to another. The broader such generalizations are, however, the more risky they become, and the facts probably do not support the assumptions of broad trait consistency which are part of the folklore of popular psychology. Temporal consistency is, nevertheless, the foundation upon which most applied psychology is based, and such consistency is frequently expressed in terms of probabilities.

A fifth and final characteristic of personality is that the personality is subject to progressive change as time goes on. Although the personality is constant, in that it is the same person who is involved from one age to another, and, although it is consistent over short periods of time, it is nevertheless constantly undergoing modification in one way or another. Such changes are more rapid during some periods of life than during others, and this pertains particularly to the first twenty years or so. No one has expressed these changes more eloquently than Shakespeare, although we will not quote him here. Suffice it to say that their study and understanding is one of the most fascinating areas of all psychology and embraces several special fields of interest and endeavor. These five characteristics are included here in brief,

as knowing them is an essential part of being familiar with the basic nature of the human personality [pp. 21–23].

James:
The fluidity of personality*

2

Many people have realized the complexity and manysidedness of personality, but the following quotation from William James (1913) has been selected because it illustrates his delightful style and shows his full grasp of the richness and variety manifested by human personality.

Properly speaking, *a man has as many social selves as there are individuals who recognize him* and carry an image of him in their mind. To wound any one of these his images is to wound him. But as the individuals who carry the images fall naturally into classes, we may practically say that he has as many different social selves as there are distinct *groups* of persons about whose opinion he cares. He generally shows a different side of himself, to each of these different groups. Many a youth who is demure enough before his parents and teachers, swears and swaggers like a pirate among his "tough" young friends. We do not show ourselves to our children as to our club-companions, to our customers as to the laborers we employ, to our own masters and employers as to our intimate friends. From this there results what practically is a division of the man into several selves; and this may be a discordant splitting, as where one is afraid to let one set of his acquaintances know him as he is elsewhere; or it may be a perfectly harmonious division of labor, as where one tender to his children is stern to the soldiers or prisoners under his command [pp. 179–180]. . . .

A man's *fame,* good or bad, and his *honor* or dishonor, are names for one of his social selves. The particular social self of a man called his honor is usually the result of one of those splittings of which we have spoken. It is his image in the eyes of his own "set," which exalts or condemns him as he conforms or not to certain

requirements that may not be made of one in another walk of life. Thus a layman may abandon a city infected with **cholera;** but a priest or a doctor would think such an act incompatible with his honor. A soldier's honor requires him to fight or to die under circumstances where another man can apologize or run away with no stain upon his social self. A judge, a statesman, are in like manner debarred by the honor of their cloth from entering into pecuniary relations perfectly honorable to persons in private life. Nothing is commoner than to hear people discriminate between their different selves of this sort: "As a man I pity you, but as an official I must show you no mercy"; "As a politician I regard him as an ally, but as a moralist I loathe him"; etc., etc. What may be called "club-opinion" is one of the very strongest forces in life. The thief must not steal from other thieves; the gambler must pay his gambling-debts, though he pay no other debts in the world. The code of honor of fashionable society has throughout history been full of permissions as well as of vetoes, the only reason for following either of which is that so we best serve one of our social selves. You must not lie in general, but you may lie as much as you please if asked about your relations with a lady; you must accept a challenge from an equal, but if challenged by an inferior you may laugh him to scorn: these are examples of what is meant [pp. 180–181]. . . .

Rivalry and conflict of the different me's

With most objects of desire, physical nature restricts our choice to but one of many repre-

---

**Quoted material is from William James, *Psychology* (New York: Holt, 1913).

sented goods, and even so it is here. I am often confronted by the necessity of standing by one of my empirical selves and relinquishing the rest. Not that I would not, if I could, be both handsome and fat and well dressed, and a great athlete, and make a million a year, be a wit, a **bon-vivant,** and a lady-killer, as well as a **philosopher;** a **philanthropist,** statesman, warrior, and African explorer, as well as a "tone-poet" and saint. But the thing is simply impossible. The millionaire's work would run counter to the saint's; the **bon-vivant** and the philanthropist would trip each other up; the philosopher and the lady-killer could not well keep house in the same tenement of clay. Such different characters may conceivably at the outset of life be alike *possible* to a man. But to make any one of them actual, the rest must more or less be suppressed. So the seeker of his truest, strongest, deepest self must review the list carefully, and pick out the one on which to stake his salvation. All other selves thereupon become unreal, but the fortunes of this self are real. Its failures are real failures, its triumphs real triumphs, carrying shame and gladness with them. This is as strong an example as

there is of that selective industry of the mind on which I insisted some pages back. Our thought, incessantly, deciding, among many things of a kind, which ones for it shall be realities, here chooses one of many possible selves or characters, and forthwith reckons it no shame to fail in any of those not adopted expressly as its own [p. 186].

The preceding passage is instructive in its implicit pointing to the importance of objects and other persons in the individual's surroundings as factors that restrict and organize personality responses into certain classes or categories. It is possible, of course, to translate James' outmoded formulation into more acceptable terminology. Still, dated as it is, his statement points to the earthbound nature of personality, its relationship to what today we call stimulus objects. James stresses the many facets of personality, a characteristic that writers often grasp with penetrating insight.

3 Bandura: Learning through imitation*

Parents are often perplexed about the origin of their children's behavior. They may remark that the child could not have learned a certain reaction from them. Still, they may unknowingly be teaching the child that very response. For example, in this article Albert Bandura notes that while a parent may verbally instruct his child not to strike another child, the parent himself may serve as an effective model when he spanks or "clobbers" his children. The article shows how social learning, or

*Quoted material is from Albert Bandura, "The Role of Imitation in Personality Development," *Journal of Nursery Education,* April 1963, **18**(3), 207–215. By permission of the author and publisher.

learning through imitation, works subtly but rapidly in shaping children's behavior by furnishing them with real-life models, plus models from television or movies.

I remember reading a story reported by Professor Mowrer about a lonesome farmer who decided to get a parrot for company. After acquiring the bird, the farmer spent many long evenings teaching the parrot the phrase, "Say Uncle." Despite the devoted tutorial attention, the parrot proved totally unresponsive and finally, the frustrated farmer got a stick and struck the parrot on the head after each refusal to produce the desired phrase.

But the visceral method proved no more effective than the cerebral one, so the farmer grabbed his feathered friend and tossed him in the chicken house. A short time later the farmer heard a loud commotion in the chicken house and, upon investigation, found that the parrot was pommeling the startled chickens on the head with a stick and shouting, "Say Uncle!" "Say Uncle!"

While this story is not intended as an introduction to a treatise on parrot-training practices, it provides a graphic illustration of the process of social learning that I shall discuss in this paper.

One can distinguish two kinds of processes by which children acquire attitudes, values, and patterns of social behavior. First, the learning that occurs on the basis of direct tuition or instrumental training. In this form of learning, parents and other socializing agents are relatively explicit about what they wish the child to learn, and attempt to shape his behavior through rewarding and punishing consequences.

Although a certain amount of socialization of a child takes place through such direct training, personality patterns are primarily acquired through the child's active imitation of parental attitudes and behavior, most of which the parents have never directly attempted to teach. Indeed, parental modeling behavior may often counteract the effects of their direct training. When a parent punishes his child physically for having aggressed toward peers, for example, the intended outcome of this training is that the child should refrain from hitting others. The child, however, is also learning from parental demonstration how to aggress physically, and this imitative learning may provide the direction for the child's behavior when he is similarly frustrated in subsequent social interactions.

Research on imitation demonstrates that, unlike the relatively slow process of instrumental training, when a **model** is provided, patterns of behavior are rapidly acquired in large segments or in their entirety (Bandura, 1962). The pervasiveness of this form of learning is also clearly evident in naturalistic observations of children's play in which they frequently reproduce the entire parental role-behavior including the appropriate mannerisms, voice inflections and attitudes, much to the parents' surprise and embarrassment. Although the process whereby a person reproduces the behavior exhibited by real-life or symbolized models is generally labeled **"identification"** in theories of personality, I shall employ the term

imitation because it encompasses the same behavioral phenomenon and avoids the elusiveness and surplus meanings that have come to be associated with the former concept.

Let us now consider a series of experiments that both illustrates the process of learning through imitation, and identifies some of the factors which serve to enhance or to reduce the occurrence of imitative behavior.

Transmission of aggression

One set of experiments was designed primarily to determine the extent to which aggression can be transmitted to children through exposure to aggressive adult models (Bandura, Ross, and Ross, 1962). One group of children observed an aggressive model who exhibited relatively novel forms of physical and verbal aggression toward a large inflated plastic doll; a second group viewed the same model behave in a very subdued and inhibited manner, while children in a control group had no exposure to any models. Half the children in each of the experimental conditions observed models of the same sex as themselves, and the remaining children in each group witnessed opposite sex models.

This investigation was later extended (Bandura, Ross, and Ross, 1963b) in order to compare the effects of real-life and film-mediated or televised aggressive models on children's behavior. Children in the human film-aggression group viewed a movie showing the same adults, who had served as models in the earlier experiment, portraying the novel aggressive acts toward the inflated doll. For children in the cartoon-aggression groups, a film in which the female model costumed as a cartoon cat exhibiting the aggressive behavior toward the plastic doll was projected on a glass lens-screen in a television console.

After exposure to their respective models, all children, including those in the control group, were mildly frustrated and tested for the amount of imitative and nonimitative aggression.

The results of these experiments leave little doubt that exposure to aggressive models heightens children's aggressive responses to subsequent frustration. As shown in Fig. 9.1, children who observed the aggressive models exhibited approximately twice as much aggression as did subjects in the non-aggressive

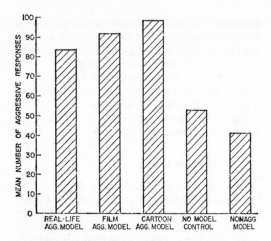

Figure 9.1 Mean number of aggressive responses performed by children in each of five groups. (From Albert Bandura, "The Role of Imitation in Personality Development," *The Journal of Nursery Education,* April 1963, **18**(3). Reproduced by permission of author and publisher.)

model group or the control group. In addition, children who witnessed the subdued nonaggressive model displayed the inhibited behavior characteristic of their model and expressed significantly less aggression than the control children.

Some evidence that the influence of models is partly determined by the sex appropriateness of their behavior is provided by the finding that the aggressive male model was a more powerful stimulus for aggression than the aggressive female model. Some of the children, particularly the boys, commented spontaneously on the fact that the female model's behavior was out of character (e.g., "That's no way for a lady to behave. Ladies are supposed to act like ladies...").

In contrast, aggression by the male model was generally viewed as appropriate and approved by both the boys ("Al's a good socker, he beat up Bobo. I want to sock like Al.") and the girls ("That man is a strong fighter. He punched and punched, and he could hit Bobo right down to the floor and if Bobo got up he said, 'Punch your nose.' He's a good fighter like Daddy.").

The data furthermore reveal that aggressive models are highly influential not only in reducing children's inhibitions over aggression, but

also in shaping the form of their behavior. Children who observed the aggressive models displayed a great number of precisely imitative aggressive acts, whereas, such responses rarely occurred in either the non-aggressive model group or the control group. Illustrations of the way many of the children became virtually carbon copies of their models are presented in Fig. 9.2. The top frames show the female model performing four novel aggressive responses; the lower frames depict a boy and a girl reproducing the behavior of the female model whom they had observed in the film presentation.

Although the children were somewhat less inclined to imitate precisely the cartoon character than the real-life aggressive model, all three experimental conditions — real-life, film-mediated, and cartoon-aggressive models — produced equivalent increases in overall aggressive behavior based on a variety of measures of both imitative and non-imitative aggression.

The finding that film-mediated models are as effective as real-life models in eliciting and transmitting aggressive responses indicates that televised models may serve as important sources of behavior and can no longer be ignored in conceptualizations of personality development. Indeed, most youngsters probably have more exposure to prestigeful televised male models than to their own fathers. With further advances in mass media and audio-visual technology, pictorially presented models, mainly through television, are likely to play an increasingly influential role in shaping personality patterns, and in modifying attitudes and social norms.

It has been widely assumed on the basis of psychoanalytic theory and other hydraulic energy models of personality, that children's vicarious participation in film-mediated aggression or the direct expression of aggressive behavior will serve to discharge "pent-up energies" and affects. Guided by this **catharsis** hypothesis, many parents, educators, and mental health workers encourage hyperaggressive children to participate in aggressive recreational activities, to view highly aggressive televised programs, and to aggress in psychotherapeutic playrooms and other permissive settings.

In contrast to this "drainage" view, social learning theory (Bandura & Walters, in press) would predict that the provision of aggressive

Figure 9.2 Imitative aggressive responses. The top frames show a female "model" engaged in four different aggressive activities. The lower frames show a boy and a girl reproducing the "model" behavior with shocking accuracy. (Photographs from the film *Social Learning of Aggression Through Imitation of Aggressive Models*. Photos courtesy of Dr. Albert Bandura.)

models and the inadvertent positive reinforcement of aggression, which inevitably occurs during the encouragement of cathartic expressions, are exceedingly effective procedures for enhancing aggressive response tendencies. It is not surprising, therefore, that studies in which children or adolescents have been exposed to film-mediated aggressive models (Bandura, Ross, and Ross, 1961, 1963b, c; Lovaas, 1961; Mussen and Rutherford, 1961; Siegel, 1959; Walters, Llewellyn, Thomas, and Acker, 1962) have uniformly demonstrated that vicarious participation in aggressive activity increases, rather than decreases, aggressive behavior.

On the other hand, providing aggressive children with examples of alternative constructive ways of coping with interpersonal frustration has been found to be highly successful in modifying aggressive-domineering personality patterns (Chittenden, 1942). Additional comparisons of social theory and the traditional approaches to personality development will be presented later.

It is apparent that children do not reproduce the personality characteristics of every model with whom they come into contact, nor do they imitate every element of behavior exhibited even by models whom they may have selected as their primary sources of social behavior. The experiments that I shall discuss in the remaining sections of this paper are mainly concerned with some of the psychological variables determining the selection of models, and the degree to which their behavior will be imitated.

Response consequences to the model and imitation

The manner in which rewarding or punishing consequences to the model's behavior influences imitation is demonstrated in an experiment in which nursery school children observed either an aggressive model rewarded, an aggressive model punished, or had no exposure to the models (Bandura, Ross, and Ross, 1963b). The models were two adults presented to the children on film projected into a television console.

In the aggression-rewarded condition, Rocky, the aggressive model appropriates all of Johnny's attractive play possessions and tasty foodstuffs through aggressive-domineering means. The film shown to the children in the aggression-punished condition was identical with that shown to the aggression-rewarded group except for a slight rearrangement of the film sequence so the aggression exhibited by Rocky resulted in his being severely punished by Johnny. Following exposure to the models the children were tested for the incidence of post-exposure aggressive behavior.

Children who observed Rocky's aggressive behavior rewarded readily imitated his physical and verbal aggression, whereas, children who saw him punished exhibited relatively little imitative behavior and did not differ from a group of control children who had no exposure to the models.

At the conclusion of the experiment each child was asked to evaluate the behavior of Rocky and Johnny and to select the character he preferred to emulate. These data yielded some interesting and surprising findings. As might be expected, children who observed Rocky's aggressive behavior punished both failed to reproduce his behavior and rejected him as a model for emulation.

On the other hand, when Rocky's aggression was highly successful in amassing rewarding resources, he was chosen by most of the children as the preferred model for imitation. The surprising finding, however, is that without exception these children were highly critical of his behavior (e.g., "Rocky is harsh...." "Rough and bossy...." "Mean...." "Wicked...." "He whack people....").

It was evident from the children's comments that the successful payoff of aggression rather than its intrinsic desirability served as the primary basis for emulation (e.g., "Rocky beat Johnny and chase him and get all the good toys ..." "He came and snatched Johnny's toys. Get a lot of toys..."). The children resolved the conflict by derogating the unfortunate victim, apparently as justification for Rocky's exploitive-assaultive behavior. They criticized Johnny for his inability to control Rocky ("He's a crybaby.

Didn't know how to make Rocky mind."), for his miserliness ("If he'd shared right in the beginning, Rocky might have played nice."), and generally described him as, "sulky", "mean", and "sort of dumb."

This study clearly demonstrates the way rewarding consequences to the model's behavior may outweigh the value systems of the observers—children readily adopted successful modeling behavior even though they had labeled it objectionable, morally reprehensible, and publicly criticized the model for engaging in such behavior.

In many televised and other mass media presentations antisocial models amass considerable rewarding resources through devious means but are punished following the last commercial on the assumption that the punishment ending will erase or counteract the learning of the model's antisocial behavior.

The findings from a recently completed experiment (Bandura, 1963) reveal that, although punishment administered to a model tends to inhibit children's performance of the modeled behavior, it has virtually no influence on the occurrence of imitative learning. In this experiment children observed a film-mediated aggressive model who was severely punished in one condition of the experiment, generously rewarded in a second condition, while the third condition presented no response-consequences to the model.

Consistent with the findings cited earlier, a postexposure test of imitative behavior showed that children who observed the punished model performed significantly fewer imitative responses than children in the model-rewarded and the no-consequence groups. Children in all three groups were then offered attractive incentives contingent on their reproducing the model's behavior. The introduction of the rewards completely wiped out the previously observed performance differences, revealing an equivalent amount of learning among the children in the model-rewarded, model-punished and the no-consequences groups. Similarly, girls exhibited approximately as much imitative aggression as did the boys.

It might be concluded from these findings that exposure of children to punished antisocial or other types of models is likely to result in little overt imitative behavior. Nevertheless, the observed behavior is learned and may be exhibited on future occasions given the appropriate instigations, the instruments necessary for performing the imitative acts, and the prospect of sufficiently attractive positive rewards contingent on the successful execution of the behavior.

Nurturance and imitation

The role of nurturance in facilitating imitative learning has been emphasized in most theories of identification. Through the repeated association of the parent's behavior and attributes with warm, rewarding, and affectionately demonstrative caretaking activities, it is assumed that the parent's behavioral characteristics gradually take on positive value for the child. Consequently, the child is motivated to reproduce these positively valenced attributes in his own behavior.

Some empirical support for the nurturance hypothesis is provided in an experiment in which the quality of the rewarding interaction between a female model and nursery school children was systematically varied (Bandura and Huston, 1961). With one group of children, the model behaved in a warm and rewarding manner, while a second group of children experienced a distant and non-nurturant relationship with the model. Following the experimental social interactions the model and the children played a game in which the model exhibited a relatively novel pattern of verbal and motor behavior, and the number of imitative responses performed by the children was recorded.

Children who had experienced the rewarding interaction with the model displayed substantially more imitative behavior than did children with whom the same adult had interacted in a non-rewarding way. Exposure to a model possessing rewarding qualities not only elicited precisely imitative verbal responses but also increased the level of non-imitative verbalization. These results are essentially in agreement with those of Milner (1951), who found that children receiving high reading readiness scores had more verbal and affectionately demonstrative maternal models than children in the low-reading ability group.

The importance of attaching positive valence to the activities and behavior which the parent or teacher wishes the child to reproduce is dramatically illustrated in a case report by Mowrer (1960). A two-year-old girl, who suffered from an auditory defect, was seriously retarded in language development, a condition that resulted primarily from her refusal to wear a hearing aid. In analyzing the mother-child verbal interaction, it became readily apparent that the girl was hearing only language responses of high amplitude, which the mother uttered in a raised voice during disciplinary interventions. Considering the repeated association of the mother's verbal behavior with negative emotional experiences, it was not surprising that the child refused to wear a hearing aid, and exhibited little interest in, or desire for, vocalization.

The mother was instructed to follow a remedial program in which she deliberately and frequently associated her vocalizations with highly positive experiences, and refrained from using language punitively. Within a brief period of time the child began to show an active interest in the mother's verbalizations, was quite willing to wear the hearing aid, and made rapid progress in her language development.

In discussions of the process of education and socialization, considerable emphasis is generally placed on direct training procedures. As the above case illustrates, however, the attachment of positive valence to modeling behavior may be an important precondition for the occurrence of social learning. Indeed, once the behavior in question has acquired positive properties, the child is likely to perform it in the absence of socializing agents and externally administered rewards.

Social power and imitation

In the studies to which reference has been made, children were exposed to only a single model. During the course of social development, however, children have extensive contact with multiple models, particularly family members, who may differ widely in their behavior and in their relative influence. Therefore, a further study, designed to test several different theories of identificatory learning, utilized three-person groups representing prototypes of the nuclear family (Bandura, Ross, and Ross, 1963a).

In one condition of the experiment, an adult assumed the role of controller of highly rewarding resources, including attractive play material, appetizing foods, and high-status objects.

Another adult was the recipient of these resources, while the child, a **participant observer** in the triad, was essentially ignored. In a second condition, one adult controlled the resources; the child, however, was the recipient of the positive resources, while the other adult was assigned a subordinate and powerless role.

An adult male and female served as models in each of the triads. For half the boys and girls in each condition, the male model controlled and dispensed the rewarding resources, simulating the husband-dominant home; for the remaining children, the female model mediated the positive resources as in the wife-dominant home. Following the experimental social interactions the adult models exhibited divergent patterns of behavior in the presence of the child, and measures were obtained of the degree to which the child patterned his behavior after that of the models.

According to the status envy theory of identification proposed by Whiting (1959, 1960), where a child competes unsuccessfully with an adult for affection, attention, food, and care, the child will envy the consumer adult and consequently identify with him. This theory represents an extension of the psychoanalytic defensive identification hypothesis that identification is the outcome of rivalrous interaction between the child and the parent who occupies an envied consumer status. In contrast to the status envy hypothesis, the social power theory of identification (Maccoby, 1959; Mussen and Distler, 1960) predicts that children will reproduce more of the behavior of the adult who controls positive resources than that of the powerless adult model.

The results of this experiment reveal that children tend to identify with the source of rewarding power rather than with the competitor for the rewards. In both experimental triads, regardless of whether the rival adult or the children themselves were the recipients of the rewarding resources, the model who possessed rewarding power was imitated to a considerably greater extent than was the competitor or the ignored model. Moreover, power inversions on the part of the male and female models produced cross-sex imitation, particularly in girls. These findings suggest that the distribution of rewarding power within the family may play an important role in the development of both appropriate and deviant sex-role behavior.

Although the children adopted many of the characteristics of the model who possessed rewarding power, they also reproduced some of the response patterns exhibited by the model who occupied a subordinate role. The children's behavior represented a synthesis of behavioral elements selected from both models, and since the specific admixture of elements varied from child to child, they displayed quite different patterns of imitative behavior. Thus, within the one family even same-sex siblings may exhibit different personality characteristics, owing to their having selected for imitation different elements of their parents' attitudes and behavior. Paradoxical as it may seem, it is possible to achieve considerable innovation through selective imitation.

Social learning,
psychoanalytic, and stage
theories of personality

It was pointed out in preceding sections of this paper that laboratory data have failed to support predictions derived from several widely accepted psychoanalytic principles of personality development. Research generated by modern social learning theory also raises some questions about the validity of stage theories that typically depict the developmental process as involving a relatively spontaneous emergence of age-specific modes of behavior as the child passes from one stage to another. According to Piaget's theory of moral development (1948), for example, one can distinguish two clear-cut stages of moral orientations demarcated from each other at approximately seven years of age.

In the first stage, defined as objective morality, children judge the gravity of a deviant act in terms of the amount of material damages and disregard the intentionality of the action. By contrast, during the second or subjective morality stage, children judge conduct in terms of its intent rather than its material consequences. The sequence and timing of these stages are presumably predetermined and, consequently, young children are incapable of adopting a subjective orientation while objective moral judgments are rarely encountered in older children.

However, in an experiment designed to study the influence of models in transmitting and modifying children's moral judgments (Bandura and McDonald, 1963), objective and subjective moral judgments were found to exist together rather than as successive developmental stages. The vast majority of young children were capable of exercising subjective judgments and most of the older children displayed varying degrees of objective morality.

Children who exhibited predominantly objective and subjective moral orientations were then selected and exposed to adult models who consistently expressed moral judgments that ran counter to the children's orientations. The provision of models was highly effective in altering the children's moral judgments. Objective children modified their moral orientations toward subjectivity and, similarly, subjective children became considerably more objective in their judgmental behavior. Furthermore, the children maintained their altered orientations in a new test situation in the absence of the models. It is highly probable that other personality characteristics generally viewed as predetermined age-specific phenomena can also be readily altered through the application of appropriate social learning principles.

Despite the voluminous clinical and theoretical literature pertaining to child development, the available body of empirically verified knowledge is comparatively meager. The recent years, however, have witnessed a new direction in theorizing about the developmental process, which has generated considerable laboratory research within the framework of social learning theory. These studies are beginning to yield relatively unambiguous statements about the influence of particular antecedent events on the behavior and attitudes of children. This approach evidently holds promise of providing both more reliable guidelines for educational practice and the type of evidence necessary for discarding procedures that prove to be ineffective in, or even a hindrance to, the successful realization of desired developmental, educational, and psychotherapeutic objectives.

---

*Lovaas, Schaeffer,
and Simmons:
Building social behavior in
autistic children by use of
electric shock*

4

To use punishment on a child who is psychotic and already disturbed and wretched seems heartless and cruel. But would you resort to use of punishment (i.e., electric shock) if it were a choice between that child's lifelong institutionalization and possible recovery? After careful consideration, O. Ivar Lovaas, Benson Schaeffer, and James W. Simmons (1965) decided to take a chance with punishment. It seemed certain in any case, that their two patients, 5-year-old identical twins diagnosed as childhood schizophrenics, would be doomed to spend the rest of their days in a mental hospital. Besides their failure to respond to conventional treatment administered over the preceding year, the twins were extremely unresponsive socially. They showed no reaction even to each other, let alone other people. They had no speech, nor did they react when spoken to. They were not toilet-trained, and handled toys and other objects in a disinterested, mechanical, apathetic fashion. Screaming, throwing things, and hitting themselves were observed frequently, but the twins spent 70 to 80 percent of their days in such autistic action as senselessly rocking, fondling themselves, and in making repetitious, aimless movements. Thus the situation looked hopeless at the time it was decided to use electric shock in three separate studies to see if the subjects' pathological behavior could be modified.

Study 1:
The "come here" study

In the first study, Lovaas wondered if he could train the twins to come to him at the verbal command, "Come here." The experiment was carried out in a 12 by 12-foot laboratory that permitted observation via a one-way vision mirror and sound equipment. The floor of the room was electrified by means of closely placed metallic tapes that prevented escape of shock. The subjects' behaviors during the experiment were recorded by using a panel of push buttons.

No-shock sessions

As a control for the first study, Lovaas held two pre-experimental sessions so as to establish a base. Subjects were put barefooted into the experimental room but they were not shocked in the first sessions. However, about five times a minute, one of two participating experimenters would say, "Come here." A record was made of the number of approaches the subjects made under no-shock conditions (see Fig. 9.3).

Escape sessions

Three shock sessions were then held on three consecutive days. In this escape-training series, the two experimenters faced each other about 3 feet apart. The child stood between them facing one *E* who would lean toward the subject, hold out his arms as if to receive him, and say, "Come here." Simultaneously, shock was turned on and stayed on until the child moved toward the open-armed experimenter. If he failed to move within 3 seconds, the experimenter behind him gave

him a push forward. Either type of movement terminated the shock.

Avoidance sessions

In this series, the children could avoid shock entirely by approaching the experimenter within 5 seconds. However, if the child did not give the expected response within 5 seconds or if he did not reach within one foot of the experimenter inside of 7 seconds, he was shocked as in the previous escape-training sessions. In these avoidance trials, another factor was introduced, namely, the distance between the experimenters was gradually increased until eventually they stood at opposite

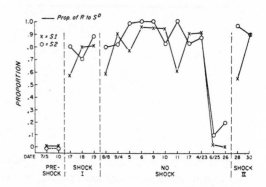

Figure 9.3 Results of the "Come here" phase of Lovaas' study. In the pre-shock phase, the command "Come here" elicited no response from either of the two subjects. However, only three shock sessions (Shock I) brought the response up to an efficiency of six to nine responses out of every ten. The subjects avoided shock entirely in this phase. The lesson was effective for the subsequent nine months without shock presentation! On June 23 and 25 there was extinction but one shock reinstated the former response as shown in Shock II. (From O. Ivar Lovaas, Benson Schaeffer, and James W. Simmons, "Building Social Behavior in Autistic Children by use of Electric Shock," *Journal of Experimental Research in Personality*, October 1965, **1**(2), 99–109. Reproduced by permission of author and publisher.)

sides of the room. Furthermore, they decreased the number of cues accompanying the command "Come here" until the bare command sufficed. And, as a last resort, if tantrum behaviors or self-stimulatory actions occurred, the subjects were instantly shocked.

Extinction sessions

After the three shock sessions described above, the experimenters followed the efficacy of their training in an extinction series over the subsequent 10 months. That is, shock was no longer given, only the command "Come here."

The second shock sessions

As a conclusion to Study 1, the experimenters now brought the children into the laboratory and first gave them a 2-second shock regardless of what the children did, as if to remind them of their previous training. From here on, these sessions were like the extinction series, that is they were without shock.

How about "No" as a secondary negative reinforcer? As an addition to the first shock session. Lovaas and his collaborators tested the efficacy of the command "No" as **a secondary reinforcer.** Prior to the first shock sessions, subjects were trained to press a lever for M & M candy, until a stable rate was obtained. Then "No" without shock was introduced, followed by "No" simultaneous with shock, and, finally, "No" without shock again.

Results and discussion

The accompanying figure (Fig. 9.3) shows concretely the results obtained dur-

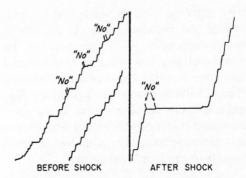

BEFORE SHOCK   AFTER SHOCK

Figure 9.4 Effect of the command "No" on bar pressing for M & M candy. The "before shock" sessions had no effect as indicated by the cumulative response curves for both subjects. The experimenter might as well have not spoken. But after the command "No" was paired with shock, the curve (representative of both Ss' performance) shown in the "after shock" portion of the figure showed that "No" even without shock had a suppressing effect on bar pressing for the candy reward. (From O. Ivar Lovaas, Benson Schaeffer, and James W. Simmons, "Building Social Behavior in Autistic Children by use of Electric Shock," *Journal of Experimental Research In Personality,* October 1965, **1**(2), 99–109. Reproduced by permission of author and publisher.)

ing the "Come here" phase of the experiment. Note that the children failed to respond to the verbal command during the two pre-shock sessions. Not so in the three following shock sessions, which show a relatively high level of response that carries over for many months (from August to April 23) of the no-shock phase. June 23 and 25 records do show a sudden extinction, but, following a single noncontingent shock reinforcement on June 28, the social response to "Come here" is as strong as ever.

What was the fate of the children's pathological behaviors? Briefly, prior to the shock sessions, self-stimulation and tantrum behavior occurred 65 to 85 percent of the time and physical contacts did not exist. However, shock immediately suppressed the pathological activities, which stayed suppressed for 11 months. On the other hand, physical contact was reinforced during the first shock session and it endured 10 to 11 months, finally extinguishing. But, again, the one noncontingent shock reinforcement reinstated the social responsiveness and suppressed the pathological components of the twins' behavior.

Effect of "no"

If the experimenter said "No" during the initial no-shock phase of the experiment when the child was pressing a lever that delivered candy, he might as well have kept silent. There was no effect on the child's performance until the verbal command was paired with shock. After such pairing, the word "No" was effective in suppressing the bar-pressing response.

Other effects of the experimental procedure

Within minutes of introducing shock, the previously aloof, uncommunicative, autistic twins showed a beneficial generalization effect. "In particular, they seemed more alert, affectionate, and seeking of E's company. And, surprisingly, during successful shock avoidance they appeared happy [p. 103]." During the first 2 weeks there was a partial generalization of desirable effect beyond the confines of the laboratory. The children appeared to **discriminate** between the shocking laboratory and nonshocking ward; physical contact soon extinguished although responses to "Come here" and "No" persisted for several months. These observations challenged Lovaas and his coworkers to shape more enduring and generalized affectionate

responses in their subjects, thus leading to further studies.

Study 2: The kiss and hug study

Briefly, the investigators attempted to evoke affectionate responses to the experimenter, who invited the subjects to kiss and hug him. Every 5 seconds during the experiment, E would face each child, hold him by the waist with outstretched arms, bow his head toward the child and alternately request him to "Hug me" and "Kiss me." Each of the 6 sessions lasted 6 minutes.

Results

During the control or no-shock sessions (Sessions 1, 2, and 4), the amount of time that the Ss embraced or hugged and kissed E was extremely low. Rather, they withdrew from him. However, during the shock-relevant sessions (Sessions 3, 5, and 6), the Ss' behavior changed markedly toward increased affection. In a situation where they had received shock-avoidance training, the Ss responded with affection to E's verbal command alone (without shock) and did not withdraw from him. The fact that this affectionate behavior maintained itself in Session 6 demonstrates that the remotely controlled shock can produce transfer of behavior change to a wide variety of situations (p. 104). See Fig. 9.5 for a graphic presentation of results.

Nurses' ratings

After the termination of the "Kiss and hug" series, four nurses, who were acquainted with the children but ignorant of the experiment and of its use of shock, were asked to rate the subjects on a number of relevant behavior traits. Without going into the details of the rating procedures, there was "an increase in the ratings of all behaviors following the shock treatment, except for pathological behaviors and happiness-contentment, which both decreased. Only the ratings on dependency and affection-seeking behaviors increased more than one point [pp. 104–105]."

Study 3: Reinforcing power of adults

If the sight of an adult terminates painful shock that is contingent upon the child's approach toward the adult, will sight of the adult in the future, without shock, reinforce approach behavior on the part of the child? This study was done in two parts. During the first or "pretreating" phase, if the children pressed a lever, they received M & M's and simultaneously saw the experimenter's face. When they acquired this response, the candy reinforcement was discontinued. In the second part of the study, the children were trained to come to *E* to escape shock. If a child responded, *E* fondled, caressed, and comforted it. A change in the rate of lever-pressing in order to obtain a view of the experimenter was used to measure the experimenter's acquired reinforcement. Results showed "a substantial increase in rate of lever-pressing accompanying shock escape training for both subjects [p. 106]."

How can we be sure that the shock-escape training had increased the twins' responsiveness to people as people? Could it be that the shock acted as a general energizer or that it effected the arousal of behaviors in general, social or asocial? To

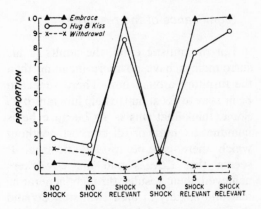

Figure 9.5 The Kiss and Hug Study. Note the low proportion of embraces, hugs and kisses in the "no shock" sessions, 1, 2, and 4. "Shock" sessions, 3 and 5, were conducted in a room in which Ss had received shock-avoidance training. They responded with a high proportion of affectionate responses showing that "you have to learn to love." It is important to point out that Session 6 was conducted in the same room as the previous control sessions. However, just before the session, Ss were given five shock-escape trials. Note the resultant maintenance of affectionate behavior. (From O. Ivar Lovaas, Benson Schaeffer, and James W. Simmons, "Building Social Behavior in Autistic Children by use of Electric Shock," *Journal of Experimental Research in Personality,* October 1965, **1**(2), 99–109. Reproduced by permission of author and publisher.)

check this possibility, the investigators looked for a relationship between shock and no-shock sessions and amount of time that the children spent in vocalization and climbing. There was no such increase in these additional behaviors during shock-escape training. Hence it was concluded that the approach behavior toward *E* came about as the specific result of his acquisition of a reinforcing function because it was paired with shock reduction. Such an interpretation was also consistent with the results of the first two studies, both of which showed an increase in social and affectionate responses.

Significance of the research

For the autistic child, the adults in his surroundings have no more meaning than the furniture around him. There seems to be no way to get at him to help him improve. Some think that this is so because he is immune to hurt or discomfort, without which there can be no modification. It seems that Lovaas and his coworkers achieved their results through generating fear and anxiety in their twin subjects and then introduced adults who became socially meaningful through reducing or eliminating that fear and anxiety.

Their study is also important because of its relationship to fundamental psychological principles. In the same way as a loving parent rescues an infant from pain and distress when he cries, so the experimenters in the present study saved the twins from pain, and added consolation and comfort. Both situations lead to the cumulative development of meaningful relationships of affection, love, trust, obedience, and so forth. Thus "No" in the present experiment, as in the normal family situation, came to have a secondary reinforcing function. Similarly, the "Kiss and Hug" study showed the reinforcing value of the sight of the adult on affectionate behavior. Finally, let us not overlook the fact that the behavior of the autistic twins investigated illustrates **escape conditioning.** First, the experimenters introduced an aversive stimulus (i.e., electric shock), cessation of which was made contingent upon the child's performing the expected, desirable response. Through secondary reinforcement, the sight of adults became social reinforcers of previously nonexistent "normal" reaction to previously meaningless persons. Thus nonpathological responses were brought under **stimulus control,** displacing the former pathological behavior. The treatment that Lovaas used differs radically from extended psychoanalysis by going to work on a small segment of behavior instead of the patient's life span. There is much controversy over the relative merits of the different methods.

5

Stewart:
How to perpetuate psychosis*

Let us now consider Horace Stewart's ironic description of how we, intentionally or not, perpetuate psychosis in mental patients. This pungent article describes actual practices that not only do not return the patient to his home, job, and community, but actually increase his chances of lifelong residence in the mental institution.

The methods employed in keeping a mental patient chronic are becoming clearer as scientific investigation continues. A long step forward was made by Heckel and Salzberg (1964) in elaborating the more commonly observed techniques. J. L. Bernard (personal communication, 1965) reported that **chronicity** can be established within a week of admission to a state hospital. The report by Kissinger (1963) on "The untherapeutic community: a team approach that failed" gives invaluable insight into the powerful

*Quoted material is from Horace Stewart, "On Keeping Mental Patients Chronic," *Psychological Reports*, 1965, 17, 216–218. By permission of author and publisher.

role of interdisciplinary disharmony in reinforcement of chronicity. The following rules are a resume of current research reported by observers located in treatment centers for the mentally disordered throughout the world.

Rules

1. The institutions's general appearance. The importance of over-crowding, under-staffing, and poorly maintained buildings and grounds cannot be overestimated. They immediately impress upon the patient the utter hopelessness of his situation. The fight is taken out of him, preparing the way for treatment. Also, the importance of a good name cannot be set aside lightly. The old names were the best, e.g., The Institution for Lunatics, Insane Asylum, The Asylum for the Relief of Persons Deprived of the Use of Their Reason.

2. In all decisions, play it safe. Never allow the patient freedom that may, in any way, give him an opportunity to kill himself, fall in love, interact with normal, honest, God-fearing folk, or simply be alone. Never believe the patient's account of any event. Decisions are best put off for several weeks, and longer if possible. The effects of a positive experience can be completely reversed by careful timing.

3. Supply only the bare necessities of life. The mental patient requires very little of the luxuries of life. The Spartan life was best. Some observers (notably state legislators) have made this observation and have attempted to make luxuries impossible through parsimonious budgeting commitments. Actually, the money is better spent on public highways, an impressive governor's mansion, and foreign aid.

4. Keep all records strictly confidential. Under no circumstances discuss a diagnosis with the patient. The records of commitment and conversations with relatives should be completely inaccessible to the patient. **Knowledge of results** has been known to lead to a complete remission.

5. Insist on physical disease. The patient should have his attention continually drawn to any physical defects or illnesses. Not only can many of these disorders be successfully treated, but this keeps the patient's mind on the fact that his mental problems are basically physical. The whole idea of pills and medical treatment

precludes any thought of the possibility of underlying psychological processes.

6. Never mention any interpersonal dynamics. This only confuses the patients. Also, it tends to undermine the good work of the physician, often making an alert patient doubt the ability of the professionally trained person to cure mental illness. Any allusion to social factors, emotional conflicts, or sibling rivalry is detrimental, as would be such foolish projects as ward government.

7. Liberally mix the patient population with criminals, addicts, and prostitutes. This helps the patient identify himself with the proper element of society. It also adds to his confusion concerning the real status of his illness. The introduction of a psychopathic criminal has been known to frighten schizophrenics into complete withdrawal for a period of weeks. A pretty prostitute enlivens a drab ward considerably and furnishes young trainees with candidates for dynamic psychotherapy. However, the sexes must be strictly segregated.

8. Special care for children and adolescents. The institution is in a unique position to teach these young impressionable minds lessons that will never be forgotten. Children placed on a back ward with several hundred regressed patients are furnished with remarkable lessons in futility. If several children or adolescents are allowed to band together, they are able to learn to steal, lie, cheat and practice sexual perversions that otherwise may take a lifetime to learn.

9. Maintain the patient's identity. The old custom of photographing mental patients considerably helped to remind the patient that he was potentially dangerous. It is well to continually remind the new attendants of the early reporting of possible escapes and bring to their attention the classic case of various crimes that have been committed by escaped mental patients. Above all, do not allow patients to become friendly with staff personnel. I need not point out the problems which arise with male staff members and certain female patients.

10. Encourage relatives to lie to the patient. This is especially important during commitment procedures. Never tell the patient where he is going to be taken. They often just become resistive and fight. A small lie enables you to have them safely transported to the institution where they can be properly managed by hospital

personnel. The doctor-relative relationship should not include the patient.

Conclusions

The results of careful observation indicate that there are time-honored methods of establishing and maintaining chronicity in the mental patient. That these principles may be generalized to other situations is not denied. It should be pointed out that there are certainly other methods available. However, with some refinement and further research other procedures may well become acceptable.

Stewart's article deals with several of the commonly practiced methods that reinforce and perpetuate the condition of mental illness. The studies mentioned early in the article discuss some current undesirable factors evident in many treatment centers and mental hospitals of this country. The satiric but realistic account above draws attention to a deplorable situation.

6

Dyer:
Problems in personality assessment*

In the newspapers and popular magazines there has recently been a rash of articles on tests and testing. Many of these articles are profoundly disturbing to a professional tester like me. It is not that the writers occasionally lambaste testing and all its works. Some of the criticism is cogent and healthy, and may serve a useful purpose in deflating the wild claims of wrongheaded optimists who have lately wandered into the testing business. What does worry the conscientious **psychometrician** (psychometrician is simply the $64 word for a person who puts the most serious part of his mind on the making of tests and all the paraphernalia that goes with them) is that the typical hostile critic of testing berates the tester for ideas he (the tester) does not hold and for a point of view he regards as fanciful if not fallacious. What worries him even more is that his very defenders have a curious habit of unwittingly ascribing to him opinions and attitudes that he himself regards as intellectually impossible.

I believe this predicament comes about, at least in part, from the fact that the psychometrician's view of human ability is basically different from the ordinary view held by people in general, including most teachers, guidance

counselors, and other educators. Accordingly, I shall try to tell you how I, as one psychometrician, look at human ability in the hope that we may approach a meeting of minds.

Superstitions about aptitude

First I shall comment on a few widely held superstitions about mental ability as measured by aptitude tests, and these include IQ tests. One of the most persistent superstitions is that an aptitude test measures something called "native ability." When people speak of native ability, they usually seem to mean something fixed and immutable inside the human being, some constant quantity of something that is born in the individual and that determines how well he does on tests and ought to do in school or college or in a career.

The notion that such an inherent entity exists is not unreasonable, although nobody has ever seen it under a microscope. Studies in genetics support the idea, and so do certain psychological studies, especially those tracing the development of twins reared separately under different conditions. But (and this is a big but) even though native ability may be a reasonable concept — or rather a construct growing out of a multitude of observations, just as the gene itself is a construct — it is certainly not reasonable to suppose that any test of mental ability measures

*Quoted material is from Henry S. Dyer, "A Psychometrician Views Human Ability," *Teachers College Record,* April 1960, **61**(7), 394–403. By permission of the author and publisher.

the construct in any meaningful way. In itself a score on an aptitude test tells you literally nothing about a particular child's native ability.

What an aptitude test does measure is the quality of a pupil's performance on a number of mental tasks. It tells how well he can cope with tasks like those on the test at the time he takes the test, and it tells nothing more. Everything beyond this datum is pure inference. And the inference of "native ability" is a particularly shaky one. It is shaky because the tasks that appear in aptitude tests are invariably of a sort that a child (or an adult) has had to *learn* to perform as a result of his experience in the world around him—experience at home, at school, on the playground, on the job, in front of a TV set, at the movies, and elsewhere.

The amount of learning that has taken place by the time the child meets the questions on a test depends on a number of things that can vary enormously from one individual to another—the vividness of his experiences, the contexts within which they have occurred, the frequency with which a given experience has been encountered, the receptiveness of the child to what is going on in the world, and so on. With all this variability in experience between the time of birth and the time of taking the test, it is absurd to suppose that an aptitude score measures some fixed entity that the child was born with.

Let me cite a small but revealing example. At an early age my son was interested in fishing and was particularly intrigued at the sight of fish leaping out of the water to catch flies. One of the questions in a standard intelligence test for children is this:

Birds fly; fish_____.

The correct answer, of course, is "swim." My son's answer was "jump." A good answer, perhaps, but atypical and therefore wrong—wrong not because he is innately stupid but because his experience with fish differed from that of the general run of children. This incident is not intended to suggest that all intelligence tests are a snare and a delusion but merely to emphasize that aptitude test scores are inevitably determined in considerable measure by what the child has seen and heard and done.

Let me re-emphasize that the psychometrician thinks of ability not as a constant entity inside the individual but simply as the quality of his behavior with respect to any set of tasks that may confront him at the moment. If these tasks constitute a test, then the individual's score on the test *is* his ability with respect to the kinds of tasks the test contains. The ability is always a construct derived from the test score. We don't measure the construct; we arrive at it through the measurement of behavior. Under this definition, which I suppose you might call an **operational definition,** an individual's ability may vary with time and with the kinds of tasks that make up the test. He may get one score on Test X one day and a different score on the same test another day. To the psychometrician this means that the individual's ability as defined by the tasks on Test X has *changed* from one time to another.

This point of view, as contrasted with the ordinary point of view about human ability, has important consequences in the way one interprets test scores.

The fallacy of the "underachiever"

To think that an aptitude test measures something fixed in the pupil's internal mechanism, something unaffected by his learning and experience, can, in the psychometrician's view, lead to confused thinking about the student himself. One fallacious notion that comes out of such thinking is that a student with high ability scores and low marks in school is an **underachiever**—one who is not working up to capacity. The reasoning implicit in such a statement goes something like this: (1) Johnny's ability score, and therefore his ability, is high; (2) this means that Johnny is equipped by nature with ability to do good school work; (3) he is not doing it; (4) therefore he is not using the ability with which nature endowed him. The fallacy in this reasoning occurs in the assumption that a high ability score means that Johnny is equipped by nature with ability to do good school work. It may mean nothing of the sort. What it does mean is that Johnny has done well on the kinds of questions that the test poses. The fact that Johnny does not also do well on the kinds of questions his teachers pose may be merely an indication that the questions in the two situations are different—that his teachers are expecting one kind of performance (or ability) from him and the test expects a different kind of performance (or ability).

In building a scholastic aptitude test, of course, the psychometrician puts into it a series of tasks that he hopes will correlate high with the kinds of tasks a student is expected to perform in school. But the correlation is never perfect because schools vary and teachers vary in their demands on pupils, and because pupils vary in their perceptions of the tasks required of them.

Nevertheless, the notion of the under-achiever—the child who is not working up to ability—has taken deep roots in spite of the efforts of some psychometricians to kill it. We thought we had it buried back in the 1930's, but in the past few years it has again raised its ugly head. The customary, and ordinarily fallacious, diagnosis is that the student with a high ability score and low marks in school is *ipso facto* unmotivated or lazy or suffering from some emotional disturbance traceable perhaps to faulty toilet training. Granted that these are possibilities, nevertheless, it is a vast mistake to assume that they can be inferred solely from the discrepancy between the scores and the marks. The first question to ask is, Why has Johnny learned how to answer the test questions better than the teacher's questions? Perhaps the trouble is not in Johnny at all but in the kinds of questions on the test, or in the kinds of questions the teacher asks, or even in the teacher's skill as a teacher.

"Culture free" tests?

Some people are wedded to the idea that ability tests *ought* to measure an unchanging native ability and that failure to do this represents a serious weakness in the tests. This point of view leads to the frequent demand that such tests should be "culture free"; that is, unaffected by the cultural milieu in which a child has been brought up. It is plainly impossible to satisfy such a demand. Consider what any test essentially is. It is made up of a series of pieces of the environment to which the pupil is expected to react in one way or another. These pieces of the environment are questions, problems, situations which, no matter how cute or original or apparently novel, are inevitably drawn from the culture. In selecting pieces of the environment for a test, the testmaker tries to sample the common culture as broadly as possible, but

even so he cannot make his test equally appropriate to all the subcultures in American life. There are too many differences between the environment of the city child and that of the farm child or between the environment of the child of foreign-born parents and that of the child of native-born parents. If the tester, on the other hand, attempts to eliminate from his test all elements which are not perfectly common (or perfectly uncommon) for all groups—and this has been tried—he is likely to find himself with a test whose scores may not be very helpful in predicting school success, for most schools and colleges reflect the dominant culture in the society of which they are a part. If a child does poorly on an aptitude test because he comes from the wrong side of the tracks, it isn't the test that is being "unfair"; it is the hard facts of social circumstance that are unfair. Anyone who is seriously interested in improving the lot of the culturally underprivileged should direct his attention not to changing the tests—which would accomplish literally nothing—but to improving the quality of educational opportunity for all children.

Wobbly test scores

Another unreasonable demand that people seem to make of tests—whether they are aptitude tests or any other kind—is that the scores they yield should be absolutely accurate measures of whatever it is they purport to measure. Take an intelligence test, for example. Some people are shocked to discover that a pupil's IQ—his score on the test—can change with time and with the test. He can get an IQ of 100 this year and one of 120 next year. If he takes two different brands of an intelligence test on the same day, he may score an IQ of 110 on one and an IQ of 95 on the other.

Teachers, guidance counselors, parents, and others find this wobbly quality of the IQ disconcerting. It destroys the notion that the IQ is an unchanging personal possession; that you can decide once and for all what a child's IQ is; or that if a child at age twelve turns up with an IQ of 115 or better he ought to be steered toward college, but if his IQ is less than that, any college plans he or his parents may be toying with should be permanently discouraged. Test scores are slippery things, and anyone who uses them without realizing how slippery they are can make serious errors in judgment and do considerable damage to a child's education.

Wobbliness in test scores is no news to the tester. It is something that he accepts as inevitable for all tests of every description: **aptitude tests** or **achievement tests, interest tests** or **personality tests,** paper-and-pencil tests or performance tests, objective tests or essay tests. No test ever devised or given is more than a *sample* of a pupil's reactions. If you give a pupil a spelling test of 100 words drawn from among the thousands he has encountered in his studies and he gets 75 out of a 100 correct, what do you have? You have an *estimate,* based on a sample, of how he would do on all the words to which he has been exposed. If you draw another sample of 100 from the same pool of words, the number of words the pupil spells correctly on this second test will in all probability be different. He may get 63 right, he may get 92 right, or anything in between or outside these limits. You now have a different estimate of his ability to spell all the words he is supposed to know.

But the difficulty does not end here. Suppose that, without allowing the pupil any opportunity for study in between, you ask him to spell the *same* sample of 100 words two days in succession. Would he get the same number correct each time? Probably not, because his response to any given word can change. Today he spells *irresistible* correctly; tomorrow he leaves out one of the *r*'s or uses *a* instead of *i* in *ible.* Today he spells *scissors* incorrectly by omitting the *c*; tomorrow he gets it right. What a pupil does with a particular word on one occasion is thus only a sample of what he would do with the same word on other occasions. What a pupil does in any test situation — a word to spell, an arithmetic problem to solve, a story to write, a cake to bake — is never more than a sample of all the possible responses he might make to the situation if given the opportunity.

Tests as samples

In a nutshell, this means that every test is two kinds of sample — a sample of the situations to which a student is expected to respond and a sample of the kinds of responses he is likely to make to each situation. Taken together, this double sampling inevitably makes for uncer-

tainty in test results, uncertainty rooted in the fact that whenever we deal with a sample we have to cope with errors of sampling.

The brutal fact about errors of sampling is that they are not the kinds of errors you can rectify. You cannot "correct" for errors of sampling. The sampling error in a pupil's test score does not mean that the score is "off" by some ascertainable amount; it simply means that we have to face the fact that it is clouded with uncertainty, that it could have been different, that if we use it to estimate a pupil's ability we run the risk of making the wrong estimate. If Johnny gets a mark of 70 on a history examination and Joe gets a mark of 55, we cannot be dead sure that Johnny passes and Joe does not. If we had given them a different sample of history questions, Joe might have got 70 and Johnny 55.

Many people, probably most, find this uncertainty hard to take. Too many of them close their eyes to it, and among those who do are many teachers, guidance counselors, college admissions officers, and others who make frequent use of test results. They seem to feel that the professional test-maker has let them down by allowing **sampling error** to creep into his tests. Every year after the results of the College Board examinations come out, I receive a rash of telephone calls from dismayed school officials or parents or college admissions officers who say, in effect, "Johnny took your Scholastic Aptitude Test last May and got a score of 550. He took it again this January and his score dropped to 475. What's happened to your crazy test?" Under the circumstances it is a little difficult to persuade the party at the other end of the line that nothing has happened to the test, that nobody has made a terrible mistake, that Johnny, bless his soul, is merely a victim of sampling error — as are all the other Johnnies and Marys who submit to *any* kind of test whatsoever. To an anxious parent or a harried admissions officer, this sort of answer is hardly comforting. Uncertainty is always uncomfortable, despite the fact that in the assessment of human ability it can never be avoided.

Inevitability of the sampling error

In defense of the testmaker, be it said that if he is worth his professional salt he is acutely aware of the sampling error in his tests, and although he knows he can never get rid of it (and wishes everybody could understand this fact), he also knows how to do something about it. He knows how to get a good estimate of the amount of sampling error (that is, the amount of uncertainty) in any test, and he knows what to do to reduce the size of this error.

Professional ethics require him to make known to his customers how much sampling error a given test contains. If he fails to report this and other matters faithfully, there are professional associations that may call him to account for unethical practice. In other words, testers take very seriously the matter of knowing, and letting the public know, how much sampling error a test contains. They only wish the public would pay more attention to this information and not go on being surprised every time the sampling error in a test becomes painfully apparent.

In the testmaking business one of the aims is to make the uncertainty of measurement as small as possible. Other things being equal, the sampling error in a test becomes smaller as the size of the sample becomes larger. Obviously a 100-word spelling test will surpass a 10-word test as an estimate of a pupil's ability to spell. But the size of the sample, though of prime importance, is not the only consideration. One has to worry also about the composition of the sample: Is it truly representative of all the different kinds of tasks a student could meet in a particular field — hard ones, easy ones, simple ones, complex ones? The sampling error in a test can also be affected by the manner in which the test is presented. How nearly uniform are the conditions of testing from sample to sample? If a child takes a test while a pile driver is pounding in the next block, the sampling of his responses may not be typical. All such matters the tester does his utmost to control, and the result is that the best of his tests if properly used provide as reliable a sample of pupil performance as can be found anywhere. Even so, looked at critically, a highly **reliable** test still has a lot of uncertainty in it.

*Imprecision in casual
observation*

People who have been generally aware of the wobbliness in test scores are often surprised,

even shocked, to realize the extent of the wobbliness. If this is the best that the best of ability tests can do, they say, why not go back to the old-fashioned tried and true ways of sizing up students? Why not rely on teachers' judgments and direct observation in face-to-face contact? Well, these old ways have long been tried, but their results are far less precise than those of a well-made test. When it is possible to check up on unfettered observation and judgment, one wonders whether the old methods can be relied upon at all.

I once witnessed such a checking up which occurred more or less by accident. A youngster was applying for a scholarship at a well-known university. He had been interviewed by three people independently — an alumnus and two assistant deans. The alumnus rated him "satisfactory," one of the assistant deans rated him "top-notch," and the other rated him "impossible." As for teachers' judgments, there is the instance of a student who had one English teacher during the first semester and another the second semester. The first one gave him an F; the second one gave him an A. As instances like these multiply, one cannot escape the impression that good tests, for all their lack of precision, give vastly less wobbly results than do the "old-fashioned" ways of assessing human performance.

Tests as predictors

The principle of uncertainty in testing extends to matters beyond the wobbliness in the scores themselves. It applies also to the use of tests for predicting how well students are likely to do in school and college. Among the most important purposes that tests can serve is that of helping the guidance counselor or the college admissions officer predict what kinds of marks Johnny is going to get if he takes a certain course or enrolls in a certain college. Such predictions are the stuff of which vital educational decisions are made.

But some people seem to have funny ideas about prediction. Johnny's mathematical aptitude score suggests that Johnny will get a B in advanced algebra. Johnny takes the course and turns up with a C. "You see," they say, "the test was wrong! You can't trust it." This attitude strikes the tester not only as unreasonable but as one that grows out of the mistaken idea that prediction must always be an all-or-none, right-or-wrong business. It would be fairer to the test and would contribute to better decision-making if prediction were thought of as a matter of calculating the chances; of figuring the risks rather than of asserting an on-the-nose expectation. We should not say the aptitude score predicts an A for Johnny; we should say it shows that Johnny has 6 chances in 10 of making an A in algebra, 8 chances in 10 of making a B or better, 9 chances in 10 of making a C or better, only 1 chance in 10 of flunking the course. This approach underlines the uncertainty that is always involved in the prediction of events. It also provides information about the amount of uncertainty with which the interested parties will have to cope when making up their minds whether Johnny should take advanced algebra.

To recapitulate briefly, I have said that an individual's ability is the quality of his performance on a series of tasks, which we may call a test. I have said that our estimate of an individual's ability from any particular test is always clouded with uncertainty because of the inevitable sampling error in any test. I have suggested that in attempting to predict an individual's ability to cope with some situation in the future, there is also an unavoidable amount of uncertainty. This is because the kinds of tasks we can reasonably expect an individual to perform at one point in time may be, and usually are, to some extent different from the kinds of tasks we may reasonably expect him to perform at a later time, after he has had new learning experiences. That is, the kinds of tasks with which you test a student's mathematical ability before he takes algebra cannot be the same as those with which you would test his mathematical ability after he has taken algebra. He has learned and his ability has changed, and the remarkable thing is that in a given field we can predict future performance from past performance as well as we do.

Diverse abilities

Let us now look at another aspect of the matter, namely, the different *kinds* of human ability. To say of an individual that he has a large amount of ability is essentially meaningless to the psychometrician. He will counter with the question, "Ability in doing what?" A person may have a large amount of ability in spelling, (that is, he may get high scores on spelling tests), but he may have only a small amount of ability to solve problems in arithmetic (meaning he may score low on an arithmetic test).

During the past forty years psychometricians have devoted a good deal of effort to identifying different kinds of ability through the technique known as **factor analysis.** Factor analysis is essentially a form of experiment in which the psychometrician tries to discover how all the different kinds of mental tasks tend to cluster. As might be expected, psychometricians have found that tasks having to do with words, their meanings, and their combinations tend to form one homogeneous cluster; tasks having to do with numbers and their manipulation form another homogeneous cluster. A homogeneous cluster of tasks is defined empirically as one in which the performance of students on any task in the cluster is highly correlated with their performance on all other tasks in the cluster. Thus, students who test high on vocabulary knowledge tend to test high also in reading comprehension, in grammatical usage, in theme writing, and so on. Such a cluster of tasks is called the verbal factor, and students who test high on the tasks constituting this factor are said to have high verbal ability. Similarly, the cluster of tasks dealing with numbers is called the mathematical or quantitative factor, and students who test high on this factor are said to have high mathematical ability. Other clusters of tasks define such things as the mechanical factor, the memory factor, and the perceptual factor. And the correlatives of these factors are mechanical ability, memory ability, perceptual ability, and so on.

Factor analysis is a fascinating and powerful technique that has done much to tease out the dimensions of human ability, but we must not make the mistake of supposing that it has somehow penetrated the mystery of mind and uncovered hidden determiners of human performance. It has, however, made possible the classification of human performance into various categories of ability. It is nevertheless **culture bound** in the sense that the categories it defines might appear quite different if the rewards accorded by society to various kinds of performance were radically changed and if such changes were reflected in a fundamental reorganization of school curricula. It is conceivable, for instance, that verbal ability and mathematical ability. which now appear so different, might merge into a single new ability if reading and arithmetic in the elementary schools were taught not as two separate subjects but as a single subject called, let us say, logical analysis.

Pitfalls in profiles

The availability of tests for several different kinds of ability has led, as you probably well know, to the development of what are known as multiaptitude test batteries for use in guidance. These test batteries have within them rich possibilities, but they have not been an unmixed blessing. For one thing, they have encouraged the oversimplified notion that a profile of ability scores summarizes clearly and efficiently a large amount of reliable information about most of the important abilities of an individual. Psychometricians have been worrying about this problem for a long time. They have inveighed repeatedly against the overconfident use of profile charts, on the ground that such charts are often grossly misleading; that the differences in ability they depict—even when they appear large—may be, and usually are, unreliable; that the score scales used for the several tests in the profile may not be comparable; that the several measures which show on the profile may appear to be highly independent measures when, in fact, many of them may be highly correlated—in short, that the apparent clarity and efficiency of an ability profile are really illusions covering up all sorts of pitfalls in score interpretation which even the most wary can scarcely avoid. Yet the profile chart is still in wide use, primarily I suppose because it is extraordinarily convenient.

Within the past few years there have been several attempts by psychometricians to develop data on which a more or less fool-proof type of profile chart could be based. This research falls into the category of what are known as differential prediction studies. We have one such study going on at ETS. The studies in connection with the General Aptitude Test Battery of the USES are another example. But probably the largest and best known is the differential prediction study being conducted at the University of Washington under the direction of Paul Horst. The goal of all these studies is to provide a profile of probable success in each of several educational or vocational fields rather than a profile showing simply where a student stands on a series of tests whose predictive validity is unknown or at least unstated in the profile itself. That is, the elements in the probability profile are *fields,* not tests, and probability that a student will succeed in a given field is based on test scores and other data.

Problems in differential prediction

The probability profile chart, as contrasted with the ability profile chart, would, I take it, be very helpful in guidance if it could actually be produced. But the differential prediction studies that must underlie such a chart are surrounded by a number of difficult problems. In the first place, such studies are extraordinarily expensive. In the second place, since they require a follow-up of student performance over several years, they take a long time. In the third place, since it is obviously impossible for every student in the study sample to try himself out in each of the fields open to him, it is difficult, though not methodologically impossible, to get data *across* fields which are meaningful and comparable. In the fourth place, the probability data obtained in such studies are interpretable only for a particular setting, that is, only for the school or college or specific occupational group for which the original data were developed.

All these problems, difficult though they may be, are surmountable if the money and time are forthcoming to surmount them. But it is still, in my judgment, an open question whether we shall ever in the nature of things be able to get test score data or any other kind of data that will permit us to draw the kind of probability profile the differential prediction studies are aiming at. To me, the University of Washington results as well as our own are discouraging. They provide reasonably good overall prediction, but so far they do not provide much *differential* prediction. That is, the probability that a given student will succeed in any one field is not so greatly different from the probability that he will succeed in most other fields, and one wonders whether such differences as there are can be considered real and reliable. The hope is, of course, that by introducing better and more sharply differentiated tests, more sharply differentiated probability statements will become possible. But this is still only a hope, and it is a moot question, it seems to me, whether *any* tests can ever be found that will separate very far in advance the student more likely to succeed in biology from the one more likely to succeed in history. Despite all the work of the factor analysts over the past forty years, I think it is possible that human abilities are sufficiently fluid over time so that, if circumstances are right, the person who today looks like a good biologist and a poor historian may undergo experiences which will convert him into a good historian and a poor biologist. You see, the trouble with the well-known square-peg-in-round-hole analogy is that it is completely static. It assumes that neither the peg nor the hole can ever change shape, when we know perfectly well that the patterns of people's abilities change as they adapt to circumstances, and circumstances change as people adapt to them. In other words, I suspect that there are dynamic elements in the relation of an individual to his changing environment which are not being taken into account in the differential prediction studies and which may, indeed, prevent them from ever arriving at any very fruitful results. But in any case, the question is still open, the problems are enormous, and the need for vast quantities of research is dire.

I suppose my basic worry about the use of profile charts, whether they are ability profiles or probability profiles, is that they tend to conceal the very great and complex problems of human functioning about which we actually know so little, and make them seem so much simpler than they really are. I doubt that we are likely to get very far in improving the guidance process or any other educational process by adopting devices which lure us into thinking we know more about human ability than is at the present knowable.

Importance of doubt

I realize that this discussion has been appallingly negative. I have suggested that the concept of native ability has little if any practical utility. I have suggested that any ability as defined by the tasks on which a student performs can be highly variable and elusive. I have pointed to the unreliability of measures of ability and to the uncertainties involved in using them for prediction purposes. I have tried to show that the categories of performance which constitute different kinds of ability are subject to change as the dominant elements in our culture and in the educational process change. I have cast doubt on the utility of ability profiles as used in guidance and have questioned whether the differential prediction studies as at present constituted may not be based upon a false assumption about the ways in which human abilities develop under training.

If I have plunged you into unrelieved doubt, I am not sorry, really, for I believe that if we are ever going to get anywhere in trying to understand human behavior, we must always realize that it comprises the most complicated phenomena on the face of the earth. And we must approach it with a healthy skepticism toward all gimmicks and with a humility that encourages caution but never gives up hope.

*Radin:
Personality and
drug addiction**

Not much sophistication is required to realize that drugs affect personality. As a matter of fact, today, more than ever before, people (young and old) are experimenting with a wide variety of drugs in an attempt to find as-yet-undiscovered dimen-sions of their personality. They seek mystical and religious insights as well as

*Quoted material is from Sherwin S. Radin, "Psychosocial aspects of drug addiction," *Journal of School Health,* December 1966, **36**(10), 481–487. By permission of the author and publisher.

sensuous experiences. Some of the problems of drug usage and drug addiction are described by Radin in the following article.

Drug addiction is a complex issue involving physiological, sociological, psychological, medical, and legal parameters. There are many questions raised by this problem:

What is drug addiction?

Why does it occur?

Where and under what circumstances does one become addicted?

Who is most likely to become addicted?

What is the relationship to genetics and to developmental phenomena?

Are there specific personality characteristics of drug addicts?

Is narcotic addiction a crime or a disease, or neither, or both?

What is the natural course?

How do the cultural and personality aspects relate to one another?

What are the problems of treatment?

Is there anything to be done to prevent drug addiction?

Many papers have been written by persons from a variety of disciplines attempting to answer these questions. Unfortunately far too few answers have emerged. The complexity of the problem itself makes it difficult to arrive at valid conclusions. I will stress some of the psychosocial phenomena related to drug usage.

From time immemorial man has sought to ease his tensions of living and to make life more bearable. His adaptive maneuvers may be sanctioned or not. People utilize realistic endeavors or resort to magic and to phantasy.

The adaptive challenge may be met by the alteration of the environment. If one is unable to accomplish this or elects not to, he may alter his perception of the environment, or alter himself or his perception of himself. There are available a variety of drugs that enable one to alter his perceptual stage. How tempting for someone with a depreciated self image to resort to a magical potion! The effortless miracle is accomplished simply by introducing a foreign object into the body. The ability to change one's private world by altering one's view of it is reminiscent of the state of infantile omnipotence. The cry of the helpless infant signals the feeding mother whose ministrations rapidly alter his state of tension and hunger to one of calmness, satiation and perhaps blissful drowsiness or sleep. It is postulated that this is the paradigm for drug addiction. Just as the infant is dependent upon his mother for need gratification the addict is dependent upon his drug. Not everyone is tempted to try drugs and of those who do or are required to for medical reasons, only a relatively small percentage become addicted. It is thus postulated that there must be some physical and/or psychological predisposition necessary for addiction to take place. Drug addiction includes a compulsive need for the drug; an increase in tolerance and in intake; a withdrawal syndrome. The addict believes he cannot function without the drug and strives to obtain it regardless of the price. The period of elation during which the sense of self is grossly expanded and the individual's problems minimized lasts for a period of time and is then generally followed by depression as the drug wears off and the harsh realities of life are magnified. The addict vigorously seeks drugs to alter the depression and regain elation as rapidly as possible. Painful reality plus the memory of the state of bliss motivates him strongly to seek the drug. There has been a shift in the population using narcotics and in the cultural reasons for addiction in this country during the past 150 years. During the early part of the 19th century the addictive powers of **opium** and other drugs were not recognized. People of all ages and from all social strata were exposed to a variety of patent medicines as well as to doctors' prescriptions containing opium. These remedies were sold without restraint and were publicized as being a "cure-all" for practically "anything that ails you." Opium, **morphine, codeine,** and **cocaine** were the main drugs. By the middle of the 19th century some 3 to 4 percent of the population were addicted. During the 1890's the dangers of addiction were recognized and institutions were opened to treat the patients. Toward the turn of the century **heroin** was discovered and promoted as a cure for morphine addiction. Heroin did relieve the withdrawal symptoms of morphine but was even more of a pernicious addictive agent in its own right.

Thus the first group of addicts in this country were predisposed persons who were medically or quasi-medically exposed via perfectly legal channels. During the past 50 years a series of events, both legal and social, have resulted in a shift in the nature of the problem.

The early addicts were considered patients and were primarily under medical care. Dr.

Charles Towns of New York was one of the early doctors who realized how dangerous addiction was and used his influence to help control it. He helped draft the Boylan Law in 1904 designed to enable physicians to assist in the control of the narcotic problem. Although this law was passed, the section drafted by Towns concerning treatment was dropped. The Harrison Narcotic Act passed by Congress in 1914 was primarily for the purpose of control of production, manufacture, and distribution of narcotic drugs. It, too, minimized the physician's role in treatment. The enforcement of the revenue act was placed under the Bureau of Internal Revenue within its Bureau of Narcotics.

The essence of this change was that not only enforcement of production and distribution but also medical treatment came under the sway of the Bureau. The enforcement of the law was quite severe so that doctors were even imprisoned for administering to their patients, now considered criminals. The net effect of all this was that many persons who previously, while using the drug under medical supervision, lived a fairly regular life, now had to go underground in order to obtain illegally that which had become necessary for their psychosocial and even physiological survival. The criminal associations and traffic in narcotics are familiar to everyone. Since the drugs have become more valuable and more difficult to obtain, forbidden-fruit connotations in defiance of authority have provided additional motivation to obtain drugs. Thus there is a shift from patients to criminals and from all social strata to a preponderance of addicts in high incidence lower socio-economic areas: where in order to gain acceptance amongst one's peers it is necessary to join in. The few cigarettes of marijuana in the 9- to 10-year-old frequently give way to heroin in the teen-ager. Recently another shift is under way: to the college campus where morphine, marijuana, L.S.D. and other drugs are currently in vogue as youth seeks psychedelic experiences.

The incidence of narcotic addiction in the United States today is difficult to determine because of its illegal aspects. Estimates vary from 60,000 to 1 million. The majority [of addicts] are found in the larger cities, particularly New York, Los Angeles, Detroit, and Chicago. The number of addicts has increased some 5 to 10 fold over the past 15 years. Males outnumber females by 5 to 1. These figures are based upon the number of arrests. The majority are young adults from 21 to 30, but there is a significant increase in addiction in children.

Even though many people from deprived areas become addicted, others exposed to the same socio-economic milieu do not. Apparently these sociological conditions help to produce addiction only in those with physical or psychological vulnerabilities. Since addiction is flourishing in a variety of colleges, it is inaccurate to accent the lower socioeconomic area as the breeding place for addiction. Some authors have stated that boredom, hopelessness, and the need for immediate gratification frequently seen in slum areas lead to addiction. These traits might be prevalent upon a college campus despite the intellectually stimulating atmosphere with its abundant opportunities for creative endeavors and discourse. A number of college students disregard this atmosphere and seek answers in a world of altered self-perceptions, created by their ingestation of drugs. Proponents of a mystique, such as Timothy Leary and Allen Ginzberg, reinforce and promote drug cults. Young sensitive people are particularly susceptible since their natural developmental dilemma is to search for a true sense of identity. When authority purports to be able to delve into the depths of the mind and to uncover the essence of mental revelations, a ray of hope is afforded to many which may become their religion or philosophy of life. It thus appears that the social milieu per se is not a crucial determinant of addiction; although it may provide the individual with the opportunity to obtain the drug, it doesn't guarantee that he will.

Is there an addict personality type? Are there qualities that all or most addicts possess? Does addiction itself lead to the development of characteristics such as impulsive, aggressive behavior or **passive dependent behavior?** There are studies in the literature where traits of character as diverse as those indicated are thought to be related in some way to drug addiction. The overall consensus, however, is that there isn't any succinct pattern that is readily identifiable as the "Narcotic Character."

Most studies indicate that the addict may be in one of several psychiatric diagnostic categories: psychotic, neurotic, **character disorder.** There are common personality qualities which are described in many studies. However, they are not exclusively found in addicts or are not in any way **pathognomonic** of narcotic addiction.

During the addiction phase, most addicts reveal emotional blunting, immaturity, and a **narcissistic** orientation primarily related to the drug rather than to his family. His mind is usually clear, rational, logical, and coherent. These qualities may be drastically altered during periods of overdose or withdrawal.

Many studies of hospitalized male addicts describe non-aggressivity, sociability, closeness to mother, interests in the arts and in creativity, passivity, omnipotent ideals and narcissism, orality with regressive tendencies as the significant qualities of addicts. These traits refer primarily to opium and its derivatives.

Drugs such as marijuana and alcohol act by releasing inhibitions, and therefore aggressive and sexual behavior is much more common than in the case of opium, where relaxation of tensions usually results in a state of pleasure, euphoria, and relaxation. **Dexedrine** is an exhilarating stimulant. Cocaine stimulates the central nervous system and may produce wild excitement with hallucinations and paranoid ideas. The latter may lead to retaliatory aggression and even to homicide. **Peyote** or **mescaline** produces colored geometric hallucinations. **Barbiturates** may lead to poor motor control and speech that may be inarticulate. Emotional lability is common. [The barbiturate-user] may suddenly change from a warm and friendly demeanor to an outburst of violence. His judgment is poor; resorting to inner fantasies is common.

Lysergic acid diethylamide (LSD-25) is a drug which recently has been the subject of much concern. Like mescaline or **psilocybin,** it is a **hallucinogenic drug.** Some persons, such as Timothy Leary, advocate it as a mind stimulant enabling one to experience fantastic sensory impressions. Their influence has been primarily upon the college campus. The potential of this drug to induce an underlying psychosis has been frequently reported. Some claim that no permanent damage to the brain results from LSD, while others state the contrary. At any rate it is a dangerous drug, which is still in its experimental stage and should be primarily reserved for the laboratory. It may have its prime function in action upon the integration mechanisms of the mind.

Lauretta Bender has found that addicts under 16 years of age are more disturbed in the psychosocial areas than are those from 16 to 21. In some hospitalized adolescents there is the possibility that addiction to opiates protects against the development of underlying psychosis.

In her informative book, *The Drug Addict as a Patient,* Dr. Marie Nyswander reviews several formulations which are related to drug addiction. She notes that addiction usually begins during adolescence and spends itself by the middle forties. These 30 years or so are the most active and productive ones for most people. It is postulated that morphine serves to quell the anxiety associated with normal sexual and aggressive drives. This enables the addict to avoid sexuality and aggression. His history generally reveals disappointment and failure in ordinary sexual experiences. Morphine provides in many a substitute orgastic experience. It obviates the need for sexual relations. When addicts indulge in opiates sexual activity is not sought. In some addicts sexual feelings are enhanced but at the expense of sexual performance. This not only refers to opiates but other drugs such as LSD, alcohol, and marijuana. "Whether this avoidance of sexuality is a cause or a result of addiction is open to question. But regardless of this aspect, the addict's life does not include what could by any stretch of the imagination be called normal sexuality" (Nyswander, 1956).

According to the Avoidance of Aggression theory, the drug prevents the addict from assuming his normal role in life associated with mature assertive strivings toward responsible behavior. The diminished interest in aggression and in sexuality in the addict predates adolescence and reflects distorted family life and developmental phenomena.

Many of the addict's qualities are reminiscent of early childhood, such as immaturity, omnipotent strivings, narcissism, inability to give, etc. The closeness and the identification of the addict with the opposite sex parent forge a personality that is poorly equipped to deal with life's problems. Through the vehicle of the drug and the providers of the same he fashions for himself an illusory world where his infantile strivings are gratified. He triumphs in his magical drug dependency as his self expands in omnipotent grandeur.

It is no mystery that the relapse rate is well over 90 percent in most studies regardless of the treatment, ambulatory or hospitalized, and with or without vigorous case work and psychiatric treatment. It is extremely difficult to substitute reality which is painful for pleasurable fantasy.

There is apparently greater success in dealing with the management of this problem in England than in the United States. The legal problems are minimized and the treatment is primarily in medical hands. This enables a greater number of people to function effectively while under medical supervision. The person is not considered a criminal and motivations such as defiance of authority are eliminated. Those suggestible persons who are influenced by "dope peddlers" are no longer fair bait. Thus in all the total number of addicts is less and those who are still addicted function in the mainstream of life to a greater extent than those in this country who are forced to wear the criminal label. Since many of the drugs, when properly supervised, do not constitute a health hazard to the user or a menace to society, the English approach is a warranted one. These comments, of course, do not exclude a psychosocial and educational program to aid those addicted.

Freedman and Wilson outline an educational approach to the prevention of addiction (1964). They stress a program for the 16-year-olds who leave schools in slum areas where they are frequently exposed to narcotics. According to these authors group and recreation workers should provide an opportunity for the children to identify with an attitude counter to the narcotic one. This is particularly important when the child's family provides little direction or education.

An informative approach to the use of drugs in the schools is readily implemented. Small discussion groups rather than formal lectures are more effective. "Two kinds of attack through environmental change are indicated: first, a general strengthening of population resistance to the addictive disorders, and, second, amelioration or elimination of the contributary environmental factors [Freedman and Wilson, p. 427]." Since the addiction problem seems to flourish under conditions of frustration and failure, and since the schools might inadvertently provide such experience for some disadvantaged children, special programming is indicated for them, in which a positive and non-frustrating environment is created.

Many of these children have emotional problems of great severity. It isn't theoretical that such children can be helped. My experiences with the Syracuse Scholastic Rehabilitation Program for children with emotional problems has dramatically demonstrated how educators and clinicians working together can effect the rehabilitation of many children

with emotional and learning problems. The overall approach is both clinical and educational. The two reinforce each other. The teacher learns to utilize the clinical knowledge of the child, his development, and his family to aid him in overcoming his learning problems. The child may simultaneously be receiving psychotherapy. His family may be involved if they appear to be playing a significant role. Usually they do and it is necessary to treat a child-family unit, rather than the child alone. Both clinician and educator working together are able to accomplish what either alone might not. The child's sense of self-worth expands as he succeeds in school. He now enjoys learning. The clinician helps free those parts of his mind which were directed at containing the emotional problems. The teacher learns from the clinician the best way of approaching the child and presenting the academic program. The end result of this is that many children who were chronic failures in school are now able to learn. A number of these children come from the same areas where drug addiction is a problem. Many of these children enter the program at a very early age, 6 to 9 or 10. This perhaps is early enough to prevent their later developing such psycho-social problems as addiction and delinquency.

This approach is not adequate enough to prevent these problems. We are dealing with only a small number of children. It is necessary to enrich the normal child's academic program by utilizing proper mental health principles and personnel. The child must be viewed as a total person in order to accomplish this task. He has social and psychological needs as well as educational ones. How can we enable children to utilize their native equipment optimally? This is the area where new approaches are warranted. How much of the pressure on young people brought to bear today for the purpose of enabling them to learn and enter colleges is exacting an unnecessary and deleterious effect? The argument that we are living in a competitive world and they might as well start now may be valid for some but not for all. In addition, this extra stress might lead to a variety of emotional disorders and breakdowns and possibly to drug addiction. If the sense of self-worth is diminished significantly, and drugs serve to elevate the sense of self, then the latter possibility must be considered.

Let us use the potential inherent in the school structure for all children, not just for those with emotional problems. The days of teaching just the 3 R's are long past. This means more than just a quantitative change to the 20, 50, or 100 R's. The effectiveness of our educational systems must be broadened by the utilization of psychological knowledge in collaboration with educators. A more effective model for children to learn, develop, and flourish under will emerge. Only then will psycho-social problems such as addiction be remedied.

Chapter summary

The first problem this chapter deals with is pinpointing the meaning of personality. A concrete, objective definition is proposed in which personality is seen as the organized totality of a given individual's responses to his related stimulus objects. We also stress the dynamic and fluid nature of personality.

A block of studies in personality modification convincingly illustrates how the behavior of children can be manipulated by providing them with models. Even moral conduct is subject to subtle, unwitting modification without prescribing the specific response to be performed. By contrast, Lovaas reports what can be done by dealing with aversive conditioning of specific undesirable responses of autistic children. Both studies show the rapidity with which learning takes place in contrast to such traditional methods as the psychoanalytic couch. The latter may require months or years in modifying undesirable behavior. Stewart's ironic article on chronic psychosis points out how we may actually be reinforcing undesirable personality traits in the wards of our mental institutions. The main point of this section is the rich potentiality for personality change via learning procedures that have been discovered in recent years.

The article by Dyer on personality measurement reveals the alertness, sophistication, and humility demanded by the difficult job of personality assessment. It stands as a warning to self-appointed "mental testers" who make facile judgments about human characteristics.

The final selection on drug addiction, included in part because of its recent connection with the college campus, shows the complexity of the drug problem. It is an appropriate selection to close the chapter with because it demonstrates how drug addiction, like personality itself, finds its controlling factors in the biological, psychological, social, legal, and economic milieu of the individual concerned.

Intelligence

The **nature-nurture controversy** pervades most categories of psychology simply because psychologists have not yet settled this basic problem. However, the question of **intelligence** need not be ignored in the meantime. Intelligence deserves to be considered separately in its own right. At least, we give it an independent status in the present chapter in order to inquire into its essential nature. What is intelligence? Can we make any deductions about it? Is it some inherent *general* ability that limits or facilitates learning? Or is it a practical, though poorly defined, cluster of certain acquired reactions?

With the foregoing remarks as a background, we turn first to an article by Joseph Cautela that exposes some common errors about intelligence, after which we examine Piaget's uncommon way of viewing intelligence. A spoof by Bowles and Pronko, which describes how the authors set about devising a genetic scheme to show "how IQ *could be* inherited," follows next. One should by no means neglect the footnote to this article.

A possible classic in the field of intelligence research is examined in a report of "longitudinal studies" of intelligence at the Fels Research Institute of Human Development at Antioch College in Ohio. These studies focus on such questions as the following: Is the IQ constant over the years? Is motivation involved in intelligence development? How about personality characteristics of the child? Its parent? Their interrelationship? Any other personality correlates? The Fels study is followed by a discussion of Terman's interesting research on "gifted" children.

A certain classic comes as close as we have yet attained to a controlled experiment on the effects of early experience and IQ. This is Harold Skeel's study of two groups of orphanage children. In a novel experiment, one group was transferred to a mental institution where, it received care, attention, and affection, plus eventual adoption. The second group of children remained in the orphanage. Here, predictably, conditions were grim and lacking in any human warmth or stimulation. The two groups were rediscovered and their progress assessed in a follow-up 30 years later. The findings are exciting and throw light on the nature of intelligence.

The Van Allen Belt was named after a contemporary physicist. Similarly, we are beginning to talk about the **"Rosenthal effect,"** which is illustrated in the next selection. Suppose you *randomly* selected certain children and told their teachers that they would make great progress that school year. Would they? And would their IQ scores show much change by comparison with a control group? Whatever the findings, they are relevant to a proper definition of intelligence.

Few people see the great range of biological defectiveness in the children resident in our institutions for the mentally retarded. Therefore we shall visit a state hospital to show how severe biopathologies prevent the growth of intelligence.

Finally, Bucklew's historical and current perspective of the field of mental retardation traces changing concepts or ways of understanding the data in this area.

1

Cautela:
Some common
misconceptions of
intelligence*

The need for such a concept as "intelligence" arose when it was observed that some people seemed to perform tasks, which they encountered in everyday life, better (faster, more often correct, leading to more desirable results) than other people. In fact, it seemed that there was some type of continuum on which most people could be placed concerning their usual performance of different tasks. In other words, when the same class of stimuli (tasks) were presented, the frequency of correct responses usually varied from individual to individual, while the rate of correct responses remained fairly constant for each individual.

Once the above observation was made, it seemed logical to conclude that this difference in performance was due to some attribute within the individual. Now, when individual A is often confronted with the same tasks as individual B and A usually performs these tasks better, one can say that A has more of this attribute (which some people call intelligence) than B. If A and B are again confronted with similar tasks, then since A has more intelligence, his rate of correct responses will be greater than B's.

Intelligence

The next question that had to be asked was "What is the nature of this attribute (intelligence)"? Some of the answers given to this question have been:

1. ability to reason
2. ability to abstract
3. ability to plan ahead
4. ability to adapt to new situations

---

*Quoted material is from Joseph R. Cautela, "Misconceptions: Intelligence and the IQ," *Education*, January 1958, **78**(5), 300–303. Reprinted by permission of the author and the publishers, The Bobbs-Merrill Company, Inc.

5. ability to think
6. ability to understand
7. ability to learn
8. ability to profit from experience
9. ability to solve problems of all kinds

All the definitions given are circular; individuals are observed to differ in their ability to perform particular tasks (e.g., thinking or reasoning tasks) and then it is said that people differ in their performance of these tasks because they differ in intelligence (their ability to perform these tasks). In other words, nothing more has been said than that people differ in their ability to perform these tasks because they differ in their ability to perform these tasks. It is equivalent to saying that an **imbecile** is not able to perform a particular task because he has "low" intelligence. The above definitions accomplish nothing more than designate the particular kind of tasks involved when the term "intelligence" is used, but we are still not told anything about the nature of the ability to perform these tasks.

IQs

One of the most popular ways to express an individual's performance on an intelligence test is in terms of IQ. A common misconception held by many teachers is that IQ means

$$\frac{\text{mental age}}{\text{chronological age}} \times 100.$$

But we must remember that the Stanford-Binet way of defining IQ is only one of a number of ways now in use.

In the Terman and Merrill revision of the Stanford-Binet, the IQ for persons 16 or under is found by computing the MA in terms of the person's performance on certain tasks compared with different age groups. The subject is assigned a certain number of months credit for each item successfully passed. The mental age is then divided by the actual age of the subject and multiplied by 100 to compute the IQ. For adults (individuals over 16 years of age) the formula is

$$\frac{14 \text{ months earned}}{15}.$$

In the **Wechsler test** the individual's performance is also expressed in terms of IQ; but the IQ is not computed in the same way as in the Binet scale. In the Wechsler test the IQ is computed by expressing the individual's score in terms of its deviation from the mean of his particular age group. The mean IQ is arbitrarily set at 100 and the standard deviation is 15. If an individual score is one standard deviation above the mean of his age group, his IQ is given as 115. If the subject scores two standard deviations above the mean, then his IQ is set at 130. The IQ is not determined by dividing the credits earned by the chronological age.

In other tests, such as the **Otis Quick Scoring Mental Ability Tests,** the IQ is also determined in a manner different from the Binet formula. Even when the Binet formula is used, such as in the **Kuhlmann-Anderson tests,** the MA is not computed in the same way, so that the IQs really mean different things. Even if a test did use the IQ in exactly the same way as the Binet scale, the IQs would still mean different things, since the tasks used would have to be somewhat different (otherwise you would have the same test).

In view of the above statements concerning the tests that used the term IQ to express the individual's score, I think the following definition of IQ to be more realistic and less misleading:

IQ is a quantitative index of an individual's performance on an intelligence test (however you define intelligence) compared to other individuals who took the test.

Is IQ normally distributed?

We often hear the statement that IQs are normally distributed or follow the normal curve distribution. This statement can be quite misleading, since the intelligence tests are so constructed that the scores have to be normally distributed. One of the bases for the selection and rejection of items and subjects for standardization is that the scores have to be normally

distributed. It is not a surprise, then, to discover that if the finished (standardized) test is given to a random group of subjects, the IQs will be normally distributed; the test was constructed that way.

Does IQ remain constant?

When we ask if IQs are constant, we are really asking will the individual's scores on a particular intelligence test remain relatively stable throughout his life.

It is generally agreed that IQ scores do remain relatively constant throughout life. But why is this so? It is certainly not because the individual's capacity remains relatively stable throughout his life.

It is so because the scales are so constructed that if an individual's score deviates by a certain amount from the "typical" score of the group with which he is compared, he will always deviate by the same amount when he is compared, with certain age groups when he grows older. In the case of adults, where the CA is made constant for all adults, the items are so selected that age will not be a factor in influencing the subject's score.

The important point to remember in trying to find out some characteristics of the IQ is that the test constructors make certain assumptions concerning its nature from studies using a different variety of tasks given to many individuals in different age groups. From these preliminary studies the test constructors came to certain conclusions about the distribution and constancy of the IQ, then worked at constructing a test until the scores fit these conclusions. They do not use the actual intelligence tests to come to conclusions about the nature of the IQ (as defined by their tests).

If we remember that IQ is merely a way of expressing a test score on a particular type of test, we are less apt to think of IQ as something we have in us; something we carry around with us, that never changes, and falls somewhere in a certain distribution.

Some other misconceptions
concerning the IQ

Three other common misconcepts concerning the IQ are the following:

1. A child of eight with an IQ of 120 is brighter than an adult with an IQ of 100. Of course this is not necessarily so. A child with an IQ of 120 can perform certain tasks much better than his own age group as compared to the adult and his own age group; but the child is probably not better at these tasks at the present time. In all probability the child will perform better on similar tasks than that same adult once he becomes an adult.

2. IQ scores reveal the degree of native intellectual capacity of an individual. Actually, this is not so. All we can say is that the person's present ability on certain tasks compares in such and such a way with other people who attempt these tasks.

3. There is a tendency for some teachers to use the IQ as the explanation of the educational problems of most children. Sometimes we pay only lip service to the notion that educational problems may arise from poor teaching, emotional problems, and physical disabilities as well as from lack of ability. We must ask ourselves if such academic behavior as reading performance is as poor as it is only because of low ability.

Due to the difficulties that arise in the use of the IQ concept, other ways to express intelligence tests scores, such as percentile ranks, standard scores and stanines, have been used.

Summary

The concept of intelligence is used to account for the difference in performance of certain tasks by different individuals. The definitions of intelligence really only designate the tasks involved where individuals differ. They do not tell us anything about the nature of that ability to perform these tasks.

Intelligence tests were devised to provide a quantitative way of estimating an individual's performance on certain tasks as compared to other individuals who are confronted with similar tasks.

One of the most popular ways to express the individual's performance, on these tasks designated as intellectual, is in terms of IQ. IQ does not always mean

$$\frac{MA}{CA} \times 100.$$

This definition is only one of a number of ways that IQ is defined in actual practice by test constructors. It is more realistic to define IQ as a quantitative index of an individual's performance on an intelligence test as compared to other individuals who took the test.

A great deal of misunderstanding concerning the interpretation and use of IQ has arisen because of the lack of knowledge, by many people who use these tests, as to how the test constructor develops and defines the IQ.

Because of some of the difficulties in the use of the concept of an IQ, other methods of expressing intelligence test scores have been suggested.

2 *Piaget on intelligence*

It is possible that if a medical man spent 40 years of his life studying **arthritis,** he might command attention from colleagues having interests in the same area. Yet a Swiss psychologist, Jean Piaget, who devoted four decades to the study of intelligence, has largely been ignored. Recently, however, his writings have won recognition, and hence a brief overall view of his work is given here.

The uninitiated reader of Piaget would find his basic work on intelligence (Piaget, 1952) a difficult book to understand, for its language is ponderous and obscure. However, two books offer guides to Piaget's system: the excellent and thorough *The Developmental Psychology of Jean Piaget* by John Flavell (1963) and a shorter work, *A Guide to Reading Piaget,* by Brearley and Hitchfield (1966). An experimental study of some of Piaget's concepts is available in a work by Decarie (1965). Decarie's book gives an account of an experimental study on 90 subjects. In the foreword (p. *xii*) by Piaget, he expresses pleasure in Decarie's findings in support of his own theories derived mainly from an intensive study of three infants. "This shows moreover...that by means of a longitudinal study in which three subjects are observed daily over a period of several months, sometimes as many facts can be noticed as in a transversal comparative study of a larger number of subjects [Decaries, p. *xii*]."

The origins of intelligence

Piaget has at least one attribute in common with Gesell (see Chapter 6), one that concerns the origin of matter. Piaget's stress on beginnings and his biological training result in a biological orientation. He sees **cognitive** development as a "mental embryology" (Flavell, p. 42) that derives from biological characteristics.

Intelligence as a biological derivative

Piaget's attempt to trace intellect to its source brings him to its biological substrate. Intelligence is always found in the presence of life. I believe Piaget is saying that an organism encounters its physicochemical conditions by breathing through gills in water and by means of lungs in air. This is one type of adaptation. However, the organism also develops a different kind of adaptation during its life history.

When we examine the later stages of verbal or cogitative intelligence, we find that they derive from sensorimotor intelli-

gence. The latter, in turn, presupposes reflexes that have an intimate connection "with the organism's anatomical and morphological structure....A certain continuity exists, therefore, between intelligence and the purely biological processes of morphogenesis and adaptation to the environment [Piaget, 1952, p. 1]."

The preceding statement is appealing to someone who has learned to see the processes of biological growth, maturation, and decline, and the processes of digestion, respiration, and so on—all as one type of phenomenon. With such an outlook, one can also see the underlying continuity that unites such diverse processes as a person's adapting to gravity, assimilating and digesting food, and solving problems. This view is in harmony with the reactional biography hypothesis developed earlier.

Heredity and intelligence

It should be obvious that men can't fly in the air and birds don't make the best deep-sea divers. Heredity fixes the structures that permit the development of flying, walking, running, grasping, and so forth. Thus heredity partly determines what varieties of intelligent responses can be developed. Even so, as Flavell points out (1963, p. 42) man can transcend the limitations imposed by his organic equipment. Although he cannot detect infrared, ultraviolet, or radio waves by his senses, nevertheless he can know, predict, and control them through mechanical contrivances that are essentially extensions of his sense organs.

Piaget thinks that, in addition to the specific limitations that hereditary structures impose upon the kinds of intelligence that an organism can develop, there is a *general* effect of heredity on intelligence. My own view is that Piaget is confused on this point because his closest explicators (Flavell, 1963, pp. 42–43) have difficulty in explaining this point. All they can do is quote him. According to Flavell, this is "a mode of intellectual functioning. We do not inherit cognitive structures as such; these come into being only in the course of development. What we do inherit is a **modus operandi,** a specific manner in which we transact business with the environment [p. 43]." I wonder if I am like the child who blurted out that the Emperor had no clothes on when I suggest that perhaps Piaget's *general* heredity effect means nothing more than the following: If an organism is alive and biologically normal, then it is capable of interacting with the sights, sounds, and smells of things in its surrounds and of evolving specific reactions to them. If so, then Piaget is only saying that the general living properties of an organism constitute *necessary* but not *causal* conditions for intelligence development. These properties do not guarantee intelligence but only make it possible to develop. By contrast, a stillborn child lacks the general hereditary factors requisite to behavior or intelligence development. Older points of view held that different individuals started out in life with different amounts of *a priori* or "head-start" potentialities for intelligence. Piaget rejects all such psychological "givens," as further discussion of his theory illustrates.

Piaget's conception of the earthbound nature of intelligence and the fact that it must be developed is substantiated in the following quotation:

> From its beginnings, due to the hereditary adaptations of the organism, intelligence finds itself entangled in a network of relations between the organism and the environment. Intelligence does not therefore appear as a power of reflection independent of the particular position which the organism occupies in the universe but is linked, from the very outset, by biological apriorities. It is not at all an independent absolute, but is a relationship among others, between the organism and things. [Piaget, 1952, p. 19].

In my opinion Piaget's statement is a model of an interactional view of intelligence. According to it, intelligence is not an entity residing within the organism, prior to birth, helping or hindering the organism. Intelligence comes into being only during the succession of organism-object interactions. Piaget's conception of intelligence as "adaptation" is harmonious with the above quotation.

Assimilation and accommodation

Again we must emphasize that for Piaget "intelligence" is simply an *extension* and *elaboration* of primitive biological functioning. Let us take nutrition as an example. To continue as a living thing, it *adapts* to its environment by incorporating certain plants and/or animals. Furthermore, it assimilates these substances unto and into itself and transforms them into skin, muscle, bone, and surplus energy. In adapting, the organism also *adjusts* — perhaps by climbing trees, grasping bananas, and chewing and swallowing them. The first aspect of adaptation has been called **assimilation,** the second **accommodation.** Both operate on the biological level, but they also function on the psychological level as in the development of intelligence.

Assimilation and accommodation in intelligence

"Adaptation is an equilibrium between assimilation and accommodation [Piaget, 1952, p. 6]." When a child incorporates all the data of its experience into a pre-existing framework, it shows assimilation. Shaking a rattle, banging with a spoon, and scribbling with a pencil illustrate successive stages of assimilation. Each action in the sequence incorporates the newer elements into prior meaning systems of the organism.

Each act of assimilation imposes modifications on previously learned responses. There can be no such thing as a literal **"regression."** We can only "act" like crawling infants; infantile crawling has made many accommodations to walking, running, skipping that have transformed it radically. Thus we can creep and crawl only once in a lifetime because, at some point of development, *accommodation* sets a point of no return. Another way of stating the same is to say that behavior is not static. On the contrary, it is a highly dynamic process *changing* and *being changed* during its continuous evolution.

There is no such thing as pure accommodation. Where you see one, you see the other. Adaptation can occur when the complementary processes of assimilation and accommodation are in equilibrium.

The concept of schema

Assimilation and accommodation strongly imply some sort of order or organization, some enduring interrelationship between the developing responses. After all, "objects are assimilated *to* something [Flavell, 1963, p. 52]." This connectedness of certain sequences of development is related to Piaget's concept of **schema.**

A clear-cut definition of schema is impossible to find anywhere in Piaget and yet it is an important aspect of his system. Let us try to understand it. First of all, schema is a psychological concept. Perhaps psychological *structure* will help. The given structure relates certain similar action sequences. After a child learns to suck its mother's breast, its future responses to bottle nipples, lollipops, drinking a soda through a straw are all assimilated to the schema of sucking. Skipping, hopping, and bicycle riding would be related to the schema of walking and still earlier ones of kicking, stepping, and so on.

It would seem that a schema refers to nothing more than a related sequence of similar actions, but Piaget leaves the term more vague than that. As Flavell (1963, p. 53) puts it, assimilation "has generated a specific cognitive *structure,* an organized *disposition* to grasp objects on repeated occasions." Schema for Piaget thus appears to be something beyond the successive actions, a kind of *controlling* entity. But the concept can be reinterpreted to refer to the fact that behavioral trends under similar conditions generate similar behavioral trends. A child's start in speaking its native language generates more of the same and, possibly, a second or even third language. Piano lessons can generate a complex series of piano-playing responses.

Adaptation and schema in Piaget's system lead naturally to *organization.* In the usage most pertinent to our purposes, "organization" is a term which suggests the general continuity and interrelatedness of a given individual's learned responses; a manic patient, for example, raves in the language he learned at his mother's knee.

With regard to intelligence, in its reflective as well as in its practical form, this dual phenomenon of functional totality and interdependence between organization and adaptation is again found. Concerning the relationships between the parts and the whole which determine the organization, it is sufficiently well known that every intellectual operation is always related to all the others and that its own elements are controlled by the same law. Every schema is thus coordinated with all the other schemata and itself constitutes a totality with differentiated parts. Every act of intelligence presupposes a system of mutual implications and interconnected meanings [Piaget, 1952, p. 7].

The preceding sketch of Piaget's view of intelligence is surely inadequate and perhaps even unjust. Like psychoanalysis, Piaget's approach is too elaborate and complex to be compressed into a few pages. His foremost exponent, Flavell (1963), required 472 pages to explain Piaget's developmental psychology. We have, however, presented some of his improvements over traditional theories of intelligence.

Summary

We have examined Piaget's theory of intelligence, which is essentially an adaptational view. It is similar to, and derived from, a biological analogy, but superimposed upon a biological substrate. We examined the relation of heredity to intelligence and found heredity to be a limiting or facilitating set of conditions but only relatively so. However, according to Piaget, heredity does not furnish any *a priori* contributions.

For Piaget, "intelligence" is the evolution of a psychological relationship between organism and stimulus object. The relationship is adaptational, one that shows assimilation and accommodation. The relationship also shows schemata — or a framework of lawful interrelationships of parts to parts and of parts to the totality. The theory is offered as an illustration of an interactional view of intelligence in contrast to the self-actional theory, which considers intelligence as an entity resident within an organism and acting in and of itself like "a man within the man."

3

Bowles and Pronko:
"A new scheme for the
inheritance of intelligence"*†

---

*Quoted material is from J. W. Bowles, Jr. and N. H. Pronko "A new scheme for the inheritance of intelligence." *The Psychological Record,* 1960, **10,** 55–57. By permission of the authors and publisher.

†With so many competing genic explanations to account for the inheritance of intelligence, the writers decided to try their hand at the game. We achieved our results in the manner of our predecessors; no more than they, did we study successive generations of humans by relating their test performances to relevant variables. This is what we did *not* do. What we did do was to simply sit down and construct a purely hypothetical scheme, which works so well that it can encompass a wide range of facts. Furthermore, it is, in a theoretical sense, more economical than other theories. The worst thing to be said against it is that it is free theoretical construction, a kind of science fiction.

Even a superficial survey of the literature dealing with the inheritance of "intelligence" and "feeblemindedness" reveals a certain vagueness and confusion. A great variety of genetic systems has been postulated by various writers. Jennings (1930, pp. 12–25), for one, assumes feeblemindedness to be a **homozygous recessive** condition. To explain how two defective parents may have a superior offspring, he assumes that the defective genes are located in different pairs. When a defective offspring results from defective parents, it is assumed that the parental genes were in the same position. In addition, he assumes unusual combinations of supplementary genes to explain the superiority of genius of offspring of mediocre or inferior parents.

Martin and Bell (1943, pp. 154–157) have published a pedigree which they believe shows that the mental defect is due to a sex-linked recessive gene with the minor exception of slight mental deficiency in two females, in which case the causal gene was said to be incompletely recessive.

Limiting himself to the heredity of **phenyl-pyruvic oligophrenia,** Jervis (1939) suggests the operation of an **autosomal recessive gene** in the manifestation of this particular type of defectiveness.

Penrose (1941, pp. 359–364) believes that severe cases of mental deficiency may be due to recessive factors or fresh gene mutations. However, some mild types may be the result of incomplete dominance and variable expressivity of genetic factors (Penrose, 1938, p. 291).

According to Gates (1946, p. 1150):

"While mental and physical abnormalities are generally inherited as unitary differences, normal physical and mental characters appear to depend largely on multiple factors which run in series."

Hurst (Gates, 1946, 1151) assumes that in addition to a pair of dominant genes, *five* minor genes acting cumulatively determine the grade of intelligence; that is, human intelligence is hexagenic.

The foregoing genic theories may be criticized on several grounds. First, they do not show much agreement. It should be noted that the range of genic explanation includes such vastly different hereditary mechanisms as **autosomal dominant,** autosomal recessive, sex-linked recessive, gene mutation, and multiple factors. Second, it imputes separate entities where none exist. Note, for example, Penrose's fragmentation of mental deficiency into "severe" and "mild" types with different genetic explanations for each. Such treatment is not in line with recent advances in psychology. Modern psychologists view "intelligence" as a continuous behavioral range extending from total lack of behavior at one extreme to superiority of performance at the other. There is the same graduation of individual difference in behavior as exists for the data of systematics in biology.

In line with the above criticism, the authors propose the genetic explanation illustrated in Fig. 10.1. Let us take the case of both parents of dull normal intelligence. If we assume four

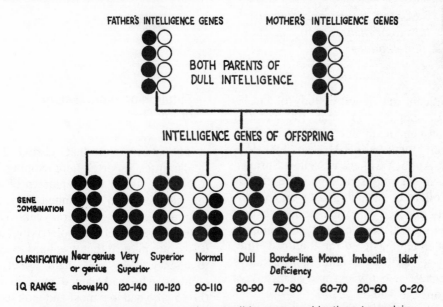

Figure 10.1 Schema representing possible gene combinations to explain how dull normal parents may have children ranging from idiot through various gradations to genius. (From J. W. Bowles, Jr. and N. H. Pronko, "A New Scheme for the Inheritance of Intelligence," *The Psychological Record,* 1960, **10**(55), 57. Reproduced by permission of author and publisher.)

pairs of genes acting cumulatively, we can readily explain the intelligence of the offspring *whatever that might be*. Note that our scheme would explain the possibility of the derivation of an **idiot**, IQ 0 to 20; **imbecile**, IQ 20 to 60; **moron**, IQ 60 to 70; borderline, IQ 70 to 80; dull normal, IQ 80 to 90; normal, IQ 90 to 110; superior, IQ 110 to 120; very superior, IQ 120 to 140; up to near genius or **genius**, IQ above 140. There is no need to make additional assumptions proposed by various authors (e.g., differential positions of gene pairs, variability in "expressivity," etc.). In other words, the explanation here proposed is scientifically more conservative. It is simplicity itself, and yet it covers the full range of facts, an achievement which the variety of theories considered above makes at the expense of discrepant or contradictory handling of *segments* of that range of facts.

Within the general framework of traditional genetic theory, the genic explanation for the inheritance of intelligence here presented is believed to be deserving of consideration alongside those with which it has been compared. At least, it is no less hypothetical than the others, and, after all, it does handle the data, no matter what those data might be. We offer this schema, then, as the last word in genetic explanations of the relationships between the IQs of parents and their offspring.

Summary

A variety of theories pertaining to the inheritance of intelligence is examined and criticized and a new scheme is presented. This assumes four pairs of genes acting cumulatively and accounts for the possibility of offspring ranging from the idiot to the genius level when the parents are dull normal. The schema is offered as the last word in genic explanations of the relationships between the IQs of parents and their offspring.

4 Sontag, Baker, and Nelson: Recent research on intelligence*

A significant and lengthy study of intelligence development in some 300 children has been conducted since 1929 at the Fels Research Institute of Human Development at Antioch College in Yellow Springs, Ohio. An enormous amount of data has been collected, including data on the offspring of children who were studied several decades ago. Among other tests, children have been administered the Stanford-Binet forms at birthdays and half-birthdays between 2½ and 6 years and at birthdays only from age 3 to 15 years.

*Quoted material is from L. W. Sontag, Charles T. Baker, and C. T. and Virginia L. Nelson, "Personality as a Determinant of Performance," *American Journal of Orthopsychiatry,* July 1955, **25**(3), 555–562. Copyright, the American Orthopsychiatric Association, Inc., reproduced by permission.

Patterns of improvement or decline

The observation that started the particular study reported here (Sontag, Baker, & Nelson, 1955) was a pattern of gradual but definite and continued increase or decrease in IQ over several years. The consistency was what was so striking; it was a deliberate pattern that was hard to attribute to chance. Why not, then, select the 35 children who had gained most in IQ and the 35 who had lost most and look for possible factors. This 25 percent of the top and bottom of the total group of 140 children constituted the subjects of the Fels study.

In attempting to account for the patterns of change in IQ, the Fels workers considered statistical factors, possible **practice effects,** atypical patterns of maturation, anxiety, test artifacts, and **motivation.** It was the last factor that turned out to be the significant one.

Motivation and IQ change

When Sontag and his co-workers considered how motivation worked, they related it to the personality structure of the child in the following manner. The child is normally born into a sheltering, protective, loving atmosphere. However, at the same time that parental love offers comfort and support, it is also a threat; for example, when the vulnerable child is of necessity at least temporarily deprived of it as a result of parental attention to siblings, discipline, and so on. As a compensatory source of comfort, the child may build up independence and reliance on self and mastery of problems. Soon self-approval and group approval through competition sustain and comfort the child as substitutes of parental love.

The picture sketched so far is a somewhat idealized one, but things don't always go as smoothly. Mothers may overprotect and infantilize the child and keep him dependent or overdependent upon parental love, thus inhibiting him in his social maturation toward developing resources of emotional reassurance stemming from "independence, mastery of problems, and competition with peers [p. 560]." As a consequence, he continues to look to his parents for emotional comfort, support, attention, and sustaining love rather than to competitive solution of problems. There is no need to compete.

Support from the data

If, then, we consider the problem of the child with an early declining IQ, we may hypothesize

that he may have failed to perform as adequately as we might expect because he isn't motivated to approve himself and secure the approval of adults by mastering tasks. Since the child with excessive dependent need feels anxiety because of his vulnerability, we should expect that in some children this anxiety level might be so high as to affect performance. We might expect the performance effect of this unresolved dependency to reach its height just before entrance into school. The drastically different environment of school, with its enforced attainment and mastery of tasks and inherently competitive nature, should change this dependency pattern at least to some degree and offer other satisfactions and therefore motivations.

Case M. J. (Fig. 10.2), the second child in a rural family, has little opportunity to play with

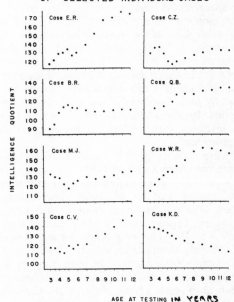

Figure 10.2 Personality as a determinant of intelligence. The striking changes in IQ of the cases shown above (discussed in the text) are related to motivational and familial conditions (L. W. Sontag, Charles T. Baker, and Virginia L. Nelson, "Personality as a Determinant of Performance," *The American Journal of Orthopsychiatry,* July 1955, **25**(3), 555–562. Copyright, the American Orthopsychiatric Association, Inc., reproduced by permission.)

other children except her sister, 8 years older. The mother is overprotective, and father and sister share in idolizing and pampering M. J. She is demanding of adult attention, indulges in almost no self-initiated play, and when with other children constantly turns to adults for reassurance. Her base Binet score is about 133. It drops until at 60 months it is about 117. By 84 months it has recovered most of its loss and by 10 years is back to its base of 133.

Case K. D. (Fig. 10.2) is that of a child who failed to respond to the competitive and problem-solving aspect of school. If our hypothesis about sources of emotional satisfactions as they influence motivation has validity, then we would expect that the children who in the school situation find a greatly *expanded* opportunity for mastery of problems, for competitiveness, and for approval for attainment, would perform progressively better on the Stanford-Binet test. They would, because of the competitiveness and problem-solving motivation, acquire more proficiency in the kind of tasks involved in the Stanford-Binet test. The satisfactions they attained should ensure a lowered anxiety level and they should approach the test situation itself as a challenging problem, the solution of which would make them emotionally more comfortable and give them satisfaction. It should be an opportunity to reassure themselves rather than a threat to their reassurance.

Case E. R. (Fig. 10.2) shows a child whose score rose from a base of 118 at 3 years to 129 at 4 years. We attributed this to the fact that he was a slow maturer in motor development. Then, after no consistent change for 3 years, his scores began an ascent which carried them almost to 180. This boy, while not aggressive, is intensely competitive in school, gets great satisfaction from mastery of such subjects as mathematics and chemistry, and spends his free hours absorbed in a book. He depends relatively little on human relationships, either family or peers, for reassurance.

A final aspect of motivation is represented by what appears to be a characteristic of the late "downers," all of whom are girls. As girls pass through their **latency period** into adolescence, they are, of course, approaching their adult feminine role. Women's perceptions of their feminine role differ tremendously. Children range all the way from those anticipating admiration and approval for charm, beauty, and golden curls to those with an almost complete failure of feminine identification and anticipation of little or no warmth and admiration for femininity. The girl with the least satisfaction from such possible femininity should have the most need to reassure herself by the ability to compete and attain in masculine or duosexual areas of achievement. A scanning of our material shows that the majority of late "downers," almost all girls, are undergoing what we call a "flight into femininity." By this we mean that competition and achievement are of primary importance only in being more feminine, more charming, more subject to admiration. School attainment or other successful competition is not necessary for emotional comfort.

Discussion

We should like to suggest to you that while we have been in a sense discussing constancy or rather inconstancy of IQ we have also been doing something very different. We have, in addition, been discussing three different patterns of emotional adjustment (or personality structure) and how effective they are individually, as measured by the individual's progressive ability to perform in a test situation. Insofar as the Stanford-Binet test samples abilities used in everyday life, application of experience to novel tasks, use of words and numbers, comprehension and reason, we are attempting to appraise the life-performance effectiveness of these personality or adjustment patterns. We have described them as: (1) the passive infantile-dependency pattern, which we believe leads to decreasing level of Binet performance; (2) the aggressive self-reassuring mastery of tasks, competitive, independent pattern, which leads to progressively advanced performance; (3) the passive feminine role, which, like the dependency pattern, offers no motivation to achieve.

In closing, we should like to emphasize that this paper is a preliminary report of our studies. The statistics of the number and degree of IQ changes in the group of 140 children are, of course, complete. But the analysis of causes for such changes, their possible basis in personality delineation as it may be determined from life records, interviews, school observations, and records, is an early progress report of a research problem which intrigues us [pp. 561–562].

Sontag, Baker, and Nelson:
*Intelligence and personality** 5

The earlier study spurred the Fels workers into further research on the nature of intelligence and possible personality correlates. This time Sontag, Baker, and Nelson (1958) included 200 subjects whose records were complete. They covered a span of over 20 years of the institute's history. The superiority of the Fels program has been its long-span longitudinal study of the same children, whereas earlier studies involved different groups of children over shorter and different age spans. Here repeated measurements were made on the same subjects year after year.

The findings

Individual curves drawn for 140 of the subjects are reproduced in the Appendix of the original report (p. 58 ff.). What a diversity of patterns! Perhaps the most outstanding characteristic is the *consistent* and *extensive* change in many of the subjects. The greatest amount of increase in IQ showed a gain of 73 IQ points from a raw score of 107 at age 2½ to a score of 180 at age 10. The greatest decline in IQ involved a loss of 40 points from a raw score of 142 at age 3 to a raw score of 102 at age 8 (p. 23). The changes were not necessarily linear, either. The same child's "curve" might be a V showing first a decline, then an increment. The converse was also true. Some subjects showed little change. Others, many of them, showed prominent shift in the shape of the curve at ages 5, 6, or 7, suggesting a relationship

to the early school years. The irregularity of the patterns of change in IQ caused by varying amounts of change at different age periods makes the classification of IQ change difficult. Clearly we cannot speak of individuals having a fixed increment of IQ change or a constant mental growth rate regardless of the age period during which these changes occur. Indeed the highly idiosyncratic nature of the IQ changes found is an argument in itself for possible complex environmental causes of IQ change rather than simple hereditary factors (p. 23).

Implications concerning intelligence

The authors consider that their findings concerning mental growth derived from longitudinal follow-up methods of study have "aided in dismissing the idea that the IQ is constant over any period during childhood [p. 51]." The individual cases argue against any "constant increment of IQ to be found in the majority of cases [p. 51]." Furthermore, they do not blame the tests as being unreliable, but go along with Bayley (1955) who "suspects that the failure of early tests in predicting a stable intellectual factor rests in the nature of intelligence itself [p. 30]." Viewing the

*Quoted material is from Lester W. Sontag, Charles T. Baker, and Virginia L. Nelson, "Mental Growth and Personality Development: A Longitudinal Study," *Monographs of the Society for Research in Child Development*, 1958, **23**(2), 13–143.

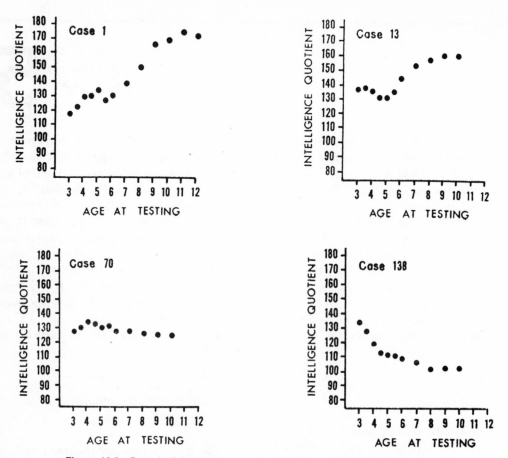

Figure 10.3 Four individual curves of intelligence development. Case 1 shows the greatest gain, one of 73 IQ points from a raw score of 107 at age 2½ to a score of 180 at age 10. Case 13 shows a decrement, then a gain. Case 70, a slight rise and a slight decline. Case 138 shows the greatest amount of loss, 40 points, from a raw score of 142 at age 3 to a raw score of 102 at age 8. (From Lester W. Sontag, Charles T. Baker, and Virginia L. Nelson "Mental Growth and Personality Development: A Longitudinal Study," *Monographs of the Society for Research in Child Development, Inc.*, 1958, **23**(2), 13–143. Reproduced by permission of the author.)

results overall, "it would appear that the extent of IQ change found during childhood has been previously underestimated [pp. 53–54]." Their conclusion follows: "From the description of the nature and amount of change in IQ and from the analysis of possible artifacts in our data, we may conclude that real changes in relative mental ability do occur in childhood [p. 54]."

Personality traits and IQ

If "real changes in relative mental ability do occur in childhood," then it seems proper to look for conditions to which they are related. Otherwise we act as if the changes were chaotic. Sontag and Baker (1958, Part II) assumed no such thing. On the contrary, they began to search for personality correlates of changes in IQ.

Capitalizing on what they had learned in a previous study, they developed personality rating scales that would help to pinpoint suspected personality traits. The following scales were eventually adopted:

1. Emotional independence from parents
2. Aggressiveness in peer relationships
3. Self-initiated behavior
4. Socialization
5. Friendliness
6. Problem-solving behavior
7. Anticipation of reward
8. General competitiveness
9. Femininity (girls only)
10. **Sibling rivalry**
11. Anxiety
12. Scholastic competition
13. Independence in scholastic achievement
14. Parental emphasis on school achievement

Hypothesis regarding personality and IQ change

For purposes of analysis, it was hypothesized that children who gained most in IQ during preschool years would be rated higher on all of the 11 scales used during this period than those who lost in IQ, with the exception of the femininity scale, where girls who ascended [in IQ] would be rated lower than [those who descended in IQ]. The children who ascended the most in IQ between the ages of 6 and 10 were expected to be rated higher on each of the 14 scales used at this period, with the exception of the femininity scale, where the ascending girls would again be expected to be rated lower. It was assumed that the scales measured personality traits which were descriptive of general avenues of personal satisfaction in dealing with meaningful persons in their environments, and in their approaches to various learning situations. The child characterized by traits of independence, aggressiveness, and competitiveness was expected to find his success on mental tasks a rewarding and challenging experience. He would therefore, not only enter the Binet testing situation with relatively high motivation, but would also increasingly benefit from increased motivation in many learning situations in life. His level of intellectual ability would increase over a period of years as a result of modification in **"learning**

to learn."** The subjects who lost most in IQ during either age period were regarded as having their basic satisfactions dependent on other persons' approval or structuring. These children could be expected to be emotionally dependent on adults, passive, and conforming. Their dependence on adults may have contributed to withdrawal or hostility in their peer relationships, or to a pattern of femininity among the girls. These various hypotheses have been reported previously by the author [pp. 103–104].

Personality ratings

In order to test their hypothesis, Sontag and Baker made their personality ratings by reading each child's central file up to age 6 and making a rating of them. The files were then read again up to age 10 and ratings made. Each of the two judges made his evaluation of the subjects independently and without knowledge of the subjects' IQs. Out of a total of 727 ratings made at age 6, only 29 ratings differed between the raters by three points or more. And, out of 938 ratings that they made at age 10, only 43 ratings differed by three or more points. A conference technique was used to resolve all differences of two or more points.

Conclusions and remarks

From the various analyses made in this chapter it would appear that our major hypotheses regarding personality factors and individual differences in mental growth rate were essentially substantiated in their broader aspects. A study of the various modes of personality by which children attempt to gain satisfaction in their experiences appeared to be of value in predicting IQ change and in understanding the nature of accelerated or decelerated mental growth rate as related to personality factors. During the preschool years, emotional dependence on parents appears to be clearly associated with the loss in IQ during this period. During the elementary school years, a cluster of personality traits with the need for achievement as a common dimension appears to be closely associated with accelerated or decelerated mental growth patterns during these years. It would also appear that during the preschool years the child who develops modes of behavior characterized by aggressiveness, self-initiation, and competitiveness is laying a basic groundwork for future acceleration in performance on mental tasks. As the child develops these pathways of behavior for satisfactorily handling his interactions with peers and adults, it is not surprising to find a generalization of these behaviors to most new learning situations. The child's motivation to learn new things appears to be enhanced by these general personality characteristics.

The mechanism involved in the pattern of IQ change manifest during the preschool years appears to be of a more complex nature. As a group, the children who gained in IQ during this period appear to be those who are venturing out of the maternal fold. Performance on mental tasks, such as those found in the Binet items given during the early years, appears to be influenced by some aspects of the personality adjustment of the child. In this instance, it does not seem economical to view the behavior of the child through a framework of an achievement motive. Rather, the curiosity and exploration which may characterize the child who has gained a relative degree of emotional independence from his parents may influence mental

growth during the early years. The variables of personality which, at age 6, were found to predict later mental development were not as clearly related to the course of mental development during the preschool years. Therefore the researcher should possibly use different frames of reference for studying mental development during these different periods of life. A number of factors could operate during the preschool years, each in a relatively small number of cases, making it difficult to predict or study factors relating to IQ change in this period of life. The low conceptual validity of preschool intelligence tests in predicting later mental behaviors also may have influenced the findings at this age [pp. 117–118].

A final word Our findings regarding the development of personality as related to the development of intellectual ability would appear to be consistent with an increasingly prevalent attitude toward problems of child development. We may regard intelligence as but one aspect of the total personality. The general motives for behavior which characterize the child's adjustment to many life situations may appropriately serve as a conceptual framework for viewing intelligence and other aspects of personality [p. 119].

6 Terman's developmental study of 1000 geniuses

Genius is next door to insanity. An intellectually superior child is bound to be physically weak. Precocious children burn themselves out early. These are some of the common misconceptions connected with early superior intellectual achievement. Because genius constituted an unknown realm, Lewis M. Terman decided to explore it. Here is how he pinpointed the problem: "What are the physical, mental, and personality traits that are characteristic of intellectually superior children and what

sort of adult does the typical gifted child become? [Terman and Oden, 1947, p. 2]." The early phase of the study took place in 1921 and 1922. A first follow-up occurred 6 years later, and further follow-up studies were made in 1936, 1940, and 1945.

From a total California school population of about a quarter million (1936), Terman and his co-workers selected over 1000 students. The average Stanford-Binet IQ of their subjects was 151. In addition to giving intelligence tests to the students,

Terman had their parents fill out detailed Home Information Blanks. Moreover, their teachers supplied additional knowledge in the form of an eight-page School Information Blank. Medical examinations, anthropometric measurements, school achievement tests, character tests, interest blanks, reading lists, and play interests furnished additional sources of highly specific information about the subjects. Numerous comparisons were made with control groups of subjects, students who averaged an IQ of 100.

The early findings

From a "physical" point of view, Terman's intellectually superior children were "above the best standards [p. 20]" in growth as revealed by both height and weight. They also excelled in lung capacity, breadth of shoulders and hips, and in muscular strength. The myth of the child prodigy as "a pathetic creature, overserious and undersized, sickly, hollow-chested, stoop-shouldered, clumsy, nervously tense, and bespectacled" (p. 24) was therefore exploded. "On the whole, the children of this group were physically superior to unselected children" (p. 24).

As for educational development, 85 percent of the subjects (p. 25) were accelerated and none was retarded. On the average, they had skipped one or more half-grades. Almost half of the subjects had learned to read before starting to school, and most had learned to read with little or no formal instruction. One girl demonstrated a reading ability at 25 months comparable to that of an average child at the end of first grade. At the time of the follow-up study, this subject had acquired a Ph.D. degree and was teaching at a state university.

Inveterate free reading characterized the superior children as a group. They read more, both in quantity and quality. In fact, "the typical gifted child of 7 years reads more books than the unselected child reads at any age up to 15 years [Terman, 1926, p. 637]." But, aside from their reading habits, there was no specialization or unevenness in the *general* abilities of the experimental group. According to Terman (1926), "the 'one-sidedness' of precocious children is mythical [p. 636]."

Popular opinion considers the intellectually precocious child as being allergic to play. On the contrary, Terman found that "the typical gifted child of 9 years has a larger body of definite knowledge about plays and games than the average child of 12 years [p. 637]." The superior children surpassed the control subjects in intellectual, social, and activity interests as well. The same held true for such character traits as honesty, trustworthiness, and truthfulness. In one respect, however, the "gifted" fell short of the controls. A test of psychotic tendencies showed that "approximately 75 percent of the gifted were above the average of unselected children [p. 638]." Does this mean that the more intellectually complex individuals are also more complex in other aspects of their personality? Perhaps.

Twenty-five years later

To what extent is superior IQ in childhood predictive of superior achievement in later life? The following is a brief summation of the superior group's attainments.

1. *Occupationally,* almost half of the men and over half of the fully employed women were engaged in professional work.

2. *Educationally,* almost 90 percent entered college and almost 70 percent graduated from college. There were about

10 times as many college graduates as in the general population, 15 times as many graduate degrees, and one or two thousand times as many Ph.D.'s (73 in all) as in the general population.

3. *Earnings, publications,* and *patents* also served to segregate experimental subjects from the controls subjects.

4. *Distinguished achievement professionally* can be found in a catalogue of concrete accomplishments (Terman and Oden, 1947, pp. 366–367). This section reads like a *Who's Who* and this was in a population nearly half of whom were below the age of 35 years, "an age when a considerable number of the most eminent persons of history were still unknown to fame" (p. 367). It would seem that precocious children do maintain their precocity instead of "burning out."

Summary

Terman's study of "a thousand gifted children" has answered several significant questions about the relationship between high IQ and other personality and character attributes. The study also illustrates the enduring character of the superior IQ these children exhibited early in life as well as the attainments which that early superiority made possible in their middle years. I believe, however, that one question needs to be asked. Terman simply assumed that the 1000 superior children were "gifted" and this is what he called them. Were they gifted or were they actually children with a head start in life? This is a question that the reader must answer for himself. A companion study to Terman's follows; perhaps it will help to clarify the subject.

7 Skeels: "Adult status of children with contrasting early life experiences"

Over thirty years ago, two mentally retarded baby girls were given up as hopeless and transferred from an orphanage to a mental institution. What then happened to them sparked a developmental study that shed new light on the concept of intelligence.

Harold M. Skeels' (1966) follow-up study of the adult status of Iowa orphan children with contrasting early life experiences deserves the status of a classic work. When Skeels did his original work in the 1930's, psychologists, educators, and **social workers** regarded intelligence as "a

fixed individual characteristic," determined genetically as inferred by the parents' occupational and educational attainments, a stable and static entity, practically uninfluenced by environmental changes (p. 1). Accordingly, plans for adoption of a child were made on the basis of the parents' occupational, economic, and educational status. It was believed that these factors provided the best prediction of his innate potentialities.

During the Depression 25 children, 20 of them illegitimate, were sent by court order to an overcrowded and understaffed Iowa orphanage. It was the practice of the institution to assign infants up to the age of 2 years to the hospital, a relatively new

---

*Quoted material is from Harold M. Skeels, "Adult Status of Children with Contrasting Early Life Experiences," *Monographs of the Society for Research in Child Development,* 1966, **31**(3), 1–65.

building. Up to about 6 months they were kept in the infant nursery, which was essentially a hospital dormitory equipped with standard hospital cribs having covered sides that limited visual stimulation. Toys were absent and human contacts consisted of changing diapers and feeding via propped bottles.

Children older than 6 months were housed in small dormitories with two to five larger cribs to a room. Movement here was a little freer, but human interactions were scarce and limited largely to "feeding, dressing, and toilet details [p. 4]."

At 2 years of age the orphanage children were transferred to cottages, where overcrowding was as marked as elsewhere. One matron, aided by three or four untrained girls, was in charge of 30 to 35 children of the same sex. In addition to having complete care of the children, she performed other tasks, such as mending their clothes and maintaining the cottage. Regimentation was the rule. For much of the day, the children sat on chairs. All of their requisite activities were carried out "in rows and in unison [p. 4]."

When children reached the age of 6, they started school, which was conducted at the orphanage. They attended elementary grades, later transferring to the public junior high school. Few, however, could maintain the level of work expected at the latter school. Although the children were treated as mentally normal, still every opportunity was seized to relieve the overcrowded condition at the orphanage — even transfer to another state institution for the mentally retarded. The story starts with Skeels' serendipitous follow-up of two little profoundly retarded patients.

How it all started

Early in the... program, two baby girls, neglected by their feebleminded mothers, ignored by their inadequate relatives, malnourished and frail, were legally committed to the orphanage. The youngsters were pitiful little creatures. They were tearful, had runny noses, and sparse, stringy, and colorless hair; they were emaciated, undersized, and lacked muscle tonus or responsiveness. Sad and inactive, the two spent their days rocking and whining.

The psychological examinations showed developmental levels of 6 and 7 months, respectively, for the two girls, although they were then 13 and 16 months old chronologically. This serious delay in mental growth was confirmed by observations of their behavior in the nursery and by reports of the superintendent of nurses, as well as by the pediatrician's examination. There was no evidence of physiological or organic defect, or of birth injury or glandular dysfunction.

The two children were considered unplaceable, and transfer to a school for the mentally retarded was recommended with a high degree of confidence. Accordingly, they were transferred to an institution for the mentally retarded at the next available vacancy, when they were aged 15 and 18 months, respectively [p. 5].

Six months after the transfer of the two children, he (the author) was visiting the wards at an institution for the mentally retarded and noticed two outstanding little girls. They were alert, smiling, running about, responding to the playful attention of adults, and generally behaving and looking like any other toddlers. He scarcely recognized them as the two little girls with the hopeless prognosis, and thereupon tested them again. Although the results indicated that the two were approaching normal mental development for their age, the author was skeptical of the validity or permanence of the improvement and no change was instituted in the lives of the children. Twelve months later they were reexamined, and then again when they 40 and 43 months old. Each examination gave unmistakable evidence of mental development well within the normal range for age [p. 6].

The transformation did not cause Skeels to doubt his original testing and evaluation, nor the subsequent test findings. He felt that the original picture was as true as the later findings, which were supported by parallel developments along social, communication, and emotional as well as general behavioral lives (p. 6).

Factors in the transformation

When Skeels searched for factors that would explain the tremendous developmental spurt that the two little girls had shown, he felt certain that he found them in their life conditions.

The two girls had been placed on one of the wards of older, brighter girls and women, ranging in age from 18 to 50 years and in mental age from 5 to 9 years, where they were the only children of preschool age, except for a few hopeless bed patients with gross physical defects. An older girl on the ward had "adopted" each of the two girls, and other older girls served as adoring aunts. Attendants and nurses also showed affection to the two, spending time with them, taking them along on their days off for automobile rides and shopping excursions, and purchasing toys, picture books, and play materials for them in great abundance. The setting seemed to be a homelike one, abundant in affection, rich in wholesome and interesting experiences, and geared to a preschool level of development.

It was recognized that as the children grew older, their developmental needs would be less adequately met in the institution for the mentally retarded. Furthermore, they were now normal and the need for care in such an institution no longer existed. Consequently, they were transferred back to the orphanage and shortly thereafter were placed in adoptive homes [p. 6].

Meanwhile, other studies were reporting the disastrous effects of psychologically impoverished environments, plus the possibility that severely retarded children so reared can attain normality if removed to an environment where affection, attention, and stimulation are provided.

A bold experiment

The striking results with the two little girls provided the impetus for a bold experiment. Since the children of this Iowa orphanage seemed destined to mental retardation anyhow, what harm would there be in sending more of them to the institution for the mentally retarded? And, who knows, perhaps results might be as therapeutic as they had been with the two girls who had returned to normal.

With understandable misgivings, the administrators of the orphanage consented to the study. To avoid the stigma of commitment to a state school for the mentally retarded, the subjects would be officially carried on the books of the orphanage but would simply be listed as "house guests" at the mental institution. Thus, in addition to the two little girls who had been transferred earlier, and another transferred to the same institution at about the same time, ten more children were moved to the institution for the mentally handicapped at Glenwood State School. Since not all wards were "elite," there was a considerable variation in the range of stimulation provided there.

The experimental and contrast groups

The experimental group consisted of the 13 "house guests," all under 3 years of age and all certified as "seriously retarded by tests and observation before transfer was considered (p. 8)."

The **contrast group**, consisting of 12 children, was so called because it was not a real control group selected in advance. Only after the data were analyzed did Skeels realize that such a group could be chosen from the records. Fortunately, tests had been given periodically to all the children and the results were available. At the time of transfer, the average age of the experimental group was 19.4 months. The range of IQs was from 35 to 89 with a mean of 64.3. Comparable data for the contrast group consisted of 16.6 months for the mean chronological age; their mean IQ was 86.7, with the range (with two exceptions, 71 and 50) varying from 81 to 103.

Their contrasting environments

The meager, impoverished conditions that prevailed in the orphanage have already been described. The conditions in the mental institution as described in the following passage from Skeels equaled or surpassed those that the two pioneer little girls and later, the third one, had experienced.

As with the first two children, who, by chance, were the first participants in the experiment, the attendants and the older girls became very fond of the children placed on their wards and took great pride in them. In fact, there was considerable competition among wards to see which one would have its "baby" walking or talking first. Not only the girls, but the attendants spent a great deal of time with "their children," playing, talking, and training them in every way. The children received constant attention and were the recipients of gifts; they were taken on excursions and were exposed to special opportunities of all kinds. For example, it was the policy of the matron in charge of the girls' school division to single out certain children who she felt were in need of special individualization and to permit them to spend some time each day visiting her office. This furnished new experiences, such as being singled out, receiving special attention and affection, new play materials, additional language stimulation, and meeting other office callers.

The spacious living rooms of the wards furnished ample space for indoor play and activity. Whenever weather permitted, the children spent some time each day on the playground under the supervision of one or more older girls. Here they were able to interact with other children of similar ages. Outdoor play equipment included tricycles, swings, slides, sand boxes, etc. The children also began to attend the school kindergarten as soon as they could walk. Toddlers remained for only half the morning and 4- or 5-year-olds, the entire morning. Activities carried on in the kindergarten resembled preschool rather than the more formal type of kindergarten.

As part of the school program, the children attended daily 15-minute exercises in the chapel, which included group singing and music by the orchestra. The children also attended the dances, school programs, movies, and Sunday chapel services.

In considering this enriched environment from a dynamic point of view, it must be pointed out that in the case of almost every child, some one adult (older girl or attendant) became particularly attached to him and figuratively "adopted" him. As a consequence, an intense one-to-one adult-child relationship developed, which was supplemented by the less intense but frequent interactions with the other adults in the environment. Each child had some one person with whom he was identified and who was particularly interested in him and his achievements. This highly stimulating emotional impact was observed to be the unique characteristic and one of the main contributions of the experimental setting [pp. 16–17].

The results

Among the "house guests," every child showed a gain from seven to 58 points. "Three children made gains of 45 points or more and all but two children gained more than 15 points [p. 18]." Their average gain was 27.5 IQ points. The contrast group showed the direct opposite. With the exception of one child who showed a gain of two points from first to last, all subjects showed losses of from nine to 45 points. Ten of the children lost 15 or more points over the course of the study. The average decline in IQ for the contrast group was 26.2 IQ points.

There was a follow-up study approximately 2½ years after the last test of the original study. Briefly, the experimental group still showed a mean increase of 31.6 points and the contrast group a mean loss of 20.6 points. Still more important, however, is the next follow-up study, which occurred 21 years later. It would seem absolutely impossible to locate all the original subjects and yet the job was done with ingenuity and heroic effort. The significant findings are stated from Skeels' own summary in the following quotation:

Summary of adult follow-up

The two groups had maintained their divergent patterns of competency into adulthood. All 13 children in the experimental group were self-supporting, and none was a ward of any institution, public or private. In the contrast group of 12 children, one had died in adolescence following continued residence in a state institution for the mentally retarded, and 4 were still wards of institutions, 1 in a mental hospital, and the other 3 in institutions for the mentally retarded.

In education, disparity between the two groups was striking. The contrast group completed a median of less than the third grade. The experimental group completed a median of the twelfth grade. Four of the subjects had one or more years of college work, one received a BA degree and took some graduate training.

Marked differences in occupational levels were seen in the two groups. In the experimental group all were self-supporting or married and functioning as housewives. The range was from professional and business occupations to domestic service, the latter the occupations of two girls who had never been placed in adoptive homes. In the contrast group, four (36%) of the subjects were institutionalized and unemployed. Those who were employed, with one exception (Case 19), were characterized as "hewers of wood and drawers of water." Using the *t* test, the difference between the status means of the two groups (based on the **Warner Index of Status Characteristics** applied to heads of households) was statistically significant ($p < .01$).

Educational and occupational achievement and income for the 11* adopted subjects in the experimental group compared favorably with the 1960 U.S. Census figures for Iowa and for the United States in general. Their adult status was equivalent to what might have been expected of children living with natural parents in homes of comparable sociocultural levels. Those subjects that married had marriage partners of comparable sociocultural levels.

Eleven of the 13 children in the experimental group were married; 9 of the 11 had a total of 28 children, an average of three children per family. On intelligence tests, these second-generation children had IQs ranging from 86 to 125, with a mean and median IQ of 104. In no instance was there any indication of mental retardation or demonstrable abnormality. Those of school age were in appropriate grades for age.

In the contrast group, only two of the subjects had married. One had one child and subsequently was divorced. Psychological examination of the child revealed marked mental retardation with indications of probable brain damage. Another male subject (Case 19) had a nice home and family of four children, all of average intelligence.

The cost to the state for the contrast group, for whom intervention was essentially limited to custodial care, was approximately five times that of the cost for the experimental group. It seems safe to predict that for at least four of the cases in the contrast group costs to the state will continue at a rate in excess of $200.00 per month each for another 20 to 40 years [pp. 54–55].

---

*Of the original 13 *S*s, one remained in the institution until adulthood and another was returned to the orphanage for several years and was then temporarily committed to an institution for the mentally retarded. Thus, the size of the sample of *adopted* *S*s was reduced to 11, although all 13 *S*s were studied in the 20-year follow-up study at which time they "were all self-supporting and none were wards of any institution—public or private [Skeels, 1966, p. 32]."

*Rosenthal and Jacobson:
Teachers' expectancies as
determinants of pupils'
IQ gains**

8

In two earlier studies Rosenthal and co-workers (Rosenthal and Fode, 1963, and Rosenthal and Lawson, 1964) showed that if student experimenters were given rats to work with, it made a difference in their findings if they were told that their rats were bred for superior learning ability than if they were told that they had been bred for inferior learning ability. The former somehow yielded higher scores than the latter without any factual biological basis. Would the same thing hold true if, instead of rats, Rosenthal were to use school children and in place of student experimenters, school teachers? This is the task that Rosenthal and Jacobson (1966) set themselves.

Procedure

Rosenthal and Jacobson's first task was to use a test that would be independent of such school-acquired skills as reading, writing and arithmetic. They eventually settled on Flanagan's (1960) **TOGA,** or **Tests of General Ability,** which involve mostly verbal and "reasoning" types of items.

The test was given to all children in an elementary school with the alleged purpose of predicting academic "bloomers." Each of the six grades contained students classified into below-average, average, and above-average levels of scholastic performances. Purely on the basis of a table of random numbers, the names of the pupils

drawn were "given to each teacher who was told that their scores on the 'test for intellectual blooming' indicated that they would show unusual intellectual gains during the academic year [p. 116]."

Nothing more was done to the children thus randomly selected or to their classmates who were destined to serve as a control group. The experimental group had been merely identified to their teachers as pupils who were expected to make great gains that year. Eight months later Rosenthal and Jacobson had the same teachers administer the same IQ test, but the investigators themselves computed a change score for each subject.

Results

"For the school as a whole those children from whom the teachers had been led to expect greater intellectual gain showed a significantly greater gain in IQ score than did the control children [p. 116]." However, the effect of teachers' expectations did not produce a uniform effect throughout the six grades. Interestingly enough, the theme noted throughout recent research work,— namely, greater effects in the earlier years— manifested itself here, too, for the most

*Quoted material is from Robert Rosenthal and Lenore Jacobson, "Teachers' Expectancies: Determinants of Pupils' IQ Gains," *Psychological Reports,* 1966, **19,** 115–118. Reprinted by permission of author and publisher. For further discussion of this topic, see Rosenthal and Jacobson's *Pygmalion in the Classroom* (New York–Holt, 1968).

significant results occurred in the first two grades.

The largest gain among the three first-grade classrooms occurred for experimental Ss, who gained 24.8 IQ points *in excess* of the gain (+16.2) shown by the controls. The largest gain among the three second-grade classrooms was obtained by experimental Ss, who gained 18.2 IQ points in excess of the gain (+4.3) shown by the controls [p. 116].

The amount of gain made by different proportions of control versus experimental subjects provides another basis of comparison of the effect of teachers' expectancies. Forty-nine control subjects gained 10 points, but 79 experimental subjects made the same gain. Only 19 control subjects gained 20 points, but 47 experimental subjects made comparable gains. A 30-point gain was achieved by only five experimental subjects, but 21 alleged "bloomers" made gains of the same magnitude. These comparisons and still others show that the gains made by the experimental subjects were not made at the expense of the controls.

Retesting of three classes was done by an outside school administrator who was naive about the identity of the control and experimental subjects. Results were not significantly different from those obtained by the teacher's retesting of their pupils, thus ruling out any influence on differential test results from that source.

There are a number of possible explanations of the finding that teachers' expectancy effects operated primarily at the lower grade levels, including (1) Younger children have less well-established reputations so that the creation of expectations about their performance would be more credible. (2) Younger children may be more susceptible to the unintended social influence exerted by the expectation of their teacher. (3) Younger children may be more recent arrivals in the school's neighborhood and may differ from the older children in characteristics other than age. (4) Teachers of lower grades may differ from teachers of higher grades on a variety of dimensions which are correlated with the effectiveness of the unintentional communication of expectancies [pp. 117–118].

Can a teacher's high expectations of a student raise the student's own level of aspiration? The findings seem to so indicate. But as to how such teacher expectancy "becomes translated into behavior in such a way as to elicit the expected pupil behavior [p. 118]," that answer must wait for the future.

 Groso: Mental retardation*

The overall concept of mental retardation involves not only intellectual functioning but, as the types presented below demonstrate, other criteria as well. Mental retardation may include several or all of the

following factors: (1) biological or physical, (2) psychological, and (3) sociological.

Concerning the biological or physical aspects, this can be presented in the sensorial areas of human reactions. Sometimes the senses are not well developed and do not reach maturity. At other times the individual may have been born without certain anatomical and physiological formations, thus leaving him blind, mute, or deaf. Other retarded types are born without eyes, without a mouth cavity, or show similar gross anatomical defects.

Psychologically, the subaverage are classified on the basis of intellectual functioning, interpersonal relationships, feelings of rejection, feelings of inferiority, frustrations, lack of warmth, or lack of self-concept. Sociologically, familial deprivation, educational deprivation, or social incompetence in the competitive environment may be factors. The mentally deficient population may be grouped into as many categories as those in which average children or adults can be grouped.

Some reports from the American Medical Association Conference on Mental Retardation, April 9 to 11, 1964, assert that approximately five million individuals diagnosed at some time in their lives as retarded now live in the United States. Some 126,000 more are born yearly. Thus retardation may be viewed as a national problem, a problem, however, now eliciting a national upsurge of interest in all aspects of work on behalf of the mentally retarded and their families. This spurt may be viewed most graphically via the experience of the President's Panel on Mental Retardation named in 1961 to explore "possibilities and pathways to prevent and cure mental retardation."

Mental deficiency is not a "disease" or a single "entity." It is rather a term applied to a condition of subnormal mental development present in early childhood and characterized mainly by limited intelligence (Mayer-Gross, Slater, and Roth, 1954). E. A. Doll attempts a definition of mental retardation by the use of six criteria, all of which must be satisfied to make the concept workable. Retardation, according to Doll, must be (1) associated with social incompetence, (2) due to mental subnormality, (3) show developmental arrest, which must (4) obtain at maturity, (5) be of constitutional origin, and (6) be essentially incurable.

In the United States the term "mental retardation" is coming to be used in a generic sense to describe the mentally subnormal. The *American Association on Mental Deficiency Manual* defines mental deficiency as a synonym for mental retardation.

Heber, who prepared the *Manual on Terminology and Classification in Mental Retardation* (1961) presents the etiologic groupings used in the classification as follows:

1. Diseases due to infection.
2. Diseases due to intoxication.
3. Diseases due to trauma or physical agent.
4. Diseases due to disorder of metabolism, growth, or nutrition.
5. New growths.
6. Diseases due to (unknown) prenatal influence.
7. Diseases due to unknown or uncertain cause with the structural reaction.
8. Diseases due to unknown or uncertain cause with the functional reaction alone manifest.

Classification of mental retardation

The same monograph gives the classification of measured intelligence, a dimension scaled into five levels in terms of standard deviation units. Responsibility in selecting the tests used will result in the most reliable and valid assessment of the general intellectual functioning of the individual. Personally, the writer feels that present methods used in measuring the intelligence of the mentally retarded are not adequate. Nevertheless, the five levels as shown in the monograph are

    −1 Borderline
    −2 Mild
    −3 Moderate
    −4 Severe
    −5 Profound

Scale of adaptive behavior

The adaptive behavior classification is helpful in assessing how the mentally retarded individual copes with the social demands of his environment. In the above-mentioned monograph, the adaptive behavior dimension is categorized in terms of four levels:

    −I Mild
    −II Moderate
    −III Severe
    −IV Profound

A special 5-year project is being conducted at Parsons State Hospital and Training Center, at Parsons, Kansas, in the application and use of the concept of adaptive behavior in planning rehabilitation for the mentally retarded.

Clinical types

Research in mental retardation includes the wider field—how to classify the retarded, how to improve their lives, how to help them—but research on how to prevent mental retardation is most promising and interesting. At the present time some types of mental retardation due to metabolic abnormalities have almost been eliminated. Cretinism is one. **Phenylketonuria** is another condition that may some day be eliminated.

Phenylketonuria (PKU) is due to inability to properly metabolize the **amino acid phenylalanine.** Since this essential amino acid is present in all natural protein foods, ingested phenylalanine soon accumulates in the blood, and phenylketone bodies (phenylpyruvic acid, phenyl-lactic acid, phenyl-acetylglutamine) are excreted in the urine (hence the designation phenylketonuria). As the condition progresses, biological development is arrested and severe mental retardation results. This condition is easily diagnosed by simple urine and blood tests. The condition is not present at birth but is detectable by the first or second week of life. Clinical experience to date indicates that if controlled by a special diet, there is a good chance of preventing mental deficiency.

Several case histories

Through medical records and photographs, we shall now observe several mentally retarded patients at a state hospital. These cases show how serious biological defects operate to preclude normal or superior behavioral development.

Case CH. 11.2

Date of birth: 26 June 1963

Etiological medical diagnosis: mental retardation associated with diseases or conditions due to infection; microcephaly, secondary; hearing handicapped; visually handicapped; major motor seizures; **spasticity, quadriplegia,** moderate; measured intelligence −5; adaptive behavior −V.

The mother stated that she felt good during her pregnancy but was exposed to German measles at 6 weeks.

Developmental history: Pregnancy was of 9-months duration and labor lasted 7 hours. The birth weight was 5 pounds, 4 ounces, and no surgical procedures were used. No breathing difficulty was noted. Besides a small head and difficulty in feeding, nothing was obvious at the time of birth. It was not until the child was 1-year-old that she was diagnosed. The child has been a feeding problem.

Physical development: She is growing and she doesn't like to be in bed. She enjoys physical therapy. She is a moderately hyperactive child.

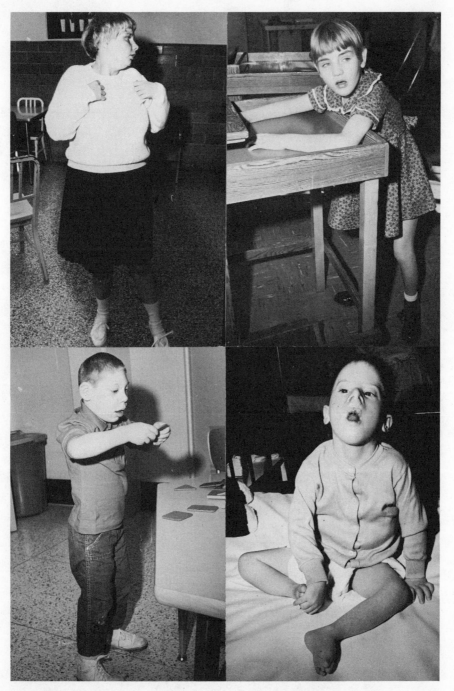

Figure 10.4 *Upper left:* Case J 42, *Upper right:* Case PV 31, *Lower left:* Case GW 62.5, *Lower right:* Case BP.

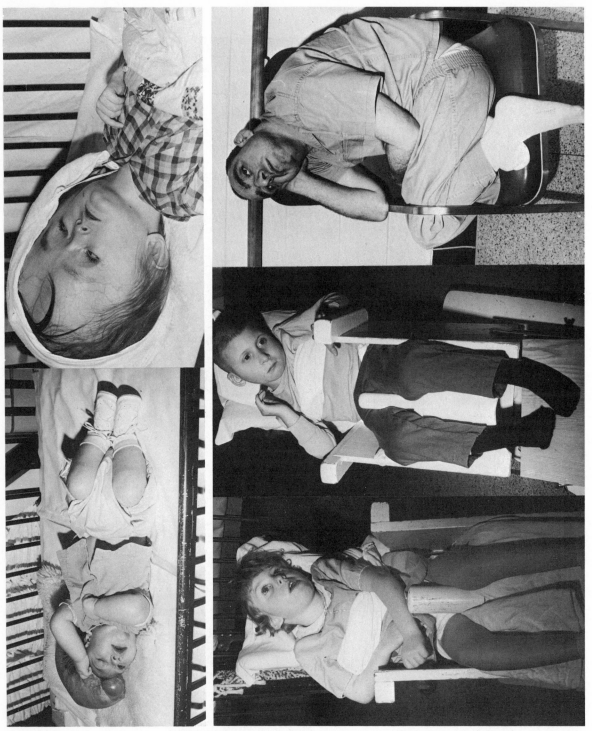

Figure 10.5 *Upper left: Case BB 625, Upper right: Case JC 62, Lower left: Case CH 11.2, Center: Case LB 69, Lower right: Case AL 11.3.*

Behavior reaction: She is aware of her environment and is improving in her behavior reactions. She likes toys and plays with them.

Case J-42

Date of birth: 9 October 1944

Etiological medical diagnosis: mental retardation associated with phenylketonuria; single recessive type transmission; with other psychiatric impairment but not further specified; measured intelligence −5; adaptive behavior −IV; personality description: psychotic reaction.

Developmental history: The mother reported that the gestation period was 10 months and that she almost lost the baby twice. The child was breast fed for 12 days, the period that the mother was in the hospital. The mother's milk was found to be lacking in nutritive values. The baby continued to have feeding trouble and bowel trouble. The baby cried practically none in the early weeks. She slept all the time and they had difficulty in getting her to eat. She was a nervous baby and jumped at the slightest noise. She could not walk until she was past 2 years old. She has never said a word.

Physical development: She is well developed physically.

Behavior reaction: She can take care of her toilet needs, but sometimes she has "accidents." She doesn't play with others. She wants to sit up, and she walks very fast without purpose, almost runs. When she goes outside, she spends her time on a bench. She doesn't interact in any way with the others. Autistic nature.

Case AL 11.3

Data of birth: 20 June 1926

Etiological medical diagnosis: **syphilis,** congenital; major motor seizures; spastic **paraplegia,** severe; measured intelligence −5; adaptive behavior −IV.

Developmental history: The child's birth was normal except that labor was long and difficult. Peculiarities were noted at 5 months, at which time the baby could not hold its head up. Early physical development was quite retarded.

Physical development: Although he grew physically, his social development is quite low. He cannot walk but crawls on the floor. He cannot talk. He is crippled from the knees down. He is not toilet trained.

Behavior reaction: He is mute, but he makes some sounds. He attracts attention by making loud noises. This man has very little ability to follow directions and instructions. He is quarrelsome, and he tries to harm other patients at times.

Case B-62.9

Date of birth: 5 March 1959

Etiological medical diagnosis: cerebral defect congenital with primary cranial anomaly (multiple anomalies of face, including nose, eyes, mouth and palate, and extremities); **hydrocephalus,** secondary; hearing and visually handicapped; measured intelligence −5; adaptive behavior −V.

This 7-year-old white female is a hydrocephalic and has some spasticity. She attempts crawling and actually gets up on her hands and knees and holds her head up. She enjoys the massage and personal attention.

Developmental history: B was born at 7½ months. Weight at birth was 4 pounds 6 ounces. The pregnancy was normal and delivery normal. She had multiple anomalies of the face, involving the nose, eyes, mouth, and palate. During the pregnancy, for approximately 3 weeks the mother had severe ear infection, necessitating treatment with antibiotics, principally **acromycin,** over a long period. At 5 months she was involved in a minor auto accident in which she was thrown against the steering wheel. She was not bruised and there was no bleeding; however, on the advice of the doctor she remained in bed a week.

Physical development: This child has many deformities. She has two eyes, but she is only able to look out of the left one. She has no nose, a hole for the mouth. She has upper teeth on the left side and lower teeth on the right side. She has one foot and one hand which are not developed.

Behavior reaction: The child responds well to auditory and visual stimuli. When she is spoken to, she lifts her head completely up to see the speaker. She is able to follow objects with her eyes and can grasp objects with her left hand. Responds well to those that work with her.

Case GW-62.5

Date of birth: 12 April 1963

Etiological medical diagnosis: microcephaly —

primary diagnosis; measured intelligence −2 (moderate); adaptive behavior −IV.

Developmental history: The mother stated her health was good during pregnancy. Labor lasted 24 hours, slowed down due to the smallness of the head. The doctor realized at birth that this child had brain damage but did not realize how extensive.

Physical development: Rolled over at 4 months. crawled at 8 months, sat at 9 months, and walked at 20 months. He is nonverbal. His hearing sensitivity is normal.

Behavior reaction: He has a very pleasant disposition and shows appropriate emotional responses. He responds to others and enjoys toys. He likes movies and bus rides. He is attending a speech therapy program.

Case BB-62.5

Date of birth: 19 May 1967

Etiological medical diagnosis: microcephaly; **encephalocele,** herniation of brain; measured intelligence not tested; adaptive behavior not tested.

Developmental history: A full-term spontaneous delivery took place. There were no complications at delivery. There were no abnormalities in his body except that examination of the head revealed the exteriorization of the brain.

Physical development: Increased motor movements progressed but not at a normal rate. The baby took oral feedings well without difficulty and has gained weight.

Behavior reaction: No behavior reactions, very limited due to his physical condition.

Case JC-62

Date of birth: 24 May 1962

Etiological medical diagnosis: cerebral defect congenital associated with primary cranial anomaly; hydrocephalus, congenital; measured intelligence not tested; adaptive behavior not tested

Developmental history: This child was born by Cesarean section because of a big head. The diagnosis of hydrocephalus was made at birth.

Physical development: The severity of this patient's medical problem obscures the behavior reaction.

Case LR-69

Date of birth: 1 October 1961

Etiological medical diagnosis:

Primary diagnosis: mental retardation associated with diseases and conditions due to prenatal influence.

Supplementary diagnoses: single dominant gene type transmission; single recessive gene type transmission; microcephaly, secondary; visually handicapped; spasticity, quadriplegia, moderate; measured intelligence −5; adaptive behavior −V.

Developmental history: This child of 7 did not breathe for 45 minutes to an hour after birth. He was placed in a respirator all night and spent the next 3 days in an incubator. At 3 or 4 months he had either **meningitis** or **encephalitis.**

Physical development: He doesn't walk, doesn't talk, but does grasp objects within reach, rolls over, reaches for nearby objects, and sits unsupported.

Behavior reaction: He laughs, follows simple instructions, demands personal attention, and likes to play with other children.

Case PV-31

Date of birth: 12 June 1959

Etiological Medical Diagnosis:

Primary Diagnosis: mental retardation associated with **encephalopathy** due to prenatal injury.

Supplementary diagnoses: microcephaly, secondary; major motor seizures; spasticity, mildly without deformities; quadriplegia; measured intelligence −5; adaptive behavior −IV.

Developmental history: The mother's labor was normal and lasted about 6 hours. No surgical procedures were used. At the age of 5 or 6 months, she began having seizures. The doctor reported that this child suffered damage during the early prenatal stage of development.

Physical development: She is an active child. She scoots around on the floor very rapidly. At the present time she is at the level of the standing table. This child could ultimately be made to walk. There are no deformities of extremities.

Behavior Reaction: She interacts well with other children. She enjoys music therapy and the recreation activities. Her attitude is friendly and she smiles often. She can see and hear and responds to her name.

Case BP-64-1x

Date of birth: 3 December 1962

Etiological medical diagnosis: mongolism, trisomy, mental retardation associated with diseases and conditions due to prenatal influence; undetermined genetic mechanism present; microcephaly, secondary; hearing handicapped; visually handicapped; **hypotonia,** quadriplegia moderate; measured intelligence −5; adaptive behavior −V.

Developmental history: This child weighed only approximately 4 pounds at birth due to prematurity. Multiple congenital defects were observed, including a double **hairlip,** a **cleft palate,** and six digits in the left hand.

Physical development: He has grown but he doesn't walk. He moves about on the floor by scooting. He grasps objects within reach and reaches for nearby objects.

Behavior reaction: This patient now reacts minimally to his environment, especially in responding to those with whom he has become familiar.

Evaluative comments It is important to point out the significance of the preceding cases for medical versus psychological purposes. For example, in treating the patient *medically,* one must determine whether the causal factor is a remediable phenylketonuria, thyroid deficiency, microcephaly, or incipient hydrocephaly. However, in a *psychological framework,* such biologically specific factors take on a more general significance, namely, that they *preclude* the organism from contacting and acquiring reactions to stimulus objects. Thus, in our framework, a lack of thyroid functioning can be equated with blindness, deafness, anatomical defectiveness, or destruction by disease.

In this context, readers might recall the case of Nigel Hunt (Chapter 7). They might also refer to the story of Helen Keller, who lost both sight and hearing, and even the sense of smell, by illness at the age of 19 months. Miss Keller, who was educated by Anne Sullivan Macy, became a famous lecturer and writer.   −N.H.P.

Bucklew:
The current status of theory
in mental retardation*

10

Mental retardation is now the most widely accepted term for what was once called feeblemindedness in America and **amentia** in England. It is a diagnostic term used to classify those individuals who fail to achieve levels of intellectual functioning appropriate to their age and adaptive to their surroundings, regardless of the causes of their subnormal functioning. The modern term calls attention to the fact that the condition is a developmental failure, and it is sometimes proposed that the term "developmental retardation" would for this reason be better (Bijou, 1963). The defining phrase "intellectual function" is understood to

---

*Written for inclusion in this volume by John Bucklew, Lawrence University. All rights reserved.

apply broadly to those basic skills in language, motor functioning, learning, problem solving, remembering, abstracting, and related activities that human beings acquire as they mature. In the following discussion, the word feeblemindedness will be used only in its appropriate historical context, and the phrase mental retardation elsewhere.

A historical perspective

The earlier scientific explanation of feeblemindedness, completed during the first decade of this century, may be summarized approximately as follows. Feeblemindedness was considered to be an arrested development of the intellectual capacity of the mind, manifested in the individual by subnormal intelligence. On the basis of certain evidence (to be explained later in our discussion), the chief cause was thought to be a paucity of cells in some layers of the cerebral cortex ("lack of gray matter" became the popular expression of the idea); and for most feebleminded individuals this cortical defect was presumed to be a hereditary condition. A. F. Tregold (1949), one of the chief architects of this theory, created the classification of **"primary amentia"** to describe constitutional or congenital cases of retardation. For those numerous cases in which the defect seemed to have originated through accidental maldevelopments in the embryonic or postnatal environment, he created the term **"secondary amentia"** (environmentally acquired). On the basis of clinical observations and tests, feeblemindedness was classified into observable types (e.g., mongolism, microcephaly, hydrocephaly, etc.) and by severity of condition into morons, the milder cases; imbeciles, the intermediate cases; and idiots, the severest cases. What will interest us most is the classification of feeblemindedness into primary and secondary types because this reflects the theory of causation of the time. On the whole, we might say that the scientific orientation towards feeblemindedness was biological and medical. Approaches to it in terms of personality theory, learning theory, and social theory were only beginning and had not yet made much impact.

Assumed irreversibility of feeblemindedness

One consequence of this general theory was the feeling that feeblemindedness was, for the most part, irreversible; that is, it was not possible to alter its development in the individual in any significant manner. As a matter of fact, most efforts to retrain the feebleminded who were at all capable of education met with rather limited results. They might be made more competent or useful, but rarely were they released from institutional care or close supervision. Thus the rather fatalistic view of hereditary influence held at the time served to give an intellectual rationale to what in fact seemed to be the case. The more severe cases of feeblemindedness were given permanent custodial care in institutions, and the less severe ones were kept in the protective atmosphere of the home and family.

Hereditary causation

Despite the simplicity and clarity of the original theory, specialists in the field have always recognized that the causation of feeblemindedness was complex and individually different. Each case had to be evaluated independently and carefully if one hoped to benefit the individual in any way. Those cases classifiable in the milder range of retardation often showed no demonstrable organic defects at all, either in the central nervous system or in the rest of the body. For them, unless one could show a gross environmental deprivation in their life history, it was assumed that the retardation was hereditary in origin, but that the manner in which the genetic influence worked in the development of the organism was, as yet, undiscovered. In only a small percentage of the cases could one find a high incidence of feeblemindedness in the relatives of the individual, and these studies usually were lacking in adequate scientific control. Modern population genetics, which uses elaborate statistical techniques of analysis, had not yet developed. The theory that these individuals were suffering from an inherited low intellectual *capacity* localized in the cortex had very little evidence to support it beyond the obvious fact that they achieved a rather limited intellectual development and were resistant to special help.

Organic cases

Another rather substantial group of cases, often referred to as **"organic"** cases (see Figs. 10.4 and 10.5) and falling mainly in the more severe range of retardation, displayed numerous gross defects, which, however, were not always or even usually found in the cortex. Sometimes the defects were located in other parts of the nervous system and very often in other regions of the body altogether. In some instances, noticeable asymmetrical maldevelopments of organs or structures on one side of the body or the other were evident. In other instances, parts of limbs might be missing or developed in only a rudimentary fashion. Similarly, the various internal organs could be grossly maldeveloped. Recognizable patterns of maldevelopment gave rise to various clinical classifications, but little was known of their actual causation. Per-

haps most important, disorders of endocrine function came to be recognized and diagnosed. One type of case, cretinism, was discovered to be due to insufficient thyroid-gland functioning resulting from low intake of iodine. If detected soon enough, it could be remedied.

Shift to an organismic theory

Thus there was a gradual shift of interest away from preoccupation with the presumed role of the cortex and toward an interest in the possible effect of maldevelopments in the whole organism. The connection between the facts of mental retardation and the original theory of a defective cortex, proposed originally by Tredgold (1949), Berry and Gordon (1931), and others, became increasingly inferential and tenuous. During the 1930's some scientists began to speak of a total **organismic approach** to the problem because they thought that the organism as a whole played an essential role in the development of intelligent behavior (Flory, 1936). Others, however, continued to look on certain organic impairments as only *simulating* "true" or inborn retardation (Fay and Doll, 1949).

In 1951 the writer and A. J. Hafner reviewed the evidence for a cerebral localization theory of feeblemindedness and decided that the organismic theory had much more to recommend it. Beyond this, it seemed apparent to them that more attention should be paid to life-history factors. Psychoanalysts in the tradition of Alfred Adler had succeeded in curing some cases of "stupid" children by techniques of individual counseling. Experimental techniques in learning were beginning to be applied to problems of training the mentally retarded (Stevens and Heber, 1964).

The contemporary period

All of which brings us to the contemporary period in the theory, research, and alleviation of mental retardation. The many changes and innovations can best be understood by reference to the early theory summarized above. After the **behaviorist** revolution in psychology in the United States, psychologists were no longer content to define their subject matter in terms of a private "mind" whose operations were inaccessible to direct observation. Consequently, the intellectual functions were restated in behavioral terms, were measured by means of intelligence scales, and were subjected to objective experimental analysis. They were also related more closely to variations in motivation, emotional and attitudinal development, the development of perceptual and motor skills, language development—in fact, to the growth of the personality as a whole. Intelligence became, not a detached separable function but an integral part of the behavior equipment acquired by the individual as he matured. More attention is now paid to the total personality development of the mentally retarded and to the socioeconomic environments in which they are born and reared. Specialists recognize that their defects can lie in many more directions than the intellectual functions proper, and that scientific reeducation techniques, such as operant conditioning, may at least increase their functioning to a more useful level.

Experimental trends

An illustration taken from recent experimental research will clarify the shift in point of view that has occurred. It had long been recognized that mentally retarded individuals **perseverated** at routine, dull tasks and did not switch readily to new ones. Their intellectual level was considered to make them rigid in their activities and unresponsive to changes in task. Edward Zigler and his associates (Green and Zigler, 1962; Shepps and Zigler, 1962; Zigler, 1963), however, questioned this interpretation because they noticed that the mentally retarded tended to respond this way when positively reinforced by the prolonged contact with a supervisor. They labeled this variable as *support versus nonsupport* conditions for doing dull work and showed in a series of experiments that institutionalized individuals, who are usually deprived of sufficient contact with normal adults, would perseverate under support conditions significantly more than noninstitutionalized cases living in their own family homes. In order to ensure that the two groups were comparable, they matched them for mental age. The difference held true for both organic and nonorganic cases of retardation.

The role of social motivation

Notice that the significant variable, support *versus* nonsupport, has to do with social motivation—the need for recognition, approval, and sympathy—rather than with intellectual factors per se. However, the task on which they were tested was an intellectual task, although a simple one. Behind the neutrally reported scientific results, one senses the striving human being whose intellectual performance is very much a product of diverse regions of his personality, and who is adapting to specific environmental situations as best he can. The functions we define as intellectual do not exist in splendid isolation!

A new perspective on an old problem

The essential shift in point of view we

have been discussing may be summarized in the following three statements. (1) Mental retardation is evaluated in terms of the individual's whole personality and of the concrete situations in which he lives. (2) The life history of the afflicted individual is regarded as a possible important determinant of his intellectual status even though he may have disabling organic deficiencies. (3) Genetic causation of mental retardation is also evaluated specifically in terms of the various environments, biochemical, ecological, psychosocial, in which the individual has matured. This last point requires explanation and leads us to the second great change that has taken place since the original theory was proposed.

Modern genetics

Although the scientific period in genetics began in the last century with the contributions of Mendel, who established the presence of dominant and recessive "genes" as agents for the transmission of traits, the story of what these agents actually were chemically, and how they exercised their influence during the long growth period in human beings, was still very much a mystery. Only in recent years, with the discovery of how genetic information is stored and transmitted by means of deoxyribonucleic acid (DNA) and messenger ribonucleic acid (RNA), has the story begun to be complete. There is a long period of elapsed time between the biological conception of the individual and the point at which we can determine by his responses that he is intellectually retarded. We have to consider both a complex biological development and a history of learned reactions. Early theorists of feeblemindedness merely supposed that somehow or other, either directly or indirectly, the original genetic endowment of the individual came to influence his cortical

development and thus the capacity of his mind. Popular thinking continued to regard heredity as a rather vague "power," which exerted its effect on the individual in mysterious ways.

Genetic "errors of metabolism" and mental retardation

The modern breakthrough in the science of genetics is probably one of the major scientific accomplishments of this century and its consequences for the understanding and amelioration of mental retardation must still be worked out. It seems probable now that some of the defective **biochemistry** found with such high frequency in mental retardates is traceable to inborn "errors of metabolism." What is needed is more information on the intricate biochemical development of these metabolic errors in order to determine how they cause deviations in the subsequent behavioral development.

The example of phenylketonuria

Information on one rather infrequent type of mental retardation, phenylketonuria (PKU), is becoming rather extensive (Anderson, 1964). It has been established that this condition is due to **homozygosity** in a rather rare recessive gene. Its presence is detectable from an unusual composition of the urine, and this, in turn, is caused by an enzyme deficiency. If treated by dietary control, the life expectancy of the child is increased, and he may achieve an intelligence quotient of 30 or less and may exhibit certain physical symptoms such as **dermatitis.** Another recognizable type of mental retardation, mongolism (now called *Down's syndrome*), is now known to be due to the accidental production of an extra chromosome, but the reasons for the accidental duplication are somewhat obscure.

Inheritance of "fixed traits" versus "norms of reaction"

The shift in point of view, which is our primary interest, occurred *before* many of the major discoveries we have been describing. It is best signalized by a paper published by the geneticist, Theodore Dobzhansky, in *Science* in 1944. Dobzhansky maintained that our knowledge of the manner in which genetic factors worked no longer permitted us to think of them as independent, unchangeable determiners of our "fate." The effect of genetic factors can be altered by changes in some aspect of the environments (biochemical, ecological, behavioral) in which the organism develops, as we have just seen in PKU, which responds favorably to dietary control. Some developed traits, such as our height or weight, are genetically based but quite modifiable, according to Dobzhansky, while others are less so. Only a few traits, such as blood type, are invariant in all known environments. As for such psychological variables as intellectual status, he thought that the genetic influences on them were quite indirect and plastic, depending on the psychological and sociological environments in which the person happened to be reared. In his view, what was inherited was a "norm of reaction" to the environment, not a fixed trait.

Better knowledge of the actual process of hereditary transmission and increasing knowledge of the biochemistry of development have greatly amplified our understanding of what these norms of reaction might be and how they may be affected by environmental changes. Still, a great deal more remains to be discovered.

The present status

How shall we characterize the present status of the theory of mental retardation? What we see are many lines of investigation, pursuing causal factors in many different directions across the boundaries of several fields of science. If any cases of mental retardation are singly caused, they must be very few in number and probably lie at the extreme lower end of the distribution of intelligence. Inasmuch as the organismic view favored a theory of multiple causation, it was pointing in the right direction. Even the classification of cases into organic and nonorganic types probably should not be taken to mean that the causal factors lie in different domains for the two categories. In their book on mental subnormality, Masland, Sarason, and Gladwin (1958) make the following remarks on this point.

Only in the most extreme cases of organic disorder can we say that psychological and environmental factors are not relevant to treatment and development, while there are equally few retarded individuals in whom we can be certain *no* biological factors (broadly conceived) are affecting their intellectual performance [p. 5].

Brain localization as a residual theory

Generally speaking, modern research in mental retardation has been oriented toward the solution of specific problems and the elucidation of new facts. For the past several years, mental retardation has assumed the dimensions of a national problem and the economic resources of society have been increasingly directed toward the subsidization of research and treatment. An air of optimism pervades the field. In interpreting the results of their research, specialists still tend to refer to the cerebral hemispheres as the locus of the difficulty, as if to make a passing reference to the traditional localization theory. However, this theory no longer serves to orient the direction of research, and the classifications of mental retardation based on it are no longer observed. It might be termed a residual theory*; it no longer performs the functions that a scientific theory should perform.

A large part of the perplexities over the theory of mental retardation depends on what we expect from a theory in the behavioral sciences. The broad and unencumbered mathematical generalizations of the physical sciences seem impossible to obtain elsewhere. But by developing very specific mathematical models for very restricted domains of data (e.g., a special form of learning or of immediate memory), psychologists have been able to attain some mathematical rigor and predictiveness. Although mathematical models for intelligence, and for other variables important in mental retardation, may prove to be valuable, they can hardly be expected to provide a general theory for something as complex as mental retardation and its

---

*By a residual theory we mean that, in historical perspective, there has been an increasing divergence of the discovered facts and relationships from those one might, on the basis of the theory, have reasonably expected to ensue. The term bears some resemblance to Pareto's (1966) "persistence of aggregates," which he also calls a *residue*. In the physical sciences, the definition of residuals is much more precise and bears no historical reference. By way of contrast to the physical sciences, theories in the behavioral sciences are rarely disproved and set aside; they merely fall into disuse and are half-forgotten. The student of these sciences might well ponder why this is true.

causes. For this task, specialists in mental retardation must develop their own theory.

A look ahead

The techniques and theory of multivariate analysis should be ideal tools for the analysis of mental retardation because of the complexity of its data and the many causal influences that seem to be operating. With the use of modern methods of psychological measurement and the valuable aid of the high-speed computer, the interaction among matrices of data can be statistically analyzed for their relationships. It is feasible now to employ factor analysis and cluster analysis to isolate basic, stable patterns of variables whose detection can, in turn, lead to newer and better classifications of mental retardation more precisely related to their causes.

Coda

The older theories of mental retardation were concerned with scientific orientation and definition in place of the mixture of folklore and tradition inherited from a prescientific period. In retracing their development, the student of the history of psychology will recognize that we have been retracing the development of systematic psychology during the present century. We have moved from mind-body dualism to organism-environment-behavior categories, from an overconcern with presumed cortical functions subserving intelligence to a perspective on human beings living and behaving in a natural and social world.

Chapter summary

Instead of trying to solve the problem of intelligence by appeal to logic or armchair speculation, we considered the facts. First we noted Cautela's discourse on some common misconceptions about IQ. Prominent among them is circular reasoning, which declares that

"A has a higher IQ than B."
"How do you know?"
"Well, because he performs better on an intelligence test than B."
"Why?"
"Because he has a higher IQ," etc.

Is it possible to show how IQ can be "transmitted" through the genes, regardless of the IQs of parents and children? Yes, this is demonstrated in a new scheme for the inheritance of intelligence. In other words, it is possible to talk nonsense about intelligence. But, in an attempt to talk sense about it, we extracted some of the most basic concepts of Piaget's interactional theory of intelligence.

Longitudinal studies of intelligence show that the IQ is anything but constant. Better still, we learn that the changes are not chaotic but show patterns similar to such changes in the biological realm as birth, growth, disease and death. A developmental study of 1000 geniuses presents a naturalistic picture of how geniuses are made.

A 30-year follow-up study shows predictable results in IQ dependent on enriched or deprived circumstances of the children involved. Even experimenter effects on IQ can be demonstrated, as we noted in "the Rosenthal effect."

Then we took a figurative walk through the wards of an institution for the mentally retarded and observed a multitude of biological defects which preclude normal psychological development.

Finally, with Bucklew's help, we offered a perspective on mental retardation, one that localizes the problem beyond the victim's brain or even total organism—and places it in the total life circumstances that confront the person. As to the innate versus acquired character of intelligence, let the reader draw his own conclusion.

Cognitive processes: Perceiving and thinking

People see, taste, hear, touch, and smell things in their surroundings. Consequently, they learn how to adapt to many conditions: escaping gas on a kitchen range, a scorched shirt on the ironing board, the screech of a jet, a counterfeit coin, and a singer "off key." These reactions are adaptive in the same way (except more so) that heavy breathing while jogging or a cat's "righting" itself after a fall from a tree is adaptive. The difference is that the former sense perceptions require learning—that is, a series of learning experiences during the individual's life history—whereas the latter responses are built-in reactions. Certainly no one was born with a "gift" for smelling gas, detecting scorched shirts, or spotting counterfeit coins. Similarly, **thinking** or implicit action, evolves from the bits and pieces of everyday perceptions.

We turn now to a consideration of the cognitive processes of **perception** and implicit action or thinking.

One way to learn about a phenomenon is to disrupt it or interfere with it radically. For example, let us take the sense of sight and turn it upside down. We see what happens in a study in which a subject wore lenses for 30 days, a procedure that forced him to live in a topsy-turvy world. Then there is the question of so-called "perfect pitch," a response that calls for such accurate perception as to reproduce or match a given note. Even more remarkable is the person who, in absence *of any standard,* can vocally hum a given note on demand and do it accurately. The latter

is clearly a case of implicit action.

We continue to selections that emphasize how perceptions develop. The first discusses **discrimination learning.** The second reports what happens when a monkey reaches for objects with an arm that was shielded from its view from birth by a circular screen permitting motor reactions but not visuo-motor ones. The third article describes an electronic method for "translating" visual patterns into tactile or touch perceptions or, as it has been dubbed, "tickle talk." A form of visual perception that resembles extrasensory perception, Psi phenomena, and a new "impossible" figure are next described to show how an apparently simple line drawing causes perceptual impasse.

What effect does starvation have on the perceptions and thought processes of the subjects in a starvation experiment? Twenty-six volunteer patients, all severely overweight, were studied under hospital conditions; the findings are reported here. The relationship between subvocal speech and thinking which has long been suspected, is examined next. A study reports how silent reading was reduced to a vestigial and, therefore, more rapid form by a method of feedback. The chapter ends with a description of research on **body image, phantom limbs** and **phantom sensations,** studies that belong to the category of thinking or implicit action. They focus on the question: Can pain, touch, and so forth survive amputation of certain organs? If so, how?

1 The nature of perception

Suppose that by some mischievous circumstance I were allowed one and only one visual aid to use in my teaching. I am sure that without the least hesitation I would choose the blotch shown in Fig. 11.1. It speaks eloquently on the essential attributes of perception.

Let us assume that the reader has never before seen this particular figure. (If he has seen it before, then he has to recall his first contact with it, the time when it *was* a meaningless blotch.) There it is before his eyes then, a meaningless blotch.

Figure 11.1   A cow. If the reader doesn't see a cow instantly, let him persist. Patience will repay him with an interesting experience. Out of the left side of the blotch, there eventually emerges the head of a cow staring straight at you, the muzzle toward the bottom and dome of her head at top. The right side of her head is in deep shadow. Her left side has some black spots on an otherwise white flank.

A perceptual response is born

Let the reader continue to look at the nonsense figure from different angles. In the typical classroom demonstration, the following event occurs. The students keep looking at the figure projected on the screen via a transparency on the overhead projector. Nothing happens for several minutes. Then one hears a succession of surprised "Ohs" and "Ahs." The students now see a cow where there was nothing a moment before. I immediately point out that the moment the meaningless blob took on the dimensions of a cow a perceptual response was born. The event is parallel to a stellar explosion that gave rise to a **super nova** somewhere in the universe. From that moment on the blob will remain a cow (perhaps forever, depending on how well the organism and cow-stimulus object are organized). Ordinarily, the two are wedded indissolubly and no man can tear them asunder. No matter whether the figure is placed upside-down or on either end, it remains a "cow."

Significance of the cow picture

The cow figure shows certain properties of perception. First, it demonstrates that perception is not something naturally inherent in the stimulus object or guaranteed by it. Perception results from the organism-object interaction. It emerges or has a beginning just like a plant or animal, or like the child's first utterance has a development and a point of origin.

Second, it is an active process, a seeking, a striving from slightly different stances or perspectives until one aspect endows the pattern with cowness and there it is henceforth forevermore. (In some cases, apparently from lack of tight organization of stimulus-response, the perceptual union is dissolved and the operation must be repeated. However, with continued active seeking, "cowness" once more triumphantly emerges.)

A third striking feature of the cow perception is its relative stability. Once the cow is there, I challenge you to *not* see the cow. The cow cannot be abolished (or willed out of existence). It continues to be cow. Look away for a few minutes, or even go away for an hour. The moment you see the figure again it is still "cow," instantaneously, effortlessly, and undeniably. In other words, the pattern is recognized as cow, which leads to the fourth point, recognition.

Recognition is another essential characteristic of perception. This term stresses the fact of *re-cognizing* or knowing a thing *again* after having known it on a prior occasion. To state it another way, once the meaningless blob takes on the property of a cow, one cannot easily return to his former state of innocence—his pre-"cow" naïveté. He sees the object now as he did then. He recognizes it. The perceptual event that took place in the past is nevertheless having its effect now. It is contributing to the immediate perception of the cow at the present time. As a test, at the next meeting of the class, ask those students who missed the previous class to identify the figure on the screen. They cannot. Next, ask those who were present at the last session to name the blob and you will get a chorus of "cow"! The present cognition is a *re-cognition*. The present perception is a function of a previous perception. This fact is what Kantor (1933) discusses with his characterization of perception as "semi-implicit" (p. 153). By this term he means that the individual does not react to the stimulus object as if for the first time. In his words:

In performing a perceiving response, we do not merely react to a thing as it stands before us, but rather to what the object means—in other words, to its possibilities as a behavior object [p. 153].

I would add that we do not react to the object as it stands before us but as it stood before us on a past occasion. We react to it now in terms of our prior reactions to it. We *re-cognize* it.

There are other ways to understand perception. This is the way I understand it.

---

2 The nature of "thinking" or implicit action

With the semi-implicit character of perception established, we are ready for a brief explanation of "thinking" as fully implicit action. In my opinion the term *thinking,* in its sharpest usage, refers to reactions performed to absent stimulus objects.

To illustrate, let us use the story of Romeo and Juliet. First, we view them in a perceptual event at the moment when they come within sight of each other. Obviously they do not "see" each other in the same way as any neutral boy sees any neutral girl. All their past interactions enrich the present moment and make it the intense emotional experience that it is. This is perception.

Now, let us observe the lovers after their parting. The striking aspect of their behavior is their expression of love for one another. Their sighings and anguish at parting are intense and continue when they are apart. These are obviously reactions to absent stimulus objects. How? Via **substitute stimuli.** Their own reactions, plus the surroundings (e.g., the moon going behind a cloud), provide the stimulation and conspire to remind Romeo of Juliet and vice versa.*

---

*For a more detailed account of implicit activity, see J. R. Kantor, *A Survey of the Science of Psychology.* Bloomington, Ind.: Principia Press, 1933.

---

3 Snyder and Pronko: Vision with spatial inversion*

Preface to an upside-down experiment

Suppose that we attached lenses to the eyes of a newborn child, lenses having the

*A condensed version of a report published by F. W. Snyder and N. H. Pronko, *Vision with Spatial Inversion.* Wichita: University of Wichita Press, 1952. A film of the same title is available from Pennsylvania Cinema Register, Pennsylvania State University, State College, Pa.

property of reversing right-left and up and down. Suppose, also, that the child wore the lenses through childhood, boyhood, and young manhood. What would happen if these inverting lenses were finally removed on his twenty-fifth birthday? Would he be nauseated and unable to reach and walk and read?

Such an experiment is out of the question, of course. Yet, another experiment was made: a young man was persuaded to wear inverting lenses for 30 days, and his experiences are reported here. His continued progress, after an initial upset, suggests that new perceptions do develop in the same way as the original perceptions did. Life situations suggest the same thing. Dentists learn to work via a mirror in the patient's mouth until the action is automatic. In the early days of television, cameramen had to "pan" their cameras with a reversed view. Later the image in the camera was corrected to correspond with the scene being panned. The changeover caused considerable confusion to cameramen until they learned appropriate visual-motor coordinations. Fred Snyder, the subject of our upside-down experiment, found himself in a similar predicament, at least for a time.

An extended study of spatial inversion (30 days) showed the relative facility with which a human adult S could reorient to a visual spatial field rotated 180 degrees (Snyder and Pronko, 1952). The study was designed to answer these questions: (1) How are visual-motor coordinations modified when the visual field is inverted up-down and right-left? (2) What features of performance during the period of wearing the inverting lenses and after their removal are related to visual-motor habits developed before the experiment or in preceding experimental periods?

Procedure

The lens system was essentially a unit-power inverting telescope. Two of these were used, making the total system binocular. Each telescope was placed inside a tube receptacle, which, in turn, was fastened to an adjustable headgear. The headgear is shown as worn by the S in Fig. 11.2.

The original experiment was divided into three periods: practice without inverting

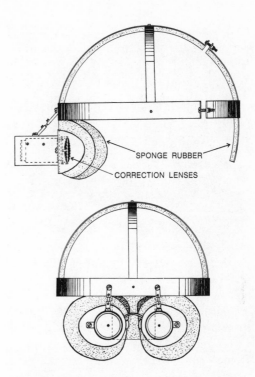

Figure 11.2 Front and side view of head gear showing placement of lens system. (From F. W. Snyder and N. H. Pronko, *Vision with Spatial Inversion.* Wichita, Kansas: University of Wichita Press, 1952. Reproduced by permission of author and publisher.)

lenses, practice with inverting lenses, and continued practice after their removal. In each of these three periods, continuous training in card sorting, a **manipulation test,** a **pegboard test,** and a **mirror-tracing** task were carried out. Observations were made of S's walking, language activities, visual-motor activities, auditory-visual conflicts, and other behaviors. S kept a diary of his observations of daily happenings in the laboratory and in daily living.

Conclusions

The conclusions from the performance of the experimental tasks (sorting, manipulation, mirror tracing) for periods

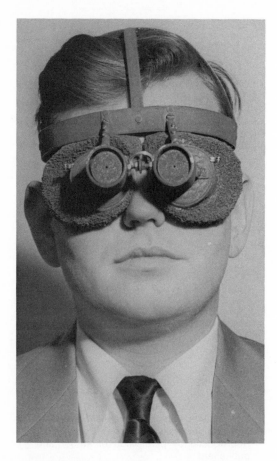

Figure 11.3 Front view of subject wearing inverting lenses. Note small hole in lens covering which drastically restricted field of vision. (From F. W. Snyder and N. H. Pronko, *Vision with Spatial Inversion.* Wichita, Kansas: University of Wichita Press, 1952. Reproduced by permission of author and publisher.)

before, during, and after disorientation are

1. The past experience of the subject was related to the initial and succeeding performance on the tasks.

2. Restriction of the visual field alone did not appreciably influence the quantitative or qualitative results for this aspect of the experiment.

3. When the inverting lenses were first put on, the subject's visual-motor coordi-

nations were in every way seriously disrupted.

4. During the 30-day period that the inverting lenses were worn, the visual-motor coordinations were refashioned so that the subject performed even better than before the lenses were put on.

5. Upon removal of the lenses, the visual-motor coordinations were again mildly disrupted for a short time.

6. The experimental tasks served as a learning situation in which there was a rapid rate of learning at first, followed by a slower one.

7. Introducing the inverted visual field for 30 days and subsequent "normalization" (lenses removed) modified the learning situation. However, the subject went on learning despite these disrupting factors.

The general conclusions for the extraexperimental tasks (walking, steadiness tests, sketching, car driving, eating, reading, writing, and typing) are as follows:

8. The visual-motor coordinations for the extraexperimental tasks were disrupted at first by inverting the visual field. These effects gradually diminished during the 30-day period. In a general way, the rate of improvement was fastest with well-practiced activities, such as walking or eating.

9. For these activities, requiring a range of vision much greater than 20 degrees, restriction of the field was a disrupting factor.

Considerable insight into the process of perceptual reorientation is available from a review of excerpts from the diary kept daily by the subject.

The subject's diary

The first reactions of the subject were recorded during the 5-day period in which tubes (minus inverting lenses) were worn which restricted the field to 20 degrees, but did not invert the visual field.

I observed difficulty in performing tasks that required a visual field larger than that allowed by the tubes. For example, it was difficult to locate an object which I knew was somewhere on the table. I also found it quite a problem to climb stairs with this restricted view. I attempted to read a newspaper and also to play Chinese checkers and found that both required much head movement.

The restricted field of view hampered the operation of the experimental tasks slightly.

The next reactions were selected from diary records kept during the interval in which the inverting-lens headgear was worn continuously except upon retiring, when a blindfold was used.

July 20. First day. Today I put on the inverting lenses. After 25 years of visually perceiving things in the usual way, in a brief moment everything was inverted. In addition, the visual field was noticeably restricted. When I turned my head, I observed that objects appeared to move at the normal rate. There was no swing effect, which both Stratton (1896, 1897) and Ewert (1930) had mentioned. One important variable involved in this phenomenon may have been the magnification of the lenses they used. Stratton and Ewert both reported upsetting effects, nausea, and giddiness. None of these effects was noticed at the time I put on my lenses.

Laboratory tasks

The first task I performed while wearing the lenses was card sorting. When I looked at the card-sorting box, I noticed it was inverted. Then I was handed the cards and told to start. I could not decide at first in what compartment I should place the card. The motions I made were awkward and somewhat embarrassing. In order to bring the upper and lower end boxes into view, it was necessary to make numerous head movements. These movements were usually inappropriate.

With the **Purdue pegboard** I found that I could pick up and place a peg in a washer with little difficulty. The operation of placing the peg in a hole, however, was extremely difficult. When my right hand moved out, it appeared to come toward me. Movements in a direction which I perceived to be correct proved to be opposite to those that I intended. Left was right and right was left in this new orientation.

The chief difficulty I found in mirror tracing with the lenses on was that I could find no appropriate movement out of all my behavior repertoire. After I had started along the star path, I moved the stylus into one of the sawtooth notches. I devoted much time trying all the possible directions that might lead me out of the notch. The first movements were usually the wrong ones.

Walking the painted-line floor maze was equally as difficult as following the star pattern. When I looked down, it seemed as though my feet belonged to someone who stood in front, facing me. At the starting signal, I stepped out. Then I could not decide which foot I was to move next. I looked at my right foot, but as I stepped, instead of moving it, I moved the wrong foot. In the course of walking the maze line, I retraced my steps many times.

When I finished my session in the laboratory, I walked into the hallway and was quite astonished to perceive the lights on the floor. In attempting to avoid an object in the hall, I only succeed in coming closer to it.

By the third day I was much better oriented toward experiences, both in experimental and life situations. In addition, I noticed many differences from my preinversion perceptions.

All perceptions with the lenses on resulted in objects seen as reversed from top-to-bottom and right-to-left. When I looked straight ahead, an object, such as the floor, normally seen at the lower part of the field was now in the upper part. If an object, a door for example, was normally on the right, it was on the left in the new spatial field.

If I moved in the downward direction so that I perceived the ceiling, this brought into view not the ceiling but the floor. Thus when I looked forward, none of the locations of objects agreed with my previous perception of them. I particularly noticed that distances of objects were not reversed. In addition, when I looked directly at the floor, I noted that objects were displaced 180 degrees, that is, those normally closest were farthest away and vice versa. These objects were reversed from right-to-left.

Progress continues

I found it easiest to understand and describe what I perceived in the different head positions by relating them to a position with my head facing straight forward. If I saw part of an object on the left of my visual field and wanted to bring this object more fully into view, I had to turn my head to the right. For objects on the right of my visual field, I had to turn my head to the left. However, if I had my head already turned to the left, to the right, upward or downward, the position of objects agreed with the positions they had with normal vision. The only difference was that these objects were inverted.

By the fourth day places that I have seen several times have become familiar scenes. I am now seldom aware that objects are inverted.

By the sixth day card sorting was much easier. On mirror tracing, the stylus was caught in the notches less frequently.

Placing a fan on a table several feet from where I was working, I plugged it in but felt no air. I realized after a few seconds that I must have turned it in the opposite direction. This may be explained by the fact that as I looked at the fan it was disoriented 180 degrees, although, as it looked to me, the fan appeared in the proper position to blow air on me.

I took a 2-hour automobile trip today. The lenses became almost unbearable so I rested my eyes by taking off the lenses and wearing the blindfold. I wore the lenses for a total time of 45 minutes during the trip. During this time I noticed some interesting experiences. In approaching cars I still perceived the sound on the left but saw the cars pass us on the right. At times I have heard the sound on the same side on which I saw it. Once or twice I seemed to see it where I heard it.

Occasionally I went to the wrong end of the **Minnesota Rate of Manipulation Test** on the seventh day. Sometimes I moved too fast to the left to get to the starting position. I believe I followed my movements much better than on the first trials with lenses.

On the evening of the eighth day I attended my first movie with inverting lenses on.

Watching an "upside-down" movie

The most striking observation was that the movie was upside down and reversed from right to left. On the screen I also noticed the same exaggerated walking movements that I noted in everyday situations. At first I did not perceive such details as facial expressions, which are so important in movie art. This was not because of definition, for the picture was in perfect focus. It seemed to be the novel position of people in relation to the way I usually see them without the lenses. Before the movie was over, I was able to perceive these facial expressions. At first I did not understand part of what was said. All my attention was directed toward the new visual experience. However, after an hour of viewing the movie, I was no longer aware of the inverted position.

By the eleventh day my reading was improving. I read about four pages per hour. The letters that gave me the most difficulty were the p's, q's, b's, and d's. This confusion was largely due to my previous reading history. A d looked like a p in the inverted position. The b looked like a q in the normal position. The q looked like b and the p like a d. The a, which is so familiar in the normal position, was difficult to discriminate when inverted.

Midway through the experiment

By the thirteenth day I observed that I was decreasingly aware of the inverted position of objects. The new position of things related to my preinversion period was brought to my attention in at least two ways: (1) when I saw something new and striking or (2) when someone called my attention to inversion by asking me a question about it.

I drove an automobile for the first time on the twentieth day. A companion drove us to a traffic-free country road. Altogether I drove nearly 2 miles and made two turns to the right. My companion aided me several times by verbally correcting mistakes.

The automobile appeared to be traveling down the left side when actually it was in the right lane. If I turned the automobile in the direction of the ditch (i.e., on the left in my visual field), I had to turn to the left. My first thought was to turn to the right to miss the ditch on my visual left; however, this would have guided the automobile *into* the ditch.

The two turns I made were done at very slow speeds. I needed verbal instructions at this point more than at any other time. In turning to my actual right, the automobile appeared to me to turn to the left.

At the swimming pool

The outstanding event of the twenty-fifth day was a visit to a swimming pool. Most of the time I waded or sunbathed and watched others swim. However, I did swim several yards without submerging the lenses. We watched a group of acrobat clowns diving. I was not aware of any upside-downness of this view until my companion asked me if things were upside down! Even then it was difficult to imagine that there was anything peculiar about the scene. What I saw appeared quite "natural." Just as much so as did my preinversion seeings. When one of the clowns jumped off the diving board, he appeared to move downward into the pool. Upon carefully checking the direction in which he passed by the lenses, I found that he appeared to move upward. Thus the way that he seemed to move depended on whether or not I made reference to my memory of the pre-experimental way of seeing things without the lenses.

Driving an auto "upside-down"

On the twenty-sixth day I drove an automobile again for a short distance between parked automobiles along a narrow street on the campus. There was no one in the vehicle with me. Altogether I drove about a block. I backed for a distance of 25 feet under these same conditions. I was able to keep along a fairly straight path both forward and backward, and experienced little difficulty in turning in the proper direction to keep the vehicle along a straight path.

On the twenty-seventh day we spent several hours in the downtown district. We walked from place to place and I was not aware most of the time that I had the lenses on or that everything was inverted. I needed little guidance from my companion. In spite of this, I felt quite confident walking about the city.

Flying "upside-down"

On the twenty-eighth day we started on a plane trip to New York City. I had been a passenger on a plane several times before, but this was certainly a novel way to fly. The scenery passed by in the same direction that we were traveling in, making it appear that we were going in the opposite direction. At our change-over point, I did not know that my companion seated me in such a way that I was traveling backward. As I looked out the window, I reported that we were traveling the direction it seemed we were, which was wrong. Then when I realized my mistake, I became even more confused. Everything was cleared up when I discovered how I was seated. In the final analysis, I found that what I saw seated toward the rear of the plane with inverting lenses was what one would see seated toward the front without lenses. Evidently when I reported the direction we were going, I was not aware that I had the lenses on. Furthermore, I had ignored several cues to the correct orientation. I walked up an incline to a place near the front, sat down in a seat tilting slightly forward, and disregarded the direction of motion of the plane.

On the twenty-ninth day I saw New York for the first time in 8 years, and then with inverting lenses. I could recognize few landmarks as we rode or walked by them. I felt quite bewildered in these surroundings, whereas at home I had become well adjusted. I could not appreciate the wide expanse of buildings, since the restricted area of vision prevented me from seeing very much at one time. In spite of these difficulties, I rarely thought about objects being inverted.

On the thirtieth day I removed the inverting lenses for a minute in bright lights. The space appeared highly illuminated. As I moved my head about, I noticed that objects moved quite rapidly in the opposite direction. The objects themselves, rather than my head, appeared to be moving. The persons standing nearest seemed to lean toward me. One person, whom I only knew with the lenses on, appeared very strange. Another, whom I had known before the lenses were worn, looked quite familiar. After the lenses had been removed for a minute, I put on a blindfold which was to be worn until the experimental session next morning.

The inverting lenses were permanently removed at this point in the experiment.

Return to normal

On the first day I experienced fatigue during the first session following removal of the lenses. In addition, I felt dizzy and slightly nauseated. I frequently ran into objects because of poor control of equilibrium. The swinging movements, observed during the short time the lenses were removed the day before, were still present. The most exaggerated movement occurred when I first started to move my head. After my head was in motion, objects did not appear to swing. However, each fixation to a new object, as I rotated my head, produced the swinging effect. It also occurred during upward and downward movements of the head. Any vibratory movements of the head, which were caused by a moving automobile, for instance, produced a blurring of objects. The brightened illumination noted yesterday persisted most of the day.

I saw a water tower through a window on the left. The scene looked very strange. I had never seen this view except with lenses on. The water tower was visually on the right with the lenses on. In this same view, I located a street below. I had previously tried to locate all the varied objects with the lenses on; however, I failed to notice the street which was now very prominent.

By the fourth day there were few aftereffects of wearing the inverting lenses.

A later study

The spatial inversion period of this experiment was repeated under similar conditions 2 years later (Snyder and Snyder, 1957). The four experimental tasks performed were identical to the ones described above. However, the lenses were not worn continuously as in the first experiment. The results showed that 2 years of normal visual-motor reactions between experiments had apparently only a slight and momentary **negative transfer** effect on the progress of the tasks performed with the inverting lenses by S of this experiment.

4

Lundin: Absolute pitch*

How about absolute pitch?

The question above is a perennial one in psychology courses. Because "absolute pitch" seems so "out of this world," many people believe that it does not obey the same laws of learning that govern other perceptual reactions. Is it an exception? This is the question that Robert W. Lundin considers in the following selection:

Pitch refers to that tonal attribute of sound which we judge as being high or low. It is generally agreed that the tones of a flute or piccolo have high pitches, whereas those of the tuba or bass viol are considered low. In a general way, pitch correlates with another attribute of sound that we call

vibrational. The human ear, at best, can respond to vibrations (also called frequencies) of the sound wave within a range of about 20 to 20,000 cps (cycles per second). The slower (also called lower) frequencies correspond to the low tones on a piano and are judged low in pitch, while the upper frequencies are judged high in pitch. The highest tone on the piano is about 4000 cps. There are, of course, many higher frequencies which we can hear in both music and nature. These higher pitched tones add to the fullness or brilliance of an orchestral instrument.

Pitch discrimination

Psychologists and musicians have come to a general agreement that the ability to discriminate different pitches (tell which is higher or lower) is *one* of the attributes of

---

*Written for inclusion in this volume by Robert W. Lundin, The University of the South. All rights reserved.

a good musician. It is, of course, only one of many other necessary abilities. However, it is not necessary to read the research in the psychology of music to realize that a violinist or singer who performs "off key" (he can't tell whether he is performing sharp or flat) is going to be in a great deal of trouble if his audience has better pitch discrimination than he has. In pitch discrimination, we do not have to identify any notes on the scale by name; we merely have to report correctly that when two different pitches are played, one is higher or lower than the other. Occasionally we find people without musical training who have very acute pitch discrimination. Actually there is a great deal of individual variation among people as to how well they can discriminate pitches. Some people are so good that they can tell the differences between two pitches when the frequencies are only one or two cycles apart. Others cannot tell a difference when the two pitches are 18 cycles apart or more. Musically, we sometimes say these people have a tin ear or are tone deaf. Some psychologists, such as C. E. Seashore (1938), have maintained over many years that this ability to judge fine differences in pitch (or not so fine) is an inborn talent and will profit little by training. Many musicians share his opinion. More recent evidence, however, has shown that the ability can be vastly improved when the right training procedures are involved. In one study Wyatt (1945) at Northwestern University took several of the poorest students in pitch discrimination. By using practice with **knowledge of results** along with visual cues as to how far off the pitch differences were, he was able to improve the students' pitch ability to a rating of good or excellent as measured by the *Seashore Test of Pitch Discrimination*(1940).

Relative pitch

If one happened to be a choir director and wanted to lead his choir without accompaniment (called *a cappella*), the problem of how to start his group on the right note might arise. Frequently a pitch pipe is used or a key note struck on the piano. This note acts as a point of reference or anchorage point, allowing him to orient the singers, so that at least in the beginning they would start off on the right key. This is a kind of discrimination in which one has simply to sing correctly the note that he hears. If one is told the name of that note, with a little training, it is also possible to name *other* notes played in relation to it. Because notes on the scale are many cycles apart, the actual discrimination is not a difficult one. It merely takes some practice in naming or reproducing a note correctly so long as he is given another note as a point of reference. This is what we call relative pitch.

Absolute pitch

An ability that is much less common and considered by many to be very elite is what we call absolute pitch or perfect pitch. If our chorus has somebody with perfect pitch, he could reproduce or name a given note without having heard any prior reference note; he could pull it out of the air so to speak. We can define absolute pitch as the *ability to identify a given note on the scale correctly without having to compare that tone to any other reference tone*. Some authorities not only include this pitch naming ability but also insist one must be able to reproduce it accurately as in singing.

Theories of absolute pitch

Inheritance Many musicians (and psychologists) believe that absolute pitch, like pitch discrimination, is an inborn talent. Seashore (1938) has suggested that those so gifted "pick it up quite easily and naturally," with a minimum of practice. They have to admit that some learning is involved, however, for there is no way of inheriting the names of the notes on the scale. However, they insist that this ability is an inborn gift limited to a few who can accurately and consistently name the notes over the range of the musical scale when played and do so without any knowledge of the names of other reference tones with which they could be compared.

Learning An alternate approach, which uses the principles of modern learning theory, suggests that like any other ability absolute pitch can be acquired if the circumstances and proper training procedures are applied (Lundin, 1942). This approach insists that musical discriminations are similar to other discriminations; that is, they are acquired throughout the life history of an individual, providing his auditory mechanism is not biologically deficient (among other things, being deaf). In a later section we will present evidence in support of this view.

Imprinting A third alternative, which uses both the learning and inheritance approaches, is a kind of "imprinting" theory. One investigator (Copp, 1916) reports evidence that absolute pitch is relatively easy to develop in children during a critical period in their development. If one should wait too long, (i.e., adolescence or adulthood), it would be too late. The phenomenon of imprinting has already been demonstrated in animal studies. For example, Hess (1958) and others trained or "imprinted" ducklings and other fowl to follow some artificial object (a decoy duck or a cube) instead of their mother, provided the imprinting object was presented during a critical period shortly after hatching, usually between 13 to 16 hours. After that

period, imprinting will not occur. The evidence for imprinting in humans is far less clear. Some suggest that the critical period would extend over a longer span of time, perhaps even years. If such is the case for absolute pitch (or any other aspect of musical talent), the evidence remains to be definitely presented.

The acquisition of absolute pitch

Taking our lead from a learning theory approach to music, we ask ourselves, can absolute pitch be acquired? Neu (1944) surveyed the literature up to 1947 and concluded that it could. For example, Riker (1946) has shown that we judge most accurately the notes with which we have had the most experience: white notes on the piano are better identified than the black ones, and notes in the middle of the scale are more correctly identified than at the extremes. The timbre or quality of the tone also plays a part. Braid (1917) has listed the musical instruments in order of their difficulty. From easiest to hardest to identify according to tone, they are piano, organ, human voice, and tuning fork.

Probably the earliest attempt to study absolute pitch was made by Max Meyer in 1899, who used both the piano and tuning forks. He started with a small number of notes (10) and gradually added new ones until he reached a total of 39. At the end of this training, his subjects were 64 percent accurate in naming the piano tones and 60 percent accurate in naming the tuning forks. Unfortunately, he did not describe the details of his procedure.

Mull (1925) trained her subjects by presenting the piano tone, middle C, for several minutes. She than asked her subjects to pick out middle C from a series of alternate tones presented within a two-octave range. A subject was informed whether or not he was correct. After the end of 9 months of training, a second series was presented in which no information was given as to correctness. She concluded that the ability could be improved with practice and acquired to a reasonable degree by some.

In a more recent study, Lundin and Allen (1942) used the following technique. A subject was placed in a soundproofed room and listened through earphones to many series of piano tones, which had previously been taped. In front of him was a panel of buttons, each of which was named and corresponded to each note on a two-octave scale. Outside of the booth was an enlarged model replica of a musical staff. When a button was pressed, a light in the note corresponding to the name of the note on his panel was illuminated. The scale was placed about 10 feet from the booth and could be seen by the subject through a glass window in the booth. If the subject pressed a particular button (say middle C), that note would immediately become lighted. As a first step in the experiment, all subjects were given a pretraining accuracy test to see how well they could identify the notes they heard prior to training. During the training period of 36 sessions, subjects were given immediate knowledge of the accuracy of their responses. When a note was heard, the subject pressed the button corresponding to what he judged that note to be (for example, C, F#, A, etc.); and the note on the musical staff corresponding to the note he pressed became illuminated. In the case of an error, the correct note would then light up. If the correct note were named, that note became perceptibly brighter than any of the others, indicating to him that he had made the correct response. Thus the subject was given a visual picture of the difference in half-

steps between the note he named and the correct one. He was also given a visual **feedback** (reinforcement) when he was correct. After the 36 training trials in which different series of notes were presented each day, a post-training test was given to measure the degree of improvement. Results indicated that all five subjects made significant gains. One subject made no errors (perfect pitch?) and a second made only one error in 24 tone identifications. Both the subjects had named about 50 percent of the notes correctly in the pitch naming prior to training. For all subjects there was a significant decrease in half-step errors (an improvement in pitch naming). This was most marked for the poorer at the beginning, but then they had more room for improvement. Error analysis showed that the white notes (natural) were more accurately named than the black notes (accidentals) and that the notes in the first octave (starting with middle C) were more accurately named than the octave above.

In a later study, Lundin (1963) applied programmed learning techniques (Skinner, 1958) to the training of perfect pitch. In this subsequent study, tones were presented according to the method described above, except that the series were graded according to difficulty instead of being presented in a randomized order. The first series consisted of the tones most easily recognized. Item analyses had found that C, F, and G of the first octave were the easiest to identify. The more difficult tones to name (sharps, for example) were gradually added in later tapes. The most difficult notes to name in order were F#, C#, G#, D#, and A#. After a subject could name the easier notes without error, he moved on to tapes that contained the harder notes. A post-test showed that the subjects improved 700, 600, and 200 percent respectively. Of course, the subjects who showed the greatest improvement had started out with the fewest correct choices.

It would seem that, given the elemental knowledge of the names of notes and what lines or spaces they correspond to on the musical staff, a pitch-naming or absolute pitch ability can be learned. Experimentally, this has been demonstrated within the limits of the musical staff used. If these discriminations can be learned, there does not seem to be any reason why other ranges of the entire scale could not be similarly acquired. It is possible that the difficulties some people encounter in learning music (or anything else for that matter) do not lie in a lack of inherent potentialities, dispositions, or talents but in the failure to apply the proper principles of learning, such as immediate reinforcement (knowledge of results). Learning music, along with other abilities, is subject to the same principles of behavioral acquisition.

5 Pumroy and Pumroy: "A case study in discrimination learning"*

Introduction

This case study provides a conditioning paradigm illustrating the solution to a specific problem in child rearing. The problem arose in the following manner. When the subject was approximately 20 months of age, he would begin to call "Mommy" or "Daddy" on awakening. This call was to inform the Es he was ready to get up and to begin his day's activities. He, naturally, would awaken at different times and his calling would continue until he was allowed to get up. On the days when he would awaken early this was disturbing to the Es. On some occasions one of the Es would enter the room and tell the child it was not time to get up. Sometimes the child would go back to sleep, but on some days he would wait for 10 to 15 minutes and begin to call again. The Es decided that what was desired was to have the child call when he was ready to get up and thus be allowed sufficient sleep, but that he should not call until 8 o'clock. The problem, thus analyzed, lent itself to a discrimination learning situation.

Subject

The subject was a healthy normal male child who was 21 months old at the start of the study.

Procedures

The response used was the number of times "Mommy" or "Daddy" was called. On Days 1, 2, and 3 when the S arose before eight o'clock, he was allowed to call until eight o'clock, at which time one of the Es went into his room and picked him up. On each day the number of calls that he made was tallied. On Day 4 the same procedure was followed except that at eight o'clock a small lamp was lit in the S's room. This lamp consisted of a small white night light (7½-watt bulb), similar to Christmas tree lights. The light was situated approximately five feet from the crib and at the S's eye level and in his line of vision when he would stand up and call. On Day 4, at eight o'clock, the light was turned on by the E plugging in an extension cord outside of the room. As soon as the S called "Mommy" or "Daddy" after the light was on, the E entered the room to get him up. The E then said, "It's time to get up. When the light comes on it's okay to get up." On subsequent

---

*Quoted material is from Donald K. Pumroy and Shirley S. Pumroy, "A Case Study in Discrimination Learning," *Journal of Genetic Psychology*, 1967, **110**, 87–89. By permission of the authors and publisher.

days the light would be turned on at eight o'clock, and as soon as the *S* said "Mommy" or "Daddy" after the light came on, one of the *E*s would enter the room and get him up. Thus the calling of "Mommy" or "Daddy" was rewarded only when the light was on. On each day the number of calls of "Mommy" or "Daddy" prior to eight o'clock was tallied.

Results

The results are presented in Fig. 11.4. The number of calls per four-day blocks are plotted. Note that the curve drops following the introduction of the light, which indicates the *S* was learning to make the discrimination. On Days 29 to 32 there were 101 responses made. In that four-day block there were three days of zero responses and one day of 101 responses.

That one day was preceded by a visit of the child's grandfather. The *S*'s grandfather was not aware of or had forgotten about the experiment, so when the child called, the grandfather entered the room before the light could be turned on. The following day the child emitted 101 responses.

Discussion

The collection of data terminated at the end of 68 days even though the curve was not **asymptotic** to zero. There are three possible reasons for the training not to be complete. One is that the number of calls is related to how long the subject sleeps. Thus if he sleeps past eight o'clock, he would not call. Certainly the physiological condition of the *S* (hungry, wet, tired) would then have an effect on the number of responses. The second reason is that there were

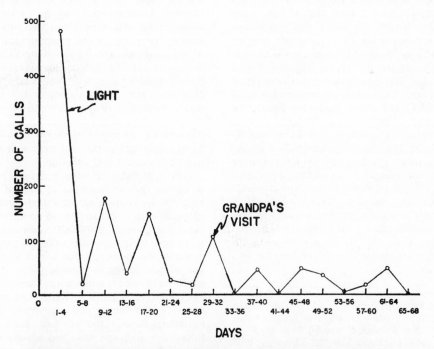

Figure 11.4 Number of calls of "Mommy" or "Daddy" per four-day blocks. (From Donald K. Pumroy and Shirley S. Pumroy, "A Case Study in Discrimination Learning," *The Journal of Genetic Psychology*, 1967, **110**, 87–89. Reproduced by permission of authors and publisher.)

stimuli other than the light to which the *S* may have been responding, e.g., the sunshine coming into the room. Lastly the response of the subject (calling "Mommy" or "Daddy") was rewarded during the day when the light was not lit.

Note that the learning did take place without the use of any aversive stimuli. The light has continued to be used by the *E*s and the *S* has trained a younger sister to obey it. The *S* is now 6 and there appear to be no adverse side effects nor long-term effects as far as his behavior is concerned.

Summary

The problem involved in this study arose when the *E*s 21-month-old son would awaken early and call "Mommy" or "Daddy." The *E*s wanted *S* to call when ready to get up, but not before 8 A.M. The number of calls prior to 8 A.M. was recorded for four days. At 8 A.M. on the fourth day the *E*s lit a light in the *S*'s room. When the *S* called after 8 A.M. he was reinforced by one of the *E*s entering his room and taking him from his crib. Results show that *S* learned the discrimination.

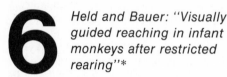

6 Held and Bauer: "Visually guided reaching in infant monkeys after restricted rearing"*

Recent research indicates that an infant primate should be unable to reach for and grasp visible objects with a limb that it has never previously viewed. To verify this prediction, one must demonstrate that the infant may be reared until its visual and motor capabilities are sufficiently mature to support visually guided reaching, but that this behavior will not appear if the relevant visual-motor interaction has been precluded. Testing the hypothesis requires an experimental subject which is normally capable of visually guided reaching and which can be reared under the necessary controlled conditions. The infant monkey satisfies both of these demands, but research on its postnatal development is difficult because the animal needs substantial maternal care. We here describe a solution of the rearing problem, as well as preliminary results that confirm our prediction.

Because it is difficult to experiment with the infant when the mother is present, the two

are separated soon after birth. The experimenter must then provide all maternal care. Human handlers can supply routine maintenance, but unless they can also furnish substitutes for some of the psychological aspects of maternal care, the infant will develop bizarre emotional behavior which interferes with controlled rearing and with subsequent testing. Harlow (1958, 1959) demonstrated that surrogate mothering devices can satisfy certain of the psychological needs of the infant monkey. Because the surrogate mother is inanimate and nonreacting, unlike the real mother, it becomes part of the controlled situation.

The apparatus we have designed (Fig. 11.5) promotes the development of normal infantile behavior by supporting the infant, surrounding its torso with a soft surface in contact with the skin, and giving it easy and continuous access to a nipple which provides milk. Furthermore, it conceals the monkey's limbs from its view and yet allows the limbs a wide range of normal exploratory and manipulatory activities. The basic unit is a metal cylinder encircling the torso of the infant and suspended above a horizontal seat. One or two baby diapers folded 7.5 to 10 cm wide and loosely wrapped around the infant's body support it snugly in the cylindrical body holder. A horizontal rod covered with a piece of fur-like rug is within easy reach of the animal. The fur serves as a sub-

*Quoted material is from Richard Held and Joseph A. Bauer, Jr., "Visually Guided Reaching in Infant Monkeys after Restricted Rearing," *Science,* 10 February 1967, **155**(3763), 718–720. Copyright 1967 by the American Association for the Advancement of Science. By permission of the authors and publisher. Various references and notes have been omitted (see original article).

stitute for the mother's hairy skin and diverts the animal's grasping response from his own body. This diversion is extremely important because a monkey who has been deprived of a real mother clings tenaciously to the hairiest object in the environment, usually itself, to the exclusion of all other activities of its limbs, including reflexive responses while falling. Three vertical aluminum rods to which the holder is attached support a circular plywood body shield with an opening in the center. The head of the infant protrudes through this opening. A cloth bib is pinned around its neck and fastened to the circumference of the shield. When bib and body shield are in place, the animal cannot view any part of its body.

The apparatus can readily be altered to accommodate infants of varying size. Routine maintenance can easily be adapted for extremely small or even premature newborns. A nursing bottle with a "preemie" nipple can be positioned so that random movement of the infant's head results in facial contact with the nipple. This

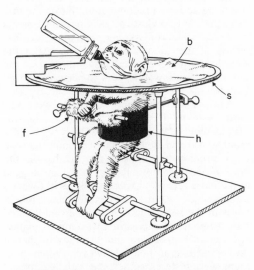

Figure 11.5 Apparatus for rearing an infant monkey without sight of its limbs. (h) metal cylinder, (f) fur-covered rod, (s) plywood body shield, (b) cloth bib. (From Richard Held and Joseph A. Bauer, Jr., "Visually Guided Reaching in Infant Monkeys after Restricted Rearing," *Science,* 10 February 1967, **155**(3763), 718–720. Copyright 1967 by the American Association for the Advancement of Science. Reproduced by permission of the authors and publisher.)

stimulation elicits the rooting response which brings mouth to nipple. Consequently, ad lib feeding can be initiated on the first day of life. The restraint placed upon the animal facilitates cleaning and routine maintenance; one or two daily changes of the diapers which cover the base are sufficient to maintain relatively odor-free conditions. Bottles need be cleaned and replaced only twice a day when fresh milk is used. Another desirable feature of this arrangement is the simplicity of its construction—only ordinary laboratory clamps, 12 mm wooden dowling, and exterior grade plywood treated with linseed oil are needed.

The apparatus also facilitates testing the infant. Since the body holder can be detached from the rest of the supporting components, it may be removed together with the animal and placed in a test apparatus with appropriate foot and seat rests. This mode of transfer retains contact between the infant and part of the rearing device when he is placed in a new environment for testing. Consequently, the animal does not exhibit the fear responses produced by the reduction of contact when separated from either a real or surrogate mother. The entire apparatus can be shifted to the test situation or, alternatively, the test apparatus can be brought to the rearing device. Thus, conditioned performance of voluntary response is easily obtained even with very young monkeys because they are not disturbed by the change. We can then assess behavioral development without waiting for the animal to adapt to a testing apparatus.

Our first subjects were two female stump-tailed macaques *(Macaca speciosa),* chosen because of the species' reputation for docility. Within 12 hours of birth, each infant was put in the rearing apparatus and for the next 34 days was not allowed to view any part of its body. The monkey was conditioned to extend its limbs on presentation of the feeding bottle during the period from Day 16 to Day 34. The rug-covered bar was removed and the bottle was hidden below the body shield while one arm was gently restrained by the experimenter. The bottle was then returned to view in front of the animal. If the monkey oriented head and eyes to the bottle and extended its unrestrained limb horizontally, the nipple was brought to its mouth for a few seconds. This procedure was repeated alternately on each arm until ten extensions had been elicited. When we first presented the bottle, the monkey made flailing responses with the free arm. In the course of daily testing, the conditioned extension became stereotyped and unrelated to the direction in which the bottle appeared. By the end of the conditioning period, presentation of the bottle elicited head and eye orientation to it and a token extension of the arm at shoulder level.

An animal that is reared under normal conditions will accurately reach for and manipulate visible objects before the age of 1 month. Our monkeys were allowed to view one of their arms for the first time on Day 35 when testing of visually guided reaching was begun. The experimenter presented a variety of visual stimuli (small objects, including the nursing bottle) within reaching distance of the animal. Testing was terminated after either ten reaches or 15 minutes. The animal was then free to view its arm for the rest of the hour-long period. During the remainder of the day, the arm was concealed as on previous days. After the first day, each subject was tested and allowed to view its arm 1 hour daily for a total of 20 days. Reaching responses during each test session were filmed to provide a permanent record of performance.

On the first day, sight of the bottle elicited arm extension; but unlike the extension response performed when the arm had been concealed, the initial reach was terminated as soon as the free hand entered the monkey's field of vision. When the hand entered the field, the animal immediately turned its gaze toward it and watched intently while moving the arm about in a manner quite unlike the stereotyped extension. The animal's fascination with the movements of its own hand resembles the hand-watching behavior of human infants described by Piaget and others.

Visual pursuit of the hand was extremely prolonged in comparison with visual following of other moving targets, including the hand and arm of another baby monkey. Occasionally sounds or movements in the test room made the infant avert its gaze from its hand, whereupon another reaching trial could be initiated. Although hand-watching occurred less frequently in the later part of the exposure hour, it was renewed with vigor during the initial test trials on the next day. As the hand-watching abated, observers found it easier to judge the accuracy of visually guided reaching, which was poorer than that of normally reared animals.

During the 20 days of testing, hand-watching gradually decreased in frequency and duration. Occasionally the monkey alternated its gaze from target to hand and back again. Concomi-

tantly, reaches elicited on presentation of a test stimulus became more obviously directed toward the target and the monkey sporadically struck the object. Only a few reaches resulted in grasping of the object. More frequently, initial contact was followed by groping, during which contact was repeatedly made and broken. After several days, reaches were executed with a continuous movement accurately directed to the target with anticipatory opening of the fist before contact. Manipulation of the objects became more delicate and precise. By the end of 20 hours of exposure, both monkeys were quite proficient in visually guided reaching and grasping with the exposed limb.

After accurate visual guidance of the initially exposed limb had been achieved, we began similar tests with the previously unexposed limb. Presentation of the visual stimulus evoked orientation of eyes and head together with limb extension, but the two responses were not integrated. As with the limb which had been exposed first, the initial extension response terminated in hand-watching behavior as soon as the limb entered the field of view. Hand-watching activity predominated, but on the first day the few awkward striking movements observed were remarkably similar to the first efforts of the initially exposed limb. After the stimulus was presented several times, the monkey was allowed to view the newly exposed limb for the remainder of an hour.

At the end of this time, both limbs were permitted to extend above the bib, and reaches for visible objects were photographed. Successful reaches were made only with the limb that had been previously exposed for 20 hours. On several occasions this limb grasped and tugged at the more recently exposed limb as if it were a foreign object. During the next few days, reaching with the second limb improved rapidly, and after 10 hours of exposure it was approximately equivalent in precision and accuracy to that of the contralateral limb. However, when both limbs were tested together, the initially exposed limb was generally used in preference to the other. At this time the infant was nearly twice the age at which the first limb was exposed and had gained considerable facility in nonvisual control of both limbs.

After the tests were terminated on Day 65, the monkeys were removed from the apparatus and placed singly in cages. Initially they remained prone and clung tenaciously to the diapers covering the cage floor, but they remained alert and ceaselessly looked about their new environment. Within hours they were manually exploring the cage sides and a bottle holder which was suspended a few inches overhead. By the end of the first week both monkeys could walk and climb with near normal ease. By the age of 4 months their locomotor behavior was indistinguishable from that of a monkey of comparable age reared under normal laboratory conditions.

The results show that an infant primate initially fails to reach accurately for attractive visible objects with a limb that it has never previously viewed. Yet the animal demonstrates both its interest in the objects and its ability to control movements of its limbs and hands with respect to its body. Integration of visuomotor control of head movement and of nonvisual control of limb movement resulting in the ability to perform a visually directed reach appears to require the specific experience of viewing the moving hand. Sight of the moving hand enables the adult to adapt coordination of the eye and hand to the changes produced by optical rearrangement; likewise, sight of the moving hand perfects accurate visual control of reaching in the neonate.

The act of reaching for a visible target by an adult primate appears to depend upon his capability first to orient his eyes and head to the target and, second, to match the direction of reaching by the hand with the actual or potential orientation of the head to the target. The match is altered when adults adapt to displaced vision of the arm, and the alteration shows little or no transfer to the contralateral unexposed arm either in man or monkey. We believe that the earliest experience of watching the moving limb provides the information necessary for the infant to match orientations of head to target and directions of reaching of the arm, and this information integrates the two control systems. If both of these systems are permitted to develop independently, as in the present experiment, handwatching becomes the prepotent activity when the hand is first seen. Since no more effective means of integrating the systems could be devised, we regard this behavior as a dramatic manifestation of an adaptive mechanism.

Addendum

Since the publication of the article, one improvement of consequence has been made in the apparatus. It consists of a vertical rug-covered cylinder about 5 cm in diameter extending from the footrest to the bottom of the body shield in front of the hand hold. This addition allows the monkey to cling with its feet as well as its hands and to support itself independently of the seat. An enlarged version of the seat may then be positioned so that the monkey can either sit on it or place its feet on it and sit on its haunches. This allows the monkey more freedom to exercise its lower extremities.

A new kind of "vision" for the blind 7

Historically the blind man has been symbolized with his cane tapping the cobblestone streets to provide supplementary auditory cues as to his location, cues that serve the sighted with instantaneous orientation of their location, obstacles, and so on. Everyone recognizes how inadequately hearing compensates for the blind person's visual sense. But if Dr. Carter Collins and his associates at the Presbyterian Medical Center of San Francisco succeed in their research work, the blind may discard their white canes. Instead, the blind may wear a miniaturized TV camera on their head that will scan the scene before them and translate it (in detail) into what someone has called "tickle talk." Their portable camera will *translate* the visual images into tactile images on the skin of the back! The general setup is shown in Fig. 11.6.

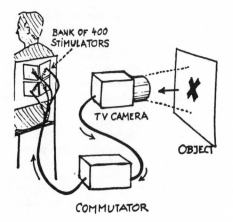

Figure 11.6 Experimental set-up for skin "vision." Essentially the technique involves a transducing of screen image upon subject's skin.

Figure 11.7a Experimental configurations of projector.

The TV camera picks up the X on the screen and sends it to a specially designed **commutator.** In turn, the commutator transmits the pattern, point for point, to a bank (originally) of nine tips in contact with the subject's skin on his back. This matrix acts mechanically by impressing a two-dimensional, vibrating **facsimile** of the outlines of a visible object onto a large area of the skin. A more complicated matrix is shown in Fig. 11.7a and b. A brief inspection shows the experimental possibilities inherent in the greater variety of pattern transmission. But the ultimate in skin discrimination so far possible is shown in the 20-line or 400-point matrix by comparing the original (Fig. 11.8a) and its translated or digitized versions (Fig. 11.8b). A number of salient features are recognizable in the point-for-point conversion of the original and its translation.

Work to date, with blindfolded subjects as shown in Fig. 11.9, reveals that with the three-by-three matrix accurate perception of direction of movement has been made when the bank of skin stimulators were

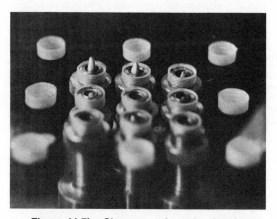

Figure 11.7b Close-up of early 9-point tactile projector matrix.

successively stimulated. Such letters or forms as T, L, X, and + have been successfully "read" on the skin when they were "written" there in correspondence with the visual signal picked up by the TV camera. Relative size of an area and tracking have also been achieved.

The possibilities of projecting visual images into patterns of mechanical vibrations applied to the skin of the back opens up exciting possibilities for the blind as well as others; for example, those engaged in space exploration. Research shows that, in addition to the eye, the skin is an accurate organ that can be organized to discriminate two-dimensional patterned arrangements of light-dark stimulation.

In a supplementary communication (mimeographed), Collins (1968) refers to literature already available that shows considerable sensory plasticity, one that permits the substitution of one sensory modality for another. Tactual perception, in particular, has been found to be "as fast and accurate as that of the eye. The skin can detect movement across its face faster than the finger can follow [p. 2]." Even reading has been explored with achievement of "tactile communication of printed words at rates of up to 30 words per minute

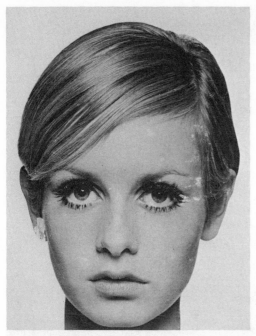

Figure 11.8a An original photo.

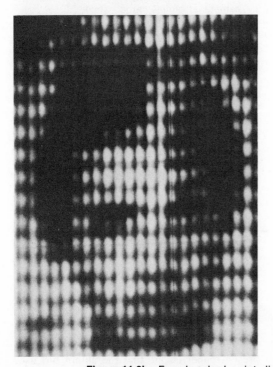

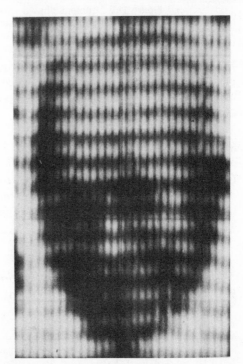

Figure 11.8b Four-hundred point digitized pictures of photos like 11.8a.

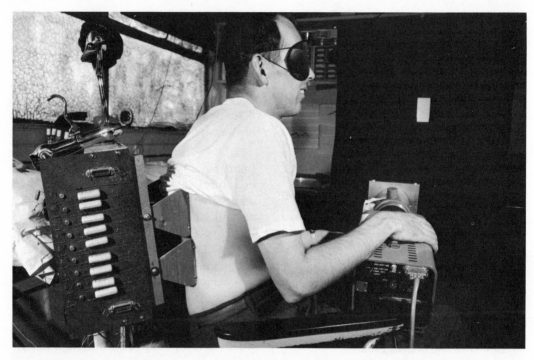

Figure 11.9 Subject shown directing TV camera at simple target while tactile image converter impresses the form of the target on his back. (Drawing and photos courtesy of Carter Collins.)

[p. 2]." In the future Braille may be learned via skin of the back rather than by finger. Touch may yet provide the most direct avenue to the replacement of vision.

Summary Research by Collins and his associates at the Presbyterian Medical Center of San Francisco has explored use of a system that translates a visual pattern into a tactual one applied to the skin of the back. Achievements to date suggest the technique's suitability as a replacement for the visual sense. Yet perhaps even more significant is the implication of the relativity and flexibility of perception. The great potentiality of human perception is shown when one realizes that we can "see" objects and movement and that we can even "read" with the skin on our back.

8 *"A classroom demonstration of 'extrasensory perception'"*

*Quoted material is from N. H. Pronko, "A Classroom Demonstration of 'Extrasensory Perception,'" *The Psychological Record*, October 1961, **11**(4), 423–426. By permission of the publisher.

The demonstration to be described in the present paper is one that the author has used successfully in his classes for a number of years. It is always presented as a problem-solving situation that the students are urged to come to grips with and to solve with the analytic tools of scientific psychology (such as stimulus-response, setting factors, etc.). As an introduction to the demonstration, students are told that, just as engineering or chemistry has questions that must be answered and as algebra or geometry has its problems that demand solution, what they are about to witness must be studied so that they understand *what* has happened and *how* it happened.

The instructor then takes a deck of **ESP** cards, preferably of the earlier edition, and hands them to a student at random in the first row of the class. He requests the student to shuffle the cards thoroughly and to ask one or more other students to cut the deck. He then asks the student who shuffled the cards to place the deck face down on the table that is usually found at the front of a lecture room. He further instructs this same student to sit close by the cards and to keep his hands off the deck until the experimenter calls each card in turn, at which point the card handler must hold up the card so that the class may clearly note each hit (or miss) of the instructor's call.

After the instructor surrenders the deck of cards to his assistant, at no time must he come into contact with the cards until after the demonstration is over. In fact, to be most effective, after he hands the cards over to the assistant, the instructor walks about 6 feet away from the table and stays in this position. (See Fig. 11.10.) He then calls the cards properly, practically as fast as his assistant can turn them, to the complete amazement of his audience.

How the trick is done

A number of years ago the writer stumbled across the fact of his "ESP powers" as he looked at a deck of ESP cards, face down, several feet away, on his desk. To his surprise he found that under the existing conditions of illumination he could make out the symbol on the back of the card. Analysis of the situation showed that the light reflected from the back of the card reflected differentially from the area in which the symbol had been imprinted on the underside (i.e., the face of the card). See Fig. 11.11. Continuing with the rest of the deck, he had equal success, predicting the symbol on each card before turning it face up. Fired with such quick success, he continued practice

Figure 11.10 A representation of the relationships that must obtain among the three variables, (a) illumination source, (b) position of ESP cards viewed face down, and (c) the human observer in order to obtain "ESP." (From N. H. Pronko, "A Classroom Demonstration of 'Extra Sensory Perception,'" *The Psychological Record,* 1961, **11,** 423–426. Reproduced by permission of author and publisher.)

Figure 11.11 A photographic artifact which attempts *to represent* how the symbols of the ESP cards appear on the back of the card as they are perceived when placed face down. However, it was impossible to capture photographically the subtle stimulus configuration on the back of the card nevertheless perceivable by the human subject. (From N. H. Pronko, "A Classroom Demonstration of 'Extra Sensory Perception,'" *The Psychological Record,* 1961, **11,** 423–426. Reproduced by permission of author and publisher.)

under varied conditions permitting him to build up quick and subtle (nonextra) sensory perceptions. The only precaution necessary prior to demonstration (i.e., before the class or group assembles) is to make a quick check of the illumination for best placement of the cards and the demonstrator. With these conditions fulfilled, no amount of card shuffling or cutting the deck can confound the experimenter's "powers." Perfect runs are the rule and even a single miss out of 25 calls is aggravating. The problem has been consistently difficult for the class to solve.

It should be stressed that the earlier printing of the ESP cards is preferable to the more recent issue. However, the writer is making progress in developing reaction sensitization to cards of the later printing.

Summary A classroom demonstration of what *appears to be* extrasensory perception achieved through inapparent, plain "sensory perception" is described. The demonstration illustrates the subtlety of visual perception. The cues may be so subtle as to be undetected by the viewing audience.

9 Psi phenomena

The preceding article would be offensive to the serious student of extrasensory phenomena or, more broadly yet, of **parapsychology (psi phenomena).** "A Classroom Demonstration of 'Extrasensory Perception'" actually depends on subtle sensory cues. The term *extrasensory perception* was purposely put in quotes to indicate that it was being used in a different context from the ordinary. At any rate, the article serves to introduce a field that has grown tremendously in the last 60 years. It is commonly referred to as ESP, less commonly as parapsychology or psi.

Varieties of psi

The easiest introduction to parapsychology is offered by J. Gaither Pratt (1966), a student of J. B. Rhine, founder and director of the Institute for Parapsychology. The institute is an outgrowth of the former Parapsychology Laboratory of Duke University at Durham, North Carolina.

In his book Pratt defines parapsychology in the following brief statement: "as physics is the science which deals with matter, so parapsychology is the science of mind

[p. 3]." As to the range of phenomena encompassed by *parapsychology,* five terms cover the varieties of psi experiences. They appear in outline form below, but are not offered as a complete definition of the boundaries of parapsychology (p. 34).

1. Extrasensory perception (ESP)
   Telepathy
   Clairvoyance
   Precognition
2. **Psychokinesis** (PK)

A definition of terms

The exact usage of the above terms is spelled out in Pratt's book. In the interest of accuracy, this quotation is offered as a brief dictionary of basic psi terms:

ESP is the act of becoming aware of, or otherwise responding to, an external object, event, or situation which is beyond the reach of the sense organs. PK is the act of exerting an influence upon an outside physical object, event, or situation without the direct use of the muscles or any physical energy or instruments. Further study of the wide range of psi experiences that occur under natural conditions reveals that three kinds or modes of ESP are distinguishable on the basis of the relation between the experiencing *subject* and the nature or condition of the experienced object or *target.* Telepathy is the ESP of another person's thought or purely subjective state. Clairvoyance is the ESP of a physical object, event, or situation that is not known to any person at the time. Precognition is the ESP of a future event that is beyond the reach of logical inference and that is not in any way later influenced or produced to make the target fit the prediction [Pratt, 1966, pp. 33–34].

The findings

In 1940 Rhine, Pratt, Stuart, and Smith (1966) published a critical appraisal of the research on extrasensory perception, a book entitled *Extrasensory Perception after Sixty Years.* Of the 145 papers published, 80 appeared in print between 1920 and 1940 showing a cumulative interest and labor in this field.

The four investigators believe that "by one criterion or another, the summarized results taken as a whole definitely favored the conclusion of the occurrence of ESP [p. 88]." The results occurred beyond chance under conditions that apparently excluded sensory cues, clerical errors and cheating, statistical artifacts, and poorly designed experiments. Furthermore, the authors invited critical comments (which would be included within their book) from seven of their most severe psychologist critics. The response was neither unanimous nor enthusiastic. Two critics sent extended criticisms and one a brief letter. These are reprinted in the book, referred to and answered.

Parapsychology since 1940

Work in parapsychology since 1940 is contained within the pages of the *Journal of Parapsychology* and certain books mentioned below. The Parapsychology Foundation in New York publishes a bimonthly Newsletter, Parapsychological Monographs, and *The International Journal of Parapsychology,* the last appearing quarterly. A special issue of the international publication published in the autumn of 1965 is particularly interesting because it is devoted entirely to parapsychology in the Soviet Union. Because the majority of papers concern "finger vision," we shall now take a closer look at this seemingly inexplicable psi phenomenon.

Can blindfolded people detect colors by means of their fingertips? In 1962, a Soviet neurologist, I. M. Goldberg (Novomeiskii, 1965), discovered a 25-year-old woman, Roza Kuleshova, who perceived colors with her fingertips. The phenomenon has been named the **dermo-optic sense,** skin vision or "eyeless" vision. Certainly this looks like extrasensory perception.

Certain theories were immediately produced to explain the strange phenomenon. A structural hypothesis suggested that Roza distinguished the different colors through the differences in structure inherent in the different dyes. Others suggested a thermal hypothesis, according to which Roza discriminated the differences by means of differences in the heat given off by various colored substances. A **photoreceptor** hypothesis explained Roza's performance by suggesting that Roza had sight in her fingertips.

However, Roza could recognize large letters and numbers with her fingers through cellophane, glass, tracing paper, and cigarette paper. Out went the structural hypothesis. The thermal hypothesis was discarded when Roza could differentiate colored light beams after they passed through a glass prism and water lens and after they were reflected by a system of mirrors and passed through a linen screen. That either daylight or artificial light had something to do with Roza's peculiar ability was shown by her inability to distinguish colors in the dark.

It was difficult to explain the nature of the dermo-optic sense in a single individual. Therefore Soviet workers carried out research with a large number of subjects. They soon discovered that one in every six persons could learn to discriminate pairs of colors, while blindfolded, after only 20 or 30 minutes of practice. Briefly, further work seemed to support an electrical basis for the color discrimination. Different colors appear to have different electrical fields, which Roza and the other subjects *sensed* through their fingertips. This was the final explanation.

An ESP explanation of "eyeless vision"

The same special issue referred to (*International Journal of Parapsychology,* Autumn 1965) has some comments by J. G. Pratt on the Russian research. Particularly interesting are Pratt's (1965) remarks on the explanation of Roza's performance and that of others. He is of the opinion that an ESP explanation should not be ruled out. The fact that the subjects "believed" that they were sensing through their fingers does not make it so. Their very efforts to learn to "see" through their fingertips "may have been ideally suited to developing a remarkably high level of ESP skill [p. 444]." Similarly, their failure to distinguish colors in the dark would not rule out ESP because they considered light favorable or necessary for their performance and therefore it worked that way. And because the physiological explanation favored by the Soviets is so difficult to reconcile with known facts, Pratt is of the opinion that "extraordinary care to exclude ESP would be required before the skin-vision explanation could properly be regarded as established [p. 445]."

Before ending the discussion on the parapsychology literature, two books should be mentioned. One by Rhine and Pratt (1957) offers "a convenient one-volume summary of present knowledge about psychology [p. v]." It is nontechnical in nature and is meant as a handbook for various professional groups or as a textbook in parapsychology. In it Rhine and Pratt offer a more specific definition of parapsychology. The distinctive feature that identifies a psychical phenomenon as parapsychical is that "there is always some distinct point at which a completely physical interpretation is manifestly inadequate [p. 6]." Thus, when a person "influences" dice to stop at a certain combination without the use of his muscles ("mind over matter") or receives knowledge of an event without the intervention of his senses, the events are said to be parapsychical.

The second book, written by Mrs. Rhine (1967) and meant for popular consumption, records both instances of "spontaneous ESP" and studies conducted at the Duke University laboratories. It offers an up-to-date account of parapsychology in an easy-to-read style.

Criticism of parapsychology

Both the facts and the theories of parapsychology have been strongly resisted for a number of reasons, particularly by academic psychologists. If a census were taken, it is probable that few psychologists would be neutral about psi. Most would either praise or condemn it, with the majority leaning toward the latter position.

No reader who is interested in evaluating parapsychology for himself should ignore Hansel's (1966) volume, *ESP: A Scientific Evaluation*. After surveying the entire field of psychical research, including spiritualism, psychic mediums, and ESP research, Hansel concludes:

> Extrasensory perception is not a fact but a theory put forward to account for observations consisting of high scores obtained during the course of experiments (p. 239).

In briefest fashion and stripped of expanded statement, Hansel's criticisms of ESP research are condensed to the following eight points. They should be read completely, in the context of Hansel's book, for a clearer specification.

1. Inadequacy of experimental design.
2. Lack of criticism during the experiment.
3. Inadequacy of the experimental report.
4. Excessive claims made by experimenters.
5. Failure to report essential features of the experimental conditions.
6. Inability to survey the evidence impartially.
7. Inability to confirm a result.
8. Inability to predict.

Schuster:
"A new ambiguous figure:
*A three-stick clevis"**

10

The accompanying figure (Fig. 11.12) recently printed in the advertising section of an aviation journal† is reproduced here because it is, as I believe, a new type or kind of ambiguous figure.

Unlike other ambiguous drawings and geometrical figures—Jastrow's (1900) "Duck-Rabbit"; Hill's "Wife and Mother-in-Law"; Botwinick's (1961) "Father and Father-in-Law," a duplication of Hill's drawing with a masculine motif; and Necker's Cube; Schroder's Stairway; and Mach's Book‡—an actual shift in visual fixation is involved in its perception and resolution.

When an observer fixates, at reading distance, the left end of the figure, he sees three rods with the right end indistinct and foggy; when he fixates the right end, he sees a U-shaped figure or clevis.

It is only when he fixates the center or allows his fixation to sweep slowly across the figure

that he realizes he is viewing an "impossible figure." It is "impossible" like the illusory figures described by Penrose and Penrose (1958) and by the authors to whom they refer (Escher, 1954; and Kilpatrick, 1952).

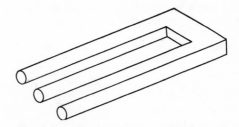

Figure 11.12 A three-stick clevis. (From D. H. Schuster, "A New Ambiguous Figure: A Three-Stick Clevis," *The American Journal of Psychology*, December 1964, **77**(4), 673. Reproduced by permission of author and publisher.)

---

†*Aviation Week and Space Technology,* 23 March 1964, **80**, 5.

‡For illustrations of these ambiguous geometrical figures see E. B. Titchener, *Experimental Psychology, Students' Manual Qualitative,* New York: Macmillan, 1901, p. 154.

---

*Quoted material is from D. H. Schuster, "A New Ambiguous Figure: A Three-Stick Clevis," *The American Journal of Psychology,* December 1964, **77**(4), 673.

11

Grumpton, Wine, and Drenick:
The effect of starvation
on cognitive processes

What effect does a continuous need have on how and what a person perceives and thinks about? For example, what about gnawing hunger for 1 month, 2 months, or longer? Postman and Crutchfield (1952) used skeleton words (words with two letters omitted) in order to study the effect of up to as many as 6 hours of food deprivation. Within the time interval studied, they found increasingly more food-related responses to the incomplete words.

Crumpton, Wine, and Drenick (1967) used the same technique "to study the effect of prolonged extreme food deprivation [p. 179]." They reasoned that if hunger had any

persistent effect on perception, cognition, imagination, fantasy, or whatever, one would expect that subjects deprived completely of food for long periods of time would give an increasingly higher proportion of food-related responses when asked to identify incomplete words [p. 179].

Procedure

The subjects, 26 obese male veterans, voluntarily entered a hospital in order to undergo radical treatment by starvation of a severe, refractory obesity. Such a setup, imposing controlled starvation, is rare in experimental circles. The average weight of the subjects, most of whom had been on an unlimited diet, was 312 pounds (p. 179). The experimental conditions required no food, and routine administration of multivitamins, water, mineral supplements, and a uricosuric agent. Sixteen subjects fasted

2 months and all of them fasted 1 month. The average weight loss amounted to 58 pounds or about a pound a day (p. 180).

For the present study, subjects were required to complete skeleton words consisting of letters and blanks, such as __IN__ER, which can be "winner" as easily as "dinner," S__AK, which does not have to be "steak," BU__ER, PICK__, __E__LY, and so on. The set consisted of 189 incomplete words, one third of which had a low (1 to 10 percent), one third a medium (21 to 35 percent), and one third a high (41 to 80 percent) probability of eliciting food-related responses [p. 180].

(For a description of standardizing procedures, see Postman and Crutchfield, 1952.)

Results and discussion

Crumpton, Wine, and Drenick developed a hypothesis that "obese men would make more food-related responses to incomplete words after being deprived of food for a long time, and, furthermore, that the relative frequency of food-related responses would increase as the length of deprivation increased [p. 180]." Results supported the hypothesis for both the 1-week and the 1-month fasting intervals but not for the 2-month period. The secondary hypothesis did not show an increase in the relative frequency of food-related responses with increasing length of the deprivation period but the frequency was greater in the initial stages of deprivation.

On initial testing, while the subjects were still eating but anticipated fasting, they gave an average of 59 percent of food-related responses, such as "activities involved in eating, names of meals, and terms referring to food deprivation [p. 180]." After one week of fasting, they showed a statistically significant increase of 8 percent more food-related responses. One month of fasting still gave a 7 percent increase over the initial response. However, after 2 months the percentage dropped to a nonsignificant statistical difference of 2 percent (p. 181).

The investigators did show an effect of need on perception, although not as cumulatively as they had guessed. However, only a very mechanistic view would conceive of hunger as building up continuously much like the pressure in a boiler. Attitudes and **sets** (such as those which must have operated during Ghandi's hunger strikes)

can negate craving for food. This suggests that as a man approaches death from starvation, he may have fewer and fewer food-related responses. Anyone who has witnessed real-life starvation would tend to hypothesize similarly.

Summary Twenty-six obese veterans were observed during a crash starvation hospital treatment of severe, chronic obesity. Comparison of their food-related responses to skeleton words showed an increase over initial test for the 1-week and 1-month but not for the 2-month fasting interval. This finding supports the hypothesized effect of the hunger drive on perception; it does not support the notion that such an effect increases cumulatively. The results also show the behavioral effects of organismic and extraorganismic conditions.

Hardyck, Petrinovich, and Ellsworth: Rapid extinction of speech muscle activity during silent reading*

12

How silently, subtly, and unwittingly reaction systems can get incorporated into responses and operate without calling attention to themselves is illustrated in silent reading. We learn to read by reading aloud, which is a relatively cumbersome and slow process. To perform silent reading rapidly, one must reduce the gross motor activity that was a part of reading aloud to a minimum. But how? There is only one way—that is, to make the person aware of crude motor activity that is participating in his response. The clever means by which Hardyck (1966) and his associates provided their subjects with the necessary feedback and how the subjects utilized it

in speeding up their silent reading is illustrated in the following article.

Effect of subvocalizing on reading

The phenomenon of **subvocal speech** has been of great interest to educators concerned with the teaching of reading. It has, however,

---

*Quoted material is from Curtis D. Hardyck, Lewis F. Petrinovich, and Delbert W. Ellsworth, "Feedback of Speech Muscle Activity During Silent Reading: Rapid Extinction," *Science,* 1966, **154**(3755), 1467–1468. By permission of the authors and publisher. Copyright 1966 by the American Association for the Advancement of Science.

received little systematic study, with the exception of the work by Sokolov (1959) and by Edfeldt (1961). Subvocalization is considered one of the most difficult problems to overcome in increasing reading speed. An individual who subvocalizes to any great extent is limited to a top reading speed of approximately 150 words per minute—a maximum attainable while reading aloud. We use the term subvocalization to include a wide range of activity, from inaudible articulations and vocalizations to audible whispering while reading. If subvocal activity includes movements of the lips and jaw, some corrective measures are possible. However, if the activity is limited to the vocal musculature, eliminating the response becomes more complex, especially since individuals are often not aware they are subvocalizing.

The initial study of subvocalization required the examination of several subjects with strong subvocalization patterns to determine whether subvocalization during silent reading could be detected by surface **electromyograms** recorded from the throat. A successful technique was developed with mesh electrodes placed over the thyroid cartilage. An ink-writing **oscillograph** was used to record the electromyogram (EMG). At maximum sensitivity of the oscillograph unit, the electrical activity of the vocal muscles can be detected while the subject is reading (if subvocalization is present), in contrast to a minimum signal (approximately 3 μv) obtained when the subject is relaxed, and to an extremely strong signal (approximately 1 μv) obtained when the subject speaks during normal conversation. To determine the presence or absence of subvocalization, the subject first selects reading material which he reads for 30 minutes, and during this time an oscillograph record of the EMG is obtained.

Detection of subvocalization

The presence of subvocalization is determined by asking the subject to stop reading, then to begin reading, and then to stop reading. Each time, the changes in the EMG record are noted. The presence of subvocalization can be detected quite reliably, there being a large increase in action potentials when reading begins and an immediate cessation of this activity when reading stops.

Treatment of subvocalization

Treatment of subvocalization is done in the following manner. The subject is asked if he is aware that he subvocalizes or reads aloud to himself. A brief discussion is held with the subject, informing him of his response tendencies while reading. The feedback technique is then introduced. The subject is told that he will be able to hear the activity of his vocal muscles as he reads, and that this will help him to eliminate the problem. The manner in which signals emanating from the vocal muscles are detected is explained to him. The subject is then given earphones to wear, and is asked to remain relaxed. Feedback is introduced by channeling the output of the oscillograph amplifier to an audio-amplifier, and then to earphones. When the subject is relaxed, the audio-circuit is opened and the subject is asked to swallow. The swallow results in an immediate burst of static in the earphones. The subject is then requested to experiment with the sound to satisfy himself that he can control it (stop it and start it) by such actions as talking, swallowing, turning his head, clenching his jaw muscles, and so forth. The subject is allowed to continue experimenting with the feedback, and with its control, until he states that he is able to control its presence or absence. The subject then begins reading while attempting to keep the EMG feedback to a minimum, that is, to maintain silence in the earphones.

The subjects

A total of 50 college students from a reading improvement class were tested; it was found that 17 subvocalized. All subjects who subvocalized were treated in the manner described above. Originally, it was planned to administer the feedback treatment over several sessions to determine the number of feedback treatments necessary to establish normal reading patterns. This was found to be unnecessary. The feedback treatment was remarkably effective (Fig. 11.13). In all cases one session of the feedback was sufficient to produce complete cessation of subvocalization.

Rapid extinction

Most of the subjects showed a reduction of speech muscle activity to resting levels within a 5-minute period. At the end of the 30-minute experimental session in which feedback was given, all subjects were able to read with speech muscle activity at the same level as during relaxation. (See Fig. 11.13.) The level of speech muscle activity was monitored at the end of 1 month, and again after 3 months. During these tests the subject read for 30 minutes; no feedback was used. None of the subjects gave any evidence of subvocalization in either of these tests.

How extinction occurred

In many ways, this is a surprising phenomenon. One does not expect the extinction of a

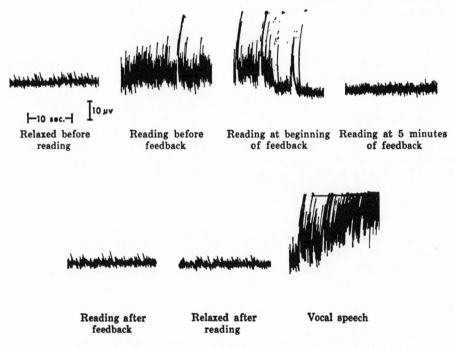

Figure 11.13 Electromyograms recorded from the laryngeal muscles. This record is typical of those obtained from the 17 subjects who received feedback treatment. Portion of record at top left may be considered a kind of baseline. The next one shows comparative involvement of one subject's speech musculature during silent reading before auditory feedback was introduced. The next recording to the right, with its prominent spikes, shows speech muscle involvement in silent reading at beginning of auditory feedback. The beneficial effect of feedback is shown in the record at top (extreme right) after reading silently only five minutes under such conditions. Compare this record with the first relaxed or baseline one. Compare also the two bottom recordings and note that *reading after feedback* is quite similar to *relaxed after reading.* Neither is like the record for *vocal speech* which resembles *reading before feedback.* (From Curtis D. Hardyck, Lewis F. Petrinovich and Delbert W. Ellsworth, "Feedback of Speech Muscle Activity during Silent Reading: Rapid Extinction," *Science,* 1966, **154**(3755), 1467–1468. Copyright 1966 by the American Association for the Advancement of Science. Reproduced by permission of author and publisher.)

habit—especially a habit which presumably had existed during the entire time the subject had been reading—to occur so quickly and easily. However, if the overlearned response of subvocalization is placed in conflict with a second, even more strongly overlearned response, extinction should be quite rapid. Such a second response is the ability to make a fine motor adjustment of the speech musculature on the basis of auditory cues. Exactly this response is involved under conditions of feedback of **laryngeal EMG** activity. The subject is required to make fine motor adjustments on the basis of auditory cues. Attempts to reduce the speech muscle activity by instructions alone were not successful. The subjects were not aware of their subvocal activity even when told they were subvocalizing, and were unable to reduce it without the feedback.

Supporting research

This ability to make fine motor adjustments of restricted muscle groups has been reported by Basmajian (1963) who found that subjects can control the contractions of single motor units on the basis of auditory and visual cues. His subjects also achieved stable control of the muscles within 15 to 30 minutes. He reports, however, that the aural feedback in all subjects is more useful than visual display on a **cathode** ray tube monitor; the visual display served a subsidiary purpose.

The motor-auditory feedback loop as a cue produced by response might well be of considerable importance. Such phenomena as the marked disruption of speech under conditions of delayed auditory feedback provide ample evidence for the importance of this cue to normal speech. Consequently, the evocation of this overlearned response-produced cue may result in the rapid extinction of subvocalization under the conditions of auditory feedback.*

Summary

Surface electromyograms of the laryngeal muscles were made while subjects read silently. Those who showed an increase in electrical activity over that at relaxation were provided with auditory feedback of the muscle activity. This treatment resulted in immediate and long-lasting cessation of the subvocalization. This method should prove valuable in treating some reading problems.

---

*The above article elicited two critical letters from McGuigan (1967) and Camacho (1967), which, in my opinion, Hardyck (1967) and his colleagues rebutted successfully. The debate is to be found in *Science,* 4 August 1967, **157**(3788), 579–581.

13 Phantom limb and phantom sensations

Amputation of a limb does not necessarily mean "psychological amputation." Just as certain songs or scenes remind us of people or events of the past a person's behavior repertoire can survive the anatomical loss of a hand, arm, foot, leg, or breast. According to Kolb, Frank, and Watson (1952) of the Mayo Clinic, 98 percent of amputees have reported **phantom limb,** phantom breast, or phantom sensations, although others have reported much smaller percentages in the literature. The discrepancy is due to variations in procedure, reluctance of patients to volunteer such information for fear of being thought queer, or, as one patient said when asked why he had not reported his phantom, "No one asked me."

Body image

Psychologists have used the concept of **body image** to help explain **phantom phenomena.** From his earliest interactions with stimulus objects, the organism is also interacting with its own spatial aspects or, we might say, its own geography. Just as a rat's whiskers permit him to gauge the width of an escape hole, so a human's vision allows him to duck his head to avoid hitting a low doorway.

Although research to support this view is lacking, I would venture to guess that the "body image" would include the hunter's gun, the surgeon's rubber gloves and scalpel, the teamster's whip, the cowboy's lasso, the Britisher's umbrella, the walking stick or cane, the smoker's pipe, and even the tip of the long feather on a woman's hat. Each is an extension of the person. Little wonder, then, that a person who has walked 20 or 30 years and has had a leg amputated still has the illusion that the leg is present. In fact, the feeling is sometimes so realistic that he may actually try to stand. Only visual inspection convinces the amputee that an amputation was actually performed on him. His body image or the way he thinks, or feels, or reacts in reactions that *used to* involve the missing organ have survived the amputation. In a sense, the reactions involved have declared their independence of the anatomy involved. Does this mean that we are such creatures of habit that some of our habits can transcend their anatomical components, that, once built up, the anatomical portion in question is not required? Perhaps an examination of the clinical and laboratory findings will help to answer that question.

Haber's findings concerning reactions to loss of limb*

William B. Haber (1958) studied 24 male World War II veterans with unilateral above-elbow amputations. Here are his findings.

All 24 men reported phantom sensations, with only one describing it as sometimes painful. The majority described the feeling as "tingling," "pins and needles," "as if asleep," "vibrating," or "electricity." Itching was reported by 7 men who, at times, attempted to scratch some phantom part. Coexisting sensations of throbbing, pulsating, warmth, tenseness, clenching, clutching, gripping, and numbness also were reported. One subject volunteered "a tingling sensation, tingling in finger and thumb. Compact and smaller in size all around, still feels like a hand. Pins and needles effect." Another said, "ticklish mostly, phantom hand as though it were there—feel tips of fingers— pins and needles. The ring on my finger feels tight and bent. Pins and needles and drawing sensation—gripping too." Still another said, "I can feel my hand. I can't get thumb out— hand is dangling below stump. Pins and needles, it goes to sleep on me." One man stated "a certain numbness, sometimes sensation of itching. But if you face realities, there is no hand there. However, don't let anybody tell you, like M.D.'s, that's in your mind. No figment of imagination. The sensation—like burning from a match and yet asleep, a combination of these two." Another reported "...the hand is right in front of my face. I'm looking at it."

In general, the outstanding feature of these reports is their marked uniformity, which makes it difficult to attribute the origin of the phantom to unusual conditions of the stump or special conditions before or after amputation. An analysis of the nature of the original trauma of presence or absence of **gangrene,** or various

*Quoted material is from William B. Haber, "Reactions to Loss of Limb: Physiological and Psychological Aspects," *Annals of the New York Academy of Science,* 30 September 1958, **74**(1), 14–24. By permission of the author.

other factors connected with the amputation, reveals a great variety of conditions before and after trauma, a variety in marked contrast to the relative uniformity of phantom sensations.

All of our patients except two reported shrinkage of the phantom and varying amounts of decreasing distance between phantom fingers and the tip of the stump. We have mentioned already that 12 of the men reported phantoms in the stump (telescoped) and 12 reported that their phantoms seemed "extended in space." Five men claimed that a gap remained between **"proximal"** parts and **distal** portions of their extended phantoms; 7 reported extended phantoms without a gap. It will be recalled that better stump sensitivity was found in amputees who reported telescoped phantoms, as compared with those whose phantoms were described as extended.

The gradual fading of a phantom takes place in a definite sequence; for example, proximal portions vanish first, then intervening areas, and finally the distal parts. Similarly, the distal regions are felt most vividly, even soon after amputation; the elbow is sometimes present, the forearm rarely, the upper arm almost never. The rank order of parts, in terms of frequency reported on a 6-point scale of vividness, corresponds closely to the size of cortical representation allotted to these parts. Fingertips, thumb, and all five fingers were ranked as most vivid with almost equal frequency; next in order were palm, wrist, and back of hand; forearm and elbow were infrequently mentioned and were least vivid.

My observations show that the range of movements in the phantom is more restricted than the awareness of stationary phantom parts. In other words, the ability to "move" phantom parts fades faster than the ability to experience these parts. Ability to call up phantom sensations at will was reported by 21 amputees (88 percent), while 12 reported the ability to move phantom parts, although this movement was limited to the distal parts. Five of the 12 could move the fingers in their telescoped phantoms, while 7 reported movements in the extended phantoms. All of these men could make a fist, and 7 maintained that flexor movements were easier to make than extensor; the position of the phantom also was reported as slightly flexed. None of the subjects with telescoped phantoms claimed to be able to penetrate solid matter with their phantoms; by contrast, 6 of the 12

who had extended phantoms reported they could move the phantom through solid objects. In the remaining 6 cases the extended phantom temporarily disappeared whenever the stump was moved close to some solid object.

Spontaneous "reaching" movements often appear in phantoms immediately after amputation, and 9 of the 21 who reported such inclinations said this tendency still persisted. As one subject said, "I often attempt to catch a ball with my phantom." Such illusory movements are related to the finding that phantoms, under certain conditions, may change positions, whether extended or telescoped. When the experimenter made a sharp perpendicular movement with a ruler through the air near the stump, 4 men said their extended phantoms recoiled closer to the stump, while 4 with telescoped phantoms felt a temporary lengthening of their phantom. One amputee stated he felt a desire to "pull away"; another wanted to "grasp the ruler."

As we have stressed, we found no significant relationship between the characteristics of the phantom and the conditions at the time of the loss of the limb, either in the position of the phantom or in the amount of pain. However, there were 8 cases (7 had extended phantoms) where similarities appeared between the posture of the phantom and that of the limb prior to the loss. One patient said, "the hand is right in front of my face"; previously he had described how he had attempted to protect his face from flying shrapnel. Even more interesting were the reports of 3 men who claimed they felt imprints of rings and one man said, "I know . . . because I had two watches on my wrist and . . . I was irritated because they were not returned." He related that he continued to feel the pressure of the watches on his phantom wrist.

There was no relation between the wearing of an artificial limb and the location or vividness of the phantom, although the prosthetic devices were quite varied. Eighteen wore a **prosthesis;** of these, 7 wore a mechanical hook or glove, 9 wore a nonfunctional cosmetic glove, and 2 sometimes wore a functional and sometimes a cosmetic prosthesis. Neither did we find a relationship between vividness of the phantom, or type of prosthesis worn (functional or cosmetic) with better sensitivity on the stump. Prosthetic devices do not appear to influence reorganization of tactile functions on the stump [pp. 19–21].

Postmastectomy
breast phantoms

It is not surprising that such highly mobile parts as legs or arms continue to be represented in the amputee's behavior repertoire. However, phantoms from such stabile portions as the breast, have also been commonly observed. In a question-naire study involving 104 breast amputees, Jarvis (1967) found that 24 of them (23 percent) reported phantom breast sensa-tions. Sixty-two percent reported itching either singly or in addition to other sensa-tions. Thirty-three percent complained of pain, whether "pressure, dullness, sore-ness, or aching. Less frequently reported sensations included tightness, tingling, fullness, burning, numbness, emptiness, and heaviness [p. 267]."

Other reports concerned the size of the phantom breast, its weight, the amount (which ranged from the whole breast to the nipple only), pleasantness or unpleasant-ness, frequency (which ranged from a fleeting occurrence to frequent reoccur-rence), and length of time over which the phantom was experienced. Forty-two per-cent still had these phantom images at the time the questionnaire was completed, the range extending up to 10 years.

Laboratory study of sensory
changes in amputee's stumps

Additional work on amputees has uncov-ered several interesting findings concerning the sensitivity of the stump. Three different techniques can be used to test, for example, the sensitivity of the stump compared with homologous or matching portions of the intact limb: (1) light touch threshold; (2) 2-point discrimination (how close together can two points be on the skin and still be

perceived as two points rather than one, i.e., by a blindfolded subject?); and (3) point localization (while blindfolded, how accurately can the subject localize by pointing to a point just touched on his skin?). All are traditional measures of accuracy of perception.

Haber's work

Haber (1958) carried out the preceding tests on the same 24 World War II ampu-tees in a comparison of their accuracy of stump versus intact limb. Here is his report.

Touch threshold

The average touch threshold (measured in log milligrams necessary to bend the graded Nylon filaments) was 2.42 for the stump in our 24 amputees and 3.37 for the intact arm. The average 2-point discrimination threshold (the minimum distance in millimeters at which two compass points were perceived as two and not one) was 42.86 on the stump and 60.70 on the intact limb. Finally, the **average error** of point localization (also measured in millimeters) was 6.34 on the stump and 14.07 on the sound limb. **Variance** ratios and t's were computed for each comparison between sound limb and stump. All differences were significant at a level of con-fidence better than 0.001. Furthermore, in each individual, the skin on the stump showed signifi-cantly lower thresholds for tactile stimuli on all three measures — light touch, 2-point discrimi-nation, and point localization.

Alteration of performance was found over the entire stump and was not restricted to the distal portion. Figure 11.14 shows the thresholds on the distal and proximal regions of the stump (areas 1 and 2) and in the corresponding distal and proximal regions of the sound limb (areas 3 and 4). The touch thresholds, in log milli-grams, are shown at the right of the diagram. At the 1/10 percent level of confidence, stump thresholds were significantly better than sound-limb thresholds. The distal stump threshold (area 1) also was significantly better than the

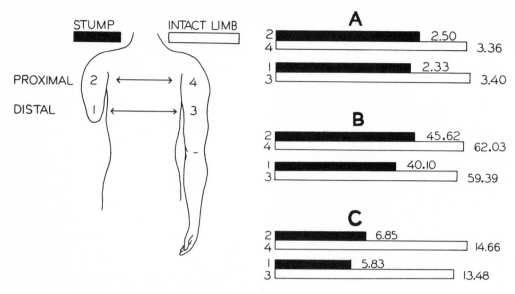

Figure 11.14 Mean thresholds in millimeters for point localization on proximal and distal portions of stump and intact limb. (From William B. Haber, "Reactions to Loss of Limb: Physiological and Psychological Aspects," *Annals of the New York Academy of Sciences*, 30 September 1958, **74**(1), 14–24. Reproduced by permission of author.)

proximal stump threshold (area 2) at the 1 percent level, but there was no significant difference between the distal threshold (area 3) on the intact limb and the proximal threshold (area 4) on the intact limb. (See Fig. 11.14.)

Two-point discrimination

Similar results were obtained for 2-point discrimination. Again, comparisons of stump to sound limb thresholds in millimeters were significant at the 1/10 percent level, while the distal threshold (area 1) on the stump also was significantly better than the proximal (area 2) at the 1 percent level. Again, there was no significant difference between area 3 and area 4, the distal and proximal regions on the intact limb.

Point localization

Similarly, comparisons for average errors of point localization, also measured in millimeters, once more point up the superior performance

of the stump and the proximodistal gradient, which was significant at the 5 percent level for the stump (1-2) but failed to reach significance for the sound limb (3-4).

Right stumps versus left stumps

Comparisons of thresholds on right stumps with those on left stumps showed no significant difference, nor did right differ from left intact limbs. The thresholds of the sound limbs of our amputees did *not* differ from either arms of our 12 control subjects (without amputation), but all stump thresholds (right or left) were better than corresponding control thresholds at the 1/10 percent level of confidence.

The steeper proximodistal gradient on the stump suggests that the distal portion of the stump has taken over some of the sensory functions of the hand. Another singular finding supporting this suggestion shows a significantly smaller number of errors of localization on the stumps of men with "telescoped" phantoms than of those with "extended" phantoms.

Figures 11.15 and 11.16 show some of these extended phantoms drawn by 12 patients and a few of the telescoped phantoms drawn by the remainder (12) of the group. The term extended phantom covers those instances where the subject reported his phantom outside his stump, while telescoped refers to those reports where the phantom hand is either completely inside the stump or with fingers partially protruding from the stump [pp. 15–17].

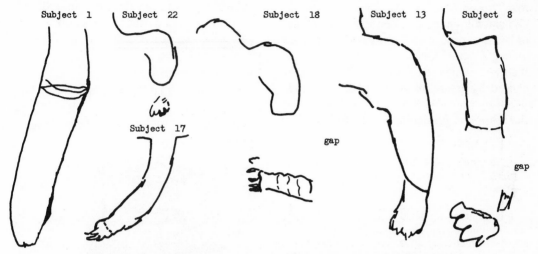

Figure 11.15 Extended phantoms—drawings made by six amputees to illustrate their phantom experience. (From William B. Haber, "Effects of Loss of Limb on Sensory Functions," *The Journal of Psychology*, 1955, **40**, 115–123. Reproduced by permission of author and publisher.)

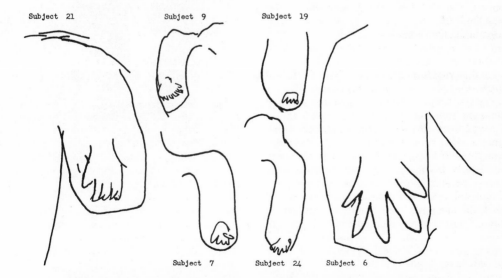

Figure 11.16 Telescoped phantoms—drawings made by six amputees to illustrate their phantom experience. (From William B. Haber, "Effects of Loss of Limb on Sensory Functions." *The Journal of Psychology,* 1955, **40,** 115–123. Reproduced by permission of author and publisher.)

The problem of phantom pain

How can the hand or foot that is no longer there cause a person excruciating pain in a locale that is plainly "off the map"? The fact is it can and does. Some explain all phantom phenomena in terms of "central processes." Haber appears to be among them. Others resort to peripheral theories, which explain the effects as if caused by irritation at the point of amputation by scar tissue, and so on, stimulating the brain and producing the pain there.

Kolb's comments on peripheral theories of phantom pain

...it is common knowledge that repeated surgical treatment of the stump and peripheral nerves, which should make such peripheral excitation unlikely is ineffective in relieving the phantom of pain in the majority of patients who come with this complaint. I have seen patients who have undergone, singly and successively, reamputation at higher levels, exploration of the stump, removal of the terminal **neuroma,** plastic operations on the stump, **rhizotomies, sympathectomies, cordotomies,** injections of alcohol into the neuroma, paravertebral anesthetic block of the sympathetic **ganglia,** spinal anesthesia and resection of the postcentral cerebral cortex, and have remained unrelieved of their painful symptoms. The importance of extended follow-up as a means of assessing the therapeutic effect must not be underestimated. Some patients have been reported as successfully treated in follow-up studies of short duration, only later to be found again suffering from the same symptom. One such patient had undergone 27 surgical and anesthetic procedures in 30 years, the last a resection of the somatosensory cortex, without modification of his painful phantom. In my series of cases less than 20 percent presented clinical symptoms or signs indicative of a physical lesion involving the stump or its vascular or nervous supply [Kolb, 1954, pp. 17–18].

An alternative, transactional, approach would be to consider the event known as a phantom limb as having developed out of interactions with stimulus objects much as other reactions to stimulus objects. Then at some point the response continued despite the diminution of the reaction systems involved. After all, reactions continue despite their diminution on the stimulus object side. The following sketch (see Fig. 11.17) is an illustration of the point.

Summary The facts of phantom limb and phantom pain were examined and related to the concept of "body image,"

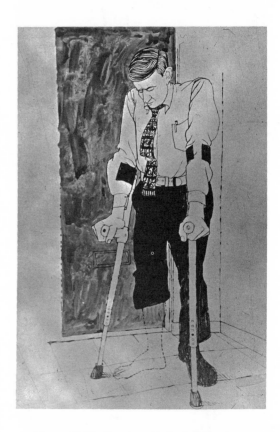

Figure 11.17 Phantom limb. Artist's representation of phantom limb. In terms of the patient's "body image," his right leg and foot feel just like the left, sometimes requiring a visual check, and sometimes causing falls. (Photo courtesy of CIBA Pharmaceutical Company, Summit, N. J.)

which was explained developmentally as a habitual response that could continue minus a missing organ even though such an organ was once an essential component of the response when it was acquired. The laboratory study of the sensitivity of stumps versus homologous parts of intact limbs then concerned us. Finally, we turned to the problem of phantom pain, applying central and peripheral theories toward their explanation. An alternative would be a transactional approach.

Chapter summary

The significant points of our examination of cognitive processes and illustrative articles follow. We presented the cognitive processes of perception and "thinking" as closely related psychological activities. I suggested that perception is semi-implicit, whereas thinking is fully implicit.

The "upside-down" experiment points to the relativity of perception and to its developmental nature, a point also illustrated by Lundin's article on absolute pitch. The role of visual-motor reactions in perception is emphasized in the experiment with the monkey reared under conditions in which it could not see its body. The study underlines how reachings, head turnings, and other movements help to *locate* objects perceptually. The article on "tickle talk" stresses the translatability of visual into tactile perceptions, the relativity of perceptions, and their modifiability. The demonstration of "extrasensory perception" illustrates the subtlety of cues in perception, while the article on psi phenomena entertains the possibility of perceiving without intervention of sense organs.

The last three selections relate to "thinking." The first article, which is a study of 26 obese men participating in a crash starvation program, indicates that organismic conditions or needs have an effect on how men perceive words and what they imagine or fantasy. Reading, which is crude and overt in the beginner, must become a vestige of its former self in the speed reader. The action must be reduced to a minimum in thinking, which is a short-hand way of reacting in small quantities. When speech muscle activity was fed back to subjects, they were able to extinguish it and make the act more vestigial by contrast with its earliest, crude phase. The final selection shows how reactions can transcend the participating anatomical organs originally involved in their acquisition. Once acquired, reactions continue after the surgical removal of arm, leg, or breast, thus requiring an explanation that involves a psychological dimension rather than a purely anatomical one.

12

Feelings and emotions

Many psychologists treat **feelings** and **emotions** as one kind of response. And many would place them both on a continuum, with feelings toward the gentler end, emotions toward the stronger. Some psychologists maintain that emotions and feelings serve to energize or motivate action. To add interest and novelty to our discussion, I am going to define feelings and emotions separately and treat them as two different types of response.

Feelings (Selections 1 through 6)

We shall assume that "feelings" constitute a broad class of responses that are predominately hidden from view. We shall call these responses "affective" to distinguish them from effective responses, which involve obvious movement by the organism in relation to a stimulus object.

We need special tools and techniques to study feelings because they are far less accessible to study than effective responses like pressing a button or turning right or left in a maze. The first selection in this chapter deals with the promising field of biotelemetry, which enables contemporary researchers to study physiological functions and processes within an organism by means of ingested or implanted radio devices.

In the next selection, we look at pupillometry, a technique that Eckhard H. Hess and his co-workers have developed at the University of Chicago. This technique permits the measurement of pupillary changes in affective responses. Would you expect men looking at pictures of women to have a smaller or larger pupil than when they look at pictures of men? Hess found

a difference here as well as in other situations.

Some people have a soothing, calming, or relaxing effect on us. Others irritate us, raise our blood pressure, make us tense and angry. At the Pavlovian Laboratory of Johns Hopkins University, W. Horsley Gantt has studied the effect that different people have on the heart action of laboratory animals, particularly dogs.

How long can affective responses survive the original learning situation? The **galvanic skin response,** to consider one example, showed a 20-year-long viability in a study by Allen E. Edwards and Loren E. Acker.

A discussion of L. S. Ewing's recent work on tension in the cockroach concludes our study of research on affective responses, or feelings.

Emotions (Selections 7, 8, and 9)

We shall describe atypical, aborted, and disruptive behaviors as "emotional." Selection 7 includes discussions of fainting, speech disturbances, and panic. In Selection 8, Stanley Milgram reports on an experiment in obedience. Milgram's subjects were asked to administer what they thought to be dangerous electric shocks to a subject who was actually the experimenter's confederate. We include the Milgram study under the heading of emotions because of the focus on the emotional behavior of the subjects. Then, in Selection 9, we examine a series of medical experiments in which human beings were actually tortured and put to death. Again, our immediate focus is on the emotional behavior in the situation.

1

"The response side of affective, or feeling, interactions"*

Feeling "blue," depressed, resentful, anxious, angry, afraid, being in love, jealous, and so on are only a few of the rich variety of affective reactions in which humans are involved. Not only are they important as reactions proper to objects that "move" us, but they occur concurrently as phases of such interactions as fighting, working, playing, eating, dancing, skating, and waiting. In fact, we doubt if they are ever totally absent in the behavioral repertoire of organisms.

Apparent and inapparent
feeling action

Some of these affective acts are quite apparent—a grief-stricken individual, for example. The person trembling from fear or perspiring freely, breathing rapidly or weeping, is quite obviously "doing something." The difference between these activities and those called "effective" is that in the latter the organism is "doing something" with respect to some object or person, such as picking up an object or writing on paper with a pencil or striking keys, as on a piano or typewriter. In affective interactions, the action is concentrated within the organism, although the preposition "within" should not imply an alleged "mind." The examples above include gross or crude affective action, but many subtle affective responses are not so readily open to inspection. Anxieties and tensions are two examples.

Affective interactions
are diffuse

Inquiry into further details about affective interactions shows one prominent feature, namely, the widespread involvement of the

organism. Sweat glands, tear glands, adrenal glands, stomach, intestines, heart and lungs, and many other organs in a diversity of patterns participate in these interactions. The everyday phrase, "He (the organism) was greatly moved," is descriptive of the essential features of the activity centered on the organism's side of the picture. Effective interactions, in contrast, would be those which might be described as *"Organism moves something,"* that is, performs some movement with respect to something.†

Since the action in affective behavior is rather difficult to observe, understanding it is not as easy as understanding overt reactions such as key pressing. In fact, mysticism has held tenaciously to this department of psychology with the result that these reactions have been thought of as "states," "mental states," "states of mind," and so forth. The primary reason for this state of affairs has been a traditional "body-mind" type of theory. Then, too, it has been easier for the man in the street to think of "action" when someone pushes or pulls something, and subtler forms of activity have usually gone by some other name.

Affective reactions
are concrete

It is our contention that affective behavior may be treated as concretely as any of the most overt acts. Let us assume that a human animal is born as transparent as a jellyfish. Imagine at what a disadvantage such an organism would be! By using a number of provocative stimuli, one could observe many dramatic shifts in its activity. Now the **spleen** muscles clamp down and push out a tremendous amount of reserve blood into the circulatory system. Such changes in the distribution of the blood supply effect blushing and paling. Increased or decreased

---

*Quoted material is from N. H. Pronko, "The Response Side of Affective or Feeling Interactions," In N. H. Pronko and J. W. Bowles, Jr., *Empirical Foundations of Psychology,* New York: Rinehart, 1951, pp. 302–306.

---

†Although some behavioral events are not readily classifiable into either of the above categories, the two classes used here serve to bring affective action into sharp focus.

lung action is immediately observable as our transparent animal becomes excited or calm and relaxed again. Provoke him again, and you can comment literally, "Your blood pressure is rising, old man!" At still another time the heart rate (pulse) is sharply and suddenly increased. Tear secretion and sweat-gland action occur. Stomach and intestinal contractions are speeded up or inhibited. (See, for example, the variety of affects illustrated in Fig. 12.1.)

Our hypothetical animal could not have a single affective secret from us. Everything would be aboveboard and immediately observable. But humans are not transparent, and therein lies the crux of the matter. Just because they are not is no reason why we should become mystical and introduce "minds" into the picture to confuse us further. These visceral acts need not be considered as bodily changes either "accompanying" or "causing" feelings. The gland, skin, and **visceral** activities *are* the psychological responses of the organism! That's all there is; there is no more. It is in this fashion, among others, that the organism responds to stimulus objects.

Affective action as acquired behavior

These activities have been built up during his reactional biography just as his walking, talking, skills, and so on have been acquired. It so happens that walking, talking, and skill reactions are performed with more or less discrete or integrated but *movable* portions of an animal's hands, arms, legs, and head. In affective reactions, *nonmovable* organs predominate. While it is possible for the arms to be stretched and moved so as to embrace the beloved, the heart (and other visceral organs) cannot do so because they are stationary. Because of the fixed position of the visceral organs, only very limited action is possible. Consequently, when the sentry sees an enemy, he shoots the gun with his hands and arms. His heart, lungs, and other visceral organs cannot manipulate the gun. It is true that the organism reacts to the sight of the enemy soldier with the viscera, but only insofar as they are anchored within the visceral region. These reactions are in terms of accelerated or inhibited normal action of the specific structures involved and constitute affective behavior when they occur in psychological events. The manipulation of the gun constitutes the effective class of response.

The role of the autonomic nervous system

One more point should be made regarding the diffuseness of the organismic action during affective behavior. The question might be put thus: How is it that the organism responds in the widespread, diffuse fashion observed in

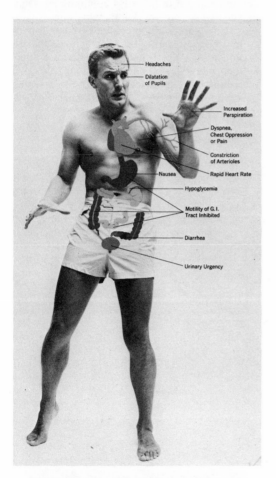

Figure 12.1 Feeling, or affective responses. A concrete illustration of the diffuseness of autonomically-mediated affective or feeling responses. These are the well-known or common components seen in anxiety or "tension" reactions. Countless others are not illustrated here. (Photo courtesy of CIBA Pharmaceutical Company, Summit, N. J.)

feeling events? Some light on the answer to this question comes from the diagram of the **autonomic nervous system** and its connection with the organs and systems that we have been discussing. The reader will note how heart, liver, stomach, adrenal glands, and so on, are interconnected by this network of nerves. When the uninitiated public speaker reacts to his audience in the affective way commonly called "stage fright," his sweat glands, heart, and salivary glands are active in certain ways. The first two systems show more rapid action, while the salivary glands show an inhibition of salivary secretion. For this reason, the speaker may pour himself a glass of water from the pitcher traditionally placed before him.

The important point concerns the reason for the involvement of these widespread organismic portions. Undoubtedly, it is because they are connected with each other that these organs participate in a particular coordinated activity. In a sense, it is correct to say that the heart is connected with the tear glands, with the surface arteries, with the spleen, and so on. (See the interconnection made possible by the autonomic nervous system in Fig. 12.2.) The total action, involving as it does widely separated organs, is made possible as a result of the intricate connections between those parts. The specific coordination of visceral action occurring in the case of any particular individual can only be understood in terms of what configuration of action occurred in his early conditioning. Only in this way can we know why one person blushes, whereas another shows cessation of stomach action, and so on. Finally, even though organisms are not transparent, affective interactions can be studied by such instrumental techniques as lie detection and fluoroscopic observations. Perhaps twentieth-century psy-

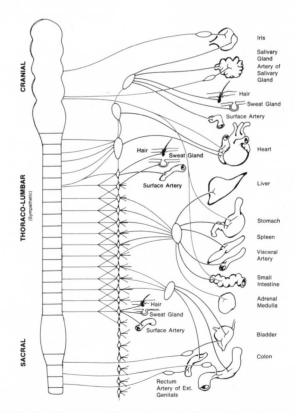

Figure 12.2 Significance of the interconnection of the visceral organs. Since the variety of organs is intimately connected via the autonomic nervous system there is little wonder that they can all "fire off" in unison in the widespread action apparent in affective behavior. Thus, increased heart, lung, adrenal, tear, and skin gland action can occur simultaneously in a variety of patterns.

chology will put an end to the "mental-states" treatment previously accorded affective interactions and will handle them as naturalistically and concretely as it has handled conditioned reflexes.*

Feelings differentiated from emotions

One final point: Many psychologists have used the terms "feelings" and "emotions" synonymously. We prefer to follow sound semantic principles and have used these two terms for rather different behaviors. The term feelings will be used to designate the behavior described above, while the term emotion will be used as a label for disrupted or disorganized behaviors as treated in the last two selections in this chapter. Since some textbooks talk about "feeling responses" when the use of the word "emotions" would be more apt, this word of caution is necessary. However, the student need not be confused, for the usage here is clearly designated and consistent [pp. 302–306].

The opulence and diversity of the feelings

Pathos, aesthetics, comedy, and tragedy are deeply imbued with feelings. Successful writers of fiction and drama adroitly depict and play on a variety of human affective responses. However, psychology has yet to inventory the exact number or variety of these reactions.

Byron L. Barrington has, at great expense of time and effort, compiled a comprehensive list of suitable descriptive words for the gamut of affective responses. An abbreviated version of his list is included here (1) for handy reference and (2) to show the wide extent and variety of feeling reactions.

*With instrumental techniques, we do no more than the physiologist does when he applies such methods to the study of nervous action, heart activity, or bone conditions with the aid of **galvanometer,** oscilloscopes, or X-ray photography. All are similarly inapparent.

Words relating directly to affective reactions†

It will be noted that the [words in the list reprinted here] are divided into various subgroups. These are rather arbitrary categories set up to permit more rapid localization of a word on the list. Because of their arbitrary nature, the value of these subcategories for any other purpose is questionable.

Unhappiness	mixed up
blue	perplexed
bad	puzzled
dejected	shocked
depressed	surprised
despondent	torn up
disappointed	uncertain
disconsolate	unsure
discouraged	
dismal	*Impatience*
distressed	dissatisfied
gloomy	fed up
miserable	frustrated
mournful	impatient
sad	restless
sorry	
sullen	*Liking*
unhappy	admired
	appreciated
Personal worth	affection
conceited	cared
good	craving
important	desiring
needed	friendly
proud	liked
worthy	interested
	loved
Disorganization	preferred
amazed	respected
astonished	wanted
baffled	
bewildered	
confused	*Empathy*
dismayed	empathizing
disorganized	pitying
distressed	sympathetic
dizzy	
foggy	
fuzzy	*Disliking*
light headed	antagonistic

†Quoted material is from Byron L. Barrington, "A List of Words Descriptive of Affective Reactions," *Journal of Clinical Psychology,* April 1963, **19**(2), 259–262. By permission of author and publisher.

bitter
contemptuous
despised
despising
detesting
disdainful
disgusted
hating
hostile
loathing
resentful
vengeful

Worry
alarmed
bothered
concerned
disturbed
doubting
suspicious
troubled
worried

Happiness
amused
cheerful
delightful
enjoying
gay
glad
grateful
gratified
happy
joyful
jolly
pleased

Anger
aggravated
angered
annoyed
exasperated
furious
indignant
infuriated
ired
irked
mad
provoked
resentful

Tiredness
apathetic

bored
exhausted
fatigued
indifferent
lazy
lethargic
listless
sleepy
tired
wearied
worn out

Strength
brave
capable
competent
confident
courageous
hopeful
independent
secure
strong

Weakness
awed
bashful
dependent
helpless
hopeless
inadequate
inferior
inhibited
impotent
shy
timid
trapped
weak

Energetic
alert
alive
eager
enthusiastic
excited
inspired
optimistic
peppy
wide awake

Jealousy
envious
jealous

Fear
afraid
apprehensive
dreading
fearful
frightened
horrified
panicky
scared
terrified

Guilt
ashamed
embarrassed
guilty
humiliated
regretting
shameful

Anxiety
anxious
moody
nervous
on edge
tense
upset

Comfort
at ease
calm
comfortable
contented
peaceful
pleased
relaxed
satisfied
untroubled

Discomfort
discontented
self-conscious
uncomfortable
unpleasant

Rejection
loneliness
rejected
unloved

Acceptance
accepted
consoled
loved
wanted

Worthlessness
useless
unimportant
worthless

Patience
patient
resigned

Determination
certain
determined
sure

Others
anticipating
cynical
sensitive
sick
tempted
reluctant

Pain
hurt

Summary Barrington's catalogue furnishes eloquent testimony of the richness and diversity of affective, or feeling, responses. The amount and range of data precludes easy ordering and categorization. However, the following article suggests some recently developed, ingenious techniques for discovering what goes on inside the opaque organism during affective responses.

A lizard sentenced to serve as a subject in physiological experiments eventually adjusts to his prisonlike laboratory existence. At rest in his home cage, his gut activity proceeds at its customary slow rate. Then humans enter the laboratory; instantly, gut activity stops. The visitors leave and gradually the activity resumes, once more reaching base level.

Yet, how could anyone possibly detect the intestinal activity of a lizard? If he were transparent, like a jellyfish, one might visually detect the onset and cessation of intestinal activity, but the lizard in question was opaque, not transparent. Actually, the activity of the **gastrointestinal tract** was perceived *audibly* via electronic equipment. The lizard subject was "persuaded" to swallow a tiny container, the size of a vitamin capsule. The inside of the capsule contained what is essentially a minuscule radio broadcasting station. Once the capsule enters the gut, we are ready for our observations. A sensitive element in it— the **transducer**—translates the power generated by gut action into a pattern of radio waves that are "broadcast." Now, the only other apparatus that we need is an ordinary, cheap radio to receive the signal broadcast from within the lizard. Once tuned in on the proper frequency emitted by the transmitter in the lizard's gut, we are also tuned in on any increase or decrease of its activity. In fact, all we have to do is listen and note the rate at which clicks are emitted by the radio receiver.

Gut activity is only one of many kinds of physiological functions that can be detected electronically. Other types of measurements achieved by similar electronic devices include the following: temperature, pressure, breathing pattern, **pH level,** the electromyogram **electrocardiogram,** and the **electroencephalogram.** Since the basic instrument is so small, it can be surgically implanted either under the skin or on or within various organs, such as the bladder, brain, or heart.

The birth of the endoradiosonde

The tiny capsule referred to above made biotelemetry possible, only, however, because the transistor made the experiment feasible. Before the extreme miniaturization that the transistor permitted, no one would have dreamt of asking man or beast to swallow a piece of equipment containing radio tubes! The replacement of tubes by the tiny transistor was the first step toward telemetry. The next step was the miniaturization of battery power into cells of the size that operate a hearing aid or a wrist watch for a whole year. It was the ingenuity of Stuart Mackay (1957) that brought the two together in a device which he christened the **"endoradiosonde."** His first device was 2.8 cm in length and 0.9 cm in diameter. Mackay could then measure the physiological activities mentioned above, plus many others.

Range of applications made possible with the endoradiosonde

The **pacemaker**, which gives a heart an artificial but life-sustaining beat, is perhaps the best-known application of the implanted transistor. However, the principle of the pacemaker is the reverse of that of the endoradiosonde in the lizard discussed above. The pacemaker, located in a human patient, *receives* an impulse generated outside the person and delivers a rhythmic shock to the heart.

Of most interest to psychologists is the information-gathering potential of the endoradiosonde. Suppose we wished to know about the action of the stomach or its acidity. We would simply develop a small transmitter and introduce it into the stomach by having the subject swallow. Normally it would pass through the organism, but to prevent this we would attach a fine nylon thread to the endoradiosonde. When the string and instrument are swallowed, we hold on to the outer end of the string and tether the apparatus to the organism's tooth. If we want to locate a moving transmitter, which may take 9 days to pass through a lizard, we can locate it by X rays. The range of organisms that have been studied physiologically or biochemically includes fish, dolphins, dogs, monkeys, tortoises, cockroaches, warm-blooded as well as cold-blooded animals, aquatic and terrestrial.

The Boston exhibit*

Figure 12.3 shows Mackay luring a dolphin with a fish that has a transmitter

*This exhibit was part of an intensive course in biomedical telemetry sponsored by Boston University, Boston, Massachusetts, 27–30 September 1967, and taught by Dr. Stuart Mackay.

installed in it. If all goes well, the transmitter will end up in the dolphin's stomach and Mackay can measure whatever the transmitter is geared to sense and broadcast. Figure 12.4 shows a 375-pound tortoise with an ingested capsule transmitting to Dr. Mackay on Galapagos Island. He also made temperature observations here on an iguana that had terrestrial as well as aquatic habits. For the latter, he developed a 500-kilocycle radio transmitter.

A rabbit with a built-in electrocardiograph One of Mackay's prize exhibits is a rabbit that 2 years ago underwent a simple operation permitting the implantation of an electrocardiograph under the skin at the region of the breast. An oscilloscope nearby receives a continuous electrocardiogram and has done so for the past 2 years. The important point is that the oscilloscope can be moved any distance from the rabbit, depending only on the strength of the power cell inside the transmitter or on booster stations outside. Imagine the possibilities for the physician to keep in constant touch with his perambulating patient. The clinical psychologist, too, might use an audio transmitter to enable him to relate the patient's cardiac crises to possible emotional, interpersonal crises.

A lizard with an implanted thermometer Another exhibit that draws many observers is a green lizard in a ventilated plastic cage. On a table outside the cage is an ordinary radio that gives a series of clicks. The accompanying instructions tell one to count the number of clicks per minute and consult an adjoining graph. A simple operation and one knows the lizard's internal temperature and can monitor it. Again, the significant point is that neither lizard nor radio need be under the same roof. The radio can be in one's headquarters and the lizard roaming freely in his natural habitat.

Figure 12.3 A fish with a temperature transmitter planted inside it is being fed to a dolphin. (Photo courtesy of R. S. Mackay and Boston University News Bureau.)

Figure 12.4 Telemetering deep body temperatures from an ingested transmitter in a 400-pound tortoise on Galapagos Islands. (Photo courtesy of R. S. Mackay and Boston University News Bureau.)

The use of multiple channels One is not limited to one transmitter per animal. Only practical considerations set the limit to the usable number. One display shows eight-channel tracing secured from a free-roaming rabbit with miniature transmitting implants yielding the following measures: electrocardiogram, electroencephalogram, respiration, blood pressure, temperature, acceleration (i.e., movement), a recurrent light flash (or any other possible stimulus pattern), and the rabbit's electroencephalographic response to the light flash. Other arrangements, limited only by the needs and ingenuity of the experimenter, are possible.

Still another display looks so undramatic as to be easily overlooked. It is merely a tracing a few inches long that was secured from a pinhead-sized transmitter implanted within the eye of a male rabbit without, incidentally, interfering with vision. The experiment was motivated by a desire to study **glaucoma,** which is caused by increased intraocular pressure. An interesting feature of the tracing is the sudden rise in pressure within the eye of the male rabbit. The initial part of the record shows (by inspection of the tracing) a base of approximately 22 millimeters mercury pressure, measured the same way the physician measures a patient's blood pressure. At a certain point indicated on the tracing, the male is shown a female; the pressure then rises to approximately 32 on the scale. Removal of the female causes a subsidence of pressure once more. Could it be that assiduous visual attention to female bunnies is hard on the male's eyes?

Implications of biotelemetry for psychological investigation

In the laboratory

First, the chief advantage that bio-telemetry offers the psychologist is a higher degree of control than ever attained before. The one-way-vision window has been useful, and will continue to be, but for some types of investigation it will yield to bio-telemetry. In addition to freeing the experimenter from continuous visual monitoring, it will permit recording and storing of the desired information. Another control is found on the subject's side. For example, no longer will it be necessary to attach the subject to cumbersome wires for recording the **EKG, EEG,** and blood pressure. Uncontrolled variables will be transformed into controlled variables. Experiments on sleep and dreams will allow the subjects concerned to sleep more normally than they have in the past. Almost any measure obtained in the past via a wire will go wire*less* just as the jet engine is displacing the wheel (i.e., the propeller).

Bykov (1957), a Russian psychologist concerned with the conditioned reflex, attempted to condition the internal organs, such as the stomach, bladder, and kidney, and was successful. However, he used extreme measures in order to get conditioning. For example, in order to be sure of a conditioned kidney response, he had to *destroy* an animal's bladder in surgically shifting the kidney to a position outside the organism so he could observe it. Today he would simply anesthetize the dog subject and attach a tiny radio to the kidney without traumatizing the animal.

In the field

Because nature offers many more dimensions than the laboratory, the opportunities for biotelemetry are enormous. Here are the possibilities that occurred to me: tracing the migration of birds (such as the swallows of Capistrano), salmon, and eels; exploring the habitats of animals in the sea or on the land. Jane Goodall had to track her chimps and Schaller his gorillas visually via field glasses in order to establish territoriality. Biotelemetry offers an additional technique. Now it is possible to temporarily "knock out" a chimp, gorilla, or a grizzly bear, with a tranquilizer gun, place a transmitting collar around his neck, and follow him by radio (or radar screen) wherever he goes. By assigning different frequencies to different individuals, one can identify the actions of specific individuals in a group. Bird song and animal calls can also be transmitted, received, and recorded for later analysis just as easily as any other signal. Accelerometers that monitor an animal's activity can give information about its diurnal cycle. Surely the revolutionary technique of biotelemetry will have many other uses in the future. The interested reader is urged to explore the possibilities in *The Cerebral Cortex of the Internal Organs* by Konstantin Bykov (1957),

Biomedical Telemetry by Cesar Caseres (1965), "Implant Biotelemetry and Microelectronics" by W. H. Ko, and M. R. Neuman (1967), "Endoradiosonde" by R. Stuart Mackay (1957), and *Biomedical Telemetry: Sensing and Transmitting Biological Information from Animals to Man* by R. Stuart Mackay (1968).

Summary We have described the radio transmission of various physiological measures by means of the miniature endoradiosonde. We have discussed present accomplishments and have considered the full range of possible applications in psychological laboratory and field investigation. We have indicated advantages of the technique in the way of providing finer controls and of extending areas of investigation to once unavailable data.

Hess, Seltzer, and Shlien: "Pupil response of hetero- and homosexual males to pictures of men and women: A pilot study"*

3

Change in the size of the pupil of the human eye has been reported to vary with a subject's interest in various pictorial stimuli (Hess and Polt, 1960). Male subjects had a larger pupil while looking at pictures of women than when looking at pictures of men. The reverse was true for female subjects: they had larger pupils looking at men. Unpublished work with a large number of subjects has continued to substantiate the finding of this difference between the sexes.

If this difference in pupil response is truly a reflection of interest in the male or female figure as a sexual object, then homosexuals would be expected to show a larger pupil response to pictures of their own sex. In the course of our work a few subjects have given a larger response to pictures of their own sex; as measured by pupil size, same-sex pictures

seemed more interesting to them. Review of these anomalous cases increased the plausibility of the idea that this same-sex response might be typical of **homosexuals.** The present report, a pilot study of a small group of overt male homosexuals, strongly supports that hypothesis.

Method

Subjects Ten young adult male subjects were tested. Five of these, students or workers

---

*Quoted material is from Eckhard H. Hess, Allan L. Seltzer, and John M. Shlien, "Pupil Response of Hetero- and Homosexual Males to Pictures of Men and Women: A Pilot Study," *Journal of Abnormal Psychology,*" June 1965, **70**(3), 165–168. Copyright 1965 by the American Psychological Association and reproduced by permission.

in our laboratory—the **heterosexual** group— were well known to us over a period of several years. Their sexual outlet was judged to be exclusively heterosexual. The other five were known, through observation, interview, and in every case by their own voluntary admissions to one of the authors who had gained their trust, to have overt homosexuality as their sole or primary sexual outlet. All 10 were of roughly the same age (between 24 and 34 years), same education (all but one were graduate students), and same social level. None was hospitalized or in therapy.

Procedure and apparatus In a dimly lit room, a subject was seated before a viewing aperture, fitted with a headrest, which was inserted in a large plywood panel. The panel concealed the working of the apparatus from the subject. Resting his head against the aperture, the subject faced a rear-projection screen, set in an otherwise black box, at a distance of 2½ feet from his eyes. A 35-mm slide projector behind this screen projected a 9 by 12-inch picture onto it. Changing of slides was controlled by the experimenter from his position behind the panel, where he also operated a concealed 16-mm camera fitted with a frame counter. As the slides were being viewed, a half-silvered mirror placed at a 45-degree angle across the subject's line of vision permitted unobtrusive filming of the eye, at the rate of two frames per second. Illumination for this photography was furnished by a 100-watt bulb on rheostat control.

Stimuli Fifteen picture slides, representations of the human figure, were shown in the following order:

	Slide content	Scoring category
A.	Painting, cubist, five figures	Art
B.	Painting, realistic, crucifixion	Art
C.	Painting, two nude males	Male
D.	Painting, reclining female nude	Female
E.	Photograph, nude man, head and upper torso	Male
F.	Painting, seated nude female, rear view	Female
G.	Painting, sailor, nude upper torso	Male
H.	Painting, nude male and nude female	Art
I.	Photograph, nude female torso	Female
J.	Photograph, nude man, rear view	Male
K.	Painting, nude female, head and upper torso	Female
L.	Painting, two partly clothed males	Male
M.	Painting, nude female, head and torso	Female
N.	Painting, abstract, three figures	Art
O.	Painting, cubist, three figures	Art

The presentation of each of these stimulus pictures was preceded by the presentation of a medium gray "control" slide. The total sequence was 30 slides in this order: Control A, Stimulus A, Control B, Stimulus B, etc., each shown for 10 seconds, with a total viewing time of 5 minutes for the entire sequence.

From the list of slides it can be seen that five were scored as being pictures of females and five were scored as pictures of males. The "male" pictures (C, E, G, J, and L), considered the homosexual equivalent of pinups, were culled from physique magazines and were generally more crude artistically than the pictures of females. These latter (D, F, I, K, and M) represented a rather lush concept of the female figure: for example, "D" was a Titian "Venus," "K" an Ingres "Odalisque."

The five "art" slides (A, B, H, N, and O) ranged in style and period from a Michelangelo to a Picasso. None of these was a clearly "male" or clearly "female" picture; the abstracts (A, N, and O) were ambiguous sexually, "H" showed both sexes, "B" had a strong religious connotation. This group of slides was included in the series for several reasons. Firstly, it was deemed desirable to place the sexual pictures in an artistic setting to reduce the threat to some subjects that might inhere in the obviously sexual material. Secondly, an abnormally high response is frequently given to the first stimulus shown to a subject. By placing art slides "A" and "B" first in the sequence, the male and the female slides, which were of major interest, were protected from this artifact. Thirdly, homosexuals are often thought to have artistic interests and, indeed, most of the homosexuals in this study did verbally indicate such interests. It was useful, therefore, to include a group of slides which would permit appraisal of response to the artistic quality of pictures separate from their representation of sexual objects. Such a separation of pictorial content from its artistic mode of expression appears feasible since (a) the homosexuals, as a group, showed a high response to the artistically good but sexually ambiguous art slides but (b) they also showed a high response to the artistically crude male pictures yet (c) they showed a low response to the artistically good female pictures. Thus, in addition to the use made of it in this report, the data point also to the potential value of the pupil technique in esthetics research.

Measurement and Scoring The processed 16mm film was projected, frame by frame, onto the underside of an opal-glass insert in a table, to a magnification of approximately 20 times. The diameter of the pupil in each frame was measured with a millimeter rule and recorded, giving a set of 20 measurements for each control presentation and a set of 20 for each stimulus. Averages were then computed for each stimulus set and for each preceding control set. In order to compare average pupil size during viewing of a picture to the pupil size during the preceding control this method was used: for each control-stimulus pair the percentage of increase or decrease in average pupil size was computed by dividing the difference between stimulus average and control average by the control average. A positive percentage indicated a larger pupil size when the subject was viewing the stimulus than when he viewed the preceding control. A

negative percentage meant a smaller average pupil size during stimulus viewing. For each subject, the five percentages of his response to each of the male pictures (C, E, G, J, and L) were added together to give his "response to 'male' picture" score (Table 12.1, first column). The total of percentages of his response to the female pictures (D, F, I, K, and M) gave his "response to 'female' picture" score (Table 12.1, second column). The algebraic subtraction of each subject's male picture total from his female picture total (column two minus column one) gave each subject's relative male-female response measure (Table 12.1, third column). Using this order of procedure for the table, a positive figure in the third column indicates that the subject had a greater total response to pictures of females than to pictures of males; a negative figure indicates lesser response to pictures of females but greater response to pictures of males.

Results

These male-female response measures clearly discriminate between the subject groups, as is shown in the last column of Table 12.1. Figure 12.5 shows this last column graphically.

Table 12.1

Pupil-size increase or decrease when comparing stimuli to controls
(expressed in percentage totals)

Subject	Total response to "male" pictures	Total response to "female" pictures	Relative "male-female" response score
Heterosexuals			
1	−00.4	+05.9	+06.3
2	−54.5	−22.4	+32.1
3	+12.5	+19.2	+06.7
4	+06.3	+39.0	+32.7
5	−01.5	+23.1	+24.6
Homosexuals			
6	+18.8	+11.2	−07.6
7	−04.6	−38.0	−33.4
8	+18.9	+18.1	−00.8
9	+18.2	−05.6	−23.8
10	+15.8	+21.5	+05.7

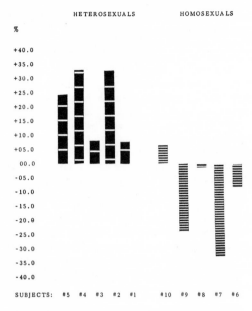

Figure 12.5 Differences in percentage of pupil-size change in response to male and female pictures. A positive score shows higher response to pictures of females; a negative score shows higher response to pictures of males. (From E. H. Hess, and J. M. Polt, "Pupil Size as Related to Interest Value of Visual Stimuli," *Science*, 1960, **132**, 349–350.)

There is no overlap between the groups in that the lowest heterosexual response is +06.3, whereas the highest homosexual response is no higher than +05.7. All heterosexual males show a larger response to pictures of women than to pictures of men (positive scores). Four of the homosexuals show a larger response to pictures of men (negative scores).

Discussion

Some of the female pictures drew a high-positive response from some of the homosexuals and some of the male pictures drew a high-positive response from some of the heterosexuals. Therefore response to any single stimulus did not serve to categorize individuals. The total response of a group of subjects to any single stimulus, however, usually served to categorize that stimulus. Total heterosexual response to

three of the five female pictures was positive. Total homosexual response to each of the five male pictures was positive. The pictures used in this pilot study were chosen on an a priori basis. The information they have given us and more recent advances in our technique—especially in the matter of brightness matching of pictures—may now permit the formulation of a test battery of pictorial stimuli designed to give a more absolute reflection of a single subject's sex-object interest. It should be emphasized, however, that since all subjects in this study saw identical stimuli, the brightness factor could not in any way account for the reported difference between individuals and the resultant groups.

The cooperation of the homosexual subjects, it should be noted, was an unusual relaxation of their customary defense against identification as homosexuals. They were all effectively operating in a normal living environment, in school, at work, with friends. Their sexual preferences were not obvious, and they were ordinarily most reluctant to talk about or reveal them; yet the pupil technique, using a response that is nonverbal and beyond the voluntary control, was able to differentiate them from the heterosexual subjects. This is not to say that the pupil response as an index of preference is a predictive substitute for the ultimate criterion of the behavior itself. It does mean that where both preference and behavior are homosexual, even though socially concealed, the pupil response has been shown in this sample to have discriminating power.

Pupil response has already seen application in the area of studies of cognition (Hess & Polt, 1964). In the study of some aspects of personality, compared with projective tests and other instruments and techniques that have been used, this technique appears to us to open up entirely new dimensions.

Summary

The pupil response of each individual in a group of heterosexual males was greater when looking at pictures of women than when looking at pictures of men. Homosexual male *S*s responded in the opposite direction. Measurement of changes in pupil size permitted clear-cut discrimination between the two groups.

The pupillary response is another example of the variety of the organism's response repertoire that can be involved in affective or feeling responses.

Affective effects of interpersonal action 4

The effect of one person on another is widely recognized and constitutes the area of interpersonal relations. Bennis, Schein, Berlew, and Steele (1964) have recently produced a heavy tome in this field. Its main concern is with searching for the lawful relationships that govern interpersonal relations in all their richness. Gantt, Newton, Royer, and Stephens (1966) have extended the definition of *effect of person* to include the effect of any organism upon any other organism's response. The term would cover the condition imposed on any laboratory worker who uses gregarious animals like sheep as subjects. Such a worker realizes that he must have another sheep in the vicinity of his sheep subject. Should he try to work with a solitary sheep, his disrupted experiment would soon convince him of the "effect of person" that one sheep has on another. A disturbing effect appears to be one result of a failure to supply the required experimental variable. This is what the term, effect of person, will mean.

Effect of person in nature

Observations scattered throughout this book offer naturalistic or field data illustrating effect of person. For example, biotelemetric study of a lizard alone in a laboratory shows a distinct reaction the instant that humans enter. The initial effect of Jane Goodall on the wild troops of chimpanzees that she attempted to study in Tanzania was an avoidance response. Gradually the effect changed to tolerance, acceptance, and even body contact—a *reversal* of effect of person. Schaller's experience with the mountain gorilla and Van Kortlandt's encounter with the chimpanzees, referred to earlier, are additional illustrations. A more ubiquitous example is furnished by most wild animals, who tend to avoid mankind and possible trouble with him.

Laboratory investigation of effect of person

Gantt and his associates, in the study mentioned earlier, had a small menagerie of mammals in order to make a comparative study. A rabbit, opossum, cat, monkey, guinea pig, and puppies did not respond in the same way affectively. When petted, some showed an increase and some a decrease in heart rate.

Conditioning of effect of person

During their laboratory studies, Gantt, Newton, Royer, and Stephens (1966) made some interesting observations that demonstrated the conditionability of effect of person. For example, the quieting effect of petting on heart action could be readily conditioned to other neutral or even contradictory stimuli. Figure 12.6 shows such a conditioning effect in a dog. Note the marked acceleration of heart rate when the bell was sounded prior to conditioning. Note also the decelerating effect of petting prior to conditioning; petting alone produced a 10 percent decrease of heart rate. Note, however, that after the bell was followed by petting ten times, the following 20 trials gave a 13 percent decrease in heart rate to bell and 18 percent to petting (p. 28).

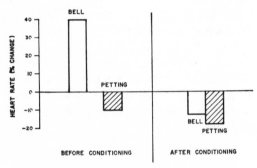

Figure 12.6 Cardiac conditional reflex based on "effect of person." Left, before conditioning: 20 trials of bell alone produced 40% increase in HR, 20 trials of petting alone produced 10% decrease in HR. Right, after bell had immediately preceded petting 10 times, next 20 trials of bell plus petting produced HR decrease of 13% to bell and 18% to petting. (From W. Horsley Gantt, Joseph E. O. Newton, Fred L. Royer, and Joseph H. Stephens, "Effect of Person," *Conditional Reflex*, January-March 1966, **1**(1), 28. Reprinted by permission of author and publisher.)

Effect of person in neurotic dogs

The laboratory setup described provided excellent opportunities for comparing the effect of person on neurotic versus normal dogs. In general, results with neurotic dogs showed extreme variability, such as cardiac acceleration on cessation of petting or during petting or marked changes in respiratory rate during petting (p. 23).

One neurotic dog, V3, showed a serious depressing effect of heart action and respiration to the mere presence of a person in the room. On one occasion V3's heart rate dropped from a level of 140 to 180 beats per minute while alone to 20 beats per minute when someone entered the room. "On several occasions, moreover, petting produced a sudden **cardiac arrest** of 6 to 8 seconds in V3 as well as a profound drop in **systolic blood pressure** for 8 minutes—from 140 to 75 mm Hg [p. 23]."

Perhaps the findings of greatest interest and significance to evolve from the research by Gantt and associates concerns a lack of concordance between motor and affective responses, a topic that we turn to next.

Schizokinesis

In conditioning motor or salivary reflexes in the dog, Gantt (1966) observed that often a generalized conditioned response of the heart or respiratory system might occur on the first trial even before the motor or salivary reflex became thoroughly conditioned (pp. 61–62). Another interesting finding showed that although cardiac and respiratory reflexes formed readily, they were nevertheless peculiarly resistant to extinction. In fact, they might continue for years after the motor or salivary reflexes disappeared. This led Gantt to formulate the concept of schizokinesis, which called attention to the split between the more general and the more specific functions (p. 62).

The fact that conditional reflexes are so often difficult to eradicate once formed makes the individual a museum of antiquities as he grows older, as I have pointed out previously (Gantt, 1952). He is encumbered with many reactions no longer useful or even...detrimental to life. This is especially true for the cardiovascular function, and it is these conditional reflexes that are the most enduring. A person may be reacting to some old injury or situation [with his **cardiovascular system**] which no longer exists, and he is usually unconscious of what it is that is causing an increase in heart rate or blood pressure. The result may be chronic hypertension. This may be the explanation of many cardiac deaths [p. 62].

An experimental demonstration of schizokinesis

The effect of person has already been discussed above. In the study considered briefly here, Anderson and Gantt (1966) tested the effect of the person variable experimentally. Their customary isolation of the dog in conditioning studies favored the use of the person factor as an independent variable. They had also noted that when a person entered the laboratory, a dog's heart rate speeded up; when that person petted the dog by rubbing behind the ears, the heart rate went down. They decided to work with cardiac deceleration in response to petting as a measure of effect of person. And, since previous work had shown that an electric shock to the foreleg of a dog increased heart rate, they also incorporated this response into their experimental setup. The fundamental question was: What would these two contradictory responses show?

Procedure

The subjects selected for the study were four, naive mongrel dogs, Dolly, Lucy, Lady, and Spook. The subjects were habituated to their new environment and then given 50 petting trials, which tended to decrease but not elim, ate the cardiac acceleration caused by the experimenter's entrance into the conditioning room. The petting-alone trials lead to ten trials of one-

second shock at 5-minute intervals on 3 consecutive days (p. 185).

The experiment proper consisted of two control conditions and one experimental situation. The first control condition required the experimenter to enter the chamber, pet the dog for 60 seconds, then leave. The second control involved administering a one-second shock to the dog's foreleg in the absence of the experimenter. The experimental condition called for a one-second shock to the dog's foreleg 12 seconds after the experimenter entered the laboratory and started to pet the animal, which he continued to do for 48 seconds; at the end of that time the experimenter left. The experimenters gave a total of 40 trials over 10 days.

Results

Cardiac data

The over-all results for the cardiac data are shown in Fig. 12.7. The increase or decrease is shown as a change from the base rate recorded during the 30-second

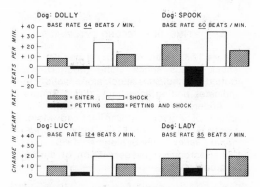

Figure 12.7 Absolute change in heart rate beats per minute. (From Sandra L. Anderson, and W. Horsley Gantt, "The Effect of Person on Cardiac and Motor Responsivity to Shock in Dogs," *Conditional Reflex*, July-September, 1966, **1**(3), 182. Reproduced by permission of author and publisher.)

period before each trial for each of the three different experimental situations. The first bar represents the 6-second interval between the experimenter's entrance into the experimental chamber and the point at which he began to pet the animal. The second bar represents amount of change in heart rate as a function of petting, the third bar, the effect of shock on heart rate, and four, petting plus shock or the suppressing effect of petting on heart rate acceleration. "It is clear that for each dog the heart rate increase which follows shock is reduced if he is being petted during the shock [p. 187]."

An individual graph showing the results for Dolly are represented in Fig. 12.8.

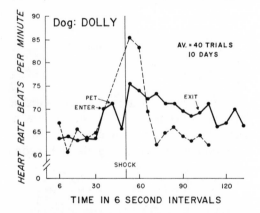

Figure 12.8 Heart rate during petting and shock versus shock alone (dog: Dolly). Dotted line indicates shock alone; solid line indicates petting and shock. (From Sandra L. Anderson, and W. Horsley Gantt, "The Effect of Person on Cardiac and Motor Responsivity to Shock in Dogs," *Conditional Reflex*, July-September 1966, **1**(3), 183. Reproduced by permission of author and publisher.)

Leg flexions

The data from conditioned leg flexion could hardly have differed more from those derived for the heart action. The motor data showed no statistically signifi-

cant differences in magnitude or number of leg flexions between the petting during shock and shock alone trials. The number of **unconditioned responses** to shock was the same for all four dogs under both conditions. Furthermore, three of the four dogs showed leg flexions in over one-half of the petting trials in which no shock was given. In fact, the experimenter's entrance into the room served as a signal for the shock. The number of leg responses that occurred in the 12 seconds after the experimenter's entrance into the room *before* shock was given also harmonizes with the above assumption.

From the data it appears that petting served as a conditional stimulus for the motor response to shock, while at the same time it suppressed the cardiac response to shock. The fact that the reactions of these two systems of responding—motor and cardiac—within the same dog were dissimilar is an example of the principle of *schizokinesis*. Measurement of one system or the other, therefore, would have given a less complete indication of the reaction to the simultaneous presentation of petting and shock. Measurement of leg flexion alone would have indicated that petting had no suppressive effect upon the response to shock, whereas measurement of heart rate alone would have suggested a marked suppression of response which could not be generalized to the specific motor reaction [pp. 187–188].

Summary

Observations at the Pavlovian Laboratory of Johns Hopkins University showed a long-lasting effect of cardiac and respiratory reactions that even survived extinction of motor responses which the organism had acquired simultaneously. These results lead to the formulation of the concept of schizokinesis, which calls attention to the differential effect of time on the component reaction systems of a complex response. Anderson and Gantt did an experimental study of schizokinesis which showed that when a person entered the conditioning laboratory, a dog's heart rate accelerated, but when the person petted the dog, his heart rate went down. On the other hand, electric shock alone accelerated the heart rate, but a person petting the dog during shock decelerated its heart rate without any effect on the dog's leg flexions. Shock alone and petting during shock showed no statistically significant difference in the latter case. In other words, the "same" variable (in a physical sense), namely, presence-of-person, functioned one way on the organism's cardiac reaction system and in another way on the components involving its leg reaction systems.

Schizokinesis should cause us no surprise *if* we recognize the necessity for handling psychological and physiological events on their own levels. The surprise comes *only* when we find that psychological events do not follow the same laws as physiological ones. But why should we expect them to do so? Perhaps the fulfillment of each discipline will come when it works out the relationships between its data and the laws governing them without transforming or reducing them to the data or principles of some other discipline. After all, why should we expect an organism's learned reactions involving its heart to show the same properties as its reactions involving its legs? *Why?*

Edwards and Acker:
"A demonstration of the
long-term retention of a
conditioned galvanic
*skin response"**

5

The long-term retention of conditioned autonomic responses has been investigated chiefly by utilizing animals in laboratory conditions. Anderson and Paramenter (1941) contributed data which support the persisting character of a conditioned response of almost 4-years duration in the sheep. Gantt (1944) reported the case of "Nick," an amiable mongrel dog who maintained conditioned cardio-respiratory responses for 10 years. To account for this, and other cases like it, he developed the concept of schizo-kinesis (Gantt, 1953), that is, the persistence of inappropriate conditioned visceral responses long after the somatic motor components disappear. ("The dog remembers with his heart 'emotionally,' but not with the specific movements.") [We have discussed schizokinesis in the previous article.]

The persistence of a conditioned response can be studied by two methods: first, by examination of the extinction process, that is, the number of times the **conditioned stimulus** (CS)

can elicit the **conditioned response** (CR) when the CS is presented without the unconditioned stimulus (UCS); and second, by the measurement of spontaneous recovery of the CR after a specified duration of time. An experimenter describing the extinction process might condition a group of subjects with a bell-shock technique, then continue the procedure, studying the responses when only the bell (the CS) is presented. If retention were being studied, the experimenter would let a known period of time elapse between the last reinforced CS presentation, then present the CS and observe whether the CR occurs. Here, under optimal conditions, an experimenter would train a group of subjects with the "bell-shock" conditioning,

---

*Quoted material is from Allan E. Edwards and Loren E. Acker, "A Demonstration of the Long-Term Retention of a Conditioned Galvanic Skin Response," Psychosomatic Medicine, 1962, 24, 459–463. By permission of the author and publisher.

arrange their environment such that they would never hear anything like a bell for perhaps 10 years, then compare their responses to the bell after that time with an appropriate control group. While both these designs are feasible with animals, time and control restrictions usually preclude the latter [design] from human research even though the demonstration of persisting conditioned visceral responses in humans is central to formulations such as Gantt's. In this study a reasonable approximation to these conditions was reached by using the U.S. Navy "Battle Stations" (General Quarters) signal for World War II as the CS. It was assumed (1) the Battle Stations signal was experienced more by Navy veterans than by Army veterans; (2) the Battle Stations signal, during the period 1941–1945, was often immediately followed by stimuli aversive to its auditors; (3) the Battle Stations signal has been rarely experienced by the subjects since 1946. It is recognized that the possibility of the subjects hearing this signal in the context of entertainment is present, but this could only weaken the effect, tending to bring the response under extinction.

Method

Subjects The subjects were 11 pairs of hospitalized male World War II veterans. These pairs were composed of an Army and a Navy veteran, both of whom had been in the service for at least 2 years during World War II, and who were separated from the service prior to 1946. An added condition was that the Navy subjects had to have shipboard service during hostilities. Each pair was selected from the same ward, thus assuring similar diagnosis for both members.

Apparatus The subject was seated in a sound-attenuated room 4 by 4 by 8 feet with electrodes fastened to each palm. Skin resistance was measured through a **Darrow Bridge** and recorded by an Offner Oscillograph. The stimuli were presented through earphones by means of a magnetic tape recorder. Twenty sounds were selected from a sound-effects library on the basis of the following criteria: (1) The sounds were judged by the experimenter to be identifiable within a 4-second presentation interval and to be discriminable among themselves. (2) All sounds were nonverbal. (3) One

of the sounds would be the Battle Stations (General Quarters) signal heard aboard ship. The stimuli used were

1. Battle Stations, U.S. Navy, World War II – a repetitive gong, approximately 100 percussions per minute.
2. Rifle and machine gun fire – a small-arms engagement between two small forces.
3. Riveting gun – the staccato reports of an air hammer.
4. Locomotive – heavy steam engine going at approximately half-throttle.
5. Cattle – large herd lowing.
6. Blacksmith forge – heavy hammer striking anvil at irregular rate.
7. Crowd – large and excited – vocalization indiscriminable.
8. Train – rapid approach of fast-moving freight.
9. Burglar alarm – rapid percussion alarm bell.
10. Handsaw – fast cutting through resonant wood.
11. Model plane – high rpm one-cylinder gas motor.
12. Airplane – diving single engine.
13. Jet – single motor, takeoff.
14. River rapids – water cascading and gurgling.
15. Surf – irregular crashing onto sandy beach – almost indistinguishable from irregular white noise.
16. Ship whistle – sudden blast of steam whistle.
17. Electric drill – high rpm electric motor under strain.
18. Dog barking – excited barking of small dog.
19. Truck maneuvering – heavy diesels, backing, stopping, and starting.
20. Printing press – running at operating speed.

Procedure Each subject was treated individually. Before being placed in the sound-attenuated room, he was told that the procedure was not unpleasant, that it had nothing to do with his hospitalization, and that it was voluntary. He was instructed: "I'm interested in what your skin does when you hear sounds. After we start you will hear a series of sounds; some you will probably recognize, some you won't. Your task is to remember, if you can, when you last heard them or what they are. When we are all finished, I'll ask you some questions about them." (No attempt was made to analyze these verbalizations; the procedure was followed only for maintaining rapport.) The subject was then seated in the room, the electrodes and ear-phones affixed, the door closed, and a 5-minute period of relaxation and stabilization of skin conductance allowed. After this period the sounds were administered with a frequency of every 50 to 80 seconds. (This was determined to be sufficient time to allow the skin con-ductance to return to the prestimulus level or below.) Each sound commenced at zero decibel, increased to approximately 70 decibels peak amplitude in 2 seconds, remained at this inten-sity for 4 seconds, and then returned to zero decibel during the last second. The skin-con-ductance measurements were made throughout the total experiment. Each *pair* of subjects received a different sequence of the 20 sounds, the first five of which were for habituation with no measurements taken. The sequences were constructed utilizing a table of random numbers with the qualifications that (1) no sound would appear more than once and (2) the Battle Sta-tions sound would not appear among the first five sounds. Skin conductance was measured at the point of onset for each stimulus, and the biggest deflection in either direction within 8 seconds after the onset of the stimulus was taken as the criterion score.

Results

It was decided, a priori, to exclude any pair of subjects where at least one showed no measurable deflection to at least 8 of the 15 stimuli upon which data were taken—two pairs were unresponders in this sense, thus reducing the *N* to 18, nine in each group.

All responses of each subject were trans-formed into **standard scores** from the responses he alone generated. Thus each standard score represents the degree of *effect* a given stimulus has upon a given subject solely in relation to the other stimuli he experienced. This procedure controls for any possible differences between Army and Navy men as regards their palmar conductance to sounds in general and makes each subject's scores comparable to all other subjects.

Because of the necessary unequal numbers in each cell, an overall analysis of variance could not be performed without possibly biasing the within-cell (error) variance. Accordingly, a simple **analysis of variance** was performed on each stimulus comparing the Army and Navy

men's **GSRs** (as expressed in standard scores representing conductance changes), the specific hypothesis being, of course, that the Navy men would respond more to the Battle Stations signal than the Army veterans. Table 12.2 shows the results.

Discussion

The results show that Navy veterans of World War II manifest conditioned autonomic response to a stimulus paired with an aversive situation between 15 and 20 years prior to testing. Since all the subjects left military service by 1946, the obtained difference on the Battle Stations signal must be interpreted as dating back to the differential experiences dur-ing this period only, that is, the selection criterion for the subjects. Little can be asserted about any other differences obtained, for no hypotheses were made beforehand. The Battle Stations effect was, however, the largest obtained.

Gantt's formulation of schizokinesis involves the persistence of responses of organs regulated by the autonomic nervous system. The findings of the present study suggest that, in addition to the persistence of cardio-respiratory condi-tioned responses, other responses which are also indicants of autonomic activity may show the same persistence; furthermore, the data are extended to include humans. In this case persistence of a conditioned GSR was demon-strated; however, further work on such indi-cants of autonomic activity as finger volume, body temperatures, and stomach motility could possibly increase even further the generality of findings to date. Since longitudinal studies over 10-, 20-, or 30-year periods have inherent diffi-culties, the present line of approach seems to be the most practical way of measuring the per-sistence of learned autonomic responses.

Summary Galvanic skin responses to the General Quarters (Battle Stations) signal, which often preceded enemy attack aboard ship during World War II, were recorded from Navy veterans. This sound was presented along with 19 other randomly selected sounds, and GSRs to all sounds were recorded and compared to a control group of World War II Army veterans. The

Table 12.2

Means and F ratios comparing Army
and Navy men on all stimuli

Stimuli	Army		Navy		F
	n	Mean	n	Mean	
Battle Stations	9	0.30	9	−0.79	11.63 †
Electric drill	1	0.14	4	0.49	4.24
Train	6	−0.07	5	0.00	0.01
Crowd	4	−0.56	4	−0.49	0.01
Saw	5	−0.66	7	0.16	1.54
Jet plane	7	−0.66	7	0.22	2.76
Truck maneuvering	6	0.97	6	−0.16	2.53
Anvil	3	0.22	4	−0.15	0.34
Gas engine plane	8	−0.54	8	0.23	2.10
Burglar alarm	6	−0.37	4	0.78	4.08
Ship whistle	6	0.41	7	0.10	0.40
Surf	5	0.36	6	−0.23	1.08
Model plane	7	0.40	6	0.20	0.26
Riveting	9	−0.29	9	0.67	5.76*
Rapids	8	0.47	9	−0.21	3.76
Locomotive	8	−0.09	8	0.83	6.92*
Cows	5	0.05	6	−0.77	0.38
Printing press	5	0.49	6	0.37	0.08
Small-arms engagement	9	0.13	9	−0.10	0.24
Dog	9	−0.52	6	−1.14	1.19

$*p$ .05
$†p$ .01

The F ratio is a statistical measure which compares the variation between a set of measures with the variation within a set of measurement. Applied to the present case, the F ratio shows that the GSR measures varied significantly more between soldiers and sailors than it did within either group, thus proving that the difference is statistically significant, which means (in still other terms) that such a difference could not occur by chance.

results showed that Navy men gave significantly greater responses than their Army controls even though 15 to 20 years had elapsed since the original conditioning.

Implications for **psychosomatic** theory and Gantt's theory of schizokinesis are discussed.

*Ewing: The stress reaction
in the cockroach* **6**

In a report to *Science* Leonard S. Ewing (1968) made some interesting and significant field observations on stress in the cockroach. The response in question is an equivalent to anxiety tension in the human.

Elsewhere in this book we have discussed fighting among members of various species, fighting that seldom if ever attains the kind of mortal combat prevalent among members of the human species. The cockroach also fights in less deadly fashion. Its purpose is to settle questions of status.

Dominance-submission fighting

When two males with ambiguous or pretty evenly matched status meet, a dominance-submission test occurs. Both animals go at each other with heads lowered in order to get under the adversary and throw him into the air, sometimes on his back. In such a case, the problem is solved. Another solution is withdrawal or flight. Whatever the outcome, it establishes dominance-subordinate relationships in future encounters of a given pair of male roaches. The inferior one will not attack the victor and, if attacked by the latter, will "prostrate himself" before the aggressor.

Ewing tested young roaches in different combinations for dominance-subordinate status and made an interesting discovery. He found that the death rate among young adult males who fought was quite high. The observation stimulated Ewing to set up a controlled experiment which, without going into details, showed that death in the sub-ordinate animal occurred in 80 percent of the cases.

The situation bears striking resemblance to the social stress found in mammals. Male rats, in particular, show a well-marked dominant-subordinate behavior. Prolonged aggression produces stress in the subordinate, and ultimately a disease state, characterized by the stress syndrome, leading to death, which cannot be attributed to external damage. Subordinate cockroaches may die from some internal changes comparable to those accompanying the stress syndrome in mammals [p. 1036].

In addition to its specific findings, Ewing's study is important because it emphasizes the need for research on the factual level. Valid theory is undoubtedly necessary, but much work remains to be done on the raw data.

Figure 12.9 Top, a male cockroach assumes a dominant position. Bottom, a cockroach "prostrates himself" before a dominant male. (Photos courtesy of Leonard S. Ewing, University of Edinburgh.)

7 Emotions defined

I am suggesting here that emotional behavior takes the form of nonfunctional, inappropriate, and aborted action. I would list the following behaviors as generally falling into this class: panicking, running amok, stuttering, freezing in the path of a car, and fainting. It would seem that such behaviors occur when an organism perceives a threatening or harmful situation and for some reason cannot react appropriately to the situation.

For help in defining the term emotion, we rely on Kantor (1933), who first distinguished between emotions and feelings. For Kantor, an emotional response is atypical (p. 219). It starts out like any other reaction, with attention and perception, but never gets completed with a final "reaction system." Instead of performing a final response, the person freezes (as mentioned above) or may even die from fright. Less severe disruptions include urinating or defecating in fright. Thus, emotional reactions are incomplete or truncated actions.

Fainting

A nonmedical observer is invited to watch an operation. *As he sees* the flow of blood in the incision, he faints. I believe that what happens in this behavior segment is as follows. First, the observer attends in the direction of the surgeon's operation and he perceives. So far this behavior segment is like any other. But at the point at which the observer falls to the floor, his response stops being normal and

becomes a nonadaptive, in fact, a disruptive, atypical reaction. Instead of making a comment or taking any other action, he passes out, thus functioning only on a physiological level. Nothing happens on a psychological plane. During this interval you are safe in offering him a million dollars on the condition that all he needs to do is say that he will accept it. Several minutes later he revives, asks what happened, and resumes his psychological life. In terms of the proposed definition, he was involved in an emotional response from the instant of collapse until he again saw, talked, and otherwise behaved following the psychological gap. His action really constituted an aborted or truncated response because it failed to go on to completion the way his (and our) behavior customarily does.

Speech disturbances

Stuttering

There are a number of theories in explanation of stuttering. This socially discomforting phenomenon can also be understood as emotional behavior. Consider what happens to the stutterer. Let us say that he wants to tell you about a little boy. All goes well until he gets to the dreaded *b* sound of *boy,* which he anticipated with anxiety long before he ever got to it. When he finally reaches the *b,* he gets "hung up." He finds himself in another painful "block" of interminable duration. Over and over he compulsively repeats the *b* sound and cannot get on with the sentence. His "block" is another variety of emotional disruption, during which the stutterer is reduced to mere reflex functioning. Observe the force and tension in the cyclic behavior during which one *b* elicits another *b*, and so on. The rigid, anatomical functioning of his speech organs has much in common with a continuous series of knee jerks evoked by repetitive stimulation with a reflex hammer. When our hypothetical victim is finally delivered from his plight (by a distracting stimulus, for example), he continues speaking normally until the next "block" precipitates another emotional behavior segment.

"Normal" speech disturbances

A most interesting study of "normal" speech disturbances by Mahl (personal communication and Progress Report of Research, mimeo) belongs to the field of emotional behavior although Mahl does not label it as such. He studied 200 varied individuals in different situations for speech disturbances, the majority of which, despite their relatively great frequency, escaped the awareness of speaker and listener! Apparently the disturbances in question are mild and therefore not as attention compelling as a convulsive fit might be. However, as disruptions of the ongoing speech sequence, they meet the proposed definition of *emotion*.

From his survey of recorded interviews Mahl developed the following categories of "normal" speech disturbance: the use of "ah" (the all-too-frequent vocal punctuation mark of the professor), sentence change, repetitions, omissions, stutters, tongue slips, sentence incompletion, and intruding incoherent sounds. Table 12.3 provides a concrete definition and specification of faulty speech patterns. Their

frequent occurrence has evidently adapted us to them. In Mahl's study, "anxiety interviews" in the experimental group yielded increased palmar sweating and also increased significantly the experimental subjects' (but not the controls') speech disturbance levels. His results would tend to fit the theory of emotion being developed here in that faulty speech is closely related to anxiety.

Panic

When people are "on the spot," their behavior may not show the same uninterrupted continuity and integration that it does when they operate under conditions more appropriate to effective functioning.*

Panic as emotional behavior

If...there is a fire in a theatre and everyone files through the exits in orderly fashion, all or most of the group will escape. Here, the behavior of each individual involves consideration of the other people and is adaptive to the situation. If, however, a few members of the group do not wait their turn to file through the exit but rather rush to the door and cause a jam, these people would be considered to be evidencing a lack of concern for the other members of the group. Further, their jamming of the escape exit may reduce the escape possibilities of the other people involved. If other group members observe these few individuals jamming the escape exit, they may also engage in similar behavior as they perceive their own chances of escape being reduced.

The only empirical information available on the behavior of the individual in a panic situation comes from interviews of approximately one thousand people who had been

*Quoted material is from Duane P. Schultz, "An Experimental Approach to Panic Behavior: Final Report to the Group Psychology Branch. Office of Naval Research, August 15, 1966." (Mimeograph)

participants in disasters (Quarantelli, 1957). Quarantelli noted that in a disaster situation the individual finds himself highly and per-

sonally threatened, with the threat source being highly tangible and readily localized. The person becomes self-conscious and fearful and gives

Table 12.3

Definitions and illustrations of the speech disturbance categories*

Category	Examples
1. *"Ah."* Wherever the "ah" sound occurs, it is scored. Less frequent variants are "eh," "uh," "uhm."	Well...ah...when I first came home.
2. *Sentence change.* A correction in the form or content of the expression while the word-word progression occurs. To be scored, these changes *must be sensed by the listener* as interruptions in the flow of the sentence.	Well she's...already she's lonesome. That was...it will be 2 years ago in the fall.
3. *Repetition.* The serial, superfluous repetition of one or more words—usually of one or two words.	'Cause they...they get along pretty well together. He was...he was sharing the office.
4. *Stutter.*	It sort of well l..l..leaves a memory.
5. *Omission.* Parts of words or, rarely, entire words may be omitted. Contractions not counted. Most omissions are of final one or two parts of words and are associated with sentence change and repetition.	She mour...was in mourning for about 2 years before. Then their anni...wedding anniversary comes around.
6. *Sentence incompletion.* An expression is interrupted, clearly left incomplete, and the communication proceeds without correction.	Well I'm sorry I couldn't get here last week so I could...ah...I was getting a child ready for camp and finishing up swimming lessons.
7. *Tongue slips.* Includes neologisms, the transposition of entire words from their "correct" serial position in sentence and the substitution of an unintended for an intended word.	We spleat the bitches (for "split the beaches") He was born in their hou(se)...hospital and came to their house. The reason that I don't...didn't seem to feel the love for him (son) that I felt for J... (daughter).
8. *Intruding incoherent sound.* A sound that is absolutely incoherent to the listener. It intrudes without itself altering the form of the expression and cannot be clearly conceived of as a stutter, omission, or neologism (though some may be such in reality).	If I see a girl now I'd like to take out I just ...dh...ask her.

*Reproduced from George F. Mahl, USPHS Grant M-1052: "The patient's language as expressive behavior." Mimeograph. Used with author's permission.

overt expression to his fear when he perceives that he and others are powerless to cope with the impending danger. Quarantelli also suggested that such an individual's behavior is nonsocial; he thinks only of saving himself.

Thus we may define panic behavior as a fear-induced flight behavior that is nonsocial, nonrational, and nonadaptive from the standpoint of total group survival because it reduces the survival possibilities of the group as a whole.

Two panic incidents

Let us examine two "classic" panic incidents that have occurred in this country. In 1903, in the Iroquois Theatre in Chicago, a fire began with the following disastrous consequences.

Somebody had, of course, yelled "Fire!"— there is almost always a fool of that species in an audience; and there are always hundreds of people who go crazy the moment they hear the word...

The horror in the auditorium was beyond all description. There were thirty exits, but few of them were marked by lights; some had heavy portieres over the doors, and some of the doors were locked or fastened with levers which no one knew how to work.

It was said that some of the exit doors... were either rusted or frozen. They were finally burst open, but precious moments had been lost—moments which meant death for many behind those doors. The fire-escape ladders could not accommodate the crowd, and many fell or jumped to death on the pavement below. Some were not killed only because they landed on the cushion of bodies of those who had gone before. But it was inside the house that the greatest loss of life occurred, especially on the stairways leading down from the second balcony. Here most of the dead were trampled or smothered, though many jumped or fell over the balustrade to the floor of the foyer. In places on the stairways, particularly where a turn caused a jam, bodies were piled 7 or 8 feet deep... An occasional living person was found in the heaps, but most of these were terribly injured. The heel prints on the dead faces mutely testified to the cruel fact that human animals stricken by terror are as mad and ruthless as stampeding cattle. Many bodies had the clothes torn from them, and some had the flesh trodden from their bones (Foy & Harlow, 1928, pp. 104–113).

It took an incredibly short 8 minutes from the moment the fire was first noticed until all the occupants were either dead, injured, or safely outside. In those 8 minutes over 500 people were killed—but the theatre itself did *not* burn. Actually, little more than the upholstery on the seats was destroyed and performances could have been given in the building just a few days after the fire.

In a nightclub called the Coconut Grove in Boston, over 800 people crowded every available table when

...a girl, her hair ablaze, hurtled across the floor screaming "Fire!"

That shriek heralded catastrophe. Some 800 guests, insane with panic, lunged in a wild scramble to get out the only way they knew— the revolving-door exit. Flames flashed with incredible swiftness...Smoke swirled in choking masses through hallways. The revolving doors jammed as the terror-stricken mob pushed them in both directions at the same time. Blazing draperies fell, setting women's evening gowns and hair on fire. Patrons were hurled under tables and trampled to death. Others tripped and choked the 6-foot-wide stairway up from the Melody Lounge. Those behind swarmed over them and piled up in layers— layers of corpses...

The fire was quickly brought under control, but the fatal damage was done (*Newsweek*, December 7, 1942, pp. 43–44).

In a very short time approximately 500 people were killed—the second greatest disaster of its kind (the first being the Iroquois Theatre fire). Only 100 people escaped unhurt, and half of these were employees of the club who were familiar with alternative exits. In both situations the fire was brought rather quickly under control and did relatively little physical damage to the buildings. Thus it seems that the fire was not the major *direct* cause of such high loss of life. Rather, it seems to have been the nonadaptive behavior of the participants in response to the fire which caused the high death rate.

Consider several of the specific behaviors exhibited in these two disasters—pushing *both* sides of a revolving door in both directions, for example. Escape is rendered impossible by this action of the people in their efforts to escape— they cut off the escape route themselves. Consider the choking and jamming of stairways where people were knocked down and trampled and others swarmed over them and piled up in layers. This behavior, too, is self-defeating and nonadaptive, for it serves to reduce the effectiveness of the escape-route stairway [Schultz, 1966, pp. 5–9].

Experimental study of panic

Difficult as it is to simulate panic in the laboratory, Schultz (1966) made an attempt to do so. His study is particularly pertinent because it focuses on individual panic behavior.

Briefly, Schultz put his subjects in a dangerous situation which threatened them with an electric shock three times stronger than an actual sample shock of 50 volts given the subject if escape did not take place within a specified time period. No subject saw the other subjects in closed cubicles, thus simulating the relationship between individuals in a burning theatre. He could "escape" from the threatening shock situation by operating a lever on the panel before him for 2 seconds. However, only one subject could escape because only one subject at a time could operate the lever. If more than one tried to escape, the mechanism jammed and no one could escape. There was no way of knowing when the mechanism became unjammed; the only thing the subject knew at a given time was whether or not escape was possible at the moment.

The subject was told he had one way out, for he could press an emergency button at any time. The button would release him but would at the same time trap the others and give them a severe electric shock. This alternative was analogous to the person jamming ahead of the rest in the theatre fire. Both could save themselves at the expense of the rest.

Schultz conducted a number of pilot studies testing the effect of such variables as group size and knowledge of escape time. But our interest is a more general one. Did the subjects panic? Yes, anywhere from one-fourth to one-half of the subjects pushed "out of turn and so eliminated the escape possibilities of the others involved [p. 21]." Comparison of "pressers" in their responses to a personality test showed some personality differences. For example, more "only-born" subjects (that is, subjects without brothers or sisters) pressed the emergency button and more pressed it earlier than late.

Subjects' comments on their panic reaction

The success of Schultz's design in simulating a real-life panic situation in the laboratory is revealed in subjects' comments following the experiment when they were asked why they pressed the emergency button or why they had not. Two representative answers follow:

I was panicked at the thought of the increased shock, knowing—or rather imagining—the pain involved. My first thought was "out." I would have gone to nearly any lengths to avoid the pain I was anticipating. (Subject pressed emergency button at 6 seconds.)

I considered the emergency button a last resort. Someone in the experiment had to receive the punishment—no sense in saving one person with the risk of punishing four others (Subject who did not press the emergency button) [pp. 29–30].

Some button pressers were embarrassed, ashamed, and guilty over their panicky behavior and considered themselves "immature, selfish, and expressed disappointment in themselves [p. 31]."

Milgram's study might just as easily have been placed in a chapter on social behavior, for it concerns uniformity reactions or, as some might call them, mass action. But the powerful emotional responses of the subject administering punishing doses of electric shock to his "victim" are what concern us here. "Nervous and [inappropriate] laughter," "full blown and uncontrollable seizures," and subjects who were "observed to sweat, tremble, stutter, bite their lips, groan, and dig their fingernails into their flesh ... characteristic rather than exceptional responses to the experiment [p. 375]," these are the primary data to be examined.

Background

Obedience is as basic an element in the structure of social life as one can point to. Some system of authority is a requirement of all communal living, and it is only the man dwelling in isolation who is not forced to respond, through defiance or submission, to the commands of others. Obedience, as a determinant of behavior, is of particular relevance to our time. It has been reliably established that from 1933 to 1945 millions of innocent persons were systematically slaughtered on command. Gas chambers were built, death camps were guarded, daily quotas of corpses were produced with the same efficiency as the manufacture of appliances. These inhumane policies may have originated in the mind of a single person, but they could only be carried out on a massive scale if a very large number of persons obeyed orders.

Obedience is the psychological mechanism that links individual action to political purpose. It is the dispositional cement that binds men to systems of authority. Facts of recent history and observation in daily life suggest that for many persons obedience may be a deeply ingrained behavior tendency, indeed, a prepotent impulse overriding training in ethics, sympathy, and moral conduct. C. P. Snow (1961) points to its importance when he writes:

"When you think of the long and gloomy history of man, you will find more hideous crimes have been committed in the name of obedience than have ever been committed in the name of rebellion. If you doubt that, read William Shirer's *The Rise and Fall of the Third Reich.* The German Officer Corps were brought up in the most rigorous code of obedience ... in the name of obedience they were party to, and assisted in, the most wicked large-scale actions in the history of the world [p. 24]."

While the particular form of obedience dealt with in the present study has its antecedents in these episodes, it must not be thought all obedience entails acts of aggression against others. Obedience serves numerous productive functions. Indeed, the very life of society is predicated on its existence. Obedience may be ennobling and educative and refer to acts of charity and kindness as well as to destruction.

General procedure

A procedure was devised which seems useful as a tool for studying obedience (Milgram, 1961). It consists of ordering a naive subject to administer electric shock to a victim. A simulated shock generator is used, with 30 clearly marked voltage levels that range from 15 to 450 volts. The instrument bears verbal designations that range from Slight Shock to Danger: Severe Shock. The responses of the victim, who is a trained **confederate** of the experimenter,

*From Stanley Milgram, "Behavioral Study of Obedience," *Journal of Abnormal and Social Psychology,* 1963, **67**(4), 371–378. By permission of the author and publisher.

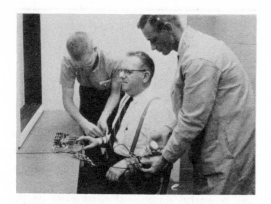
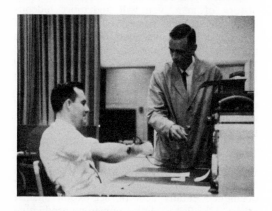

Figure 12.10 Photograph of general set up of Milgram's experiment. Reading from left to right and from top to bottom: (1) shock generator, (2) learner is strapped into chair, (3) subject receives sample shock, (4) subject breaks off experiment, (5) post-experimental interview, (6) reconciliation of subject and learner. (From Stanley Milgram, "Behavioral Study of Obedience," *Journal of Abnormal and Social Psychology,* 1963, **67**(4), 371–378. Copyright 1963 by the American Psychological Association, and reproduced by permission.)

are standardized. The orders to administer shocks are given to the naive subject in the context of a "learning experiment" ostensibly set up to study the effects of punishment on memory. As the experiment proceeds, the naive subject is commanded to administer increasingly more intense shocks to the victim, even to the point of reaching the level marked Danger: Severe Shock. Internal resistances become stronger, and at a certain point the subject refuses to go on with the experiment. Behavior prior to this rupture is considered "obedience," in that the subject complies with the commands of the experimenter. The point of rupture is the act of disobedience. A quantitative value is assigned to the subject's performance based on the maximum intensity shock he is willing to administer before he refuses to participate further. Thus for any particular subject and for any particular experimental condition the degree of obedience may be specified with a numerical value. The crux of the study is to systematically vary the factors believed to alter the degree of obedience to the experimental commands.

The technique allows important variables to be manipulated at several points in the experiment. One may vary aspects of the source of command, content and form of command, instrumentalities for its execution, target object, general social setting, etc. The problem, therefore, is not one of designing increasingly more numerous experimental conditions but of selecting those that best illuminate the *process* of obedience from the sociopsychological standpoint.

Method

Subjects The subjects were 40 males between the ages of 20 and 50, drawn from New Haven and the surrounding communities. Subjects were obtained by a newspaper advertisement and direct mail solicitation. Those who responded to the appeal believed they were to participate in a study of memory and learning at Yale University. A wide range of occupations is represented in the sample. Typical subjects were postal clerks, high school teachers, salesmen, engineers, and laborers. Subjects ranged in educational level from one who had not finished elementary school to those who had doctorate and other professional degrees. They were paid $4.50 for their participation in the experiment. However, subjects were told that payment was simply for coming to the laboratory, and that the money was theirs no matter what happened after they arrived. Table 12.4 shows the proportion of age and occupational types assigned to the experimental condition.

Personnel and Locale The experiment was conducted on the grounds of Yale University in the elegant interaction laboratory. (This detail is relevant to the perceived legitimacy of the experiment. In further variations, the experiment was dissociated from the university, with consequences for performance.) The role of experimenter was played by a 31-year-old high school teacher of biology. His manner was impassive, and his appearance somewhat stern throughout the experiment. He was dressed in a gray technician's coat. The victim was played by a 47-year-old accountant, trained for the role; he was of Irish-American stock, whom most observers found mild mannered and likable.

Procedure One naive subject and one victim (an accomplice) performed in each experiment. A pretext had to be devised that would justify the administration of electric shock by the naive subject. This was effectively accomplished by the cover story. After a general introduction on the presumed relation between punishment and learning, subjects were told:

"But, actually, we know *very little* about the effect of punishment on learning, because almost no truly scientific studies have been made of it in human beings.

"For instance, we don't know how *much* punishment is best for learning—and we don't know how much difference it makes as to who is giving the punishment, whether an adult learns best from a younger or an older person than himself—or many things of that sort.

"So in this study we are bringing together a number of adults of different occupations and ages. And we're asking some of them to be teachers and some of them to be learners.

"We want to find out just what effect different people have on each other as teachers and learners, and also what effect *punishment* will have on learning in this situation.

"Therefore, I'm going to ask one of you to be the teacher here tonight and the other one to be the learner.

Table 12.4

*Distribution of age and occupational types
in the experiment*

Occupations	20–29 Years n	30–39 Years n	40–50 Years n	Percentage of Total (Occupations)
Workers, skilled and unskilled	4	5	6	37.5
Sales, business and white-collar	3	6	7	40.0
Professional	1	5	3	22.5
Percentage of total (Age)	20	40	40	

Note: Total $N = 40$

"Does either of you have a preference?"

Subjects then drew slips of paper from a hat to determine who would be the teacher and who would be the learner in the experiment. The drawing was rigged so that the naive subject was always the teacher and the accomplice always the learner. (Both slips contained the word "Teacher.") Immediately after the drawing, the teacher and learner were taken to an adjacent room and the learner was strapped into an "electric chair" apparatus.

The experimenter explained that the straps were to prevent excessive movement while the learner was being shocked. The effect was to make it impossible for him to escape from the situation. An electrode was attached to the learner's wrist, and electrode paste was applied "to avoid blisters and burns." Subjects were told that the electrode was attached to the shock generator in the adjoining room.

In order to improve credibility, the experimenter declared, in response to a question by the learner: "Although the shocks can be extremely painful, they cause no permanent tissue damage."

Learning task The lesson administered by the subject was a **paired-associate learning** task. The subject read a series of word pairs to the learner, and then read the first word of the pair along with four terms. The learner was to indicate which of the four terms had originally been paired with the first word. He communicated his answer by pressing one of four switches in front of him, which in turn lit up one of four numbered quadrants in an answer box located atop the shock generator.

Shock generator The instrument panel consists of 30 lever switches set in a horizontal line. Each switch is clearly labeled with a voltage designation that ranges from 15 to 450 volts. There is a 15-volt increment from one switch to the next going from left to right. In addition, the following verbal designations are clearly indicated for groups of four switches going from left to right: Slight Shock, Moderate Shock, Strong Shock, Very Strong Shock, Intense Shock, Extreme Intensity Shock, Danger: Severe Shock. (Two switches after this last designation are simply marked XXX.)

Upon depressing a switch: a pilot light corresponding to each switch is illuminated in bright red; an electric buzzing is heard; an electric blue light, labeled "voltage energizer," flashes; the dial on the voltage meter swings to the right; various relay clicks are sounded.

The upper left-hand corner of the generator is labeled Shock Generator, Type ZLB, Dyson Instrument Company, Waltham, Mass. Output 15 Volts–450 Volts.

Details of the instrument were carefully handled to ensure an appearance of authenticity. The panel was engraved by precision industrial engravers, and all components were of high quality. No subject in the experiment suspected that the instrument was merely a simulated shock generator.

Sample shock Each naive subject is given a sample shock on the shock generator, prior to beginning his run as teacher. This shock is always 45 volts, and is applied by pressing the third switch of the generator. The shock is applied to the wrist of the naive subject, and has its source in a 45-volt battery wired into the generator. This further convinces the subject of the authenticity of the generator.

Shock instuctions The subject is told to administer a shock to the learner each time he gives a wrong response. Moreover—and this is the key command—the subject is instructed to "move one level higher on the shock generator each time the learner flashes a wrong answer." He is also instructed to announce the voltage level before administering a shock. This serves to continually remind subjects of the increasing intensity of shocks administered to the learner.

Preliminary and regular run Pretests revealed that the procedure of reading words and administering shocks requires some practice before it can be handled smoothly. Therefore, immediately preceding the regular run, the teacher is given a preliminary series of 10 words to read to the learner. There are three neutral words in the practice series (i.e., words that the learner answers correctly), so that shocks are administered for seven of the words, with the maximum shock at 105 volts (moderate shock). Almost all subjects master the procedure by the time the preliminary run is over.

Subjects are then presented with a second list and are told that the procedure is the same as for the first list; the experimenter adds, however:

"When you get to the bottom of the list, repeat it over again, and continue giving shocks, until the learner has learned all the pairs correctly."

The experimenter instructs the subject to start from 15 volts and increase the shock level one step each time the learner gives a wrong answer.

Feedback from the victim In all conditions the learner gives a predetermined set of responses to the word pair test, based on a schedule of approximately three wrong answers to one correct answer. In the present experimental condition, no vocal response or other sign of protest is heard from the learner until Shock Level 300 is reached. When the 300-volt shock is administered, the learner pounds on the wall of the room in which he is bound to the electric chair. From this point on the learner's answers no longer appear on the four-way panel.

At this juncture subjects ordinarily turn to the experimenter for guidance. The experimenter instructs the subject to treat the absence of a response as a wrong answer and to shock the subject according to the usual schedule. He advises the subjects to allow 5 to 10 seconds before considering no response as a wrong answer and to increase the shock level one step each time the learner fails to respond correctly. The learner's pounding is repeated after the 315-volt shock is administered; afterward he is not heard from, nor do his answers reappear on the four-way signal box.

Experimenter feedback At various points in the experiment the subject may turn to the experimenter for advice on whether he should continue to administer shocks. Or he may indicate that he does not wish to go on. It was important to standardize the experimenter's responses to these inquiries and reactions.

If the subject indicated his unwillingness to go on, the experimenter responded with a sequence of "prods," using as many as necessary to bring the subject into line.

Prod 1: "Please continue" *or* "Please go on."
Prod 2: "The experiment requires that you continue."
Prod 3: "It is absolutely essential that you continue."
Prod 4: "You have no other choice, you *must* go on."

The prods were always made in sequence: Only if Prod 1 had been unsuccessful, could Prod 2 be used. If the subject refused to obey the experimenter after Prod 4, the experiment was terminated. The experimenter's tone of voice was at all times firm, but not impolite. The sequence was begun anew on each occasion that the subject balked or showed reluctance to follow orders.

Special Prods If the subject asked if the learner was liable to suffer permanent physical injury, the experimenter said:

"Although the shocks may be painful, there is no permanent tissue damage, so please go on." (Followed by Prods 2, 3, and 4 *if* necessary.)

If the subject said that the learner did not want to go on, the experimenter replied: "Whether the learner likes it or not, you must go on until he has learned all the word pairs correctly. So please go on." (Followed by Prods 2, 3, and 4 *if* necessary.)

Dependent measures The primary dependent measure for any subject is the maximum shock he administers before he refuses to go any further. In principle, this may vary from 0 (for a subject who refuses to administer even the first shock) to 30 (for a subject who administers the highest shock on the generator). A subject who breaks off the experiment at any point prior to administering the thirtieth shock level is termed a *defiant* subject. One who complies with experimental commands fully, and proceeds to administer all shock levels commanded, is termed an *obedient* subject.

Further records With few exceptions experimental sessions were recorded on magnetic tape. Occasional photographs were taken through one-way mirrors. Notes were kept on any unusual behavior occurring during the course of the experiments. On occasion additional observers were directed to write objective descriptions of the subjects' behavior. The latency and duration of shocks were measured by accurate timing devices.

Interview and dehoax Following the experiment, subjects were interviewed; open-ended questions, projective measures, and attitude scales were employed. After the interview, procedures were undertaken to ensure that the subject would leave the laboratory in a state of well-being. A friendly reconciliation was arranged between the subject and the victim, and an effort was made to reduce any tensions that arose as a result of the experiment.

Results

Preliminary notions Before giving an account of the experimental results, it is instructive to consider how persons predict others will perform when commanded to administer powerful shocks to another person. Fourteen Yale seniors, all psychology majors, were provided with a detailed description of the experimental situation. They were asked to reflect carefully on it and to predict the behavior of 100 hypothetical subjects. More specifically, they were instructed to plot the distribution of obedience of "100 Americans of diverse occupations, and ranging in age from 20 to 50 years," who were placed in the experimental situation.

There was considerable agreement among the respondents on the expected behavior of hypothetical subjects. All respondents predicted that only an insignificant minority would go through to the end of the shock series. (The estimates ranged from 0 to 3 percent; i.e., the most "pessimistic" member of the class predicted that of 100 persons, 3 would continue through to the most potent shock available on the shock generator—450 volts.) The class mean was 1.2 percent. The question was also posed informally to colleagues of the author, and the most general feeling was that few if any subjects would go beyond the designation Very Strong Shock.

Result of experiment I: Subjects accept situation. With few exceptions subjects were convinced of the reality of the experimental situation, that they were administering shocks to another person, and the most potent shocks were extremely painful. In the postexperimental interview subjects were asked: "How painful to the learner were the last few shocks that you administered to him?" Subjects were instructed to indicate their answers on a printed 14-point scale ranging from "Not at all painful" to "Extremely painful." The modal response was 14 (Extremely painful) with the mean at 13.42.

Signs of extreme tension Many subjects showed signs of nervousness in the experimental situation, and especially upon administering the more powerful shocks. In a large number of cases the degree of tension reached extremes that are rarely seen in sociopsychological laboratory studies. Subjects were observed to sweat, tremble, stutter, bite their lips, groan, and dig their fingernails into their flesh. These were characteristic rather than exceptional responses to the experiment.

One sign of tension was the regular occurrence of nervous laughing fits. Fourteen of the 40 subjects showed definite signs of nervous laughter and smiling. The laughter seemed entirely out of place, even bizarre. Full-blown, uncontrollable seizures were observed for 3 subjects. On one occasion we observed a seizure so violently convulsive that it was necessary to call a halt to the experiment. The

Table 12.5

Distribution of break-off points

Verbal designation and voltage indication	Number of subjects for whom this was maximum shock
Slight Shock	
15	0
30	0
45	0
60	0
Moderate Shock	
75	0
90	0
105	0
120	0
Strong Shock	
135	0
150	0
165	0
180	0
Very Strong Shock	
195	0
210	0
225	0
240	0
Intense Shock	
255	0
270	0
285	0
300	5
Extreme Intensity Shock	
315	4
330	2
345	1
360	1
Danger: Severe Shock	
375	1
390	0
405	0
420	0
XXX	
435	0
450	26

subject, a 46-year-old encyclopedia salesman, was seriously embarrassed by his untoward and uncontrollable behavior. In the postexperimental interviews subjects took pains to point out that they were not sadistic types and that the laughter did not mean they enjoyed shocking the victim.

Distribution of scores   It had been conjectured that persons would not, in general, agree to administer shocks beyond the level designated as Very Strong Shock. The distribution of maximum shocks for this experiment is shown in Table 12.5. The obtained distribution of scores deviates radically from the prediction.

Upon command of the experimenter, each of the 40 subjects went beyond the expected break-off point. No subject stopped prior to administering Shock Level 20. (At this level—300 volts—the victim kicks on the wall and no longer provides answers to the teacher's multiple-choice questions.)

Of the 40 subjects, 5 refused to obey the experimental commands beyond the 300-volt level; 4 more subjects administered one further shock, and then refused to go on. Two broke off at the 330-volt level, and 1 each at 345, 360, and 375 volts. Thus a total of 14 subjects defied the experimenter. It is instructive to reprint their remarks at the point of defiance, as transcribed from the tape recordings:

(0124) "I think he's trying to communicate, he's knocking...Well it's not fair to shock the guy...these are terrific volts. I don't think this is very humane...Oh, I can't go on with this; no, this isn't right. It's a hell of an experiment. The guy is suffering in there. No, I don't want to go on. This is crazy." (Subject refused to administer more shocks.)

(0123) "He's banging in there. I'm gonna chicken out. I'd like to continue, but I can't do that to a man...I'm sorry I can't do that to a man. I'll hurt his heart. You take your check... No really, I couldn't do it."

These subjects were frequently in a highly agitated and even angered state. Sometimes verbal protest was at a minimum, and the subject simply got up from his chair in front of the shock generator and indicated that he wished to leave the laboratory.

Of the 40 subjects, 26 obeyed the orders of the experimenter to the end, proceeding to punish the victim until they reached the most potent shock available on the shock generator. At that point the experimenter called a halt to the session. (The maximum shock is labeled 450 volts and is two steps beyond the designation. Danger: Severe Shock.) Although obedient subjects continued to administer shocks, they often did so under extreme stress. Some expressed reluctance to administer shocks beyond the 300-volt level and displayed fears similar to those who defied the experimenter; yet they obeyed.

After the maximum shocks had been delivered and the experimenter called a halt to the proceedings, many obedient subjects heaved sighs of relief, mopped their brows, rubbed their fingers over their eyes, or nervously fumbled cigarettes. Some shook their heads, apparently in regret. Some subjects had remained calm throughout the experiment and displayed only minimal signs of tension from beginning to end.

Discussion

The experiment yielded two findings that were surprising. The first finding concerns the sheer strength of obedience tendencies manifested in this situation. Subjects have learned from childhood that it is a fundamental breach of moral conduct to hurt another person against his will. Yet 26 subjects abandon this tenet in following the instructions of an authority who has no special powers to enforce his commands. To disobey would bring no material loss to the subject: no punishment would ensue. It is clear from the remarks and outward behavior of many participants that in punishing the victim they are often acting against their own values. Subjects often expressed deep disapproval of shocking a man in the face of his objections, and others denounced it as stupid and senseless. Yet the majority complied with the experimental commands. This outcome was surprising from two perspectives: first, from the standpoint of predictions made in the questionnaire described earlier. (Here, however, it is possible that the remoteness of the respondents from the actual situation, and the difficulty of conveying to them the concrete details of the experiment, could account for the serious underestimation of obedience.)

But the results were also unexpected to persons who observed the experiment in progress, through one-way mirrors. Observers often uttered expressions of disbelief upon seeing a subject administer more powerful shocks to the victim. These persons had a full acquaintance with the details of the situation and yet systematically underestimated the amount of obedience that subjects would display.

The second unanticipated effect was the extraordinary tension generated by the procedures. One might suppose that a subject would simply break off or continue as his conscience dictated. Yet, this is very far from what happened. There were striking reactions of tension and emotional strain. One observer related:

"I observed a mature and initially poised businessman enter the laboratory smiling and confident. Within 20 minutes he was reduced to a twitching, stuttering wreck, who was rapidly approaching a point of nervous collapse. He constantly pulled on his earlobe and twisted his hands. At one point he pushed his fist into his forehead and muttered: 'Oh God, let's stop it.' And yet he continued to respond to every word of the experimenter and obeyed to the end."

Any understanding of the phenomenon of obedience must rest on an analysis of the particular conditions in which it occurs. The following features of the experiment go some distance in explaining the high amount of obedience observed in the situation.

1. The experiment is sponsored by and takes place on the grounds of an institution of unimpeachable reputation, Yale University. It may be reasonably presumed that the personnel are competent and reputable. The importance of this background authority is now being studied by conducting a series of experiments outside of New Haven, and without any visible ties to the university.

2. The experiment is, on the face of it, designed to attain a worthy purpose—advancement of knowledge about learning and memory. Obedience occurs not as an end in itself but as an instrumental element in a situation that the subject construes as significant, and meaningful. He may not be able to see its full significance, but he may properly assume that the experimenter does.

3. The subject perceives that the victim has voluntarily submitted to the authority system of the experimenter. He is not (at first) an unwilling captive impressed for involuntary

service. He has taken the trouble to come to the laboratory presumably to aid the experimental research. That he later becomes an involuntary subject does not alter the fact that, initially, he consented to participate without qualification. Thus he has in some degree incurred an obligation toward the experimenter.

4. The subject, too, has entered the experiment voluntarily, and perceives himself under obligation to aid the experimenter. He has made a commitment and to disrupt the experiment is a repudiation of this initial promise of aid.

5. Certain features of the procedure strengthen the subject's sense of obligation to the experimenter. For one, he has been paid for coming to the laboratory. In part this is canceled out by the experimenter's statement that:

"Of course, as in all experiments, the money is yours simply for coming to the laboratory. From this point on, no matter what happens, the money is yours."

6. From the subject's standpoint, the fact that he is the teacher and the other man the learner is purely a chance consequence (it is determined by drawing lots) and he, the subject, ran the same risk as the other man in being assigned the role of learner. Since the assignment of positions in the experiment was achieved by fair means, the learner is deprived of any basis of complaint on this count. (A similar situation obtains in Army units, in which—in the absence of volunteers—a particularly dangerous mission may be assigned by drawing lots, and the unlucky soldier is expected to bear his misfortune with sportsmanship.)

7. There is, at best, ambiguity with regard to the prerogatives of a psychologist and the corresponding rights of his subject. There is a vagueness of expectation concerning what a psychologist may require of his subject, and when he is overstepping acceptable limits. Moreover, the experiment occurs in a closed setting and thus provides no opportunity for the subject to remove these ambiguities by discussion with others. There are few standards that seem directly applicable to the situation, which is a novel one for most subjects.

8. The subjects are assured that the shocks administered to the subject are "painful but not dangerous." Thus they assume that the discomfort caused the victim is momentary, while the scientific gains resulting from the experiment are enduring.

9. Through Shock Level 20 the victim continues to provide answers on the signal box. The subject may construe this as a sign that the victim is still willing to "play the game." It is only after Shock Level 20 that the victim repudiates the rules completely, refusing to answer further.

These features help to explain the high amount of obedience obtained in this experiment. Many of the arguments raised need not remain matters of speculation but can be reduced to testable propositions to be confirmed or disproved by further experiments.

The following features of the experiment concern the nature of the conflict which the subject faces.

10. The subject is placed in a position in which he must respond to the competing demands of two persons: the experimenter and the victim. The conflict must be resolved by meeting the demands of one or the other; satisfaction of the victim and the experimenter are mutually exclusive. Moreover, the resolution must take the form of a highly visible action, that of continuing to shock the victim or breaking off the experiment. Thus the subject is forced into a public conflict that does not permit any completely satisfactory solution.

11. While the demands of the experimenter carry the weight of scientific authority, the demands of the victim spring from his personal experience of pain and suffering. The two claims need not be regarded as equally pressing and legitimate. The experimenter seeks an abstract scientific datum; the victim cries out for relief from physical suffering caused by the subject's actions.

12. The experiment gives the subject little time for reflection. The conflict comes on rapidly. It is only minutes after the subject has been seated before the shock generator that the victim begins his protests. Moreover, the subject perceives that he has gone through but two-thirds of the shock levels at the time the subject's first protests are heard. Thus he understands that the conflict will have a persistent aspect to it and may well become more intense as increasingly more powerful shocks are required. The rapidity with which the conflict descends on the subject and his realization that it is predictably recurrent may well be sources of tension to him.

13. At a more general level, the conflict stems from the opposition of two deeply ingrained behavior dispositions: first, the disposition not to harm other people and, second, the tendency to obey those whom we perceive to be legitimate authorities.

Summary

This article describes a procedure for the study of destructive obedience in the laboratory. It consists of ordering a naive S to administer increasingly more severe punishment to a victim in the context of a learning experiment. Punishment is administered by means of a shock generator with 30 graded switches ranging from Slight Shock to Danger: Severe Shock. The victim is a confederate of the E. The primary dependent variable is the maximum shock the S is willing to administer before he refuses to continue further. [Out of 40 subjects,] 26 Ss obeyed the experimental commands fully and administered the highest shock on the generator; 14 Ss broke off the experiment at some point after the victim protested and refused to provide further answers. The procedure created extreme levels of nervous tension in some Ss. Profuse sweating, trembling, and stuttering were typical expressions of this emotional disturbance. One unexpected sign of tension—yet to be explained—was the regular occurrence of nervous laughter, which in some Ss developed into uncontrollable seizures. The variety of interesting behavioral dynamics observed in the experiment, the reality of the situation for the S, and the possibility of parametric variation within the framework of the procedure, point to the fruitfulness of further study.

Comments on "behavioral study of obedience"

The implications of Milgram's experiment, with its reference to gas chambers and death camps, are shocking. But Milgram's experiment itself has raised questions of propriety and ethics. Baumrind (1964) has criticized Milgram's study for a number of reasons. For example, she considers the laboratory an unsuitable setting for studying obedience which occurs in natural social settings. Secondly, she objects to the fact that the participating subjects were made anxious, embarrassed, or otherwise hurt. Thirdly, she feels that the public reputation of psychology could be damaged by such procedures. Certainly Milgram's study has raised many eyebrows as well as generating a wide variety of affective reactions.

Shirer: Dr. Rascher's
experiments*

Man's capacity for cruelty and destructive obedience manifests itself in the following account from William L. Shirer's *The Rise and Fall of the Third Reich.* In Germany during World War II, Dr. Sigmund Rascher conducted decompression and freezing experiments on human subjects at the Dachau concentration camp. A large number of people, including many medical doctors, cooperated or acquiesced in his research. In the context of our discussion of emotion, our immediate focus is on the responses of Rascher's victims, but the broader implications of this report will not escape the reader.

It was this Dr. Sigmund Rascher who seems to have been responsible for the more sadistic of the medical experiments in the first place. This horrible quack had attracted the attention of Himmler, among whose obsessions was the breeding of more and more superior Nordic offspring, through reports in S.S. circles that Frau Rascher had given birth to three children after passing the age of forty-eight, although in truth the Raschers had simply kidnaped them at suitable intervals from an orphanage.

In the spring of 1941, Dr. Rascher, who was attending a special medical course at Munich given by the Luftwaffe, had a brain storm. On May 15, 1941, he wrote Himmler about it. He had found to his horror that research on the effect of high altitudes on flyers was at a stand-still because "no tests with human material had yet been possible as such experiments are very dangerous and nobody volunteers for them."

Can you make available two or three professional criminals for these experiments ... The experiments, by which the subjects can of course die, would take place with my co-operation.

The S.S. Fuehrer replied within a week that "prisoners will, of course, be made available gladly for the high-flight research."

They were, and Dr. Rascher went to work. The results may be seen from his own reports and from those of others, which showed up at Nuremberg and at the subsequent trial of the S.S. doctors.

Dr. Rascher's own findings are a model of scientific jargon. For the high-altitude tests he moved the Air Force's decompression chamber at Munich to the nearby Dachau concentration camp where human guinea pigs were readily available. Air was pumped out of the contraption so that the oxygen and air pressure at high altitudes could be simulated. Dr. Rascher then made his observations, of which the following one is typical.

*Quoted material is from William L. Shirer, *The Rise and Fall of the Third Reich* (New York: Simon and Schuster, 1960), 984–991. Copyright © 1959, 1960 by William L. Shirer. Reprinted by permission of Simon & Schuster, Inc. Source notes have been omitted (see original).

The third test was without oxygen at the equivalent of 29,400 feet altitude conducted on a 37-year-old Jew in good general condition. Respiration continued for 30 minutes. After four minutes the TP [test person] began to perspire and roll his head.

After five minutes spasms appeared; between the sixth and tenth minute respiration increased in frequency, the TP losing consciousness. From the eleventh to the thirtieth minute respiration slowed down to three inhalations per minute, only to cease entirely at the end of that period...About half an hour after breathing had ceased, an autopsy was begun.

An Austrian inmate, Anton Pacholegg, who worked in Dr. Rascher's office, has described the "experiments" less scientifically.

I have personally seen through the observation window of the decompression chamber when a prisoner inside would stand a vacuum until his lungs ruptured...They would go mad and pull out their hair in an effort to relieve the pressure. They would tear their heads and face with their fingers and nails in an attempt to maim themselves in their madness. They would beat the walls with their hands and head and scream in an effort to relieve pressure on their eardrums. These cases usually ended in the death of the subject.

Some two hundred prisoners were subjected to this experiment before Dr. Rascher was finished with it. Of these, according to the testimony at the "Doctors' Trial," about eighty were killed outright and the remainder executed somewhat later so that no tales would be told. This particular research project was finished in May 1942, at which time Field Marshal Erhard Milch of the Luftwaffe conveyed Goering's "thanks" to Himmler for Dr. Rascher's pioneer experiments. A little later, on October 10, 1942, Lieutenant General Dr. Hippke, Medical Inspector of the Air Force, tendered to Himmler "in the name of German aviation medicine and research" his "obedient gratitude" for "the Dachau experiments." However, he thought, there was one omission in them. They had not taken into account the extreme cold which an aviator faces at high altitudes. To rectify this omission the Luftwaffe, he informed Himmler, was building a decompression chamber "equipped with full

refrigeration and with a nominal altitude of 100,000 feet. Freezing experiments," he added, "along different lines are still under way at Dachau."

Indeed they were. And again Dr. Rascher was in the vanguard. But some of his doctor colleagues were having qualms. Was it Christian to do what Dr. Rascher was doing? Apparently a few German Luftwaffe medics were beginning to have their doubts. When Himmler heard of this he was infuriated and promptly wrote Field Marshal Milch protesting about the difficulties caused by "Christian medical circles" in the Air Force. He begged the Luftwaffe Chief of Staff to release Rascher from the Air Force medical corps so that he could be transferred to the S.S. He suggested that they find a "non-Christian physician, who should be honorable as a scientist," to pass on Dr. Rascher's valuable works. In the meantime Himmler emphasized that he

personally assumed the responsibility for supplying asocial individuals and criminals who deserve only to die from concentration camps for these experiments.

Dr. Rascher's "freezing experiments" were of two kinds: first, to see how much cold a human being could endure before he dies; and second, to find the best means of rewarming a person who still lived after being exposed to extreme cold. Two methods were selected to freeze a man: dumping him into a tank of ice water or leaving him out in the snow, completely naked, overnight during winter. Rascher's reports to Himmler on his "freezing" and "warming" experiments are voluminous; an example or two will give the tenor. One of the earliest ones was made on September 10, 1942.

The TPs were immersed in water in full flying uniform...with hood. A life jacket prevented sinking. The experiments were conducted at water temperatures between 36.5 and 53.5 degrees Fahrenheit. In the first test series the back of the head and the brain stem were above water. In another series the back of the neck and cerebellum were submerged. Temperatures as low as 79.5 in the stomach and 79.7 in the rectum were recorded electrically. Fatalities occurred only when the medulla and the cerebellum were chilled.

In autopsies of such fatalities large quantities of free blood, up to a pint, were always found inside the cranial cavity. The heart regularly showed extreme distention of the right chamber. The TPs in such tests inevitably died when body temperature had declined to 82.5, despite all rescue attempts. These autopsy findings plainly prove the importance of a heated head and neck protector for the foam suit now in the process of development.

A table which Dr. Rascher appended covers six "Fatal Cases" and shows the water temperatures, body temperature on removal from water, body temperature at death, the length of stay in the water and the time it took the patient to die. The toughest man endured in the ice water for one hundred minutes, the weakest for fifty-three minutes.

Walter Neff, a camp inmate who served as Dr. Rascher's medical orderly, furnished the "Doctors' Trial" with a layman's description of one water-freezing test.

It was the worst experiment ever made. Two Russian officers were brought from the prison barracks. Rascher had them stripped and they had to go into the vat naked. Hour after hour went by, and whereas usually unconsciousness from the cold set in after sixty minutes at the latest, the two men in this case still responded fully after two and a half hours. All appeals to Rascher to put them to sleep by injection were fruitless. About the third hour one of the Russians said to the other, 'Comrade, please tell the officer to shoot us.' The other replied that he expected no mercy from this Fascist dog. The two shook hands with a 'Farewell, Comrade'...These words were translated to Rascher by a young Pole, though in a somewhat different form. Rascher went to his office. The young Pole at once tried to chloroform the two victims, but Rascher came back at once, threatening us with his gun...The test lasted at least five hours before death supervened.

The nominal "chief" of the initial cold-water experiments was a certain Dr. Holzloehner, Professor of Medicine at the University of Kiel, assisted by a Dr. Finke, and after working with Rascher for a couple of months they believed that they had exhausted the experimental possibilities. The three physicians thereupon drew up a thirty-two-page top-secret report to the Air Force entitled "Freezing Experiments with Human Beings" and called a meeting of German

scientists at Nuremberg for October 26–27, 1942, to hear and discuss their findings. The subject of the meeting was "Medical Questions in Marine and Winter Emergencies." According to the testimony at the "Doctors' Trial," ninety-five German scientists, including some of the most eminent men in the field, participated, and though the three doctors left no doubt that a good many human beings had been done to death in the experiments there were no questions put as to this and no protests therefore made.

Professor Holzloehner and Dr. Finke bowed out of the experiments at this time but the persevering Dr. Rascher carried on alone from October 1942 until May of the following year. He wanted, among other things, to pursue experiments in what he called "dry freezing." Auschwitz, he wrote to Himmler,

is much better suited for such tests than Dachau because it is colder there and because the size of the grounds causes less of a stir in the camp. (The test persons yell when they freeze.)

For some reason the change of locality could not be arranged, so Dr. Rascher went ahead with his studies at Dachau, praying for some real winter weather.

Thank God, we have had another intense cold snap at Dachau [he wrote Himmler in the early spring of 1943]. *Some people remained out in the open for 14 hours at 21 degrees, attaining an interior temperature of 77 degrees, with peripheral frostbite...*

At the "Doctors' Trial" the witness Neff again provided a layman's description of the "dry-freezing" experiments of his chief.

A prisoner was placed naked on a stretcher outside the barracks in the evening. He was covered with a sheet, and every hour a bucket of cold water was poured over him. The test person lay out in the open like this into the morning. Their temperatures were taken.

Later Dr. Rascher said it was a mistake to cover the subject with a sheet and to drench him with water...In the future the test persons must not be covered. The next experiment was a test on ten prisoners who were exposed in turn, likewise naked.

As the prisoners slowly froze, Dr. Rascher or his assistant would record temperatures, heart action, respiration and so on. The cries of the suffering often rent the night.

Initially [Neff explained to the court] *Rascher forbade these tests to be made in a state of anesthesia. But the test persons made such a racket that it was impossible for Rascher to continue these tests without anesthetic.*

The TPs (test persons) were left to die, as Himmler said they deserved to, in the ice-water tanks or lying naked on the ground outside the barracks at Dachau on a winter evening. If they survived they were shortly exterminated. But the brave German flyers and sailors, for whose benefit the experiments were ostensibly carried out, and who might find themselves ditched in the icy waters of the Arctic Ocean or marooned in some frozen waste above the Arctic Circle in Norway, Finland or northern Russia, had to be saved if possible. The inimitable Dr. Rascher therefore took to performing on his human guinea pigs at Dachau what he termed "warming experiments." What was the best method, he wanted to know, for warming a frozen man and thus possibly saving his life?

Heinrich Himmler, never backward in offering "practical" solutions to his corps of busy scientists, suggested to Rascher that warming by "animal heat" be tried, but at first the doctor did not think much of the idea. "Warming by animal heat—the bodies of animals or women—is much too slow," he wrote the S. S. chief. But Himmler kept after him.

I am very curious [he wrote Rascher] *about the experiments with animal heat. Personally I believe these experiments may bring the best and the most sustained results.*

Though skeptical, Dr. Rascher was not the man to ignore a suggestion from the leader of the S.S. He promptly embarked on a series of the most grotesque "experiments" of all, recording them for posterity in every morbid detail. Four inmates from the women's concentration camps at Ravensbrueck were sent to him at Dachau. However there was something about one of them—they were classified as prostitutes —that disturbed the doctor and he so reported to his superiors.

One of the women assigned showed impeccably Nordic racial characteristics...I asked the girl why she had volunteered for brothel service and she replied, "To get out of the concentration camp." When I objected that it was shameful to volunteer as a brothel girl, I was advised, "Better half a year in a brothel than half a year in the concentration camp..."

My racial conscience is outraged by the prospect of exposing to racially inferior concentration camp elements a girl who is outwardly pure Nordic...For this reason I decline to use this girl for my experimental purposes.

But he used others, whose hair was less fair and the eyes less blue. His findings were duly reported to Himmler in a report marked "Secret" on February 12, 1942.

The test persons were chilled in the familiar way—dressed or undressed—in cold water at various temperatures...Removal from the water took place at a rectal temperature of 86 degrees.

In eight cases the test persons were placed between two naked women on a wide bed. The women were instructed to snuggle up to the chilled person as closely as possible. The three persons were then covered with blankets...

Once the test persons regained consciousness, they never lost it again, quickly grasping their situation and nestling close to the naked bodies of the women. The rise of body temperature then proceeded at approximately the same speed as with test persons warmed by being swathed in blankets...An exception was formed by four test persons who practiced sexual intercourse between 86 and 89.5 degrees. In these persons, after coitus, a very swift temperature rise ensued, comparable to that achieved by means of a hot-water bath.

Dr. Rascher found, somewhat to his surprise, that one woman warmed a frozen man faster than two women.

I attribute this to the fact that in warming by means of one woman personal inhibitions are avoided and the woman clings more closely to the chilled person. Here too, return of full consciousness was notably rapid. In the case of only one person did consciousness fail to return and only a slight degree of warming was recorded. This test person died with symptoms of a brain hemorrhage, later confirmed by autopsy.

Summing up, this murderous hack concluded that warming up a "chilled" man with women "proceeds very slowly" and that hot baths were more efficacious.

Only test persons [he concluded] *whose physical state permitted sexual intercourse warmed up surprisingly fast and also showed a surprisingly rapid return of full bodily well-being.*

According to the testimony at the "Doctors' Trial" some four hundred "freezing" experiments were performed on three hundred persons of whom between eighty and ninety died directly as a result thereof, and the rest, except for a few, were bumped off subsequently, some of them having been driven insane. Dr. Rascher himself, incidentally, was not around to testify at this trial. He continued his bloody labors on various new projects, too numerous to mention, until May 1944, when he and his wife were arrested by the S.S.—not for his murderous "experiments," it seems, but on the charge that he and his wife had practiced deceit about how their children came into the world. Such treachery Himmler, with his worship of German mothers, could not brook—he had sincerely believed that Frau Rascher had begun to bear her three children at the age of forty-eight and he was outraged when he learned that she had kidnaped them. So Dr. Rascher was incarcerated in the political bunker at his familiar Dachau camp and his wife was carted off to Ravensbrueck, from which the doctor had procured his prostitutes for the "warming" tests. Neither survived, and it is believed that Himmler himself, in one of the last acts of his life, ordered their execution. They might have made awkward witnesses.

A number of such awkward witnesses did survive to stand trial. Seven of them were condemned to death and hanged, defending their lethal experiments to the last as patriotic acts which served the Fatherland. Dr. Herta Oberheuser, the only woman defendant at the "Doctors' Trial," was given twenty years. She had admitted giving lethal injections to "five or six" Polish women among the hundreds who suffered the tortures of the damned in a variety of "experiments" at Ravensbrueck. A number of doctors, such as the notorious Pokorny, who had wanted to sterilize millions of the enemy, were acquitted. A few were contrite. At a second trial of medical underlings Dr. Edwin Katzenellenbogen, a former member of the faculty of the Harvard Medical School, asked the court for the death sentence. "You have placed the mark of Cain on my forehead," he exclaimed. "Any physician who committed the crimes I am charged with deserves to be killed." He was given life imprisonment.

Chapter summary

In the present chapter I have described two classes of psychological events, feelings and emotional reactions. I suggested that the terms *feelings* and *affective reactions* describe the diffuse, autonomic responses, such as blushing, breathing, blood pressure, and heart rate involvement. I have treated feelings as being largely adaptive and functional. **Emotions** were designated as disruptive, atypical, aborted activities, such as stuttering or panic.

Studies showed that biotelemetry opens up vast areas of the organism for possible psychological involvement in his milieu in the same way that the X-ray did for medical research. Hess's pupillometry research adds another valuable instrumental technique for affective study. Even at this stage, both lines of work demonstrate how every nook and cranny of the organism can participate in research on the feelings.

Gantt's work on "effect of person" proves the ubiquity and specificity of the stimuli that elicit affective responses. His concept of schizokinesis shows the specificity of affect on the response side. Different components of a conditioned response do not necessarily share the same destiny, for we saw the survival of a cardiac response and extinction of its motor component. The long-time retention of a conditioned galvanic skin response has been demonstrated, and even the lowly cockroach was seen to suffer from anxiety tension.

A simulated panic situation, Milgram's daring laboratory investigation of destructive obedience, and a grim excerpt from Shirer's *The Rise and Fall of the Third Reich* concluded our study of the area of emotions.

13

Learning: Theory and application

Anyone attempting to keep up with the proliferation of learning studies in recent years must inevitably succumb to a feeling of hopelessness. The diversity and specificity of the studies frustrate efforts to acquire even a nodding acquaintance with the field, let alone a thorough knowledge of it. In the past five years, psychologists have produced thousands of articles based on studies of learning—naturalistic studies, laboratory studies, clinical studies, studies involving various organisms from flatworms to people.

When I began to organize material for the present chapter, the mere size of my collection of articles overwhelmed me. Then it occurred to me that I could exclude those articles expounding such basic matters as the principles of operant and classical conditioning. These topics, after all, are adequately covered in introductory texts and/or lectures. But after that happy thought, I had a *déjà vu* experience as I went through the remaining material and recalled how every prior chapter in the present volume was permeated with learning. How could I organize a meaningful separate chapter on the topic? Indeed, isn't learning truly co-extensive with psychology?

Abandoning myself to **free association** and random observation, I spotted on my book shelves a number of volumes that forced me to focus on the tremendous explosion of research work not only in learning but also in applications of learning research, particularly in the **behavior therapies.** Here are the titles of those books —a fragmentary sampling of the literature: *Social Learning and Personality Development* by Albert Bandura and Richard H. Walters (1963), *Conditioning Techniques in Clinical Practice and Research* by Cyril M. Franks (1964), *Early Behavior: Comparative and Developmental Approaches* by Harold W. Stevenson, Eckhard H. Hess, and Harriet L. Rheingold (1967), *Learning and Instinct in Animals* by W. H. Thorpe (1964), *Control of Human Behavior* by Roger Ulrich and Thomas Stachnik (1966), *The Experimental Analysis of Behavior* by Thom Verhave (1966), and *The Conditioning Therapies* by Joseph Wolpe, Andrew Salter, and L. J. Reyna (1964).

Further thought along this line made me realize how the recent, rapid expansion of research in learning, particularly operant conditioning, permitted applications never before imagined, especially in the behavior therapies. This realization set the theme for the present chapter: the interplay of theory and practice. So, starting with an experiment on "learning to learn," we go on to studies that show applications of learning theory to behavior modification and to studies that lead finally, to the development of a psychological technology derived from established principles.

1

*Dixon: Pattern discrimination
and learning-to-learn
in a pony**

America's horse population is increasing and has now surpassed its preautomobile level. The majority of these horses have been trained to make many complex behavioral responses under human control. It is not particularly difficult to establish such responses in horses, mules, and donkeys. However, closely related species, such as the wild ass and the zebra, are extremely resistant to similar training. Despite the academic interest inherent in behavioral study of the horse family and the increasing availability of subjects, modern psychology has largely ignored this area in experimental research. An examination of *Psychological Abstracts* for 1946 through 1965 reveals only 12 studies of horses and related species; all but 3 are unavailable in English. Such neglect is surprising when one considers that the horse's economic value, unlike that of other domestic animals, lies in the ease with which its natural behavior can be modified and adapted to human purposes. The frequent appearance of "trick" horses in the entertainment field suggests that horses readily learn to respond to subtle visual, auditory, and tactile cues. Yet there is little formal

knowledge of the extent of these perceptual abilities. The following brief account of pattern discrimination, learning set, and retention in a pony is above all an attempt to show the feasibility of equine behavioral research.

Subject and procedure

The subject was Pecos, a 7-year-old gelding, who stands only 43 inches at the shoulder. He had previously been used only for occasional riding and driving, having proved too spirited for a child's mount.

The patterns that I required him to learn were those used by Rensch (1956) for his studies of the intellectual capacity of a young Indian elephant. Figure 13.1 shows the 20 pairs of patterns used. The pony was taught to choose the one on the left in each pair. Thirteen of the patterns were entirely black and white, 2 had additional small areas of color, and 5 were mostly in color. The stimuli ranged from a cross versus a circle and narrow bands versus wide bands to the letter L versus the letter R and a green leaf versus a yellow crescent.

The stimuli, mounted on an 8- by 10-inch illustration board, were presented to the pony in a pair of wooden frames, each of which had a white plastic ball attached to one corner by a short wire. The cards slid into place easily and could be changed rapidly. Figure 13.2 shows the experimental setup.

Testing was generally conducted outdoors in a large paddock, with the pony

*Published here for the first time. By Jane C. Dixon, Behavior Genetics Laboratory, Department of Psychology, Western Reserve University. All rights reserved. (Presented at the Midwestern Psychological Association Convention, Chicago, May 1966. This research was supported in part by training grant 5T1 MH-675807 from the National Institute of Mental Health, U.S. Public Health Service.)(I would like to thank Mr. and Mrs. Albert Hennig of Happy Hill Farm, Chagrin Falls, Ohio, for their generous cooperation in making their pony and facilities freely available to me for this study.   J.C.D.)

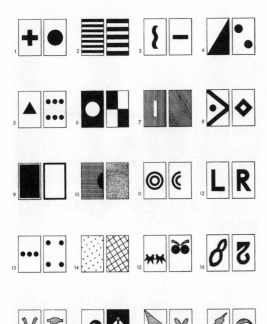

Figure 13.1 Twenty pairs of stimuli that Pecos was required to discriminate. The one on the left of each pair shown had to be selected. Note the difficult discrimination demanded in some pairs. (From B. Rensch, "The Intelligence of Elephants," Copyright © 1957 by *Scientific American,* Inc. All rights reserved.)

separated from the apparatus by a bar at about his chest level. On rainy days sessions were held in the barn. The frames were laid flat on a low bench just beyond the restraining bar so that the pony could reach them easily. Pecos indicated his choices by touching one of the balls with his nose. A pair of patterns was presented simultaneously, with the correct pattern alternating from right to left according to a Gellermann series (Gellermann, 1933). Between trials I removed the frames and cards from the bench and out of the pony's reach.

When Pecos made a correct choice, I rewarded him with a small piece of carrot before removing the stimuli; when his

choice was incorrect, I removed the stimuli immediately. After about 30 sessions the pony attended to the testing voluntarily, and it was no longer necessary to tie him to the restraining bar to prevent him from leaving the field.

Pecos was taught the 20 pairs in 87 daily sessions, each of which consisted of about 100 trials and lasted from 15 to 20 minutes. The criterion for learning was set at less than eight errors, that is, 15 percent in 50 consecutive trials. I gave him periodic reviews of the pairs he had already learned.

Results

Figure 13.3 shows the number of errors the pony made on the first 100 trials for each pair of stimuli. The improvement in Pecos' learning performance was impressive. He needed almost a thousand trials to reach the learning criterion for the first pair, but he learned each successive pair more rapidly until, from the sixth pair on, he made less than 15 percent errors in the first 50 trials. After the first 2 months of training (70 sessions), Pecos had learned 10 pairs, but it took him only 17 sessions to learn the remaining 10 pairs. We see that at first Pecos' performance was erratic; after the fourth pair, however, his performance improved markedly, and his errors soon stabilized at about 10 percent.

After Pecos had learned the twentieth pair of patterns to criterion, he was given a final test on all the pairs at once. For six sessions of 100 trials each, he was presented with the 20 pairs of stimuli, one after the other, in random order. He made 92.5 percent correct choices in the 600 trials, and his errors were distributed rather evenly among the six sessions.

The pony was retested after 1 month, 3 months, and 6 months on all the pairs. He was still rewarded for correct choices to

Figure 13.2 Learning to learn. Pecos making the proper pattern discrimination. (Photo courtesy of Miss Jane C. Dixon.)

prevent extinguishing his responses through nonreinforcement. His rate of correct choices decreased to 81 percent after 1 month, 78 percent after 3 months, and 77.5 percent after 6 months. Thus his greatest learning loss occurred in the first month after learning. In the subsequent 5 months his accuracy rate dropped only 3.5 percent. His total learning loss over 6 months was 15 percent. His errors on the retests were distributed among all the pairs. However, comparing his performance on the first five pairs to that on the last five, we find that he made 24 percent errors on the first group and only 17 percent errors on the last group.

Discussion

Pecos' learning performance conforms to Harlow's (1949) description of the phenomenon he called **"learning set** formation." He observed that animals learn not only specific tasks but also that they "learn to learn"; that is, they learn general solutions to frequently encountered problems. In the present case the pony had to learn the rules of the game: he had to learn that only one of a pair of stimuli was positive and consistently led to reward, and that where the positive stimulus was placed — left or right — was irrelevant. Pecos appears to have arrived at this general solution

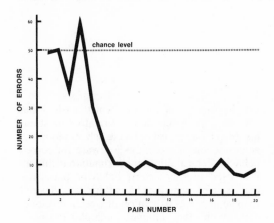

Figure 13.3 Number of errors made on the first 100 trials on each pair, indicating the formation of a learning set between pairs 4 and 7.

after learning the sixth pair of stimuli. From then on he recognized the positive pattern after the first or second trial: The 10 percent errors he continued to make were distributed over the test session and were probably the result of distractions and inattention.

During the learning of new stimulus pairs, the pony could rely on short-term retention, for a wrong choice on one trial could be corrected on the next. The final series of 600 trials tested for long-term retention, both because each pair appeared only once in a series of 20 trials and because the testing covered 6 days. His error rate of 7.5 percent during these trials does not differ from his error rate when single pairs were presented repeatedly, demonstrating that he was able to distinguish the positive stimulus from the negative stimulus in each of the 20 pairs from memory.

Pecos' tendency to make somewhat more errors after an extended period of time on those pairs which he had learned first suggests that perhaps superior retention accompanies an increase in efficiency in learning. He required from 5 to 20 times as many learning trials to reach criterion on the first five pairs as on the last five. In addition, he received reviews of the early pairs every week or so throughout the learning of the later pairs. On the memory test immediately following learning of all 20 pairs, his error rate on the first five pairs was slightly lower than that on the last five. Perhaps in being presented with the same pair many hundreds of times, he learned irrelevant cues that interfered with his performance, but only after some forgetting had occurred. However, it is also possible that the last five pairs of patterns provided a richer array of discriminative cues and thus were more easily remembered.

Conclusion

In conclusion, the set of pattern discriminations that Rensch's elephant had learned were learned by a pony with equal success. Rensch implied that the performance of his subject was related to the size of the brain of this largest of all land mammals. The small pony of this study, however, was not inferior to the elephant. The pony was able to perceive the difference between the members of each pair, and in the process of learning the 20 pairs, arrived at a general conceptual solution to the problems he was required to solve. Moreover, he was able to remember all 20 discriminations when he was tested on all the pairs in random order, and continued to be able to do so at least 6 months after the original learning.

2

Norris: Domestication of the porpoise*

Kenneth S. Norris, a zoologist at U.C.L.A. and a researcher at the Oceanic Institute at Oahu, Hawaii, controlled the behavior of a porpoise sufficiently to make it a useful subject of study. Norris's particular interest was in the swimming speed of the porpoise; our main interest here is in the psychological implications of the porpoise's training. Norris found the answer to his biological question, but only after first going through a certain psychological procedure with the animal—the procedure of **reinforcement,** or operant conditioning. Also worth noting is the interplay of science and technology revealed in the following article.

The experimental porpoise, named Keiki (Hawaiian for "child"), was caught 24 March 1964 on Penguin Bank 45 km from the Oahu coast. The animal was taken from a school of approximately 80 animals, including at least four other young.

When the porpoise was feeding well, after a few days of captivity at the Oceanic Institute, trainers established the sound of a police whistle as a conditioned reinforcing stimulus by pairing the stimulus with the presentation of food. The conditioned stimulus, followed by food, was used to establish some simple conditioned behavior, including stopping in front of the trainer. No further training was undertaken until 15 June 1964, when a variety of trained behaviors related to the projected speed tests were shaped by standard conditioned-response techniques. Throughout the tests behavior desired by the experimenter was reinforced

first by the use of a police whistle, which had become a strong conditioned reinforcing stimulus, then by a reward of whole fish. No food was given the animal except as a reward for correct behavior. The multiple approximation technique was used to shape most behavior patterns— that is, if a complicated pattern was desired, the simplest approximation of it was developed first, with the ultimate complexity being developed gradually through prolonged training. Thus the first approximation of response to the recall signal consisted of requiring the stationary porpoise to touch the speaker [a loudspeaker] held very close to its rostrum [snout] when the sound signal was turned on. Gradually the speaker was taken farther and farther from the animal, thus requiring the porpoise to move toward it. Ultimately, in the open sea, the animal responded to the loud underwater sound signal by swimming toward the submerged speaker and stopping directly in front of it.

Punishment Punishment consisted of moving away from the animal after an erroneous performance, for a time period set approximately 1 minute longer than the animal required, on the average, to station himself spontaneously in front of the trainer in anticipation of further work.

Keiki refuses to leave his cage

The [major part] of training was performed in the semienclosed lagoon, 300 meters in length, that fronts the University of Hawaii Marine Laboratory at Coconut Island. Here the cage was set up and half the length of the lagoon was blocked off by a net barrier. After the porpoise had spent 2 days within the cage, one side was let down. The animal at first refused to leave the cage and had to be escorted by swimmers into the lagoon. These swimmers led the animal the full length of the netted lagoon. The porpoise refused to enter the cage again and was finally forced back into the cage by the use of a

*Quoted material is from Kenneth S. Norris, "Trained Porpoise Released in the Open Sea," *Science,* 26 February 1965, **147**(3661), 1048–1050. Copyright 1965 by the American Association for the Advancement of Science. By permission of author and publisher.

Figure 13.4 Keiki, a trained Pacific bottlenose porpoise, swims free in the ocean near Oahu, Hawaii but does not escape. Its movements are being controlled via conditioned sound signals and standard food rewards. (Photo courtesy of Kenneth Norris by Camera Hawaii, Honolulu.)

crowder net. This behavior was repeated three times and then the porpoise began, voluntarily, to return to his cage upon command of the recall signal. After that the porpoise was given full run of the blocked lagoon, but seldom ventured beyond the immediate area within which his swimming speed was being timed (about one-third the area available). Keiki's entire food intake consisted of approximately 6.75 kg [kilograms] per day of frozen surf smelt (daily intake was varied somewhat according to the requirements of training), except that the porpoise was seen, on two occasions, swallowing masses of colonial **hydroids** found floating in the lagoon. The animal's dependence on us to provide food obviously continued into the open sea situation; he was not observed to make any attempt to catch the numerous fish available in the lagoon. Furthermore, the requirements of the speed tests at sea allowed the porpoise little free time in which to hunt.

During the first 3 weeks of August, daily training sessions were carried out in which the animal was required to leave the cage on cue (a 3 kilocycles per second constant tone), swim a 60-meter course at high speed, and return to his cage upon hearing the recall signal. At the end of each daily session, the animal was recalled, the gate closed, and the animal left in confinement overnight.

Behavior in the open sea

On 20 August restraining nets were removed so that Keiki had easy access to the open sea, but he never attempted to venture out alone. On 23 August the recall-signal speaker and instrument console were placed in a skiff powered by a small outboard motor, and the animal was led by periodic recalls into all parts of the lagoon, and finally into the open waters of Kaneohe Bay. The porpoise at first hung behind the boat and seemed reluctant to leave the lagoon. Once we had ventured past the entrance and into the deep channel, the animal became visibly nervous, exhibiting jaw chattering and tail slapping, and showing the whites of the eyes—behavior patterns which have been associated with agitation in **cetaceans** [whales, dolphins, porpoises, etc.]. After several recalls had been performed in the open water, Keiki disappeared momentarily and when next seen was plunging very rapidly away from our skiff, along the edge of the reef that fringes Coconut Island. When the animal was an estimated 195 meters away, the recall was switched on. The animal stopped at once and returned directly to the speaker. After several more recalls were performed, Keiki was led back into the lagoon and caged.

On 25 August the porpoise was moved to the floating pen in the lee of Manana Island. A week-long series of speed trials was performed, in which the porpoise spent an average of 3 hours a day swimming unfettered in open water. Keiki was required to follow a fast skiff that towed a surfboard with a streamlined speaker pod suspended beneath, through which the recall signal could be transmitted. The tests were performed along a 320-meter calibrated buoy line. Throughout these tests the porpoise remained near one of the small craft, even in the absence of the recall signal, and never strayed away farther than about 90 meters. The operation became quite routine after the first day, and little attention was given to holding the animal close to the skiff with the recall signal. The porpoise reentered the floating cage upon hearing the recall signal (with the portable speaker hooked over the rear of the cage) and allowed us to close the door without any attempt to rush from the cage.

The exact components of our control over the porpoise cannot be listed categorically. It seems probable that the trainer's control has multiple bases, among which are controlled feeding, social ties between the scientist and the porpoise, the porpoise's fear of unknown waters or situations, coupled with the porpoise's isolation as an individual and the formal conditioning process through which the animal was led.

Captive cetaceans, in general, are notable for the ease with which they become habituated to a single kind of food, which may be wholly foreign to them in nature, often to the exclusion of all others. This may assume ridiculous proportions, such as occurred with the captive **beluga** [whale] that would eat nothing but tiny **killifish.** Captive cetaceans may often be kept in the same tank with living fish of various varieties and often may completely ignore them.

Keiki's tameness

In nature, most porpoise species form tightly knit schools. The social structure of such schools is complex and may involve much dependence of young upon adults. Young bottlenose porpoises orient to their mothers, or to "auntie" porpoises, for an extraordinarily long time (as long as 6 years), particularly in times of stress. To remove a young animal from such a social order and to place it in captive isolation may induce starvation. In some oceanariums a docile well-tamed animal is maintained that can be held with such a newcomer until the new animal is tamed and feeding. Even after a porpoise is tamed, isolation is stress-producing, and extended periods may cause a decline in health. For these reasons, during the training described here, about an hour a day was devoted to swimming with the isolated animal. Keiki quickly became very tame and solicited bodily contact of various sorts from the swimmer. Porpoises frequently stroke each other with their flippers. The members of the investigating team often responded to Keiki's solicitations by stroking and patting him during and after work sessions. It is possible that this bodily contact constitutes a reward for which the presence of human beings becomes a conditioned reinforcing stimulus, increasing the probability that the animal will stay near people under most circumstances. Keiki's high degree of tameness allowed us to perform many manipulations, such as transport, that otherwise would have frightened him severely. Whether we did more than develop a high degree of tolerance, and whether we pressed into the realm of dependence, is a moot point.

A porpoise afraid of the open sea?

Fear is expressed in porpoises by the visible signals mentioned before, and may also be indicated by abrupt cessation of feeding and a sudden lack of clear response to learned signals. All of these things suggest that from time to time Keiki was frightened. Such fright occurred whenever the animal was led into a new situation, such as when the porpoise was taken for the first time beyond the limits of the measured course, or when he was led out of the cage for the first time. Bottle-nose porpoises in captivity are notable for refusing to go through gates where they cannot see or for refusing to pass under unfamiliar objects above water or over newly placed obstacles on the bottom. Before an animal can be induced to do these things, it may literally have to be driven by force once or twice. This marked fear of new situations

may also have been an important part of our control over the lone animal in the open sea.

The possibilities

The development of a trained porpoise that can be manipulated in the open sea opens the way to a variety of experimental possibilities. Several captive porpoises have been broken to harnesses, which not only allows an additional degree of control but also permits the attachment of a variety of instruments to the animal that can record physiological parameters, such as heart rate, lung configuration, and blood pressure. It may prove possible to insinuate a trained animal in schools of wild animals and to observe and record various kinds of behavior. Such animals could also be used to perform a variety of human-directed tasks in the sea.*

---

*Keiki continues to be trained for open sea work. He now does a variety of jobs for divers, such as carrying new air bottles down to them, sampling gear, messages, and even hauls a diver back to the surface on command. He is to be used to support an underwater chamber going down this fall off the Oceanic Institute (Kenneth S. Norris, personal communication).

On ways of
looking at response **3**

James J. Asher (1964) has introduced the total physical response to the learning of foreign languages. Asher's experimental subjects do not passively pair together symbolic equivalents from Japanese and English, like "kokuban = blackboard." Instead, they copy their instructor's physical responses to commands in Japanese to do things like "run to the blackboard" or "Walk to the desk and put down the pencil and book."

Asher (1964, p. 90) considers his strategy of the total physical response as a hypothesis. He thinks it may be more

effective than traditional, more passive methods, but notes that highly controlled experiments must still be carried out and many questions are still awaiting answer. Even so, the work he has done is quite striking. First, let us note what his strategy involves and then examine some of the results obtained.

The strategy of the total physical response

As worked out by Asher, the strategy

Figure 13.5 The strategy of the total physical response: an application to learning Japanese. When the boys and the adult model heard the Japanese command "Tobe" played on a tape recorder, they jumped. Similar commands were also learned in a format approximating one-trial learning with excellent retention. (*Iral,* 1965, **3**(4), 277–289. Photo courtesy of James Asher.)

of the total physical response involved a Japanese instructor who (as shown in Fig. 13.5) would call out a command in Japanese, for example, *tobe* meaning *jump*. He would execute the order, expecting his subjects to do the same. The first session called for simple commands that elicited such total physical responses as *tate* (stand up), *aruke* (walk), *tomare* (stop), *maware* (turn around), *sagare* (walk backward), *suware* (sit down), and *kagame* (squat) (p. 91).

Before training, the only instructions to the subjects were these: When you hear the noise (or utterance in Japanese) automatically make a physical response without thinking. Please remember to respond immediately with no attempt to translate. We will not ask you to make the noises yourself. Just be silent, listen to the Japanese, and execute the physical response to the command. Now the instructor will demonstrate what you are to do. Please listen to him, then do exactly what he does [p. 91].

After the instructor, as leader of the group, felt that his "students" were ready to respond alone, he sat down and gave oral commands to each subject in turn. With every session, the length of the utterance increased gradually in length and complexity. The instructions reinforced students, from time to time, to carry out the commands *in action* without translation. Pilot studies showed that 12-year-old boys could learn and retain for a fairly long time quite a number of Japanese sentences learned in a session as short as 20 minutes. A 15-minute motion picture, *A Demonstration of a New Strategy in Language Learning,* shows how the learning actually takes place.

Since his theoretical formulation and pilot studies, Asher (1965) has published two papers applying the method to the learning of Japanese and Russian. The former will serve our purpose in describing his work.

An application of the strategy of the total physical response to learning Japanese

Subjects consisted of 88 volunteer college students who were divided into three experimental groups and three control groups. They were without prior training or exposure to Japanese, without fluency in any language besides English, and they were nonlanguage majors.

For the experimental group, the procedure required subjects to listen to a tape recording that would utter a command in Japanese which they were to execute by following the example of their leader (instructor). They were warned against translating the Japanese into English; instead they were told to carry out the order "as fully, automatically, and spontaneously as possible" (p. 278). The first command was "tate" (stand), to which instructor and subjects stood with alacrity. Similar one-word commands delivered in a random order continued for 8 minutes; then the subjects took a retention test.

They returned 24 hours later and took a retention test, following which they underwent 10½ minutes of training with more complex commands. Here are two examples: (1) "To ni aruite ike." (Walk to the door.) (2) "Tsukue ni hashitte ike." (Run to the desk.) (p. 279). The second training series consisted of about 40 different commands of such complexity. The subjects again returned 24 hours later, and submitted to another retention test and a third and final training session of 7½-minutes duration. This time the subjects gave the total physical response to 16 different utterances, still more complex than the last set and spoken at a normal conversational rate.

"Tsukue ni aruite itte enpitsu to hon ooke." (Walk to the desk and put down the pencil and book). "Mado ni hashitte itte hon o motte tsukue ni oite isu nu suware." (Run to the window, pick up the book, put it on the desk, and then sit on the chair). Immediately following the test, subjects took a retention test and were requested to return 2 weeks later to take a final retention test. So much for the experimental group.

There were three control groups. Group 1 consisted of 15 subjects who listened to the same tape as the experimental group but without executing a total physical response. All they did was sit and observe the instructor carrying out each command uttered in Japanese to walk, turn around, run, squat, and so on. The 18 subjects of Group 2 sat and listened to each Japanese utterance and then heard its English translation.

The 18 subjects of Group 3 sat still and, following each Japanese command, were instructed to read (silently) its English translation in a book.

Results

No matter how Asher measured retention, whether immediately after training, 24 hours later, or 2 weeks later, "the experimental group was superior to the control groups [p. 281]." This superiority held true for single words and for short, long, or novel utterances and gave "significantly better" results than traditional language teaching methods (p. 288).

Generally the control groups did not show statistically significant differences among themselves, thus demonstrating a togetherness among themselves but a separateness from the experimental group. Response of the experimental group on *novel utterances* sets them far apart from the control groups (.005 level of significance). Translated into psychological terms, this means that when the experimental group students were subjected to recombinations of elements in a series they had not previously heard in that order, they responded much more effectively than control groups. In other words, they were gaining *fluency* in Japanese. Without going into further specific details, Asher seems to have demonstrated the superiority of the total physical response.

Significance of Asher's research

Is it possible that our traditional view of stimulus and response is impeding our progress? Perhaps Asher's work will jolt us into a fresh look at response, which a traditional theory has viewed as a passive, static process. If supported by further research, his formulation of the strategy of the total physical response may require a revision of theory and practice with possible beneficial consequences to both.

Summary

As a critic of traditional learning theory's ineffectualness in applications of learning to everyday life situations, Asher has proposed the strategy of the total physical response. The technique calls for total physical response in language learning, not unlike the responses demanded of small children, beginning to learn their mother tongue. He has demonstrated the superiority of his method experimentally. His work calls attention to a need for a reexamination of our concept of response with possible benefits to theoretical as well as practical applications.

Asher's method has been criticized because its usefulness appears to be limited to the concrete situations described above. People have to run or squat or carry something from here to there. The objection is that the student cannot talk about justice or infinity. To me, this is carping criticism. Any saving of effort or time in language learning should be welcomed. And does not every child learn its native language in concrete situations? Cannot the abstract (which is semantically slippery at best) be learned later by the child as well as the adult who learns via Asher's procedure?

Shortly after the turn of the century a German physician by the name of Pfaundler (Wickes, 1958) ingeniously devised a simple electrical apparatus that would notify the parents of an **enuretic** child that its bed was wet and needed changing. To his astonishment, quite a few of his patients stopped wetting the bed. Thus he became serendipitously the father of the conditioning method of treating bed wetting. But despite its long-time availability in many versions and variations, the public, particularly the medical profession, has been reluctant to adopt the method.

Background of research

Werry (1966) reports approximately 20 studies in the literature covering well over 1000 children. A summary of the studies, some of them hard to correlate with one another, reports an average rate of success of about 75 percent (p. 228), although Werry (p. 228) reports cures in about one-third of his cases. At the same time Werry reports on investigators (e.g., Friedell in the 1920s) who achieved a rate of cure in 80 percent of their subjects by the simple muscular injection of sterile distilled water. Another investigator, with encouragement and a star chart (on which the child's successes were recorded with little gold stars), attained a 50 percent recovery, results not too different from Werry's one-third recovery for his series. Werry appears to scoff at "the Mowrers who were able to obtain 100 percent cure [p. 228]." Perhaps the discrepant results

by various workers are partly explained by their own attitudes and their effect on the subjects.

Ordinary toilet training

Micturition in infancy is a reflex process. Pressure within the bladder builds up until it becomes an adequate stimulus for the opening of the **sphincter.** Relief of the pressure automatically closes it. Ordinarily, in normal toilet training, the parent judges the proper interval that calls for urination and places the child in the usual posture, which is adequate to trigger the response. But this act is itself preceded by some word used by the parent or nurse to signal the next step and, in time, comes to be adopted by the child itself as a request to be taken to the toilet. Eventually bladder tension causes either restlessness, standing on one foot first and then the other (especially if facilities are not at hand), or actual independent walking to the toilet by himself. This success causes no problem between parent and child, but misfiring of the normal learning process does, and calls for treatment, one form of which is conditioning. We examine how it works in the following pages.

The conditioned response method

The goal of the conditioning treatment of enuresis is to substitute walking to the toilet for wetting the bed. Basically most techniques use a pad large enough to cover the middle of the child's bed. The pad consists of three thicknesses of cloth; the bottom one, next to the sheet, is wired with wires placed in parallel about an inch apart. A single lead-off wire connecting all of them exits at one corner. An absorbent layer of muslin or some other cloth goes on top of the one just described. And, on top of it, a duplicate of the bottom one is fitted with its own lead-off wire. Now, the two lead-off wires are ready for connecting via a relay that operates a bell or buzzer. Sometimes a tensor light is also connected so that the tiniest moisture acts to "close the switch" and start the bells ringing and lights lighting. This serves as an unconditioned stimulus to start the child going to the toilet with instructions to empty his bladder as completely as possible, change the wet pads for dry ones and to reset the signal system.

How it works

Deduction from conditioning theory would indicate that "cure" can come in only one way. The response of walking to the toilet and micturating there must acquire another signal, a conditioned stimulus. Fortunately, one is already built into the organism, namely, the tension in the bladder building up prior to reflex micturition. The hope is that this increased pressure will become an adequate substitute stimulus to the child since, during the conditioning procedure, it has been the immediately preceding condition just prior to the bed wetting. When it has become a signal in its own right to elicit the expected reaction, then the child is in the same situation as the trained adult who responds properly to the bladder tension out of the soundest sleep.

A transistorized signal-package for toilet training of infants

Obviously toilet training beyond the time and place when children are asleep would extend opportunities for toilet training. The transistor has helped to achieve the proper device. Van Wagenen and Murdock (1966) have reported a miniature transmitter system with built-in speaker, all contained within a cigarette

Figure 13.6 Application of conditioning principles to treatment of enuresis. When the slightest moisture is expelled, a circuit is closed which activates a speaker that emits a signal audible throughout the average-sized home. Its useful range is extended far beyond the much more limited treatment of bed wetting. Positioning of the signalling device showing the grid is of exaggerated size. Note also miniature packaging. (From R. Keith Van Wagenen and Everett E. Murdock, "A Transistorized Signal-Package for Toilet Training of Infants," *Journal of Experimental Child Psychology*, 1966, **3**, 312–314. Reproduced by permission of the author.)

case sewed into the waist of the toddler's clothing. A tone signal is emitted when urine or moisture from fecal matter comes in contact with a grid sewn into the child's training pants, thus closing the speaker circuit. The signal "can be heard throughout an average-sized home [p. 312]."

The apparatus has been tried on both a male and a female subject of about 16 months of age and was found to function well. The authors employed a discrimination hierarchy based on proximity to the toilet facility. That is, the infant was initially reinforced at the occurrence of any expulsion, but on subsequent urinations or defecations, movement in the direction of the toilet was reinforced with confections, and the most distal areas of the house successively removed from the possibility of reinforcement. Aspects of the response as movement toward the toilet and restraining of the expulsion were the focus of reinforcement [p. 314].

Toilet training that applies conditioning principles and biotelemetry is successfully treating enuresis.

Gericke:
Operant conditioning
in the treatment
*of behavior pathology**

5

The following article is only one out of scores of reports on similar work being done in behavior therapy. It focuses on the specific undesirable behavior in question and attempts to eliminate it. O. L. Gericke works in a radically different way from those therapists who first want to find "the cause" of the troublesome behavior.

The plan

The over-all plan as to what operant conditioning procedures were to be used was determined entirely by practical considerations. We knew that with only 10 nurses or psychiatric technicians per unit (and usually fewer than 5 of these on duty) it would be impossible to give close attention to more than 10 or 15 patients. Yet each unit contained at least 70 and sometimes as many as 90 patients. Consequently, we decided to have three groups of patients on each unit: an orientation group of approximately 60 percent of the total unit population, a therapy group of approximately 20 percent, and a "ready to leave" group of another 20 percent. The staff would work intensively only with the therapy group. They were to obtain behavioral base lines from patients in the orientation group. The habits, idiosyncrasies, and details of behavior of these patients were to be noted as time allowed, but no action was to be taken on this information until a patient was transferred into the therapy group. Each nurse was to be responsible for 2 or 3 patients in the therapy group, for three times as many patients in the orientation group. At first there were, of course, no patients in the "ready to leave" group, but when a patient entered it following successful therapy, the nurse who had previously controlled his behavior would continue to work with him until he left the hospital. Other forms of group therapy and, of course, individual supervision of medication through the unit physician continued concurrently with the program.

---

*Quoted material is from O. L. Gericke, "Practical Use of Operant Conditioning Procedures in a Mental Hospital," *Psychiatric Studies & Projects,* June 1965, 3(5), 3–10. Reproduced by permission of author and publisher.

The reinforcers

The next step was to list the reinforcers available to us. The food the patient eats, the bed he sleeps on, the minor privileges he enjoys on the unit, such as watching TV or being permitted to go to the cafeteria, were obvious variables that we felt we could use within limits to control the behavior of patients. In order to have some versatility in granting these primary reinforcers, we decided to introduce tokens (poker chips) into the program. Patients could exchange these tokens for desired minor privileges.

The behaviors to be shaped

We then drew up a list of the desirable behaviors that we expected to influence through these reinforcers. We required each member of the nursing staff to make up his list independently. Making this list gave individuals much insight into the purposes of our plan. The immediate behaviors listed were "getting to the dining room on time," "maintaining personal hygiene" (these are open units and the patients are expected to be able to perform adequately in these respects), "performing simple household duties on the unit," and, as appropriate, "seeking off-the-unit jobs in the patient laundry, the kitchen, the cafeteria, the grounds crew, or in offices within the hospital."

The staff quickly grasped that such global statements of goals are of little value to the **behavioral engineer.** Personal hygiene means many things to many people. We demonstrated that to make this term meaningful we must be more specific. For "personal hygiene" we arrived at the following list: (1) no **desquamatus** between the toes, (2) no dirt on the instep or heels of the feet, (3) no dirt on legs and knees, (4) no evidence of body odor, (5) no residue in the naval, (6) clean hands and fingernails, (7) neat and recent shave (or neatly trimmed beard) for the man, (8) nicely combed hair, and (9) a daily change of underwear. A separate list for the women included appropriate use of cosmetics.

Figure 13.7 Elegant type of dining facility that patients could enjoy by earning tokens through operant conditioning procedure. (Photo by Bruce Duchaine, courtesy of Dr. O. L. Gericke.)

It became overwhelmingly evident that although there might be disagreement about poorly defined global goals, the items on the detailed list could be agreed upon without much difficulty and, most important for our purposes, could be selectively reinforced. Everyone understood that this was quite different from demanding "adequate personal hygiene," which society at large reinforces but which it does little to shape selectively.

Orientation group
versus therapy group

An important feature of the program was structuring the unit environment to make living in the orientation group sufficiently undesirable to motivate patients to move into the therapy group. We adhered, of course, to the minimal requirements that human dignity and common sense demand, but whereas the therapy group could watch television, visit the cafeteria (some distance away from the unit), and go to social functions, dances, and movies, the orientation group enjoyed none of these privileges. Furthermore, the therapy group enjoyed the most desirable dormitories or single rooms, equipped with night stands, curtains, and attractive bedspreads. The orientation group slept in community rooms equipped with plain beds, no bedspreads, and a "bed sack" commonly in use throughout the hospital for storing personal belongings. In the dining rooms, the therapy group could sit at tables for four, covered with a tablecloth and set with attractive china, stainless steel flatware, and flowers. The patients in the orientation group sat at a long, bare table, and their meals were served out of picnic trays. The quantity and quality of meals for both groups were, of course, the same.

As a routine procedure, the staff had daily meetings during which individual problems could be discussed and procedures considered for use with individual patients.

The last step was to screen patients for admission to the program. To be admitted to

Figure 13.8 Plain dining facilities in the same room as the elegant one but assigned to patients who hadn't earned enough tokens to "pay" for them. Note sharp contrast. (Photo by Bruce Duchaine, courtesy of Dr. O. L. Gericke.)

the units, patients must have been hospitalized for more than 6 months, have no brain damage, and be able to function on an open unit. There were no other restrictions.

Because we knew that our procedures were likely to elicit strong letters of concern from relatives, we designated the units' social worker as director of the project and asked him to explain to relatives, when necessary, the basic principles underlying the operant conditioning program.

Tokens as reinforcers

Finally the day came when the program officially started. The patients received their first tokens for answering "pill call" and for doing various chores around the unit. The nurses went to some length to invent small jobs for the patients because the main purpose of this day was to establish the tokens as behavior reinforcers.

At lunchtime the patients were admitted to the dining room only if they could pay for their entry with a token. A small number only had been selected for the therapy group, and they were told that they had to pay more tokens to eat at the specially designated tables. Some patients did not have enough tokens, and they were told that although they could easily earn enough in the course of a day, since they unfortunately did not yet have enough tokens to pay for this privilege, they would have to sit with the orientation group patients at the long, bare table. Some patients, even though they had earned a token in the course of the morning, thought the hospital staff had no right to charge for entering the dining room. These patients, we well understood, were merely trying to find out how serious we were. The staff stuck to the rules, especially when they noticed that those who missed a meal could easily afford to do so because they were overweight. No male patient missed his meal.

Modifications of the plan

During this first day patients began to ask for jobs, such as emptying wastebaskets, rearranging chairs, setting the table, and helping in the kitchen, to earn tokens. It became obvious that there could be no general rule about how many tokens a patient could earn for a given job. Some worked so much that, if a standard rule had been enforced, they would have earned as many as 50 tokens in one day. Therefore we simply increased the number of responses needed to earn one token. This procedure is called a **variable ratio schedule.** The patient never knows exactly when or how much he is getting paid. Because of that, he increases his responses. Doing more instead of less under a variable ratio schedule is a somewhat unexpected empirical finding of behavioral scientists. Yet, on reflection, we can see that much of our own daily behavior is reinforced on a variable ratio. We know that after continuous reinforcement — a reward for each response — the response ceases very swiftly. (This is called *extinction* by behavioral scientists.) A good example is the continuous reinforcement we receive when we deposit a coin into a postal meter to obtain a stamp. For every coin we deposit, we obtain one stamp. If for some reason the machine breaks down, extinction (the cessation of our response) would be swift. At most we would deposit one more coin into the machine to try it out. The situation is different when we are responding to a variable ratio schedule as, for example, with a gambling machine. If such a machine is cold and does not pay off, the gambler continues to throw in coins for a long time before his responses are finally extinguished.

Since our long-term goal is to wean the patients away from the artificial support of token reinforcement, we welcomed every opportunity to introduce a variable ratio reinforcement. We replaced tokens by other types of reinforcement, such as friendly praise from the nurse to a patient for doing a job well.

The results on patients

One of the most impressive overall results of the program was that we could reach patients who had heretofore remained passive. They felt that all of a sudden something was expected of them and someone was taking them seriously. Some rebelled against the system. (While such rebellion is obviously not a desirable response to any therapeutic technique, it is better to have a patient react even negatively than not to react at all.) Many rebelled by being absent without leave from the unit. We dealt with this problem by assigning baby-sitters (who were patients themselves and earned one token an hour for this job) to patients who left the unit without authorization. The term "baby-sitter" was used deliberately to imply that absentees were acting childishly. No patient required a baby-sitter for more than 4 days, although at various times we had as many as eight baby-sitters assigned.

Some patients did not earn enough tokens even for the plainest beds on the unit. Theoretically these patients should sleep on the floor or on cots. We felt that if the secondary reinforcers, the tokens, were to have any value at all, we would have to tie them strongly to such primary reinforcers as food and a place to sleep. We knew from previous experience that none of the patients would have to go without meals or without a bed for any length of time. However, we were mindful of possible public criticism of a hospital procedure that might appear to deprive patients of basic rights.

In the light of this consideration, we agreed that no patient would be denied adequate sleeping facilities or a meal if he was not able to "pay" for these services with a token. At that time we also drafted a statement to ourselves to clarify our own thinking.

Rejection of use of punishment

The basic premise on which operant conditioning procedures rest is that there are reinforcers which, as a consequence of some behavior, will strengthen or weaken that behavior. The details are that the removal of a negative reinforcer will strengthen the behavior which removed it; appearance of a positive reinforcer will strengthen the behavior which brought it about. Thus both negative reinforcers and positive reinforcers can be used to bring about reinforcement of a behavior. Withholding of a positive reinforcer constitutes extinction or weakening of a behavior. The granting of a negative reinforcer as a consequence of some behavior constitutes punishment and does not have the same result, that is, a weakening or extinction of that behavior. What happens in that case is that the behavior in question is *temporarily* suppressed, only to emerge more strongly when the aversive consequences no longer follow. Hence, while there are negative

and positive reinforcers, it is not correct to speak of negative and positive reinforcement. To change a behavior *permanently,* to strengthen or to weaken it, it is necessary to employ the procedures of reinforcement or extinction but not procedures of punishment.

There are some reinforcers which are very general, such as food, water, and a place to sleep. Interestingly, these reinforcers play a relatively minor role in our daily lives. Much more important to all of us are such conditioned reinforcers as social approval, praise, money in all its forms, social privileges, and so on. A particularly useful conditioned general reinforcer for the operant conditioning project are tokens. These tokens would have, however, no reinforcing value if they were not paired with primary reinforcers, that is to say, if they had not acquired the status of being conditioned reinforcers. It was on the basis of such deliberations that we originally planned making a patient's meals and bed ("room and board") contingent on the presence of carefully selected behaviors. The patient would earn tokens by having these types of behavior and "buy" his room and board, as it were, with the tokens.

In general, the tokens have now been established successfully as conditioned reinforcers. From now on the tokens will be made to maintain their reinforcing status by careful manipulation of social prestige privileges (often of very minor apparent nature) which exceed minimum services to which the patient ethically, or by law, is entitled. Thus a meal served from handsome china, on a tablecloth decked with tasteful silverware, is more reinforcing than one served from a stainless-steel mess tray. A bed in a room with drapes, bed stands, and minor conveniences is more desirable than a bed in an otherwise barren room."

As it developed, the final solution of the sleeping question was to provide military cots, which conformed entirely to minimum standards but were sufficiently disliked by the patients to motivate them to respond to our therapy program.

As anyone who has slept on such cots knows, they are not uncomfortable. But in comparison with a full-sized bed that could be obtained with tokens earned by socially acceptable behavior, the cots achieved the purpose of reinforcing such behavior.

On the men's unit, from the beginning, the main source of token income was passing

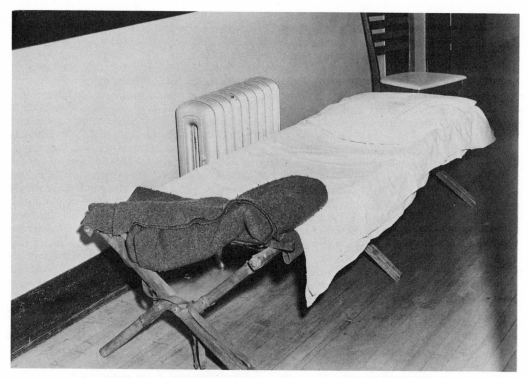

Figure 13.9 Cots like this one were provided for patients who did not have tokens to pay for standard hospital bed with innerspring mattress. (Photo by Bruce Duchaine, courtesy of Dr. O. L. Gericke.)

inspection for personal cleanliness. Two technicians shared the task of carrying out the inspection. The effect was that the men patients quickly learned that in order to be somebody on this unit, they merely had to do regularly a few things which they did (or knew they should do) anyway, such as bathing and shaving. All the coaxing, admonishing, and helping that had heretofore required much of the nurses' time was now no longer necessary.

The case of Susan

One of the most gratifying aspects of the project was the personal interest the nursing staff took in working with individual patients. There was, for example, the patient named Susan, who for months had sat seclusively in a corner by herself. The token system had moved her slightly. She began to earn enough tokens for her bed and meals, but beyond that did

nothing much. Susan is a 26-year-old Mexican girl, the youngest of four children. Her mother and father are still living, although they are not physically well. Susan was educated formally to the third grade and quit school because she disliked one of her teachers. She preferred to stay at home. As a teen-age girl she had occasionally worked as a housekeeper and baby-sitter. She was married 9 years ago, when she was 17. After her marriage she stayed home as a housewife.

About a year later her husband noticed that her behavior became odd, while she was going to a **gynecologist** for treatment of a female disorder. She became increasingly nervous, tore her clothing, and threw things. She also expressed **paranoid ideation** and had many **somatic** complaints. Over the years she began a sequence of periods during which she was hospitalized and then discharged again to return to her husband.

Every time she returned to the hospital she

seemed more depressed. The nursing staff noticed that milk was the only nourishment she would take and that she would dress only in white or light-colored clothing. The nurse assigned to her mentioned this preference, and we decided to use white clothing as a positive reinforcer for acceptable behavior. When Susan's white dress was taken away from her, and institution dark olive-drab clothing substituted, she reacted for the first time in the course of her current hospitalization: she tore the institution dress, sat on her bed, and refused to dress. The nurses left her and waited to see what would happen next. After about 2 hours, Susan called the nurse and asked for a needle and thread to fix the dress that she had ripped. The nurse complied and immediately gave her a white scarf to wear with her dark dress.

The resulting change in Susan's behavior was dramatic. After she had mended the clothing, she asked for odd jobs in the kitchen. Each time she completed a task, she received a token and some of her white clothing back. During the next few days she earned the right to get all her clothing back. She added white ice cream and mashed potatoes to her diet, after being satiated by increasing portions of milk daily. The next goal of the staff was to condition her to wearing dark clothing and to eating foods that were not white.

During discussions between the charge nurse and Susan, it emerged very clearly that the color white was an irrationally powerful control stimulus for Susan. She associated white with purity, goodness, and the worth of life. Black and dark colors symbolized the devil, sin, and everything undesirable. She felt that God had punished her by giving her black hair and that she would have to bear this burden. Her first reaction to the milk satiation program was to gorge herself with milk. After a few days the nurse began to charge extra tokens for extra glasses of milk but not for other food. Since Susan, until then, had not earned sufficient tokens to stay with the program, one of two things was expected to happen. She would either have to work more and interact more with patients (a behavior that was, of course, sought for her) or she would have to choose other foods that would cost her no tokens. The second alternative happened. Susan began to eat bacon and toast for breakfast. Although Susan's troubles were not over, some communication had been established between this withdrawn girl and the staff.

Effect on women patients

It is interesting to read the report that the charge nurse of the women's unit wrote at the end of the first month of the program: "The project goes extremely well. We no longer have to call individuals for meals or coax them to go into the dining room. This used to require considerable time. Patients are taking the responsibility now of getting to the dining room on time. It sometimes seems to us today that this came about automatically with the use of tokens. Other by-products are that at mealtimes the general atmosphere seems more relaxed. There is no longer the mad rush to eat and get out. Patients get up without being called. Many of the patients we had to look out for in the beginning are now looking out for themselves. We hope this will continue. The night technician no longer has to go from bed to bed, calling the patients to get up for breakfast, get dressed for breakfast, and so on. She merely turns on the light and in 3 minutes goes back, and the patients who are up get their tokens. The ones who are not up get nothing. Very few are *not* up by then.

"We have a much larger percentage of patients turning up for breakfast now than we did before the program. In the beginning our plans were to more or less ignore the orientation group. But the orientation patients refuse to be ignored, and they are getting as much attention as any other patients. I feel that the visibility of progress is also much more evident in the orientation group than it is with those in the therapy group. The patients in the orientation group very much dislike eating at the big community table and from the mess dishes. This is, of course, exactly what we wanted, and it provides excellent motivation for them to try to get into the therapy groups. I have known some of the patients for 5 years, and for the first time I am seeing real progress made with them. I feel quite encouraged with our program, and we are learning as we go along. We understand fully now that we must reinforce good behavior when it occurs. Reinforcement is not as effective if it is given too long after the behavior has occurred. All the staff are extremely enthusiastic and feel that their own thinking is tremendously stimulated by what they are learning in this project."

Figure 13.10 Patients earning tokens for passing inspection. Note the well kept man on the right being handed several tokens. The man on the left did not shave and his shirt is disordered. He will earn one token, however, for having bathed. (Photo by Bruce Duchaine, courtesy of Dr. O. L. Gericke.)

Effect on male patients

Although the problems are different on the men's unit, the results are the same. Perhaps the most striking difference on the men's unit is that the men are undoubtedly now the cleanest group of men on an open unit anywhere in the hospital. There is none of the stale odor frequently encountered when large numbers of men live in one unit. Everyone wears neatly pressed clothes and is shaved and well-scrubbed.

The creation of special schedules of reinforcement for individual patients is practiced on the men's unit, too. The following is an example.

The case of Cecil

Cecil is a 61-year-old single patient who has been at Patton State Hospital since 1930. He was brought to staff attention for placement in the men's open unit because he required no medication, displayed no psychotic symptoms, and had been known for many years as a dependable worker in the print shop. But he had come to accept being in the hospital as a normal way of life.

Cecil is a mild-mannered, apologetic, white-haired, balding man. He is considered a loner in his relations to other patients and his distant relatives. In accepting this patient in the program, we surmised that transferring him to a less comfortable setting in an environment that offered choice and competition might trigger some change in his attitude and perhaps renew his interest in the world outside. We also assumed that the change to a new unit would be difficult and upsetting to this patient.

After experiencing the new life for a short time, Cecil sought the social worker and expressed an interest in seeing downtown Los Angeles again. He also asked for an interview with the unit physician, with whom he discussed the problems of his situation. He said that he had been worried about the change in units, but found the new procedure something he could cope with.

After only 3 weeks in the orientation group, Cecil was accepted in the therapy group. This step, the physician had told him, was necessary if he was to visit his brother in Los Angeles. Two interviews with staff members from social service preceded this planned visit. During these interviews he said that if he could keep up with the young fellows on the unit under the therapy program, he could probably make it on the outside. "I felt pushed around," he said, "but now they promoted me, and I have no one to thank for that but myself." This increase in self-confidence was striking compared to the stolid and indifferent attitude Cecil had shown before entering the program.

The 5-day visit was a complete success. In the course of it, Cecil made tentative plans to live at his brother's house with the brother's family, who are happy at the thought of having their uncle back. Presently plans are being made for Cecil to receive funds from the aid to the totally disabled program when he is discharged. In view of his 34 years of hospitalization and because of his age it will be difficult, although not impossible, for him to obtain remunerative employment.

Another patient, Rudy, has no family, and his only friend is a male volunteer who visited him regularly for the last 8 years. This volunteer expressed his amazement at the change the program has brought about in Rudy. "Christmas meant something to him for the first time since I have known him," he told us after visiting Rudy. He felt that Rudy had become a person, that he responded with feeling to his questions, that, in short, he was a new man.

Behavioral engineering
evaluated

In these cases, we know exactly what variables we manipulated to bring about the changes. These and other instances give us great confidence in the unorthodox techniques we are now using, and we point to them whenever we are called upon to explain and justify a therapy that requires the patient to pay for what he used to regard as his due.

Not the least benefit of a program involving behavioral science techniques is that everyone involved is often forced to ask, "Why am I doing what I do, and how does it affect the patient's behavior?" Ever since mental hospitals came into being, the great leaders in psychiatry have asked this question. But in the course of time, as routine and habit make it easy to move along the path of least resistance, perhaps many of us do not really question as seriously as we should our roles in the recovery of patients. Some even defend the view that technicians and nurses should never ask questions. To be sure, there are situations in life, such as with the military, where the success of an operation depends on a person's ability, not to reason *why*, but to *do,* if necessary without understanding. But such situations hardly apply to the problems we face in the mental institution. Operant procedures rest primarily on the analysis of behavior and thus on questioning our own responses.

With the complexity of human behavior it is, however, no task for one single person to explore all the reinforcers, all the control stimuli, and all response contingencies even for a single patient. A team is needed to provide base lines of the behavioral repertory of the patient, to structure the physical environment, and to arrange schedules of reinforcement that lead to acceptable behavior and to recovery. Nurses and psychiatric technicians are a vital part of this team.

In initiating this project we questioned whether behavioral techniques are practical and useful in a mental hospital. We are now satisfied that this question has been affirmatively answered. As our knowledge increases, we are beginning to ask to what degree these techniques can be applied to deal with individual problems and, in particular, how *permanently* we can change a pattern of behavior. The discharged patient usually returns to an environment that is not very different from that which prevailed when his difficulties began. This environment is not under our control. Our job must be to prepare the patient to cope with this environment. Will behavioral techniques enable us to do this? We shall try to provide empirical answers to this question by continuing and expanding our project.

6

*Breland and Breland:
A new psychological
technology is born*

If you are ever in Hot Springs, Arkansas, do not fail to visit *IQ Zoo,* where for a small admission fee you can observe Rufus, the racoon, shooting a basketball into a basket, hens participating in miniature baseball games, a pig depositing "coins" (wooden disks) into a piggy bank, or a hen walking a tightrope. The originators of this clever assemblage of live-animal acts are two behavioral engineers, Keller and Marian Breland who, as former students of Skinner, have applied what they learned to an expanding and profitable technology. The following article tells the story of their enterprise.

*Breland and Breland:
"A field of applied
animal psychology"**

Recent developments in behavior theory have made possible a new field of **applied psychology.** This new field has yet to be finally christened. It might be called the field of applied animal psychology or the field of behavioral engineering. We consider it an excellent example of how the findings of "pure" research can be put to practical use.

The core of the field is the work of the **neo-behaviorists,** which has so ordered the facts of

---

*Quoted material is from Keller Breland and Marian Breland, "A Field of Applied Animal Psychology," American Psychologist, June 1951, 6(6), 202–204. By permission of the authors and publisher. A more detailed account of their work with over 8000 animals representing more than 60 species is available in Keller Breland and Marian Breland, Animal Behavior, New York: Macmillan, 1966.

behavior that many of their experimental data and those of earlier workers have become immediately applicable to the engineering of animal behavior. We have found most useful the systematic formulation presented by B. F. Skinner in *The Behavior of Organisms.* This body of theory has made it possible for us since the spring of 1947 to develop a flourishing and expanding business concerned with the mass production of conditioned operant behavior in animals.

Applied animal psychology brings together the two formerly unrelated fields of professional animal training and modern behavioral science. The field is new in that it represents, we believe, the first application of systematic behavior theory to the control of animal behavior. We are now in a position to outstrip old-time professional animal trainers in speed and economy of training. In many instances we can use automatic training methods. We can apply to our training the data of **comparative psychology,** utilizing new tricks, new animals. We can turn out multiple units — 200 "Clever Hanses" instead of one. Furthermore, the systematic nature of the theory puts us in a position to advance to new and more elaborate behavior patterns, to predict results and forestall difficulties. So far, all our applications have been made for the purpose of advertising exhibits for General Mills, Inc. We developed first a series of trained chicken acts, which were used for county-fair booth exhibits in the Midwest, for the purpose of advertising farm seeds. These acts were performed by a group of 2-year-old hens which had been culled from a neighbor's flock and were destined for the stew pot. We used a hen-sized stage, some specially constructed props, and a solenoid-driven automatic feed hopper for dispensing reinforcements in the form of scratch grain.

One hen played a 5-note tune on a small piano, another performed a "tap dance" in costume and shoes, while a third "laid" wooden eggs from a nest box; the eggs rolled down a trough into a basket—the audience could call out any number of eggs desired, up to eight, and the hen would lay that number, nonstop.

Principle of successive approximations

The basic operation in all these acts was reinforcement at the proper moment in the behavior sequence, by presenting the chicken with a small amount of scratch grain from the solenoid-operated hopper. During the training period, **successive approximations** to the desired behavior, and component parts of the final pattern, were reinforced. During performances longer ratios or more elaborate completed patterns were reinforced to keep the behavior at a high level of strength.

During the ensuing year three sets of these acts were prepared and shipped all over the United States and placed in the hands of men who had had only 1 or 2 days' training. The birds played thousands of performances without a single failure, except for an occasional sluggish performance due to ill health or overfeeding. The acts proved to be unprecedented crowd-stoppers at the fairs and feedstore "open-house" events where they played, showing to as many as 5000 people in a day.

Priscilla, the fastidious pig

The success of these acts led to the development of a trained pig show, "Priscilla, the Fastidious Pig," whose routine included turning on the radio, eating breakfast at a table, picking up the dirty clothes and putting them in a hamper, running the vacuum cleaner around, picking out her favorite feed from those of her competitors, and taking part in a quiz program, answering "Yes" or "No" to questions put by the audience, by lighting up the appropriate signs.

Priscilla was similarly shown at fairs and special feedstore events and conventions throughout the country. She also appeared on television. She was even more successful than the chicken acts at jamming fair booths and feedstores with spectators. The pig act was in use almost steadily from the fall of 1948 to the summer of 1950. It was necessary to train a replacement about every 3 to 5 months, for the pigs rapidly became too large for easy shipping. After training, the pigs were turned over to their handler, usually a General Mills' feed salesman, who had had 1 or 2 days' instruction at our farm or in the field under our supervision.

In addition to teaching handlers to manage the animals on the road, we have twice taught instructors to do the basic training of the animals and assist with the instruction of the handlers. Both experiences in training instructors were successful and demonstrated clearly that people with no special psychological background can learn the methods and theory behind our animal training procedures. One instructor was a woman college graduate who had taken her degree in statistics and sociology. The other was an average male high school graduate, whose only specialty had been radio repair work. Both acquired in a few weeks most of the techniques of training the existing acts, and enough of the theory and nature of the process to train new acts on their own.

A chick act is hatched

Our next development was a baby chick act. Sixty to 100 chicks are trained for one show. Beginning at about one week of age, they are trained for about 10 days. The show is run with about 10 or 12 chicks on stage. Each runs up a ramp or inclined plane to a platform from which he can reach a feed hopper. He "roots" the top chick off, grabs a bite of feed, then in turn gets pushed off by the next in line. As he goes, he falls onto a tilting pan and is deposited onto the stage floor, accompanied by the sounding of a chime and flashing of a trade name sign. This sequence of behavior results in an endless chain of baby chicks running up the ramp and sliding off. When the group becomes sleepy, they are replaced by a fresh batch, and the show can thus go on indefinitely; it has actually been used about 12 hours a day in most cases.

This act is our first "packaged act." It is designed to run virtually automatically. It requires only the attendant to keep the feed hopper full and change the group of chicks on stage when they become sleepy. No special training is required for the attendant; mimeographed directions are shipped out with the chicks and provide the only necessary instruction. This act has been a perennial favorite and we have trained more than 2500 chicks to fill orders for this display.

We have developed two variations on the baby chick act. One uses a projector to present advertising copy, with an endless chain of baby chicks in motion around it. The other variation substitutes for the ramp a series of steps onto which the chicks must jump.

A trained calf

A calf was trained for the General Mills' booth at the International Dairy Exposition at Indianapolis. "Larro Larry" took part in a quiz program by lighting up "Yes" and "No" signs, as did Priscilla the Pig, and played "bull in the China Shop" by systemically upsetting an elaborate display of dishes, to the great alarm of the passing crowd.

A turkey act

A turkey act has been developed in which members of the audience play a game with the turkey. The bird is placed in a display case and has access through an opening to part of the miniature playing field. The turkey is trained to rake a steel ball off this field into his goal. The audience player is given a long pole with a magnet on one end and tries to guide the ball along the playing field into his goal before the turkey wins. Various barriers are placed along the playing field to make the game more difficult for both players.

Additional acts

Additional acts using grown chickens have been designed and used, two involving discrimination problems: the Card Sharp, who picks out a better poker hand than a member of the audience, and the Old Shell Game, in which the chicken picks out the shell with the bean under it; and two contests between two birds, a High Jump contest, and a Strength of Pull

test. Another automatic act was created by training a hen, on a very high fixed ratio, to beat a toy drum for hours at a time. We also trained a hen in some bizarre contortions; the hen twisted her neck to one side and over her back so that she appeared to be looking frantically in all directions at once. This was billed as "The Civilian Aircraft Spotter" or "The Atom Bomb Neurosis." We have done a few experiments and some developmental work on rats, hamsters, guinea pigs, ducks, pigeons, rabbits, cats, dogs, and crows.

There are, obviously, innumerable other possibilities in the field of advertising exhibits. One is the perfection of the "packaged act," the fully automatic unit which can be shipped anywhere, set up in a store window or convention booth, and operated day in and day out with no more instructions than are necessary for the operation of any machine designed for such use. One adaptation of the automatic act is the animated display — show window advertising in which live animals take the place of puppets and robots.

Possibilities for entertainment

However, probably the biggest applications exist in the entertainment world. Here we can take over the formal animal training involved in the standard animal act for stage, circus, and movies, and do it faster, cheaper, better, and in multiple units. It is possible to create new acts, whole new circuses, in fact, using unusual animals and unusual acts, and again do it cheaply, quickly, and in numbers limited only by time and production facilities. Television offers unusual opportunities. We can invade the field of night-club entertainment with novel small animals. We can sell or rent trained animal units to hospitals, doctors' offices, waiting rooms of various sorts, or even to private individuals, supplying instructions on care and maintenance.

Applications to training of farm animals

Another important application of animal psychology is the training of farm animals. Farm dogs and horses could be rendered much more useful to the average farmer if they were given appropriate training. Farmers could themselves be instructed in training and handling their own animals.

Training seeing-eye dogs

The training of dogs for the blind could probably be done on a larger scale, more rapidly and efficiently. One of the big problems of the "Seeing Eye" institution was obtaining instructors. The difficulty was, apparently, that the first masters of the art did not have a sufficiently precise theoretical formulation in training the dogs and hence could not pass the information on to new instructors. They then encountered another problem in instructing the blind to handle the dogs and met numerous failures here in adapting client to dog. Many of these failures could now doubtless be avoided.

Dogs, of course, can be trained more readily with the new methods in all the traditional fields of canine service to mankind: hunting, guarding children and property, and detective work. Military use of dogs in such tasks as guard duty and carrying messages can also be made more effective.

This, then, seems to be the general outline of a promising new field which we have only begun to explore. It is so vast, we feel, that we cannot begin to develop one-tenth of the projects we have considered. More psychologists, grounded in the theory, are needed to advance the technology and explore the undeveloped portions of this program. Furthermore, once the technology gets under way and the business develops, there will be active need for academic psychologists to do the background research necessary for full development of the program. And, of course, as psychologists continue to do basic research using animals as subjects, one by-product will be new and better methods of applied animal psychology.

Two types of problems have cropped up repeatedly in our efforts. (1) Apparatus problems have consumed much more time than problems connected with the behavior. The apparatus must be suited to the physique of the particular animal, must be durable enough to stand up under cross-country shipment, and must be foolproof enough to be operated by relatively untrained personnel. (2) We need to know the answers to various "academic" problems, such as "What sort of fixed ratio will an animal sustain on a response made to a disappearing manipulandum, a key available, for example, only every 3 minutes?" "What would constitute an adequate reinforcement for a hamster, to sustain performances over several hours without satiation?" "What are the emotional characteristics of rabbits and guinea pigs — to what sort and magnitude of stimuli will they adapt, and what is the nature of the curve of recovery from such an adaptation?"

The study of these and related questions — in short, the reexamination of the whole field of **comparative psychology** in this new light — by psychologists who have available the facilities of an animal laboratory, would greatly speed up the development of the applied field.

Conclusion

In conclusion, we feel that here is a genuine field of applied psychology, old as "group living" and "parenthood" in its subject matter, but new in method and approach, which psychologists can enter with promise of financial reward and a sense of accomplishment and ultimate benefit to the science. For we all know that there is nothing as convincing to the layman of the worth of a discipline as achievement, and the present field offers the psychologist a fine opportunity to demonstrate control of his subject matter.

7

Verhave: "The pigeon as a quality-control inspector"*†

Many of the operations involved in the quality-control inspection of commercial products consist of monotonous checking jobs performed by human operators. In addition to monotony, these (usually visual) inspection jobs have several other characteristics in common: (*a*) They require little if any manual skill or dexterity, (*b*) they require good visual acuity, (*c*) they require a capacity for color vision, and (*d*) they are extremely difficult to automate. There is, however, an organic device which has the following favorable properties: (*a*) an average life span of approximately 10–15 years (Levi, 1963), (*b*) an extreme flexibility in adjusting to its environment as well as an enormous learning ability (Ferster & Skinner, 1957; Smee, 1850)‡, (*c*) a visual acuity as good as the human eye (Reese, 1964), (*d*) color vision (Reese, 1964). The price for one such device is only

(approximately) $1.50; its name: *Columba livia domestica* or the pigeon.

Because of the characteristics listed above it is quite feasible to train pigeons to do all the visual checking operations involved in commercial manufacture. What follows is a brief account of an exploratory attempt to put the above suggestion into actual practice (Verhave, 1959). This paper is written partially in self-defense: Stories about the pill-inspecting pigeons have circulated for many years§— many versions containing gross inaccuracies.

In July of 1955 I was employed as a **"psycho-pharmacologist"** at one of the larger pharmaceutical companies. The main purpose of the laboratory was to develop and evaluate techniques for the experimental analysis of the effects of drugs on the behavior of animals.

Sometime, probably early in 1958, I finally took the tour of the plant, which is mandatory for all new employees. During the all-day tour of the extensive research and manufacturing facilities, I ran into the (gelatin) drug-capsule facilities. The capsules are manufactured by several very large and extremely complex machines, which together have a maximum production capacity of approximately 20,000,000 capsules per day. All of the capsules, which are made in a large number of sizes and colors, are visually inspected. This job was done by a contingent of about 70 women. After inspection the capsules go to other machines which fill them automatically with the appropriate pharmaceuticals. The capsules are inspected in batches. The number of caps in a batch depends on the volume or size of the capsule: the larger the capsule size, the smaller the number in a batch to be inspected. All of the capsules in a particular batch are of the same shape, size, and color. A big reservoir with a funnel drops the capsules at a fixed rate on an endless moving belt. The inspector, or "capsule sorter" as she

---

*By Thom Verhave, Queens College of the City University of New York. Originally written for *Control of Human Behavior,* (Ulrich, Stachnik, and Mabry, eds., 1966), this version is reprinted with changes and corrections from the one which appeared in the *American Psychologist,* 1966, **21**, 109–112.
T. Verhave.

†Opinions and conclusions contained in this article are those of the author. They are not to be construed as necessarily reflecting the views or the endorsement of either the pharmaceutical industry or any pigeon. I am indebted to John E. Owen, my former collaborator, for a critical reading of this paper, which saved me from many errors due to faulty memory.
T. Verhave.

‡It was Alfred Smee (1818–1877), a London surgeon, biologist, and biophysicist, who established that: "The various images impressed upon the mind of man and animals, according to their pleasurable or painful character, regulate ... their subsequent operations. By a pleasurable impression the most obdurate beast may, to some extent, be tamed, and led to perform various acts ... (page 72). Pigeons may be readily taught to go through a bolting wire by gently pushing them through a few times and then supplying them with food ...." (page 73).

§See, for example, C. P. Hickman. *Integrated Principles of Zoology* (1966, page 845).

is called, is located in front of the moving belt, which is illuminated from underneath. She "pattern scans" the capsules as they move by and picks up and throws out all "skags." A skag is a discard capsule because it is off-color, has a piece of gelatin sticking out, or has a dent in it. This also includes all double-cap capsules. When the capsule comes to the capsule sorter, it is already closed by putting two halves, a cap and a body, together. This step was already performed by the production machine. Sometimes, however, during transportation or in storage a second cap (the larger half of a capsule) is put on top of an already capped capsule (a cap and body may vibrate apart and a loose cap may then slide over the body of another already capped capsule). Such a "double-cap skag" produces problems later on in the filling machine. After inquiry, I was told that the double-cap skag is also one of the more difficult types to spot.

The sorters (all female) are paid off on a group-bonus schedule employing "error cost." After the inspection of a batch is completed, a supervisor (usually also female) scoops a ladleful of inspected capsules out of the barrel in which they were collected. The types of skag defects are categorized and the inspector can allow up to three or four of the more minor imperfections per sample before a batch is rejected. If she finds more than the allowed number of skags in the sample ladled from the batch, the inspector has to reinspect the entire batch of capsules. She is thus likely to reduce her bonus pay for the day since it depends partially on her own inspection output.

To come back to the main story: On seeing those women and their simple monotonous task, and knowing about Skinner's World War II project with "pigeons in a Pelican" (1960, 1965),* I said to myself, "Hell, a pigeon can do that!" Sometime later, I mentioned my bird-brain idea to a friend and fellow scientist in the **physiochemistry** department who also super-

*Skinner's project to train pigeons to guide missiles was undertaken during World War II. It was not, however, officially disclosed until September, 1959, when Skinner gave an account of it at the meeting of the American Psychological Association at Cincinnati, Ohio. The talk was subsequently published in the *American Psychologist* in 1960. Knowledge of Skinner's Kamikaze pigeons had been common lore long before official permission for disclosure had been granted by the Navy.

vised the electronics shop which supported the research division. He almost fell out of his chair and choked in a fit of laughter. However, after the joke had worn off, we talked more seriously about my odd notion, especially after I told him about Project ORCON (organic control—Skinner, 1960, 1965). Eventually the director of research and I talked about it. It so happened that I had come up with my suggestion at an opportune time. The company had recently spent a considerably sum of money on a machine constructed by an outside engineering firm designed to inspect automatically for double caps. It did not work. After some deliberation the director of research gave me the go-ahead to build a demonstration and tryout setup. With the able help and splendid cooperation of the instrument-shop people, under the direction of my friend of the physiochemistry department, a demonstration apparatus was built.

While the apparatus was being designed and built, I had plenty of opportunity to consider varying aspects of the discrimination-training problems I would be faced with. The first decision to be made was which particular "skag" problem to tackle first. I obtained samples of various sized capsules of different colors. It was tempting to tackle the most troublesome problem first: the double-cap skag, especially those involving small capsules of colorless and transparent gelatin. On the actual inspection line these were the most difficult to spot. After playing around with different ways of presenting these capsules to a pigeon behind a modified pigeon key, a simple solution to the double-cap problem was discovered by accident. One of the minor problems to be solved was the lighting of the capsules presented behind the key. I discovered that by shining a narrow beam of light at the proper angle on a three-dimensional transparent curved surface, one obtains a focal point inside the object. (The tops and bottoms of all capsules are either round or oval.) In the case of a double-cap skag, one gets two clearly distinct focal points in slightly different positions. So, even in the case of the transparent double-cap capsule, all a pigeon had to do was to discriminate between one versus two bright spots of light inside the curious objects behind his key: no problem!†

†The opaque, single-color double cap may still be a difficult discrimination problem, even for a pigeon.

For the purpose of working out the details of the actual training and work procedure, however, I decided to take the simplest discrimination problem possible. I chose a simple color discrimination: white versus red capsules. Two naive birds were selected for inspection duty. For one bird the red capsules were arbitrarily defined as skags (S). For the other bird, the white capsules were given the same status.

There were two pigeon keys. One key was actually a small transparent window, the other was opaque. The capsules could be brought into view behind the transparent key one by one at a maximum rate of about two per second. After a preliminary training phase, the birds were run as follows: A single peck on the weakly illuminated opaque key would (*a*) momentarily (.5 second) turn off the light behind the transparent key, and (*b*) weakly illuminate the window key to an extent insufficient to see much of the capsule in place behind it.

Next, a single peck on the now weakly lit window key would turn on a bright and narrow beam of light which clearly illuminated the capsule. The capsules were individually mounted in small and hollow bottlestops glued onto the metal plates of the endless belt. If the bird now pecked three more times on the window key with the new illuminated capsule exposed to view, a brief tone would sound. Next came the moment of decision. If the capsule exposed to view was judged to be a skag, the bird was required to make two more pecks on the window key. This would (*a*) turn off the beam of light illuminating the capsule, (*b*) move up the next capsule, and (*c*) produce food by way of the automatic hopper on a fixed-percentage basis (usually 100%). However, if the capsule was considered to be acceptable, the bird indicated this by changing over to the opaque key. A peck on this key would also (*a*) turn off the beam of light behind the other key (window), and (*b*) move up the next capsule. It would not, however, produce reinforcement.

A bird, then, determined his own inspection rate. A peck on the opaque key would initiate an inspection cycle. However, reinforcement came only after making the appropriate number of pecks on the window key in case of a true skag only. Skags occurred rarely; they made up 10% of all the capsules on the belt. Wrong pecks, either false alarms or misses, did not get reinforced, and produced a blackout (Ferster, 1954)

of 30 seconds. The results were very encouraging: Both birds inspected on a 99 percent correct basis within 1 week of daily discrimination training. The director of the pharmacology division, my immediate superior, who had watched the entire project with serious misgiving since its inception (he was sincerely afraid I was making a fool of myself), was delighted. In his immediate enthusiasm he called the director of research, who came over for a look. One week later the vice presidents as well as the president of the company had been given a demonstration. Everybody, including my immediate associates and co-workers, was greatly excited. The situation, as Skinner had previously discovered in a similar situation (Skinner, 1960), was a great source for jokes. There was talk about a new company subsidiary: "Inspection, Inc.!" (Company slogan: "It's for the birds!")

There were some sobering thoughts, however. One of them concerned the staggering problem of the logistics involved in getting pigeons to inspect as many as 20,000,000 separate objects each day. Although this problem did not seem insoluble to me, the details of the various possible approaches to a solution were never worked out.

After the company president had watched my feathered pupils perform, he congratulated me on my achievement. I was subsequently informed that serious consideration would be given to the further use and development of the method. I was also told that I could expect a visit from the chairman of the board and his brother, both elder statesmen of the company, who made all final policy decisions of importance. During their brief visit to the laboratory, one of them raised the question of possible adverse publicity. What about the Humane Society, and, more important, suppose salesmen from other pharmaceutical houses should tell doctors not to buy any of our company's products: "Who would trust medicine inspected by pigeons?!" I suggested that the use of pigeons was incidental, and that, for example, one could use hawks just as well; after all, what is better than a hawk's eye? This suggestion produced a wan smile.

One other problem that was brought up raised the question of the pigeons coming in contact with what was being inspected. The competition could well choose to ignore the mechanical details of the situation and exploit the more distasteful but imaginary possibilities. Even though the birds would only see the capsules at a distance through a window, the first mental picture* is usually one of a pigeon "manually" (proboscically?) sorting capsules, a thought no doubt repulsive to many people, especially to those who already have an aversion to birds as such.

After a brief stay, and a polite pat on the back, my distinguished visitors left.

Three weeks went by without any further word from HUM (Higher-Up-Management— Verhave, 1961). I concluded that probably meant that my pigeons were finished. I was right. Sometime later I was so informed. Through the grapevine I learned that the board of directors had voted 13 to 1 not to continue to explore the use of animals for quality-control inspection. The one "yes" vote presumably came from the director of research who initially had given me the green light for the preliminary demonstration.

There is one further amusing tale to the story: The company did try to patent my inspection method. The poor lawyer assigned to the case almost developed a nervous breakdown. It turned out to be "unpatentable" because, as the lawyers of the patent office put it (so succinctly), the method involved "a mental process" which is unpatentable in principle.† I tried to pin my lawyer friends down on what they meant by a "mental process." I suggested that the pigeon was merely an organic computer.‡ However, I got nowhere. Lawyers apparently want no part of either physicalism or behaviorism.§

---

*If a behaviorist may be excused for using such illegitimate terms. . . .

†On this point, I may refer the reader to a recent article in *Science* by J. H. Munster, Jr., and Justin C. Smith (1965).

‡The main advantage the pigeon has over mechanical or electronic checking or inspection devices lies both in the superiority of its eyeball as a photocell and pattern recognition device and its nervous system as a rather advanced computer. That the steadily advancing computer technology may soon catch up with our feathered friends, however, is indicated by a recent article in *Electronics* (Hattaway, Hietanen, and Rothfusz, 1966). We may in the future have to add bestiological unemployment to the many social and economic problems that challenge us.

So much as far as my own story is concerned. My efforts apparently stimulated another exploratory attempt by my friend, William Cumming, of Columbia University, who trained pigeons to inspect diodes (Cumming, 1966). Brief descriptions of his work also can be found in an article by Ferster and Ferster (1962), an anonymous article in *Factory* (1959), and a recent article in *The Atlantic Monthly* by R. J. Herrnstein (1965).‖

---

§Not even the views of St. Thomas Aquinas (1225–1274) and Rene Descartes (1596–1650) (see Verhave, 1966), concerning animals as "mere machines," seem to have penetrated these circles yet. According to Anthony LeGrand (or Legrand) ". . . A Beast is a mere Automaton or Engin: that is, an Animal destitute of all Knowledge, and consequently may be thus defined: A Beast is an Artificial Engin or Machine of God, furnished with a various and wonderful structure of Organs, containing in itself a material principle of Life, Motion and Sense." Legrand was a Franciscan Friar who died in anno domini 1699. He was at one time Professor of Philosophy and Theology at Douay in France. He was subsequently sent as a missionary to England where he taught Descartes' philosophy as well as Catholicism and was the main proponent of Cartesianism in the England of his days. The above quotation appears in his Institutio Philosophiae, secundum principia Renati Descartes, nova methodo adornata et explicata ad usum juventutis academicae London, (1672, 4th ed. 1680). An English translation by Richard Blome appeared in 1694 at London. It also has a grand title: "An Entire Body of Philosophy, according to the Principles of the Famous Renate des Cartes. . . . Written originally in Latin by the Learned Anthony le Grand, Now carefully Translated from the Last Corrections, Alterations, and Large Additions of the Author, Never yet Published. . . ." The quote appears in this 1694 edition in Part VII on page 254. I quote Legrand's statement because it suggests a more plausible reason why, even today, animals are, by the general public, considered to be "stupid" and not capable of showing intelligence: according to Legrand animals are "destitute of all knowledge." Do we have here one more illustration of the truth of Fred Keller's remark that "Descartes' views were nearly identical with the 'commonsense' opinion of most of the persons who will read this account—proof convincing enough of his influence upon the thought of later generations" (Keller, 1937, pages 2–3)?

‖Herrnstein (with D. H. Loveland, 1964) is also the author of an interesting and relevant article on the formation of a complex visual concept in the pigeon. Concerning this topic, see also Lubow, Siebert, and Carr-Harris (1966).

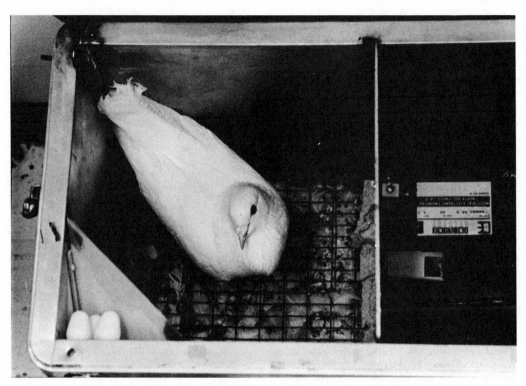

Figure 13.11 Pigeon at work in pill-inspection apparatus. (Photo courtesy of Thom Verhave.)

One problem not yet touched on deserves some discussion. In the demonstration apparatus the capsules were coded as to whether they were acceptable or skags. In this way the automatic programming (relay) circuit could set up and enforce the appropriate discriminatory behavior of the birds. However, on an actual inspection line, this aspect of the training procedure could no longer be maintained. There would be no way of knowing which capsules are skags except by actual inspection. Consequently on a real inspection line there would be no way of knowing when to reward or not to reward the animal inspector! As a result, due to the lack of differential reward, the animal's discriminations would rapidly deteriorate.* There are two solutions. I discarded the

first and most obvious one because it seemed mechanically cumbersome and not as interesting as the other solution.

The first solution would involve the use of known skags. A certain percentage of the capsules inspected would consist of such labeled duds, and be used to check up on the discriminatory behavior of the birds. This is similar to the use of catch tests in human **psychophysical** experiments. This solution to the problem of guaranteeing that the animal inspector conforms to the values of his human employers makes it necessary to determine what minimum percentage of the objects inspected have to be planted skags in order to keep the inspecting behavior at an acceptable level of reliability.†

As a solution to the conformity-enforcement problem, however, this general solution is

---

*Skinner, in his World War II project to train pigeons to home missiles, did not face this problem. His birds were meant to "extinguish" after a brief period of duty. Blough (1961), however, did run into the same obstacle in his attempt to adapt his beautiful

threshold-determination procedure to the study of brightness contrast.

†This question was investigated experimentally by Cumming. See his 1966 article.

expensive and awkward. The on-line inspection equipment would need special machinery to insert in a random manner a fixed percentage of "stool-pigeon skags" and after inspection remove them again automatically for later reuse. The slightest observable difference between the "planted" objects and the other ones would lead to the development of a conditional discrimination (Lashley, 1938), and reintroduce the problem one set out to solve initially.

The second solution is simpler from a purely mechanical point of view. It also is of more theoretical or philosophical interest.

Briefly, it would involve the use of a minimum of two animals to simultaneously inspect each object. Initially, each animal would be trained to inspect capsules by using a training apparatus such as the one I had already constructed. In this apparatus all the capsules would be labeled as to whether they were skags or not and thus control the reward circuit.

After the desired discriminatory performance was well established the two birds would be removed to the on-line inspection situation. From then on the birds would only be rewarded if they *both* agreed on whether a particular object was a skag or not. Such an agreement-contingency setup would most likely be quite adequate to maintain the desired behavior. There is, of course, the possibility that both birds would indeed, once in a while, agree to treat a skag as an acceptable object. However, the probability of this happening for any particular object on a particular inspection trial is the product of the error frequencies (the probability of such an error) of each bird. If, therefore, each bird independently has an error frequency as high as 1 out of 100, the probability of both birds being wrong but still rewarded would be 1 out of 10,000! Hooking additional animals into the agreement-contingency circuit would make the possibility of the development of a "multiple folly"* very unlikely.

The solution is of some philosophical interest because it makes the pigeon observers act according to Charles Peirce's (1923, orig. publ. 1878) **pragmatic theory** of truth: "The opinion which is fated to be ultimately agreed to by all who investigate, is what is meant by the truth, and the object represented in this opinion

is real [pp. 56–57]." It also appears to me that the agreement-contingency type of arrangement provides a basic paradigm for the experimental analysis of social behavior, a terra incognita so far hardly even explored by a systematic experimental investigation (Verhave, 1966; 1967).

In conclusion, let me point out that the idea of using trained animals for the dubious purposes of Homo sapiens is very old indeed (Gudger, 1923).† Since antiquity man has domesticated many animals (Hahn, 1896; Shaler, 1896; Thevenin, 1947; Wood-Gush, 1959, Zeuner, 1954). It seems an obvious development to apply our modern knowledge of behavior theory to the task of training some of our animal companions for the performance of various, hopefully peaceful, and more sophisticated tasks (Bertrand, 1967; Breland and Breland, 1951; Clarke, 1958; Gudger, 1923; Herrnstein, 1965).

The obstacle in the way of such developments is not our ignorance of behavior, though it is still large, but mainly, it seems, the obstinate belief of man in his intellectual superiority over other creatures‡ as well as a generalized fear of the imagined consequences of novel developments.

---

*"folie a deux, trois, . . . *n*."

---

†As far as "dubious purposes" are concerned: Skinner (1960) has mentioned the use of sea gulls to detect submarines in the English Channel during World War I. Elsewhere (1956) he has referred to the use, by Russians, of dogs to blow German tanks during World War II. Such practices seem to have a long and curious history. An English author writing ca. 1850 states that: "Many animals are trained to perform certain actions under the influence of fear. At one period, in Belgium, dogs were taught to carry smuggled goods across the frontier into France. After having been frequently beaten by a person dressed up in the uniform of a Custom-house Officer, they acquired such a dread of anyone in that dress, that they were always on their guard, and could not be caught by the real officials. In the same manner the Russian Soldiers in the Caucasus have trained their dogs to keep watch against any surprise by the Circassians. When the dogs are being fed, a man in a Circassian dress takes their food from them and beats them, and thus the dogs, having acquired a deadly animosity against the whole tribe, give instant alarm as soon as they perceive the presence of one of them" (Thompson, 1851, page 406).

‡See the quotation from Anthony Legrand! (fourth footnote, page 465).

14

Retrospect and prospect

Here are a few propositions and tentative conclusions that can be derived from our present perspective, as we look out over the broad terrain of animal and human behavior.

1 Some slants, perspectives, and basic considerations: Science is a human activity, a procedure for making accurate observations and deriving valid propositions about them. Science presents (avoidable) pitfalls as does any human endeavor. Among them are the scientist's own silent assumptions and beliefs, which must be searched out and identified because they affect the outcome of his inquiry. Scientific procedures contrast sharply with nonscientific procedures.

2 The nervous system and psychology: Recent research on the functioning of the nervous system leaves the relationship between the nervous system and behavior far from settled, but it does cast doubt on many hoary notions about that relationship. Contemporary work hints at the plausibility of fresh insights into the true function of the nervous system. The "hollow organism" theory is one such newer view.

3 Race and psychology: The fact that humans vary in skin color, hair texture, and size is beyond dispute. But do these anatomical properties correlate with the obvious psychological variation among human groups? Recent contributions in this area by students of man point out the dangers of stereotyping. They warn against drawing any conclusions about racial causes of differences among various populations of the single human species. Consider the far-reaching implications of Japan's invisible race or of the black Jews of Harlem.

4 Heredity and psychology: Starting with a clear definition of heredity in its proper biological setting, we examined its intrusion into psychological inquiry. Recent theory exposes the many fallacies connected with psychoheredity. While some psychologists think it a dead issue and act accordingly, others consider the heredity-environment question proper matter for a lively and as yet unsettled debate.

5 Instincts(?), tropisms, and imprinting: A correct understanding of behavior demands a distinction between unlearned and learned acts. Are organisms ushered into the world with ready-made psychological reactions? This is a crucial question. On this point, recent work explodes many myths, such as the alleged punctual return of the swallows of Capistrano, the instinctive mass suicide of lemmings, and the ferocity of "wild" animals. Also, the work of the young ethologists appears to show the cultural transmission of tool-using, grooming, and other traditions through learning. On the other hand, migration (as of salmon) is apparently a simple, unlearned response to a physicochemical condition. Thus, we see a gradient ranging from rigid, reflexive, and tropismic or pheromonic activities to more flexible and uniquely adaptive responses. We may debate where to draw the boundary between the unlearned and the learned, but we find no difficulty in distinguishing between them at the extremes of the continuum.

6 Beginnings, origins, nascencies, and sequences: Does behavior spring forth full blown or does it have a natural history of its own? At the embryological stage of organismic development, we might expect to find only uncoordinated and diffuse mass activity. Continued observation, however, has revealed the development of specific responses to specific conditions which involve learning. Thus, acts which appear at birth as genuine psychological responses have been shown to have evolved prior to birth. Imprinting of the duck embryo confirms such an interpretation, and recent discoveries of rapid behavior development of infants offer exciting vistas of the tremendous potentialities in very early learning. The detrimental effects of early infantile mishandling are eloquently illustrated by such exhibits as the wolf children of India and autistic children in America. Both attest to the "great plasticity in infantile and early child development," a a fairly recent finding.

7 *The reactional biography, or psychological history:* A realization of the significance of specific conditions in the early development of behavior leads us naturally to the conception of a reactional biography, or psychological history, which encompasses every one of a person's reactions to every stimulus object with which he ever interacts. This concept, with its stress on past interaction as the key to present behavior, implies a tremendous human potential for selecting and modifying stimulus objects and stimulus situations and thus affecting human behavior. This newer view of human nature contrasts sharply with the pessimism of traditional views which hold characteristics like "personality" and "intelligence" to be inborn and virtually immutable. If the newer view is the more correct, then psychology has not yet come into its own.

8 *Conformity, or shared responses:* Few animals are solitary; most live with other animals. What effect do social factors have on the developing organism? The excerpts from recent research reports examined in Chapter 8 show the inevitable force with which culture shapes diet, clothes, voice, posture, even anatomy (e.g., Chinese "club foot"), and starvation. And newer studies show that man is not the sole possessor of culture. He shares this trait with monkeys, chimps, and even birds.

9 *Personality:* Newer objective approaches make personality more fluid and complex but also more concrete and manageable than do older conceptions. Proof of the pudding lies in personality transformations seen when children imitate models in social learning experiments. Building social behavior in hopelessly autistic children by means of shock is another test of the validity of newer conceptions of personality. The way to perpetuate psychosis has been spelled out, and, in fact, the prescription is being followed every day in mental hospitals operating under the old banners. There are many implications of the newer approaches to personality in the area of personality assessment.

10 *Intelligence:* An older, still extant view holds intelligence to be a native and permanent fixed quality of some sort that limits the possessor's development. Recently, longitudinal studies of children's intelligence development over many years show anything but constancy of IQ. The 30-year follow-up study of orphanage children with contrasting early life experiences argues against the immutability of the IQ. Rosenthal's study shows that IQ is apparently susceptible to teachers' expectancies. Groso's report outlines the role of biological defectiveness in mental retardation. Altogether, the newer work calls for a broader view of mental retardation, like that offered by Bucklew.

11 *Cognitive processes: Perceiving and thinking:* Cognitive processes, as described in Chapter 11, include perceiving and thinking responses. Studies using upside-down lenses that totally disrupt vision show the developmental nature of visual perception. While absolute pitch has traditionally been considered an innate gift, recent work tends to upset that notion by showing that such pitch discrimination can be acquired. That

visual perception is tied to and derived from reachings, turnings, and other movements is indicated by the study in which a monkey was prevented from seeing its hands. Studies on "tickle talk" demonstrate the possibility of translating visual images into touch images on the skin of the back, for example. A technological device to aid the blind may be in the offing as the result of such work. Is there a form of perception that is not dependent on the sense organs? The answer depends on whether a proponent or opponent of ESP is talking.

Does thinking occur in a vacuum or is it earthbound and influenced by setting factors? The thinking of obese patients on a starvation diet gives a partial answer to the question. The relation of speech muscle activity to reading is shown in a study by Hardyck; reading can be speeded up by active stepping down or elimination of the muscle action concerned. Finally, studies of phantom limbs, phantom breasts, and phantom sensations show that once certain reactions are built up, they can survive amputation of the anatomical portion involved. Here is another instance in which the psychological response transcends or triumphs over the biological, even though the phantom reaction could not have evolved without the biological substrate. Once established, however, a psychological response can declare its independence of anatomy.

12 Feelings and emotions: The most up-to-date and exciting development in the area of feelings has been biotelemetry, which has vastly extended the possible dimensions of psychological investigation. Another promising technique, pupillometry, shows the variety of organismic involvement in affective response. Experimental and clinical studies with dogs, as with humans, demonstrate the easy conditionability and long retention of affective reac-

tions. Tests on cockroaches indicate that they, too, are involved in establishing dominance–submission relationships. Furthermore, death may result from changes that are comparable to those that manifest themselves in the stress syndrome of humans.

Emotions are treated in Chapter 13 as aborted, atypical, fragmented responses, very different from feelings. Though studies of emotion are difficult to perform in the laboratory, we nevertheless considered a fairly successful experimental investigation of simulated panic, as well as a more realistic experiment by Milgram of destructive obedience. The inhuman experiments performed in the concentration camps have many rich implications for the study of human nature.

13 Learning: Theory and application: The literature on learning is represented in every chapter of the present book, since learning is the very hallmark of psychology. In Chapter 13 we saw that even a horse can learn how to learn, and that a porpoise can be so domesticated as to be afraid of the open sea. The importance of the response in learning is indicated by the ease with which language learning occurs when the correct strategy is worked out. Further applications of recent developments of learning theory are illustrated in toilet training via conditioning using biotelemetric devices. More striking still are achievements in the treatment of behavior pathology via operant conditioning. The possibility of behavioral engineering is illustrated in Breland and Breland's development of a rich variety of animal acts for either pedagogical or entertainment purposes. And, last but not least, we have the possibility of the pigeon as a quality-control inspector in a drug manufacturing plant. Such applications of psychology only hint of the shape of things to come.

Glossary*

abnormal psychology   An area of specialization within psychology which concerns itself with the study of behavior disorders.

abortion   The giving of birth (accidentally, artificially, or embryonally) to a nonviable embryo or fetus prior to the fourth month of pregnancy.

accelerometer   An instrument used for measuring acceleration.

accommodation   The effect of a new experience in modifying characteristic ways of thinking, perceiving, feeling, and behaving.

achievement test   Any test which measures the testee's general level and rate of academic accomplishment.

Acromycin (Achromycin)   A brand name for the drug Tetracycline Hydrochloride.

adrenal glands   Ductless endocrine glands located near or upon the kidneys (one on each side of the body) which secrete adrenaline, a kind of emergency hormone secreted in greater supply by sympathetic nervous system activity.

affective reaction   A kind of reaction in which the organism does not do anything with respect to any stimulus object other than itself. Feelings such as hate, love, fear, etc.

alcoholic hallucinosis   A psychiatric disorder where disturbing hallucinations result from a heavy indulgence in alcohol. This condition may also develop in a predisposed person after only moderate intake.

Amblystoma   A genus of tailed amphibians.

amentia   Subnormal development particularly in the area of intellectual capacities, with the implication that such incapacity has been prevalent since birth or early infancy.

amino acid   An organic compound which is commonly found in proteins and is a fundamental constituent of living matter.

amniotic membrane   The membrane that surrounds the fetus. *See amniotic sac.*

amniotic sac   The sac that envelops the fetus as it develops in the uterus. *See amniotic membrane.*

amphibia   A class of vertebrates, including frogs, toads, newts, and salamanders, which generally begins life in the water, but later develops lungs.

anaclitic depression   A term for the syndrome of withdrawal that characterizes infants who have been separated from their mothers for a considerable period of time.

analysis of variance   A statistical method for determining whether the differences found between experimental groups, who have been differentially exposed to the influence of the experimental variable or variables, are greater than what may be expected by chance.

anatomy   A field of science which studies the structure of plants and animals.

androgen   A generic term for any substance which stimulates the develop-

---

*Prepared by Marvin J. Parrish.

ment and maintenance of male sexual characteristics.

anthropocentric bias   Showing partiality to the idea that man is the central fact or final aim and purpose of the universe.

anthropoid   Resembling man. Pertains especially to the larger, more highly developed apes. *See Anthropoidea.*

Anthropoidea   The classification, or suborder of primates that includes monkeys, apes, and man.

anthropologist   *See anthropology.*

anthropology   A field of science which concerns itself with the comparative study of human civilizations.

anthropomorphic   Excessive ascription of human characteristics to non-human beings, and interpretation of the behavior of such non-humans as if they were, in fact, human.

antibiotic   A chemical substance which is destructive to some forms or aspects of life. A dilute solution can be used to fight infectious diseases in man, animals, and plants.

anticonvulsant therapy   A drug therapy which attempts to prevent or relieve convulsions.

anxiety attack   (Also called *anxiety reaction*). A neurosis characterized by a generalized fear that something dreadful is about to happen, such fear having no apparent cause or object.

Apgar score   A simple and quick assessment made by a pediatrician within one minute of an infant's birth on the infant's heart rate, respiratory efficiency, reflex irritability, muscle tone, and color. Since the score on each item ranges from 0 to 2, the highest possible total score is 10.

aphasia   An impairment or loss of one's ability to use any form of language, generally thought to be due to lesions in the brain.

apoplexy   A condition caused by acute vascular lesions in the brain which involves a coma followed by paralysis.

applied psychology   A general area comprising the many practical applications of psychology, that is, in education, industry, and clinic.

aptitude test   Any test which attempts to assess the testee's potential for success in one or more tasks or fields of endeavor.

archaeological   *See archaeology.*

archaeology   A field of science and branch of anthropology which concerns itself with the study of the life and culture of ancient peoples by gaining its knowledge of such peoples through the excavated artifacts of earlier civilizations.

archetype   The original type or model.

Armenoid "race"   An early Caucasoid racial type that was mainly concentrated in the Middle East.

arthritis   Inflammation of a joint, which may be accompanied by pain, swelling, heat and redness.

artificial insemination   The artificial injection of semen into a female.

assimilation   The principle that an organism's response to a new situation will be like his responses to similar situations of the past.

astronomer   *See astronomy.*

astronomy   A field of science that concerns itself with the study of stars and other celestial bodies.

asymptote   A straight line which constantly approaches a regular curve, but never reaches it. *Asymptotic* may refer to the relationship of either line to the other.

asymptotic   *See asymptote.*

attention   The focusing on selected aspects of a current experience.

attention span   The length of time a person can devote his attention to a single thing. Also, the number of objects that can be distinctly perceived within a momentary presentation.

attic children   Children raised in seclusion with little opportunity to relate to other human beings on a social level.

audio-oscillator   An instrument capable of emitting a highly variable audio output.

autism   A severe psychotic behavior disorder in children which is characterized by extreme social withdrawal, proclivities toward repetitious activities, and lack of basic communication skills.

autistic   *See autism.*

autistic children   *See autism.*

autonomic nervous system   A major division of the nervous system which is the motor nerve supply of the smooth muscles and glands.

autosomal dominant gene   A dominant gene on a chromosome that is not a sex-chromosome.

autosomal recessive gene   A recessive gene on a chromosome that is not a sex-chromosome.

average error   The average amount of difference between separate judgments of a stimulus and the standard stimulus or between separate individual responses and the correct response.

aversive conditioning   Conditioning which uses some form of punishment as an aid to learning.

aviary   A large cage, house, or enclosure which houses many birds.

axolotl   A larval salamander of the genus Amblystoma.

barbiturate   A salt of barbituric acid. The *barbiturate* drugs are commonly used for sedation and anesthesia.

baseline   The measured status of a behavior before direct experimental manipulation has occurred.

behavior therapies   *See behavior therapy.*

behavior therapy   A behavior modification system which applies the principles of learning theory to the treatment of behavioral problems and anomalies.

behavioral engineer   A behavior therapist. *See behavior therapy.*

behaviorism   A school or viewpoint in psychology which contends that psychology as a science should study only *observable* behavior.

behaviorist   *See behaviorism.*

beluga   A white whale, also a white sturgeon which is found in the Black and Caspian Seas.

Binet IQ   An intelligence quotient as measured by the Stanford-Binet Intelligence Scale. *See Stanford-Binet Intelligence Scale.*

biopsy   The examination and diagnosis of tissue or other material which has been excised from the living body.

biotelemetry The study of physiological functions and processes via messages transmitted from radio devices ingested or implanted in an organism's body.

biped Any animal with only two feet.

bipedally *See biped.*

blastopore A temporary opening on the surface of the embryo which occurs during the gastrula stage of development.

body image The mental picture or representation one has of his own body, whether stationary or in motion.

bolus A small, round mass of some material such as food, pills, or fecal material.

bon vivant (French) A person having cultivated or refined tastes.

borderline case A case that diagnostically falls between broad classificatory levels of intelligence rating or behavior pathology. It is used most often as "borderline mental deficiency" and "borderline psychotic."

brain The anterior mass of nerve tissue of the central nervous system which is housed in the cranium.

brain trace The supposed locus of a specific "brain-recorded" learning.

card reading A practice whereby it is claimed by the performing psychist or medium that future events can be predicted by his reading and interpretation of cards.

cardiac arrest Cessation of heart function. Arterial blood pressure disappears.

cardiovascular system Pertaining to the heart and blood vessels.

castration The surgical removal of the testes, or of the penis and testes. In psychoanalysis *castration* or *castration complex* refers to the repressed fear of one's losing his genitals and the consequent anxiety which accompanies such a fear.

cataplexy A temporary state of weakness, immobility, and rigidity resulting from emotional strain or certain other forms of stimulation.

catharsis The purging or purification of one's emotional self by releasing tensions and anxieties through artistic expression, psychoanalysis, or some other kind of expressive or symbolic reaction.

cathode ray Streams of electrons projected from the surface of a negatively charged electrode. *Cathode rays* produce x-rays when they strike a solid surface.

Caucasian Of or belonging to the racial strain which is loosely called the "white race."

cell body The mass of cytoplasm and nucleus which gives rise to the branches of a nerve cell. *See neuron.*

cerebellum The division of the brain lying behind the cerebrum. It consists of two lateral hemispheres and serves the function of coordinating movements.

cerebral Of or pertaining to the cerebrum. *See cerebrum.*

cerebral cortex The gray matter on the surface of the cerebral hemispheres. *See cerebral hemisphere.*

cerebral hemisphere The large mass of brain tissue on either side of the cerebrum. *See cerebrum.*

cerebrum The principle portion of the brain which occupies the upper part of the cranium. It is the major division of the brain and the largest part of man's central nervous system.

Cetacea   An order of aquatic placental mammals which includes whales, porpoises, and dolphins.

Cetacean   *See Cetacea.*

chance   A name given to the combined effects of uncontrolled, perhaps unknown, variables in an experiment or other well-defined situation.

character disorder   A disorder marked by sporadic changes and inconstancy in one's volitional behavior.

chemosensory perception   Capacity to perceive changes in the chemical composition of substances.

chemotropic   *See chemotropism.*

chemotropism   A tropism which has some form of a gradient of chemical concentration as its stimulus. *See tropism.*

child   Any human being who is between one and twelve years of age. Childhood is an arbitrary division in the life span of human beings which covers year 1 to year 12.

cholera   An acute epidemic infectious disease which is characterized clinically by severe diarrhea, nausea, muscular cramps, and extreme physical exhaustion.

chromosomes   Small bodies within cells that contain the genes that are responsible for the organism's hereditary traits.

chronicity   A prolonged state of any disease, disorder, or habit.

clairvoyance   In parapsychology, the alleged power or ability to perceive objective events without the use of known sensory processes.

classical biology   The traditional approach in biology which advocates the study of biological processes without appealing to molecularistic or reductionistic explanations.

classical conditioning   A learning procedure whereby a new stimulus (conditioned stimulus) is made to acquire the response-eliciting properties of the original "natural" stimulus (unconditioned stimulus) by pairing the two stimuli in close temporal proximity.

cleft palate   A congenital condition where the roof of the mouth has a fissure along its median line due to incomplete development.

clinal   *See cline.*

cline   Continuous gradual change of characteristics within a population of species which is correlated with its ecological distribution.

clinician   One who offers assistance to individuals who have specific problems of one kind or another. Such aid is offered in a nonexperimental setting.

cocaine   A drug used as a local anesthetic, sedative, and narcotic; made from coca leaves.

codeine   An analgesic drug obtained from opium or artificially made from morphine.

cognition   A generic term for any process whereby an organism obtains knowledge and gains awareness. Loosely speaking, *cognition* refers to a thought or idea.

cognitive   *See cognition.*

commutator   A device used for changing the direction of an electric current.

comparative psychology   An area of specialization within psychology that concerns itself with the study of similarities and differences in the behavior of different animal species.

conditioned response   A new or modified response created by conditioning, either purposefully or accidentally. It is used more specifically in classical conditioning than in operant conditioning, but, strictly speaking, applies to both. *See classical conditioning and operant conditioning.*

conditioned stimulus   The stimulus that is made to acquire the response-eliciting properties of an unconditioned "natural" stimulus by presenting the two stimuli in close temporal proximity.

conditioning   A general term referring to either of the two systematically defined learning techniques of *classical conditioning* and *operant conditioning.*

confederate   An accomplice to the experimenter in a psychological experiment. The confederate's role as an experimenter "plant" is not known by the subject.

consanguineous   Having descended from the same ancestor, generally from an ancestor not greatly remote.

conscious   In psychoanalysis, a division of the psyche or mind that includes those aspects of mental life that are part of a person's awareness at a given point in time. The *conscious* exists in a dynamic relationship with the *preconscious* and the *unconscious.*

contrast group   Any group whose performance or condition is contrasted with that of another group which received some kind of experimental treatment or manipulation. In essence, a *contrast group* is a *"control" group* which, usually because of extenuating circumstances, did not receive adequate experimental control.

control group   A specific group of experimental subjects which does not receive the treatment of the *independent variable* and whose performance is contrasted with that of the experimental group.

convolution   One of the prominent irregular folds of the outer surfaces of the brain.

cordotomies   *See cordotomy.*

cordotomy   The surgical sectioning of a vocal cord. Also, the surgical interruption of anterolateral nervous pathways in the spinal cord for the purpose of pain alleviation.

corpus callosum   The commissure of the brain which lies at the bottom of the longitudinal fissure and connects the two cerebral hemispheres.

cortex   The outer portion of an organ as distinguished from its inner portion (medulla).

cortisone therapy   The injection of an adrenal cortical hormone, formally known as Kendall's compound E, for purposes of relieving any one of a number of allergic conditions or systemic disorders.

CR   *See conditioned response.*

cretinism   A chronic condition due to a lack of thyroid secretion in fetal life or early infancy. It is marked by gross physical stigmata as well as a lack of psychological development.

Cro-Magnon man   A prehistoric "race" of tall, erect men who inhabited the European continent.

Crustacea   A class of Arthropoda which includes, among other animals, shrimps, crabs, and waterfleas.

CS   *See conditioned stimulus.*

cultural   *See culture.*

cultural anthropology   An area of specialization within anthropology which concerns itself with the description and study of the culture and social behavior of various peoples.

culture   The learned and shared behavior of a group of people; a way of life transmitted from one generation to the next.

culture bound   A term in psychological testing which is used to describe a test which is conspicuously partial to a testee with a specific cultural background.

cyclotron   An apparatus used in atomic research to accelerate protons or deuterons to high energy levels.

cytoplasm   A transparent, slightly viscous solution which comprises all of the protoplasm of a cell except for the nucleus.

Darrow Bridge   An apparatus for determining electrical resistance; the essential component of the galvonometer which is used to measure the galvanic skin response.

db   The abbreviation for decibel. *See decibel.*

de novo (Latin)   From the beginning.

decibel   A unit for measuring the intensity of a sound wave.

dèjá vu **experience** (French)   An experiential illusion where one falsely perceives a new scene as one that is familiar to him.

dementia praecox   An older term for what is now more generally called schizophrenia. *See schizophrenia.*

deoxyribonucleic acid   A compound consisting of a long strand of many nucleotides in the form of a double helix. It is believed to be the inherited material of almost all living things.

dependent variable   The variable whose changes are the consequence of changes in the manipulated independent variable or variables.

depression   (Also called *depressive reaction*). In general, a state of lowered initiative and unhappy thoughts. When classified as a neurosis, a *depressive reaction* is more severe and is usually precipitated by some loss. Guilt feelings and self-depreciation often accompany it. In its most severe form, a state of depression can be classified as a *psychotic depressive reaction.*

dermatitis   Inflammation of the skin.

dermo-optic sense   The ability to "see" with the skin. It is alleged to be an ability of the mollusk *Pholas dactylus.* It has been claimed by some that human beings also possess this sense.

desquamatus   The scaly epithelial elements shed by the body, particularly the skin.

deus ex machina (Latin)   A god from a machine. A reference to the custom in classical tragedy of ushering in a god by stage machinery to solve a problem. Therefore, any theoretical entity invented to explain something which itself needs explaining.

developmental psychology   An area of specialization within psychology which concerns itself with the study of how individual organisms and classes of individual organisms develop psychologically.

dexedrine sulfate A central nervous system stimulant that is sympathomimetic. Since it depresses the appetite, it is frequently used in the treatment of obesity.

Dinaric "race" An early Caucasoid subracial type, generally characterized by a long, round face and flattened head, mainly concentrated in Eastern Europe.

discriminate *See discrimination.*

discrimination A term in learning theory which means an organism has at its disposal the ability to make differentiations among stimuli.

discrimination learning Learning that is manifested by the capacity to make perceptual differentiations among stimuli.

distal Away from the center or point of reference. A *distal* stimulus is an environmental event. A *proximal* stimulus impinges directly on a receptor. A *distal* response involves an organism's alteration of the environment in some way. A *proximal* response involves actual muscular movement on the organism's part.

diurnal cycle The progression of events which occurs during the day. (contrasted with *nocturnal* cycle)

DNA *See deoxyribonucleic acid.*

dualism In psychology, a point of view which represents a distinction between mental and physical phenomena, loosely termed as the mind-body distinction.

dualistic *See dualism.*

dyadic relationship Existing or occurring in pairs.

ecological *See ecology.*

ecology An area of specialization within psychology and biology which concerns itself with the study of the relationship between living organisms and their environments.

ectoparasite An organism which lives parisitically on the outside of another organism.

ectoplasm In botany, it is synonymous with the external plasma membrane. In zoology, it refers to the outer layer of cytoplasm. It is usually semi-solid and has an important role in cell-division and other forms of cell movement.

Edison Instrument *See Edison Responsive Environment Instrument.*

Edison Responsive Environment Instrument An instrument designed to consistently feed back to its user a wide variety of responses which simulate a more or less "ideal" learning environment for the particular task at hand.

EEG *See electroencephalogram.*

effective reaction. A reaction where the behaving organism "moves something" or does something with respect to some stimulus object other than merely responding within itself.

ego The concept of self. In psychoanalytic theory, the ego functions to rationally reconcile the instinctual demands of the id with the strictures imposed by the civilized, morally conscious superego.

EKG *See electrocardiogram.*

electrocardiogram A graphic representation of the varying somatic electric currents produced by the contractions of the heart muscle.

electroencephalogram A record of brain activity made by the electroencephalograph. *See electroencephalograph.*

electroencephalograph An instrument consisting of a cathode ray oscillograph which records brain waves by means of electrodes placed on some area of the scalp or on the brain itself. It is useful in localizing brain tumors and intracranial lesions.

electromyogram A record of the subtle changes in the electrical potential of muscles made by an electromyograph.

embryo The early developmental stage of any organism. In man, the embryological stage begins the second week after conception and lasts until the end of the second prenatal month.

embryology An area of specialization within biology that concerns itself with the form and development of organisms in their rudimentary stages.

encephalitis Inflammation of the brain.

encephalocele A hernia of the brain that is manifested by brain substance protruding through a cleft in the skull.

encephalopathy Any degenerative disease of the brain.

endocrinology A field of science and branch of biology that concerns itself with the study of physiological and pathological relations of internal glandular secretions.

endoradiosonde In biotelemetry, a miniature radio transmitter which is implanted (or ingested) into an organism for purposes of studying its internal physiological reactions.

engram Any permanent mark or trace, physiologically or psychologically.

entomologist *See entomology.*

entomology An area of specialization within zoology that concerns itself with the study of insects.

enuresis The involuntary discharge of urine, particularly during sleep at night.

enuretic Of or pertaining to enuresis or any agent which causes enuresis. *See enuresis.*

epigenesis The theory that new phenomena and new properties emerge during the course of the development of an organism without their existing in miniature in the fertilized egg or germ of the organism. It is contrasted with the *preformation* theory of development.

epigenetic *See epigenesis.*

epilepsy A chronic functional nervous disorder which is characterized by one or more symptoms based on paroxysmal disturbances of the electrical activity of the brain.

equine Like or characteristic of a horse.

equipotential *See equipotentiality.*

equipotentiality In general, *equipotentiality* means equality in power, importance or effectiveness. In neurology, equipotentiality refers to the theory that all parts of the cerebrum are of equal importance with regard to specific functions.

ERE *See Edison Responsive Environment Instrument.*

eroticism   Sexual excitement. Also the preoccupation with or exaltation of sex.

escape conditioning   Any kind of conditioning which is manifested by the organism's learning to remove itself from a painful or unwanted set of circumstances.

ESP   *See extrasensory perception.*

estrogen   A generic term for any substance which stimulates the development and maintenance of female sexual characteristics.

ethnic group   Any group of persons who are believed to be biologically related. The term *ethnic group* is often intentionally used so as to avoid the problems inherent in the use of the term "race."

ethnologist   *See ethnology.*

ethnology   A field of science and branch of anthropology which studies and compares the cultures and characteristics of various peoples.

ethology   An area of specialization within psychology and biology which concerns itself with the study of an animal's behavior within its normal environment.

etiology   The causes or origins, especially in reference to a disease.

ETS   Abbreviation for Educational Testing Service.

eugenics   The attempt to improve the inborn qualities of a race or breed by selective breeding, that is, the control of hereditary factors.

Euglena   A genus of green protozoans found in fresh (especially stagnant) water, sharing characteristics of both plants and animals.

euphoria   An exaggerated mood or emotional attitude of well-being.

evirato   an Italian term for a male singer castrated in boyhood.

experimental group   That group which is treated with the independent variable or variables of an experiment and whose performance indicates the influence of that variable or variables.

experimenter bias   The tendency for an experimenter to allow his own theories or ideas to interfere with the objective collection of data.

extinction   The disappearance of a conditioned response brought about by the discontinuance of reinforcement.

extinguished   *See extinction.*

extrasensory perception   A perceptual response unavailable to normal sensory processes. Also, the ability or capacity to make these perceptions.

facsimile   A replica, reproduction or copy.

factor analysis   A method whereby intercorrelations among a set of variables are analyzed. Each original variable can then be designated as being associated with one or more of a number of underlying *factors,* the factors being preferably fewer in number than the variables.

fantasy   A kind of defense mechanism whereby one projects himself into some kind of dreamworld.

fauna   The animal population of a particular area or time.

feedback   (Also called *knowledge of results*). The return of information concerning the consequences of one's performance.

feral children   Human offspring who have purportedly been reared by animals or whose upbringing has been characterized by severe social isolation from human beings.

fetishism   In anthropology, the veneration of inanimate objects which are believed to have magical powers. In psychology, the production of sexual excitement or gratification by objects other than sexual organs and characteristics.

fetishistic   *See fetishism.*

fetus   An embryo in a later stage of development. The human embryo is considered to be a *fetus* from six to eight weeks after conception until birth.

field   All of the factors which influence a psychological event. *See field theory.*

field observer   One who makes naturalistic observations, who observes things and events as they exist in their natural settings and relationships.

field theory   A theory which maintains that the behavior of a given organism must be understood in terms of the field or environment within which the behaving organism finds itself.

fission   A kind of reproduction where the organism splits into two equal parts (binary fission) or a multiplicity of equal parts (multiple fission).

fissure of Rolando   A cleft or groove between the parietal and frontal lobes of the brain.

fixation   A habit or attitude rigidly adhered to as the consequence of repeated reinforcement or frustration.

flora   The plant population of a particular area or time.

free association   A psychoanalytic technique which requires the patient to think what he will without constraint or direction and to speak freely whatever comes to mind.

frontal   In general, pertaining to the anterior part of the body or an organ such as the brain. *See frontal lobe.*

frontal lobe   The area of the brain that includes, approximately, the front half of the cerebral hemisphere on either side.

frustration   The behavioral residue that results from the blocking of goal-oriented behavior.

frustration tolerance   The capacity to adjust to thwarted goal-seeking behavior without undue emotionality or behavior disruption.

gallinaceous   Of or belonging to a large group of birds who make their nests on the ground.

galvanic skin response   The increase in the electrical potential of the skin resulting from the autonomic nervous system's influence on the sweat glands.

galvanometer   An instrument used in measuring the intensity of an electric current. *See psychogalvanometer.*

ganglia   *See ganglion.*

ganglion   Any aggregation of nervous tissue which serves as a center of nervous influence.

gangrene   The massive putrefaction and mortification of tissue.

gastrointestinal tract   Pertaining to the stomach and intestines in continuity.

Gates Reading Test A general test of reading ability.

general paresis A psychiatric disorder due to syphilis of the central nervous system which is characterized by both mental and physical symptoms.

generalization In learning theory, *generalization* may be either the failure to discriminate between different stimuli or the failure to discriminate between different responses.

genes Chromosomal constituents which are the essential units in the transmission of hereditary characteristics.

genetic code A biochemical description of the formula of a given organism's heredity.

genetic drift A random change in the gene frequencies of a small population.

genetics An area of specialization within biology which concerns itself with the study of the transmission of inherited characteristics.

genius A generic term for one who has ability and brilliance of the highest order. The idea that a genius is a person with an IQ of 140 or more is not very prevalent today.

genocide The systematic murder or destruction of an entire people or nation.

genotype The genetic constitution of an organism as contrasted with its overt characteristics (phenotype).

genus One of the several kinds of group classifications of organisms. A *genus* consists of several similar species, although occasionally it contains only one species.

Gestalt A form, configuration or totality that possesses properties as a unified whole that could not be derived by summing its individual parts.

gestation The length of time between conception and birth in a viviparous animal.

glandular therapy Any therapeutic technique which directly influences glandular secretions.

glaucoma An eye disease wherein an increase of fluids in the eyeball leads to intense intra-ocular pressure. Atrophy of the retina, blindness and other effects may result.

Gloger's rule The rule that faces in warm and humid areas are more heavily pigmented than those in cool and dry areas. This fact as well as the pigmentation of birds and mammals is said to follow Gloger's rule, although how is not exactly clear.

gonadal *See gonads.*

gonads The gamete-producing organs in animals.

grey matter Tissue of the nervous system, especially of the brain.

GSR *See galvanic skin response.*

guidance counselor One who offers assistance and advice in matters of personal adjustment, vocational choice, and other problematic areas of every day living. A *guidance counselor* is usually employed in an educational or health-related institution.

gynecologist *See gynecology.*

gynecology An area of specialization within medicine which concerns itself with the study and treatment of diseases peculiar to women.

hallucination A false perception that is accepted as real by its perceiver, although relevant and adequate sensory stimulation is absent.

hallucinogenic drug Any drug which produces hallucinations upon intake. A *psychotomimetic drug.*

harelip A congenital or acquired defect involving a cleft in the upper lip.

Hawthorne effect The motivation for success or superior achievement which is instilled in an experimental subject by his knowledge of the fact that he is participating in an experiment.

Head Start Program A program sponsored by the Federal Government which provides school-like experiences to disadvantaged children of pre-school age.

hemispherectomy The excision of a cerebral hemisphere.

hermaphrodite A person who possesses both male and female sex organs.

heroin A powerful, habit-forming narcotic derived from morphine.

heterosexual Having sexual desire for those of the opposite sex. Also consisting of two different sexes.

hippocampus An elevated, curved structure on the floor of the middle horn of the lateral ventricle of the brain. It forms the greater part of the olfactory cerebral cortex.

histological *See histology.*

histology A subdivision of anatomy which concerns itself with the study of the minute structure, composition, and function of the tissues.

holistic orientation A point of view that maintains that the properties of a living organism belong to its totality rather than to its separate constituent parts.

hollow-organism theorist A psychological theorist who maintains that the psychologist's contribution to science lies in his ability to impart information about behavior qua behavior rather than by his appealing to complex within-the-organism phenomena in an attempt to explain such behavior.

homo erectus (Latin) Those animals of the genus *homo* which walk upright.

homosexual Having sexual desire for those of the same sex.

homozygosity A condition in genetics where the two corresponding loci of a pair of chromosomes have identical genes.

homozygous recessive A condition in genetics where the two corresponding loci of a pair of chromosomes have identical recessive genes.

hormone An organic substance which is produced in one part of the organism and transported to other parts where it has a profound effect.

hybrid A plant or animal which results from a cross between two parents that are genetically different.

hydrocephalus A condition characterized by an excessive collection of fluids in the cerebral ventricles. It causes convulsions, atrophy of the brain, and gross enlargement of head.

hydroid A member of one of the orders of Hydrozoa. A *hydroid* commonly forms a tuft-like growth on a seaweed or some other similar variety of plant life.

hypothalamus A region of the forebrain or diencephalon which serves as a primary brain center for autonomic functions.

hypothesis   An admittedly tentative explanation of some relationship within a complex set of data.

hypothetical construct   An entity or process inferred to actually exist and influence behavior but which cannot be directly observed.

hypothyroidism   A deficiency of thyroid activity.

hypotonia   A reduction of tension in any part of the body, or a reduction of muscle tonicity.

id   In psychoanalysis, that division of the human psyche which is governed by the pleasure principle and occupied by instinctual impulses.

identification   A process whereby one individual outwardly imitates the behavior of another individual while inwardly accepting the purposes and values of the one with whom he identifies.

idiosyncrasy   A behavior or mannerism which is peculiar to a particular person or group.

idiosyncratic   *See idiosyncrasy.*

idiot   A classificatory term denoting a person with an IQ of 20 or less. It is being used with decreasing frequency as a diagnostic label of intelligence.

imbecile   A classificatory term denoting a person with an IQ between 20 and 60. It is being used with decreasing frequency as a diagnostic label of intelligence.

imitation   Copying or patterning the outward behavior of another.

imprinting   The very rapid learning which occurs with some animals at a critical stage in development.

in utero   Within the uterus.

infant   Any human being who is between one and sixteen months of age. Infancy is the arbitrary division in the life span of a human being which covers approximately month one through month sixteen.

inferiority complex   A generalized resentment of being inferior that permeates and distorts one's behavioral repertoire. Psychoanalytic theory would maintain that an *inferiority complex* is composed of *repressed* feelings of inferiority.

infrahuman   Below the human (*homo sapiens*) on the phylogenetic scale in animal classification.

instinct   A complex, unlearned behavior pattern which appears in complete form once the proper stimulus has been presented and which may persist beyond the duration of the instigating stimulus.

intelligence   A general term which represents a person's level of competence in performing a wide variety of both verbal and performance tasks.

intelligence quotient   A person's recorded level of intelligence which is derived by any one of several techniques which utilizes some concept or variation of mental age divided by chronological age.

interaction   According to the interactional view, one thing is always related to something else because nothing exists by itself in absolute independence of other things. In other words, every "effect" has a "cause." To the primitive mind, rain, lightning, and land slides are mysterious in origin. Today, such events, as well as sneezes, knee jerks, and disease, are easily conceived of as interactions. In psychology, the stimulus-response framework illustrates an interactional approach.

interactional   *See interaction.*

interbehavioral theory   *See interbehaviorism.*

interbehaviorism   A theoretical approach to the study of psychology developed by Prof. J. R. Kantor, which stresses organism-stimulus object *fields* or *events* in which all the factors are held equally necessary. Their relationships are studied. This view is in contrast to organism-centered views which treat psychology as if it happened inside the organism.

interest test   Any one of several tests which attempts to assess a testee's degree of interest in a broad range of vocational and avocational fields.

ion   An atom or group of atoms carrying a charge of electricity.

IQ   *See intelligence quotient.*

irreversibility   The idea that once a certain kind of learning or experience has occurred the organism can never return to the psychological state which existed before that particular learning or experience. Also refers to irreparable tissue losses as of the brain.

isogenic   Having the same set of genes.

isolation   The state of being separated from others.

isomorphic   *See isomorphism.*

isomorphism   The view or doctrine that there is a formal point-for-point correspondence between excitatory fields in the brain and the experienced contents of consciousness.

isotope   A term applied to either of two chemically identical elements which occupy the same position in the periodic table of elements, but which have different atomic weights.

kheder   The lower school in which young Jewish boys were instructed in Hebrew and the Bible.

killifish   Any of the several small oviparous cyprinodont fishes, particularly of the genus *Fundulus*.

kinesthesis   A sense which imparts knowledge of body movements or of movements of body members.

kinesthetic   *See kinesthesis.*

knowledge of results   (Also called *feedback*). The immediate feedback to the learner of the quality and direction of his performance. It is considered necessary for quick and efficient learning.

Korah* or *Parashah   A term denoting (1) a section or paragraph of the Hebrew Bible, (2) the portion of the Torah read at public services.

Kuhlman-Anderson Test   A general test of intelligence.

laboratorian   One who works in the laboratory and purposely exercises some degree of control over the phenomena he studies. An experimentalist.

lactating   *See lactation.*

lactation   The production of milk via mammary glands.

laryngeal   *See larynx.*

larynx   In tetrapods, it is the dilated region in the upper end of the trachea which junctions with the pharynx. In man, it is commonly referred to as the "Adam's apple."

latency period In psychoanalysis, it constitutes a period from around age 4 or 5 to about age 12 when sexual interest is sublimated.

learning A relatively enduring change in behavior brought about by past experience.

learning set A kind of learning readiness which results from an organism's previous experiences with problem-solving tasks that were different in content but similar in type. A kind of *transfer of training* phenomenon.

"learning to learn" A catchy phrase for a *learning set. See learning set.*

Lee-Clark Reading Test A general test of reading ability.

lesion A wound, injury, or pathological change in tissue.

libidinal *See libido.*

libido In psychoanalytic theory, that aspect of psychic energy which concerns itself with sexual or affiliative needs.

locomotor activity Movement of the body from one place to another.

longitudinal An observational or experimental approach which involves the study of changes in individual behavior over an extended period of time.

LSD *See lysergic acid diethylamide.*

lysergic acid diethylamide A psychotomimetic drug (psychosis mimicking) which can produce a psychotic-like reaction in human subjects.

malingering Pretending to be sick, disabled, or incompetent.

mammal Any member of a class of tetrapod vertebrates known as Mammalia.

manic-depressive psychosis A kind of psychiatric disturbance which is marked by extreme emotional oscillation. Emotional excitement in the manic phase alternates with depression.

manipulation test Any test where the testee is given items or tasks which require varying degrees of finger and hand dexterity and visual-motor coordination.

marijuana The Indian hemp plant, or its leaves and flowers which are dried and smoked in cigarettes as a narcotic.

maturation Behavioral attainment which accrues from development due to hereditary factors rather than from learning.

maturational *See maturation.*

mean A computation derived by dividing the sum total of all measurements by the total number of cases.

mechanist The view or doctrine that all human activities can be fully explained in terms of the principles of physical mechanics. A reductionist. *See reductionism.*

medulla The central part of an organ.

meningitis Inflammation of the membranes which envelop the brain and spinal cord.

meningocele A hernial protrusion of the membranes of the brain or spinal cord through a defect in the skull or vertebral column.

menstruation The cyclical, physiological discharge of bloody fluid from the uterus, occurring at approximately four-week intervals in the non-pregnant uterus.

mental deficiency   A synonym for mental retardation. *See mental retardation.*

mental retardation   A general term used for all levels of intellectual subnormality.

mental telepathy   The knowledge one person has of another person's mental processes which is made possible by processes not available to normal sensory mechanisms.

mentally retarded   *See mental retardation.*

mescaline   A poisonous alkaloid which produces a psychotic-like state with delusions of color and music when ingested.

mesencephalic   *See mesencephalon.*

mesencephalon   The midbrain.

metabolism   The sum total of all chemical processes by which an organism maintains itself.

microcephaly   Abnormal smallness of the head with concomitant smallness of the cerebral hemispheres.

microcosm   A little world or universe or something which symbolically represents a little world, such as a man or community.

micturition   Urination.

mind   A hypothetical construct which represents the organized totality of all mental processes of an individual organism.

Minnesota Rate of Manipulation Test   A specific manipulation test which was developed at the University of Minnesota. *See manipulation test.*

mirror tracing   A task which involves one's tracing of a design while viewing his hand and the design to be traced only in a mirror.

miscarriage   The expulsion of a nonviable fetus any time between the fourth and sixth months of pregnancy.

modal   Of or pertaining to the mode. *See mode.*

mode   The most frequently occurring score or value in a group of different scores or values.

model   A designed mathematical, logical or physical replica or description of some system or relationship that demonstrates the working principles of that which it represents. A *model* may also be one human being whose behavior is copied by another, the latter usually being a child.

modus operandi (Latin)   Method of working.

molecular biology   A relatively recent development in modern biology which emphasizes the study of biological macromolecules and their functions.

mongolism   A congenital condition which is characterized by a flat skull, a short thick neck, stubby fingers and thumbs, an oblique eye slit, and a fissured tongue. Mental retardation commonly accompanies *mongolism.*

Mongoloid   *See mongolism.*

monolingual   Using or having the capacity to speak only one language.

moron   A classificatory term denoting a person with an IQ between 60 and 70. It is being used with decreasing frequency as a diagnostic label of intelligence.

morphine   The principal and most active alkaloid of opium. It has opium's properties. Compared to opium, *morphine* is less likely to produce narcotism or constipation, but has a greater tendency to produce nausea and skin eruptions.

morphological   *See morphology.*

morphology   An area of specialization within biology which concerns itself with the study of the form and structure of plants and animals.

motivation   A general term that refers to an aroused state of an organism, a state maintained by need states and goals.

mulatto   Any person who has one Negro parent and one Caucasian parent.

mutation   A change in form or quality brought about by sudden alteration of the chromosomal material.

myogenic   Originating in muscle tissue.

narcissism   In general, *narcissism* means self-love. A narcissist holds his own bodily qualities in high esteem and, by extension, has high regard for his personal deeds and qualities.

narcissistic   *See narcissism.*

narcolepsy   A condition characterized by an uncontrollable desire for sleep.

natural selection   The theory that individuals having certain characteristics will produce more offspring than individuals with other characteristics. The result is a change in the composition of the population in so far as inherited characteristics are concerned.

naturalistic observation   The observation of things and events as they exist in nature. Observation which occurs without experimental manipulation of the situation.

nature-nurture controversy   The perennial disagreement over whether heredity or environment plays the predominant role in producing a particular behavior, quality, or condition.

Neanderthal man   A now extinct race of man which inhabited Europe during the paleolithic period.

negative transfer   The deleterious effect of past learning on present learning attempts.

neo-behaviorist   A psychologist who adheres to the basic premises of early behaviorism, but who has moved beyond or built upon that viewpoint in one or more aspects of theory and/or practice.

neonate   The arbitrary division in the life span of a human being which begins with birth at full term and ends with the conclusion of the first postnatal month.

nervous system   A mechanism which coordinates the various activities within the organism as well as enabling the organism to respond to environmental events by means of rapidly conducted electro-chemical messages.

neurology   An area of specialization within the field of medicine which concerns itself with the study of the nervous system in both healthy and pathological conditions.

neuroma   A tumor or growth formed chiefly from nerve cells and fibers.

neuron   A nerve cell body and its accessories.

neurosis   A nonorganic behavior disorder, less serious than psychosis, wherein a person typically experiences a general or specific anxiety, troubled interpersonal relationships, and overall unhappiness.

olfactory   Of or pertaining to the sense of smell.

oligophrenia   A condition of mental deficiency or feeble intellect. *Oligophrenia* is rather infrequently used in modern day psychology in America but is in use in Great Britain.

one-way vision window   An apparatus whereby an observer may look through a glass window at a subject without the subject's being able to see the observer.

ontogeny   The entire course of development during an individual organism's life history.

open field test   A large open area where an experimenter may observe the extent to which an organism manifests exploratory behavior.

operant   Pertaining to a response that is identified by its environmental consequences.

operant conditioning   A systematic, well-defined learning procedure wherein the desired response is selectively reinforced so as to increase the probability of the continuance of that response.

operational definition   A term defined by a statement of the operations which were involved in distinguishing the object or ideas referred to from others.

opium   A narcotic, soporific, astringent, and analgesic which is obtained from the concrete juice of the poppy, *Papaver Somniferum.*

organic case   A case is labeled *organic* when the pathology involved is thought to have some kind of physiological or anatomical etiology.

organismic approach   An approach to the study of behavior which rejects mentalistic notions and emphasizes a holistic attitude; a point of view which considers the whole organism as the behaving object.

orgasm   The climax of sexual excitement that involves a group of involuntary movements in the genital organs. The movements produce ejaculation in the male and consist of somewhat analogous rhythmic contractions in the female.

oscillograph   An instrument used for recording electrical oscillations.

Otis Quick Scoring Mental Ability Test   A group test of general intelligence.

ovary   In zoology, the female organ which produces ova. In vertebrates, the *ovary* also produces sex hormones.

pacemaker   A fixed point in the wall of the cardiac auricles where the stimulus which excites the normal heart beat originates. Also, in biochemistry, any substance whose own rate of reaction sets a pace for a series of linked reactions.

paired-associate learning   A procedure used in studies of learning and retention whereby a subject is presented paired items and told to learn them. The retention aspect enters into the procedure when the subject is later presented the first item of each pair and asked to reproduce the second.

paleolithic Of or pertaining to the Old Stone Age, which was characterized by the use of stone tools.

paleontological *See paleontology.*

paleontology A field of science and branch of geology which concerns itself with the study of prehistoric life through the examination of fossils.

paranoia A kind of psychosis that is characterized by delusions of grandeur and/or persecution which appear to be logically defended by the one affected.

paranoid Any behavior which resembles paranoia or paranoid schizophrenia. *See paranoia and paranoid schizophrenia.*

paranoid ideation Thoughts and ideas of paranoid quality, characterized by anything from oversuspicion of others and hypersensitivity to criticism in less serious instances to full-blown paranoid psychosis in more serious cases.

paranoid schizophrenia A kind of psychosis which is characterized by delusions of grandeur and/or persecution, hallucinations, and general personality disruption. Even the delusions tend to become less systematized with the passage of time. It is in this latter aspect that *paranoid schizophrenia* differs from *paranoia.*

paraplegia Paralysis of the legs and also of more or less of the trunk.

parapsychology An area of concentration within psychology which concerns itself with the study of psychological phenomena which at present are not explained, at least from parapsychology's point of view, by recognized scientific laws and principles.

parietal Of or pertaining to the middle region of the cranium which extends downward in back of the temples on each side. *Parietal* also refers to those portions of the brain which lie beneath that area of the skull. *See parietal lobe.*

parietal lobe A major division of each cerebral hemisphere comprising the area of the brain that lies between the frontal and occipital lobes and above the temporal lobe.

parsimony, principle of *See principle of parsimony.*

parthenogenesis The development of an unfertilized ovum into a new individual.

participant observer A basically scientific observer who becomes a member, to some degree, of the group he is studying, preferably without the group's knowledge of the observer's real purpose and status.

passive dependent behavior The typical behavior pattern of the personality that lacks independence and initiative.

pathognomonic *See pathognomy.*

pathognomy The recognition of the feelings and emotions of a person. Also, the diagnosis of disease.

pegboard test Any test, such as the Purdue Pegboard Test, which makes use of a flat board with designated openings into which various objects are inserted and/or manipulated as a test of manual dexterity and visual-motor coordination.

Pentateuch   The first five books of the Old Testament.

peptic ulcer   An ulcer located on the mucous membrane of the esophagus, stomach, or duodenum. It is caused by acidic gastric juice.

perception   A process comprising the organism's selection, organization and interpretation of the sensory data available to it.

peristalsis   The wave of contractions by which the various tubular organs that are supplied with both longitudinal and circular muscle fibers propel their contents.

peristaltic   *See peristalsis.*

perseverated   *See perseveration.*

perseveration   The repetition of organismic activity without any apparent associative stimulus.

personality   A person's characteristic ways of thinking and behaving; all that a person is and all that he is trying to become. The unique collection of attributes that makes up a specific human being.

personality test   Any one of several tests which attempts to assess a testee's basic personality structure.

petitio principii (Latin)   A begging of the question. In the terms of formal logic, it is the fallacy of assuming within the premise of an argument the very thing which is to be proved by the argument's conclusion.

peyote   A drug obtained from the Mexican cactus which, upon intake, produces a kind of intoxication that is characterized by feelings of ecstasy.

pH   The commonly used symbol in expressing hydrogen ion concentration. It is a measure of alkalinity and acidity.

phantom breast   *See phantom phenomena.*

phantom limb   *See phantom phenomena.*

phantom pain   *See phantom phenomena.*

phantom phenomena   The recurring sensations in amputees of such things as movement, pain, itching, and simple physical presence with regard to the amputated body member, as if it were not really missing.

phantom sensation   *See phantom phenomena.*

phemerol   An antiseptic and detergent agent used to fight infection.

phenylalanine   Phenylaminopropionic acid. *Phenylalanine* is a decomposition product of protein. It is a water-soluble amino acid which is essential to the nutrition of man and most animals.

phenylketonuria   A congenital biochemical defect consisting of the faulty metabolism of phenylalanine, a defect that results in phenylpyruvic acid appearing in the urine. If not corrected, as by diet, a condition of mental retardation often develops.

phenylpyruvic oligophrenia   A condition of mental deficiency that is due to a congenital faulty metabolism of phenylalanine.

pheromone   A chemical substance released by one animal of a species which has some influence on either the behavior or development of other members of the same species.

philanthropist   *See philanthropy.*

philanthropy   The love of mankind which culminates in altruism or benevolence.

philosopher   *See philosophy.*

philosophy   An academic discipline which concerns itself with the study of the general causes and principles of all existence.

phoneme frequency   The total number of times that any member of a group of closely similar speech sounds (though commonly regarded as being the same sound) occurs within a given speech sample.

phosphene   The sensation of light that results from pressure being placed on the eyeball. Also, in eye accommodation, the streak of light that surrounds the visual field as the eye adjusts in the dark.

photoreceptor   A receptor that is sensitive to light.

photosynthesis   The process whereby green plants synthesize organic compounds from water and carbon dioxide by using the energy from the sun which is absorbed by their chlorophyll.

phrenology   A system whereby it is claimed that one's mental abilities and personality characteristics can be analyzed by studying and interpreting the meaning of the shape and topography of one's skull.

physical anthropology   An area of specialization within the field of anthropology which concerns itself with the study of the evolutionary changes in man's bodily structure and the classification of modern racial types.

physiochemistry   An area of specialization within the fields of physiology and chemistry which concerns itself with the study of the chemical aspects of physiology.

physiological   *See physiology.*

physiology   A field of science and branch of biology which concerns itself with the study of the functions and processes of living organisms.

pièce de résistance (French)   Principal dish; therefore, the prime or most desirable item in a collection or series.

placebo   A medicineless preparation (at least relative to the complaint for which it is offered) that is given to a patient so that he will believe he is receiving treatment.

planarian   A free-swimming flatworm used rather frequently in studies investigating possible bio-chemical factors in learning.

plastic surgery   Restorative surgery which concerns itself with the rebuilding of body structures that have become damaged or defective by injury or disease. New tissues from neighboring body parts are often grafted or transferred to the defective area.

Pleistocene   An early epoch of time comprising the first epoch of the Quaternary Period in the Cenozoic Era.

pneuma   In spiritualism, it refers to the vital spirit or the soul. In theology, *pneuma* refers to the Spirit of God or the Holy Spirit.

pneumograph   An instrument used for measuring subtle changes in breathing pattern and over-all respiratory movements.

polygraph   An instrument used for simultaneously recording a number of mechanical or electrical impulses which are correlated with autonomic changes in the organism. It is sometimes loosely termed a "lie detector." In general, *polygraph* refers to any device which produces many writings or drawings.

postnatal   Occurring after birth.

practice effects   Changes in one's ability to perform a task which result from practice.

pragmatic theory   *See pragmatism.*

pragmatism   The philosophical doctrine that practical consequences are the true test of the meaning of anything.

precognition   In parapsychology, the extrasensory perception of a future event for which it is claimed that no prior logical inference existed.

preconscious   In psychoanalysis, that part of the mind or psyche which is not conscious at any given time, but which can readily become conscious when called upon by the appropriate stimulus or stimuli.

predaceous   *See predator.*

predator   In zoology, an animal which preys on another animal.

primary amentia   When mental deficiency is present at birth and is due to some inherited factor, it is called *primary amentia*. This terminology is little used today. An even older term was *congenital amentia*.

principle of parsimony   A law or principle which states that the simplest explanation or interpretation of the data is the most desirable or preferable.

projective test   A standardized test which requires the testee to respond to a number of unstructured stimuli. There are few restrictions placed upon the subject's mode of response and it is assumed that the responses will reflect the subject's psychological needs and status.

proprioceptive   *See proprioceptor.*

proprioceptor   Any receptor which is sensitive to the movement of the body or of any of its members. A *proprioceptor* gives rise to *kinesthetic* sensations.

prostate gland   A gland surrounding the bladder and the neck of the urethra in the male animal, including man. During the emission of semen, it secretes a milky fluid into the urethra.

prosthesis   Any artificial replacement of some absent part of the body.

protoculture   The earliest form or aspect of a culture, or a representative form.

provisioning   A technique whereby wants and/or necessities are provided for animal populations in the hope that these provisions will render such populations more agreeable to and available for close observation and study.

proximal   Contiguous or touching. A *proximal* stimulus impinges directly on a receptor. A *distal* stimulus is an environmental event. A *proximal* response involves actual muscular movement on the organism's part. A *distal* response involves the organism's alteration of the environment in some way.

pseudopregnancy   Any false appearance of pregnancy of either psychosomatic or physical origin.

pseudoscience   A false science. A discipline or area of study or practice that purports to be a science but which is not recognized as such by the established scientific community generally.

psi phenomena   The events and processes investigated by *parapsychology*, such as *extrasensory perception, precognition, clairvoyance, psychokinesis,* and *mental telepathy.*

psilocybin   A crystalline solid which is obtained from the mushroom, *Psilocybe mexicana.* Ingestion of the drug produces a kind of psychedelic and hallucinogenic effect.

psychiatry   An area of specialization within medicine which concerns itself with the study, diagnosis, treatment, and prevention of mental illness and behavior disorders as well as numerous problems related to personal adjustment.

psychist   In parapsychology, one who claims to have supernatural powers or abilities.

psychoanalysis   A theoretical approach in psychology which places great stress on unconscious motivation and dynamic personality processes. It is also a system of psychotherapy which is based on psychoanalytic theory.

psychoanalytic   *See psychoanalysis.*

psychogalvanometer   An instrument used to measure changes in the electrical resistance of the skin as the sweat glands are influenced by the action of the autonomic nervous system.

psychoheredity   The inheritance of psychological characteristics.

psychokinesis   In parapsychology, *psychokinesis* is the direct influence of intentional thought on a physical system without any intermediating physical instrumentation.

psychology   A field of science which concerns itself with the study of the behavior of living organisms.

psychometrician   A psychologist who is skilled in the administration and interpretation of psychological tests.

psychomotor   Of or pertaining to the motor effects of psychological processes.

psychomotor epilepsy   A condition which is characterized by intentional motor and/or psychological activity which has no relevance for the time and place of its occurrence. After the seizure the patient is usually amnestic with regard to what transpired during the seizure.

psychopathology   An area of specialization within psychology and psychiatry which deals with the systematic investigation of behavior disorders.

psychopharmacologist   *See psychopharmacology.*

psychopharmacology   An area of specialization within psychology which concerns itself with the study of the effect of drugs on behavior.

psychophysical   *See psychophysics.*

psychophysics   A kind of subspecialty within experimental psychology which studies the relationship between the physical attributes of the stimulus and the quantitative attributes of the sensation which it arouses.

psychosis A serious behavior disorder which is marked by major personality disruption, delusions and hallucinations.

psychosomatic Pertaining to a phenomenon or reaction which is both psychological and somatic.

psychotherapy The treatment of psychological or behavioral disorders by patient-therapist communication and interaction.

puberty The age at which the sexual reproductive organs become functionally operative, accompanied by the development of secondary sexual characteristics.

pupa The developmental stage between larva and adult of the endopterygate insect, during which locomotion and feeding cease and great developmental changes take place.

pupate *See pupa.*

pupillometry The measurement of subtle changes in the size of the pupil of the eye for purposes of correlating such changes with emotional, attitudinal, and interest dispositions in the human subject.

Purdue Pegboard A specific type of pegboard test which was developed at Purdue University. *See pegboard test.*

quadriplegia A condition of paralysis in all four limbs.

radioisotope An isotope which is radioactive. *See isotope.*

rat psychologist A non-technical term used to designate experimental psychologists generally because they often use white rats as experimental subjects. The term is sometimes applied somewhat indiscriminately in light of the fact that experimental psychologists use many different kinds of animal species as well as humans as experimental subjects.

reactional biography An individual organism's entire history of psychological reactions.

recluse A hermit; a person who lives secluded from other people.

reductionism A general view taken by some scientists which holds that all complex phenomena are ultimately explained and understood by analyzing them into increasingly simpler and supposedly more elementary components. Under reductionism, psychology is reduced to physiology, physiology to chemistry, chemistry to physics, etc.

reductionist *See reductionism.*

reductionistic *See reductionism.*

regression The act of returning to an earlier and more immature form or level of behavior.

reinforce *See reinforcement.*

reinforcement Any action or substance which increases the probability and stability of a given response.

reliability The stability and consistency of a test or measurement over multiple administrations.

reliable *See reliability.*

research psychologist A psychologist who concentrates on gathering psychological data from systematic experimental investigations and observations of behavior.

respondent A term used to characterize behavior that is elicited by a specific stimulus, as in *classical conditioning.*

response   Any psychological event which is the consequence or result of stimulation. *Response* is one of psychology's most widely used terms.

reticular formation   A network of cells that lie deep in the center of the brain stem which are said to function significantly with regard to the alertness or lethargy of the organism.

reticular system   See reticular formation.

rhinencephalic   *See rhinencephalon.*

rhinencephalon   The *olfactory* area of the brain.

rhizotomies   *See rhizotomy.*

rhizotomy   A surgical operation where a section of the motor or sensory nerve-roots is interrupted for the purpose of relieving intractable pain or spastic paralysis. It is also called Dana's operation.

ribonucleic acid   An important constituent of the chromatin material of a cell. It is essential in protein production.

RNA   *See ribonucleic acid.*

rod-divining   The use of a rod to locate water. Those who believe that the technique is valid claim that the water exerts some kind of influence on the rod as it is held in the diviner's hand, pulling the rod downward in some characteristic fashion.

Rosenthal Effect   The result of an experimenter or teacher unwittingly giving performance-enhancing advantages to subjects or students whom the experimenter or teacher has prematurely judged to be superior.

sampling error   (Also called *sample bias*). Any factor or procedure in the method of selecting a sample that renders the sample less representative of the population from which it was drawn.

schema   An established pattern of meaningful psychological behavior, especially with regard to intelligence and its prerequisites.

schizoidia   A psychiatric disorder which is marked by a person's separating himself from his surroundings and confining his interests to his own person. The schizoid individual may become schizophrenic, but *schizoidia* should not be confused with schizophrenia.

schizokinesis   A situation in which, for example, a foot withdrawal and accelerated heart action which have both become aspects of a conditioned response show a differential extinction as when the heart action continues following a complete disappearance of the conditioned foot withdrawal. Thus, a fragmentation or splitting off of two or more acts that had once been a unified conditioned response, each having a different outcome.

schizophrenia   A group of clinically distinguishable psychotic reactions which are marked by fundamental disturbances in reality relationships with accompanying disturbances in the affective, intellectual, and behavioral spheres.

schizophrenic   *See schizophrenia.*

science   Originally, the word simply meant knowledge. Today, it is more specifically defined as that kind of knowledge which is derived from some systematic collection of data, as by observation, study, and experimentation.

scientific method A systematic procedure which demands the objective and accurate observation and collection of data along with a permissible interpretation of the same.

secondary amentia A kind of mental deficiency which results from a lack of neurological development due to adverse environmental effects.

secondary reinforcement Reinforcement which is derived from the primary or original reinforcement. In essence, a *secondary reinforcement* is any reinforcement which does not directly alleviate a biological need.

secondary reinforcer *See secondary reinforcement.*

self-action The view according to which, a thing is the cause of itself; in a sense, an uncaused cause. The primitive, pre-biological notion of "spontaneous generation" explained the presence of bugs and worms in rain puddles as being self-generated. A common example from psychology is the conception that ideas just "pop" into the head; in other words, they are unrelated to other factors and just generate themselves.

self-actional *See self-action.*

self-fulfilling prophecy The principle that a participant's belief, prediction, or expectations about an event will influence its outcome in the direction of the participant's expectations.

seminal fluid The thick, whitish secretion of the male reproductive organs.

senile dementia A condition of chronic mental deterioration in older people.

septal *See septum.*

septum Any one of several dividing walls or partitions which are located at various points throughout the body.

serology A branch of medicine which concerns itself with the study of serum, especially antigen-antibody reactions in vitro.

servo-mechanism A control system for another system that maintains the operation of the latter system at prescribed rates and strength.

set A predisposition to respond in a certain way.

setting factors The complex of environmental or ecological variables wherein a behavioral act occurs, such factors influencing and giving meaning to the response.

sexual selection The principle that the members of a species which have the most desirable characteristics will be selected for mating.

shtetl A Jewish community or settlement that existed in Eastern Europe until World War II.

sibling rivalry Competition between brothers and/or sisters.

sinusitus Inflammation of a sinus, especially of one of the accessory sinuses of the nose.

sitzfleisch A word borrowed from the German expression, *"er hat kein sitzfleisch,"* meaning "he can't sit still." A sitzfleisch would be a sedentary person.

Skinner Box An enclosure within which are located one or more devices that will provide some kind of reinforcement to the organism contained therein upon that organism's correct operation of the device.

social psychology   An area of specialization within psychology which concerns itself with the study of individual behavior within social settings.

social selection   Selectivity based on social acceptability.

social worker   In general, any person who works professionally to improve the activities, services, and social conditions of a community. This attempt at community improvement may involve work with individuals, families, or larger social groups.

sociology   A branch of the social sciences that concerns itself with the study of group life and social processes.

sociopathy   Any abnormality which characterizes a social group. Also, a complex of abnormal attitudes about the social environment.

somatic   Of or pertaining to the physical body.

sonagram   A photograph or representation of a spectrum.

spasticity   A condition characterized by spasms, muscle stiffness, and awkwardness of movement.

species   Disregarding geographical separation, a species is roughly defined as any group of individuals able to breed among themselves, but not with members of other groups of organisms, each group comprising a species.

spectrograph   An instrument used for photographing or producing a representation of a spectrum.

sphincter   A ring of smooth muscle which closes a natural orifice.

spleen   A large ductless, glandlike organ situated in the upper portion of the abdominal cavity on the left side. It functions in the disintegration of red blood corpuscles and the release of hemoglobin. The full scope of its functions is not yet clearly understood.

stabilimeter crib   A crib that contains an instrument that measures the amount of bodily sway in a subject who tries to stand erect and hold perfectly still.

standard score   Any derived score which uses the standard deviation of a criterion group as its unit.

Stanford-Binet Intelligence Scale   A general test of intelligence developed at Stanford University from an earlier test compiled by a Frenchman named Binet. The *Stanford-Binet* has undergone several revisions.

startle reflex   Any rapid reaction to a sudden, unexpected stimulus. It shows little variation among different individuals.

statistical significance   A concept meaning that a given experimental finding has not occurred by chance with respect to a prescribed level of confidence.

statistically   *See statistics.*

statistically significant   *See statistical significance.*

statistics   A mathematical and logical procedure whereby the variable collected data of an experiment are numerically displayed, coordinated, and interpreted, particularly in contrast with the probability of the data's occurrence by chance.

stereotropism   A tropism which has some solid body as its stimulus. *See tropism.*

stereotype   A rigid and oversimplified conception of some aspect of reality, with particular reference to social groups or persons.

stereotyping   *See stereotype.*

stimulus   A general term which represents that something which provokes a response from an organism.

stimulus control   The regulation of the stimuli which are available to the organism to the degree that the regulator also gains control of the organism.

stimulus function   The specific meaning, application, or use of a stimulus object in psychological action. The functional role of a stimulus object.

stimulus object   An object which has acquired one or more stimulus functions.

stimulus-response learning   A general approach to learning which makes use of explicit stimuli and explicit responses and the intentional binding of the two together so that a specific stimulus will evoke a specific response.

substitute stimulus   Any stimulus which is sufficiently representative of the original stimulus to the degree that

it calls forth the same response (or similar response) as did the original stimulus.

subvocal speech   The subtle movement of various speech mechanisms without the production of audible sound. Implicit speech.

successive approximations   In operant conditioning, the gradual shaping of the desired response by reinforcing approximations of the desired response as they grow progressively more adequate.

superego   In psychoanalysis, the *superego* is that system of the psyche which imposes restrictions on the instinctual demands of the id. The *superego* is a kind of conscience which has incorporated the moral standards of parents and society into its own essence.

super nova   In astronomy, an extremely bright nova that produces from ten million to one hundred million times as much light as the sun. It is estimated that one such nova occurs in a galaxy about once every six hundred years.

surrogate   A substitute. *Surrogate* is employed frequently in psychology to denote an object or person who is playing a substitute role.

symbiosis   The phenomenon of two species living together in a relationship that is mutually beneficial to both to the extent that neither could survive without the other. In psychology *symbiosis* quite often refers to a close mutual-aid relationship between individuals.

sympathectomies   *See sympathectomy.*

sympathectomy A surgical or chemical interruption of some portion of a sympathetic nervous pathway.

syphilis A contagious venereal disease that is marked by a variety of structural and cutaneous lesions. The disease is generally contracted by direct contact, usually coital.

systolic blood pressure The blood pressure that occurs at the time that the ventricles of the heart are contracted, driving the blood into the aorta and the pulmonary artery. *Systolic blood pressure* is the period of maximum blood pressure.

tabula rasa (Latin) A scraped tablet or a blank slate. It usually refers to a mind not yet affected by experiences or impressions.

Talmud A collection of early writings constituting the body of early Jewish religious and civil law.

taxis A synonym for *tropism*. The term *taxis* is much less frequently used in modern day biology than in an earlier era. *See tropism.*

tegmentum The grayish upper covering of that portion of the brain which is known as the pedunculus cerebri.

temporal In general, pertaining to the temples, the flat area of the head just above the cheeks. In neuroanatomy, *temporal* refers to the area of the cerebral hemispheres underlying the temples. *See temporal lobe.*

temporal lobe That portion of the cerebral hemisphere which lies in front of the occipital lobe and just below the lateral fissure of the brain.

testis The male reproductive gland. It is situated in the scrotum and produces spermatozoa.

tests of general ability Standardized tests which assess a testee's knowledge and skill over a wide variety of general areas.

thalamus The middle and larger portion of the part of the brain that is known as the diencephalon. The *thalamus* serves as a kind of relay center that transmits sensory impulses to the cerebral cortex.

theology A religious discipline that concerns itself with the study of God and religious doctrine.

theoretical construct *See hypothetical construct.*

theoretician One who coordinates and systematizes the various data of a given field and espouses theories which are based on the integration and implications of such data.

theories *See theory.*

theory A principle or group of principles that are logically deduced from existing data and that serve the purpose of integrating such data into a meaningful and predictive statement.

thinking In general, *thinking* is the ability to respond to a stimulus not physically present in its specific form in the outside environment.

thorax The chest; the part of the body between the neck and the abdomen.

thyroid *See thyroid gland.*

thyroid gland A large, ductless gland that is situated in front of the upper part of the trachea. It produces thyroxin, an organic compound that has a significant influence on body metabolism.

thyroxin A secretion of the thyroid gland. *See thyroid gland.*

T-maze A system of alleys shaped like a "T." The starting box lies at the base of the "T." The initial singular alley branches off, at a point, into a right alley and a left alley, thus giving the maze the shape of a "T." It is used frequently in animal experimentation, particularly with rats.

TOGA *See Tests of General Ability.*

tranquilizing pill A pill which contains a drug that soothes and pacifies its user.

transaction The view according to which phenomena are studied as a field or totality, every aspect of which is related to, and dependent upon, every other aspect. The layman's view of "gravity" as an independent force illustrates the self-actional view. A "gravitational field" exemplifies a transactional one. Let the reader view a picture of a galaxy and he can understand how difficult it is to "dismember" a particular sun or its planet. The "whole" sticks out like a sore thumb and can even be easily seen in relation to other galaxies. One step beyond is the cosmos. This view is difficult to apply in psychology because one must maintain the total field and yet analyze it, which requires tearing it apart.

transactional *See transaction.*

transducer Any device that receives energy from one system and retransmits it to another system.

transfer *See transfer of training.*

transfer of training The effect old learning has on new learning tasks, either of a positive (positive transfer) or negative (negative transfer) nature.

trauma Any experience that inflicts the organism with serious somatic or psychological damage.

traumatic *See trauma.*

tropism The response of a plant or animal to some stimulus, for example, gravity or light, such that the growth curvature of that plant or animal is determined by the direction from which the stimulus originates. The response may be toward (positive tropism) the stimulus or away (negative tropism) from it.

***T*-test** A specific test for statistical significance which is designed for psychologist's contribution to

unconditioned response A response that is elicited by a specific stimulus at the beginning of a learning or conditioning period.

unconditioned stimulus Any stimulus which elicits a specific response at the beginning of a learning or conditioning period.

unconscious In psychoanalysis, a division of the psyche or mind that includes those aspects of mental life that are not open to conscious scrutiny. However, the *unconscious* has a dynamic effect on conscious processes and behavior.

uncus Any hook-like structure, but particularly the hooked end of the hippocampal convolution.

underachiever Any person whose actual accomplishments or achievements are fewer in number and/or more inferior in quality than various standardized tests of ability or intelligence would predict them to be.

UR *See unconditioned response.*

US *See unconditioned stimulus.*

uterus The womb; the hollow, muscular organ in female animals where the embryo and fetus develop.

variable One of the conditions under observation in an experiment. Hence, it is measured and/or controlled. *See dependent variable and independent variable.*

variable ratio schedule A schedule of reinforcement which prescribes that a given percentage of responses be reinforced, but that the sequence be varied so that the reinforced response does not fall at the same point in the sequence each time.

variance A statistical measure of the extent to which individual scores in a set of scores differ each from each.

virus A sub-microscopic agent that infects plants and animals, usually causing disease, and is unable to multiply outside of the host tissues.

viscera The large organs enclosed within the great cavities of the body, especially the abdomen.

visceral Pertaining to the viscera. *See viscera.*

visual convergence The coordinated movements of the two eyes in aiming at objects in the visual field.

visual-motor Pertaining to the coordination of vision with muscular activity.

Warner Index of Status Characteristics A method for evaluating the prestige position of a family by rating its position with regard to four simple characteristics: occupation, source of income, house type, and dwelling area.

Wechsler Test Any one of several tests of general intelligence which were compiled by the psychologist David Wechsler.

wide range achievement test A standard test of achievement which covers a broad spectrum of academic subjects and skills.

withdrawal A defense mechanism whereby a person removes himself from a frustrating or conflict-ridden situation, either physically or psychologically.

x-chromosome The sex chromosome carried by one-half of the male gametes and all of the female gametes in all heterogametic animals.

yeshiva An orthodox Jewish higher school which educates children in both religious and secular subjects.

yolk sac An extraembryonic membrane comprising the umbilical vesicle.

zoology A field of science and branch of biology which concerns itself with the study of animals.

References

Adams, S. H. The Juke myth. *Saturday Review,* April 2, 1955.

Adamson, J. *Born free.* New York: Bartholomew House, 1960.

Adamson, J. *Living free.* New York: Harcourt, 1961.

Aebersold, P. C. Radioisotopes – new keys to knowledge. In *The Smithsonian Report for 1953.* Washington, D. C., 1954.

Anastasi, A. Heredity, environment, and the question "How?" *Psychological Review,* July 1958, **65,** 197–208.

Anderson, O. D., & Parameter, R. A long-term study of experimental neurosis in the sheep and dog; with nine case histories. *Psychosomatic Medicine Monographs,* 1941, **2** (3 & 4).

Anderson, S. L., & Gantt, W. H. The effect of person on cardiac and motor responsivity to shock in dogs. *Conditional Reflex,* July-September 1966, **1**(3), 181–189.

Anderson, V. E. Genetics in mental retardation. In H. A. Stevens & R. Heber (Eds.), *Mental retardation.* Chicago: University of Chicago Press, 1964, pp. 348–394.

Anonymous. This inspector is a bird. *Factory,* December 1959, 219–221.

Asher, J. J. Toward a new-field theory of behavior. *Journal of Humanistic Psychology,* Fall, 1964, **4** (2), 85–94.

Asher, J. J. The strategy of the total physical response: An application to learning Russian. *Sonderdruck aus IRAL,* 1965, **3**(4), 291–299.

Babich, F. R., Jacobson, A. L., & Bubash, S. Cross-species transfer of learning: Effect of ribonucleic acid from hamsters on rat behavior. *Proceedings of the National Academy of Sciences,* 1965, **54**(5), 1299–1302.

Babich, F. R., Jacobson, A. L., Bubash, S., & Jacobson, A. Transfer of a response to naive rats by injection of ribonucleic acid extracted from trained rats. *Science,* 1965, **149**(3684), 656–657.

Baldwin, A. L. Variation in Stanford-Binet IQ resulting from an artifact of the test. *Journal of Personality,* December 1948, **17**(2).

Bandura, A. Social learning through imitation. In M. R. Jones (Ed.), *Nebraska Symposium on Motivation.* Lincoln: University of Nebraska Press, 1962, pp. 211–269.

Bandura, A. The influence of response consequences to the model on the acquisition and performance of imitative responses. Unpublished manuscript, Stanford University, 1963.

Bandura, A. The role of imitation in personality development. *The Journal of Nursery Education,* April 1963, **18**(3), 207–215.

Bandura, A., & Huston, A. C. Identification as a process of incidental learning. *Journal of Abnormal Social Psychology,* 1961, **63,** 311–318.

Bandura, A., & McDonald, F. J. The influence of social reinforcement and the behavior of models in shaping children's moral judgments. *Journal of Abnormal Social Psychology,* 1963, **67,** 274–281.

Bandura, A., Ross, D., & Ross, S. A. Transmission of aggression through imitation of aggressive models. *Journal of Abnormal Social Psychology,* 1961, **63,** 575–582.

Bandura, A., Ross, D., & Ross, S. A. A comparative test of the status envy, social power and secondary reinforcement theories of identificatory learning. *Journal of Abnormal Social Psychology,* 1963, **67,** in press. (a)

Bandura, A., Ross, D., & Ross, S. A. Imitation of film-mediated aggressive models. *Journal of Abnormal Social Psychology,* 1963, **66,** 3–11. (b)

Bandura, A., Ross, D., & Ross, S. A. Vicarious reinforcement and imitative learning. *Journal of Abnormal Social Psychology,* 1963, **67,** in press. (c)

Bandura, A., & Walters, R. H. *Social Learning and Personality Development.* New York: Holt, 1963.

Barber, B. Resistance by scientists to scientific discovery. *Scientific Manpower Bulletin*, 1960, 36–47.

Bardach, J., Johnson, G., & Todd, J. A new laboratory method for tracking aquatic animals. *Medical & Biological Illustration*, April 1967, **17**(2), 108–111. (a)

Bardach, J., Todd, J., & Crickmer, R. Orientation by taste in fish of the genus ictalurus. *Science*, March 10, 1967, **155** (3767), 1276–1278. (b)

Barrington, B. L. A list of words descriptive of affective reactions. *Journal of Clinical Psychology*, April 1963, **19**(2), 259–262.

Basmajian, J. V. Control and training of individual motor units. *Science*, 1963, **141**, 440–441.

Baumrind, D. Some thoughts on ethics of research: After reading Milgram's "Behavioral study of obedience." *American Psychologist*, 1964, **19**(6), 421–425.

Bayley, N. Mental growth in young children. Factors influencing the growth of intelligence in young children. *39th Yearbook of the National Society for the Study of Education*, 1940.

Bayley, N. Some increasing parent-child similarities during the growth of children. *Journal of Educational Psychology*, 1954, **45**, 1–21.

Bayroff, A. G. The experimental social behavior of animals: I. The effect of early isolation of white rats on their later reactions to other white rats as measured by two periods of free choice. *Journal of Comparative Psychology*, 1936, **21**, 67.

Benedict, R. *Patterns of Culture*. New York: The New American Library, 1934.

Bennis, W. G., Schein, E. H., Berlew, D. E., & Steel, F. I. *Interpersonal Dynamics*. Homewood, Ill.: Dorsey, 1964.

Bensberg, G. J. (Ed.) *Teaching the mentally retarded*. Atlanta, Georgia: Southern Regional Education Board, 1965.

Bentley, A. F. *Inquiry into inquiries*. Boston: Beacon, 1954.

Bernstein, L. A note on Christie's "experimental naivete and experiential naivete." *Psychological Bulletin*, January 1952, **49**, 38.

Berry, R. J. A., & Gordon, R. G. *The mental defective*. New York: Whittlesey House, 1931.

Bertrand, M. Training without reward: Traditional training of pig-tailed macaques as coconut harvesters. *Science*, 1967, **155**, 484–486.

Bettelheim, B. *Love is not enough*. Glencoe, Ill.: Free Press, 1950.

Bettelheim, B. *Truants from life*. Glencoe, Ill.: Free Press, 1955.

Bettelheim, B. Feral children and autistic children. *American Journal of Sociology*, 1959, **64**, 455–467.

Biel, W. C. The effects of early inanition of a developmental schedule in the albino rat. *Journal of Comparative Psychology*, 1939, **28**, 1.

Bijou, S. W. Theory and research in mental (developmental) retardation. *Psychological Record*, January 1963, **13**, 95–110.

Bloom, B. Early learning in the home. The first B. J. Paley Lecture, U.C.L.A., July 18, 1965.

Blough, D. S. Experiments in animal psychophysics. *Scientific American*, 1961, **205**, 113–122.

Botwinick, J. Husband and father-in-law — a reversible figure. *The American Journal of Psychology*, 1961, **74**, 312–313.

Brackbill, Y. Extinction of the smiling response in infants as a function of reinforcement schedule. *Child Development*, March 1958, **29**(1), 115–124.

Braid, J. W. Memory for absolute pitch. In *Studies in psychology: Titchener commemorative volume*. Worcester, Mass: Louis H. Wilson, 1917.

Brearley, M., & Hitchfield, E. *A guide to reading Piaget*. New York: Shocken Books, 1966.

Breland, K., & Breland, M. A field of applied animal psychology. *American Psychologist*, 1951, **6**, 202–204.

Brotz, H. *The black Jews of Harlem*. New York: Free Press, 1964.

Bucklew, J., Jr. Conceptions of social psychology. In N. H. Pronko & J. W.

Bowles, Jr. (Eds.), *Empirical foundations of psychology.* New York: Holt, 1951.

Bucklew, J., Jr. The social psychological response. In N. H. Pronko & J. W. Bowles, Jr. (Eds.), *Empirical Foundations of Psychology.* New York: Holt, 1951.

Bucklew, J., Jr. & Hafner, A. J. Organismic versus cerebral localization of biological defects in feeblemindedness. *Journal of Psychology,* July 1951, **32**, 69–78.

Bykov, K. M. *The cerebral cortex of the internal organs* (Ed. and trans. by W. Horsley Gantt). New York: Chemical Publishing, 1957.

Byrne, W. L. Memory transfer. *Science,* 1966, **153**(3736), 658–659.

Calvin, G. J., & Calvin, M. Wanted: A star. *Main Currents In Modern Thought,* 1967, **23**(3), 59–64.

Cameron, N. A. *The psychology of behavior disorders.* Boston: Houghton Mifflin, 1947.

Caras, R. A. *Dangerous to man: Wild animals: A definitive study of their reputed dangers to man.* Philadelphia: Chilton, 1964.

Caseres, C. A. (Ed.) *Biomedical telemetry.* New York: Academic Press. 1965.

Cautela, J. R. Misconceptions: Intelligence and the IQ. *Education,* January 1958, **78**(5). 300–303.

Chittenden, Gertrude E. An experimental study in measuring and modifying assertive behavior in young children. *Monographs of Social Research and Child Development,* 1942, **7**(1), (Serial no. 31).

Clarke, A. C. Our dumb colleagues. *Harper's Magazine,* 1958, **216**, 32–33.

Clarke, A. M. & Clarke, A. D. B. (Eds.) *Mental deficiency.* (Rev. ed.) New York: Free Press, 1965.

Cochran, W. G. & Cox, G. M. *Experimental designs.* New York: Wiley, 1950.

Collins, C. C. Ancillary communication by tactile image visualization education. (Mimeograph) 1968.

Commoner, B. Roles of deoxyribonucleic acid in inheritance. *Nature,* June 6, 1964, **202**(4936), 960–968.

Coon, C. S. *The origin of races.* New York: Knopf, 1962.

Coon, C. S., & Hunt, E. E., Jr. *The living races of man.* New York: Knopf, 1965.

Copp, E. F. Musical ability. *Journal of Heredity,* 1916, **7**, 297–305.

Crumpton, E., Wine, D. B., & Drenick, E. J. Effects of prolonged food deprivation on food responses to skeleton words. *Journal of General Psychology,* 1967, **76**, 179–182.

Cumming, W. W. A bird's eye glimpse of men and machines. In R. Ulrich, T. Stachnik, & J. Mabry (Eds.), *Control of human behavior.* Glenview, Ill.: Scott, Foresman, 1966, pp. 246–256.

Decarie, T. G. *Intelligence and affectivity in early childhood.* New York: International Universities Press, 1965.

DeVos, G., & Wagatsuma, H. *Japan's invisible race.* Berkeley: University of California Press, 1966.

Dewey, J., & Bentley, A. F. *Knowing and the known.* Boston: Beacon, 1949.

Dobzhansky, T. What is heredity? *Science,* November 3, 1944, **100**(2601), 406.

Dyer, H. S. A psychometrician views human ability. *Teachers College Record,* April 1960, **61**(7), 394–403.

Ebert, E., & Simmons, K. The Brush Foundation study of child growth and development. *Monographs of Social Research and Child Development,* 1943, **8**(2), 1–49.

Edfeldt, A. W. *Silent speech and silent reading.* Chicago: University of Chicago Press, 1960.

Edwards, A. E., & Acker, L. E. A demonstration of the long-term retention of a conditioned galvanic skin response. *Psychosomatic Medicine,* 1962, **24**, 459–463.

Eisner, T., & Davis, J. A. Mongoose throwing and smashing millipedes. *Science,* February 3, 1967, **155**(3762), 577–579.

Enesco, H. E. Rate of ^{14}C-RNA injected into mice. *Experimental Cell Research,* 1966, **42**, 640–645.

Engel, G. L. *Psychological development in health and disease.* Philadelphia: Saunders, 1962.

Engel, G. L. Anxiety and depression-withdrawal: The primary effects of unpleasure. *International Journal of Psychoanalysis,* 1962, **43**, 89.

Engel, G. L., & Reichsman, F. Spontaneous and experimentally induced depression in an infant with a gastric fistula; a contribution to the problem of depression. *Journal of American Psychoanalytic Association,* 1956, **4**, 428–452.

Escher, M. C. *Catalogue 118.* Amsterdam: Stedelijik Museum, 1954.

Ewert, P. H. A study of the effect of inverted retinal stimulation upon spatially coordinated behavior. *Genetic Psychological Monographs,* 1930, **7**, 177–363.

Ewing, L. S. Fighting and death from stress in a cockroach. *Science,* 1967, **155**, 1035–1036.

Farson, R. E. Can science solve human dilemmas? In R. E. Farson (Ed.), *Science and human affairs.* Palo Alto, California: Science and Behavior Books, 1965.

Fay, J., & Doll, E. A. Organic impairment simulating mental deficiency. *American Journal of Orthopsychiatry,* January 1949, **19**, 112–119.

Fenichel, O. *The psychoanalytic theory of neurosis.* New York: Norton, 1945.

Ferreira, A. J. Emotional factors in prenatal environment. *Journal of Nervous and Mental Disease,* 1965, **141**(1), 108–118.

Ferster, C. B. Use of the blackout in the investigation of temporal discrimination in fixed-interval reinforcement. *Journal of Experimental Psychology,* 1954, **47**, 69–74.

Ferster, C. B., & Skinner, B. F. *Schedules of reinforcement.* New York: Appleton-Century-Crofts, 1957.

Ferster, M. B., & Ferster, C. B. Animals as workers. *New Scientist,* 1962, **15**, 497–499.

Flanagan, J. C. *Tests of general ability: Technical report.* Chicago. Science Research Associates, 1960.

Flavell, J. H. *The developmental psychology of Jean Piaget.* Princeton, N. J.: Van Nostrand, 1963.

Flory, C. D. The physical growth of mentally deficient boys. *Monographs of Social Research in Child Development,* 1936, **1**(6).

Foy, E., & Harlow, A. F. *Clowning through life.* New York: Dutton, 1928.

Franks, C. M. *Conditioning techniques in clinical practice and research.* New York: Springer, 1964.

Fredericson, E. Competition: The effects of infantile experience upon adult behavior. *Journal of Abnormal and Social Psychology,* 1951, **46**, 406.

Freedman, A. M., & Wilson, E. A. Childhood and Adolescent Addictive Disorders. *Pediatrics,* September 1964, 425–430.

Fried, M. H. Disastrous definition. *Science,* 1964, **146**, 1526.

Fried, M. H. A four-letter word that hurts. *Saturday Review,* October 2, 1965, 21–23.

Friedell, A. A reversal of the normal concentration of urine in children having enuresis. *American Journal of the Disturbed Child,* 1927, **33**, 717–721.

Fuller, J. L., & Thompson, W. R. *Behavior genetics.* New York: Wiley, 1960.

Gantt, W. H. *Experimental basis for neurotic behavior.* New York: Hoeber, 1944.

Gantt, W. H. Postscript to experimental induction of psychoneuroses by conditioned reflex with stress. In Milbank Memorial Foundation, *The biology of mental health and disease.* New York: Hoeber, 1952.

Gantt, W. H. Principles of nervous breakdown in schizokinesis and autokinesis. *Annals of the New York Academy of Science,* 1953, **56**, 143–163.

Gantt, W. H. Reflexology, schizokinesis, and autokinesis. *Conditional Reflex,* January-March 1966, **1**(1), 57–68. (a)

Gantt, W. H., Newton, J. E. O., Royer, F. L., & Stephens, J. H. Effect of person. *Conditional Reflex,* January-March 1966, **1**(1), 18–35. (b)

Gates, R. R. *Human genetics.* New York: Macmillan, 1946.

Gellerman, L. W. Chance orders of alternating stimuli in visual discrimination experiments. *Journal of Genetic Psychology,* 1933, **42,** 206–207.

Gesell, A. *The embryology of behavior.* New York: Harper, 1945.

Gesell, A., & Ilg, F. L. *Child development: An introduction to the study of human growth.* New York: Harper, 1949.

Goodall, J. Tool-using and aimed throwing in a community of free-living chimpanzees. *Nature* (London), March 28, 1964, **201**(4926), 1264–1266.

Goodall, J. Chimpanzees of the Gombe Stream Reserve. In Irven DeVore (Ed.), *Primate behavior.* New York: Holt, 1965.

Goodall, J. *My friends the wild chimpanzees.* Washington, D. C.: The National Geographic Society, 1967.

Goodall, J., & Goodall, H. Use of tools by the Egyptian vulture, Neophron percnopterus. *Nature,* December 24, 1966, **212,** 1468–1469.

Gottlieb, G., & Kuo, Zing-Yang. Development of behavior in the duck embryo. *Journal of Comparative and Physiological Psychology,* 1965, **59**(2), 183–188.

Gray, P. H., & Howard, K. I. Specific recognition of humans in imprinted chicks. *Perceptual and Motor Skills,* 1957, **7,** 301–304.

Green, C., & Zigler, E. Social deprivation and the performance of retarded and normal children in a satiation type task. *Child Development,* June 1962, **33,** 499–508.

Green, R., & Money, J. Incongruous gender role: Nongenital manifestations in prepubertal boys. *Journal of Nervous and Mental Disease,* August 1960, **130**(8), 160–168.

Gresham, W. L. Fortune tellers never starve. *Esquire,* November 1949, **32**(5).

Grier, J. B., Counter, S. A., & Shearer, W. M. Prenatal auditory imprinting in chickens. *Science,* March 31, 1967, **155**(3770), 1692–1693.

Griffiths, B. The sacred cow. *Commonweal,* February 3, 1967, **85,** 483–484.

Gross, C. G., & Carey, F. M. Transfer of learned response by RNA injection: Failure of attempts to replicate. *Science,* 1965, **150**(3704), 1749.

Gudger, E. W. Monkeys trained as harvesters: Instances of a practice extending from remote times to the present. *Natural History,* 1923, **23,** 262–279.

Haber, W. B. Effects of loss of limb on sensory functions. *Journal of Psychology,* 1955, **40,** 115–123.

Haber, W. B. Reactions to loss of limb: Physiological and psychological aspects. *Annals of the New York Academy of Sciences,* September 30, 1958, **74**(1), 14–24.

Hahn, E. *Die Haustiere und ihre Beziehungen zur Wirtschaft des Menschen.* Leipzig: Duncker and Humblot, 1896.

Hall, C. S., & Whiteman, P. H. The effects of infantile stimulation upon later emotional stability in the mouse. *Journal of Comparative Physiological Psychology,* 1951, **44,** 61.

Handy, R. *Methodology of the behavioral sciences: Problems and controversies.* Springfield, Illinois: Charles C Thomas, 1964.

Hansel, C. E. M. *ESP: A scientific evaluation.* New York: Scribners, 1966.

Harlow, H. F. The formation of learning sets. *Psychological Review,* 1949, **56,** 51–65.

Harlow, H. F. The nature of love. *American Psychologist,* 1958, **13,** 673–685.

Harlow, H. F., & Zimmerman, R. R. Affectional responses in the infant monkey. *Science,* 1959, **130,** 421–432.

Harris, M. *Patterns of race in the Americas.* New York: Walker, 1964.

Harris, M. The cultural ecology of India's sacred cattle. *Current Anthropology,* February 1966, **7**(1), 51–66.

Harrison, G. A., et al. *Human biology.* New York: Oxford, 1964.

Hart, B. M., Allen, K. E., Buell, J. S., Harris, F. R., & Wolf, M. M. Effects of social reinforcement on operant crying. *Experimental Child Psychology,* July 1964, **1**(2), 145–153.

Hartry, A. L., Keith-Lee, P., & Morton, W. D. Planaria: Memory transfer through cannibalism reexamined. *Science,* 1964, **146**(3641), 274–275.

Hasler, A. D. *Underwater guideposts: Homing of salmon.* Madison: University of Wisconsin Press, 1966.

Hattaway, D. P., Hietanen, E. D., & Rothfusz, R. W. Training a machine to read with nonlinear threshold logic. *Electronics,* August 22, 1966, 86–93.

Hazelwood, J. Electronic eyes for the blind. *Science News,* May 1967, **91**(13), 456–457.

Heath, R. G. Electrical self-stimulation of the brain in man. *The American Journal of Psychiatry,* 1963, **120**(6), 571–577.

Heckel, R. V., & Salzberg, H. C. How to make your patients chronic. *Mental Hospitals,* 1964, **15,** 37–38.

Henderson, W. J. *Early history of singing.* New York: Longmans, Green, 1921.

Herrnstein, R. J., & Loveland, D. H. Complex visual concept in the pigeon. *Science,* 1964, **146,** 549–551. Reprinted in R. Ulrich, T. Stachnik, & J. Mabry (Eds.), *Control of human behavior.* Glenview, Ill.: Scott, Foresman, 1966, pp. 239–241.

Hess, E. H. Effects of meprobamate on imprinting in waterfowl. *Annals of the New York Academy of Sciences,* 1957, **67,** 724–732.

Hess, E. H. Imprinting in animals. *Scientific American,* 1958, **198**(3), 81–90.

Hess, E. H., & Polt, J. M. Pupil size as related to interest value of visual stimuli. *Science,* 1960, **132,** 349–350.

Hess, E. H., & Polt, J. M. Pupil size in relation to mental activity during simple problem solving. *Science,* 1964, **143,** 1190–1192.

Hess, E. H., & Ramsay, A. O. A laboratory approach to the study of imprinting. *Wilson Bulletin,* 1954, **66,** 196–206.

Hess, E. H., Seltzer, A. H., & Shlien, J. M. Pupil response of hetero- and homosexual males to pictures of men and women: A pilot study. *Journal of Abnormal Psychology,* June 1965, **70**(3), 165–168.

Hewes, G. W. World distribution of certain postural habits. *American Anthropologist,* April 1955, **57**(2), 231–244.

Hewes, G. W. The domain posture. *Anthropological Linguistics,* November 1966, **8**(8), 106–112.

Hickman, C. P. Integrated principles of zoology. (3rd ed.) St. Louis: C. V. Mosby Co., 1966.

Hilden, A. H. A longitudinal study of intellectual development. *Journal of Psychology,* 1949, **28,** 187–214.

Hilgard, E. R., & Atkinson, R. C. *Introduction to psychology.* (4th ed.) New York: Harcourt, 1967.

Hodgins, E. *Episode: Report on the accident inside my skull.* New York: Atheneum, 1964.

Holt, E. B. *Animal drive and the learning process.* Vol. 1. New York: Holt, 1931.

Hunt, J. McV. The effects of infant feeding-frustration upon adult hoarding in the albino rat. *Journal of Abnormal and Social Psychology,* 1941, **36,** 338.

Hunt, J. McV. The psychological basis for using pre-school enrichment as an antidote for cultural deprivation. *Merrill-Palmer Quarterly of Behavior and Development,* July 1964, **10**(3), 209.

Hunt, J. McV. Competence in the light of psychological and social development. An address at a symposium at The American Psychological Association Meeting in Washington, D. C., September 2, 1967.

Hunt, N. *The world of Nigel Hunt.* New York: Garrett Publications, 1967.

Hydén, H. Biochemical changes in glial cells and nerve cells at varying activity. *Biochemistry of the central nervous system,* in *Proceedings of the Fourth International Congress of Biochemistry.* Vol. 3. London: Pergamon Press, 1959.

Hydén, H., & Egyhâzi, E. Glial RNA changes during a learning experiment in rats. *Proceedings of the National Academy of Sciences,* 1963, **49,** 618–624.

Irwin, O. C. Reliability of infant speech sound data. *Journal of Speech and Hearing Disorders,* 1945, **10,** 227–235.

Irwin, O. C. Development of speech during infancy: curve of phonemic frequencies. *Journal of Experimental Psychology,* 1947, **37,** 187–193.

Irwin, O. C. Infant speech: The effect of family occupational status and of age on sound frequency. *Journal of Speech and Hearing Disorders,* 1948, **13**, 320–323.

Irwin, O. C. Correct status of a third set of consonants in the speech of cerebral palsy children. *Cerebral Palsy Review,* 1957, **18**(3), 17–20.

Irwin, O. C. Infant speech: Effect of systematic reading of stories. *Journal of Speech and Hearing Research,* June 1960, **3**(2), 187–190.

Irwin, O. C., & Chen, H. P. Development of speech during infancy: Curve of phonemic types. *Journal of Experimental Psychology,* 1946, **36**, 431–436.

Irwin, O. C., & Curry, J. Vowel elements in the crying vocalization of infants under ten days of age. *Child Development,* 1941, **12**, 99–109.

Itani, J. The society of Japanese monkeys. *Japan Quarterly,* 1961, **8**(4).

Jacobson, M. *Insect sex attractants.* New York: Wiley, 1965.

James, W. *Psychology.* New York: Holt, 1913.

Jarvis, J. H. Postmastectomy breast phantoms. *Journal of Nervous and Mental Disease,* 1967, **144**(4), 266–272.

Jastak, J. F., MacPhee, H. M., & Whitemen, M. *Mental retardation.* Newark, Delaware: University of Delaware Press, 1963.

Jastrow, J. *Fact and fable in psychology.* New York: Houghton Mifflin, 1900.

Jastrow, J. *The story of human error.* New York: Appleton-Century-Crofts, 1936.

Jennings, H. S. Heredity and environment. *The Scientific Monthly,* September 1924, **19**(15), 225–238.

Jennings, H. S. *The biological basis of human nature.* New York: Norton, 1930.

Jervis, G. A. A contribution to the study of the influence of heredity on mental deficiency. The genetics of phenylpyruvic oligophrenia. *Proceedings of the American Association of Mental Deficiency,* 1939, **44**(2), 13–24.

Jones, E. How to tell your friends from geniuses. *Saturday Review,* August 10, 1957, **39**.

Jordan, T. E. *The mentally retarded.* Columbus, Ohio: Merrill, 1961.

Kagan, J., & Lewis, M. Studies of attention in the human infant. *Merrill-Palmer Quarterly of Behavior and Development,* 1965, **11**(2), 95–127.

Kahn, M. W. The effect of severe defeat at various age levels on the aggressive behavior of mice. Unpublished Master's thesis, Pennsylvania State College, 1949.

Kallmann, F. *The genetics of schizophrenia.* New York: J. J. Augustin, 1938.

Kantor, J. R. *Principles of psychology,* Vol. 2. New York: Knopf, 1926.

Kantor, J. R. *Survey of the science of psychology.* Bloomington, Ind.: Principia Press, 1933.

Kantor, J. R. *Problems of physiological psychology.* Bloomington, Ind.: Principia Press, 1947.

Kantrow, R. W. An investigation of conditioned feeding responses and concomitant adaptive behavior in young infants. *University of Iowa Studies in Child Welfare,* 1937, **13**(3).

Karelitz, S., Karelitz, R. F., & Rosenfeld, L. S. Infants' vocalizations and their significance. *Mental Retardation,* 1965, 439–446.

Kaufman, I. C., & Rosenblum, L. A. Depression in infant monkeys separated from their mothers. *Science,* February 24, 1967, **155**(3765), 1030–1031.

Keller, F. S. *The definition of psychology* (1937). New York: Appleton-Century-Crofts, 1962.

Kellogg, V. L. *Mind and heredity.* Princeton: Princeton University Press, 1923.

Kessen, W. Research in the psychological development of infants: An overview. *Merrill-Palmer Quarterly of Behavior and Development,* 1963, **9**, 83–94.

Kilpatrick, F. P. Elementary demonstrations of perceptual phenomena. *Human Behavior from the Transactional Point of View.* Hanover, N. H.: The Institute for Associated Research, 1952.

Kinsey, A. C., Pomeroy, W. B., & Martin, C. E. *Sexual behavior in the human male.* Philadelphia: Saunders, 1948.

Kinsey, A. C., Pomeroy, W. B., Martin, C. E., & Gebhard, P. H. *Sexual behavior in the human female.* Philadelphia: Saunders, 1953.

Kissinger, R. D. The un-therapeutic community: A team approach that failed. Paper read at the Eastern Psychological Association meeting in Philadelphia, 1963.

Klopfer, P. H. Is imprinting a cheshire cat? *Behavioral Science,* March 1967, **12**(2), 122–129.

Kluckhohn, C. *Mirror for man.* New York: Fawcett, 1960.

Ko, W. H., & Neuman, M. R. Implant biotelemetry and microelectronics. *Science,* April 21, 1967, **156**(3773), 351–360.

Kolb, L. C. *The painful phantom.* Springfield, Ill.: Charles C Thomas, 1954.

Kolb, L. C., Frank, L. M., & Watson, E. J. Treatment of the acute phantom limb. *Proceedings Staff Meetings, Mayo Clinic,* 1952, **27,** 110–118.

Kortlandt, A. Reply. *Current Anthropology,* 1967, **8,** 255–257.

Kortlandt, A., & van Zon, J. C. J. Experimentation with chimpanzees in the wild. (Summary from a lecture delivered at the International Ethological Conference, April 1967.)

Krebs, C. J. *The lemming cycle at Baker Lake, Northwestern Territories, during 1959–1962.* Arctic Institute of North America Technical Paper No. 15, September 1964.

Kunihira, S., & Asher, J. J. The strategy of the total physical response: An application to learning Japanese. *Sonderdruck aus IRAL,* 1965, **3**(4), 277–289.

Kuo, Zing-Yang. Genesis of cat's responses to rats. *Journal of Comparative Psychology,* October 1930, **2,** 1.

Lashley, K. S. Conditional reactions in the rat. *Journal of Psychology,* 1938, **6,** 311–324.

Lee, D. *Freeing capacity to learn.* Washington, D. C.: Association for Supervision and Curriculum Development, 1960.

Lehrman, D. S. A critique of Konrad Lorenz's theory of instinctive behavior. *Quarterly Review of Biology,* 1953, **28,** 337–363.

Lehrman, D. S. Interaction of hormonal and experiential influences on development of behavior. In E. L. Bliss (Ed.), *Roots of behavior.* New York: Harper, 1962.

Levi, M. *The pigeon.* (Rev. ed.) Sumpter, S. C.: Levi Publishing Co., 1963.

Levy, D. M. Experiments in the sucking reflex and social behavior of dogs. *American Journal of Orthopsychiatry,* 1934, **4,** 203.

Levy, D. M. On instinct: An experiment in the pecking behavior of chickens. *Journal of Genetic Psychology,* 1939, **18,** 327.

Levy, H. S. *Chinese footbinding: The history of a curious erotic custom.* New York: Walter Rawls, 1966.

Lewis, M. The meaning of a response, or why researchers in infant behavior should be Oriental metaphysicians. *Merrill-Palmer Quarterly of Behavior and Development,* 1966.

Lewis, M., Bartels, B., Campbell, H., & Goldberg, S. Individual differences in attention: The relation between infants' condition at birth and attention distribution within the first year. *American Journal of the Disturbed Child,* in press.

Lewis, M., Campbell, H., Bartels, B., & Fadel, D. Infants' responses to facial stimuli during the first year of life. *Developmental Psychology,* in press.

Lewis, M., Kagan, J., Campbell, H., & Kalafat, J. The cardiac response as a correlate of attention in infants. *Child Development,* March 1966, **37**(1), 63–71. (a)

Lewis, M., Kagan, J., & Kalafat, J. Patterns of fixation in the young infant. *Child Development,* June 1966, **37**(2), 331–341. (b)

Lipsitt, L. P. Learning processes of human newborns. *Merrill-Palmer Quarterly of Behavior and Development,* 1966, **12**(1), 45–71.

Lipsitt, L. P., Engen, T., & Kaye, H. Developmental changes in the olfactory threshold of the neonate. *Child Development,* 1963, **34,** 371–376.

Lipsitt, L. P., & Kaye, H. Conditioned sucking in the human newborn. *Psychonomic Science,* 1964, **1,** 29–30.

Lipsitt, L. P., Kaye, H., & Bosack, T. N. Enhancement of neonatal sucking through reinforcement. *Journal of Experimental Child Psychology,* 1966, **4**(2), 163–168.

Lipsitt, L. P., & Levy, N. Electrotactual threshold in the neonate. *Child Development,* 1959, **30,** 547–554.

Livingstone, F. B. On the nonexistence of human races. *Current Anthropology,* 1962, **3**(3).

Lorenz, K. Z. *King Solomon's ring.* New York: Crowell, 1952.

Lovaas, I. O., Schaeffer, B., & Simmons, J. W. Building social behavior in autistic children by use of electric shock. *Journal of Experimental Research in Personality,* October 1965, **1**(2), 99–109.

Lovaas, O. J. Effect of exposure to symbolic aggressive behavior. *Child Development,* 1961, **32,** 37–44.

Lubow, R. E., Siebert, L. E., & Carr-Harris, E. The perception of high order variables by the pigeon. *Technical Report AFAL-TR-66-63.* March 1966. Wright-Patterson Air Force Base, Ohio.

Lundin, R. W. Can perfect pitch be learned? *Music Education Journal,* 1963, **49,** 49–51.

Lundin, R. W., & Allen, J. D. A technique for training perfect pitch. *Psychological Record,* 1942, **12,** 139–146.

Luttges, M., Johnson, T., Buck, C., Holland, J., & McGaugh, J. An examination of "transfer of learning" by nucleic acid. *Science,* 1966, **151**(3712), 834–837.

Maccoby, Eleanor E. Role-taking in childhood and its consequences for social learning. *Child Development,* 1959, **30,** 239–252.

Mackay, R. S. Endoradiosonde. *Nature,* June 15, 1957, **179,** 1239–1240.

Mackay, R. S. *Biomedical telemetry: Sensing and transmitting biological information*

from animals to man. New York: Wiley, 1968.

MacLeod, Robert B. The teaching of psychology and the psychology we teach. *American Psychologist,* 1965, **20,** 344–352.

Mahan, H. C. *The interactional psychology of J. R. Kantor: An introduction.* San Marcos, Calif.: Palomar College, Project Socrates Press, 1968.

Manual on terminology and classification in mental retardation. (2nd ed.) A monograph supplement to the *American Journal of Mental Deficiency* (prepared by Rick Heber), 1961.

Marler, P. Bird songs and mate selection. *Animal Sounds and Communication,* 1960, **7,** 348–367.

Marler, P., & Tamura, M. Song dialects in three populations of white-crowned sparrows. *The Condor,* September–October 1962, **64**(5), 368–377.

Marler, P., & Tamura, M. Culturally transmitted patterns of vocal behavior in sparrows. *Science,* December 11, 1964, **146**(3650), 1483–1486.

Marquis, D. P. Can conditioned responses be established in the newborn infant? *Journal of Genetic Psychology,* 1931, **39,** 479–492.

Martí-Ibáñez, F. *Centaur.* New York: MD Publications, 1960.

Martin, J. H. Freeport Public Schools experiment on early reading using the Edison Responsive Environment Instrument. New York: *Responsive Environments Corporation.*

Martin, J. P., & Bell, J. A pedigree of mental defect showing sex-linkage. *Journal of Neurological Psychiatry,* 1943, **6,** 154–157.

Masland, R. L., Sarason, S. B., & Gladwin, T. *Mental subnormality.* New York: Basic Books, 1958.

Mauss, M. Les techniques du corps. *Journal de Psychologie Normale et Pathologique,* 1935, **32,** 271–293.

Mayhew, W. W. The biology of the cliff swallow in California. *The Condor,* 1958, **60**(1), 7–37.

McConnell, J. V. Memory transfer through cannibalism in planaria. *Journal of Neuropsychiatry,* 1962, **3,** 45.

McConnell, J. V., Jacobson, A. L., & Kimble, D. P. The effects of regeneration upon retention of a conditioned response in the planarian. *Journal of Comparative and Physiological Psychology,* 1959, **52**(1), 1–5.

McNiven, M. A. Social-releaser mechanisms in birds: A controlled replication of Tinbergen's study. *The Psychological Record,* October 1960, **10**(4), 259–265.

Melvin, K. B., Cloar, F. T., & Messingill, L. S. Imprinting of bobwhite quail to a hawk. *The Psychological Record,* 1967, **17,** 235–238.

Mental retardation: A family crisis — the therapeutic role of the physician. Formulated by the Committee on Mental Retardation. New York: Group for Advancement of Psychiatry, 1963. Report No. 56.

Mental retardation (handbook). Report of the American Medical Association Conference on Mental Retardation, April 9–11, 1964.

Meyer, M. Is the memory of absolute pitch capable of development by training? *Psychological Review,* 1899, **6,** 514–516.

Milgram, S. Dynamics of obedience. Washington, D. C.: *National Science Foundation,* January 25, 1961. (Mimeograph)

Milgram, S. Some conditions of obedience and disobedience to authority. *Human Relations,* 1964.

Millikan, G. C., & Bowman, R. I. Observations on Galapagos tool-using finches in captivity. *The Living Bird,* 1967, **6,** 23–41.

Milner, E. A study of the relationship between reading readiness and patterns of parent-child interaction. *Child Development,* 1951, **22,** 95–112.

Moltz, H., & Rosenblum, L. A. Imprinting and associative learning: The stability of the following response in Pekin ducks. *Journal of Comparative Physiological Psychology,* October 1958, **51**(5), 580–583.

Money, J. Hermaphroditism. In A. Ellis (Ed.), *The encyclopedia of sexual behavior.* New York: Hawthorne Books, 1961.

Money, J., Hampson, J. G., & Hampson, J. L. An examination of some basic sexual concepts: The evidence of human hermaphroditism. *Bulletin of the Johns Hopkins Hospital,* October 1955, **97**(4), 301–319. (a)

Money, J., Hampson, J. G., & Hampson, J. L. Hermaphroditism: Recommendations concerning assignment of sex, changes of sex, and psychologic management. *Bulletin of the Johns Hopkins Hospital,* October 1955, **97**(4), 284–300. (b)

Money, J., Hampson, J. G., & Hampson, J. L. Sexual incongruities and psycho-pathology: The evidence of human hermaphroditism. *Bulletin of the Johns Hopkins Hospital,* January 1956, **98**(1), 43–57.

Montagu, A. *The direction of human development.* New York: Harper, 1955.

Montagu, A. *Biosocial nature of man.* New York: Grove Press, 1956.

Montagu, A. *Race, science, and humanity.* Princeton, N. J.: Van Nostrand, 1963.

Montagu, A. *The concept of race.* New York Free Press, 1964.

Montagu, A. *Man's most dangerous myth: The fallacy of race.* (4th rev. ed.) Cleveland: World, 1964.

Moore, B. P. Isolation of the scent-trail pheromone of an Australian termite. *Nature,* August 13, 1966, **211**(5050), 746–747.

Morison, R. S. Where is biology taking us? *Science,* January 27, 1967, **155**(3761), 429–433.

Mowrer, O. H. *Learning theory and the symbolic processes.* New York: Wiley, 1960.

Mowrer, O. H., & Mowrer, W. M. Enuresis — an etiological and therapeutic study. *Journal of Pediatrics,* 1965, **67,** 436–459.

Mull, H. K. The acquisition of absolute pitch. *American Journal of Psychology,* 1925, **36,** 469–493.

Munster, J. H., Jr., & Smith, J. C. The care and feeding of intellectual property. *Science,* 1965, **148,** 739–743.

Mussen, P., & Rutherford, E. Effects of aggressive cartoons on children's aggressive play. *Journal of Abnormal Social Psychology,* 1961, **62,** 461–464.

Neu, D. M. A critical review of the literature on "absolute pitch." *Psychological Bulletin,* 1944, **47**, 249–266.

News of Van Nostrand Books, July 17, 1964.

Nielsen, J. M., & Sedgwick, R. P. Instincts and emotions in an anencephalic monster. *Journal of Nervous and Mental Disease,* 1949, **110**(5), 387–394.

Novomeiskii, A. S. The nature of the dermo-optic sense. *International Journal of Parapsychology,* 1965, **7**(4), 341–367.

Nyswander, M. *The drug addict as a patient.* New York: Grune & Stratton, 1956.

Olds, J. Self-stimulation of the brain. *Science,* 1958, **127**(3294), 315–324.

Pareto, V. *Sociological writings,* selected by S. E. Finer. New York: Praeger, 1966.

Pastore, N. The genetics of schizophrenia. *Psychological Bulletin,* July 1949, **46**(4), 285–302.

Patrick, J. R., & Laughlin, R. M. Is the wall-seeking tendency in the white rat an instinct? *Journal of Genetic Psychology,* 1934, **44**, 378.

Pattie, F. A. The gregarious behavior of normal chicks and chicks hatched in isolation. *Journal of Comparative Psychology,* 1936, **21**, 161.

Penfield, W. *The excitable cortex in conscious man.* Springfield, Ill.: Charles C Thomas, 1958.

Penfield, W. The interpretive cortex. *Science,* 1959, **129**(3365), 1719–1725.

Penrose, L. S. Genetical problems and mental deficiency. *Eugenics Review,* 1938, **30**, 291.

Penrose, L. S. Inheritance of mental defect. *Scientific Monthly,* 1941, **52**, 359–364.

Penrose, L. S., & Penrose, R. Impossible objects: A special type of illusion. *British Journal of Psychology,* 1958, **49**, 31–33.

Phenylketonuria. Evansville, Ind.: Mead Johnson & Company, 1958.

Piaget, J. *The moral judgment of the child.* Glencoe, Illinois: Free Press, 1948.

Piaget, J. *The origins of intelligence in children.* New York: International Universities Press, 1952.

Pierce, C. S. How to make our ideas clear. *Popular Science Monthly,* 1878, **12**, 286–302. Reprinted in C. Hartshorne and P. Weiss (Eds.), *Collected papers.* Cambridge, Mass.: The Belknap Press of Harvard University Press, 1934, Vol. 5, pp. 248–271. Also in M. R. Cohen (Ed.), *Chance, love and logic.* New York: Harcourt, 1923. Also in P. Kurtz (Ed.), *American philosophy in the twentieth century,* New York: Macmillan, 1966.

Planck, M. *Scientific autobiography* (translated by F. Gaynor). New York: Philosophical Library, 1949.

Poincaré, H. *The foundations of science.* Lancaster, Pennsylvania: Science Press, 1946.

Postman, L., & Crutchfield, R. S. The interaction of need, set, and stimulus-structure in a cognitive task. *American Journal of Psychology,* 1952, **65**, 196–217.

Pratt, J. G. *Parapsychology: An insider's view of ESP.* New York: Dutton, 1966.

Pronko, N. H. "Heredity" and "environment" in biology and psychology. *The Psychological Record,* 1957, **7**, 45–54.

Pronko, N. H. *Textbook of abnormal psychology.* Baltimore: Williams & Wilkins, 1963.

Pronko, N. H., & Bowles, J. W., Jr. (Eds.) *Empirical foundations of psychology.* New York: Holt, 1951.

Pronko, N. H., & Snyder, F. W. Film: *Vision with spatial inversion.* State College, Pa.: Psychological Cinema Register, Pennsylvania State University, 1951.

Quarantelli, E. The behavior of panic participants. *Sociology and Social Research,* 1957, **41**, 187–194.

Radin, S. S. Mental health problems of school children. *Journal of School Health,* December 1962, **32**(10), 250–257.

Radin, S. S. The teacher and the rehabilitation of the emotionally disturbed child. *Journal of School Health,* 1965, **35**(3), 481–487.

Radin, S. S. Psychological aspects of drug addiction. *Journal of School Health,* December 1966, **36**(10), 481–487.

Reese, E. P. *Experiments in operant behavior.* New York: Appleton-Century-Crofts, 1964.

Rensch, B. Increase of learning capability with increase of brain size. *American Naturalist,* 1956, **90**, 81–95.

Rensch, B. The intelligence of elephants. *Scientific American,* February 1957, **196**, 44–49.

Rheingold, H. L., Gerwitz, J. L., & Ross, H. W. Social conditioning of vocalizations in the infant. *Journal of Comparative and Physiological Psychology,* February 1959, **52**(1), 68–73.

Rhine, J. B., & Pratt, J. G. *Parapsychology: Frontier science of the mind.* Springfield, Ill.: Charles C Thomas, 1957.

Rhine, J. B., Pratt, J. G., Stuart, C. E., & Smith, B. M. *Extrasensory perception after sixty years.* Boston: Bruce Humphries, 1966.

Rhine, L. E. *ESP in life and lab.* New York: Macmillan, 1967.

Richards, B. W. (Ed.) with the assistance of A. D. B. Clarke and A. Shapiro. *Proceedings of the London Conference on the scientific study of mental deficiency,* July 24–29, 1960. Vols. 1 & 2. Dagenham, England: May and Baker, Ltd., 1962.

Riese, W. *A history of neurology.* New York: MD Publications, 1959.

Riesen, A. H. Stimulation as a requirement for growth and function in behavioral development. In D. W. Fiske & S. R. Maddi (Eds.), *Functions of varied experience.* Homewood: Dorsey Press, 1961.

Riker, B. L. The ability to judge pitch. *Journal of Experimental Psychology,* 1946, **36**, 331–346.

Robinson, H. B., & Robinson, N. M. *The mentally retarded child.* New York: McGraw-Hill, 1965.

Rosenthal, R. The effect of the experimenter on the results of psychological research. In B. A. Maher (Ed.), *Progress in experimental personality research.* Vol. 1. New York: Academic Press, 1964, pp. 79–114.

Rosenthal, R. *Experimenter effects in behavioral research.* New York: Appleton-Century-Crofts, in press.

Rosenthal, R., & Fode, K. L. The effect of experimenter bias on the performance of the albino rat. *Behavioral Science,* 1963, **8**, 183–189.

Rosenthal, R., & Lawson, R. A longitudinal study of the effects of experimenter bias on the operant learning of laboratory rats. *Journal of Psychiatric Research,* 1964, **2**, 61–72.

Rosenzweig, S. Babies are taught to cry: A hypothesis, *Mental Hygiene,* January 1954, **38**(1), 81–84.

Rostand, J. *Can man be modified?* New York: Basic Books, 1959.

Rothschild, B. F. Incubator isolation as a possible contributing factor to the high incidence of emotional disturbance among prematurely born persons. *Journal of Genetic Psychology,* 1967, **110**, 287–304.

Saetveit, J. G., Lewis, D., & Seashore, C. E. Revision of the Seashore measures of musical talents. *University of Iowa Studies Aims Program,* **65**, 1–66.

Salapatek, P., & Kessen, W. Visual scanning of triangles by the human newborn. *Journal of Experimental Child Psychology,* May 1966, **3**(2), 155–167.

Sanford, N. Will psychologists study human problems? *American Psychologist,* March 1965, **20**(3), 192–202.

Sarason, S. B. *Psychological problems in mental deficiency.* (2nd ed.) New York: Harper, 1953.

Schaller, G. B. *The mountain gorilla.* Chicago: University of Chicago Press, 1963.

Schaller, G. B. *The year of the gorilla.* New York: Ballantine Books, 1965.

Schneirla, T. C. Interrelationships of the "innate" and the "acquired" in instinctive behavior. In P. P. Grasse (Ed.), *L'Instinct dans le comportement des animaux et de l'homme.* Paris: Masson et Cie, 1956.

Schneirla, T. C., & Rosenblatt, J. S. "Critical periods" in the development of behavior. *Science,* March 15, 1963, **139**(3559), 1110–1115.

Schultz, D. P. An experimental approach to panic behavior: Final report to the Group Psychology Branch, Office of Naval Research, August 15, 1966. (Mimeograph).

Scott, J. P. Social behavior, organization and leadership in a small flock of domestic sheep. *Comparative Psychology Monographs,* 1945, **18,** 96.

Scott, J. P. Critical periods in behavioral development. *Science,* November 30, 1962, **138**(3544), 949–958.

Scott, J. P., Fredericson, E., & Fuller, J. L. Experimental exploration of the critical period hypothesis. *Personality,* 1951, **1,** 162.

Seashore, C. E. *Psychology of music.* New York: McGraw-Hill, 1938.

Seitz, P. F. D. The effects of infantile experiences upon adult behavior in animal subjects: I. Effects of litter size during infancy upon adult behavior in the rat. *American Journal of Psychiatry,* 1954, **110,** 916–927.

Shaler, N. S. *Domesticated animals.* London: Smith Elder & Co., 1896.

Shepps, R., & Zigler, E. Social deprivation and rigidity in the preference of organic and familial retardation. *American Journal of Mental Deficiency,* September 1962, **67,** 262–268.

Sherman, J. From the ashes: A personal reaction to the revolt of Watts. *The Antioch Review,* Fall 1967, **27**(2), 285–293.

Shirer, W. L. *The rise and fall of the Third Reich.* New York: Simon and Schuster, 1960.

Shirley, M. M. *The first two years.* Minneapolis: University of Minnesota Press, 1931–1933. 2 Vols.

Siegel, A. E. Film-mediated fantasy aggression and strength of aggressive drive. *Child Development,* 1956, **27,** 365–378.

Silverstein, R. M., Rodin, J. O., Burkholder, W. E., & Gorman, J. E. Sex attractant of the black carpet beetle. *Science,* July 7, 1967, **157**(3784), 85–87.

Singer, C., Holmyard, E. J., & Hall, A. R. (Eds.) *A history of technology,* Vol. 1. New York: Oxford University Press, 1954.

Singh, J. A. L., & Zingg, R. M. *Wolf children and feral man.* New York: Harper, 1940.

Siqueland, E. R. Operant conditioning of head turning in four-month infants. *Psychonomic Science,* 1964, **1,** 223–224.

Siqueland, E. R., & Lipsitt, L. P. Conditioned head turning in human newborns. *Journal of Experimental Psychology,* 1966, **3,** 356–376.

Skeels, H. M. Adult status of children with contrasting early life experiences. *Monographs of the Society for Research in Child Development,* 1966, **31**(3) 1–65.

Skinner, B. F. *The behavior of organisms.* New York: Appleton-Century-Crofts, 1938.

Skinner, B. F. *Science and human behavior.* New York: Macmillan, 1953.

Skinner, B. F. Teaching machines. *Science,* 1958, **128,** 969–977.

Skinner, B. F. A case history in scientific method. *American Psychologist,* 1956, **11,** 221–233. Reprinted in S. Koch (Ed.), *Psychology: A study of a science.* Vol. 2. New York: McGraw-Hill, 1958. Also in B. F. Skinner, *Cumulative record* (enlarged edition). New York: Appleton-Century-Crofts, 1961, pp. 76–100.

Skinner, B. F. Pigeons in a pelican. *American Psychologist,* 1960, **15,** 28–37. Reprinted in B. F. Skinner, *Cumulative record* (enlarged edition). New York: Appleton-Century-Crofts, 1961, pp. 426.01–426.18.

Skinner, B. F. Stimulus generalization in an operant: A historical note. In D. I. Mostofsky (Ed.), *Stimulus generalization.* Stanford: Stanford University Press, 1965, pp. 193–209.

Skorpen, E. The whole man. *Main currents in modern thought,* September-October 1965, **22**(1), 10–16.

Sluckin, W. *Imprinting and early learning.* Chicago: Aldine, 1965.

Smee, A. *Instinct and reason.* London: Reeve, Benham & Reeve, 1850.

Smith, A., & Burklund, C. W. Dominant hemispherectomy: Preliminary report on neuropsychological sequelae. *Science,* 1966, **153**(3741), 1280–1282.

Snow, C. P. Either-or. *Progressive,* February 1961, **24.**

Snyder, F. W., & Pronko, N. H. *Vision with spatial inversion.* Wichita, Kansas: University of Wichita Press, 1952.

Snyder, F. W., & Snyder, C. W. Vision with spatial inversion: A follow-up study. *Psychological Record,* 1957, **7,** 20–30.

Sokolov, A. N. In *Psikhologicheskaya Nauka V SSSR, 1,* Akas. Pedag. Nauk RSFSR, Moscow, 1959, p. 488. (Translation in *Psychological Science in the USSR, 1,* U. S. Joint Publications Res. Serv. No. 11466, Washington, D. C., 1961, p. 669.)

Sontag, L. W., Baker, C. T., & Nelson, V. L. Personality as a determinant of performance. *American Journal of Orthopsychiatry,* July 1955, **25**(3), 555-562.

Sontag, L. W., Baker, C. T., & Nelson, V. L. Mental growth and personality development: A longitudinal study. *Monographs of the Society for Research in Child Development,* 1958, **23**(2), 13–143.

Spalding, D. A. Instinct, with original observations on young animals. *Macmillan's Magazine,* 1873, **27,** 282–293.

Sperry, R. W. Brain mechanisms in behavior. *Engineering and Science Monthly,* May 1957.

Spitz, R. A. *Psychoanalytic study of the child,* 1946, **2,** 313.

Stevens, H. A., & Hever, R. (Eds.) *Mental retardation.* Chicago: University of Chicago Press, 1964.

Stevenson, H. W., Hess, E. H., & Rheingold, H. L. *Early behavior: Comparative and developmental approaches.* New York: Wiley, 1967.

Stewart, H. On keeping mental patients chronic. *Psychological Reports,* 1965, **17,** 216–218.

Stratton, G. M. Some preliminary experiments in vision without inversion of the retinal image. *Psychological Review,* 1896, **3,** 611–617.

Stratton, G. M. Vision without inversion of the retinal image. *Psychological Review,* 1897, **4,** 341–360.

Taylor, W. S. Letter. *Science,* August 27, 1965, **149,** 910.

Terman, L. M. *Genetic studies of genius.* Vol. 1. *Mental and physical traits of a thousand gifted children.* Stanford: Stanford University Press, 1926.

Terman, L. M., & Oden, M. H. *Genetic studies of genius.* Vol. 4. *The gifted child grows up.* Stanford: Stanford University Press, 1947.

Terry, C. S. *The origin of the family of Bach musicians.* London: Oxford University Press, 1929.

Thevenin, R. *Origine des animaux domestiques.* Paris: Presses Universitaires de France, 1947.

Thompson, C. V., Huff, T., & Wass, W. Migration of bullet in gunshot wound of the brain. *California Medicine,* 1957, **87**(44), 44.

Thompson, E. P. *The passions of animals.* London: Chapman and Hall, 1851.

Thompson, R., & McConnell, J. V. Classical conditioning in the planarian, Dugesia Dorotocephala. *Journal of Comparative Physiological Psychology,* 1955, **48,** 65–68.

Thorpe, W. H. *Learning and instinct in animals.* Cambridge: Harvard University Press, 1956.

Thorpe, W. H. *Learning and instinct in animals* (2nd ed.). London: Methuen, 1963.

Thorpe, W. H., & North, M. E. W. Origin and significance of the power of vocal imitation: With special reference to the antiphonal singing of birds. *Nature,* October 16, 1965, **208**(5007), 219–222.

Thorpe, W. H., & North, M. E. W. Vocal imitation in the tropical boubou shrike Laniarius aethiopicus major as a means of establishing and maintaining social bonds. *Ibis,* 1966, **108,** 432–435.

Tregold, A. F. A textbook of mental deficiency. (7th ed.) Baltimore: William Wood, 1949.

Ulrich, R., Stachnik, T., & Mabry, J. (Eds.) *Control of human behavior.* Glenview, Ill.: Scott, Foresman, 1966.

Van Wagenen, R. K., & Murdock, E. E. A transistorized signal-package for toilet training of infants. *Journal of Experimental Child Psychology,* 1966, **3,** 312–314.

Verhave, T. Recent developments in the experimental analysis of behavior. *Proceedings of the Eleventh Research Conference, American Meat Institute Foundation,* March 1959, 113–116. Reprinted in R. Ulrich, T. Stachnik & J. Mabry (Eds.), *Control of human behavior.* Glenview, Ill.: Scott, Foresman, 1966, pp. 32–42.

Verhave, T. Is the system approach of engineering psychology applicable to social organizations? *Psychological Record,* 1961, **11,** 69–86.

Verhave, T. (Ed.) *The experimental analysis of behavior: Selected readings.* New York: Appleton-Century-Crofts, 1966.

Verhave, T. The organism as a machine. *Impulse: Journal of the Tasmanian University Psychology Society,* 1966, **2,** 5–10.

Verhave, T. The inspector general...is a bird. *Psychology Today,* 1967, **1,** 48–53.

Wagatsuma, H. The pariah caste in Japan: History and present self-image. In *CIBA Foundation symposium on caste and race: Comparative approaches.* London: Churchill, 1967.

Walker, D. R., & Milton, G. A. Memory transfer vs. sensitization in cannibal planarians. *Psychonomic Science,* 1966, **5**(7), 293–294.

Walker, D. R. Memory transfer in planarians: An artifact of the experimental variables. *Psychonomic Science,* 1966, **5**(9), 357–358.

Walters, R. H., Llewellyn, T. E., & Acker, C. W. Enhancement of punitive behavior by audio-visual displays. *Science,* 1962, **136,** 872–873.

Watson, J. B. *Behaviorism.* New York: Norton, 1930.

Watson, J. S. The development and generalization of "contingency awareness" in early infancy: Some hypotheses. *Merrill-Palmer Quarterly of Behavior and Development,* 1966, **12**(2), 123–135.

Way, T. J. Chemosensory perception in the bullhead. *Research News,* March 1967, **17**(9), 1–4.

Webster's new international dictionary. (2nd ed.) Springfield, Mass.: G. C. Merriam, 1957.

Weisberg, P. Social and nonsocial conditioning of infant vocalizations. *Child Development,* 1963, **34,** 377–388.

Wenger, M. A. An investigation of conditioned responses in human infants. *University of Iowa Studies in Child Welfare,* 1936, **12**(1).

Werry, J. S. The conditioning treatment of enuresis. *American Journal of Psychiatry,* August 1966, **123**(2), 226–229.

White, B. L., & Held, R. Plasticity of sensorimotor development in the human infant. In J. F. Rosenblith & W. Allinsmith (Eds.), *The causes of behavior: Readings in child development and educational psychology.* Boston: Allyn and Bacon, 1966.

Whiting, J. W. M. Sorcery, sin, and the superego. In M. R. Jones (Ed.), *Nebraska symposium on motivation.* Lincoln: University Nebraska Press, 1959, pp. 174–195.

Whiting, J. W. M. Resource mediation and learning by identification. In I. Iscoe & H. W. Stevenson (Eds.), *Personality development in children.* Austin: University Texas Press, 1960, pp. 112–126.

Wickens, D. D., & Wickens, C. D. A study of conditioning in the neonate. *Journal of Experimental Psychology,* 1940, **26,** 94–102.

Wickes, I. G. Treatment of persistent enuresis with the electric buzzer. *Archives Disturbed Child,* 1958, **33,** 160–164.

Williamson, G., & Payne, W. J. A. *An introduction to animal husbandry in the tropics.* London: Longmans, Green, 1959.

Wolf, A. The dynamics of the selective inhibition of specific functions in neurosis. *Psychosomatic Medicine,* January 1943, **5,** 27.

Wolff, P. H. The development of attention in young infants. *Annals of the New York Academy of Science,* 1965, **118**(21), 815–830.

Wolff, P. H., & White, B. L. Visual pursuit and attention in young infants. *Journal of the American Academy of Child Psychiatry,* July 1965, **4**(3), 473–484.

Wolpe, J., Salter, A., & Reyna, L. J. *The conditioning therapies.* New York: Holt, 1964.

Woodford, P. F. Sounder thinking through clearer writing. *Science,* May 12, 1967, **156**(3776), 743–745.

Woodger, J. H. *Biological principles.* London: Kegan Paul, 1929.

Wood-Gush, D. G. M. A history of the domestic chicken from antiquity to the 19th century. *Poultry Science,* 1959, **38,** 321–326.

Wyatt, R. F. The improvability of pitch discrimination. *Psychological Monographs,* 1945, **58,** 1–58.

Zeuner, F. E. Domestication of animals. In C. Singer, E. J. Holmyard, and A. R. Hall (Eds.), *A history of technology,* Vol. 1. New York: Oxford University Press, 1954, Ch. 13, pp. 327–352.

Zigler, E., & Williams, J. Institutionalization and the effectiveness of social reinforcement: A three-year follow-up study. *Journal of Abnormal Social Psychology,* March 1963, **66**(3), 197–205.

Index of names

Index of subjects